ATLAS

DK
Penguin
Random
House

FOR THE SIXTH EDITION
Senior Cartographic Editor Simon Mumford
Designer Nimbus Design
Editors Cambridge International Reference on Current Affairs (CIRCA)
3D Globes Planetary Visions Ltd., London
Senior Producer Mandy Inness **Producer, Pre-Production** Nikoleta Parasaki

Publisher Andrew Macintyre
Publishing Director Jonathan Metcalf
Associate Publishing Director Liz Wheeler
Art Director Philip Ormerod

FOR PREVIOUS EDITIONS
Cartographic Director Andrew Heritage
Cartography Roger Bullen, Rob Stokes, Iorwerth Watkins
Project Editor Sam Atkinson **Art Editor** Karen Gregory

First published in Great Britain in 2001 by
Dorling Kindersley Limited, 80 Strand, London WC2R 0RL

Sixth edition 2015
Previously published as the Ultimate Pocket Book of the World Atlas & Factfile

10 9 8 7 6 5 4 3 2
002–265179–Apr/15

A CIP catalogue record for this book is available from the British Library
ISBN: 978-0-2411-8869-9

Printed and bound in Hong Kong

A WORLD OF IDEAS:
SEE ALL THERE IS TO KNOW

www.dk.com

Key to map symbols

ELEVATION

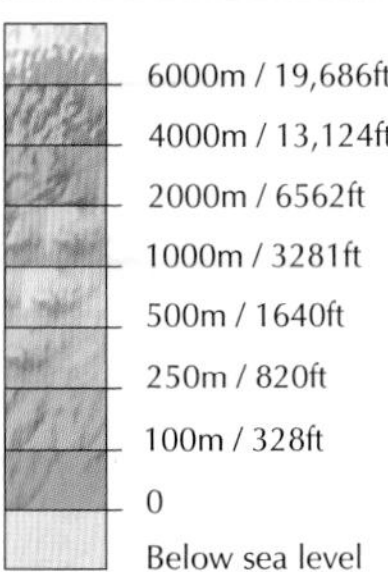
6000m / 19,686ft
4000m / 13,124ft
2000m / 6562ft
1000m / 3281ft
500m / 1640ft
250m / 820ft
100m / 328ft
0
Below sea level

▲ Mountain

• Depression

BORDERS

Full international

Disputed *de facto*

Territorial claim

Cease-fire line

Undefined

State/Province

DRAINAGE FEATURES

River

Seasonal river

Canal

Lake

Seasonal lake

SETTLEMENTS

Capital city

Major town

Minor town

Major port

COMMUNICATIONS

Major road

Rail

International airport

Insight; facts, figures, and amazing information from around the world

Atlas contents

The Political World 8-9
The Physical World 10-11
Time Zones 12-13
Atlas Opener. 14-15

North & Central America 16–17

Western Canada & Alaska . . . 18-19
Eastern Canada 20-21
USA: The Northeast. 22-23
USA: Central States 24-25
USA: The West 26-27
USA: The Southwest 28-29
USA: The Southeast 30-31
Mexico 32-33
Central America 34-35
The Caribbean. 36-37

South America 38–39

Northern South America 40-41
Peru, Bolivia, & North Brazil 42-43
Paraguay, Uruguay,
& South Brazil. 44-45
Southern South America 46-47
The Atlantic Ocean 48-49

Africa 50–51

Northwest Africa 52-53
Northeast Africa 54-55
West Africa 56-57
Central Africa 58-59
Southern Africa 60-61

Europe 62–63

The North Atlantic. 64-65
Scandinavia & Finland. 66-67
The Low Countries 68-69
The British Isles 70-71
France, Andorra,
& Monaco. 72-73
Spain & Portugal 74-75
Germany &
the Alpine States 76-77
Italy. 78-79
Central Europe 80-81
Southeast Europe. 82-83
The Mediterranean 84-85

Atlas contents

Bulgaria & Greece. 86-87
The Baltic States
& Belarus 88-89
Ukraine, Moldova,
& Romania 90-91
European Russia 92-93

North & West Asia 94–95

Russia & Kazakhstan 96-97
Turkey & the Caucasus 98-99
The Near East
& West Bank. 100-101
The Middle East 102-103
Central Asia. 104-105

South & East Asia 106–107

Western China
& Mongolia. 108-109
Eastern China & Korea. . . .110-111
Japan. 112-113
South India & Sri Lanka. . .114-115
North India & Pakistan . . .116-117
Mainland Southeast Asia . .118-119
Maritime Southeast Asia . .120-121

The Indian Ocean 122-123

Australasia & Oceania 124–125

The Southwest Pacific 126-127
Western Australia 128-129
Eastern Australia 130-131
New Zealand 132-133

The Pacific Ocean 134-135
Antarctica 136
Arctic 137

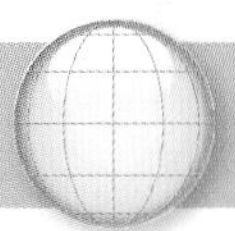

Country Factfiles 138–359

See overleaf for contents

Overseas territories 360-365
International organizations . . . 366

Abbreviations 367
Index. 368-432

Factfile contents

A

Afghanistan 153
Albania 154
Algeria. 155
Andorra. 156
Angola. 157
Antarctica 158
Antigua & Barbuda . . 159
Argentina. 160
Armenia 161
Australia 162–163
Austria. 164
Azerbaijan. 165

B

Bahamas, The 166
Bahrain 167
Bangladesh 168
Barbados 169
Belarus 170
Belgium. 171
Belize 172
Benin. 173
Bhutan. 174
Bolivia. 175
Bosnia
& Herzegovina 176
Botswana. 177
Brazil. 178-179
Brunei 180
Bulgaria. 181
Burkina Faso 182
Burma . . . . . *see Myanmar*
Burundi 183

C

Cambodia 184
Cameroon 185
Canada 186-187
Cape Verde 188
Central African
Republic 189
Chad 190
Chile 191
China 192-193
Colombia 194
Comoros 195
Congo 196
Congo, Dem. Rep. . . 197
Costa Rica 198
Côte d'Ivoire 199
Croatia 200
Cuba 201
Cyprus. 202
Czech Republic. 203

D

Denmark 204
Djibouti. 205
Dominica 206
Dominican Republic . 207

E

East Timor 208
Ecuador. 209
Egypt 210
El Salvador 211
Equatorial Guinea . . . 212
Eritrea 213
Estonia. 214
Ethiopia. 215

F

Fiji. 216
Finland 217
France 218

G

Gabon. 219
Gambia 220
Georgia 221
Germany 222
Ghana 223
Greece 224
Grenada 225
Guatemala. 226
Guinea 227
Guinea–Bissau. 228
Guyana 229

H

Haiti 230
Honduras 231
Hungary 232

I

Iceland 233
India 234-235
Indonesia. 236-237
Iran 238
Iraq 239
Ireland. 240
Israel 241
Italy. 242

J

Jamaica 243
Japan. 244-245
Jordan 246

K

Kazakhstan 247
Kenya 248
Kiribati 249
Korea, North 250
Korea, South 251
Kosovo 252
Kuwait. 253
Kyrgyzstan. 254

L

Laos. 255
Latvia 256
Lebanon 257
Lesotho 258
Liberia. 259

Factfile contents

Libya 260
Liechtenstein 261
Lithuania 262
Luxembourg 263

M

Macedonia 264
Madagascar 265
Malawi 266
Malaysia 267
Maldives 268
Mali 269
Malta 270
Marshall Islands 271
Mauritania 272
Mauritius 273
Mexico 274
Micronesia 275
Moldova 276
Monaco 277
Mongolia 278
Montenegro 279
Morocco 280
Mozambique 281
Myanmar (Burma) . . . 282

N

Namibia 283
Nauru 284
Nepal 285
Netherlands 286
New Zealand 287
Nicaragua 288
Niger 289
Nigeria 290
Norway 291

O

Oman 292

P

Pakistan 293
Palau 294
Panama 295
Papua New Guinea . . 296
Paraguay 297
Peru 298
Philippines 299
Poland 300
Portugal 301

Q

Qatar 302

R

Romania 303
Russian
Federation 304
Rwanda 305

S

St. Kitts & Nevis 306
St. Lucia 307
St. Vincent & the
Grenadines 308
Samoa 309
San Marino 310
Sao Tome & Principe . 311
Saudi Arabia 312
Senegal 313
Serbia 314
Seychelles 315
Sierra Leone 316
Singapore 317
Slovakia 318
Slovenia 319
Solomon Islands 320
Somalia 321
South Africa 322
South Sudan 323
Spain 324
Sri Lanka 325
Sudan 326
Suriname 327
Swaziland 328
Sweden 329
Switzerland 330
Syria 331

T

Taiwan 332
Tajikistan 333
Tanzania 334
Thailand 335
Togo 336
Tonga 337
Trinidad & Tobago . . . 338
Tunisia 339
Turkey 340
Turkmenistan 341
Tuvalu 342

U

Uganda 343
Ukraine 344
United Arab Emirates. 345
United Kingdom . 346-347
United States 348-350
Uruguay 351
Uzbekistan 352

V

Vanuatu 353
Vatican City 354
Venezuela 355
Vietnam 356

Y

Yemen 357

Z

Zambia 358
Zimbabwe 359

The Political World

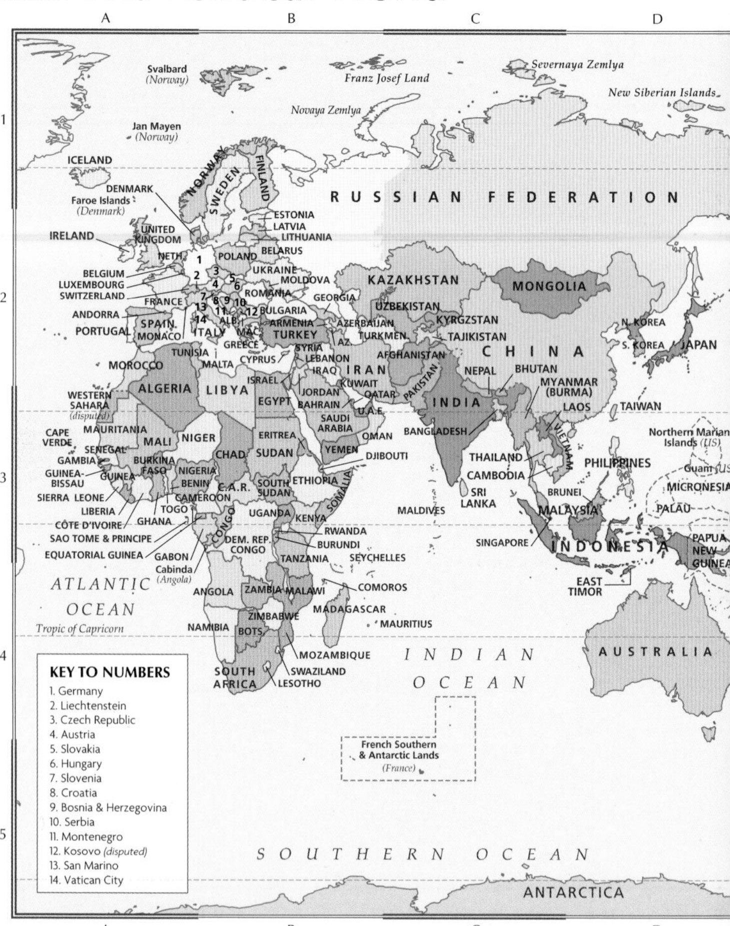

A B C D
1 2 3 4 5
Svalbard (Norway)
Franz Josef Land
Severnaya Zemlya
New Siberian Islands
Novaya Zemlya
Jan Mayen (Norway)
ICELAND
NORWAY
SWEDEN
FINLAND
RUSSIAN FEDERATION
DENMARK
Faroe Islands (Denmark)
ESTONIA
LATVIA
LITHUANIA
IRELAND
UNITED KINGDOM
NETH.
POLAND
BELARUS
BELGIUM
LUXEMBOURG
SWITZERLAND
UKRAINE
MOLDOVA
KAZAKHSTAN
MONGOLIA
FRANCE
ROMANIA
GEORGIA
UZBEKISTAN
KYRGZSTAN
ANDORRA
BULGARIA
SPAIN
PORTUGAL
MONACO
ITALY
ALB.
MAC.
ARMENIA
AZERBAIJAN
TURKEY
TURKMEN.
TAJIKISTAN
N. KOREA
S. KOREA
JAPAN
GREECE
AZ.
CHINA
TUNISIA
MALTA
CYPRUS
SYRIA
LEBANON
AFGHANISTAN
MOROCCO
IRAQ
IRAN
NEPAL
BHUTAN
ISRAEL
JORDAN
KUWAIT
PAKISTAN
ALGERIA
LIBYA
EGYPT
BAHRAIN
QATAR
INDIA
MYANMAR (BURMA)
WESTERN SAHARA (disputed)
SAUDI ARABIA
U.A.E.
LAOS
TAIWAN
CAPE VERDE
MAURITANIA
MALI
NIGER
ERITREA
OMAN
BANGLADESH
Northern Mariana Islands (US)
SENEGAL
GAMBIA
BURKINA FASO
CHAD
SUDAN
YEMEN
DJIBOUTI
THAILAND
VIETNAM
PHILIPPINES
GUINEA-BISSAU
GUINEA
NIGERIA
BENIN
C.A.R.
SOUTH SUDAN
ETHIOPIA
SOMALIA
CAMBODIA
Guam (US)
MICRONESIA
SIERRA LEONE
CAMEROON
SRI LANKA
BRUNEI
LIBERIA
TOGO
UGANDA
KENYA
MALDIVES
MALAYSIA
PALAU
CÔTE D'IVOIRE
GHANA
CONGO
RWANDA
SAO TOME & PRINCIPE
DEM. REP. CONGO
BURUNDI
SINGAPORE
INDONESIA
PAPUA NEW GUINEA
EQUATORIAL GUINEA
GABON
TANZANIA
SEYCHELLES
Cabinda (Angola)
EAST TIMOR
ATLANTIC OCEAN
ANGOLA
ZAMBIA
MALAWI
COMOROS
MADAGASCAR
ZIMBABWE
MAURITIUS
Tropic of Capricorn
NAMIBIA
BOTS.
MOZAMBIQUE
INDIAN OCEAN
AUSTRALIA
SOUTH AFRICA
SWAZILAND
LESOTHO
French Southern & Antarctic Lands (France)
SOUTHERN OCEAN
ANTARCTICA
KEY TO NUMBERS
1. Germany
2. Liechtenstein
3. Czech Republic
4. Austria
5. Slovakia
6. Hungary
7. Slovenia
8. Croatia
9. Bosnia & Herzegovina
10. Serbia
11. Montenegro
12. Kosovo (disputed)
13. San Marino
14. Vatican City

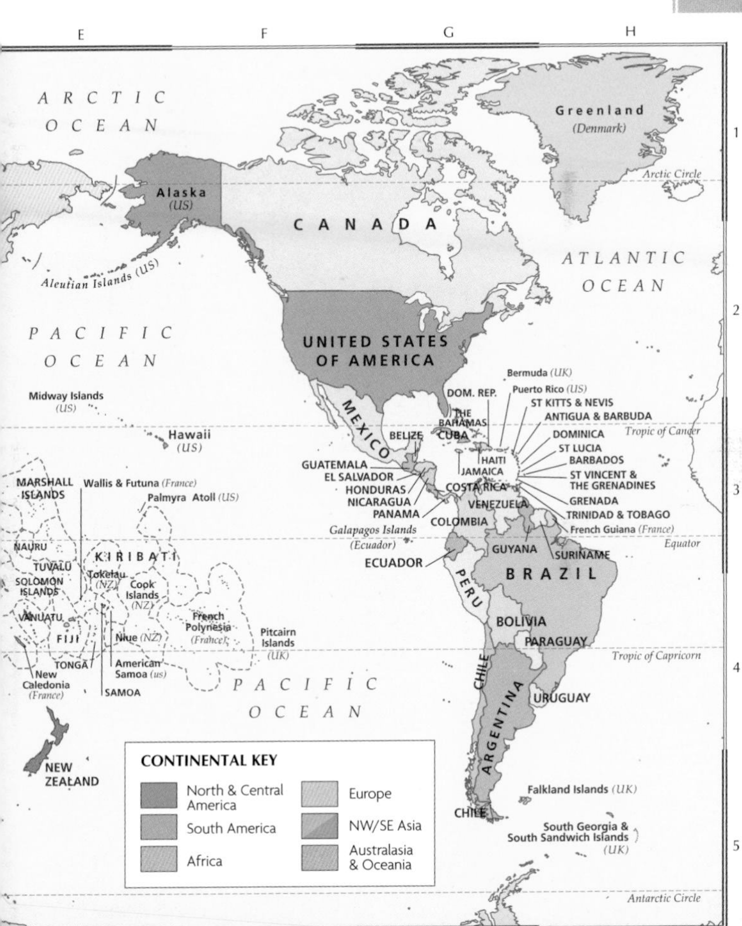

E
F
G
H
1
2
3
4
5
ARCTIC OCEAN
Greenland
(Denmark)
Arctic Circle
Alaska
(US)
CANADA
Aleutian Islands (US)
ATLANTIC OCEAN
PACIFIC OCEAN
UNITED STATES OF AMERICA
Bermuda (UK)
Puerto Rico (US)
DOM. REP.
ST KITTS & NEVIS
Midway Islands
(US)
MEXICO
THE BAHAMAS
ANTIGUA & BARBUDA
Hawaii
(US)
BELIZE
CUBA
DOMINICA
Tropic of Cancer
ST LUCIA
HAITI
BARBADOS
GUATEMALA
JAMAICA
EL SALVADOR
ST VINCENT & THE GRENADINES
MARSHALL ISLANDS
Wallis & Futuna (France)
HONDURAS
COSTA RICA
Palmyra Atoll (US)
NICARAGUA
VENEZUELA
GRENADA
PANAMA
TRINIDAD & TOBAGO
COLOMBIA
Galapagos Islands
(Ecuador)
French Guiana (France)
Equator
NAURU
KIRIBATI
GUYANA
SURINAME
TUVALU
ECUADOR
Tokelau
(NZ)
BRAZIL
SOLOMON ISLANDS
Cook Islands
(NZ)
PERU
French Polynesia
(France)
BOLIVIA
VANUATU
Pitcairn Islands
(UK)
PARAGUAY
FIJI
Niue (NZ)
Tropic of Capricorn
TONGA
American Samoa (us)
CHILE
New Caledonia
(France)
PACIFIC OCEAN
ARGENTINA
URUGUAY
SAMOA
CONTINENTAL KEY
NEW ZEALAND
North & Central America
Europe
Falkland Islands (UK)
South America
NW/SE Asia
CHILE
South Georgia & South Sandwich Islands
(UK)
Africa
Australasia & Oceania
Antarctic Circle
E
F
G
H

The Physical World

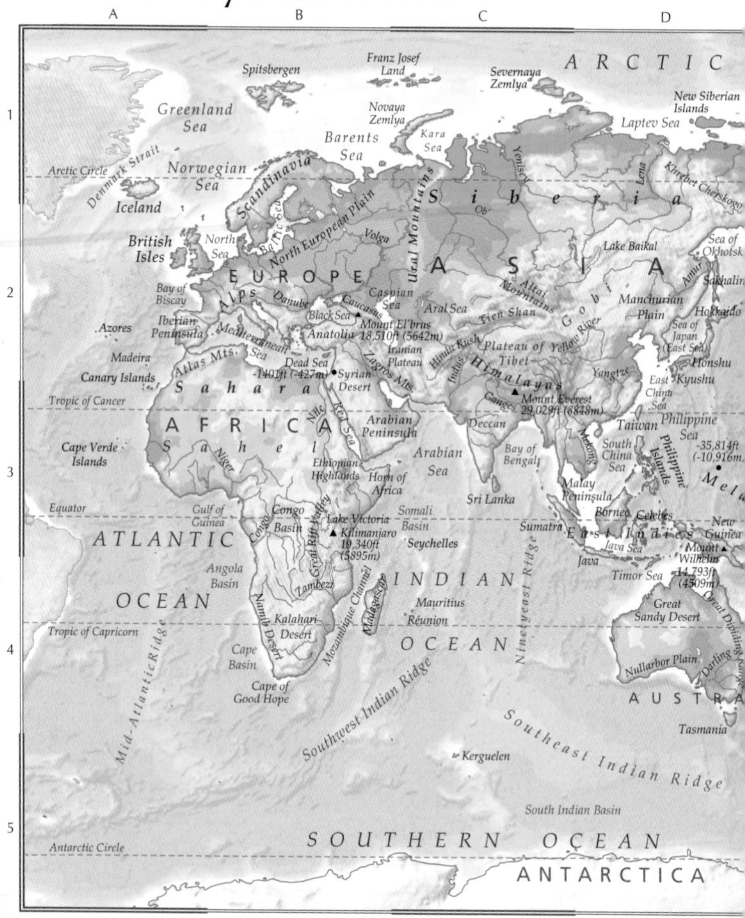
A
B
C
D
1
2
3
4
5
ARCTIC
Spitsbergen
Franz Josef Land
Severnaya Zemlya
New Siberian Islands
Greenland Sea
Novaya Zemlya
Laptev Sea
Kara Sea
Barents Sea
Arctic Circle
Denmark Strait
Norwegian Sea
Scandinavia
Yenisey
Lena
Khrebet Cherskogo
Iceland
Siberia
Ob'
British Isles
North Sea
Baltic Sea
North European Plain
Volga
Ural Mountains
Lake Baikal
Sea of Okhotsk
ASIA
EUROPE
Amur
Sakhalin
Bay of Biscay
Alps
Danube
Caspian Sea
Caucasus
Altai Mountains
Manchurian Plain
Hokkaido
Azores
Iberian Peninsula
Black Sea
Mount El'brus 18,510ft (5642m)
Aral Sea
Tien Shan
Gobi
Sea of Japan (East Sea)
Mediterranean Sea
Anatolia
Hindu Kush
Plateau of Tibet
Yellow River
Madeira
Atlas Mts.
Dead Sea -1401ft (-427m)
Iranian Plateau
Honshu
Canary Islands
Syrian Desert
Zagros Mts
Indus
Himalayas
Yangtze
Kyushu
Sahara
East China Sea
Tropic of Cancer
Mount Everest 29,029ft (8848m)
Ganges
AFRICA
Nile
Red Sea
Arabian Peninsula
Deccan
Taiwan
Philippine Sea
Cape Verde Islands
Sahel
Niger
Arabian Sea
Bay of Bengal
Mekong
South China Sea
Philippine Islands
-35,814ft (-10,916m)
Ethiopian Highlands
Horn of Africa
Malay Peninsula
Equator
Gulf of Guinea
Congo
Congo Basin
Great Rift Valley
Somali Basin
Sri Lanka
Borneo
Celebes
Lake Victoria
Sumatra
East Indies
New Guinea
ATLANTIC
Kilimanjaro 19,340ft (5895m)
Seychelles
Java Sea
Mount Wilhelm 14,793ft (4509m)
Angola Basin
Java
Timor Sea
Zambezi
Mozambique Channel
Madagascar
INDIAN
Ninetyeast Ridge
OCEAN
Mauritius
Great Sandy Desert
Namib Desert
Kalahari Desert
Réunion
Great Dividing Range
Tropic of Capricorn
Mid-Atlantic Ridge
OCEAN
Cape Basin
Nullarbor Plain
Darling
Cape of Good Hope
Southwest Indian Ridge
AUSTRA
Tasmania
Southeast Indian Ridge
Kerguelen
South Indian Basin
SOUTHERN OCEAN
Antarctic Circle
ANTARCTICA

E
F
G
H
OCEAN
East Siberian Sea
Beaufort Sea
Ellesmere Island
Queen Elizabeth Islands
Greenland
Baffin Bay
Baffin Island
Arctic Circle
Chukchi Sea
Brooks Range
Bering Strait
Kamchatka
Mackenzie
Great Bear Lake
Great Slave Lake
Hudson Bay
Labrador Sea
Mount McKinley (Denali) 20,322ft (6194m)
Bering Sea
Coast Mountains
Rocky Mountains
Gulf of Alaska
Aleutian Islands
NORTH AMERICA
Great Lakes
Great Plains
Appalachian Mts
Grand Banks of Newfoundland
Northwest Pacific Basin
Coast Ranges
Mississippi
North American Basin
Mid-Atlantic Ridge
Polynesia
Hawaiian Islands
Mid-Pacific Mountains
Micronesia
Gulf of Mexico
West Indies
Tropic of Cancer
ATLANTIC OCEAN
Caribbean Sea
PACIFIC OCEAN
Galapagos Islands
Equator
Amazon
Amazon Basin
Andes
SOUTH AMERICA
Solomon Islands
Coral Sea
Fiji
New Caledonia
Peru Basin
East Pacific Rise
Brazil Basin
Tropic of Capricorn
Easter Island
Cerro Aconcagua 22,831ft (6959m)
Gran Chaco
Paraná
Pampas
North Island
Southwest Pacific Basin
Tasman Sea
New Zealand
South Island
Patagonia
Argentine Basin
Falkland Islands
South Georgia
Tierra del Fuego
Cape Horn
Drake Passage
South Sandwich Islands
Antarctic Peninsula
Antarctic Circle
1
2
3
4
5

Standard Time Zones

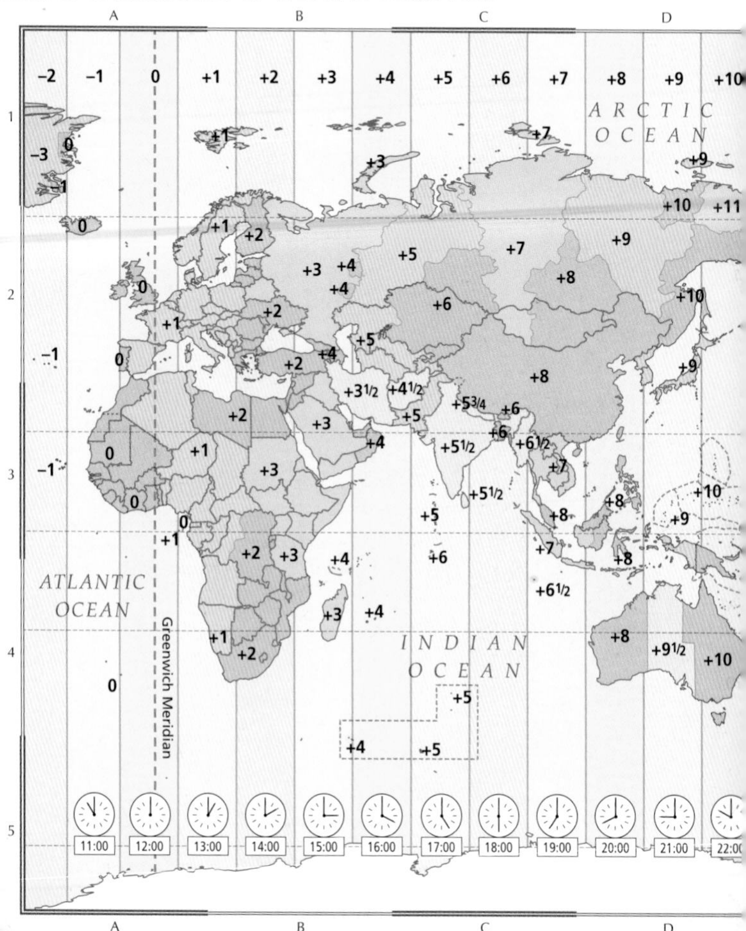
A
B
C
D
1
2
3
4
5
−2
−1
0
+1
+2
+3
+4
+5
+6
+7
+8
+9
+10
+11
ARCTIC OCEAN
ATLANTIC OCEAN
INDIAN OCEAN
Greenwich Meridian
−3
+3 1/2
+4 1/2
+5 3/4
+5 1/2
+6 1/2
+9 1/2
11:00
12:00
13:00
14:00
15:00
16:00
17:00
18:00
19:00
20:00
21:00
22:00

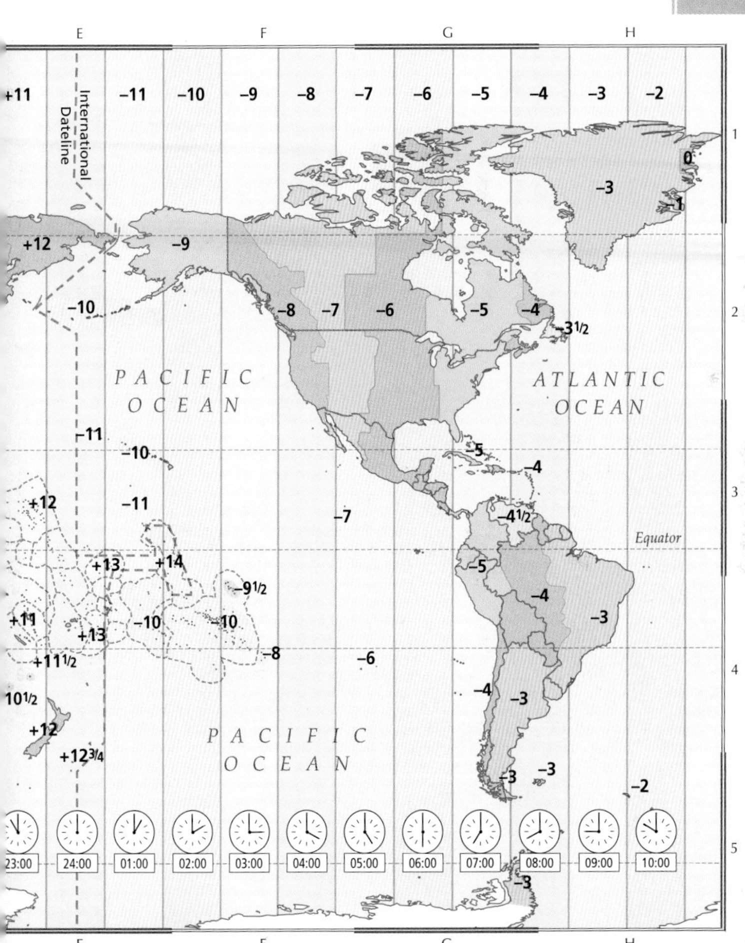
E
F
G
H
+11
–11
–10
–9
–8
–7
–6
–5
–4
–3
–2
International Dateline
1
0
–3
–1
+12
–9
–10
–8
–7
–6
–5
–4
–3½
2
PACIFIC OCEAN
ATLANTIC OCEAN
–11
–10
–5
–4
+12
–11
3
–7
–4½
Equator
+13
+14
–5
–9½
–4
+11
–10
–10
–3
+13
+11½
–8
–6
4
10½
–4
–3
+12
PACIFIC OCEAN
+12¾
–3
–3
–2
23:00
24:00
01:00
02:00
03:00
04:00
05:00
06:00
07:00
08:00
09:00
10:00
5
–3
E
F
G
H

The world's regions

North & Central America

EUROPE
Franz Josef Land
(to Russia)
Svalbard
(to Norway)
Jan Mayen
(to Norway)
ICELAND
Greenland
(Denmark)
Arctic Circle
Labrador Sea
Labrador
Laurentian Mountains
Baffin Bay
Baffin Island
Hudson Bay
CANADA
Lake Winnipeg
Reindeer Lake
Lake Athabasca
Great Slave Lake
Great Bear Lake
Mackenzie
Queen Elizabeth Islands
ARCTIC OCEAN
North Pole
Beaufort Sea
ASIA
Arctic Circle
ALASKA (US)
Mount McKinley
(Denali)
20,322ft (6194m)
Yukon
Bering Strait
Bering Sea
Aleutian Islands
Gulf of Alaska
PACIFIC OCEAN
Snake
62
94
95
134

UNITED STATES OF AMERICA
Miquelon
(France)
Mount Whitney
14,495ft (4418m)
Death Valley
-282ft (-86m)
Lake Superior
Great Lakes
Lake Huron
Lake Ontario
Lake Michigan
Lake Erie
Missouri
Colorado
Ohio
Arkansas
Mississippi
Appalachian Mountains
ATLANTIC OCEAN
Bermuda
(UK)
Sargasso Sea
Tropic of Cancer
Rio Grande
Sierra Madre Occidental
Sierra Madre Oriental
MEXICO
Gulf of Mexico
THE BAHAMAS
Turks & Caicos Islands (UK)
DOMINICAN REPUBLIC
Virgin Islands (US)
British Virgin Islands (UK)
Anguilla (UK)
ST KITTS & NEVIS
ANTIGUA & BARBUDA
Puerto Rico
(US)
CUBA
Cayman Islands
(UK)
HAITI
Guadeloupe
(France)
Montserrat (UK)
DOMINICA
ST LUCIA
JAMAICA
BELIZE
GUATEMALA
HONDURAS
Martinique (France)
ST VINCENT & THE GRENADINES
BARBADOS
Clipperton Island
(French Polynesia)
EL SALVADOR
Aruba (Neth.)
GRENADA
NICARAGUA
Curaçao
(Neth.)
Bonaire
(Neth.)
TRINIDAD & TOBAGO
COSTA RICA
PACIFIC OCEAN
PANAMA
Equator
Andes
SOUTH AMERICA
Galapagos Islands
(Ecuador)
0 km
1000
0 miles
1000
134
135
38
48
A
B
C
D
E
5
6
7
8

Western Canada & Alaska

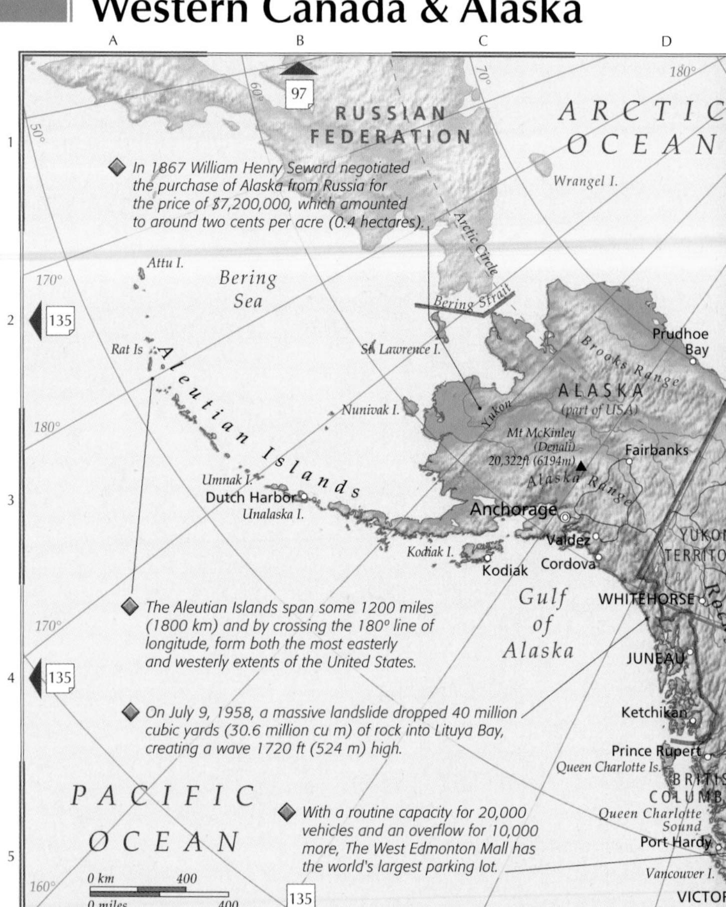

A
B
C
D
1
2
3
4
5
97
135
135
135
RUSSIAN FEDERATION
ARCTIC OCEAN
Wrangel I.
In 1867 William Henry Seward negotiated the purchase of Alaska from Russia for the price of $7,200,000, which amounted to around two cents per acre (0.4 hectares).
Arctic Circle
Attu I.
Bering Sea
Bering Strait
Rat Is
Aleutian Islands
St Lawrence I.
Nunivak I.
Prudhoe Bay
Brooks Range
ALASKA (part of USA)
Yukon
Mt McKinley (Denali) 20,322ft (6194m)
Fairbanks
Alaska Range
Umnak I.
Dutch Harbor
Unalaska I.
Anchorage
Valdez
Kodiak I.
Kodiak
Cordova
YUKON TERRITORY
Gulf of Alaska
WHITEHORSE
The Aleutian Islands span some 1200 miles (1800 km) and by crossing the 180° line of longitude, form both the most easterly and westerly extents of the United States.
JUNEAU
On July 9, 1958, a massive landslide dropped 40 million cubic yards (30.6 million cu m) of rock into Lituya Bay, creating a wave 1720 ft (524 m) high.
Ketchikan
Prince Rupert
Queen Charlotte Is.
BRITISH COLUMBIA
PACIFIC OCEAN
With a routine capacity for 20,000 vehicles and an overflow for 10,000 more, The West Edmonton Mall has the world's largest parking lot.
Queen Charlotte Sound
Port Hardy
Vancouver I.
VICTORIA
0 km 400
0 miles 400
50°
60°
70°
180°
170°
180°
170°
160°
140°
130°

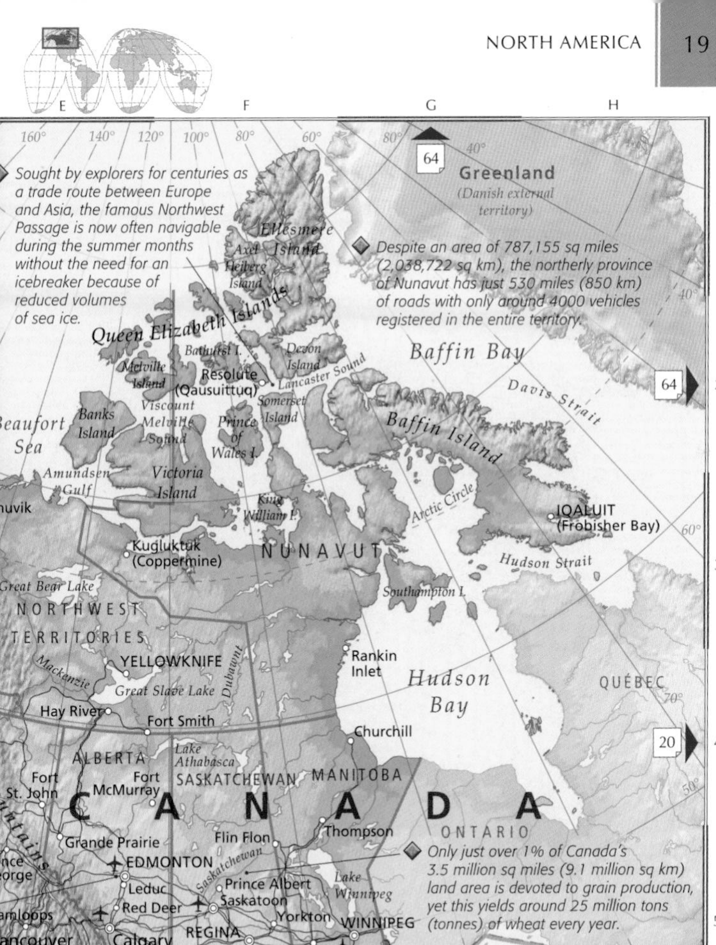
Sought by explorers for centuries as a trade route between Europe and Asia, the famous Northwest Passage is now often navigable during the summer months without the need for an icebreaker because of reduced volumes of sea ice.
Despite an area of 787,155 sq miles (2,038,722 sq km), the northerly province of Nunavut has just 530 miles (850 km) of roads with only around 4000 vehicles registered in the entire territory.
Only just over 1% of Canada's 3.5 million sq miles (9.1 million sq km) land area is devoted to grain production, yet this yields around 25 million tons (tonnes) of wheat every year.
Greenland
(Danish external territory)
Ellesmere Island
Axel Heiberg Island
Queen Elizabeth Islands
Bathurst I.
Melville Island
Devon Island
Resolute (Qausuittuq)
Lancaster Sound
Baffin Bay
Davis Strait
Somerset Island
Viscount Melville Sound
Banks Island
Prince of Wales I.
Beaufort Sea
Baffin Island
Amundsen Gulf
Victoria Island
Inuvik
King William I.
Arctic Circle
IQALUIT (Frobisher Bay)
Kugluktuk (Coppermine)
NUNAVUT
Hudson Strait
Great Bear Lake
Southampton I.
NORTHWEST TERRITORIES
Rankin Inlet
YELLOWKNIFE
Mackenzie
Dubawnt
Hudson Bay
QUÉBEC
Great Slave Lake
Hay River
Fort Smith
Churchill
Lake Athabasca
ALBERTA
Fort St. John
Fort McMurray
SASKATCHEWAN
MANITOBA
CANADA
Thompson
ONTARIO
Grande Prairie
Flin Flon
Prince George
EDMONTON
Saskatchewan
Lake Winnipeg
Leduc
Prince Albert
Saskatoon
Red Deer
Kamloops
Yorkton
WINNIPEG
REGINA
Vancouver
Calgary
Brandon
Kelowna
Lethbridge
Estevan
USA
64
20
25

Eastern Canada

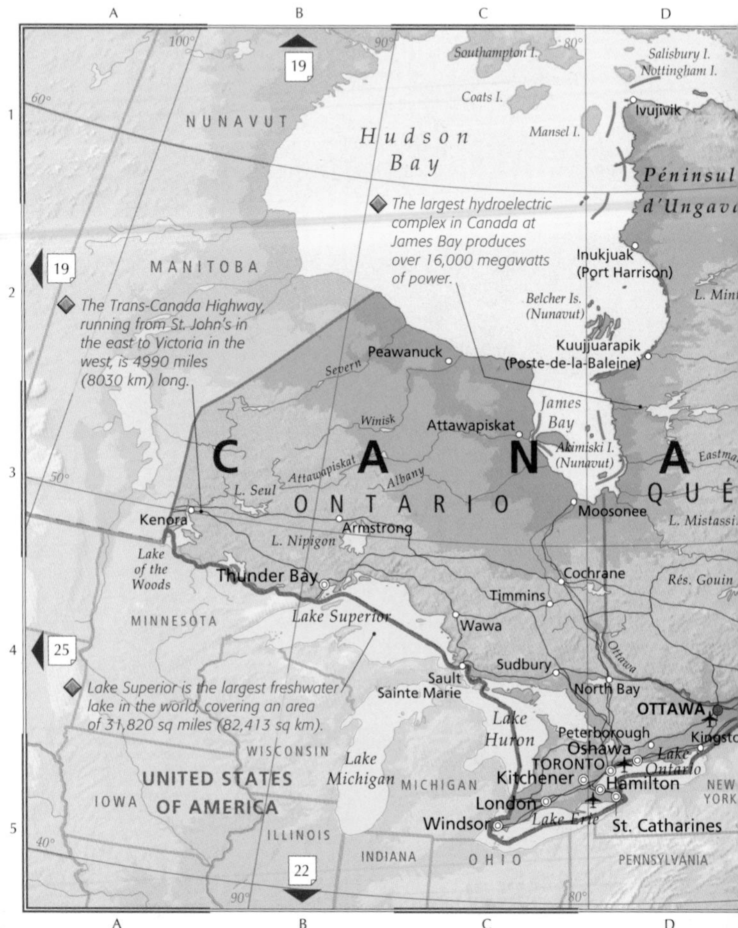

A
B
C
D
19
NUNAVUT
Hudson Bay
Southampton I.
Coats I.
Mansel I.
Salisbury I.
Nottingham I.
Ivujivik
Péninsul d'Ungava
The largest hydroelectric complex in Canada at James Bay produces over 16,000 megawatts of power.
19
MANITOBA
Inukjuak (Port Harrison)
Belcher Is. (Nunavut)
L. Mini
The Trans-Canada Highway, running from St. John's in the east to Victoria in the west, is 4990 miles (8030 km) long.
Peawanuck
Severn
Kuujjuarapik (Poste-de-la-Baleine)
James Bay
Winisk
Attawapiskat
CANADA
Akimiski I. (Nunavut)
Eastmai
Attawapiskat
Albany
L. Seul
ONTARIO
QUÉ
Kenora
Armstrong
Moosonee
L. Mistassi
L. Nipigon
Lake of the Woods
Thunder Bay
Cochrane
Rés. Gouin
Timmins
MINNESOTA
Lake Superior
Wawa
25
Ottawa
Sudbury
Sault Sainte Marie
North Bay
Lake Superior is the largest freshwater lake in the world, covering an area of 31,820 sq miles (82,413 sq km).
OTTAWA
Lake Huron
Peterborough
Kingstc
Oshawa
WISCONSIN
Lake Michigan
TORONTO
Lake Ontario
UNITED STATES OF AMERICA
MICHIGAN
Kitchener
Hamilton
NEW YORK
IOWA
London
Windsor
Lake Erie
St. Catharines
ILLINOIS
INDIANA
OHIO
PENNSYLVANIA
22
100°
90°
80°
60°
50°
40°
1
2
3
4
5

E
F
G
H
Baffin I.
Labrador Sea
Hudson Strait
Akpatok I. (Nunavut)
Ungava Bay
64
1
Formed around 210 million years ago by a 5 km (3.1 mile) diameter asteroid, the Manicouagan crater is 100 km (60 miles) across, making it the biggest visible impact crater on Earth.
Kuujjuaq
Nain
Labrador
ATLANTIC
OCEAN
Hopedale
Makkovik
48
2
Caniapiscau
Schefferville
Cartwright
Smallwood Reservoir
NEWFOUNDLAND & LABRADOR
Strait of Belle Isle
Réservoir Caniapiscau
Newfoundland
D
A
Havre-Saint-Pierre
Gander
3
E C
Réservoir Manicouagan
Grand Falls
ST JOHN'S
Île d'Anticosti
Corner Brook
Sept-Îles
St. Lawrence
Gaspé
Gulf of St. Lawrence
Channel-Port-aux-Basques
Cape Race
L. Saint-Jean
Jonquière
Cabot Strait
St Pierre & Miquelon
(French overseas collectivity)
Chicoutimi
PRINCE EDWARD ISLAND
Bathurst
NEW BRUNSWICK
Sydney
QUÉBEC
Moncton
CHARLOTTETOWN
FREDERICTON
48
4
NOVA SCOTIA
Trois-Rivières
Dartmouth
Sherbrooke
Saint John
HALIFAX
Canada has the world's longest coastline (including thousands of islands), with a total length of 151,019 miles (243,042 km).
Montréal
MAINE
Yarmouth
NEW HAMPSHIRE
VERMONT
The Bay of Fundy has the world's highest tidal range, with water's rising 20–56 ft (5–17 m) every high tide as around 115 billion tons (tonnes) of water flows into the bay.
MASSACHUSETTS
RHODE ISLAND
5
CONNECTICUT
0 km
300
0 miles
300
48
70°
60°
50°
40°

USA: The Northeast

A
B
C
D
1
2
3
4
5
20
25
25
30
MINNESOTA
Lake Superior
ONTARIO
C A
Superior
Ironwood
Marquette
Sault Ste Marie
Iron Mountain
Ladysmith
Cheboygan
Lake Huron
WISCONSIN
MICHIGAN
Eau Claire
Mississippi
Green Bay
Traverse City
La Crosse
Oshkosh
Lake Michigan
Bay City
IOWA
MADISON
Milwaukee
Grand Rapids
Saginaw
Flint
LANSING
Waukegan
Rockford
Detroit
Ann Arbor
Chicago
Lake Erie
Erie
Aurora
Joliet
South Bend
Toledo
Cleveland
Rock Island
Gary
Youngstown
Galesburg
Akron
Peoria
Fort Wayne
Mansfield
Canton
ILLINOIS
INDIANA
OHIO
Wheeling
Champaign
Muncie
SPRINGFIELD
INDIANAPOLIS
COLUMBUS
Decatur
Dayton
Effingham
Terre Haute
Cincinnati
MISSOURI
Bloomington
Ohio
East St Louis
Wabash
Mt. Vernon
Louisville
Huntington
CHARLESTON
Evansville
FRANKFORT
Lexington
WEST VIRGINIA
Carbondale
Owensboro
Richmond
Ohio
KENTUCKY
Paducah
Hopkinsville
Bowling Green
London
ARKANSAS
95°
90°
85°
80°
45°
40°

◆ *The Chicago River originally flowed into Lake Michigan, but was reversed in 1900 by the completion of a canal.*

◆ *Many US freight trains are over 2 miles (3.2 km) long, made up of almost 200 cars, and can take around 5 minutes to pass a level-crossing.*

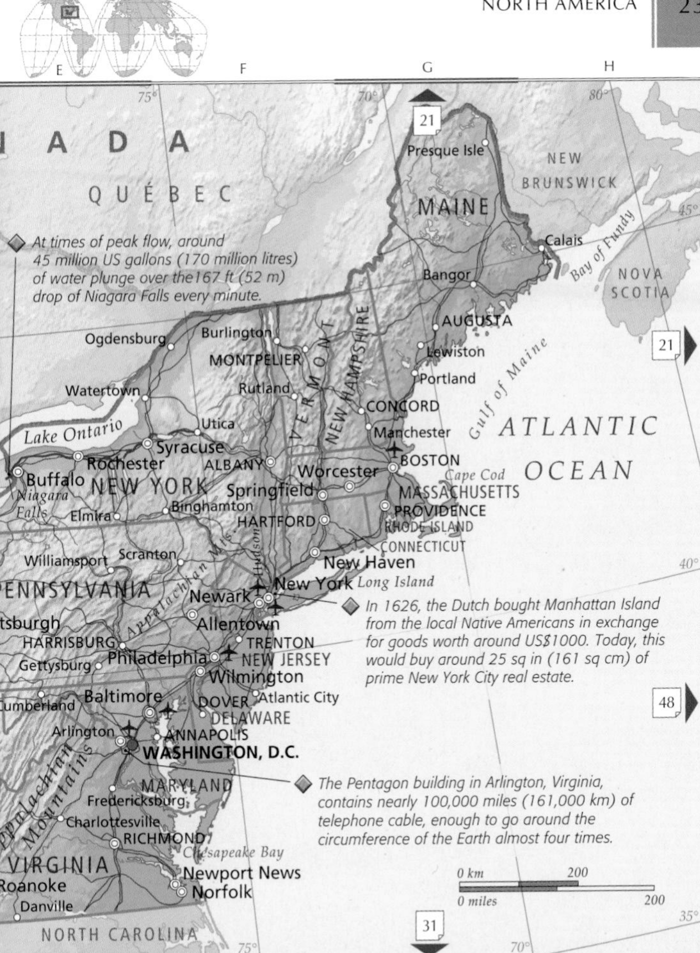
E
F
G
H
75°
70°
80°
45°
40°
35°
21
31
48
1
2
3
4
5
NADA
QUÉBEC
At times of peak flow, around 45 million US gallons (170 million litres) of water plunge over the167 ft (52 m) drop of Niagara Falls every minute.
Presque Isle
NEW BRUNSWICK
MAINE
Calais
Bay of Fundy
Bangor
NOVA SCOTIA
AUGUSTA
Lewiston
Portland
Gulf of Maine
Ogdensburg
Burlington
MONTPELIER
VERMONT
NEW HAMPSHIRE
Watertown
Rutland
CONCORD
Manchester
ATLANTIC OCEAN
Lake Ontario
Utica
Syracuse
Rochester
ALBANY
BOSTON
Cape Cod
Buffalo
NEW YORK
Worcester
Springfield
MASSACHUSETTS
Niagara Falls
Elmira
Binghamton
PROVIDENCE
HARTFORD
RHODE ISLAND
CONNECTICUT
Williamsport
Scranton
Hudson
New Haven
PENNSYLVANIA
Appalachian Mts
New York
Long Island
Newark
In 1626, the Dutch bought Manhattan Island from the local Native Americans in exchange for goods worth around US$1000. Today, this would buy around 25 sq in (161 sq cm) of prime New York City real estate.
ttsburgh
Allentown
HARRISBURG
TRENTON
Philadelphia
NEW JERSEY
Gettysburg
Wilmington
Baltimore
Atlantic City
Cumberland
DOVER
DELAWARE
Arlington
ANNAPOLIS
WASHINGTON, D.C.
Appalachian Mountains
MARYLAND
The Pentagon building in Arlington, Virginia, contains nearly 100,000 miles (161,000 km) of telephone cable, enough to go around the circumference of the Earth almost four times.
Fredericksburg
Charlottesville
RICHMOND
Chesapeake Bay
VIRGINIA
Newport News
Roanoke
Norfolk
0 km 200
0 miles 200
Danville
NORTH CAROLINA

NORTH AMERICA

USA: Central States

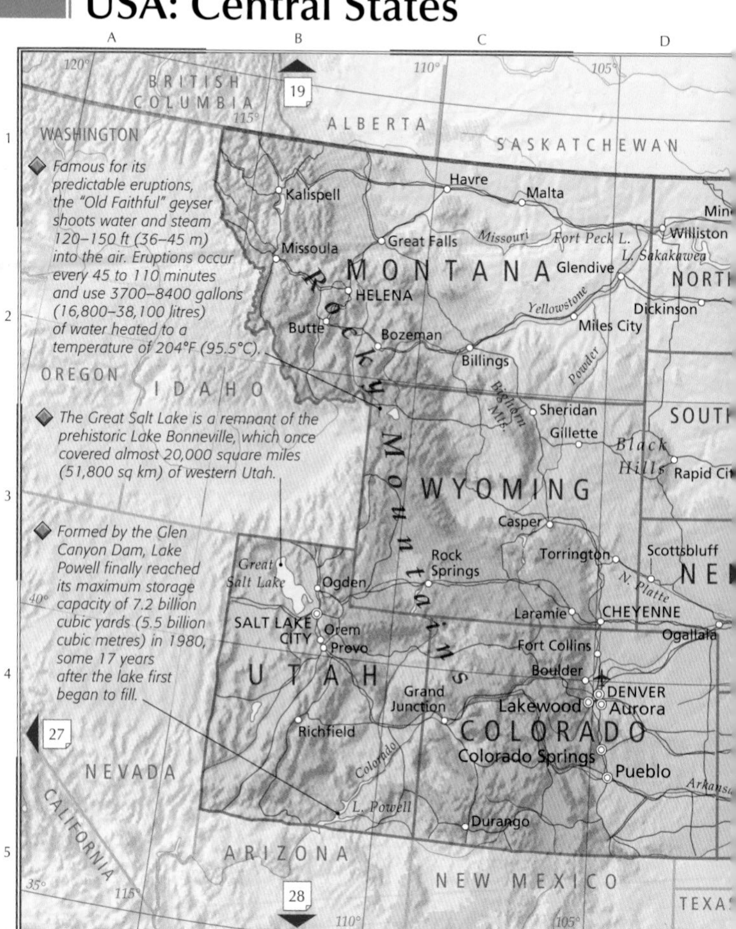
A B C D
1 2 3 4 5
BRITISH COLUMBIA
ALBERTA
SASKATCHEWAN
WASHINGTON
OREGON
IDAHO
MONTANA
WYOMING
UTAH
COLORADO
NEVADA
CALIFORNIA
ARIZONA
NEW MEXICO
TEXAS
NORTH
SOUTH
NE
Famous for its predictable eruptions, the "Old Faithful" geyser shoots water and steam 120–150 ft (36–45 m) into the air. Eruptions occur every 45 to 110 minutes and use 3700–8400 gallons (16,800–38,100 litres) of water heated to a temperature of 204°F (95.5°C).
The Great Salt Lake is a remnant of the prehistoric Lake Bonneville, which once covered almost 20,000 square miles (51,800 sq km) of western Utah.
Formed by the Glen Canyon Dam, Lake Powell finally reached its maximum storage capacity of 7.2 billion cubic yards (5.5 billion cubic metres) in 1980, some 17 years after the lake first began to fill.
Kalispell
Havre
Malta
Williston
Missoula
Great Falls
Missouri
Fort Peck L.
L. Sakakawea
Glendive
HELENA
Yellowstone
Dickinson
Butte
Bozeman
Billings
Miles City
Powder
Rocky Mountains
Bighorn Mts.
Sheridan
Gillette
Black Hills
Rapid City
Casper
Torrington
Scottsbluff
Rock Springs
N. Platte
Great Salt Lake
Ogden
SALT LAKE CITY
Orem
Provo
Laramie
CHEYENNE
Ogallala
Fort Collins
Boulder
DENVER
Aurora
Lakewood
Grand Junction
Richfield
Colorado
Colorado Springs
Pueblo
Arkansas
L. Powell
Durango
19
27
28
120°
115°
110°
105°
40°
35°

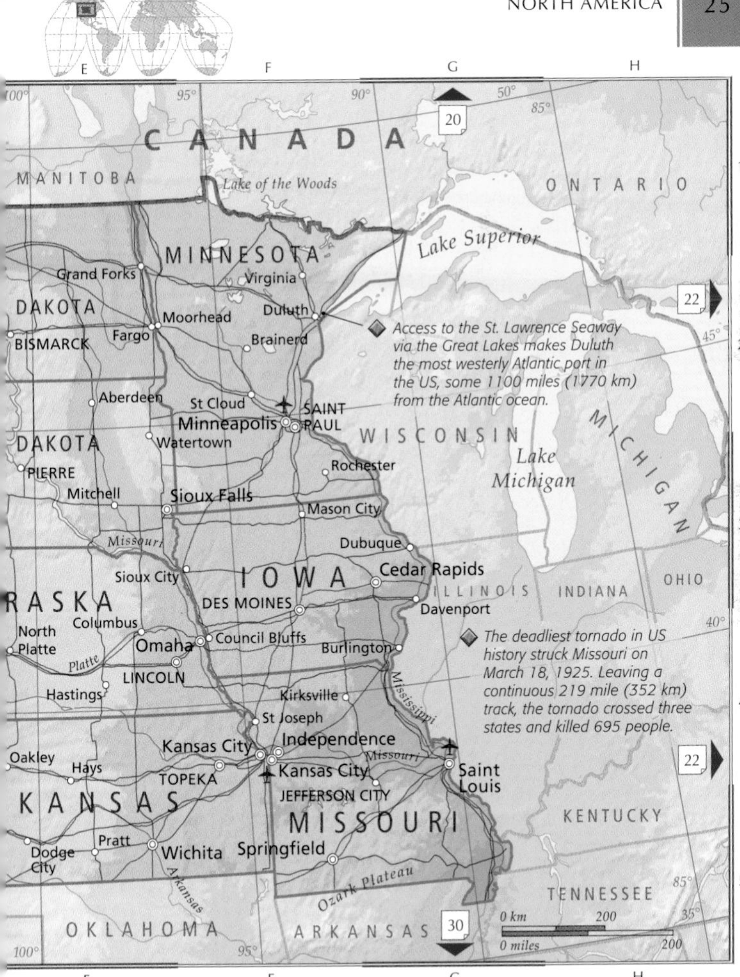
CANADA
MANITOBA
Lake of the Woods
ONTARIO
Lake Superior
MINNESOTA
Grand Forks
Virginia
DAKOTA
Moorhead
Duluth
Fargo
BISMARCK
Brainerd
Access to the St. Lawrence Seaway via the Great Lakes makes Duluth the most westerly Atlantic port in the US, some 1100 miles (1770 km) from the Atlantic ocean.
Aberdeen
St Cloud
SAINT PAUL
Minneapolis
WISCONSIN
MICHIGAN
DAKOTA
Watertown
Lake Michigan
PIERRE
Rochester
Mitchell
Sioux Falls
Mason City
Missouri
Dubuque
Sioux City
IOWA
Cedar Rapids
ILLINOIS
INDIANA
OHIO
RASKA
DES MOINES
Davenport
North Platte
Columbus
Council Bluffs
Omaha
Burlington
The deadliest tornado in US history struck Missouri on March 18, 1925. Leaving a continuous 219 mile (352 km) track, the tornado crossed three states and killed 695 people.
Platte
LINCOLN
Hastings
Kirksville
Mississippi
St Joseph
Independence
Kansas City
Missouri
Oakley
Hays
Kansas City
Saint Louis
TOPEKA
JEFFERSON CITY
KANSAS
MISSOURI
KENTUCKY
Pratt
Dodge City
Wichita
Springfield
Ozark Plateau
Arkansas
TENNESSEE
OKLAHOMA
ARKANSAS
0 km 200
0 miles 200
E F G H
1 2 3 4 5
100° 95° 90° 85° 50° 45° 40° 35°
20 22 22 30

NORTH AMERICA

USA: The West

CANADA
ALBERTA
BRITISH COLUMBIA
The Boeing aircraft factory in Everett is the world's largest building by volume at 472 million cu ft (13.3 million cu m), covering 100 acres (40 hectares).
Vancouver Island
Bellingham
Port Angeles
Everett
Seattle
Bellevue
Tacoma
Spokane
Coeur d'Alene
Cascade Range
Columbia
135
Aberdeen
OLYMPIA
Ellensburg
MONTANA
24
19
19
WASHINGTON
Yakima
Richland
Kennewick
Walla Walla
Lewiston
Bitterroot Range
Hells Canyon is the deepest in the US, with cliffs up to 7993 ft (2436 m) high.
Astoria
Longview
Vancouver
Portland
Pendleton
Blue Mts.
La Grande
SALEM
Newport
Albany
Corvallis
Baker
Snake
Hells Canyon
Coast Ranges
Eugene
Springfield
Bend
Cascade Range
IDAHO
Coos Bay
Bandon
Burns
Caldwell
Nampa
BOISE
Idaho Falls
OREGON
American Falls Res.
Pocatello
Medford
Twin Falls
Klamath Falls
Crescent City
Goose Lake
Alturas
Weed
Great Basin

At Black Rock Desert on October 15, 1997, ThrustSSC, driven by Andy Green, became the first land vehicle to break the sound barrier by achieving a speed of 763 mph (1228 km/h).
Death Valley is not only the lowest point in North America, at -282 ft (-86 m) below sea level, it is also the hottest, with a maximum air temperature of 134°F (57°C) recorded in 1913.
The Golden Gate Bridge, completed in 1937, has 80,000 miles (129,000 km) of wire in its two main cables, weighing a total of 22,200 tons (tonnes).
UTAH
NEVADA
ARIZONA
CALIFORNIA
MEXICO
PACIFIC OCEAN
Elko
Ely
Tonopah
Hawthorne
Fallon
CARSON CITY
Sparks
Reno
Susanville
Pyramid Lake
Lake Tahoe
Humboldt
Las Vegas
Lake Mead
Colorado
Death Valley
Mt Whitney 14,495 ft (4418m)
-282 ft (-86m)
Mojave Desert
Sierra Nevada
Coast Ranges
Ranges
San Joaquin Valley
Redding
Chico
Yuba City
SACRAMENTO
Stockton
Modesto
Oakland
Berkeley
San Francisco
Santa Rosa
Ukiah
San Jose
Santa Cruz
Salinas
Monterey
Merced
Fresno
Visalia
Bishop
Bakersfield
Mojave
Lancaster
Barstow
Pasadena
San Bernardino
Riverside
Palm Springs
Santa Ana
Oceanside
Salton Sea
San Diego
Chula Vista
Los Angeles
Long Beach
Huntington Beach
Oxnard
Santa Barbara
Santa Rosa I.
Channel Islands
Santa Catalina I.
San Nicolas I.
San Clemente I.
0 km 200
0 miles 200
40°
35°
120°
115°
28
32
32
135
A B C D E
5 6 7 8

USA: The Southwest

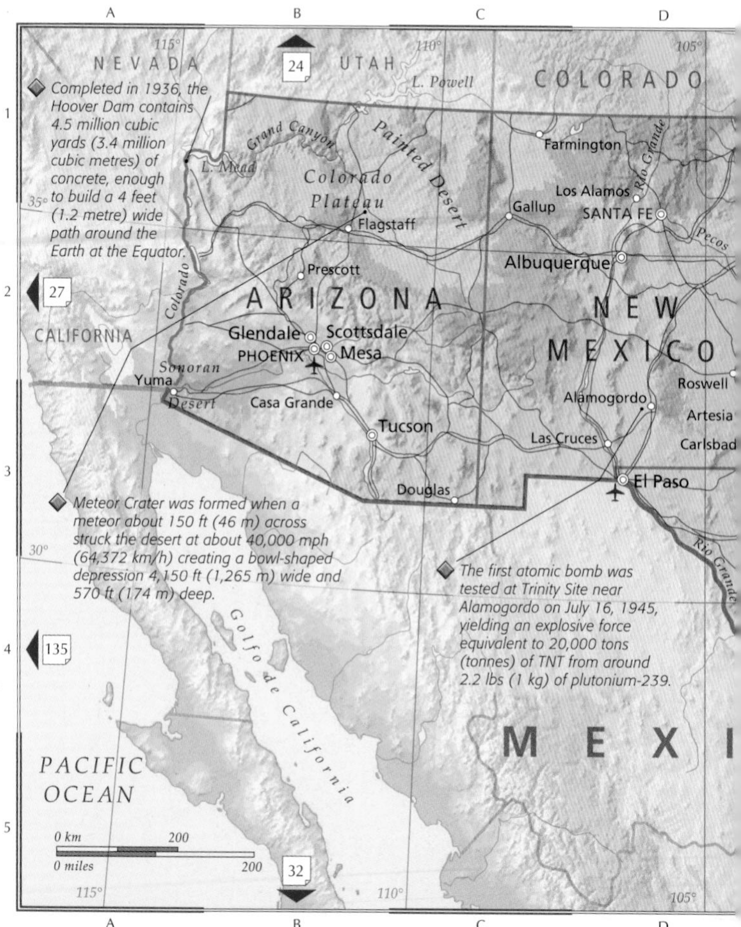
A
B
C
D
1
2
3
4
5
24
27
135
32
NEVADA
UTAH
COLORADO
CALIFORNIA
ARIZONA
NEW MEXICO
MEXI
PACIFIC OCEAN
Completed in 1936, the Hoover Dam contains 4.5 million cubic yards (3.4 million cubic metres) of concrete, enough to build a 4 feet (1.2 metre) wide path around the Earth at the Equator.
Meteor Crater was formed when a meteor about 150 ft (46 m) across struck the desert at about 40,000 mph (64,372 km/h) creating a bowl-shaped depression 4,150 ft (1,265 m) wide and 570 ft (174 m) deep.
The first atomic bomb was tested at Trinity Site near Alamogordo on July 16, 1945, yielding an explosive force equivalent to 20,000 tons (tonnes) of TNT from around 2.2 lbs (1 kg) of plutonium-239.
L. Powell
L. Mead
Grand Canyon
Painted Desert
Colorado Plateau
Colorado
Sonoran Desert
Golfo de California
Rio Grande
Pecos
Farmington
Los Alamos
Gallup
SANTA FE
Flagstaff
Albuquerque
Prescott
Glendale
Scottsdale
PHOENIX
Mesa
Yuma
Casa Grande
Tucson
Douglas
Roswell
Alamogordo
Artesia
Las Cruces
Carlsbad
El Paso
115°
110°
105°
35°
30°
0 km
200
0 miles
200

KANSAS
OKLAHOMA
OKLAHOMA CITY
Ponca City
Enid
Tulsa
Broken Arrow
Shawnee
Norman
Lawton
Borger
Pampa
Amarillo
Canadian
Clovis
Red River
Vernon
Wichita Falls
Paris
Lubbock
Brownfield
Denton
Arlington
Fort Worth
Dallas
Longview
Tyler
Hobbs
Sweetwater
Abilene
Jacksonville
Big Spring
Odessa
Midland
Brazos
Waco
Toledo Bend Res.
Colorado
San Angelo
Neches
Pecos
TEXAS
Bryan
L. Travis
AUSTIN
Edwards Plateau
Houston
Pasadena
San Antonio
Texas City
Galveston
Del Rio
Victoria
Freeport
Eagle Pass
Corpus Christi
Laredo
Kingsville
Padre Island
Rio Grande
Brownsville
ARKANSAS
LOUISIANA
Beaumont
Port Arthur
Gulf of Mexico
CO
The world's first parking meter was installed in Oklahoma City on July 16, 1935.
On January 10, 1901, the Lucas Gusher blew oil 150 ft (46 m) into the air, flowing at 100,000 barrels a day until it was eventually capped nine days later.
With winds estimated at over 145 mph (233 km/h), the 1900 Galveston Hurricane claimed over 8000 lives, making it the deadliest natural disaster in US history.
100°
95°
35°
30°
25°
E
F
G
H
1
2
3
4
5
25
30
33

USA: The Southeast

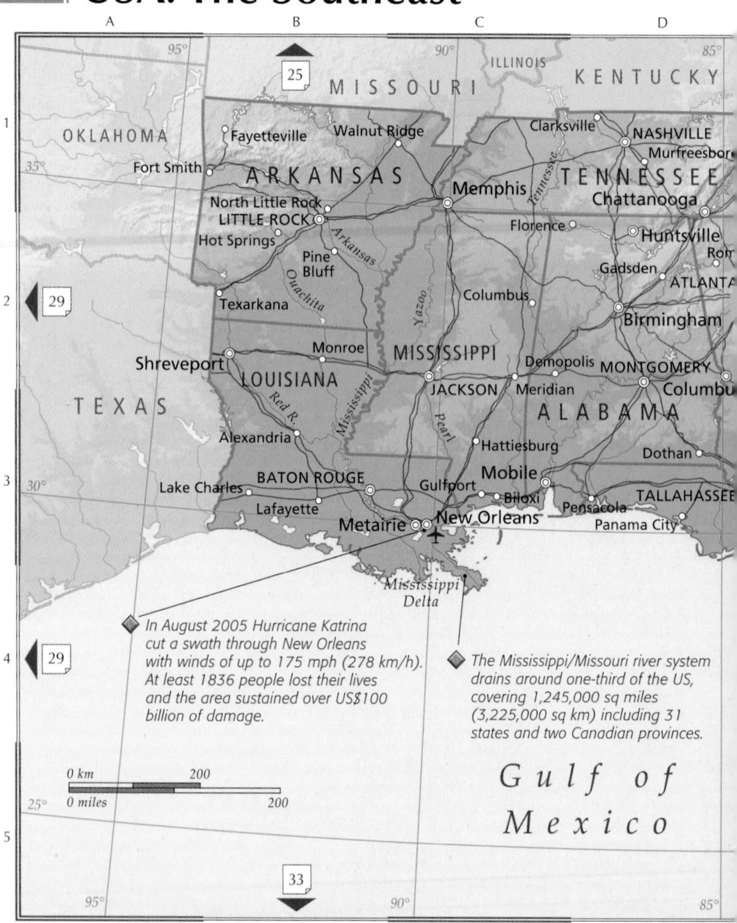

A
B
C
D
1
2
3
4
5
95°
90°
85°
35°
30°
25°
25
29
29
33
MISSOURI
ILLINOIS
KENTUCKY
OKLAHOMA
ARKANSAS
TENNESSEE
MISSISSIPPI
LOUISIANA
ALABAMA
TEXAS
Fayetteville
Walnut Ridge
Fort Smith
North Little Rock
LITTLE ROCK
Hot Springs
Pine Bluff
Texarkana
Memphis
Clarksville
NASHVILLE
Murfreesbor
Chattanooga
Florence
Huntsville
Gadsden
ATLANTA
Birmingham
Columbus
Monroe
Shreveport
JACKSON
Meridian
Demopolis
MONTGOMERY
Columbu
Alexandria
Hattiesburg
Dothan
Mobile
Lake Charles
BATON ROUGE
Lafayette
Gulfport
Biloxi
Pensacola
TALLAHASSEE
Panama City
Metairie
New Orleans
Arkansas
Ouachita
Yazoo
Tennessee
Mississippi
Red R.
Pearl
Mississippi Delta
In August 2005 Hurricane Katrina cut a swath through New Orleans with winds of up to 175 mph (278 km/h). At least 1836 people lost their lives and the area sustained over US$100 billion of damage.
The Mississippi/Missouri river system drains around one-third of the US, covering 1,245,000 sq miles (3,225,000 sq km) including 31 states and two Canadian provinces.
Gulf of Mexico
0 km
200
0 miles
200

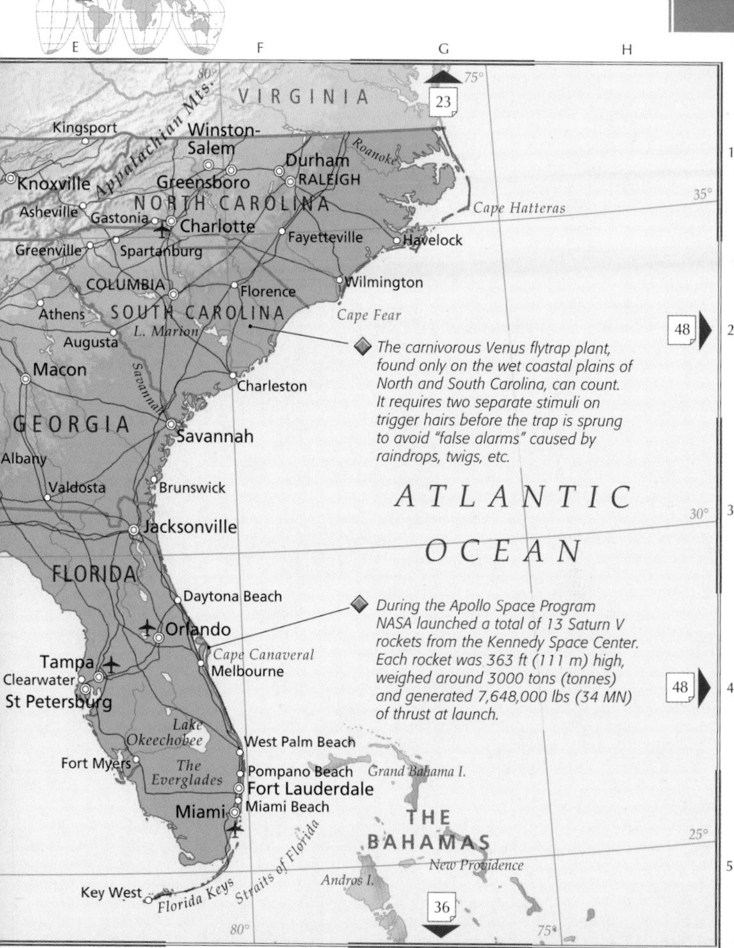
E
F
G
H
VIRGINIA
23
Appalachian Mts.
Kingsport
Winston-Salem
Roanoke
Durham
RALEIGH
Knoxville
Greensboro
NORTH CAROLINA
Asheville
Gastonia
Charlotte
Cape Hatteras
35°
Fayetteville
Havelock
Greenville
Spartanburg
COLUMBIA
Wilmington
Florence
Athens
SOUTH CAROLINA
Cape Fear
L. Marion
Augusta
Savannah
Macon
Charleston
GEORGIA
Savannah
Albany
Valdosta
Brunswick
ATLANTIC
OCEAN
Jacksonville
30°
FLORIDA
Daytona Beach
Orlando
Cape Canaveral
Melbourne
Tampa
Clearwater
St Petersburg
Lake Okeechobee
West Palm Beach
Fort Myers
The Everglades
Pompano Beach
Grand Bahama I.
Fort Lauderdale
Miami Beach
Miami
THE BAHAMAS
New Providence
25°
Andros I.
Key West
Florida Keys
Straits of Florida
36
80°
75°
48
48
1
2
3
4
5

The carnivorous Venus flytrap plant, found only on the wet coastal plains of North and South Carolina, can count. It requires two separate stimuli on trigger hairs before the trap is sprung to avoid "false alarms" caused by raindrops, twigs, etc.

During the Apollo Space Program NASA launched a total of 13 Saturn V rockets from the Kennedy Space Center. Each rocket was 363 ft (111 m) high, weighed around 3000 tons (tonnes) and generated 7,648,000 lbs (34 MN) of thrust at launch.

Mexico

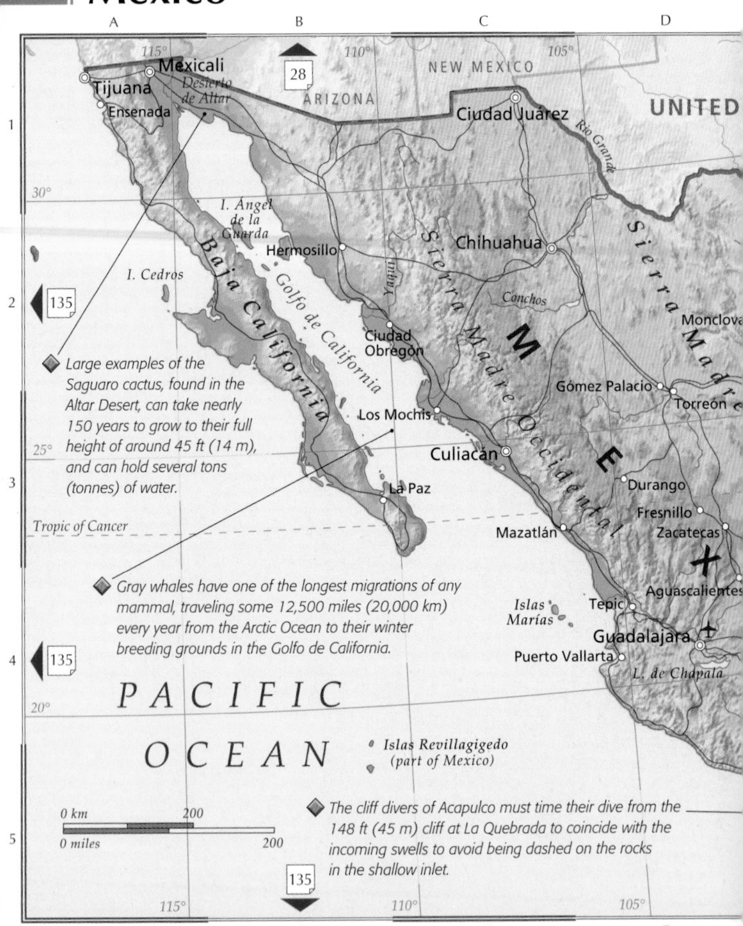
A
B
C
D
1
2
3
4
5
115°
110°
105°
30°
25°
20°
28
135
135
135
Mexicali
Tijuana
Ensenada
Desierto de Altar
ARIZONA
NEW MEXICO
UNITED
Ciudad Juárez
Río Grande
I. Ángel de la Guarda
Hermosillo
I. Cedros
Baja California
Golfo de California
Yaqui
Sierra Madre Occidental
Chihuahua
Conchos
Sierra Madre
Monclova
Ciudad Obregón
M
E
X
Gómez Palacio
Torreón
Los Mochis
Culiacán
La Paz
Durango
Fresnillo
Zacatecas
Mazatlán
Tropic of Cancer
Aguascalientes
Tepic
Islas Marías
Guadalajara
Puerto Vallarta
L. de Chapala
PACIFIC
OCEAN
Islas Revillagigedo (part of Mexico)
0 km
200
0 miles
200
Large examples of the Saguaro cactus, found in the Altar Desert, can take nearly 150 years to grow to their full height of around 45 ft (14 m), and can hold several tons (tonnes) of water.
Gray whales have one of the longest migrations of any mammal, traveling some 12,500 miles (20,000 km) every year from the Arctic Ocean to their winter breeding grounds in the Golfo de California.
The cliff divers of Acapulco must time their dive from the 148 ft (45 m) cliff at La Quebrada to coincide with the incoming swells to avoid being dashed on the rocks in the shallow inlet.

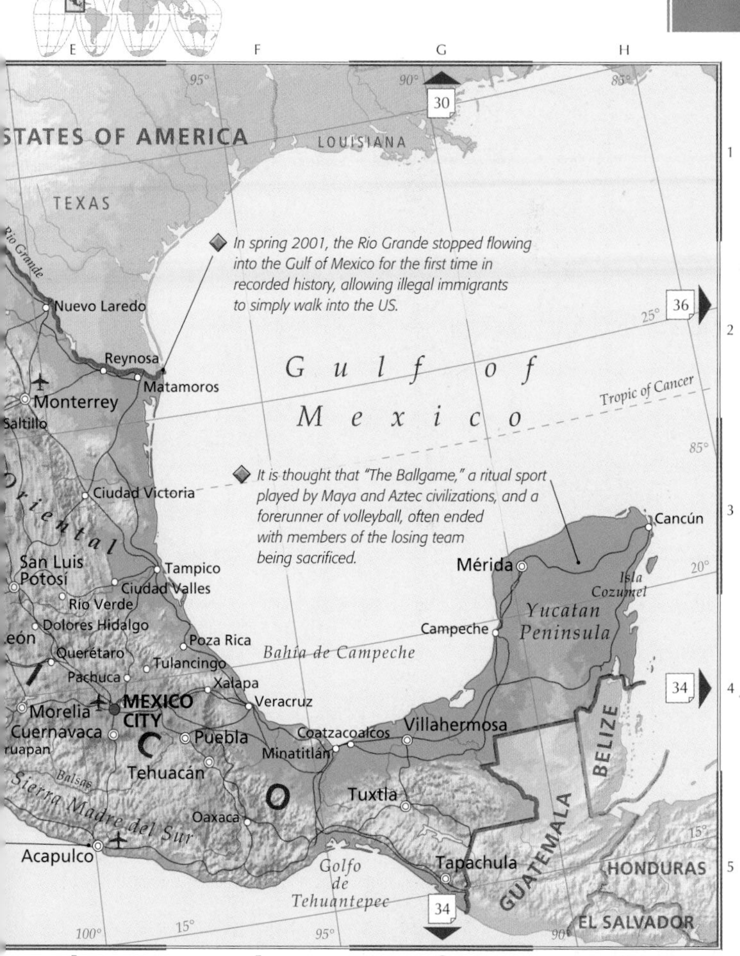
STATES OF AMERICA
LOUISIANA
TEXAS
Rio Grande
In spring 2001, the Rio Grande stopped flowing into the Gulf of Mexico for the first time in recorded history, allowing illegal immigrants to simply walk into the US.
Nuevo Laredo
Reynosa
Matamoros
Monterrey
Saltillo
Gulf of Mexico
Tropic of Cancer
It is thought that "The Ballgame," a ritual sport played by Maya and Aztec civilizations, and a forerunner of volleyball, often ended with members of the losing team being sacrificed.
Ciudad Victoria
Cancún
Mérida
Isla Cozumel
Yucatan Peninsula
San Luis Potosí
Tampico
Ciudad Valles
Río Verde
Dolores Hidalgo
León
Campeche
Poza Rica
Querétaro
Tulancingo
Bahía de Campeche
Pachuca
Xalapa
MEXICO CITY
Morelia
Veracruz
Cuernavaca
Puebla
Coatzacoalcos
Villahermosa
Minatitlán
Tehuacán
Balsas
Sierra Madre del Sur
Tuxtla
BELIZE
GUATEMALA
Oaxaca
Acapulco
Golfo de Tehuantepec
Tapachula
HONDURAS
EL SALVADOR
30
36
34
34
E F G H
1 2 3 4 5

Central America

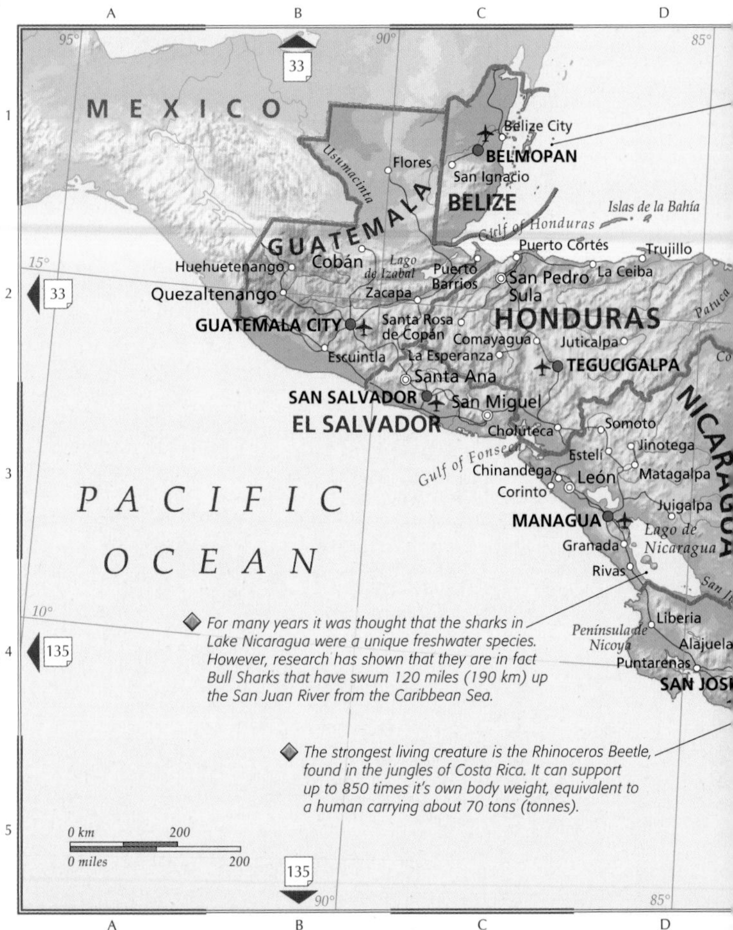
A
B
C
D
1
2
3
4
5
95°
90°
85°
15°
10°
33
135
MEXICO
GUATEMALA
BELIZE
HONDURAS
EL SALVADOR
NICARAGUA
PACIFIC OCEAN
Usumacinta
Belize City
BELMOPAN
Flores
San Ignacio
Islas de la Bahía
Gulf of Honduras
Puerto Cortés
Trujillo
La Ceiba
Cobán
Lago de Izabal
Puerto Barrios
San Pedro Sula
Huehuetenango
Quezaltenango
Zacapa
Patuca
GUATEMALA CITY
Santa Rosa de Copán
Comayagua
Juticalpa
Escuintla
La Esperanza
TEGUCIGALPA
Santa Ana
SAN SALVADOR
San Miguel
Choluteca
Somoto
Gulf of Fonseca
Estelí
Jinotega
Chinandega
León
Matagalpa
Corinto
Juigalpa
MANAGUA
Lago de Nicaragua
Granada
Rivas
Liberia
Península de Nicoya
Alajuela
Puntarenas
0 km
200
0 miles
200

For many years it was thought that the sharks in Lake Nicaragua were a unique freshwater species. However, research has shown that they are in fact Bull Sharks that have swum 120 miles (190 km) up the San Juan River from the Caribbean Sea.

The strongest living creature is the Rhinoceros Beetle, found in the jungles of Costa Rica. It can support up to 850 times it's own body weight, equivalent to a human carrying about 70 tons (tonnes).

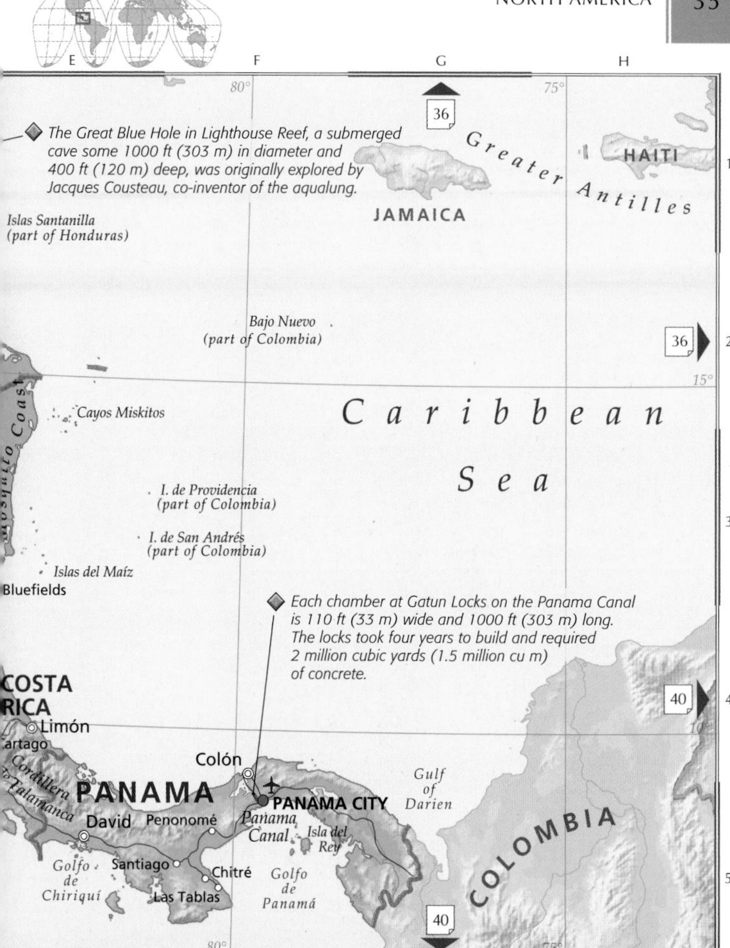
E
F
G
H
80°
75°
36
The Great Blue Hole in Lighthouse Reef, a submerged cave some 1000 ft (303 m) in diameter and 400 ft (120 m) deep, was originally explored by Jacques Cousteau, co-inventor of the aqualung.
Greater Antilles
HAITI
JAMAICA
1
Islas Santanilla (part of Honduras)
Bajo Nuevo (part of Colombia)
36
2
15°
Cayos Miskitos
Mosquito Coast
Caribbean
Sea
I. de Providencia (part of Colombia)
I. de San Andrés (part of Colombia)
3
Islas del Maíz
Bluefields
Each chamber at Gatun Locks on the Panama Canal is 110 ft (33 m) wide and 1000 ft (303 m) long. The locks took four years to build and required 2 million cubic yards (1.5 million cu m) of concrete.
COSTA RICA
40
4
Limón
artago
Colón
Cordillera de Talamanca
PANAMA
Gulf of Darien
PANAMA CITY
David
Penonomé
Panama Canal
Isla del Rey
COLOMBIA
Golfo de Chiriquí
Santiago
Chitré
Golfo de Panamá
5
Las Tablas
40
80°
75°
E
F
G
H

The Caribbean

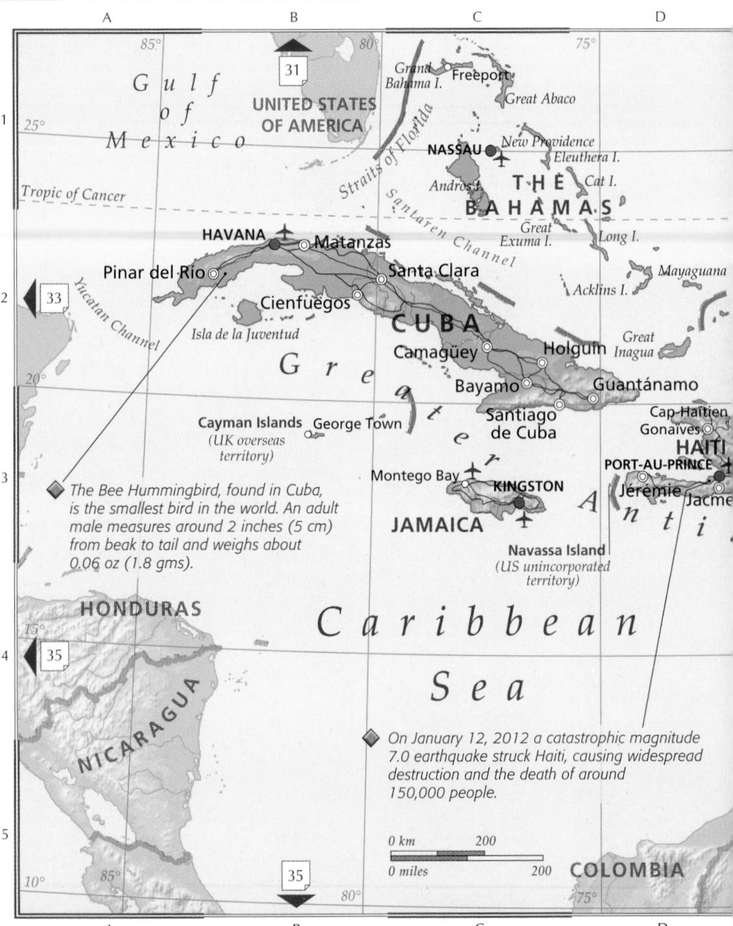
A
B
C
D
1
2
3
4
5
85°
80°
75°
25°
20°
15°
10°
31
33
35
Gulf of Mexico
UNITED STATES OF AMERICA
Straits of Florida
Grand Bahama I.
Freeport
Great Abaco
NASSAU
New Providence
Eleuthera I.
Andros I.
THE BAHAMAS
Cat I.
Tropic of Cancer
Santaren Channel
Great Exuma I.
Long I.
HAVANA
Matanzas
Pinar del Río
Santa Clara
Mayaguana
Acklins I.
Yucatan Channel
Cienfuegos
Isla de la Juventud
CUBA
Great Inagua
Camagüey
Holguín
Bayamo
Guantánamo
Greater Antilles
Cayman Islands
(UK overseas territory)
George Town
Santiago de Cuba
Cap-Haïtien
Gonaïves
HAITI
PORT-AU-PRINCE
Montego Bay
KINGSTON
Jérémie
JAMAICA
Navassa Island
(US unincorporated territory)
HONDURAS
Caribbean Sea
NICARAGUA
0 km
200
0 miles
200
COLOMBIA

The Bee Hummingbird, found in Cuba, is the smallest bird in the world. An adult male measures around 2 inches (5 cm) from beak to tail and weighs about 0.06 oz (1.8 gms).

On January 12, 2012 a catastrophic magnitude 7.0 earthquake struck Haiti, causing widespread destruction and the death of around 150,000 people.

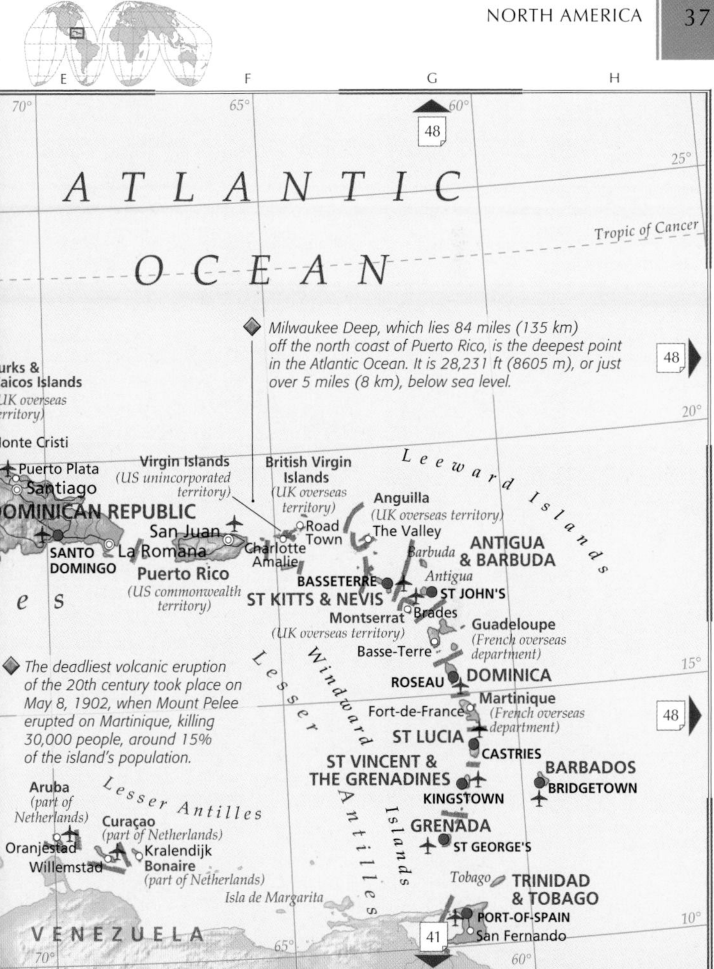
E
F
G
H
70°
65°
60°
48
25°
1
ATLANTIC
OCEAN
Tropic of Cancer
Milwaukee Deep, which lies 84 miles (135 km) off the north coast of Puerto Rico, is the deepest point in the Atlantic Ocean. It is 28,231 ft (8605 m), or just over 5 miles (8 km), below sea level.
48
2
Turks & Caicos Islands
(UK overseas territory)
20°
Monte Cristi
Leeward Islands
Puerto Plata
Santiago
DOMINICAN REPUBLIC
Virgin Islands
(US unincorporated territory)
British Virgin Islands
(UK overseas territory)
Anguilla
(UK overseas territory)
San Juan
Road Town
The Valley
3
SANTO DOMINGO
La Romana
Charlotte Amalie
Barbuda
ANTIGUA & BARBUDA
Puerto Rico
(US commonwealth territory)
BASSETERRE
Antigua
ST KITTS & NEVIS
ST JOHN'S
Montserrat
(UK overseas territory)
Brades
Guadeloupe
(French overseas department)
Basse-Terre
15°
The deadliest volcanic eruption of the 20th century took place on May 8, 1902, when Mount Pelee erupted on Martinique, killing 30,000 people, around 15% of the island's population.
Lesser Antilles
Windward Islands
ROSEAU
DOMINICA
Martinique
(French overseas department)
Fort-de-France
48
4
ST LUCIA
CASTRIES
ST VINCENT & THE GRENADINES
BARBADOS
BRIDGETOWN
KINGSTOWN
Aruba
(part of Netherlands)
Lesser Antilles
Curaçao
(part of Netherlands)
GRENADA
ST GEORGE'S
Oranjestad
Kralendijk
Willemstad
Bonaire
(part of Netherlands)
Tobago
TRINIDAD & TOBAGO
5
Isla de Margarita
PORT-OF-SPAIN
VENEZUELA
41
San Fernando
10°
65°
70°
60°
E
F
G
H

South America

Greater Antilles
Jamaica
Hispaniola
Puerto Rico
Lesser Antilles
Caribbean Sea
ATLANTIC
OCEAN
Trinidad
(claimed by Venezuela)
French Guiana (France)
VENEZUELA
GUYANA
SURINAME
COLOMBIA
Orinoco
Llanos
Meta
Cauca
Magdalena
Guiana Highlands
(claimed by Suriname)
Equator
ECUADOR
Chimborazo 20,702ft (6310m)
Putumayo
Napo
Marañón
Ucayali
Río Negro
Represa Balbina
Içá
Amazon Basin
Amazon
Juruá
Purus
Madeira
Tapajós
BRAZIL
Planalto da Borborema
São Francisco
Represa de Sobradinho
PERU
Andes
Xingu
Araguaia
Tocantins
Chapada dos Parecis
Beni
Lake Titicaca
Altiplano
Pantanal
BOLIVIA
Planalto de Mato Grosso
Brazilian Highlands

17
48
17
49

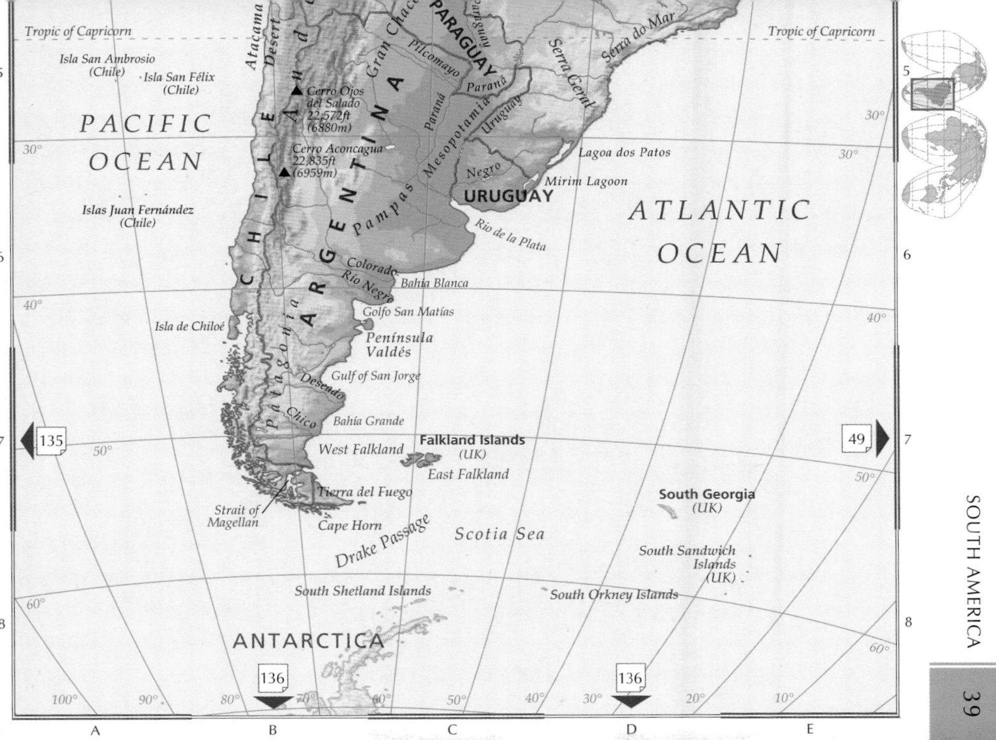

Tropic of Capricorn
Tropic of Capricorn
Isla San Ambrosio (Chile)
Isla San Félix (Chile)
Atacama Desert
Andes
Gran Chaco
PARAGUAY
Paraguay
Pilcomayo
Paraná
Serra do Mar
Serra Geral
Cerro Ojos del Salado 22,572ft (6880m)
PACIFIC OCEAN
Paraná
Uruguay
Mesopotamia
Cerro Aconcagua 22,835ft (6959m)
Lagoa dos Patos
Negro
Mirim Lagoon
URUGUAY
Islas Juan Fernández (Chile)
CHILE
ARGENTINA
Pampas
ATLANTIC OCEAN
Río de la Plata
Colorado
Río Negro
Bahía Blanca
Golfo San Matías
Isla de Chiloé
Península Valdés
Patagonia
Gulf of San Jorge
Deseado
Chico
Bahía Grande
135
49
Falkland Islands (UK)
West Falkland
East Falkland
Tierra del Fuego
South Georgia (UK)
Strait of Magellan
Cape Horn
Drake Passage
Scotia Sea
South Sandwich Islands (UK)
South Shetland Islands
South Orkney Islands
ANTARCTICA
136
136

Northern South America

Caribbean Sea
PACIFIC OCEAN
PANAMA
COLOMBIA
ECUADOR
PERU
VENE
Gulf of Venezuela
Lago de Maracaibo
Golfo de Guayaquil
0° Equator
Santa Marta
Ríohacha
Barranquilla
Cartagena
Valledupar
Maicao
Coro
Maracaibo
Cabimas
CARACA
Maracay
Valencia
Ciudad Ojeda
Barquisimeto
Acarigua
Valera
San Juan de los Morros
Mérida
Guanare
Barinas
Sincelejo
Montería
Cúcuta
San Cristóbal
San Fernando
Bucaramanga
Barrancabermeja
Arauca
Bello
Medellín
Itagüí
Quibdó
Tunja
Yopal
Puerto Carreño
Manizales
Pereira
BOGOTÁ
Armenia
Ibagué
Buenaventura
Villavicencio
Cali
Popayán
Neiva
San José del Guaviare
Florencia
Pasto
Mocoa
Esmeraldas
Tulcán
Mitú
Ibarra
QUITO
Santo Domingo de los Colorados
Manta
Ambato
Portoviejo
Riobamba
Guayaquil
Milagro
Cuenca
Machala
Loja
Cauca
Magdalena
Arauca
Apure
Guanare
Meta
Guaviare
Aguarico
Caquetá
Putumayo
Andes
36
35
135
42
The first coffee seedlings were brought to Colombia in 1804 by Jesuit missionaries; today, Colombia produces over 700,000 tons (tonnes) of coffee beans every year.
Colombia has the highest number of species by area in the world. There are over 1700 endemic bird species; more than all of Europe and North America combined.

E
F
G
H
65°
60°
55°
Antilles
GRENADA
37
Isla de Margarita
Carúpano
TRINIDAD & TOBAGO
ATLANTIC OCEAN
1
Cumaná
Barcelona
The Serpent's Mouth
10°
Maturín
Tucupita
El Tigre
Orinoco
Ciudad Guayana
Ciudad Bolívar
Embalse de Guri
(claimed by Venezuela)
ZUELA
Cuyuni
GEORGETOWN
Nieuw Amsterdam
49
2
New Amsterdam
St.-Laurent-du-Maroni
Bartica
Salto Ángel
Rockstone
Linden
PARAMARIBO
Sinnamary
Kourou
GUYANA
Caura
Caroní
Paragua
W.J. van Blommesteinmeer
5°
Guiana Highlands
CAYENNE
SURINAME
French Guiana
(French overseas department)
Orinoco
Essequibo
Courantyne
Marowijne
3
Acarai Mts.
(claimed by Suriname)
(claimed by Suriname)
Equator 0°
4
Amazon Basin
BRAZIL
43
0 km 200
0 miles 200
5
43
65°
60°
55°
5°
E
F
G
H

The Guiana Shield is one of the Earth's oldest surfaces, formed around 2 billion years ago.

Angel Falls (Salto Ángel) plunge a total of 3212 ft (979 m) to form the world's highest waterfall.

The European Space Agency launch facility at Kourou takes advantage of the Earth's spin near the equator to gain 10 percent more payload than an equivalent launch at Cape Canaveral in the US.

2.47 acres (one hectare) of Amazon rain forest can contain more than 750 types of trees and 1500 plant species, amounting to around 900 tons (tonnes) of living plant material.

Peru, Bolivia & North Brazil

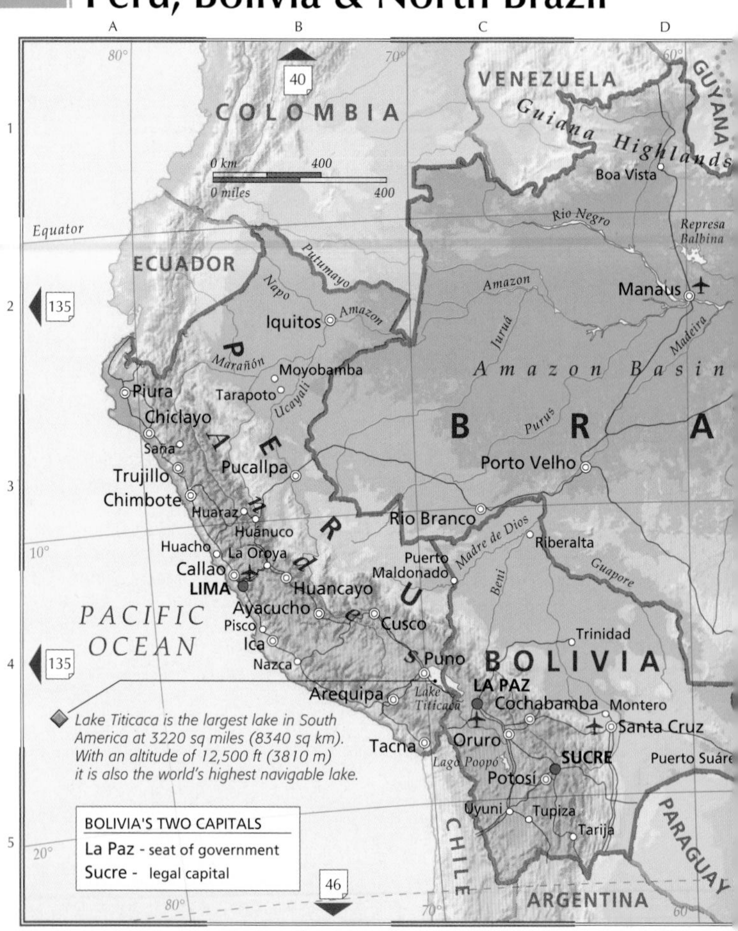

A
B
C
D
1
2
3
4
5
80°
70°
60°
40
135
46
COLOMBIA
VENEZUELA
GUYANA
Guiana Highlands
Boa Vista
0 km 400
0 miles 400
Equator
Rio Negro
Represa Balbina
ECUADOR
Putumayo
Napo
Amazon
Manaus
Iquitos
Juruá
Madeira
PERU
Marañón
Moyobamba
Amazon Basin
Piura
Tarapoto
Ucayali
Chiclayo
BRAZIL
Purus
Saña
Andes
Pucallpa
Porto Velho
Trujillo
Chimbote
Huaraz
Rio Branco
Huánuco
Madre de Dios
Riberalta
Huacho
La Oroya
Puerto Maldonado
Guapore
10°
Callao
Beni
LIMA
Huancayo
PACIFIC OCEAN
Ayacucho
Cusco
Pisco
Ica
Trinidad
Nazca
Puno
BOLIVIA
LA PAZ
Arequipa
Lake Titicaca
Cochabamba
Montero
Santa Cruz
Tacna
Oruro
Lago Poopó
SUCRE
Puerto Suáre
Potosí
Uyuni
Tupiza
PARAGUAY
Tarija
CHILE
20°
ARGENTINA

Lake Titicaca is the largest lake in South America at 3220 sq miles (8340 sq km). With an altitude of 12,500 ft (3810 m) it is also the world's highest navigable lake.

BOLIVIA'S TWO CAPITALS	
La Paz	seat of government
Sucre	legal capital

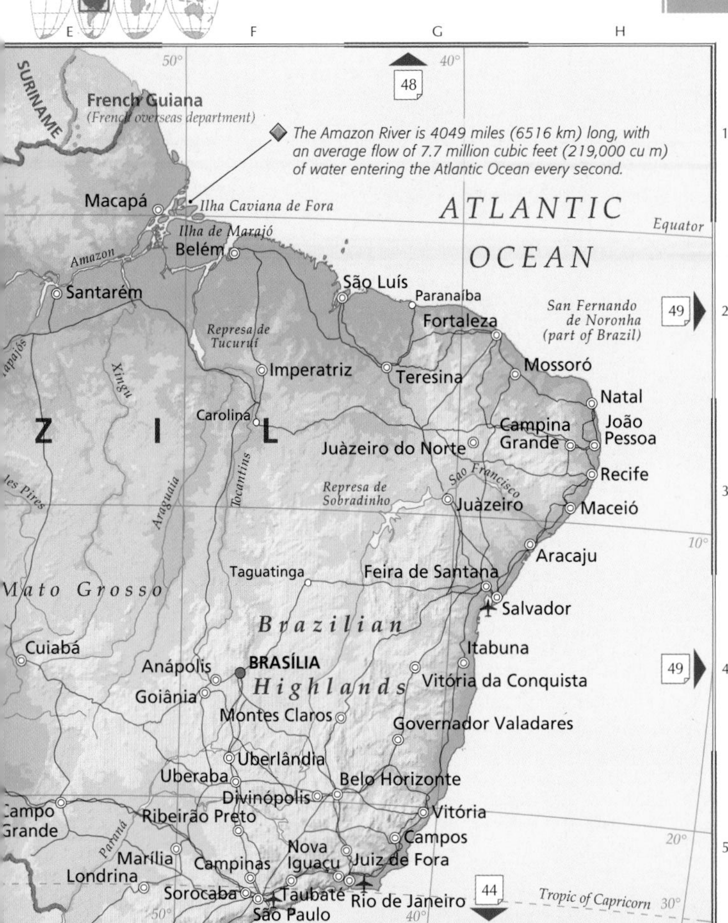
E
F
G
H
1
2
3
4
5
50°
40°
48
SURINAME
French Guiana
(French overseas department)
The Amazon River is 4049 miles (6516 km) long, with an average flow of 7.7 million cubic feet (219,000 cu m) of water entering the Atlantic Ocean every second.
Macapá
Ilha Caviana de Fora
ATLANTIC
OCEAN
Equator
Ilha de Marajó
Belém
Amazon
Santarém
São Luís
Paranaíba
San Fernando de Noronha (part of Brazil)
49
Fortaleza
Represa de Tucuruí
Tapajós
Xingu
Imperatriz
Teresina
Mossoró
Natal
Carolina
Z
I
L
Campina Grande
João Pessoa
Juàzeiro do Norte
Recife
Tocantins
Araguaia
Represa de Sobradinho
São Francisco
Juàzeiro
Maceió
Teles Pires
10°
Aracaju
Taguatinga
Feira de Santana
Mato Grosso
Salvador
Brazilian
Highlands
Itabuna
Cuiabá
Anápolis
BRASÍLIA
Vitória da Conquista
Goiânia
49
Montes Claros
Governador Valadares
Uberlândia
Uberaba
Belo Horizonte
Divinópolis
Campo Grande
Ribeirão Preto
Vitória
Paraná
Campos
20°
Nova Iguaçu
Marília
Campinas
Juiz de Fora
Londrina
44
Sorocaba
Taubaté
Rio de Janeiro
Tropic of Capricorn
30°
São Paulo
50°
40°

Paraguay, Uruguay & South Brazil

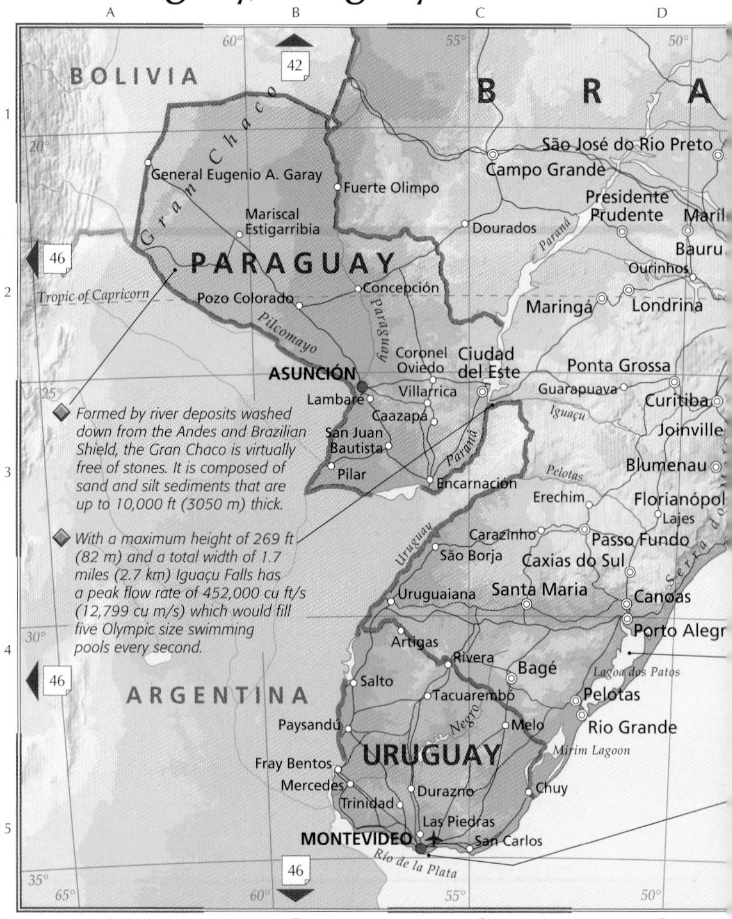
A
B
C
D
1
2
3
4
5
60°
55°
50°
65°
20°
25°
30°
35°
42
46
46
46
BOLIVIA
B R A
Gran Chaco
São José do Rio Preto
Campo Grande
General Eugenio A. Garay
Fuerte Olimpo
Presidente Prudente
Marília
Mariscal Estigarribia
Dourados
Paraná
Bauru
PARAGUAY
Ourinhos
Tropic of Capricorn
Concepción
Pozo Colorado
Paraguay
Maringá
Londrina
Pilcomayo
Coronel Oviedo
Ciudad del Este
Ponta Grossa
ASUNCIÓN
Villarrica
Guarapuava
Curitiba
Lambaré
Iguaçu
Caazapá
Joinville
San Juan Bautista
Pilar
Blumenau
Pelotas
Encarnación
Erechim
Florianópolis
Lajes
Carazinho
Passo Fundo
Uruguay
São Borja
Caxias do Sul
Uruguaiana
Santa Maria
Canoas
Porto Alegre
Artigas
Rivera
Bagé
Lagoa dos Patos
Salto
Tacuarembó
Pelotas
ARGENTINA
Negro
Melo
Rio Grande
Paysandú
Mirim Lagoon
URUGUAY
Fray Bentos
Mercedes
Durazno
Chuy
Trinidad
Las Piedras
MONTEVIDEO
San Carlos
Río de la Plata
Formed by river deposits washed down from the Andes and Brazilian Shield, the Gran Chaco is virtually free of stones. It is composed of sand and silt sediments that are up to 10,000 ft (3050 m) thick.
With a maximum height of 269 ft (82 m) and a total width of 1.7 miles (2.7 km) Iguaçu Falls has a peak flow rate of 452,000 cu ft/s (12,799 cu m/s) which would fill five Olympic size swimming pools every second.

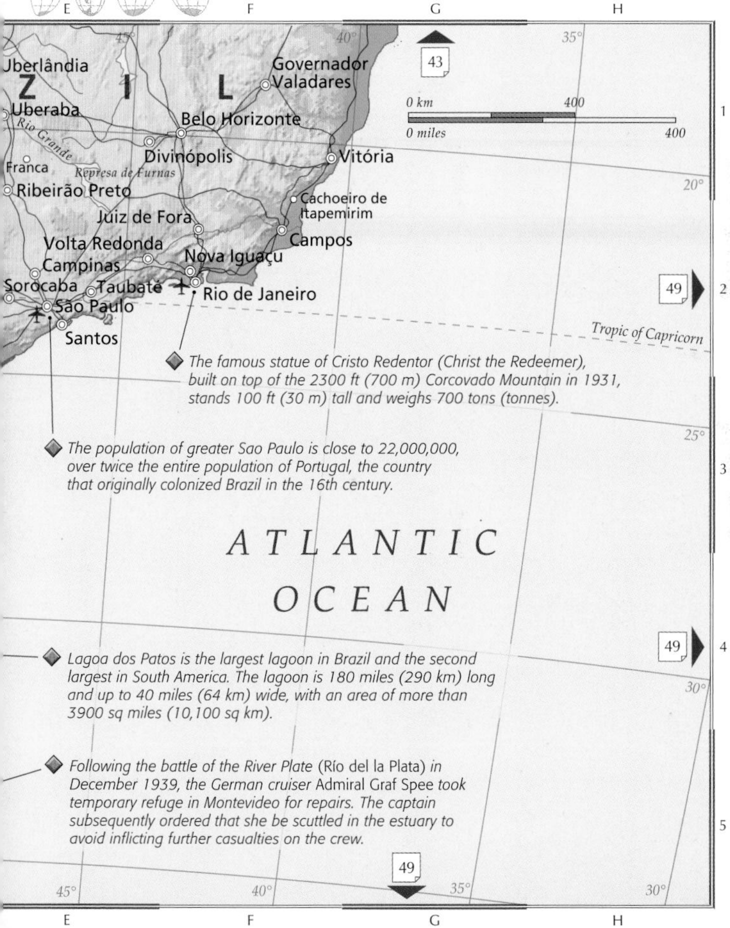

E
F
G
H
Uberlândia
Z
I
L
Governador Valadares
Uberaba
Rio Grande
Belo Horizonte
Divinópolis
Vitória
Franca
Represa de Furnas
Ribeirão Preto
Cachoeiro de Itapemirim
Juiz de Fora
Campos
Volta Redonda
Nova Iguaçu
Campinas
Sorocaba
Taubaté
Rio de Janeiro
São Paulo
Santos
Tropic of Capricorn
0 km
400
0 miles
400
43
49
49
49
1
2
3
4
5
ATLANTIC OCEAN

The famous statue of Cristo Redentor (Christ the Redeemer), built on top of the 2300 ft (700 m) Corcovado Mountain in 1931, stands 100 ft (30 m) tall and weighs 700 tons (tonnes).

The population of greater Sao Paulo is close to 22,000,000, over twice the entire population of Portugal, the country that originally colonized Brazil in the 16th century.

Lagoa dos Patos is the largest lagoon in Brazil and the second largest in South America. The lagoon is 180 miles (290 km) long and up to 40 miles (64 km) wide, with an area of more than 3900 sq miles (10,100 sq km).

Following the battle of the River Plate (Río del la Plata) in December 1939, the German cruiser Admiral Graf Spee took temporary refuge in Montevideo for repairs. The captain subsequently ordered that she be scuttled in the estuary to avoid inflicting further casualties on the crew.

Southern South America

The driest place on Earth is the Atacama Desert in Chile, with an average rainfall of 0.004 inches (0.1 mm) per year. Until recently, some places had received no rain for over 400 years.
One of the world's largest copper mines at Chuquicamata has produced around 29 million tons (tonnes) of copper over its 90-year history. The huge opencast pit is 2.6 miles (4.3 km) long, 2 miles (3 km) wide, and over 2788 ft (850 m) deep.
PERU
BRAZIL
BOLIVIA
PARAGUAY
URUGUAY
ARGENTINA
CHILE
PACIFIC OCEAN
Desierto de Atacama
Gran Chaco
Andes
Pampas
Tropic of Capricorn
Arica
Iquique
Tocopilla
Antofagasta
Chañaral
Copiapó
Vallenar
La Serena
Coquimbo
Illapel
La Ligua
Viña del Mar
Valparaíso
San Antonio
Pilchilemu
Talca
Linares
Curicó
Rancagua
SANTIAGO
Chuquicamata
Calama
San Salvador de Jujuy
Salta
San Miguel de Tucumán
Santiago del Estero
La Rioja
San Juan
Córdoba
Mendoza
Godoy Cruz
Villa Mercedes
Río Cuarto
Santa Fe
Paraná
Rosario
Junín
BUENOS AIRES
La Plata
Gualeguaychú
Concordia
Corrientes
Resistencia
Formosa
Posadas
Vera
Laguna Mar Chiquita
Cerro Aconcagua 22,831 ft (6959 m)
Pilcomayo
Bermejo
Salado
Uruguay
Paraná
Río de la Plata
Islas Juan Fernández (to Chile)

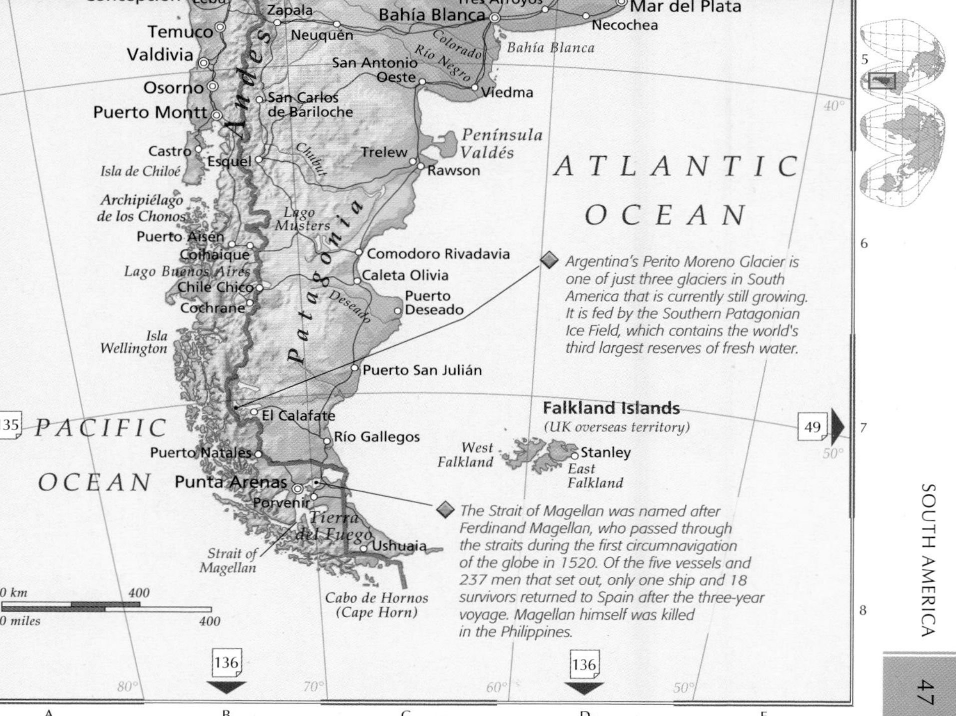

5
6
7
8
A
B
C
D
E
40°
50°
60°
70°
80°
Concepción
Lebu
Zapala
Temuco
Neuquén
Valdivia
Osorno
Puerto Montt
Andes
San Carlos de Bariloche
Tres Arroyos
Bahía Blanca
Mar del Plata
Necochea
Colorado
Río Negro
Bahía Blanca
San Antonio Oeste
Viedma
Península Valdés
Castro
Isla de Chiloé
Esquel
Chubut
Trelew
Rawson
ATLANTIC
OCEAN
Archipiélago de los Chonos
Lago Musters
Patagonia
Puerto Aisén
Coihaique
Lago Buenos Aires
Chile Chico
Cochrane
Comodoro Rivadavia
Caleta Olivia
Puerto Deseado
Deseado
Argentina's Perito Moreno Glacier is one of just three glaciers in South America that is currently still growing. It is fed by the Southern Patagonian Ice Field, which contains the world's third largest reserves of fresh water.
Isla Wellington
Puerto San Julián
Falkland Islands
(UK overseas territory)
El Calafate
PACIFIC
OCEAN
Río Gallegos
West Falkland
Stanley
East Falkland
Puerto Natales
Punta Arenas
Porvenir
Tierra del Fuego
Ushuaia
Strait of Magellan
The Strait of Magellan was named after Ferdinand Magellan, who passed through the straits during the first circumnavigation of the globe in 1520. Of the five vessels and 237 men that set out, only one ship and 18 survivors returned to Spain after the three-year voyage. Magellan himself was killed in the Philippines.
0 km 400
0 miles 400
Cabo de Hornos (Cape Horn)

135
49
136
136

The Atlantic Ocean

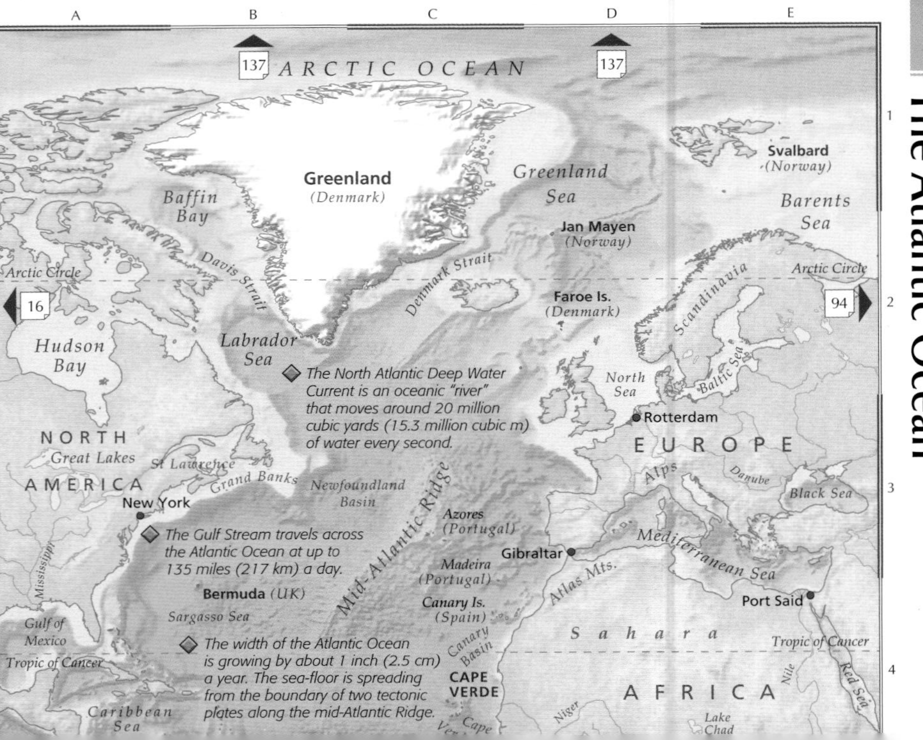

A
B
C
D
E
1
2
3
4
137
137
ARCTIC OCEAN
Greenland (Denmark)
Baffin Bay
Greenland Sea
Svalbard (Norway)
Barents Sea
Jan Mayen (Norway)
Arctic Circle
Davis Strait
Denmark Strait
Arctic Circle
Scandinavia
16
Faroe Is. (Denmark)
94
Hudson Bay
Labrador Sea
The North Atlantic Deep Water Current is an oceanic "river" that moves around 20 million cubic yards (15.3 million cubic m) of water every second.
North Sea
Baltic Sea
Rotterdam
NORTH
Great Lakes
AMERICA
St Lawrence
Grand Banks
Newfoundland Basin
EUROPE
Alps
Danube
Black Sea
New York
Mid-Atlantic Ridge
Azores (Portugal)
The Gulf Stream travels across the Atlantic Ocean at up to 135 miles (217 km) a day.
Mississippi
Gibraltar
Mediterranean Sea
Madeira (Portugal)
Atlas Mts.
Bermuda (UK)
Canary Is. (Spain)
Port Said
Sargasso Sea
Gulf of Mexico
Sahara
Canary Basin
Tropic of Cancer
Tropic of Cancer
The width of the Atlantic Ocean is growing by about 1 inch (2.5 cm) a year. The sea-floor is spreading from the boundary of two tectonic plates along the mid-Atlantic Ridge.
CAPE VERDE
AFRICA
Nile
Red Sea
Niger
Caribbean Sea
Cape Verde
Lake Chad

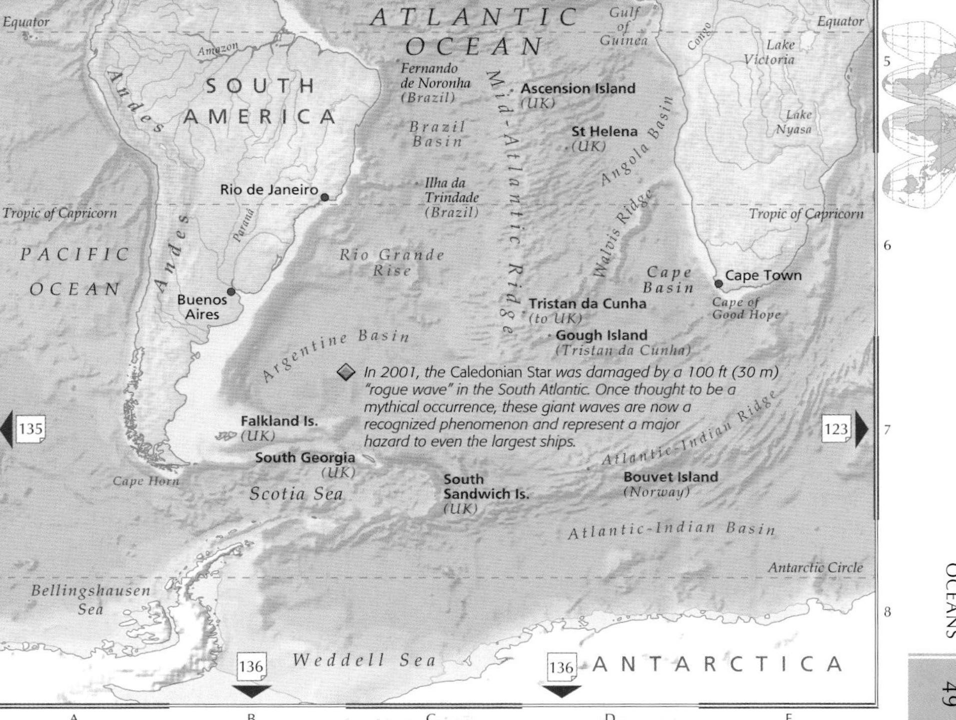
ATLANTIC OCEAN
PACIFIC OCEAN
SOUTH AMERICA
ANTARCTICA
Equator
Tropic of Capricorn
Antarctic Circle
Amazon
Andes
Paraná
Rio de Janeiro
Buenos Aires
Cape Horn
Fernando de Noronha (Brazil)
Brazil Basin
Ilha da Trindade (Brazil)
Rio Grande Rise
Argentine Basin
Mid-Atlantic Ridge
Ascension Island (UK)
St Helena (UK)
Angola Basin
Walvis Ridge
Gulf of Guinea
Congo
Lake Victoria
Lake Nyasa
Cape Basin
Cape Town
Cape of Good Hope
Tristan da Cunha (to UK)
Gough Island (Tristan da Cunha)
Falkland Is. (UK)
South Georgia (UK)
Scotia Sea
South Sandwich Is. (UK)
Bouvet Island (Norway)
Atlantic-Indian Ridge
Atlantic-Indian Basin
Bellingshausen Sea
Weddell Sea
5 6 7 8
A B C D E

In 2001, the Caledonian Star was damaged by a 100 ft (30 m) "rogue wave" in the South Atlantic. Once thought to be a mythical occurrence, these giant waves are now a recognized phenomenon and represent a major hazard to even the largest ships.

135
123
136
136

Africa

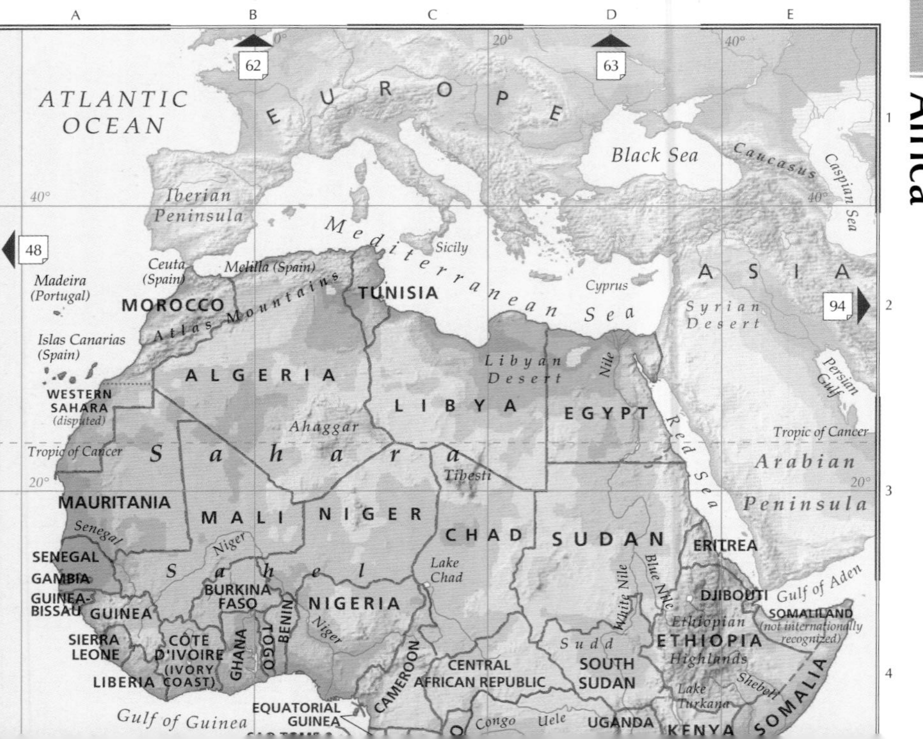

ATLANTIC OCEAN
E U R O P E
Black Sea
Caucasus
Caspian Sea
Iberian Peninsula
Mediterranean Sea
Sicily
Cyprus
A S I A
Syrian Desert
Persian Gulf
Tropic of Cancer
Arabian Peninsula
Red Sea
Gulf of Aden
Madeira (Portugal)
Islas Canarias (Spain)
Ceuta (Spain)
Melilla (Spain)
MOROCCO
Atlas Mountains
TUNISIA
ALGERIA
LIBYA
Libyan Desert
Nile
EGYPT
WESTERN SAHARA (disputed)
Ahaggar
Tibesti
Sahara
Sahel
MAURITANIA
Senegal
MALI
Niger
NIGER
CHAD
Lake Chad
SUDAN
White Nile
Blue Nile
ERITREA
DJIBOUTI
SOMALILAND (not internationally recognized)
Ethiopian Highlands
ETHIOPIA
Shebeli
Lake Turkana
SOMALIA
KENYA
UGANDA
SOUTH SUDAN
Sudd
Uele
Congo
CENTRAL AFRICAN REPUBLIC
CAMEROON
NIGERIA
BENIN
TOGO
GHANA
BURKINA FASO
CÔTE D'IVOIRE (IVORY COAST)
LIBERIA
SIERRA LEONE
GUINEA
GUINEA-BISSAU
GAMBIA
SENEGAL
EQUATORIAL GUINEA
Gulf of Guinea
62
63
94
48

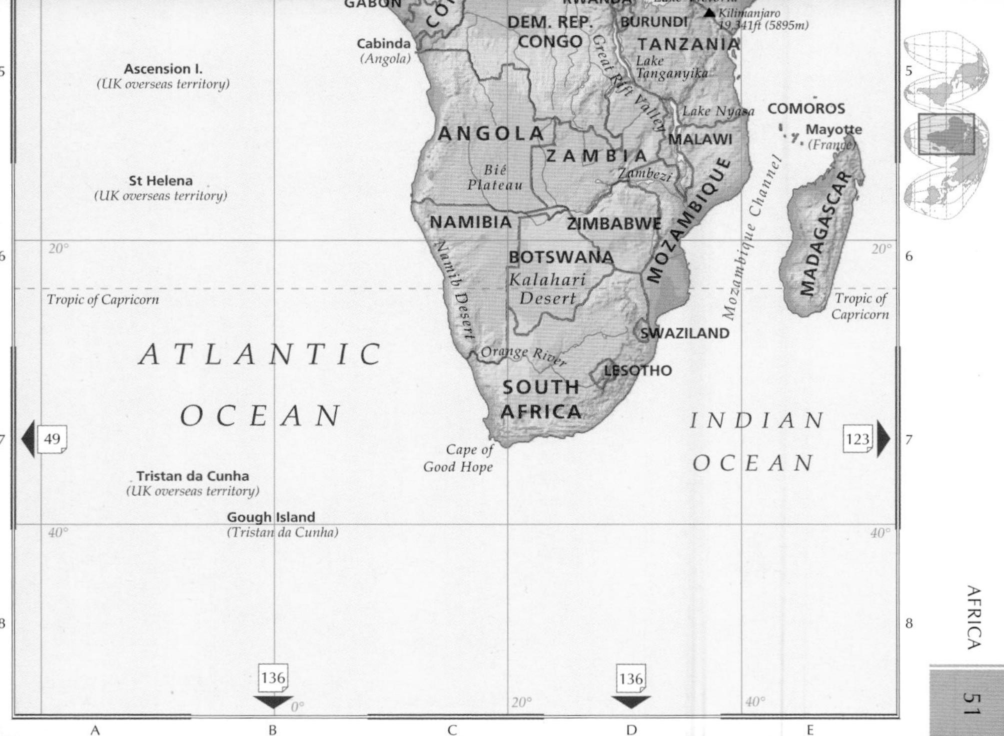
GABON
Cabinda
(Angola)
DEM. REP. CONGO
BURUNDI
TANZANIA
Kilimanjaro
19,341ft (5895m)
Lake Tanganyika
Great Rift Valley
Lake Nyasa
MALAWI
COMOROS
Mayotte
(France)
MADAGASCAR
Mozambique Channel
MOZAMBIQUE
ANGOLA
Bié Plateau
ZAMBIA
Zambezi
ZIMBABWE
NAMIBIA
BOTSWANA
Kalahari Desert
Namib Desert
Orange River
SOUTH AFRICA
SWAZILAND
LESOTHO
Cape of Good Hope
Tropic of Capricorn
ATLANTIC OCEAN
INDIAN OCEAN
Ascension I.
(UK overseas territory)
St Helena
(UK overseas territory)
Tristan da Cunha
(UK overseas territory)
Gough Island
(Tristan da Cunha)
20°
40°
0°
A
B
C
D
E
5
6
7
8
49
123
136

Northwest Africa

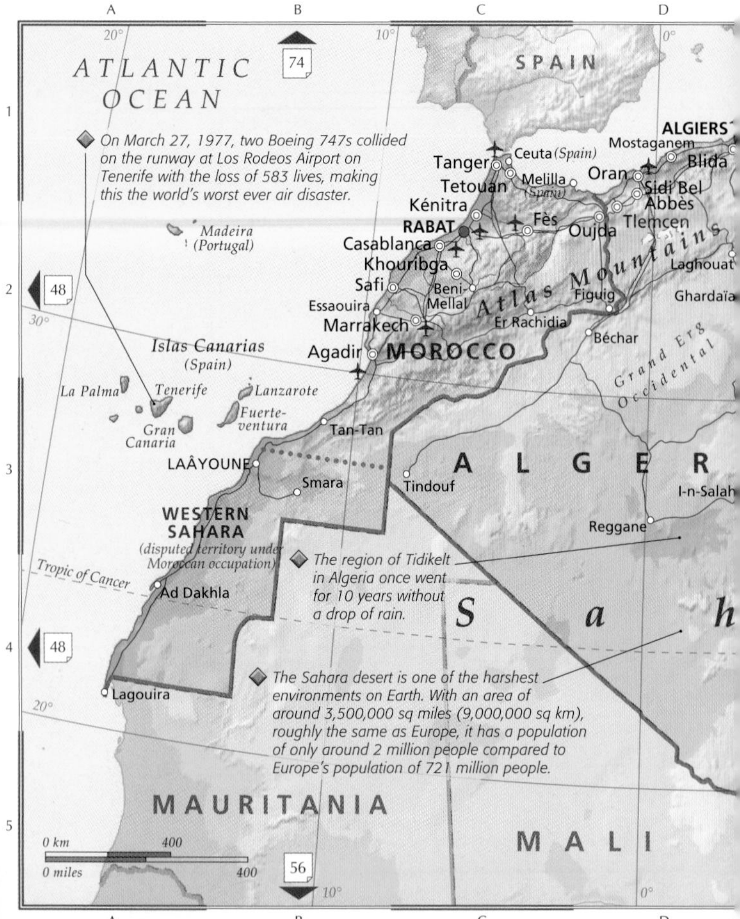

A
B
C
D
1
2
3
4
5
20°
10°
0°
30°
74
48
48
56
ATLANTIC OCEAN
On March 27, 1977, two Boeing 747s collided on the runway at Los Rodeos Airport on Tenerife with the loss of 583 lives, making this the world's worst ever air disaster.
SPAIN
ALGIERS
Mostaganem
Blida
Ceuta (Spain)
Tanger
Tetouan
Melilla (Spain)
Oran
Sidi Bel Abbès
Kénitra
RABAT
Fès
Oujda
Tlemcen
Madeira (Portugal)
Casablanca
Khouribga
Safi
Beni-Mellal
Atlas Mountains
Figuig
Laghouat
Ghardaïa
Essaouira
Marrakech
Er Rachidia
Béchar
Islas Canarias (Spain)
Agadir
MOROCCO
Grand Erg Occidental
La Palma
Tenerife
Lanzarote
Fuerte-ventura
Gran Canaria
Tan-Tan
LAÂYOUNE
ALGERIA
Smara
Tindouf
I-n-Salah
WESTERN SAHARA
(disputed territory under Moroccan occupation)
Reggane
Tropic of Cancer
The region of Tidikelt in Algeria once went for 10 years without a drop of rain.
Ad Dakhla
Sah
Lagouira
The Sahara desert is one of the harshest environments on Earth. With an area of around 3,500,000 sq miles (9,000,000 sq km), roughly the same as Europe, it has a population of only around 2 million people compared to Europe's population of 721 million people.
MAURITANIA
MALI
0 km 400
0 miles 400

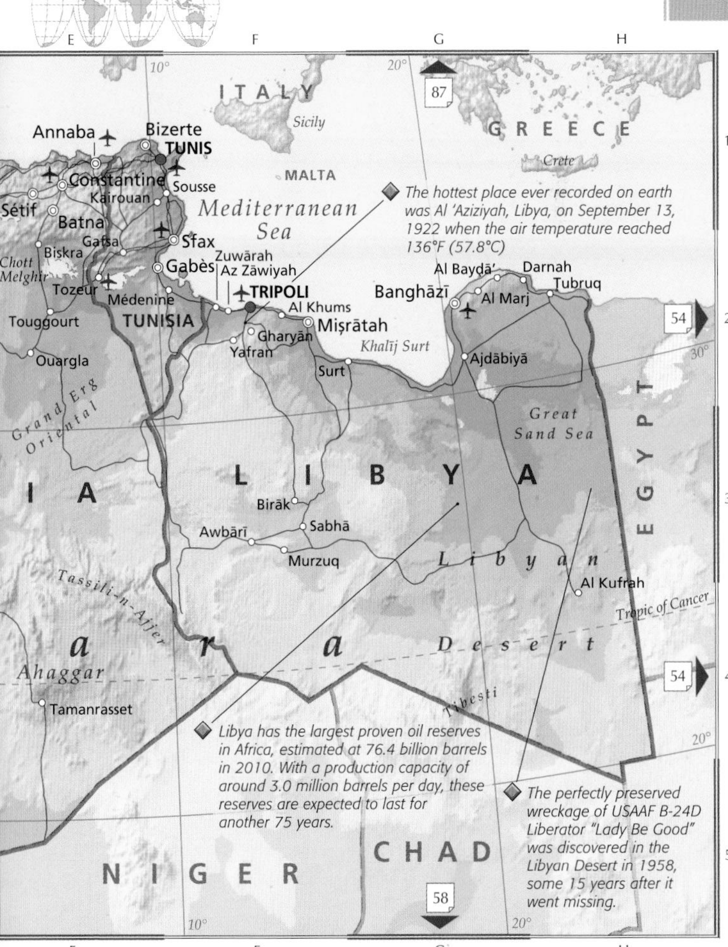
E
F
G
H
10°
20°
87
ITALY
Sicily
GREECE
Crete
1
Annaba
Bizerte
TUNIS
Constantine
Sousse
MALTA
Kairouan
Sétif
Batna
Mediterranean Sea
Sfax
Gafsa
Biskra
Chott Melghir
Gabès
Zuwārah
Az Zāwiyah
Tozeur
TRIPOLI
Médenine
Al Khums
TUNISIA
Touggourt
Gharyān
Miṣrātah
Yafran
Khalīj Surt
Ouargla
Surt
Al Bayḍā'
Darnah
Tubruq
Al Marj
Banghāzī
Ajdābiyā
54
2
30°
Grand Erg Oriental
Great Sand Sea
EGYPT
LIBYA
IA
3
Birāk
Sabhā
Awbārī
Murzuq
Libyan Desert
Al Kufrah
Tassili-n-Ajjer
Tropic of Cancer
a r a
Ahaggar
54
4
Tamanrasset
Tibesti
20°
CHAD
NIGER
5
58
10°
20°

The hottest place ever recorded on earth was Al 'Aziziyah, Libya, on September 13, 1922 when the air temperature reached 136°F (57.8°C)

Libya has the largest proven oil reserves in Africa, estimated at 76.4 billion barrels in 2010. With a production capacity of around 3.0 million barrels per day, these reserves are expected to last for another 75 years.

The perfectly preserved wreckage of USAAF B-24D Liberator "Lady Be Good" was discovered in the Libyan Desert in 1958, some 15 years after it went missing.

Northeast Africa

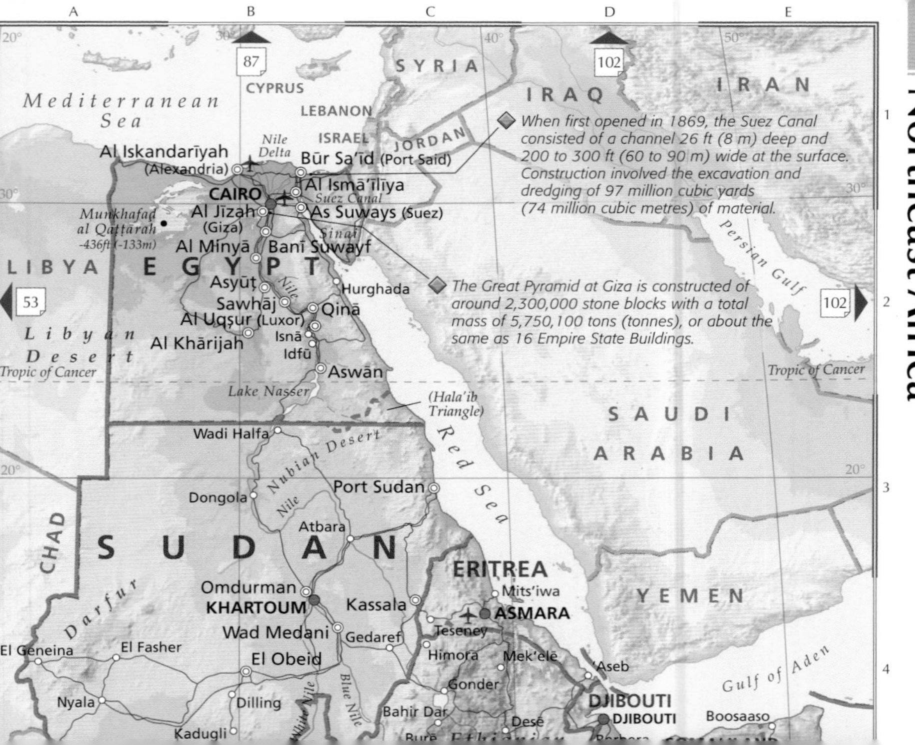
When first opened in 1869, the Suez Canal consisted of a channel 26 ft (8 m) deep and 200 to 300 ft (60 to 90 m) wide at the surface. Construction involved the excavation and dredging of 97 million cubic yards (74 million cubic metres) of material.
The Great Pyramid at Giza is constructed of around 2,300,000 stone blocks with a total mass of 5,750,100 tons (tonnes), or about the same as 16 Empire State Buildings.
Mediterranean Sea
CYPRUS
LEBANON
ISRAEL
SYRIA
JORDAN
IRAQ
IRAN
Persian Gulf
SAUDI ARABIA
YEMEN
Gulf of Aden
Red Sea
LIBYA
EGYPT
SUDAN
CHAD
ERITREA
DJIBOUTI
Libyan Desert
Nubian Desert
Darfur
Tropic of Cancer
Al Iskandarīyah (Alexandria)
Nile Delta
CAIRO
Al Jīzah (Giza)
Būr Sa'īd (Port Said)
Al Ismā'īlīya
Suez Canal
As Suways (Suez)
Sinai
Munkhafad al Qaţţārah -436ft (-133m)
Al Minyā
Banī Suwayf
Asyūţ
Sawhāj
Nile
Al Uqşur (Luxor)
Qinā
Isnā
Idfū
Hurghada
Aswān
Al Khārijah
Lake Nasser
(Hala'ib Triangle)
Wadi Halfa
Dongola
Atbara
Port Sudan
Omdurman
KHARTOUM
Wad Medani
Kassala
Gedaref
El Obeid
Dilling
Kadugli
El Fasher
Nyala
El Geneina
Blue Nile
White Nile
Mits'iwa
ASMARA
Teseney
Himora
Mek'elē
Gonder
Bahir Dar
Desē
Aseb
DJIBOUTI
Boosaaso
87
102
53

The Great Rift Valley is one of the most extensive rifts on the Earth's surface, extending from Jordan southward through eastern Africa to Mozambique. The system is some 4,000 miles (6,400 km) long and averages 30–40 miles (48–64 km) wide.
In 1954, a swarm of desert locust covering 77 sq miles (200 sq km) invaded Kenya. The swarm was estimated to contain 10 billion individual insects.
The shortest war on record, between Britain and Zanzibar in 1896, lasted just 38 minutes.
SOUTH SUDAN
CENTRAL AFRICAN REPUBLIC
DEM. REP. CONGO
ETHIOPIA
SOMALIA
KENYA
UGANDA
RWANDA
BURUNDI
TANZANIA
MOZAMBIQUE
MALAWI
ZAMBIA
MADAGASCAR
COMOROS
SEYCHELLES
INDIAN OCEAN
ADDIS ABABA
JUBA
KAMPALA
KIGALI
BUJUMBURA
NAIROBI
DODOMA
MOGADISHU
Wau
Rumbek
Yambio
Gorē
Jīma
Nazrēt
Highlands
Ogaden
Garoowe
Gaalkacyo
Beledweyne
Shebeli
Elemi Triangle (adminstered by Kenya)
Negēlē
Lokitaung
Lake Turkana
Baydhabo
Wanlaweyn
Marka
Arua
Gulu
White Nile
Lira
Lake Albert
Masindi
Mbale
Eldoret
Nakuru
Meru
Nyeri
Jamaame
Kismaayo
Garissa
Lake Edward
Entebbe
Lake Victoria
Kisumu
Great Rift Valley
Kabale
Lake Kivu
Mwanza
Kilimanjaro 19,341ft (5895m)
Arusha
Moshi
Malindi
Mombasa
Shinyanga
Masai Steppe
Tabora
Kigoma
Tanga
Zanzibar
Dar es Salaam
Lake Tanganyika
Lake Rukwa
Morogoro
Sumbawanga
Iringa
Mbeya
Lake Nyasa
Lindi
Mtwara
Songea
Equator
0 km 400
0 miles 400
59
60
61
122
10°
30°
40°
50°
A
B
C
D
E
5
6
7
8

West Africa

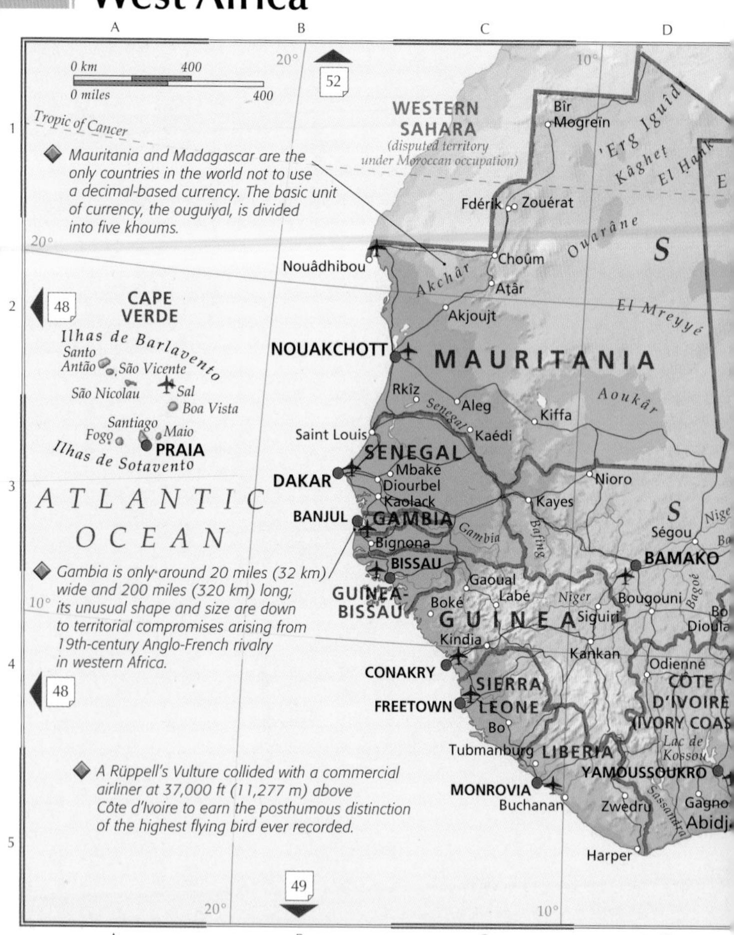
A
B
C
D
1
2
3
4
5
0 km
400
0 miles
400
20°
10°
52
48
49
Tropic of Cancer
Mauritania and Madagascar are the only countries in the world not to use a decimal-based currency. The basic unit of currency, the ouguiyal, is divided into five khoums.
WESTERN SAHARA
(disputed territory under Moroccan occupation)
Bîr Mogreïn
'Erg Iguîdi
Kâgheț
El Hank
Fdérik
Zouérat
Ouarâne
Choûm
Nouâdhibou
Akchâr
Atâr
Akjoujt
El Mreyyé
CAPE VERDE
Ilhas de Barlavento
Santo Antão
São Vicente
São Nicolau
Sal
Boa Vista
Santiago
Maio
Fogo
PRAIA
Ilhas de Sotavento
NOUAKCHOTT
MAURITANIA
Rkîz
Aleg
Senegal
Kiffa
Aoukâr
Saint Louis
Kaédi
SENEGAL
Mbaké
Diourbel
Kaolack
DAKAR
Nioro
ATLANTIC OCEAN
BANJUL
GAMBIA
Gambia
Kayes
Bafing
Ségou
Niger
BAMAKO
Bignona
BISSAU
GUINEA-BISSAU
Gaoual
Labé
Boké
GUINEA
Niger
Siguiri
Bougouni
Bagoé
Kindia
Kankan
Odienné
CONAKRY
SIERRA LEONE
FREETOWN
CÔTE D'IVOIRE
(IVORY COAS
Bo
Tubmanburg
LIBERIA
Lac de Kossou
YAMOUSSOUKRO
MONROVIA
Buchanan
Zwedru
Sassandra
Gagno
Abidj
Harper
Gambia is only around 20 miles (32 km) wide and 200 miles (320 km) long; its unusual shape and size are down to territorial compromises arising from 19th-century Anglo-French rivalry in western Africa.
A Rüppell's Vulture collided with a commercial airliner at 37,000 ft (11,277 m) above Côte d'Ivoire to earn the posthumous distinction of the highest flying bird ever recorded.

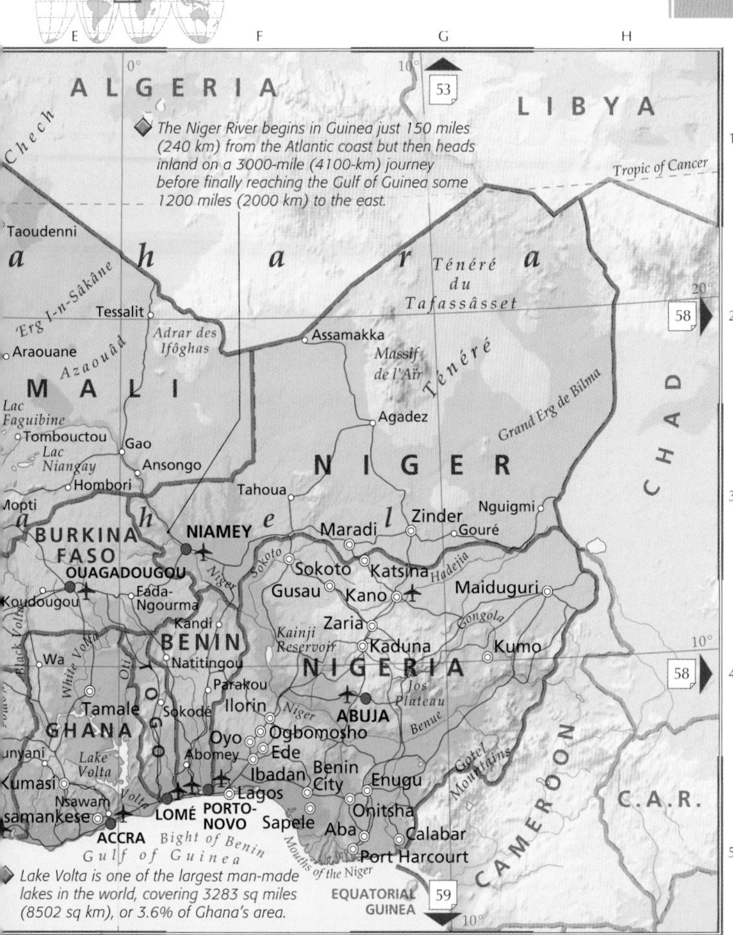

ALGERIA
LIBYA
The Niger River begins in Guinea just 150 miles (240 km) from the Atlantic coast but then heads inland on a 3000-mile (4100-km) journey before finally reaching the Gulf of Guinea some 1200 miles (2000 km) to the east.
Tropic of Cancer
Taoudenni
Ténéré du Tafassâsset
Erg I-n-Sâkâne
Tessalit
Adrar des Ifôghas
Assamakka
Massif de l'Aïr
Ténéré
Araouane
Azaouâd
MALI
Lac Faguibine
Tombouctou
Gao
Lac Niangay
Ansongo
Hombori
Agadez
Grand Erg de Bilma
NIGER
CHAD
Tahoua
Mopti
Zinder
Nguigmi
BURKINA FASO
NIAMEY
Maradi
Gouré
OUAGADOUGOU
Sokoto
Katsina
Hadejia
Koudougou
Fada-Ngourma
Gusau
Kano
Maiduguri
Kandi
Zaria
Gongola
BENIN
Kainji Reservoir
Kaduna
Kumo
Wa
Natitingou
NIGERIA
Black Volta
White Volta
Oti
Parakou
Jos Plateau
Tamale
Sokodé
Ilorin
ABUJA
Niger
GHANA
TOGO
Oyo
Ogbomosho
Benue
Abomey
Ede
CAMEROON
Lake Volta
Ibadan
Benin City
Enugu
Gotel Mountains
Kumasi
Lagos
Nsawam
Volta
LOMÉ
PORTO-NOVO
Onitsha
C.A.R.
Sapele
Aba
Calabar
ACCRA
Bight of Benin
Gulf of Guinea
Port Harcourt
Mouths of the Niger
Lake Volta is one of the largest man-made lakes in the world, covering 3283 sq miles (8502 sq km), or 3.6% of Ghana's area.
EQUATORIAL GUINEA
53
58
58
59

Central Africa

LIBYA
EGYPT
Tropic of Cancer
ALGERIA
The eye of an ostrich is bigger than it's brain. They are the largest bird on Earth. An adult male can stand 8 ft (2.5 m) tall, weigh up to 300 lbs (135 kg), and run at around 30 mph (48 km/h).
NIGER
Tibesti
Sahara
The vast sand flats surrounding Lake Chad were once covered by water. Changing climatic patterns caused the lake to shrink and desert now covers much of its previous area.
Faya
Ennedi
CHAD
SUDAN
Mao
Bol
Lake Chad
Ati
Biltine
Abéché
Mongo
Kousséri
N'DJAMÉNA
Pygmies who inhabit the Congo Basin grow to be only 3 to 4 feet (0.9 to 1.2 m) tall at adulthood. The name is derived from the Greek word "pygmê," which referred to a unit of measurement equivalent to the length of a forearm.
Am Timan
Maroua
Chari
Guider
Bongor
Laï
Garoua
Sarh
Massif des Bongo
NIGERIA
Moundou
Goré
Ndélé
Ngaoundéré
CENTRAL AFRICAN REPUBLIC
SOUTH SUDAN
Bossangoa
Bria
Banyo
Bamenda
Bouar
Sibut
Obo
53
53
57
54

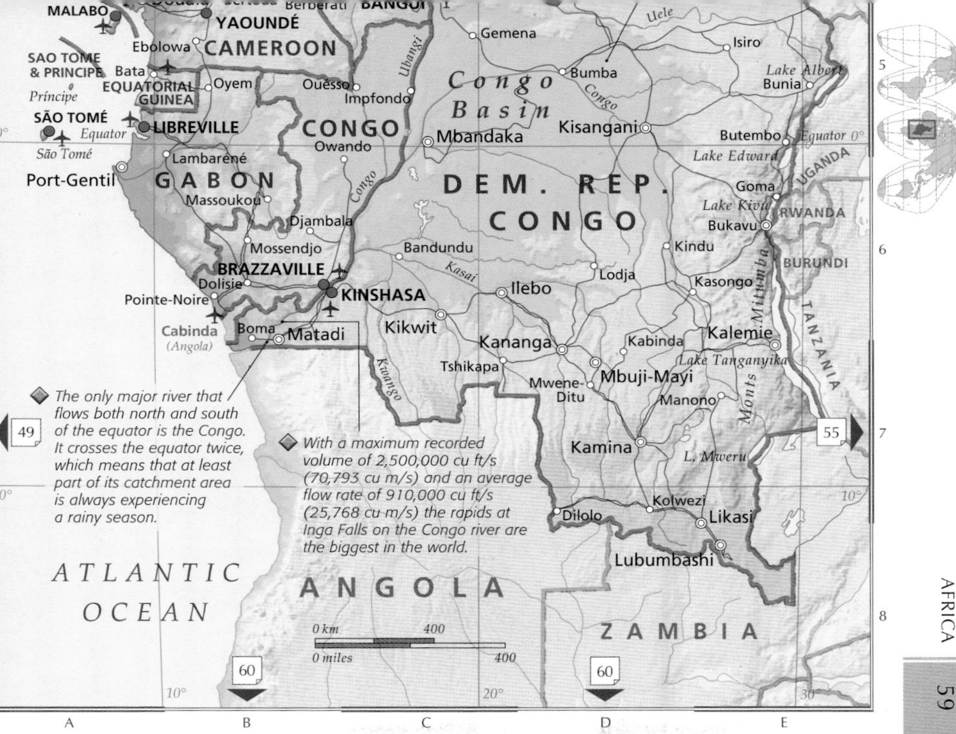
MALABO
YAOUNDÉ
Berberati
BANGUI
CAMEROON
Ebolowa
SAO TOME & PRINCIPE
Bata
EQUATORIAL GUINEA
Oyem
Príncipe
SÃO TOMÉ
LIBREVILLE
Equator
São Tomé
Lambaréné
Port-Gentil
GABON
Massoukou
Ouésso
Impfondo
Ubangi
CONGO
Owando
Congo
Djambala
Mossendjo
BRAZZAVILLE
Dolisie
Pointe-Noire
KINSHASA
Cabinda (Angola)
Boma
Matadi
Gemena
Uele
Bumba
Congo Basin
Congo
Mbandaka
Kisangani
Isiro
Lake Albert
Bunia
Butembo
Equator 0°
Lake Edward
UGANDA
DEM. REP. CONGO
Goma
Lake Kivu
RWANDA
Bukavu
Kindu
Bandundu
Kasai
Ilebo
Lodja
Kasongo
Mitumba
BURUNDI
TANZANIA
Kikwit
Kananga
Kabinda
Kalemie
Lake Tanganyika
Tshikapa
Mwene-Ditu
Mbuji-Mayi
Kwango
Manono
Monts
Kamina
L. Mweru
Kolwezi
Likasi
Dilolo
Lubumbashi
ATLANTIC OCEAN
ANGOLA
ZAMBIA
0 km 400
0 miles 400
0°
10°
20°
30°
A B C D E
5 6 7 8
49
55
60
60

The only major river that flows both north and south of the equator is the Congo. It crosses the equator twice, which means that at least part of its catchment area is always experiencing a rainy season.

With a maximum recorded volume of 2,500,000 cu ft/s (70,793 cu m/s) and an average flow rate of 910,000 cu ft/s (25,768 cu m/s) the rapids at Inga Falls on the Congo river are the biggest in the world.

Southern Africa

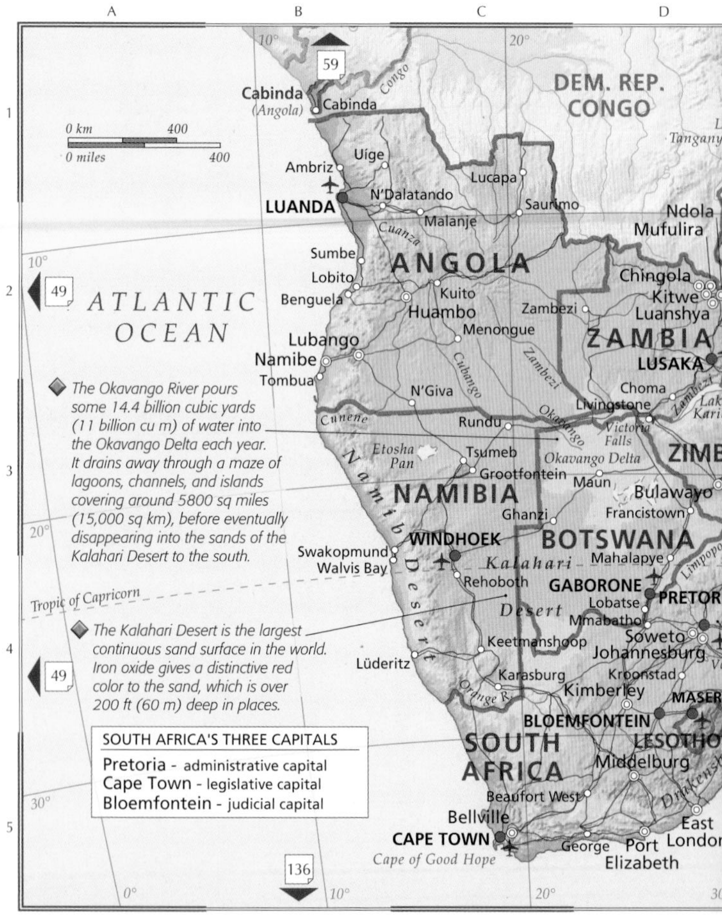
A
B
C
D
1
2
3
4
5
59
49
49
136
10°
20°
10°
20°
30°
0°
10°
20°
0 km
400
0 miles
400
DEM. REP. CONGO
Cabinda (Angola)
Cabinda
Congo
Uíge
Ambriz
Lucapa
LUANDA
N'Dalatando
Saurimo
Malanje
Cuanza
Ndola
Mufulira
Sumbe
ANGOLA
Lobito
Chingola
Kitwe
Luanshya
Benguela
Kuito
Huambo
Zambezi
ATLANTIC OCEAN
Menongue
ZAMBIA
Lubango
Namibe
LUSAKA
Tombua
Cubango
Zambezi
Choma
N'Giva
Livingstone
Cunene
Rundu
Okavango
Victoria Falls
Etosha Pan
Tsumeb
Okavango Delta
Grootfontein
Maun
NAMIBIA
Bulawayo
Francistown
Ghanzi
Namib Desert
WINDHOEK
BOTSWANA
Swakopmund
Walvis Bay
Kalahari Desert
Mahalapye
Limpopo
Rehoboth
GABORONE
Tropic of Capricorn
Lobatse
Mmabatho
Soweto
Keetmanshoop
Johannesburg
Lüderitz
Karasburg
Kroonstad
Orange R.
Kimberley
BLOEMFONTEIN
SOUTH AFRICA
Middelburg
Beaufort West
Bellville
CAPE TOWN
George
Port Elizabeth
Cape of Good Hope
East London
The Okavango River pours some 14.4 billion cubic yards (11 billion cu m) of water into the Okavango Delta each year. It drains away through a maze of lagoons, channels, and islands covering around 5800 sq miles (15,000 sq km), before eventually disappearing into the sands of the Kalahari Desert to the south.
The Kalahari Desert is the largest continuous sand surface in the world. Iron oxide gives a distinctive red color to the sand, which is over 200 ft (60 m) deep in places.
SOUTH AFRICA'S THREE CAPITALS
Pretoria - administrative capital
Cape Town - legislative capital
Bloemfontein - judicial capital

E
F
G
H
40°
50°
60°
122
123
136
1
2
3
4
5
TANZANIA
Mbala
Kasama
MALAWI
Mzuzu
Lake
Nyasa
Salima
Zomba
Blantyre
Tete
Nsanje
Rovuma
Mocímboa
da Praia
MOZAMBIQUE
Nacala
Nampula
Moçambique
Mocuba
Quelimane
Beira
Chimoio
Inhambane
Xai-Xai
MAPUTO
WAZILAND
Mozambique Channel
COMOROS
Grande Comore
MORONI
Mwali
Anjouan
Mamoudzou
Mayotte
(French overseas
department)
Inner Islands
VICTORIA
Mahé
SEYCHELLES
Amirante
Islands
Aldabra
Group
Farquhar
Group
Outer Islands
Antsirañana
Ambanja
Antalaha
Antsohihy
Mahajanga
MADAGASCAR
Fenoarivo Atsinanana
ANTANANARIVO
Toamasina
Morondava
Ambositra
Fianarantsoa
Mananjary
Ihosy
Toliara
Farafangana
Vangaindrano
Amboasary
INDIAN
OCEAN
10°
20°
30°
MAURITIUS
PORT LOUIS
Saint-Denis
Réunion
(French
overseas
department)
Mascarene Islands
Tropic of Capricorn
ietermaritzburg
urban

Coco de Mer, or the double coconut palm, produces some of the largest seeds in the plant kingdom. Weighing up to 60 lbs (27 kg), they take around 10 years to ripen.

In 1905, the world's largest rough diamond was discovered at the Cullinan Diamond Mine. Weighing 3106 carats, or about 1.3 pounds (0.6 kg), the diamond was cut into nine smaller stones, including the 530.2 carat "Cullinan I" or "Great Star of Africa," which forms part of the British Crown Jewels and is estimated to be worth over $400 million.

Thought to have been extinct for 70 million years, a living coelacanth was netted in the Indian Ocean in 1938. They are powerful predators, averaging 5 feet (1.5 m) in length and weighing about 100 lbs (45 kg).

Europe

A
B
C
D
1
2
3
4
5
137
48
48
50
40°
20°
0°
Arctic Circle
Limit of winter pack ice
ICELAND
Norwegian Sea
Faroe Islands
(Denmark)
Outer Hebrides
British Isles
Ireland
IRELAND
Britain
North Sea
DENMARK
ATLANTIC OCEAN
Celtic Sea
UNITED KINGDOM
NETHERLANDS
English Channel
BELGIUM
LUX.
GERMANY
Seine
Loire
Rhine
Elbe
Bay of Biscay
FRANCE
Massif Central
Garonne
Rhône
SWITZ.
LIECH.
Alps
Mont Blanc
15,771ft (4807m)
Po
PORTUGAL
Duero
Tagus
Iberian
Ebro
Pyrenees
MONACO
SAN MARINO
SPAIN
Peninsula
ANDORRA
Corsica
ITALY
Madeira
(to Portugal)
Strait of Gibraltar
Balearic Islands
Sardinia
VATICAN CITY
Tyrrhenian Sea
Gibraltar
(UK)
Mediterranean
Sicily
Atlas Mountains
AFRICA
MALTA
Canary Islands
(to Spain)

E
F
G
H
1
2
3
4
5
Barents Sea
North Cape
Ostrov Kolguyev
Kola Peninsula
White Sea
FINLAND
Gulf of Bothnia
Lake Onega
Lake Ladoga
Northern Dvina
Ural Mountains
Arctic Circle
137
RUSSIAN FEDERATION
94
Aland
ESTONIA
LATVIA
LITHUANIA
RUSS. FED.
European Plain
Central Russian Upland
Volga Uplands
Volga
Ural
BELARUS
POLAND
Pripet Marshes
Vistula
Bug
Dnieper Lowlands
Dnieper
Don
UKRAINE
Carpathian Mts.
Dniester
SLOVAKIA
MOLDOVA
Aral Sea
(the Ukrainian territory of Crimea was annexed by Russia in 2014)
Sea of Azov
Crimea
HUNGARY
ROMANIA
Caucasus
El'brus 18,510ft (5642m)
Caspian Sea
Black Sea
SERBIA
Danube
BULGARIA
KOS. (disputed)
Balkan Mts.
MACED.
TURKEY
ALBANIA
Aegean Sea
ASIA
Anatolia
GREECE
Peloponnese
Crete
Cyprus
20°
40°
60°
80°

The North Atlantic

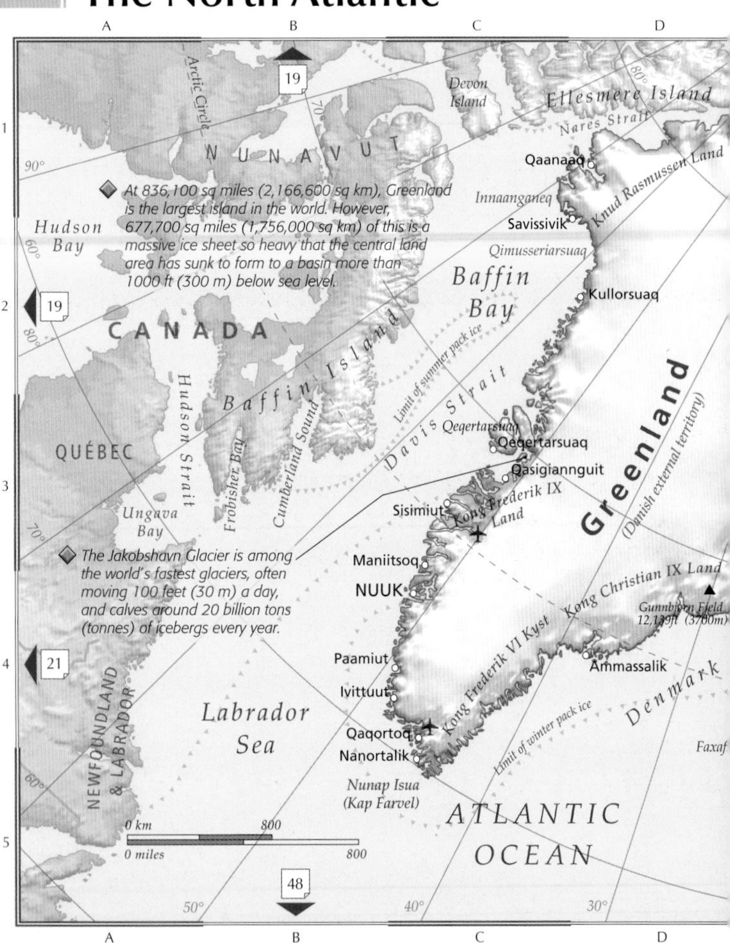

A
B
C
D
1
2
3
4
5
19
21
48
Arctic Circle
Devon Island
Ellesmere Island
Nares Strait
NUNAVUT
90°
80°
70°
60°
50°
40°
30°
Qaanaaq
Knud Rasmussen Land
At 836,100 sq miles (2,166,600 sq km), Greenland is the largest island in the world. However, 677,700 sq miles (1,756,000 sq km) of this is a massive ice sheet so heavy that the central land area has sunk to form to a basin more than 1000 ft (300 m) below sea level.
Innaanganeq
Savissivik
Hudson Bay
Qimusseriarsuaq
Baffin Bay
Kullorsuaq
CANADA
Baffin Island
Limit of summer pack ice
Davis Strait
Greenland
(Danish external territory)
Hudson Strait
Cumberland Sound
Frobisher Bay
Qeqertarsuaq
QUÉBEC
Qasigiannguit
Kong Frederik IX Land
Sisimiut
Ungava Bay
The Jakobshavn Glacier is among the world's fastest glaciers, often moving 100 feet (30 m) a day, and calves around 20 billion tons (tonnes) of icebergs every year.
Maniitsoq
NUUK
Kong Christian IX Land
Gunnbjørn Fjeld
12,139ft (3700m)
Kong Frederik VI Kyst
Ammassalik
Paamiut
Ivittuut
Denmark
NEWFOUNDLAND & LABRADOR
Labrador Sea
Limit of winter pack ice
Qaqortoq
Nanortalik
Faxaf
Nunap Isua
(Kap Farvel)
ATLANTIC OCEAN
0 km
800
0 miles
800

E
F
G
H
ARCTIC OCEAN
Lincoln Sea
Kap Morris Jesup
Wandel Sea
Nord
Svalbard
(Norwegian dependency)
Zemlya Frantsa-Iosifa
Kvitøya
Nordaustlandet
Kong Karls Land
Spitsbergen
Barentsøya
Edgeøya
Longyearbyen
Barentsberg
Storfjorden
Novaya Zemlya
Kong Frederik VIII Land
Kong Christian X Land
Greenland Sea
Bjørnøya
(Norway)
Barents Sea
Daneborg
Kong Oscar Fjord
Ittoqqortoormiit
Jan Mayen
(Norway)
Kangikajik
Norwegian Sea
Limit of winter pack ice
Strait
ICELAND
Siglufjörður
Húsavík
Seyðisfjörður
REYKJAVÍK
Selfoss
Surtsey
Faroe Islands
(Denmark)
Tórshavn
Shetland Islands
RUSSIAN FEDERATION
Arctic Circle
FINLAND
NORWAY
SWEDEN
137
62
66
70
1
2
3
4
5

With temperatures ranging from 59° F (15° C) in the summer to -40° F (-40° C) in the winter, vegetation on Svalbard consists mostly of lichens and mosses; the only trees are the tiny polar willow and the dwarf birch.

Greenland's deeply indented coastline is 24,430 miles (39,330 km) long, a distance roughly equivalent to the Earth's circumference at the equator.

During April 2010, the Icelandic volcano Eyjafjallajökull ejected an estimated 330,000,000 cu yd (250 million cu m) of ash 5 miles (8 km) into the atmosphere. This eventually caused the closure of most of Europe's airspace over a six day period, leading to around 107,000 flight cancellations.

Scandinavia & Finland

ARCTIC OCEAN
The North Cape Current warms the northern coasts of Norway, Finland, and Russia's Kola Peninsula with water temperatures of 39–54° F (4–12° C), allowing this area of the Barents Sea to remain free of pack ice throughout the winter.
The sun is continuously visible from late May to late July in Tromsø because of its position well north of the Arctic Circle.
Carved by a massive glacier during the last Ice Age, Sognefjord is 4291 ft (1308 m) deep and 126 miles (203 km) long. Cliffs rise almost vertically from the water to heights of 3,330 ft (1000 m).
Barents Sea
Norwegian Sea
Nordkapp (North Cape)
RUSSIAN FEDERATION
FINLAND
NORWAY
SWEDEN
Lapland
Arctic Circle
Vesterålen
Lofoten
Hammerfest
Vardø
Kirkenes
Tromsø
Harstad
Narvik
Bodø
Mo i Rana
Steinkjer
Trondheimsfjorden
Kiruna
Gällivare
Luleå
Piteå
Skellefteå
Kokkola
Oulu
Tornio
Kemi
Rovaniemi
Kemijärvi
Sodankylä
Kuusamo
Kajaani
Iisalmi
Deatnu
Ounasjoki
Muonioälv
Tornionjoki
Kemijoki
Oulujoki
Oulujärvi
Ångermanälven
0 km 200
0 miles 200
0° 5° 10° 15° 20° 25° 30° 35° 70° 65°
A B C D E 1 2 3 4
137 137 65 92

NORWAY
SWEDEN
FINLAND
ESTONIA
LATVIA
LITHUANIA
BELARUS
POLAND
GERMANY
DENMARK
KALININGRAD
(part of Russian Federation)
Gulf of Bothnia
Gulf of Finland
Baltic Sea
Skagerrak
OSLO
STOCKHOLM
HELSINKI
COPENHAGEN
Ålesund
Bergen
Haugesund
Stavanger
Kristiansand
Arendal
Porsgrunn
Drammen
Hønefoss
Gjøvik
Lillehammer
Hamar
Moss
Fredrikstad
Halden
Hermansverk
Sognefjorden
Setesdal
Mjøsa
Trollhättan
Göteborg
Borås
Halmstad
Helsingborg
Malmö
Kristianstad
Karlskrona
Växjö
Jönköping
Kalmar
Linköping
Norrköping
Nyköping
Örebro
Västerås
Uppsala
Karlstad
Skövde
Vänern
Vättern
Falun
Borlänge
Gävle
Sundsvall
Örnsköldsvik
Ljusnan
Visby
Gotland
Öland
Bornholm
Rønne
Mariehamn
Åland
Vaasa
Seinäjoki
Pori
Rauma
Turku
Tampere
Riihimäki
Hämeenlinna
Espoo
Vantaa
Jyväskylä
Lappeenranta
Imatra
Saimaa
Kouvola
Kotka
Varkaus
Hjørring
Frederikshavn
Aalborg
Jylland
Randers
Århus
Silkeborg
Herning
Esbjerg
Vejle
Odense
Aabenrå
Sjælland
Nykøbing
70
76
80
88
A B C D E
5 6 7 8
10° 15° 20° 25°
55° 60°

Finns consume an average of 26.5 lbs (12 kg) of coffee each per year, which is over twice the amount of most other Europeans, and makes them among the biggest coffee drinkers in the world.

The 10 mile (16 km) bridge and tunnel link across the Oresund Sound is one of the largest infrastructure projects in European history. It connects the Danish capital Copenhagen to the Swedish port of Malmö.

The Low Countries

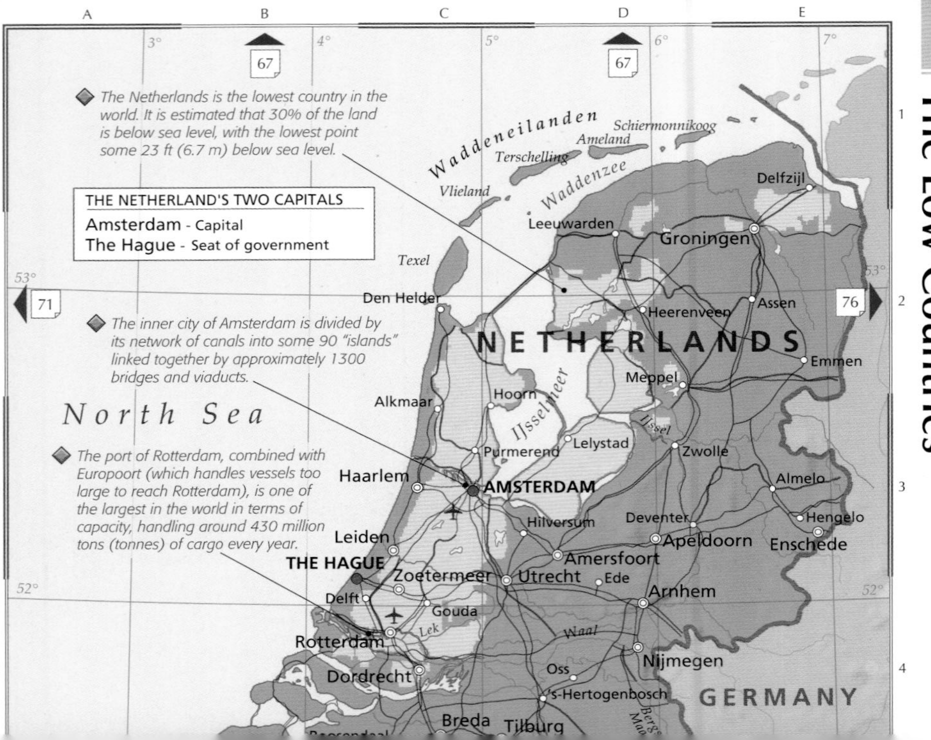
The Netherlands is the lowest country in the world. It is estimated that 30% of the land is below sea level, with the lowest point some 23 ft (6.7 m) below sea level.
THE NETHERLAND'S TWO CAPITALS
Amsterdam - Capital
The Hague - Seat of government
The inner city of Amsterdam is divided by its network of canals into some 90 "islands" linked together by approximately 1300 bridges and viaducts.
The port of Rotterdam, combined with Europoort (which handles vessels too large to reach Rotterdam), is one of the largest in the world in terms of capacity, handling around 430 million tons (tonnes) of cargo every year.
North Sea
Waddeneilanden
Waddenzee
Schiermonnikoog
Ameland
Terschelling
Vlieland
Texel
NETHERLANDS
GERMANY
Ijsselmeer
IJssel
Delfzijl
Leeuwarden
Groningen
Den Helder
Heerenveen
Assen
Emmen
Meppel
Alkmaar
Hoorn
Lelystad
Purmerend
Zwolle
Haarlem
AMSTERDAM
Almelo
Hilversum
Deventer
Hengelo
Leiden
Apeldoorn
Enschede
Amersfoort
THE HAGUE
Zoetermeer
Utrecht
Ede
Delft
Arnhem
Gouda
Lek
Waal
Rotterdam
Nijmegen
Oss
Dordrecht
's-Hertogenbosch
Breda
Tilburg
67
67
71
76
A
B
C
D
E
1
2
3
4
3°
4°
5°
6°
7°
53°
52°

Zeebrugge
Westerschelde
Terneuzen
Turnhout
Venlo
Oostende
Brugge
Scheldt
Antwerpen
Sint-
Niklaas
Flanders
Gent
Mechelen
Aalst
Roeselare
Ieper
Kortrijk
Mouscron
BRUSSELS
Leuven
Tienen
Hasselt
Genk
Heerlen
Maastricht
BELGIUM
Liège
Seraing
Verviers
Tournai
La Louvière
Mons
Charleroi
Sambre
Namur
Meuse
Ourthe
Dinant
Ardennes
Bastogne
Sûre
Our
Diekirch
LUXEMBOURG
Arlon
LUXEMBOURG
Moselle
Esch-
sur-Alzette
GERMANY
FRANCE
72
77
0 km
50
0 miles
50
51°
50°
3°
4°
5°
6°
A
B
C
D
E
5
6
7
8

◆ Over 80 percent of the world's rough-cut diamonds pass through Antwerp's (Antwerpen) Diamond Quarter every year, making it the largest diamond trading center in the world, with an annual turnover of over US$50 billion.

◆ On August 23, 1914, three weeks after Britain entered World War I, the 70,000 strong British Expeditionary Force encountered the advancing German army for the first time at the battle of Mons.

◆ Echternach is the home of the only religious dancing procession remaining in the Western world. Every year since the 15th century, thousands of pilgrims have marched down the streets of the town performing a ritual dance involving specific movements, music, and prayers.

The British Isles

A
B
C
D
E
1
2
3
4
10°
5°
0°
60°
55°
65
65
48
67
Faroe Islands
ATLANTIC
OCEAN
Shetland Islands
Lerwick
Midges have the fastest wing-beat of any insect, and are able to flap their wings at around 60,000 beats per minute.
Orkney Islands
Kirkwall
After the surrender of the German fleet in 1918 and its internment in Scapa Flow, over 50 ships were scuttled by the German crews on June 21, 1919, to prevent them falling into British hands.
Thurso
Isle of Lewis
Stornoway
Outer Hebrides
North Uist
South Uist
Barra
The Little Minch
The Minch
Ullapool
Moray Firth
Elgin
Inverness
Loch Ness
Isle of Skye
With a depth of 788 ft (240 m) and a length of about 23 miles (36 km), Loch Ness contains the largest volume of fresh water in Great Britain.
Aberdeen
SCOTLAND
Grampian Mts.
Ben Nevis 4406ft (1343m)
Fort William
The Giant's Causeway comprises approximately 37,000 interlocking dark basalt polygonal columns; they were formed by volcanic activity some 55 million years ago.
Isle of Mull
Oban
Loch Lomond
Jura
Forth
Dundee
Perth
Stirling
Firth of Forth
EDINBURGH
North
Sea
Greenock
Glasgow
Islay
Isle of Arran
Ayr
Southern Uplands
UNITED KINGDOM
Dumfries
Carlisle
Newcastle upon Tyne
NORTHERN
Londonderry

IRELAND
DUBLIN
BELFAST
Sligo
Athlone
Galway
Ennis
Limerick
Tralee
Killarney
Cork
Waterford
Wexford
Newry
Dundalk
Lough Corrib
Lough Ree
Lough Derg
Shannon
Blackwater
Barrow
Liffey
Wicklow Mts.
Bantry Bay
Irish Sea
(British Crown Dependency)
Douglas
Anglesey
Holyhead
Bangor
Snowdonia
Cardigan Bay
Aberystwyth
Fishguard
Milford Haven
Swansea
CARDIFF
Newport
Brecon Beacons
WALES
ENGLAND
LONDON
Lancaster
Blackpool
Preston
Liverpool
Chester
Bolton
Bradford
Manchester
Leeds
York
Middlesbrough
Kingston upon Hull
Grimsby
Sheffield
Lincoln
The Wash
Stoke-on-Trent
Shrewsbury
Derby
Nottingham
Leicester
The Fens
Peterborough
Norwich
Birmingham
Coventry
Worcester
Stratford-upon-Avon
Gloucester
Severn
Oxford
Cambridge
Colchester
Ipswich
Southend-on-Sea
Thames
Swindon
Bristol
Bath
Reading
Canterbury
Dover
Channel Tunnel
Barnstaple
Exmoor
Taunton
Salisbury
Southampton
Brighton
Portsmouth
Bournemouth
Isle of Wight
Exeter
Dartmoor
Plymouth
Penzance
Land's End
Isles of Scilly
English Channel
Channel Islands
St. Peter Port
Guernsey
(British Crown Dependency)
St. Helier
Jersey
(British Crown Dependency)
FRANCE
ATLANTIC OCEAN
Every year over 1.5 billion pints (850 million litres) of Guinness® Irish stout are consumed in over 120 countries around the world.
The River Severn has the second highest tidal range in the world, as much as 50 ft (15 m), often giving rise to a tidal bore. In September 1996, one such wave carried a surfer for 5.7 miles (9 km).
With evidence of teaching beginning as early as 1096, Oxford University is the second oldest university in the world.
0 km 100
0 miles 100
48
68
74
72
50°
10°
5°
0°
A B C D E
5 6 7 8

France, Andorra & Monaco

North Sea
English Channel
Bay of Biscay
UNITED KINGDOM
NETHERLANDS
BELGIUM
GERMANY
LUXEMBOURG
FRANCE
SWITZERLAND
Channel Islands
(British Crown Dependencies)
Guernsey
Jersey
Île d'Ouessant
Belle Île
Channel Tunnel
Normandie
Bretagne
Bourgogne
Vosges
Work began on the 31-mile (50-km) Channel Tunnel in 1987. Earth was removed at the rate of 2400 tons (tonnes) a day until completion, seven years later. Around 10.5 million cu yards (8 million cu m) had been excavated.
On July 1, 1916, the British suffered 58,000 casualties on the opening day of the Somme Offensive. Five months later, after advancing only a few miles, there had been 420,000 British, 200,000 French, and 500,000 German casualties.
Champagne bottles are placed neck down into a freezing brine bath (bac à glace), freezing only the bottle's neck to form a plug that keeps the wine – and the bubbles – in the bottle while sediments are removed.
PARIS
Dunkerque
Calais
Boulogne-sur-Mer
Lille
Arras
Douai
Amiens
Dieppe
Rouen
Le Havre
Cherbourg
Caen
St.-Lô
St.-Malo
St.-Brieuc
Brest
Quimper
Lorient
Rennes
Laval
Alençon
Le Mans
Angers
Nantes
St.-Nazaire
la Roche-sur-Yon
Tours
Blois
Orléans
Chartres
Versailles
Mantes-la-Jolie
Beauvais
Laon
Reims
Châlons-en-Champagne
Troyes
Auxerre
Nevers
Bourges
Poitiers
Dijon
Besançon
Vesoul
Épinal
Bar-le-Duc
Nancy
Metz
Thionville
Strasbourg
Colmar
Mulhouse
Belfort
Somme
Seine
Marne
Meuse
Moselle
Saône
Loire
71
65
76
5°
0°
50°
55°
A
B
C
D
E
1
2
3
4

In 2010, an 1869 Château Lafite, was sold at auction for US$233,972, making it the most expensive bottle of wine in the world.
The Tour de France bicycle race is typically held over some 20 day-long stages covering around 2200 miles (3600 km) for the coveted yellow jersey.
The lowest point in Andorra is Riu Runer, at 2756 ft (840m) above sea level.
The word denim comes from "de Nîmes," this being the town where the fabric was originally produced.
One of history's great leaders, Napoleon Bonaparte, was born on August 15, 1769, at Ajaccio in Corsica.
Saintes
Limoges
Vichy
Mâcon
Lake Geneva
Angoulême
Roanne
Villeurbanne
Mont Blanc 15,771ft (4807m)
Clermont-Ferrand
Lyon
Annecy
St.-Chamond
Périgueux
St.-Étienne
Chambéry
Massif Central
Bordeaux
Dordogne
Aurillac
le Puy
ITALY
Garonne
Lot
Grenoble
Alps
Cahors
Valence
Rodez
Mende
Mont-de-Marsan
Agen
Montauban
Tarn
Rhône
Bayonne
Auch
Albi
Cévennes
Avignon
Provence
Pau
Toulouse
Nîmes
Aix-en-Provence
MONACO
Tarbes
Montpellier
Arles
Cannes
Nice
Pyrenees
Carcassonne
Beziers
Marseille
Côte d'Azur
Narbonne
Perpignan
Toulon
Ligurian Sea
ANDORRA
ANDORRA LA VELLA
Golfe du Lion
Îles d'Hyères
Bastia
Corse (Corsica)
Ajaccio
SPAIN
Sardinia
Balearic Islands
Mediterranean Sea
0 km 100
0 miles 100
45°
40°
0°
5°
75
78
84
84
A B C D E
5 6 7 8

Spain & Portugal

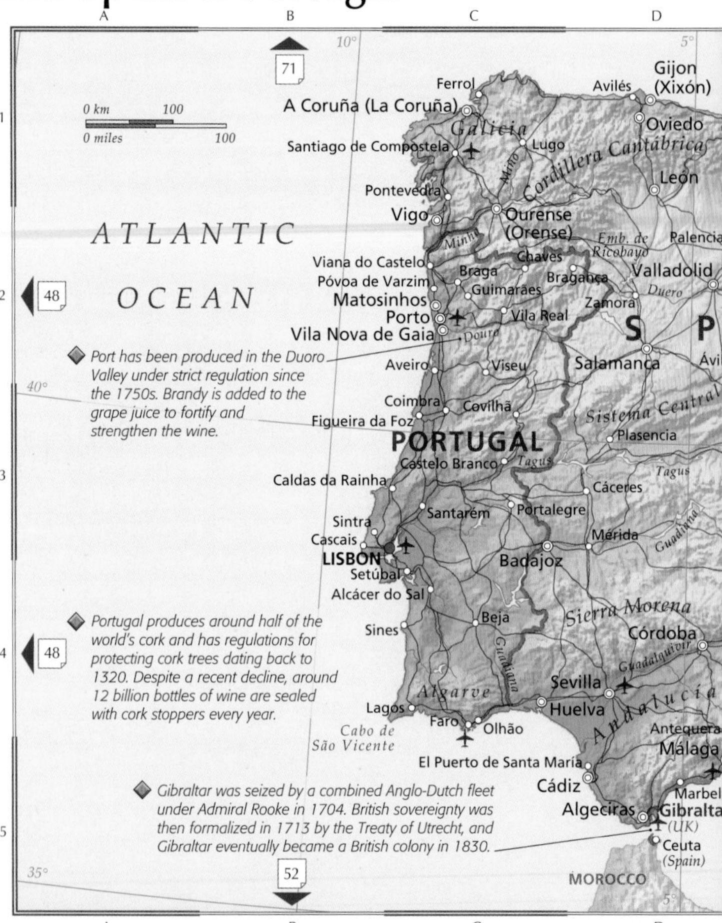

Port has been produced in the Duoro Valley under strict regulation since the 1750s. Brandy is added to the grape juice to fortify and strengthen the wine.
Portugal produces around half of the world's cork and has regulations for protecting cork trees dating back to 1320. Despite a recent decline, around 12 billion bottles of wine are sealed with cork stoppers every year.
Gibraltar was seized by a combined Anglo-Dutch fleet under Admiral Rooke in 1704. British sovereignty was then formalized in 1713 by the Treaty of Utrecht, and Gibraltar eventually became a British colony in 1830.
0 km 100
0 miles 100
71
48
48
52
ATLANTIC
OCEAN
PORTUGAL
S P
MOROCCO
Ferrol
A Coruña (La Coruña)
Galicia
Santiago de Compostela
Lugo
Miño
Cordillera Cantábrica
Avilés
Gijon (Xixón)
Oviedo
León
Pontevedra
Vigo
Ourense (Orense)
Minho
Emb. de Ricobayo
Palencia
Viana do Castelo
Braga
Chaves
Bragança
Valladolid
Póvoa de Varzim
Guimarães
Matosinhos
Zamora
Duero
Porto
Vila Real
Vila Nova de Gaia
Douro
Aveiro
Viseu
Salamanca
Coimbra
Covilhã
Figueira da Foz
Sistema Central
Plasencia
Castelo Branco
Tagus
Caldas da Rainha
Cáceres
Santarém
Portalegre
Sintra
Cascais
LISBON
Mérida
Guadiana
Badajoz
Setúbal
Alcácer do Sal
Sierra Morena
Beja
Sines
Córdoba
Guadalquivir
Sevilla
Algarve
Huelva
Andalucía
Lagos
Faro
Olhão
Cabo de São Vicente
Antequera
Málaga
El Puerto de Santa María
Cádiz
Algeciras
Gibraltar (UK)
Ceuta (Spain)

E
F
G
H
1
2
3
4
5
0°
5°
40°
73
78
79
52
Bay of Biscay
FRANCE
Santander
Bilbao
Donostia/San Sebastián
Vitoria-Gasteiz
Miranda de Ebro
Pamplona (Iruña)
Pyrenees
ANDORRA
Golfe du Lion
Burgos
Logroño
Ebro
Huesca
Figueres
Girona (Gerona)
Costa Brava
Cataluña
Soria
Lleida
Terrassa
Mataró
Zaragoza
Sabadell
Barcelona
L'Hospitalet de Llobregat
Sistema Ibérico
AIN
Reus
Tarragona
Tortosa
egovia
MADRID
Getafe
Teruel
Cuenca
Júcar
oledo
Castellón de la Plana
Valencia
País Valenciano
Gandia
Palma
Menorca
Mallorca
Ibiza
Islas Baleares
(Balearic Islands)
Formentera
Albacete
iudad Real
Elda
Benidorm
Segura
Cieza
Alicante (Alacant)
Elche (Elx)
Linares
Murcia
Costa Blanca
Jaén
Lorca
Cartagena
Granada
Sierra Nevada
Almería
Motril
Costa del Sol
Mediterranean Sea
ALGERIA
Work continues on the Sagrada Família, Gaudí's unfinished cathedral. Begun in 1882, construction passed the mid-point in 2010 and is now due to be completed in around 2025.
Seat of many great civilizations throughout history, the name Mediterranean translates as "sea between the lands."
Spain produces just under half of the world's olive oil, which amounted to around 1.2 million tons (tonnes) in 2009. Of this, roughly 30 percent is the highest quality "extra-virgin" olive oil.

Germany & The Alpine States

North Sea
Jylland
The Kiel Canal is 61 miles (98 km) long and one of the busiest canals in the world, with around 45,000 ships a year passing between the Baltic and the North Sea.
DENMARK
Sjælland
Fyn
SWEDEN
0 km 100
0 miles 100
Baltic Sea
Bornholm (Denmark)
Early in the morning of Sunday, August 13, 1961, work began on the Berlin Wall, which would eventually run for 66 miles (107 km) between east and west Berlin, cutting through 192 streets.
During what became known as "The Berlin Airlift" a total of 2,326,406 tons (tonnes) of supplies were flown into Berlin over an 18-month period to break a Soviet blockade of the city.
North Frisian Islands
Falster
Fehmarn Belt
Fehmarn
Mecklenburger Bucht
Rügen
Flensburg
Kiel
Neumünster
Lübeck
Stralsund
Greifswald
Rostock
Wismar
Schwerin
Neubrandenburg
Müritz
Cuxhaven
Bremerhaven
Emden
Hamburg
Lüneburg
Elbe
Oldenburg
Bremen
NETHERLANDS
Ems
Weser
GERMANY
Osnabrück
Hannover
Wolfsburg
BERLIN
Frankfurt an der Oder
Münster
Hildesheim
Braunschweig
Potsdam
Bielefeld
Salzgitter
Magdeburg
Dessau
Cottbus
Recklinghausen
Hamm
Paderborn
Saale
Halle
Spree
POLAND
Essen
Duisburg
Dortmund
Bochum
Göttingen
Düsseldorf
Wuppertal
Kassel
Leipzig
Dresden
Leverkusen
Erfurt
Jena
Gera

67 67 71 80

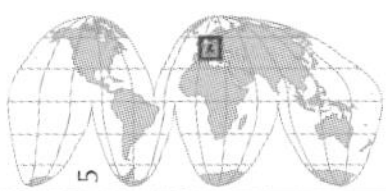

At 528 ft (161 m) high and containing 768 steps, the steeple of Ulm Minster makes it the tallest church in the world.

Born in Salzburg on January 27, 1756, Wolfgang Amadeus Mozart was already writing music by the age of five, and at eleven he produced his first opera.

When it is completed in 2016, the Gotthard Base Tunnel will run for 35.5 miles (57 km) beneath the Lepontine Alps to become the longest rail tunnel in the world.

The acrylic glass roof over the Olympic stadium in München (Munich) measures 914,940 sq ft (85,000 sq m), making it the biggest structure of its kind in the world.

CZECH REPUBLIC
FRANCE
SWITZERLAND
LIECHTENSTEIN
AUSTRIA
HUNGARY
SLOVENIA
CROATIA
ITALY
BELGIUM
LUX.
Erzgebirge
Bohemian Forest
Wiesbaden
Mainz
Frankfurt am Main
Offenbach
Darmstadt
Würzburg
Erlangen
Nürnberg
Kaiserslautern
Mannheim
Heidelberg
Saarbrücken
Karlsruhe
Heilbronn
Pforzheim
Stuttgart
Reutlingen
Fränkische Alb
Schwäbische Alb
Schwarzwald
Regensburg
Ingolstadt
Landshut
Augsburg
Ulm
München
Freiburg im Breisgau
Danube
Rhine
Mosel
Neckar
Inn
Braunau am Inn
Linz
Wels
Krems an der Donau
Hollabrunn
Sankt Pölten
VIENNA
Barden
Eisenstadt
Wiener Neustadt
Neusiedler See
Salzburg
Hellejn
Enns
Kapfenberg
Schaffhausen
Lake Constance
Bavarian Alps
Basel
Delémont
Zürich
Zürichsee
Bregenz
Innsbruck
Jura
Biel
Zug
BERN
Luzern
VADUZ
Chur
Tirol
Hohe Tauern
Alps
Judenburg
Graz
Mur
Lac de Neuchâtel
Yverdon
Lausanne
Thuner See
Berner Alpen
Lake Geneva
Genève
Sion
Brig
Monthey
Matterhorn 14,692ft (4478m)
Locarno
Lugano
Lake Maggiore
Lienz
Villach
Klagenfurt
Maribor
Celje
Sava
Kranj
LJUBLJANA
Koper
Gulf of Venice
50°
45°
10°
15°
A B C D E
5 6 7 8

73
78
78
81

Italy

In June 2011, a violin called the "Lady Blunt," made by Italian master Stradivari at Cremona in 1721, sold for a record US$16,300,000.
San Marino formed in AD 301 is the oldest, and, at 24 sq mi (61 sq km), one of the smallest republics in the world.
Established in 1088, Bologna University is the oldest in the world.
FRANCE
GERMANY
CZECH REPUBLIC
SLOVAKIA
LIECHTENSTEIN
SWITZERLAND
AUSTRIA
HUNGARY
SLOVENIA
CROATIA
BOSNIA & HERZEGOVINA
ITALY
SAN MARINO
VATICAN CITY
ROME
Alps
Lake Maggiore
Lago di Como
Lago di Garda
Alpi Dolomitiche
Appennino
Aosta
Novara
Monza
Bergamo
Milano
Brescia
Torino
Cremona
Verona
Vicenza
Treviso
Bolzano
Trento
Udine
Mestre
Trieste
Venezia
Padova
Mantova
Adige
Po
Piave
Gulf of Venice
Po Delta
Alessandria
Piacenza
Parma
Ferrara
Genova
Reggio nell' Emilia
Modena
Bologna
Savona
Golfo di Genova
La Spezia
San Remo
Ravenna
Forlì
Rimini
Viareggio
Prato
Pisa
Arno
Firenze
Livorno
Ligurian Sea
Toscana
Arezzo
Siena
Ancona
Lago Trasimeno
Isola d'Elba
Perugia
Foligno
Corsica (part of France)
Grosseto
Arcipelago Toscano
Terni
Ascoli Piceno
Viterbo
Tevere
Pescara
L'Aquila
Adriatic Sea
A B C D E
1 2 3 4
10°
15°
45°
77
77
73
82

The medical school at Salerno is the oldest in Europe, established during the 11th and 12th centuries.
Mt. Etna began some 300,000 years ago as a submarine volcano and has since grown to a cone with a base 30 miles (48 km) wide and 10,922 ft (3329 m) high.
The George cross that appears on the Maltese flag was awarded to the islanders by King George VI of Britain for their heroism during World War II.
Mediterranean Sea
Tyrrhenian Sea
Ionian Sea
Sardegna
(Sardinia)
Sicilia
(Sicily)
Calabria
TUNISIA
MALTA
VALLETTA
Gozo
Malta Channel
Strait of Sicily
Stretto di Messina
Strait of Otranto
Golfo di Taranto
Golfo di Salerno
Golfo di Gaeta
Isola di Capri
Isola d'Ustica
Isole Eolie
Isola Lipari
Isola Vulcano
Isola Stromboli
Isole Egadi
Isola di Pantelleria
Isole Pelagie
Alghero
Nuoro
Oristano
Iglesias
Cagliari
Napoli
Torre del Greco
Benevento
Salerno
Potenza
Ofanto
Bari
Altamura
Taranto
Brindisi
Lecce
Gallipoli
Crotone
Catanzaro
Cosenza
Reggio di Calabria
Messina
Palermo
Cefalù
Trapani
Marsala
Agrigento
Caltanissetta
Salso
Catania
Siracusa
Ragusa
0 km 100
0 miles 100
40°
35°
10°
15°
A
B
C
D
E
5
6
7
8
53
83

Central Europe

SWEDEN
DENMARK
LATVIA
LITHUANIA
BELARUS
GERMANY
POLAND
KALININGRAD (part of Russian Federation)
Baltic Sea
Bornholm (part of Denmark)
Courland Lagoon
Gulf of Danzig
Pomeranian Bay
Zalew Szczeciński
Mazury
Founded in Gdansk shipyard in 1980, the Solidarity trade union, and its leader Lech Walesa, played a key role in the downfall of communism across much of eastern Europe.
Built between 1747 and 1795, the Zaluski Library in Warsaw was one of the world's first public libraries.
In November 1989, the so-called "Velvet Revolution" saw Czechoslovakia split into the Czech Republic and Slovakia.
WARSAW
Słupsk
Gdynia
Gdańsk
Koszalin
Elbląg
Olsztyn
Człuchów
Grudziądz
Szczecin
Piła
Bydgoszcz
Toruń
Ostrołęka
Białystok
Gorzów Wielkopolski
Włocławek
Płock
Poznań
Zielona Góra
Kalisz
Łódź
Radom
Lublin
Legnica
Wrocław
Kielce
Ostrowiec Świętokrzyski
Děčín
Liberec
Oder
Wisła
Warta
Noteć
Narew
Bug
0 km 100
0 miles 100
67
88
76
89
15°
20°
25°
55°
A B C D E
1 2 3 4

CZECH REPUBLIC
SLOVAKIA
HUNGARY
AUSTRIA
SLOVENIA
CROATIA
BOSNIA & HERZEGOVINA
SERBIA
ROMANIA
UKRAINE
ITALY
Adriatic Sea
Carpathian Mts.
Great Hungarian Plain
PRAGUE
BRATISLAVA
BUDAPEST
Plzeň
Stratonice
České Budějovice
Tábor
Jihlava
Pardubice
Prostějov
Brno
Olomouc
Ostrava
Wodzisław Śląski
Rybnik
Bielsko-Biała
Kraków
Rzeszów
Žilina
Martin
Trenčín
Trnava
Piešťany
Nitra
Banská Bystrica
Lučenec
Poprad
Prešov
Košice
Rožňava
Ózd
Miskolc
Nyíregyháza
Debrecen
Szolnok
Kecskemét
Békéscsaba
Szeged
Győr
Sopron
Tatabánya
Székesfehérvár
Veszprém
Szombathely
Zalaegerszeg
Nagykanizsa
Kaposvár
Szekszárd
Baja
Pécs
Danube
Tisza
Drava
Váh
Morava
Rába
Balaton
Elbe
Laborec
90
82
77
77
Built in 1357, Charles Bridge was the only crossing point of the Vltava in Prague until the 19th century.
With a surface area of around 231 sq mi (598 sq km), Lake Balaton has an average depth of only 11 ft (3.25 m).
The Great Hungarian Plain (Alföld) stretches south from Budapest to the borders of Croatia and Serbia and east to Ukraine and Romania. It covers an area of 20,000 sq miles (51,800 sq km) and is almost completely flat.

Southeast Europe

SLOVAKIA
At 11:15 am, on June 28, 1914, Archduke Francis Ferdinand and his wife were shot dead by Gavrilo Princip in Sarajevo. This single act precipitated World War I, which eventually lead to the death of almost 10 million troops.
AUSTRIA
HUNGARY
Born in Zagreb in 1892, Marshall Tito was the president of the former Yugoslavia from 1953 until his death in 1980.
The Danube forms all or part of the border between nine different European nations: Germany, Austria, Slovakia, Hungary, Croatia, Serbia, Romania, Bulgaria, and Ukraine.
SLOVENIA
ROMANIA
CROATIA
VOJVODINA
BOSNIA & HERZEGOVINA
REP. SRPSKA
FED. BOSNA I HERCEGOVINA
SERBIA
Dalmacija
Dinaric Alps
Kopaonik
Danube
Drava
Sava
Drina
Bosna
Una
Morava
The modern necktie has its origins in 17th century Croatia as a knotted "cravat" that was worn by
77
81
78
90
ZAGREB
BELGRADE
SARAJEVO
Čakovec
Varaždin
Koprivnica
Bjelovar
Virovitica
Samobor
Karlovac
Sisak
Nova Gradiška
Osijek
Đakovo
Vukovar
Subotica
Kanjiža
Bačka Topola
Sombor
Zrenjanin
Novi Sad
Vršac
Pančevo
Smederevo
Rijeka
Krk
Cres
Pula
Pag
Ogulin
Prijedor
Slavonski Brod
Bosanski Šamac
Modriča
Bihać
Banja Luka
Doboj
Šabac
Loznica
Tuzla
Gospić
Ključ
Zvornik
Zenica
Jajce
Srebrenica
Kragujevac
Zadar
Knin
Dugi Otok
Šibenik
Livno
Čačak
Zaječar
Kraljevo
Konjic
Split
Aleksinac
Kruševac
Brač
Makarska
Foča
Mostar
Niš
15°
20°
45°
A
B
C
D
E
1
2
3
4

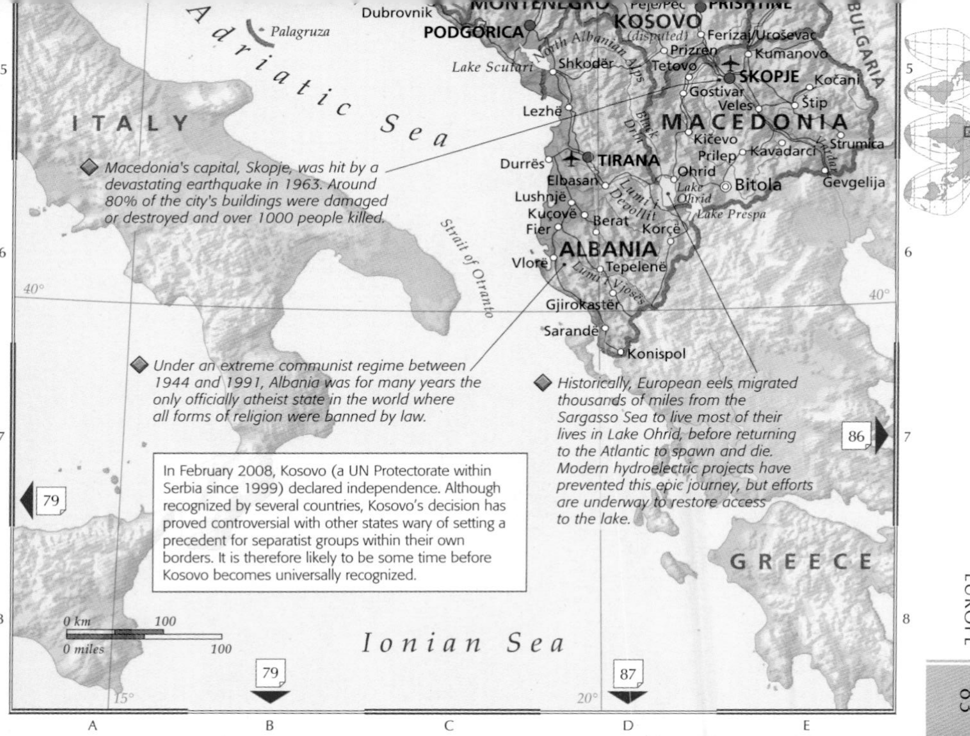
ITALY
Adriatic Sea
Palagruza
Dubrovnik
MONTENEGRO
PODGORICA
Lake Scutari
North Albanian Alps
Shkodër
Lezhë
Durrës
TIRANA
Black Drin
Elbasan
Lushnjë
Kuçovë
Berat
Fier
Lumi i Devollit
Korçë
ALBANIA
Vlorë
Tepelenë
Lumi i Vjosës
Gjirokastër
Sarandë
Konispol
Strait of Otranto
KOSOVO
(disputed)
Pejë/Peć
PRISHTINE
Ferizaj/Uroševac
Prizren
Tetovo
Gostivar
SKOPJE
Kumanovo
Kočani
Štip
Veles
MACEDONIA
Kičevo
Prilep
Kavadarci
Vardar
Strumica
Ohrid
Lake Ohrid
Bitola
Gevgelija
Lake Prespa
BULGARIA
GREECE
Ionian Sea
40°
15°
20°
0 km
100
0 miles
100
A
B
C
D
E
5
6
7
8

Macedonia's capital, Skopje, was hit by a devastating earthquake in 1963. Around 80% of the city's buildings were damaged or destroyed and over 1000 people killed.

Under an extreme communist regime between 1944 and 1991, Albania was for many years the only officially atheist state in the world where all forms of religion were banned by law.

Historically, European eels migrated thousands of miles from the Sargasso Sea to live most of their lives in Lake Ohrid, before returning to the Atlantic to spawn and die. Modern hydroelectric projects have prevented this epic journey, but efforts are underway to restore access to the lake.

In February 2008, Kosovo (a UN Protectorate within Serbia since 1999) declared independence. Although recognized by several countries, Kosovo's decision has proved controversial with other states wary of setting a precedent for separatist groups within their own borders. It is therefore likely to be some time before Kosovo becomes universally recognized.

79
86
79
87

The Mediterranean

A
B
C
D
1
2
3
4
5
50°
40°
30°
10°
0°
62
48
48
52
UNITED KINGDOM
Thames
English Channel
NETHERLANDS
BELGIUM
LUX.
GERMANY
Rhine
Seine
Danube
E U
LIECH.
SWITZ.
Loire
FRANCE
L. Geneva
Alps
ATLANTIC
OCEAN
Bay of Biscay
Massif Central
Dordogne
Rhône
Po
SAN MARINO
Garonne
Genoa
Apennines
MONACO
Marseille
Livorno
Pyrenees
ANDORRA
Golfe du Lion
Corsica
VATICAN CITY
Ebro
Iberian
Peninsula
Barcelona
PORTUGAL
SPAIN
Tagus
Balearic Is.
Sardinia
Valencia
Tyrrhenian Sea
Guadalquivir
Gibraltar (UK)
Gibraltar
Oran
Algiers
Tunis
TUNISIA
Sfax
Strait of Gibraltar
MOROCCO
Atlas Mountains
Chott el Jerid
Madeira (Portugal)
ALGERIA
Grand Erg Occidental
Grand Erg Oriental
Canary Is. (Spain)
AFRI
Saha

E
F
G
H
1
2
3
4
5
20°
30°
40°
63
94
54
POLAND
CZECH REP.
UKRAINE
(the Ukrainian territory of Crimea was annexed by Russia in 2014)
SLOVAKIA
USTRIA
HUNGARY
Hungarian Plain
Carpathian Mountains
MOLDOVA
Dnieper
Don
RUSSIAN FEDERATION
Sea of Azov
LOVENIA
CROATIA
BOS. & HERZ.
ROMANIA
Danube Delta
Crimea
SERBIA
Danube
Dinaric Alps
Adriatic Sea
KOSOVO (disputed)
BULGARIA
Balkan Mts.
Black Sea
Caucasus
MON.
Rhodope Mts.
Bosporus
GEORGIA
TALY
MACEDONIA
Pindus Mts.
Naples
ALBANIA
Aegean Sea
Lesbos
TURKEY
Anatolia
Ionian Sea
GREECE
Piraeus
Izmir
Lake Van
Sicily
Peloponnese
Kos
Taurus Mts.
MALTA
Rhodes
Euphrates
Tigris
Cyprus
SYRIA
Crete
LEBANON
Anti-Lebanon
IRAQ
Haifa
ISRAEL
Syrian Desert
Gulf of Sirte
Nile Delta
Port Said
JORDAN
ASIA
Suez Canal
LIBYA
Nile
SAUDI ARABIA
EGYPT
Libyan Desert
Red Sea
Arabian Peninsula
ROPE
CA
ranean Sea

Bulgaria & Greece

Bulgaria is one of the few countries in the world where locals shake their heads from side to side to mean "yes" and nod up and down for "no."
Sofia's skyline is dominated by the gold domes of the Alexander Nevski Memorial Church, which took craftsmen and artists some thirty years to build between 1882 and 1912.
Built between 447 and 438 BCE, the Parthenon survived almost unscathed for over 2000 years until, in 1687, a gunpowder magazine beneath the building exploded, causing considerable damage.
ROMANIA
SERBIA
KOSOVO
(disputed)
MACEDONIA
ALBANIA
BULGARIA
TURKEY
GREECE
Black Sea
Marmara Denizi
Thracian Sea
Balkan Mountains
Rhodope Mountains
Pindos
SOFIA
Vidin
Vratsa
Pernik
Pleven
Lovech
Ruse
Razgrad
Shumen
Dobrich
Varna
Burgas
Yambol
Sliven
Stara Zagora
Gabrovo
Kazanlŭk
Plovdiv
Pazardzhik
Velingrad
Khaskovo
Blagoevgrad
Petrich
Orestiáda
Alexandroúpoli
Komotiní
Xánthi
Kavála
Dráma
Sérres
Kilkís
Thessaloníki
Kalamariá
Kateríni
Véroia
Kozáni
Flórina
Lárisa
Vólos
Tríkala
Karditsa
Ioánnina
Préveza
Kérkyra
Mitilíni
Danube
Iskŭr
Yazovir Iskŭr
Kamchiya
Maritsa
Tundzha
Arda
Strymonas
Vardar
Pineiós
Lake Prespa
Samothráki
Thásos
Límnos
Lésvos
Kérkyra
Vóreies Sporádes
Akrotírio Pínes
Akrotírio Drépano
Akrotírio Palioúri
Thermaïkós Kólpos
25°
20°
40°
A
B
C
D
E
1
2
3
4
90
93
83

TURKEY
Aegean Sea
Chalkída
Pátra
Korinthiakós Kólpos
Kórinthos
Peiraías
ATHENS
Kefalloniá
Zákynthos
Iónia Nisiá (Ionian Islands)
Pelopónnisos
Trípoli
Kalámata
Spárti
Ionian Sea
Kýthira
Chíos
Ándros
Sámos
Tínos
Ikaría
Tziá
Mýkonos
Kykládes (Cyclades)
Náxos
Mirtóo Pelagos
Páros
Kos
Amorgós
Íos
Mílos
Santoríni
Astypálaia
Dodekánisa (Dodecanese)
Ródos
Ródos (Rhodes)
Kárpathos
Kritikó Pélagos (Sea of Crete)
Irákleio
Chaniá
Kríti (Crete)
Mediterranean Sea
0 km 100
0 miles 100
35°
20°
25°
A
B
C
D
E
5
6
7
8

The first Olympic athletics festival was held at Olympia in around 776 BCE.

The Corinth Canal was completed in 1893 after 11 years of work. The canal is 4 miles (6.3 km) long, 80 ft (25 m) wide, and 26 ft (8 m) deep. The central section runs along a 260 ft- (79 m-) deep cutting through solid rock.

Only about 100 of the 2000 or so Greek Islands are permanently inhabited.

The Minoans developed the first Hellenic civilization 4000 years ago, based at the luxurious palace of Knossos. Unfortunately, in 1400 BCE, this civilization came to an abrupt end, destroyed by a catastrophic event, probably a tidal wave.

79
98
53
54

EUROPE

The Baltic States & Belarus

SWEDEN
FINLAND
Gulf of Bothnia
In 2007, Estonia held the world's first general elections where people were able to vote online using the internet.
Low salinity and the shallow coastal waters cause pack ice to accumulate at the head of the Gulf of Bothnia and off Finland during most winters; occasionally the ice becomes banked up in pressure ridges that are almost 50 ft (15 m) high.
Gulf of Finland
Gotland
Baltic Sea
Hiiumaa
Vormsi
Saaremaa
Narva Bay
ESTONIA
TALLINN
Paldiski
Loksa
Haapsalu
Tapa
Rakvere
Kohtla-Järve
Narva
Paide
Virtsu
Kuressaare
Pärnu
Viljandi
Tartu
Lake Peipus
Gulf of Riga
Kolka
Ventspils
Venta
Talsi
Burtnieku Ezers
Valga
Lake Pskov
Võru
Liepāja
Kuldīga
Valmiera
Saldus
RIGA
Cēsis
Dating from the 13th century, the Latvian flag is one of the oldest in the world. It is said to have originated when a Latvian leader was wounded in battle, and the edges of the white sheet in which he was wrapped were stained with his blood.
Dobele
Ogre
Mažeikiai
Jelgava
LATVIA
Kretinga
Klaipėda
Telšiai
Plunge
Madona
Šiauliai
Jēkabpils
Western Dvina
Biržai
KALININGRAD (part of Russian Federation)
Kelmė
Šilutė
Radviliškis
Rēzekne
Courland Lagoon
Tauragė
Panevėžys
LITHUANIA
Kaliningrad
Neman
Jurbarkas
Daugavpils
Utena
Gusev
Chernyakhovsk
Kaunas
Ukmergė
Navapolatsk

POLAND
RUSSIAN FEDERATION
BELARUS
UKRAINE
Alytus
VILNIUS
Hlybokaye
Western Dvina
Druskininkai
Lyepyel'
Vitsyebsk/Vitebsk
Hrodna/Grodno
Maladzyechna
Barysaw
Orsha
Neman
MINSK
Zhodzina
Vawkavysk
Horki
Byarezina
Slonim
Baranavichy/Baranovichi
Mahilyow/Mogilev
Slutsk
Brest
Babruysk/Bobruysk
Krychaw
Kobryn
Salihorsk
Pinsk
Luninyets
Zhlobin
Pripet
Ptsich
Pripet Marshes
Svyetlahorsk/Svetlogorsk
Rechytsa
Homyel'/Gomel'
Mazyr
Kalinkavichy
Dnieper (Dnyapro/Dnepr)
Kyyivs'ka Vdskh
55°
50°
25°
30°
A
B
C
D
E
5
6
7
8
80
90
91
Formed in 1945 from the northern half of German East Prussia, and ceded to Russia under the Potsdam agreement, Kaliningrad oblast became a true enclave, completely separated from the rest of Russia, when Lithuania and Belarus achieved their independence in 1991.
Covering an area of approximately 34,000 sq miles (88,000 sq km), Pripet Marshes are the largest area of marshland in Europe.
Following the breakup of the Soviet Union, the Commonwealth of Independent States was established on December 8, 1991, by a treaty signed at Minsk, with the intent of coordinating the foreign policies of the newly independent former Soviet republics.

Ukraine, Moldova & Romania

A
B
C
D
1
2
3
4
5
20°
25°
30°
45°
50°
81
82
86
POLAND
BELARUS
SLOVAKIA
HUNGARY
SERBIA
BULGARIA
U K R
MOLDOVA
ROMANIA
On April 25, 1986, engineers accidentally initiated an uncontrolled chain reaction in the number 4 reactor of the Chornobyl' nuclear power plant. The resulting explosion released 8 tons (tonnes) of radioactive material in the world's worst-ever nuclear accident.
Vlad Dracula or Vlad the Impaler was the real-life prince upon whom Bram Stoker based his famous Count Dracula. Dracula was born in Transylvania in 1431 in the town of Sighisoara.
In 1889, Timisoara became the first city in Europe to have electric street lighting.
Pripet
Pripet Marshes
Kovel'
Luts'k
Korosten'
Rivne
Bug
Zhytomyr
L'viv
Ternopil'
Khmel'-nyts'kyy
Ivano-Frankivs'k
Vinnytsya
Uzhhorod
Carpathian Mountains
Kam"yanets'-Podil's'kyy
Dniester
Transnistri
Chernivtsi
Satu Mare
Rîbnița
Bălți
Baia Mare
Suceava
Botoșani
Oradea
Dej
Transylvania
Dubăsari
Piatra-Neamț
CHIȘINĂ
Cluj-Napoca
Iași
Tiraspol
Arad
Târgu Mureș
Bacău
Tighina (Bendery)
Alba Iulia
Sighisoara
Timișoara
Siret
Basarabeasca
Deva
Sibiu
Focșani
Carpații Meridionali
Reșița
Brașov
Galați
Reni
Râmnicu Vâlcea
Buzău
Târgoviște
Tulcea
Pitești
Brăila
Ploiești
Drobeta-Turnu Severin
BUCHAREST
Craiova
Danube
Olt
Constanța
Corabia
Giurgui
Eforie Sud
Mangalia

E
F
G
H
30°
35°
40°
RUSSIAN FEDERATION
93
1
Shostka
Chernihiv
Chornobyl'
Sumy
Kyyivs'ke Vdskh.
KIEV
Kaniv's'ke Vdskh.
Lubny
Bila Tserkva
A I N E
Kharkiv
50°
93
2
Cherkasy
Poltava
Donets
Kremenchuts'ke Vdskh.
Kremenchuk
Syeverodonets'k
Oleksandriya
Slov''yans'k
Luhans'k
Kirovohrad
Pavlohrad
Horlivka
Kostyantynivka
Dnipropetrovs'k
Yenakiyeve
Makiyivka
Krasnyy Luch
Donets'k
3
Pivdennyy Buh
Kryvyy Rih
Nikopol
Zaporizhzhya
Kakhovs'ka Vdskh.
Mariupol'
Mykolayiv
Melitopol'
Berdyans'k
Kherson
Dnieper
Kakhovka
Odesa
Sea of Azov
(the Ukrainian territory of Crimea was annexed by Russia in 2014)
93
4
Karkinits'ka Zatoka
Kryms'kyy Pivostriv
Kerch
45°
Yevpatoriya
Simferopol'
RUSSIAN FEDERATION
Black Sea
Sevastopol'
Yalta
0 km
100
0 miles
100
5
98
35°
40°
E
F
G
H

◆ A monument in central Kiev stands as testament to the 7–12 million Ukrainian peasants who died during the Great Famine, or Holodomor, of 1932–33.

◆ In 1872, an iron foundry was established at Donets'k by British industrialist John Hughes (from whom the town's pre-Revolutionary name Yuzovka was derived) to produce rails for the growing Russian transportation network.

◆ Odesa was one of the major flashpoints in the Russian Revolution of 1905, and was the scene of the mutiny on the warship Potemkin, when sailors protesting against the serving of rotten meat eventually killed several of the ship's officers.

European Russia

ARCTIC OCEAN
The port of Murmansk remains ice-free throughout the winter thanks to the Gulf Stream, whereas St. Petersburg, 600 miles (965 km) to the south on the Baltic Sea, is ice-bound between December and May.
0 km 400
0 miles 400
137
66
96
Norwegian Sea
Arctic Circle
NORWAY
SWEDEN
FINLAND
Gulf of Bothnia
Baltic Sea
Gulf of Finland
ESTONIA
LATVIA
LITHUANIA
BELARUS
Murmansk
Barents Sea
Novaya Zemlya
Karskoye More
Ostrov Kolguyev
Ostrov Vaygach
Kol'skiy Poluostrov
Beloye More
Ladozhskoye Ozero
Onezhskoye Ozero
Sankt Petersburg
Petrozavodsk
Arkhangel'sk
Vorkuta
Pechora
Mezen'
Pinega
Severnaya Dvina
Onega
Usa
(Ural Mountains)
Pskov
Velikiy Novgorod
Velikiye Luki
Cherepovets
Rybinskoye Vdkhr
Vologda
Kotlas
Ukhta
Syktyvkar
Smolensk
Tver'
Yaroslavl'
RUSSIAN FEDERATION
Dnieper

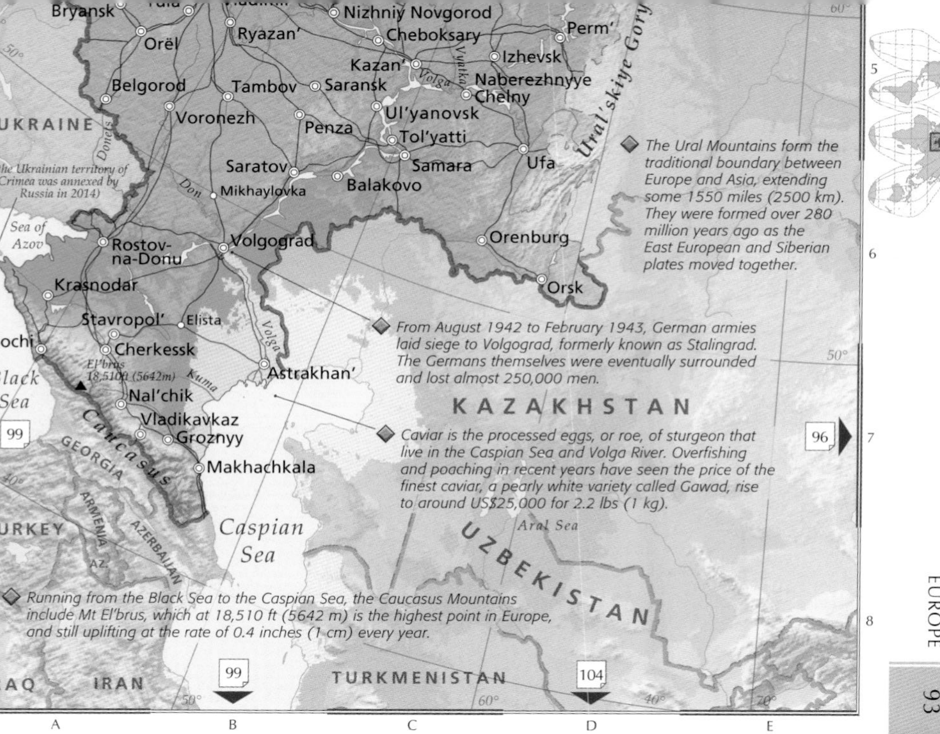
Bryansk
Orël
Belgorod
Ryazan'
Tambov
Voronezh
Nizhniy Novgorod
Cheboksary
Kazan'
Saransk
Penza
Ul'yanovsk
Tol'yatti
Samara
Saratov
Balakovo
Mikhaylovka
Perm'
Izhevsk
Naberezhnyye Chelny
Ufa
Orenburg
Orsk
Ural'skiye Gory
Volga
Vyatka
Don
Donets
UKRAINE
(the Ukrainian territory of Crimea was annexed by Russia in 2014)
Sea of Azov
Rostov-na-Donu
Volgograd
Krasnodar
Stavropol'
Elista
Sochi
Cherkessk
El'brus 18,510ft (5642m)
Kuma
Astrakhan'
Black Sea
Nal'chik
Vladikavkaz
Groznyy
Makhachkala
Caucasus
GEORGIA
ARMENIA
AZERBAIJAN
AZ.
TURKEY
Caspian Sea
KAZAKHSTAN
UZBEKISTAN
Aral Sea
TURKMENISTAN
IRAQ
IRAN
30°
40°
50°
60°
70°
A
B
C
D
E
5
6
7
8

99
96
99
104

The Ural Mountains form the traditional boundary between Europe and Asia, extending some 1550 miles (2500 km). They were formed over 280 million years ago as the East European and Siberian plates moved together.

From August 1942 to February 1943, German armies laid siege to Volgograd, formerly known as Stalingrad. The Germans themselves were eventually surrounded and lost almost 250,000 men.

Caviar is the processed eggs, or roe, of sturgeon that live in the Caspian Sea and Volga River. Overfishing and poaching in recent years have seen the price of the finest caviar, a pearly white variety called Gawad, rise to around US$25,000 for 2.2 lbs (1 kg).

Running from the Black Sea to the Caspian Sea, the Caucasus Mountains include Mt El'brus, which at 18,510 ft (5642 m) is the highest point in Europe, and still uplifting at the rate of 0.4 inches (1 cm) every year.

North & West Asia

A
B
C
D
1
2
3
4
5
20°
40°
60°
80°
137
63
50
50
A R C T I C
Franz Josef Land
Severnaya Zemlya
Novaya Zemlya
Kara Sea
Norwegian Sea
North Cape
Barents Sea
Arctic Circle
Gulf of Bothnia
Lake Onega
Northern Dvina
Lake Ladoga
Baltic Sea
North Sea
KALININGRAD
(Russ. Fed.)
Volga
Central Russian Upland
Ural Mountains
R U S S I A N
West Siberian Plain
Ob'
Irtysh
Yenisey
Ishim
KAZAKHSTAN
Ozero Zaysan
E U R O P E
(the Ukrainian territory of Crimea was annexed by Russia in 2014)
Don
Ural
Aral Sea
Lake Balkhash
Ili
Tien Shan
Caucasus
Caspian Sea
Black Sea
Danube
GEORGIA
ARMENIA
AZERB.
UZBEKISTAN
KYRGYZSTAN
TURKMEN.
Amu Darya
TAJIKISTAN
TURKEY
Lake Van
Mediterranean Sea
SYRIA
IRAQ
LEBANON
IRAN
AFGHANISTAN
Tibetan Plateau
Himalayas
Ganges
ISRAEL
JORDAN
Euphrates
Tigris
KUWAIT
BAHRAIN
Persian Gulf
QATAR
U.A.E.
Tropic of Cancer
Nile
Red Sea
SAUDI ARABIA
OMAN
Arabian Sea
Bay of Bengal
YEMEN
A F R I C A
Gulf of Aden
Socotra (Yemen)

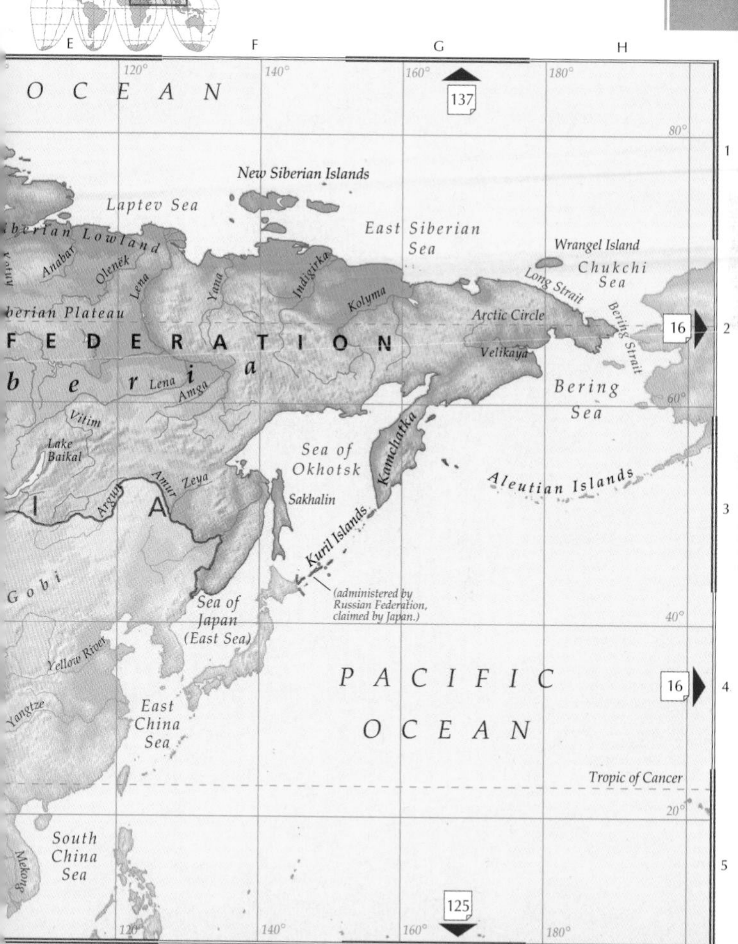
E
F
G
H
120°
140°
160°
180°
137
O C E A N
80°
1
New Siberian Islands
Laptev Sea
East Siberian Sea
Wrangel Island
Chukchi Sea
Long Strait
Bering Strait
Arctic Circle
berian Lowland
Anabar
Olenëk
Lena
Yana
Indigirka
Kolyma
berian Plateau
16
2
F E D E R A T I O N
Velikaya
b e r i a
Lena
Amga
Bering Sea
60°
Vitim
Lake Baikal
Sea of Okhotsk
Kamchatka
Aleutian Islands
Amur
Zeya
Sakhalin
Argun
I A
Kuril Islands
3
Gobi
(administered by Russian Federation, claimed by Japan.)
Sea of Japan (East Sea)
40°
Yellow River
P A C I F I C
O C E A N
16
4
Yangtze
East China Sea
Tropic of Cancer
20°
South China Sea
Mekong
5
125
120°
140°
160°
180°
E
F
G
H

Russia & Kazakhstan

A B C D
1 2 3 4 5
ARCTIC
Barents Sea
Zemlya Frantsa-Iosifa
Novaya Zemlya
Karskoye More
NORWAY
SWEDEN
FINLAND
DENMARK
GERMANY
KALININGRAD (part of Russian Federation)
POLAND
LITH.
LAT.
EST.
BELARUS
UKRAINE
MOLDOVA
(the Ukrainian territory of Crimea was annexed by Russia in 2014)
Arctic Circle
Murmansk
Sankt-Peterburg
Pskov
Velikiy Novgorod
Arkhangel'sk
Cherepovets
MOSCOW
Vologda
Yaroslavl'
Bryansk
Tula
Ryazan'
Nizhniy Novgorod
Kirov
Syktyvkar
Vorkuta
Salekhard
Nori'lsk
Yenisey
Ob'
Ural'skiye Gory
Zapadno-Sibirskaya Ravnina
Voronezh
Kazan'
Perm'
Izhevsk
Serov
Rostov-na-Donu
Volgograd
Samara
Ufa
Yekaterinburg
Nizhnevartovsk
Sochi
Stavropol'
Nal'chik
Volga
Ural'sk
Ural (Zhayyk)
Orenburg
Chelyabinsk
Kostanay
Petropavlovsk
Krasnoyarsk
Astrakhan'
Orsk
Rudnyy
Omsk
Tomsk
GEORGIA
ARM.
Groznyy
Makhachkala
Kokshetau
Novosibirsk
KAZAKHSTAN
ASTANA
Pavlodar
Kemerovo
AZ.
Aktau
Aral Sea
Barnaul
Karagandy
Novokuznetsk
Caspian Sea
Zhezkazgan
Semey
Kyzylorda
Balkhash
Ust'-Kamenogorsk
TURKMENISTAN
UZBEKISTAN
Shymkent
Taraz
Ozero Balkhash
Taldykorgan
IRAN
Almaty
KYRGYZSTAN
CHINA
RUS FED

66
91
102
104

OCEAN
Also known as the "Road of Bones," construction of the 1262 mile (2031 km) road between Yakutsk and Magadan took over twenty years and cost the lives of a huge number of prisoners from Stalin's notorious Gulag camps.
Ostrov Vrangelya
18
Arctic Circle
Pevek
Anadyr'
Vostochno-Sibirskoye More
Ambarchik
Bering Sea
Severnaya Zemlya
Novosibirskiye Ostrova
More Laptevykh
Poluostrov Taymyr
Ozero Taymyr
Tiksi
134
Ossora
Ust'-Kamchatsks
Poluostov Kamchatka
Verkhoyanskiy Khrebet
Lena
Olenëk
Magadan
Petropavlovsk -Kamchatskiy
Srednesibirskoye Ploskogor'ye
Okhotsk
Yakutsk
Sea of Okhotsk
Suntar
Sibir (Siberia)
ATION
Kuril Islands
Sakhalin
Komsomol'sk-na-Amure
Kansk
Skovorodno
134
Bratsk
Ozero Baykal
Yuzhhno-Sakhalinsk
Blagoveshchensk
Amur
Khabarovsk
Irkutsk
Chita
Ulan-Ude
CHINA
JAPAN
Vladivostok
The Trans-Siberian Railroad, completed in 1916, runs 5578 miles (9297 km) between Moscow and Vladivostok. Crossing eight time zones, the journey takes six days.
MONGOLIA
0 km 500
0 miles 500
110

Turkey & the Caucasus

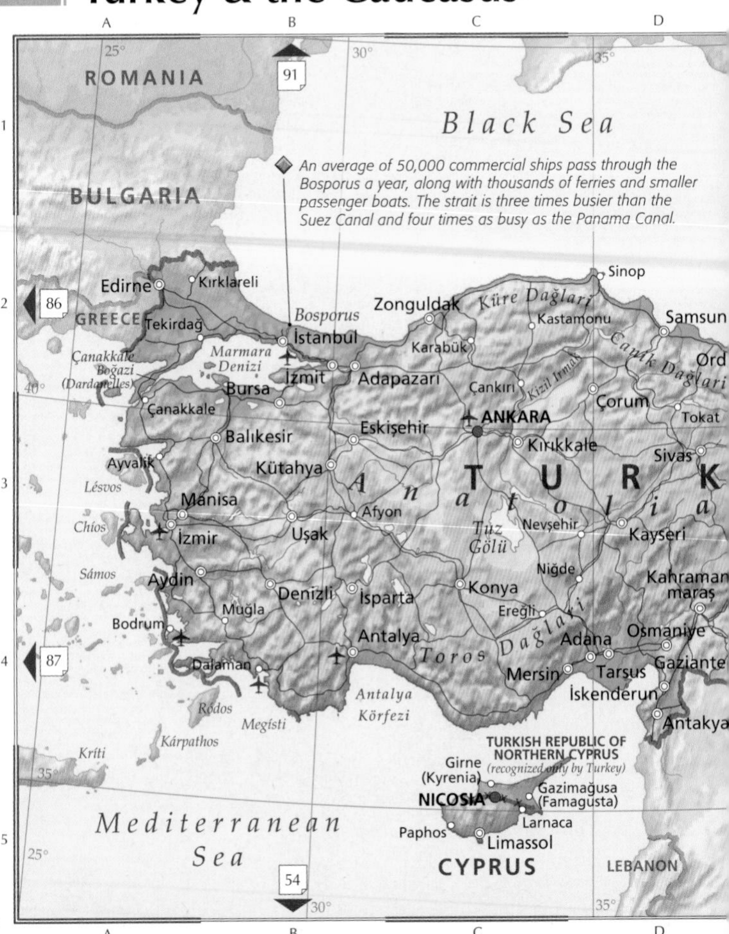
A
B
C
D
1
2
3
4
5
ROMANIA
BULGARIA
Black Sea
An average of 50,000 commercial ships pass through the Bosporus a year, along with thousands of ferries and smaller passenger boats. The strait is three times busier than the Suez Canal and four times as busy as the Panama Canal.
91
86
87
54
GREECE
Edirne
Kırklareli
Tekirdağ
Bosporus
İstanbul
Marmara Denizi
Çanakkale Boğazi (Dardanelles)
Bursa
İzmit
Adapazarı
Zonguldak
Küre Dağları
Sinop
Kastamonu
Samsun
Karabük
Canik Dağları
Ord
Çankırı
Kizil Irmak
Çorum
Tokat
Çanakkale
Balıkesir
Eskişehir
ANKARA
Kırıkkale
Sivas
Ayvalik
Kütahya
TURK
Anatolia
Lésvos
Manisa
Afyon
Tuz Gölü
Nevşehir
Kayseri
Chíos
İzmir
Uşak
Sámos
Aydin
Denizli
İsparta
Konya
Niğde
Kahraman maraş
Muğla
Ereğli
Bodrum
Antalya
Toros Dağları
Adana
Osmaniye
Dalaman
Mersin
Tarsus
Gaziante
İskenderun
Antalya Körfezi
Ródos
Megísti
Antakya
Kárpathos
Kríti
TURKISH REPUBLIC OF NORTHERN CYPRUS
(recognized only by Turkey)
Girne (Kyrenia)
Gazimağusa (Famagusta)
NICOSIA
Larnaca
Paphos
Limassol
Mediterranean Sea
CYPRUS
LEBANON
25°
30°
35°
40°

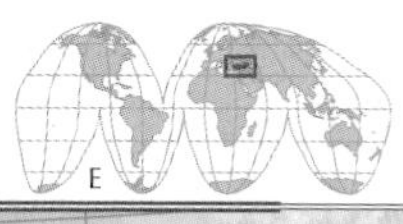

E F G H

RUSSIAN FEDERATION

93

The Spitak earthquake struck Armenia in 1988, killing at least 25,000 people and devastating the country's infrastructure.

Caucasus

Caspian Sea

Gagra
Sokhumi
Ochamchire
Enguri
Kutaisi
GEORGIA
Poti
Batumi
TBILISI
Rustavi
Quba
Hopa
Kura
Vanadzor
Gäncä
Mingäçevir
Sumqayıt
BAKU
Trabzon
Rize
Gyumri
ARMENIA
AZERBAIJAN
Kars
Doğu Karadeniz Dağları
Sevana Lich
Nagorno-Karabakh
YEREVAN
Aras
Xankändi
Erzurum
Erzincan
Büyükağri Daği (Mount Ararat) 16,853ft (5137m)
Naxçıvan
AZERBAIJAN
Länkäran
Van Gölü
Muş
Elazig
Güney Doğu Toroslar
Van
Tigris
Malatya
Siirt
Diyarbakır
Batman
Kurdistan
Adıyaman
Mardin
Şanliurfa
IRAN
SYRIA
IRAQ

104

102

102

Azerbaijan has substantial oil reserves located in and around the Caspian Sea. They were some of the earliest oilfields in the world to be exploited.

The salty water of Lake Van inhibits all animal life except the Pearl Mullet, a small fish that has adapted to the harsh conditions.

Atatürk Dam, one of the largest dams in the world, was completed in 1990. The reservoir behind the dam covers an area of 315 sq miles (816 sq km) and often requires interruptions in the flow of the Euphrates River to maintain water levels.

0 km 200
0 miles 200

40° 45° 50° 35° 40°

1 2 3 4 5

E F G H

The Near East

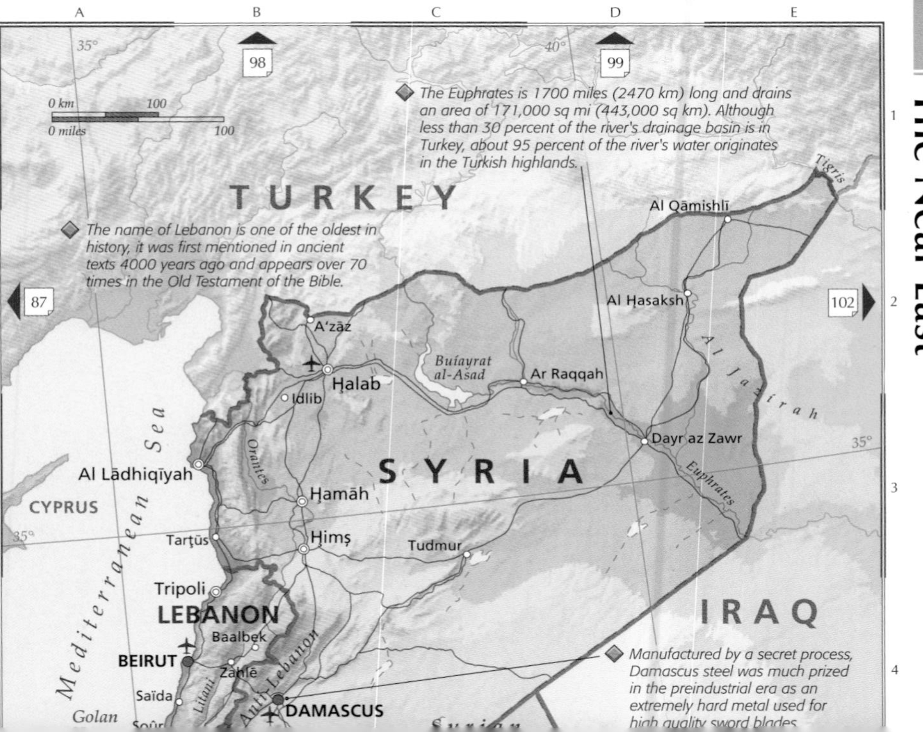
The Euphrates is 1700 miles (2470 km) long and drains an area of 171,000 sq mi (443,000 sq km). Although less than 30 percent of the river's drainage basin is in Turkey, about 95 percent of the river's water originates in the Turkish highlands.
The name of Lebanon is one of the oldest in history, it was first mentioned in ancient texts 4000 years ago and appears over 70 times in the Old Testament of the Bible.
Manufactured by a secret process, Damascus steel was much prized in the preindustrial era as an extremely hard metal used for high quality sword blades
TURKEY
SYRIA
IRAQ
LEBANON
CYPRUS
Mediterranean Sea
Al Jazīrah
Tigris
Euphrates
Orontes
Buḩayrat al-Asad
Anti-Lebanon
Litani
Golan
Al Qāmishlī
Al Ḩasaksh
Dayr az Zawr
Ar Raqqah
Tudmur
Ḩalab
A'zāz
Idlib
Ḩamāh
Ḩimṣ
DAMASCUS
Baalbek
Zahlē
Tripoli
BEIRUT
Saïda
Ţarţūs
Al Lādhiqīyah
0 km 100
0 miles 100
98
99
102
87
35°
40°
A B C D E
1 2 3 4

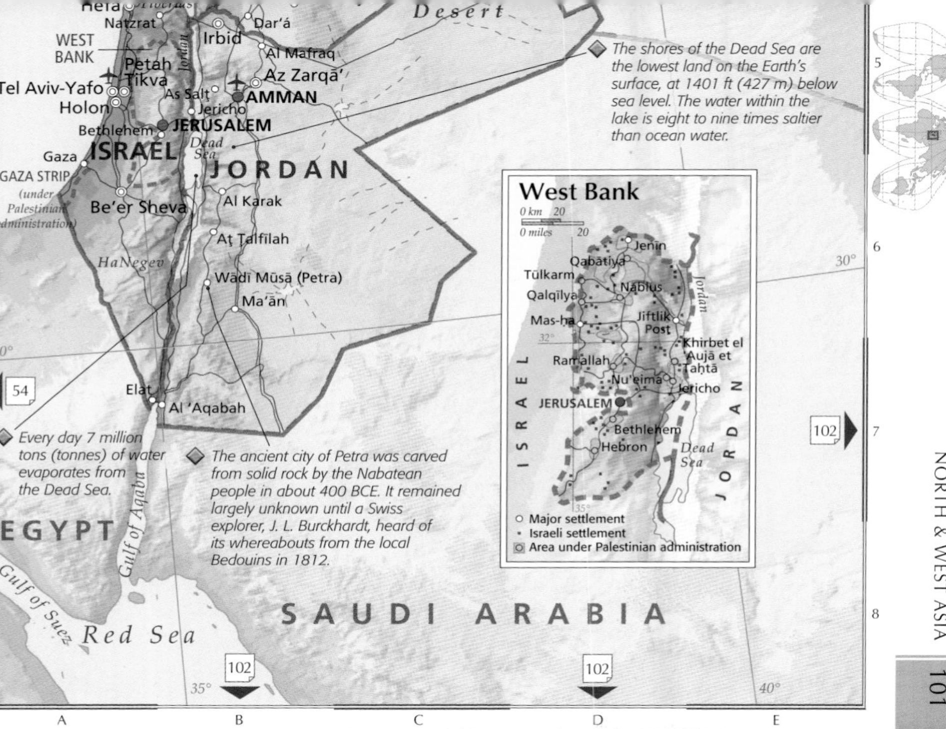

Desert
Natzrat
Dar'á
Irbid
WEST BANK
Al Mafraq
Jordan
Petah Tikva
Az Zarqā'
Tel Aviv-Yafo
As Salt
AMMAN
Holon
Jericho
Bethlehem
JERUSALEM
Gaza
ISRAEL
Dead Sea
JORDAN
GAZA STRIP (under Palestinian administration)
Be'er Sheva
Al Karak
Aṭ Ṭafīlah
HaNegev
Wādī Mūsā (Petra)
Ma'ān
Elat
Al 'Aqabah
EGYPT
Gulf of Aqaba
Gulf of Suez
Red Sea
SAUDI ARABIA
The shores of the Dead Sea are the lowest land on the Earth's surface, at 1401 ft (427 m) below sea level. The water within the lake is eight to nine times saltier than ocean water.
Every day 7 million tons (tonnes) of water evaporates from the Dead Sea.
The ancient city of Petra was carved from solid rock by the Nabatean people in about 400 BCE. It remained largely unknown until a Swiss explorer, J. L. Burckhardt, heard of its whereabouts from the local Bedouins in 1812.
West Bank
0 km 20
0 miles 20
Jenīn
Qabāṭiya
Ṭūlkarm
Nāblus
Qalqīlya
Mas-ha
Jiftlik Post
Jordan
Khirbet el Aujā et Taḥtā
Ramallah
Nu'eima
Jericho
JERUSALEM
Bethlehem
Hebron
Dead Sea
ISRAEL
JORDAN
Major settlement
Israeli settlement
Area under Palestinian administration
54
102
102
102
30°
30°
32°
35°
35°
40°
5
6
7
8
A
B
C
D
E

The Middle East

It is thought that Abdul Kassem Ismael, the Grand Vizier of Persia at the end of the 10th century, decided to take his entire library with him wherever he went. The 117,000 volume library was carried by 400 camels trained to walk in alphabetical order.
Four thousand years ago Babylonian law laid down a minimum wage for every class of workers in the kingdom.
UKRAINE
(the Ukrainian territory of Crimea was annexed by Russia in 2014)
RUSSIAN FEDERATION
KAZAKHSTAN
UZBEKISTAN
TURKMENISTAN
AFGHANISTAN
PAKISTAN
GEORGIA
ARMENIA
AZERBAIJAN
AZ.
TURKEY
SYRIA
CYPRUS
LEBANON
ISRAEL
JORDAN
IRAQ
IRAN
KUWAIT
Sea of Azov
Black Sea
Caspian Sea
Aral Sea
Caucasus
Anatolia
Tigris
Euphrates
Buhayrat ath Tharthār
Dasht-e Kavīr
Kuhhā-ye Zāgros (Zagros Mountains)
Iranian Plateau
An Nafūd
Khvoy
Tabrīz
Ardabīl
Rasht
Marāgheh
Zanjān
Qazvīn
Āmol
Sārī
Gorgān
Sabzevār
Neyshābūr
Mashhad
TEHRĀN
Qom
Kāshān
Hamadān
Arāk
Sanandaj
Kermānshāh
Arbil
Kirkūk
Al Mawşil (Mosul)
BAGHDĀD
An Najaf
Dezfūl
Ahvāz
Ābādān
Al Başrah (Basra)
KUWAIT CITY
Eşfahān
Yazd
Kermān
Zāhedān
Khāsh
Shīrāz
Bandar-e Būshehr
Sakākah
Al Jawf
Tabūk
93
96
98
104

The name "Red Sea" is probably derived from the extensive blooms of algae that occasionally occur. These change pigment when they die, turning the sea's normally intense blue-green waters a deep red.
Saudi Arabia has around 267 billion barrels of proven oil reserves, with around 60 percent of this still remaining. At maximum output, the region can produce around 10 million barrels of oil every day.
Every Muslim must make at least one pilgrimage to Mecca during his or her lifetime. Muslims regard the small shrine called the Ka'bah, located near the center of the Great Mosque in Mecca, as the most sacred place on Earth.
SAUDI ARABIA
YEMEN
OMAN
UNITED ARAB EMIRATES
QATAR
BAHRAIN
EGYPT
SUDAN
ERITREA
DJIBOUTI
ETHIOPIA
SOMALIA
INDIAN OCEAN
Arabian Sea
Red Sea
Gulf of Aden
Gulf of Oman
Tropic of Cancer
Arabian Peninsula
Ad Dahna
Wādī ar Rimah
Ar Rub' al Khālī (Empty Quarter)
Ramlat as Sab'atayn
Hadramawt
Ramlat Āl Wahībah
Jazīrat Maşīrah
Khalīj Maşīrah
Juzur al Ḩalānīyāt
Jazá'ir Farasán
Suqutrá (Socotra) (to Yemen)
RIYADH
MANAMA
DOHA
ABU DHABI
MUSCAT
SANA
Buraydah
Al Madīnah (Medina)
Makkah (Mecca)
Jiddah (Jedda)
Aţ Ţā'if
Laylā
Ḩaraḑ
Al Hufūf
Dubayy
Ash Shāriqah (Sharjah)
Şuḩār
Ar Rustāq
Nazwā
Şūr
Duqm
Şawqirah
Şalālah
Sanāw
Wuday'ah
As Sulayyil
Najrān
Abhā
Jīzān
Şa'dah
Say'ūn
Al Hudaydah
Ta'izz
'Adan
Al Mukallā
Sayḩūt
55
122
20°
10°
40°
50°
A
B
C
D
E
5
6
7
8

Central Asia

A
B
C
D
1
2
3
4
5
96
99
102
102
50°
60°
40°
50°
30°
60°
Since 1960, the Aral Sea has shrunk by 90 percent, becoming extremely saline and consequently losing all but one of its once-abundant fish species.
Aral Sea
Ustyurt Plateau
Turan Lowland
Nukus
UZBEKISTAN
Köneürgenç
Daşoguz
Urganch
To'rtko'l
Uchquduq
Zarafshon
Aydarko'l Ko'li
Türkmenbaşy
Hazar
Balkanabat
Bereket
TURKMENISTAN
Navoiy
Buxoro
Caspian Sea
Serdar
Garagum
Seýdi
Samarqand
Baharly
Gökdepe
Türkmenabat
Qarshi
Abadan
AŞGABAT
Garagum Kanaly
Amu Darya
Saýat
Mary
Baýramaly
Kaka
Atamyrat
Tejen
Murgap
Aqchah
Shibirghan
Mazār-e Sharīf
The desert of Kara Kum (Garagum) occupies over 70 percent of Turkmenistan, severely limiting human settlement across much of the country.
Maimanah
Bālā Murghāb
Serhetabat
Daryā-ye Murghāb
IRAN
Harīrūd
Herāt
AFGHANISTAN
The Kara Kum (Garagum) Canal, the world's longest irrigation canal, stretches some 850 miles (1375 km) and is known as the "River of Life," since it irrigates large areas of arid land.
Farāh
Qalāt
Gereshk
Kandahār
Zaranj
Dasht-e-Mārgow
Daryā-ye Helmand
0 km 200
0 miles 200

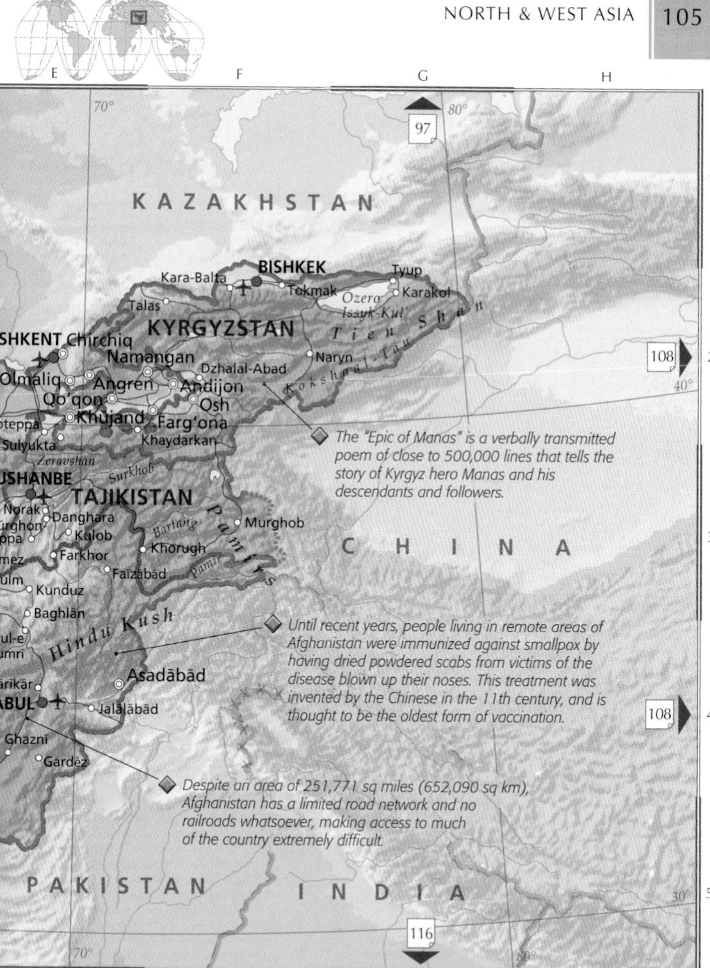
E
F
G
H
70°
80°
97
1
KAZAKHSTAN
BISHKEK
Kara-Balta
Tyup
Tokmak
Karakol
Talas
Ozero
Issyk-Kul'
KYRGYZSTAN
Tien Shan
SHKENT
Chirchiq
Namangan
Dzhalal-Abad
Naryn
108
2
Olmaliq
Angren
Andijon
Kokshaal-Tau
40°
Qo'qon
Osh
Khujand
Farg'ona
oteppa
Sulyukta
Khaydarkan
Zeravshan
Surkhob
USHANBE
TAJIKISTAN
Pamirs
Norak
Danghara
Bartang
Murghob
Kulob
3
Khorugh
CHINA
Farkhor
Pamir
Faizābād
Kunduz
Baghlān
Hindu Kush
Asadābād
ABUL
Jalālābād
108
4
Ghaznī
Gardēz
PAKISTAN
INDIA
30°
5
116
70°
80°
E
F
G
H

◆ The "Epic of Manas" is a verbally transmitted poem of close to 500,000 lines that tells the story of Kyrgyz hero Manas and his descendants and followers.

◆ Until recent years, people living in remote areas of Afghanistan were immunized against smallpox by having dried powdered scabs from victims of the disease blown up their noses. This treatment was invented by the Chinese in the 11th century, and is thought to be the oldest form of vaccination.

◆ Despite an area of 251,771 sq miles (652,090 sq km), Afghanistan has a limited road network and no railroads whatsoever, making access to much of the country extremely difficult.

South & East Asia

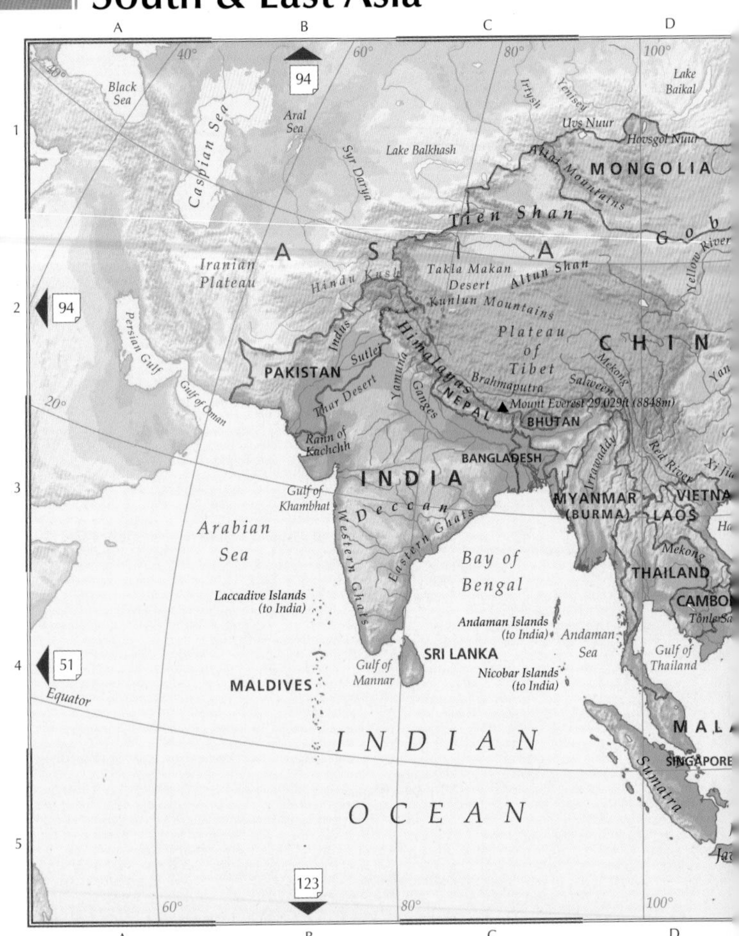

A
B
C
D
1
2
3
4
5
40°
60°
80°
100°
20°
Equator
94
51
123
Black Sea
Caspian Sea
Aral Sea
Syr Darya
Lake Balkhash
Irtysh
Yenisey
Lake Baikal
Uvs Nuur
Hovsgol Nuur
Altai Mountains
MONGOLIA
Tien Shan
Gobi
Yellow River
A S I A
Iranian Plateau
Hindu Kush
Takla Makan Desert
Altun Shan
Kunlun Mountains
Plateau of Tibet
Persian Gulf
Indus
Sutlej
PAKISTAN
Himalayas
CHINA
Mekong
Salween
Brahmaputra
Yamuna
Ganges
Thar Desert
Gulf of Oman
NEPAL
Mount Everest 29,029ft (8848m)
BHUTAN
Rann of Kachchh
BANGLADESH
Irrawaddy
Red River
INDIA
Gulf of Khambhat
MYANMAR (BURMA)
VIETNAM
LAOS
Deccan
Eastern Ghats
Western Ghats
Arabian Sea
Bay of Bengal
Mekong
THAILAND
Laccadive Islands (to India)
CAMBODIA
Tônle Sap
Andaman Islands (to India)
Andaman Sea
SRI LANKA
Gulf of Thailand
Gulf of Mannar
MALDIVES
Nicobar Islands (to India)
INDIAN OCEAN
SINGAPORE
Sumatra

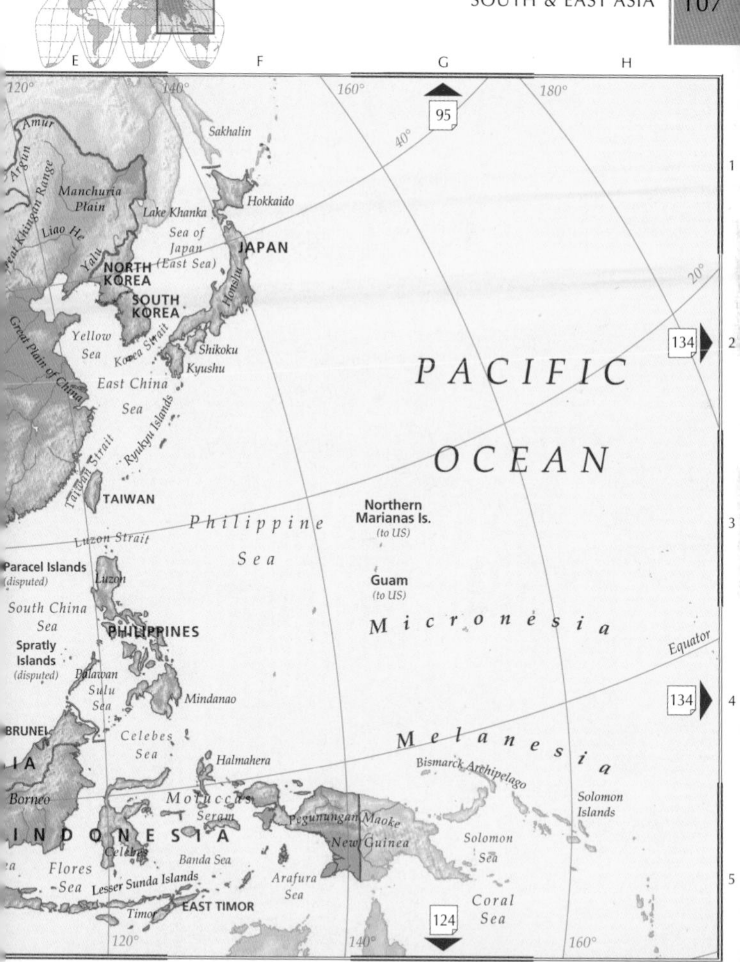
E
F
G
H
120°
140°
160°
180°
95
40°
20°
Equator
Amur
Argun
Great Khingan Range
Manchuria Plain
Liao He
Yalu
Sakhalin
Hokkaido
Lake Khanka
Sea of Japan (East Sea)
JAPAN
NORTH KOREA
SOUTH KOREA
Honshu
Great Plain of China
Yellow Sea
Korea Strait
Shikoku
Kyushu
East China Sea
Ryukyu Islands
Taiwan Strait
TAIWAN
PACIFIC OCEAN
134
Northern Marianas Is.
(to US)
Philippine Sea
Luzon Strait
Paracel Islands
(disputed)
Luzon
Guam
(to US)
South China Sea
PHILIPPINES
Micronesia
Spratly Islands
(disputed)
Palawan
Sulu Sea
Mindanao
BRUNEI
Celebes Sea
Melanesia
Halmahera
Bismarck Archipelago
Borneo
Moluccas
Seram
Pegunungan Maoke
Solomon Islands
INDONESIA
New Guinea
Solomon Sea
Celebes
Banda Sea
Flores Sea
Lesser Sunda Islands
Arafura Sea
Coral Sea
Timor
EAST TIMOR
124
1
2
3
4
5

Western China & Mongolia

The Altai Mountains provide one of the last refuges for the endangered snow leopard. There are thought to be only a few thousand animals left in the wild.
The Turpan Depression is the lowest and hottest place in China. Temperatures can exceed 117°F (47°C) around the lake of Aydingkol Hu, which lies 505 ft (154 m) below sea level.
Although forming around 20 percent of China's landmass, Tibet is sparsely populated, supporting only 1 percent of China's 1.3 billion population.
RUSSIAN FED
KAZAKHSTAN
KYRGYZSTAN
TAJIKISTAN
AFGH.
PAKISTAN
INDIA
NEPAL
BHUTAN
MONG
CHI
Ulaangom
Uvs Nuur
Hövsgöl Nuur
Ölgiy
Hyargas Nuur
Mörön
Har Us Nuur
Altay
Hovd
Tsetserleg
Hangayn Nuruu
Altay Mountains
Altay
Bayanhongor
Ulungur Hu
Junggar Pendi
Karamay
Kuytun
Yining
Shihezi
ÜRÜMQI
Qitai
Hami
Tien Shan
Turpan
Bosten Hu
Dalain Hob
Korla
Tarim He
Tarim Basin
Kashi
Lop Nur
Xingxingxia
Yengisar
Shache
XINJIANG UYGUR ZIZHIQU
GANSU
Yecheng
(claimed by India)
Ruoqiang
Qilian Shan
Taklimakan Shamo
Altun Shan
Karakoram Range
Moyu
Qira
Qaidam Pendi
Qinghai Hu
Kunlun Shan
Golmud
Dulan
Aksai Chin
(administered by China, claimed by India)
Indus
Qingzang Gaoyuan
(Plateau of Tibet)
Tongtian He
QINGHAI
Rutog
Bayan Har Shan
Demchok/Dêmqog
(administered by China, claimed by India)
Gar
(Shiquanhe)
XIZANG ZIZHIQU
(Tibet)
Tanggula Shan
Mekong
Yushu
Zanda
Amdo
Himalayas
Nyima
Tangra Yumco
Siling Co
Nagqu
Qamdo
Brahmaputra
Nam Co
Damxung
Salween
Nyainqêntanglha Shan
Jinsha Jiang
Lhazê
LHASA
Gyangzê
Arunachal Pradesh
(claimed by China)
Mount Everest
29,029ft (8848m)
0 km
400
0 miles
400
A
B
C
D
1
2
3
4
5
70°
80°
90°
100°
50°
40°
30°

96
96
116
117

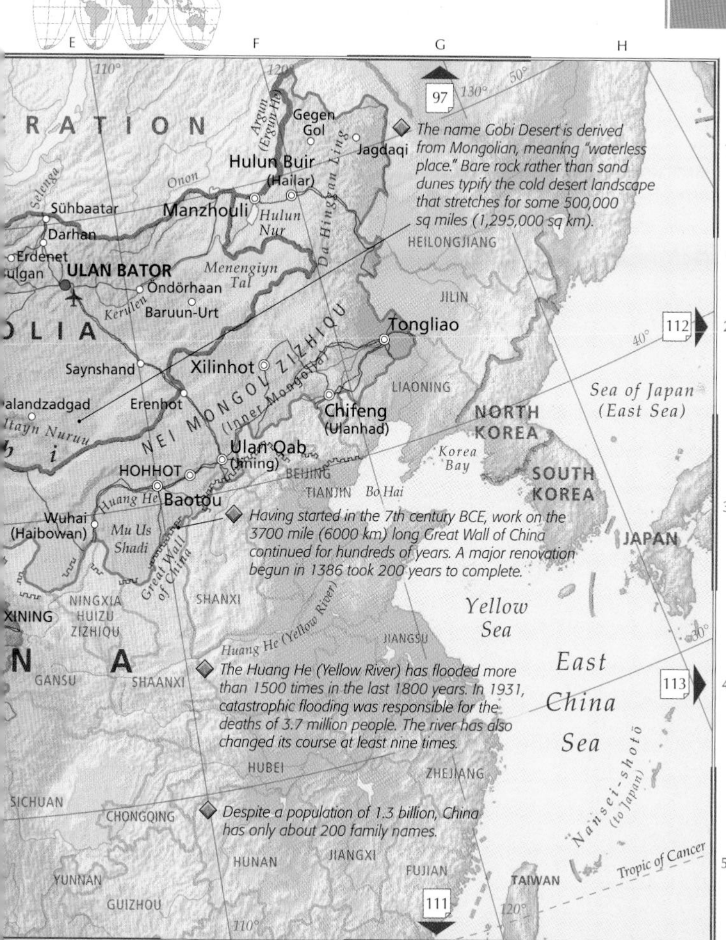
E
F
G
H
110°
120°
97
130°
50°
RATION
Argun (Ergun He)
Gegen Gol
Jagdaqi
The name Gobi Desert is derived from Mongolian, meaning "waterless place." Bare rock rather than sand dunes typify the cold desert landscape that stretches for some 500,000 sq miles (1,295,000 sq km).
1
Hulun Buir (Hailar)
Da Hinggan Ling
Onon
Selenga
Sühbaatar
Manzhouli
Hulun Nur
Darhan
HEILONGJIANG
Erdenet
ULAN BATOR
Menengiyn Tal
Öndörhaan
Kerulen
Baruun-Urt
JILIN
OLIA
Tongliao
112
2
40°
NEI MONGOL ZIZHIQU (Inner Mongolia)
Xilinhot
Saynshand
LIAONING
Sea of Japan (East Sea)
Erenhot
Chifeng (Ulanhad)
NORTH KOREA
Korea Bay
Ulan Qab (Jining)
HOHHOT
BEIJING
SOUTH KOREA
Baotou
TIANJIN
Bo Hai
3
Huang He
Wuhai (Haibowan)
Mu Us Shadi
Having started in the 7th century BCE, work on the 3700 mile (6000 km) long Great Wall of China continued for hundreds of years. A major renovation begun in 1386 took 200 years to complete.
JAPAN
Great Wall of China
NINGXIA HUIZU ZIZHIQU
SHANXI
XINING
Yellow Sea
Huang He (Yellow River)
JIANGSU
30°
East China Sea
GANSU
SHAANXI
The Huang He (Yellow River) has flooded more than 1500 times in the last 1800 years. In 1931, catastrophic flooding was responsible for the deaths of 3.7 million people. The river has also changed its course at least nine times.
113
4
HUBEI
ZHEJIANG
Nansei-shotō (to Japan)
SICHUAN
CHONGQING
Despite a population of 1.3 billion, China has only about 200 family names.
HUNAN
JIANGXI
5
FUJIAN
TAIWAN
Tropic of Cancer
YUNNAN
GUIZHOU
111
120°
110°
E
F
G
H

Eastern China & Korea

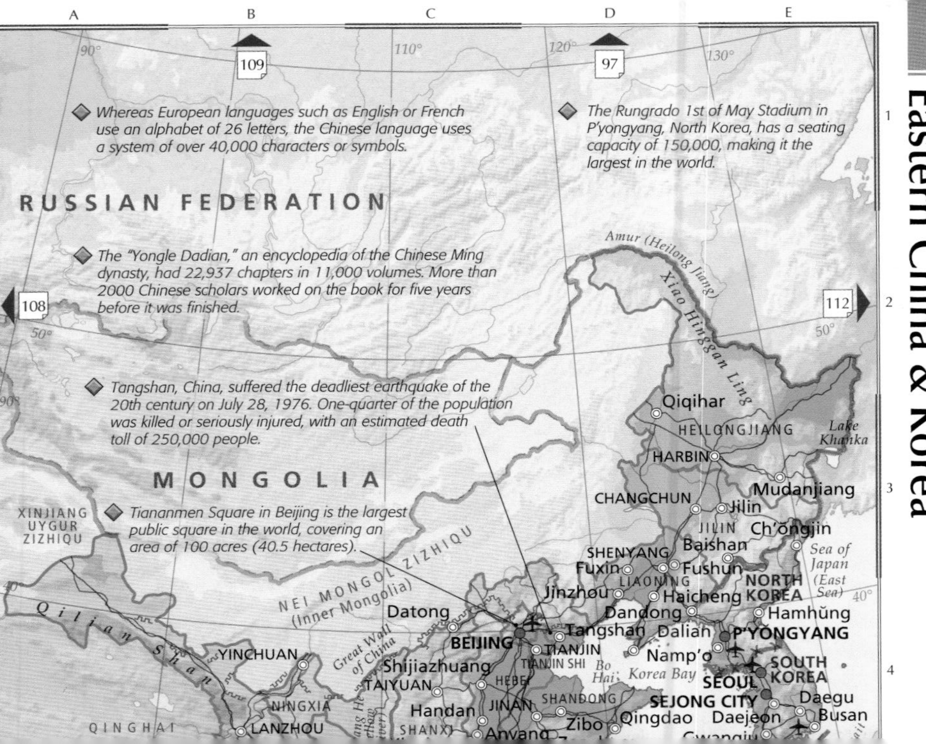
A
B
C
D
E
1
2
3
4
109
97
108
112
90°
110°
120°
130°
50°
40°
RUSSIAN FEDERATION
MONGOLIA
XINJIANG UYGUR ZIZHIQU
NEI MONGOL ZIZHIQU (Inner Mongolia)
Qilian Shan
Great Wall of China
Amur (Heilong Jiang)
Xiao Hinggan Ling
Qiqihar
HEILONGJIANG
HARBIN
Lake Khanka
Mudanjiang
CHANGCHUN
Jilin
JILIN
Ch'ŏngjin
Baishan
SHENYANG
Fuxin
Fushun
LIAONING
Jinzhou
Haicheng
NORTH KOREA
Sea of Japan (East Sea)
Datong
Dandong
Hamhŭng
BEIJING
Tangshan
Dalian
P'YŎNGYANG
YINCHUAN
TIANJIN
TIANJIN SHI
Namp'o
SOUTH KOREA
Shijiazhuang
Bo Hai
Korea Bay
SEOUL
TAIYUAN
HEBEI
SHANDONG
SEJONG CITY
Daegu
NINGXIA
Handan
JINAN
Qingdao
Daejeon
Busan
QINGHAI
LANZHOU
SHANXI
Zibo
Anyang

◆ Whereas European languages such as English or French use an alphabet of 26 letters, the Chinese language uses a system of over 40,000 characters or symbols.

◆ The Rungrado 1st of May Stadium in P'yongyang, North Korea, has a seating capacity of 150,000, making it the largest in the world.

◆ The "Yongle Dadian," an encyclopedia of the Chinese Ming dynasty, had 22,937 chapters in 11,000 volumes. More than 2000 Chinese scholars worked on the book for five years before it was finished.

◆ Tangshan, China, suffered the deadliest earthquake of the 20th century on July 28, 1976. One-quarter of the population was killed or seriously injured, with an estimated death toll of 250,000 people.

◆ Tiananmen Square in Beijing is the largest public square in the world, covering an area of 100 acres (40.5 hectares).

SOUTH KOREA'S TWO CAPITALS
Seoul - capital
Sejong City - administrative capital
Li is the family name for over 87 million people in China.
By far the biggest tidal bore in the world occurs on the Qiantang River in China. At spring tides the wave attains a height of up to 30 ft (9 m) and a speed of 25 mph (40 km/h).
The Giant Bamboo is the fastest growing plant in the world, able to grow at the rate of 3 ft (90 cm) a day.
CHINA
PACIFIC OCEAN
South China Sea
East China Sea
Yellow Sea
Nansei-shotō (part of Japan)
(China and Taiwan claim all of each other's territory)
Paracel Islands (disputed by China, Taiwan and Vietnam)
Spratly Islands (disputed by China, Malaysia, Philippines, Taiwan and Vietnam)
Hong Kong (Special Administrative Region)
Macao (Special Admin. Region)
TAIWAN
TAIBEI (TAIPEI)
Taizhong
Tainan
Gaoxiong
Taiwan Strait
Luzon Strait
Tropic of Cancer
Okinawa
Jeju-do
JAPAN
PHILIPPINES
VIETNAM
LAOS
THAILAND
CAMBODIA
MYANMAR (BURMA)
XIZANG ZIZHIQU (Tibet)
Gulf of Tongking
Hainan Dao
HAINAN
Red River
Mekong
Salween
Hengduan Shan
Wuliang Shan
Jinsha Jiang
Chang Jiang (Yangtze)
Sichuan Pendi
SHANGHAI
Nanjing
Wuxi
HANGZHOU
Ningbo
Jiaxing
Jinhua
Wenzhou
FUZHOU
Xiamen
Shantou
Dongguan
GUANGZHOU
NANNING
Liuzhou
Shangrao
Jingdezhen
NANCHANG
Fuzhou
Hengyang
CHANGSHA
Yueyang
WUHAN
HEFEI
Bengbu
Huainan
Kaifeng
ZHENGZHOU
Lichuan
CHONGQING
CHENGDU
Mianyang
Hanzhong
Leshan
Zigong
Guiyang
KUNMING
SICHUAN
SHAANXI
HENAN
HUBEI
ANHUI
ZHEJIANG
FUJIAN
JIANGXI
HUNAN
GUIZHOU
GUANGDONG
YUNNAN
GUANGXI ZHUANGZU ZIZHIQU
0 km 400
0 miles 400
118
121
134

Japan

A
B
C
D
E
1
2
3
4
130°
135°
140°
145°
45°
40°
97
110
134
CHINA
RUSSIAN FEDERATION
NORTH KOREA
Ostrov Sakhalin
La Pérouse Strait
Sea of Okhotsk
Kuril Islands
(administered by the Russian Federation, claimed by Japan)
Ostrov Iturup
Ostrov Kunashir
Ostrov Shikotan
Wakkanai
Rebun-tō
Rishiri-tō
Abashiri
Asahikawa
Kitami
Nemuro
Sapporo
Otaru
Obihiro
Kushiro
Hokkaidō
Tomakomai
Okushiri-tō
Hakodate
At 33.4 miles (53.8 km), 14.3 miles (23.3 km) of which lie under the Tsugaru Strait, the Seikan Tunnel is currently the longest tunnel in the world. Construction began in 1964 and took 24 years to complete.
Aomori
Hachinohe
Morioka
Akita
Honshū
Sea of Japan
(East Sea)
JAPAN
On Friday March 11, 2011 a 9.0 magnitude earthquake struck off the east coast of Japan triggering massive tsunami waves up to 133 ft (40 m) high that devastated coastal regions and left a death toll in excess of
The Toyota Motor Corporation was first established in 1937 as a spin-off from Toyoda Automatic Loom Works. In 2012, the company became the first in the world to produce 10 million vehicles a year, equivalent to one every 3.1 seconds.
Sendai
Sado
Niigata
Fukushima
Koriyama
Iwaki
Shinano-gawa
Toyama
Hitachi
Liancourt Rocks

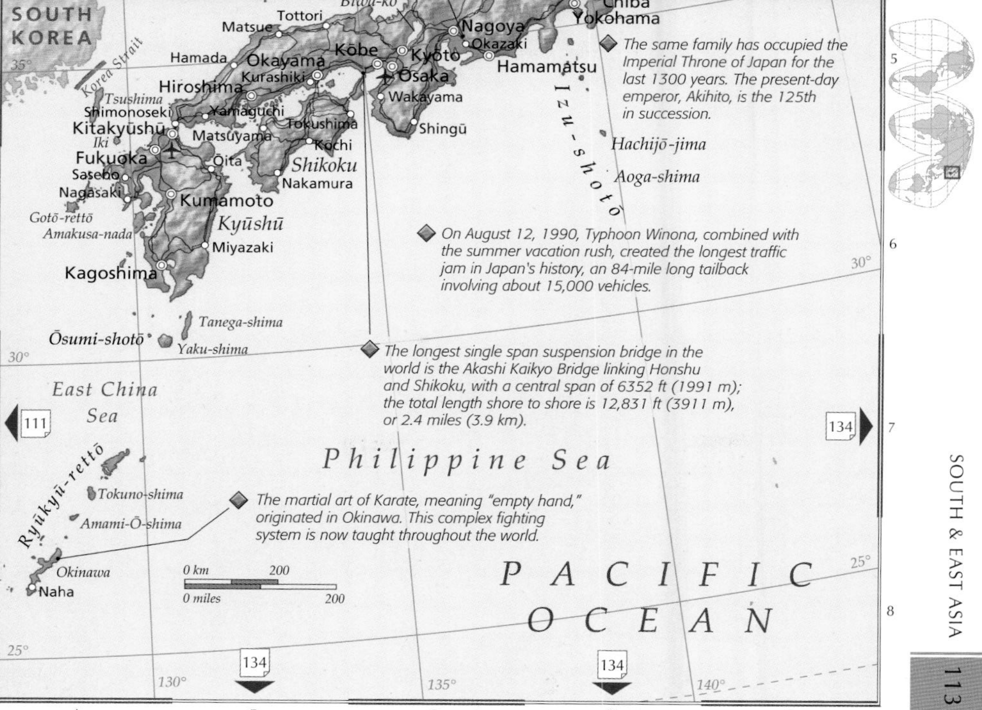
SOUTH KOREA
Korea Strait
Tsushima
Iki
Gotō-rettō
Amakusa-nada
Biwa-ko
Tottori
Matsue
Hamada
Okayama
Kurashiki
Hiroshima
Shimonoseki
Yamaguchi
Kitakyūshū
Matsuyama
Tokushima
Kōchi
Shikoku
Nakamura
Fukuoka
Sasebo
Nagasaki
Ōita
Kumamoto
Kyūshū
Miyazaki
Kagoshima
Kōbe
Kyōto
Ōsaka
Wakayama
Shingū
Nagoya
Okazaki
Hamamatsu
Chiba
Yokohama
Izu-shotō
Hachijō-jima
Aoga-shima
The same family has occupied the Imperial Throne of Japan for the last 1300 years. The present-day emperor, Akihito, is the 125th in succession.
On August 12, 1990, Typhoon Winona, combined with the summer vacation rush, created the longest traffic jam in Japan's history, an 84-mile long tailback involving about 15,000 vehicles.
Tanega-shima
Ōsumi-shotō
Yaku-shima
The longest single span suspension bridge in the world is the Akashi Kaikyo Bridge linking Honshu and Shikoku, with a central span of 6352 ft (1991 m); the total length shore to shore is 12,831 ft (3911 m), or 2.4 miles (3.9 km).
East China Sea
Philippine Sea
Ryūkyū-rettō
Tokuno-shima
Amami-Ō-shima
Okinawa
Naha
The martial art of Karate, meaning "empty hand," originated in Okinawa. This complex fighting system is now taught throughout the world.
0 km 200
0 miles 200
PACIFIC OCEAN
35°
30°
25°
130°
135°
140°
111
134
A B C D E
5 6 7 8

Southern India & Sri Lanka

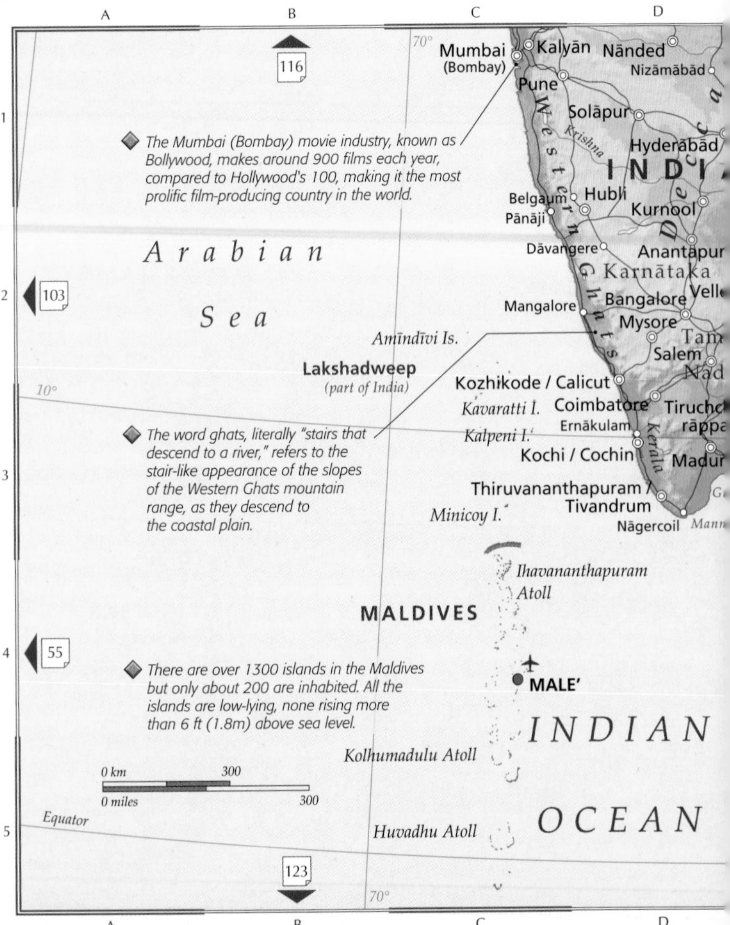
A
B
C
D
1
2
3
4
5
116
103
55
123
70°
10°
Equator
Mumbai
(Bombay)
Kalyān
Nānded
Nizāmābād
Pune
Solāpur
Krishna
Hyderābād
INDIA
Western Ghats
Deccan
Belgaum
Hubli
Kurnool
Pānāji
Dāvangere
Anantapur
Karnātaka
Bangalore
Mangalore
Mysore
Salem
Tamil Nadu
Amīndīvi Is.
Lakshadweep
(part of India)
Kozhikode / Calicut
Kavaratti I.
Coimbatore
Ernākulam
Kalpeni I.
Kochi / Cochin
Kerala
Madurai
Thiruvananthapuram /
Tivandrum
Minicoy I.
Nāgercoil
Arabian
Sea
Ihavananthapuram
Atoll
MALDIVES
MALE'
INDIAN
OCEAN
Kolhumadulu Atoll
Huvadhu Atoll
0 km
300
0 miles
300
The Mumbai (Bombay) movie industry, known as Bollywood, makes around 900 films each year, compared to Hollywood's 100, making it the most prolific film-producing country in the world.
The word ghats, literally "stairs that descend to a river," refers to the stair-like appearance of the slopes of the Western Ghats mountain range, as they descend to the coastal plain.
There are over 1300 islands in the Maldives but only about 200 are inhabited. All the islands are low-lying, none rising more than 6 ft (1.8m) above sea level.

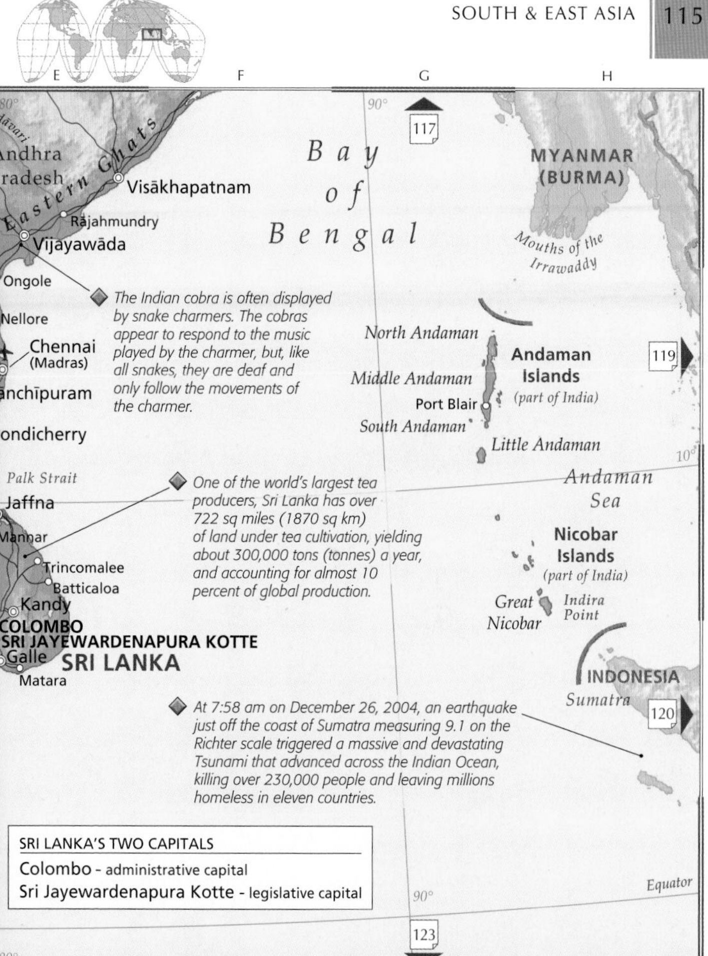
E
F
G
H
80°
Andhra
Pradesh
Eastern Ghats
Visākhapatnam
Rājahmundry
Vijayawāda
Ongole
Nellore
Chennai
(Madras)
Pondicherry
Bay of Bengal
90°
117
MYANMAR
(BURMA)
Mouths of the Irrawaddy
1
The Indian cobra is often displayed by snake charmers. The cobras appear to respond to the music played by the charmer, but, like all snakes, they are deaf and only follow the movements of the charmer.
North Andaman
Middle Andaman
Port Blair
South Andaman
Andaman
Islands
(part of India)
119
2
Little Andaman
10°
Palk Strait
Jaffna
Mannar
Trincomalee
Batticaloa
Kandy
COLOMBO
SRI JAYEWARDENAPURA KOTTE
Galle
SRI LANKA
Matara
One of the world's largest tea producers, Sri Lanka has over 722 sq miles (1870 sq km) of land under tea cultivation, yielding about 300,000 tons (tonnes) a year, and accounting for almost 10 percent of global production.
Andaman
Sea
Nicobar
Islands
(part of India)
3
Great
Nicobar
Indira
Point
INDONESIA
Sumatra
120
4
At 7:58 am on December 26, 2004, an earthquake just off the coast of Sumatra measuring 9.1 on the Richter scale triggered a massive and devastating Tsunami that advanced across the Indian Ocean, killing over 230,000 people and leaving millions homeless in eleven countries.
SRI LANKA'S TWO CAPITALS
Colombo - administrative capital
Sri Jayewardenapura Kotte - legislative capital
90°
Equator
5
123
80°
E
F
G
H

North India & Pakistan

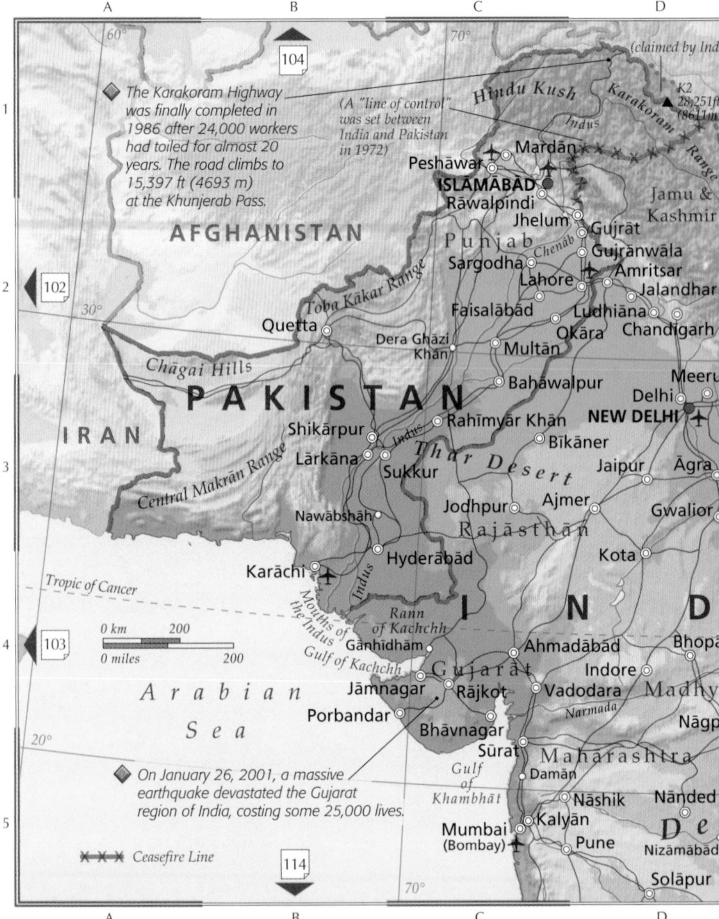

A
B
C
D
1
2
3
4
5
104
102
103
114
The Karakoram Highway was finally completed in 1986 after 24,000 workers had toiled for almost 20 years. The road climbs to 15,397 ft (4693 m) at the Khunjerab Pass.
(A "line of control" was set between India and Pakistan in 1972)
(claimed by Indi
Hindu Kush
Karakoram Range
K2 28,251ft (8611m)
Indus
AFGHANISTAN
Peshāwar
Mardān
ISLĀMĀBĀD
Rāwalpindi
Jhelum
Gujrāt
Jamu & Kashmir
Punjab
Chenāb
Sargodha
Gujrānwāla
Amritsar
Lahore
Jalandhar
Faisalābād
Ludhiāna
Chandigarh
Okāra
Toba Kākar Range
Quetta
Dera Ghāzi Khān
Multān
Chāgai Hills
PAKISTAN
Bahāwalpur
Meeru
Delhi
NEW DELHI
IRAN
Shikārpur
Rahīmyār Khān
Bīkāner
Lārkāna
Sukkur
Thar Desert
Jaipur
Āgra
Central Makrān Range
Jodhpur
Ajmer
Gwalior
Nawābshāh
Rajāsthān
Hyderābād
Kota
Karāchi
Tropic of Cancer
Mouths of the Indus
Rann of Kachchh
INDIA
0 km 200
0 miles 200
Gāndhidhām
Ahmadābād
Bhopā
Gulf of Kachchh
Gujarāt
Indore
Arabian Sea
Jāmnagar
Rājkot
Vadodara
Madhy
Porbandar
Narmada
Nāgp
Bhāvnagar
Sūrat
Mahārāshtra
On January 26, 2001, a massive earthquake devastated the Gujarat region of India, costing some 25,000 lives.
Gulf of Khambhāt
Damān
Nāshik
Nānded
Kalyān
Mumbai (Bombay)
Pune
Nizāmābād
Solāpur
Ceasefire Line
60°
70°
30°
20°

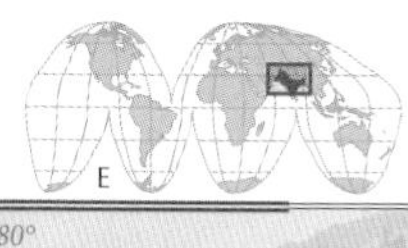

E F G H

108

80° 90°

XINJIANGUYGUR ZIZHIQU

The northern ranges of the Himalayas contain the highest mountains in the world, with average heights of more than 23,000 ft (7000 m) and many peaks higher than 26,000 ft (8000m).

Aksai Chin (administered by China, claimed by India)

CHINA

QINGHAI

Demchok/Dêmqog (administered by China, claimed by India)

Cherrapunji, 4872 ft (1484 m) above sea level, has an average annual rainfall of 450 inches (1143 cm), although most of this falls during the monsoon – the winter is a virtual drought. The highest-ever seasonal rainfall was 904 inches (2298 cm).

XIZANG ZIZHIQU (Tibet)

108

The Kingdom of Bhutan is the only country in the world to measure the happiness of its citizens.

Arunachal Pradesh (claimed by China)

30°

Himalayas

NEPAL

Mount Everest 29,029ft (8848m)

Bareilly

KATHMANDU

THIMPHU

BHUTAN

Gangtok

Uttar Pradesh

Lucknow

Birātnagar

Guwāhāti

Dispur

Kohīma

Kānpur

Saidpur

Brahmaputra

Yamuna

Vārānasi

Patna

Ganges

Jamālpur

Imphāl

Allahābād

Bihār

BANGLADESH

Sylhet

Gaya

Rājshāhi

Tropic of Cancer

INDIA

Dhanbād

West Bengal

DHAKA

Comilla

118

Jabalpur

Rānchi

Kolkata (Calcutta)

Khulna

Chittagong

Pradesh

MYANMAR (BURMA)

Raipur

Mouths of the Ganges

20°

Orissa

Mahānadi

Cuttack

Bay of Bengal

The heaviest hailstones on record, weighing about 2.25 lbs (1 kg), are reported to have killed 92 people in the Gopalganj area of Bangladesh on April 14, 1986.

Eastern Ghats

Kāveri

Warangal

Visákhapatnam

115

90°

E F G H

1 2 3 4 5

Mainland Southeast Asia

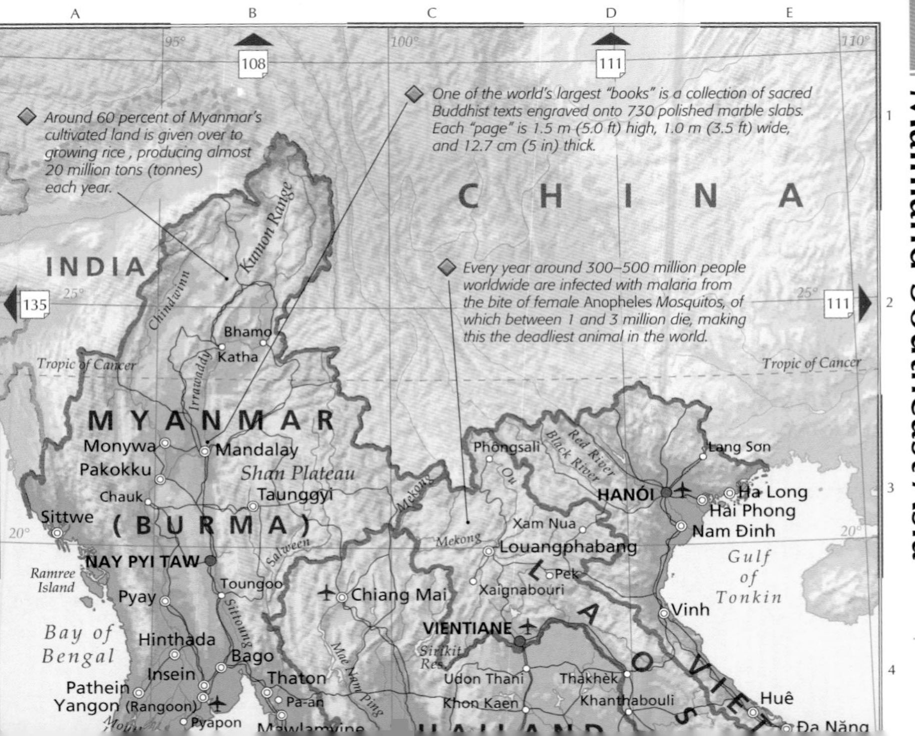
Around 60 percent of Myanmar's cultivated land is given over to growing rice, producing almost 20 million tons (tonnes) each year.
One of the world's largest "books" is a collection of sacred Buddhist texts engraved onto 730 polished marble slabs. Each "page" is 1.5 m (5.0 ft) high, 1.0 m (3.5 ft) wide, and 12.7 cm (5 in) thick.
Every year around 300–500 million people worldwide are infected with malaria from the bite of female Anopheles Mosquitos, of which between 1 and 3 million die, making this the deadliest animal in the world.
CHINA
INDIA
MYANMAR (BURMA)
LAOS
VIETNAM
Tropic of Cancer
Gulf of Tonkin
Bay of Bengal
Kumon Range
Shan Plateau
Chindwinn
Irrawaddy
Salween
Sittoung
Mekong
Red River
Black River
Ou
Mae Nam Ping
Sirikit Res.
Ramree Island
Lang Son
Ha Long
Hai Phong
Nam Đinh
HANOI
Vinh
Huê
Đa Năng
Phongsali
Xam Nua
Louangphabang
Pek
Xaignabouri
VIENTIANE
Thakhek
Khanthabouli
Udon Thani
Khon Kaen
Chiang Mai
Bhamo
Katha
Mandalay
Taunggyi
Monywa
Pakokku
Chauk
NAY PYI TAW
Toungoo
Pyay
Hinthada
Bago
Thaton
Pa-an
Insein
Pyapon
Pathein
Yangon (Rangoon)
Sittwe
108
111
135

Nakhon Ratchasima
Srinagarind Res.
Ayutthaya
BANGKOK
Dawei
Ratchaburi
Bătdâmbang
Chon Buri
Pattaya
Myeik
Ratchathani
Muang Không
Phumĭ Sâmraông
Stœng Sên
Mekong
Tônle Kông
Quy Nhon
Stœng Treng
Tônlé Sap
CAMBODIA
Nha Trang
Đa Lat
Kâmpóng Chhnăng
Kâmpóng Cham
PHNOM PENH
Svay Riĕng
Hô Chi Minh
Kâmpôt
Sihanoukville (Kâmpóng Saôm)
Rach Gia
Cân Thơ
Mouths of the Mekong
Ko Chang
Gulf of Thailand
Mergui Archipelago
Chumphon
Isthmus of Kra
Ko Phangan
Ko Samui
Surat Thani
Nakhon Si Thammarat
Ko Phuket
Phuket
Trang
Nicobar Islands (part of India)
Andaman Sea
Songkhla
Pattani
Hat Yai
Yala
South China Sea
Malay Peninsula
MALAYSIA
Strait of Malacca
INDONESIA
Sumatra
INDIAN OCEAN
0 km 200
0 miles 200
15°
10°
5°
95°
100°
105°
A B C D E
5 6 7 8

Bangkok's full ceremonial name is: Krungthepmahanakhon Amonrattanakosin Mahintharayutthaya Mahadilokphop Noppharatratchathaniburirom Udomratchaniwetmahasathan Amonphimanawatansathit Sakkathattiyawitsanukamprasit, which is the longest place name in the world.

The world's smallest mammal is the Kitti's hog-nosed bat, also known as the bumblebee bat, of Thailand, weighing less than 0.09 oz (2.5 g).

Following years of conflict, it is estimated that as many as 6 million landmines remain buried in the soils of Cambodia.

115 121 121 122

Maritime Southeast Asia

A
B
C
D
1
2
3
4
5
MYANMAR (BURMA)
THAILAND
LAOS
VIETNAM
CAMBODIA
Gulf of Tonkin
Paracel Islands
(disputed by China, Taiwan, and Vietnam)
South China Sea
Spratly Islands
(disputed by China, Malaysia, Philippines, Taiwan, and Vietnam)
0 km 400
0 miles 400
MALAYSIA'S TWO CAPITALS
Kuala Lumpur - Capital
Putrajaya - Administrative capital
Andaman Sea
Gulf of Thailand
Isthmus of Kra
Nicobar Islands
(to India)
The Rafflesia plant has the largest single flower in the world. The bloom, 3 ft (90 cm) in diameter, attracts insects by imitating the foul smell of rotting flesh.
Strait of Malacca
George Town
Kota Bharu
Kuala Terengganu
Kuantan
Bandaaceh
Taiping
Ipoh
Medan
Klang
KUALA LUMPUR
Pematangsiantar
PUTRAJAYA
MALAYSIA
Pulau Simeulue
Danau Toba
Sibolga
Johor Bahru
SINGAPORE
Pulau Nias
Equator
Sumatera
(Sumatra)
Padang
Pekanbaru
Pontianak
Pegunungan Barisan
Batang Hari
Pulau Siberut
Kepulauan Mentawai
Jambi
Bangka
Selat Karimata
Palembang
Kota Kinabalu
BANDAR SERI BEGAWAN
BRUNEI
Sibu
Sarawak
Kuching
Pegunungan Muller
Kapuas
Borneo
Kalimantan
Samarinda
Balikpapan
Banjarmasin
INDIAN OCEAN
Bengkulu
Pulau Belitung
Java Sea
Tegal
Pekalongan
Bandar Lampung
JAKARTA
Semarang
Kudus
Surabaya
Mataram
Jember
Selat Sunda
Bogor
Sukabumi
Bandung
Cilacap
Magelang
Yogyakarta
Surakarta
Madiun
Kediri
Malang
Denpasar
Bali
Jawa
(Java)
In August 1883, a devastating volcanic eruption destroyed most of the island of Krakatau and triggered a tsunami that claimed around 35,000 lives.
90°
100°
110°
10°

119
122
122
123

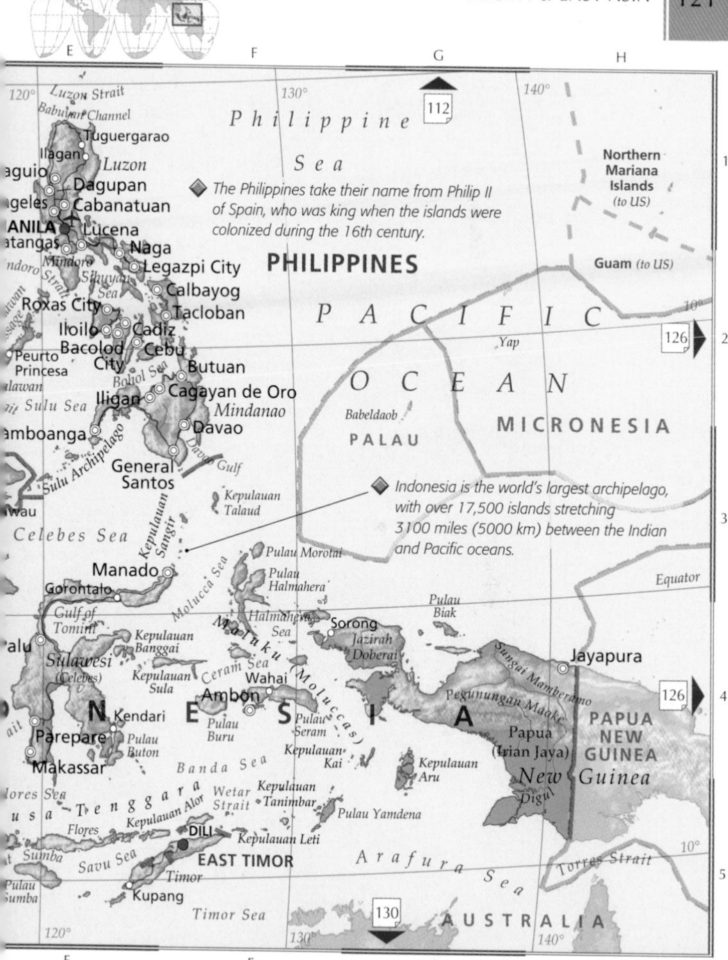

E
F
G
H
Luzon Strait
Babuyan Channel
Philippine Sea
112
Tuguergarao
Ilagan
Luzon
Dagupan
Cabanatuan
Lucena
Naga
Legazpi City
PHILIPPINES
Northern Mariana Islands (to US)
Guam (to US)
Calbayog
Tacloban
Roxas City
Iloilo
Cadiz
Bacolod City
Cebu
Peurto Princesa
Butuan
Iligan
Cagayan de Oro
Mindanao
Sulu Sea
Davao
Sulu Archipelago
General Santos
Davao Gulf
PACIFIC OCEAN
Yap
126
Babeldaob
PALAU
MICRONESIA
Kepulauan Talaud
Kepulauan Sangir
Celebes Sea
Manado
Gorontalo
Gulf of Tomini
Molucca Sea
Pulau Morotai
Pulau Halmahera
Halmahera Sea
Sorong
Jazirah Doberai
Pulau Biak
Equator
Kepulauan Banggai
Sulawesi (Celebes)
Kepulauan Sula
Ceram Sea
Maluku (Moluccas)
Wahai
Ambon
Pulau Seram
Pulau Buru
Kendari
Parepare
Makassar
Pulau Buton
Banda Sea
Kepulauan Kai
Kepulauan Aru
Sungai Mamberamo
Pegunungan Maoke
Jayapura
Papua (Irian Jaya)
New Guinea
PAPUA NEW GUINEA
Digul
INDONESIA
Flores Sea
Nusa Tenggara
Kepulauan Alor
Wetar Strait
Kepulauan Tanimbar
Pulau Yamdena
Flores
DILI
Kepulauan Leti
Sumba
Savu Sea
EAST TIMOR
Timor
Kupang
Pulau Sumba
Timor Sea
Arafura Sea
Torres Strait
130
AUSTRALIA
120°
130°
140°
10°

◆ The Philippines take their name from Philip II of Spain, who was king when the islands were colonized during the 16th century.

◆ Indonesia is the world's largest archipelago, with over 17,500 islands stretching 3100 miles (5000 km) between the Indian and Pacific oceans.

The Indian Ocean

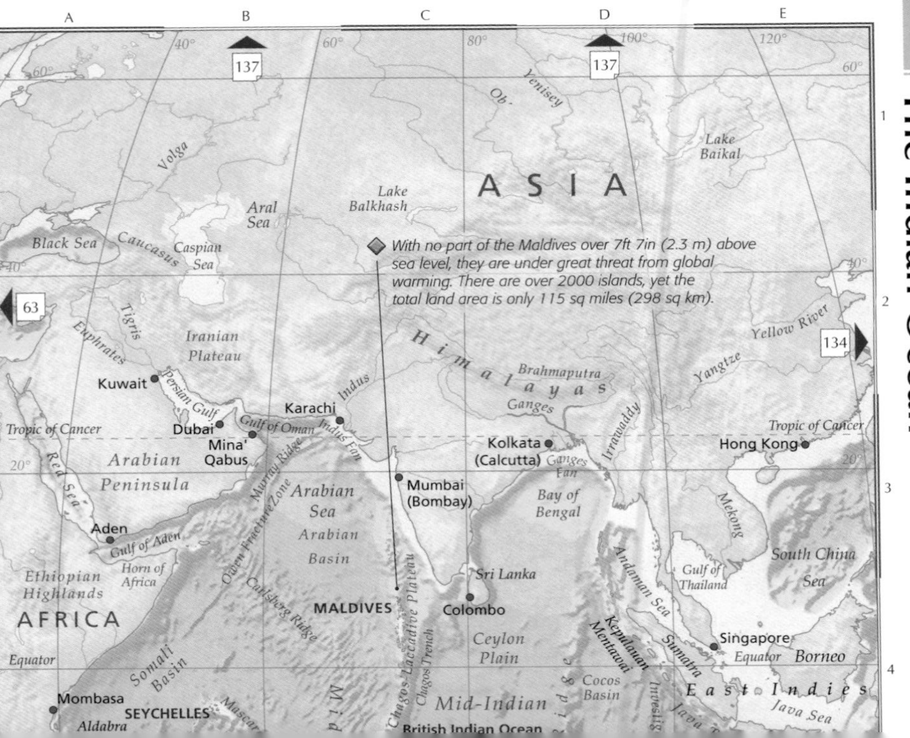
With no part of the Maldives over 7ft 7in (2.3 m) above sea level, they are under great threat from global warming. There are over 2000 islands, yet the total land area is only 115 sq miles (298 sq km).
ASIA
AFRICA
Lake Baikal
Yenisey
Ob'
Lake Balkhash
Aral Sea
Caspian Sea
Volga
Caucasus
Black Sea
Tigris
Euphrates
Iranian Plateau
Arabian Peninsula
Persian Gulf
Gulf of Oman
Kuwait
Dubai
Mina' Qabus
Karachi
Indus
Indus Fan
Himalayas
Ganges
Brahmaputra
Ganges Fan
Irrawaddy
Yangtze
Yellow River
Mekong
Kolkata (Calcutta)
Mumbai (Bombay)
Hong Kong
Tropic of Cancer
Bay of Bengal
Andaman Sea
South China Sea
Gulf of Thailand
Singapore
Equator
Borneo
Sumatra
Java Sea
East Indies
Kepulauan Mentawai
Cocos Basin
Sri Lanka
Colombo
Ceylon Plain
Mid-Indian
Chagos Trench
Chagos-Laccadive Plateau
MALDIVES
Arabian Sea
Arabian Basin
Carlsberg Ridge
Owen Fracture Zone
Murray Ridge
Red Sea
Aden
Gulf of Aden
Horn of Africa
Ethiopian Highlands
Somali Basin
SEYCHELLES
Mombasa
Aldabra
British Indian Ocean
137
134
63
20°
40°
60°
80°
100°
120°

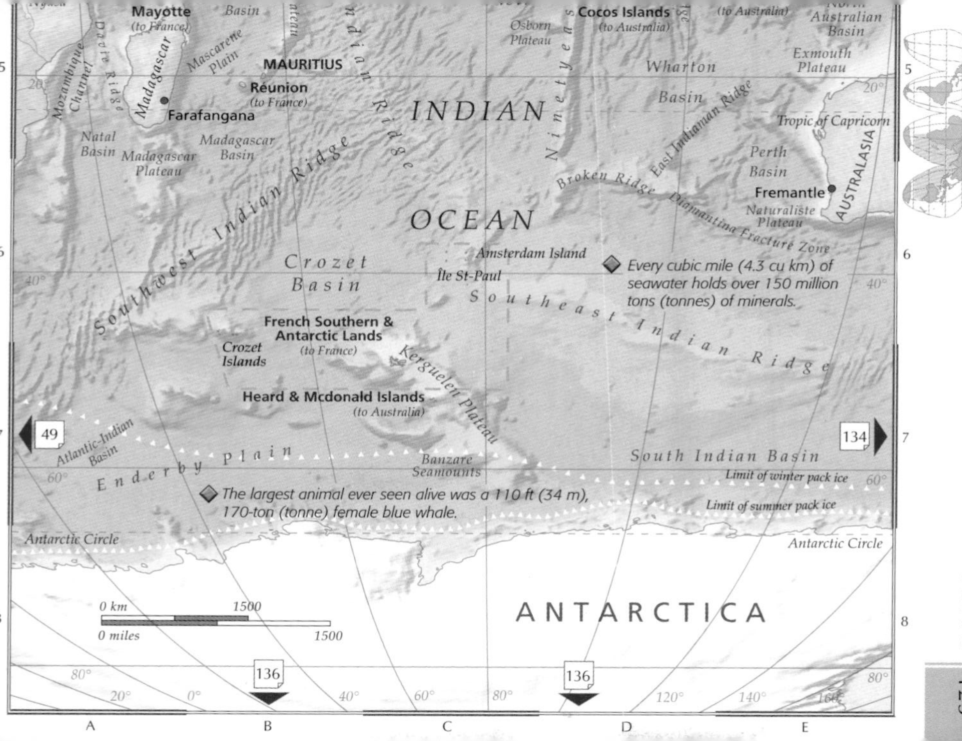
Mayotte (to France)
Mozambique Channel
Davie Ridge
Madagascar
Farafangana
Mascarene Plain
MAURITIUS
Réunion (to France)
Natal Basin
Madagascar Plateau
Madagascar Basin
INDIAN
OCEAN
Southwest Indian Ridge
Ninetyeast Ridge
Osborn Plateau
Cocos Islands (to Australia)
Wharton Basin
Australian Basin
Exmouth Plateau
East Indiaman Ridge
Tropic of Capricorn
Perth Basin
Broken Ridge
Fremantle
AUSTRALASIA
Naturaliste Plateau
Diamantina Fracture Zone
Crozet Basin
Amsterdam Island
Île St-Paul
Every cubic mile (4.3 cu km) of seawater holds over 150 million tons (tonnes) of minerals.
Southeast Indian Ridge
French Southern & Antarctic Lands (to France)
Crozet Islands
Kerguelen Plateau
Heard & Mcdonald Islands (to Australia)
Atlantic-Indian Basin
Enderby plain
Banzare Seamounts
South Indian Basin
Limit of winter pack ice
Limit of summer pack ice
The largest animal ever seen alive was a 110 ft (34 m), 170-ton (tonne) female blue whale.
Antarctic Circle
Antarctic Circle
ANTARCTICA
0 km
1500
0 miles
1500
49
134
136
136

Australasia & Oceania

Northern Mariana Islands
(to US)
Saipan
Guam
(to US)
Wake Island
(to US)
MARSHALL ISLANDS
Ratak Chain
Ralik Chain
Micronesia
Philippine Sea
Philippines
Sulu Sea
Yap
MICRONESIA
Caroline Islands
Chuuk Islands
Pohnpei
Kosrae
Babeldaob
PALAU
Tungaru (Gilbert Islands)
Celebes Sea
Borneo
Equator
Melanesia
Nauru
NAURU
Banaba
KIRIBATI
Bismarck Archipelago
Bismarck Sea
TUVA
Mount Wilhelm 14,793ft (4509m)
New Britain
New Guinea
Solomon Sea
Solomon Islands
SOLOMON ISLANDS
Santa Cruz Islands
Celebes
Banda Sea
PAPUA NEW GUINEA
Guadalcanal
Arafura Sea
Torres Strait
Timor
Flores
VANUATU
Coral Sea
Espiritu Santo
Vanua Le
Malekula
Efate
Viti Levu
Timor Sea
Arnhem Land
Gulf of Carpentaria
Cape York Peninsula
Great Barrier Reef
Coral Sea Islands
(to Australia)
New Caledonia
(to France)
Ashmore & Cartier Islands
(to Australia)
New Caledonia
FI
INDIAN OCEAN
AUSTRALIA
Great Dividing Range
Great Sandy Desert
Macdonnell Ranges
Simpson Desert
Uluru (Ayers Rock)
Grey Range
Norfolk Island
(to Australia)
Gibson Desert
L. Eyre North
Darling
Lord Howe Island
(to Australia)
North C
Great Victoria Desert
L. Torrens
North Island
Tropic of Capricorn
Nullarbor Plain
Murray
Mount Kosciuszko 7310ft (2228m)
NEW ZEALAND
Great Australian Bight
Kangaroo Island
Bass Strait
Tasman Sea
South Island
Aoraki (Mt Cook) 12,283ft (3744m)
Tasmania
Cape Leeuwin
Antipod Islan
Auckland Islands
(to New Zealand)
120°
140°
160°
20°
100°
40°
A
B
C
D
1
2
3
4
5

107
107
123
136

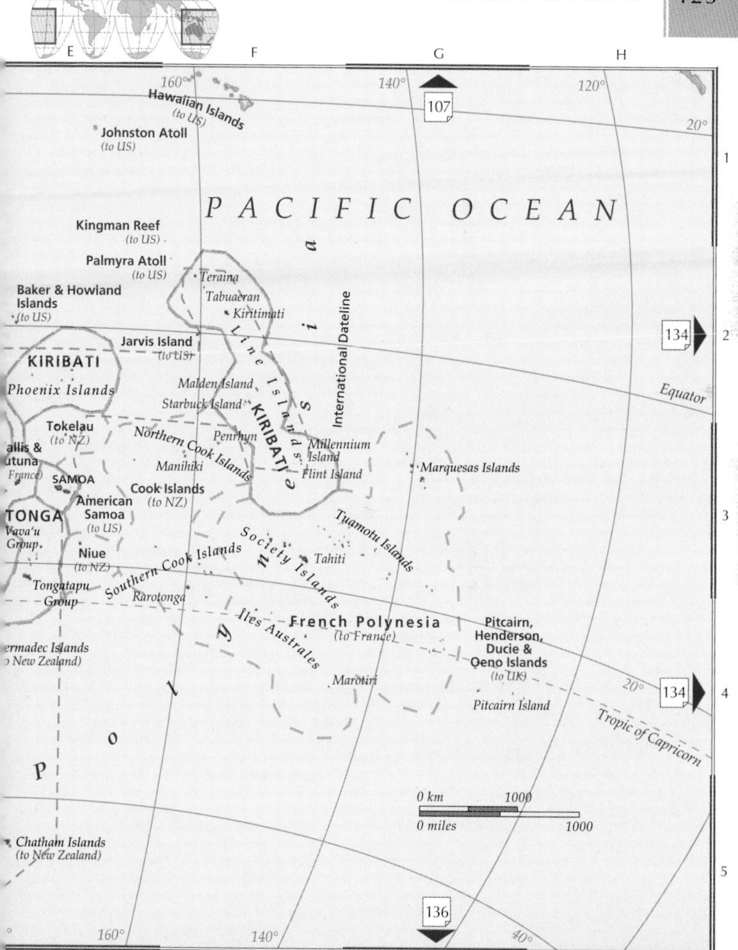
E
F
G
H
1
2
3
4
5
160°
140°
120°
20°
107
134
136
Hawaiian Islands
(to US)
Johnston Atoll
(to US)
PACIFIC OCEAN
Kingman Reef
(to US)
Palmyra Atoll
(to US)
Baker & Howland
Islands
(to US)
Teraina
Tabuaeran
Kiritimati
Line Islands
International Dateline
Jarvis Island
(to US)
KIRIBATI
Phoenix Islands
Malden Island
Starbuck Island
KIRIBATI
Equator
Tokelau
(to NZ)
Northern Cook Islands
Penrhyn
Millennium
Island
Flint Island
Marquesas Islands
allis &
utuna
France)
Manihiki
SAMOA
Cook Islands
(to NZ)
American
Samoa
(to US)
TONGA
Vava'u
Group
Tuamotu Islands
Society Islands
Tahiti
Niue
(to NZ)
Southern Cook Islands
Tongatapu
Group
Rarotonga
Polynesia
French Polynesia
(to France)
Îles Australes
Pitcairn,
Henderson,
Ducie &
Oeno Islands
(to UK)
ermadec Islands
New Zealand)
Marotiri
Pitcairn Island
Tropic of Capricorn
0 km
1000
0 miles
1000
Chatham Islands
(to New Zealand)
40°

The Southwest Pacific

A
B
C
D
1
2
3
4
5
134
121
128
131
Guam
(US unincorporated territory)
HAGÅTÑA
Marianas Trench
Yap
Micronesia
Caroline Islands
Chuuk Is.
Pohnpei
PALIKIR
NGERULMUD
PALAU
MICRONESIA
Kosrae
MARSHALL ISLANDS
Ralik Chain
Ratak Chain
Majuro
BAIRIKI
Tarawa
NAURU
Banaba
The Pitohui bird has a poison on its feathers and skin similar to the poison arrow tree frog, making it the only known example of a poisonous bird.
Equator
PAPUA NEW GUINEA
Bismarck Archipelago
New Ireland
INDONESIA
Mt Wilhelm 14,793ft (4509m)
Madang
New Guinea
Lae
New Britain
Bougainville I.
Melanesia
New Georgia Islands
PORT MORESBY
Solomon Sea
HONIARA
Santa Cruz Islands
Arafura Sea
Torres Strait
SOLOMON ISLANDS
Gulf of Carpentaria
Coral Sea
Banks Is.
VANUATU
Found only in the rainforest of New Guinea, Queen Alexandra's Birdwing, with a wingspan of 11 inches (280 mm), is the largest butterfly in the world.
Coral Sea Islands
(Australian external territory)
New Caledonia
(French special collectivity)
PORT VILA
Great Barrier Reef
AUSTRALIA
NOUMÉA
Îles Loyauté
Tropic of Capricorn
130°
140°
150°
160°
170°
10°
0°
10°
20°

E
F
G
H
180°
170°
160°
150°
135
PACIFIC OCEAN
In 1995, the International Date Line was repositioned around Kiribati territory, bringing Millennium Island 14 hours ahead of UTC, making it the first landfall for sunrise at the dawn of the new millennium.
10°
International Dateline
Kingman Reef
(US unincorporated territory)
Palmyra Atoll
(US incorporated territory)
Teraina
Tabuaeran
Kiritimati
Line Islands
Baker & Howland Is.
(US unincorporated territory)
Jarvis I.
(US unincorporated territory)
Tungaru Islands)
Equator 0°
KIRIBATI
Phoenix Islands
KIRIBATI
Samoa is home to the world's smallest known spider, the Patu marplesi, which spans a mere 0.017 inches (0.4 mm).
TUVALU
FONGAFALE
Tokelau
(NZ dependent territory)
American Samoa
(US unincorporated territory)
Vostok I.
Millennium I.
Flint I.
Polynesia
Wallis & Futuna
(French overseas collectivity)
SAMOA
ÁPIA
PAGO PAGO
Northern Cook Is.
French Polynesia
(French overseas collectivity)
FIJI
Vanua Levu
Vava'u Group
Cook Islands
(in free assoc. with NZ)
Îles de la Société
SUVA
Niue
(in free assoc. with NZ)
PAPEETE
Tahiti
Ha'apai Group
ALOFI
Southern Cook Is.
TONGA
NUKU'ALOFA
AVARUA
Rarotonga
20°
0 km 500
0 miles 500
Tropic of Capricorn
1
2
3
4
5

Western Australia

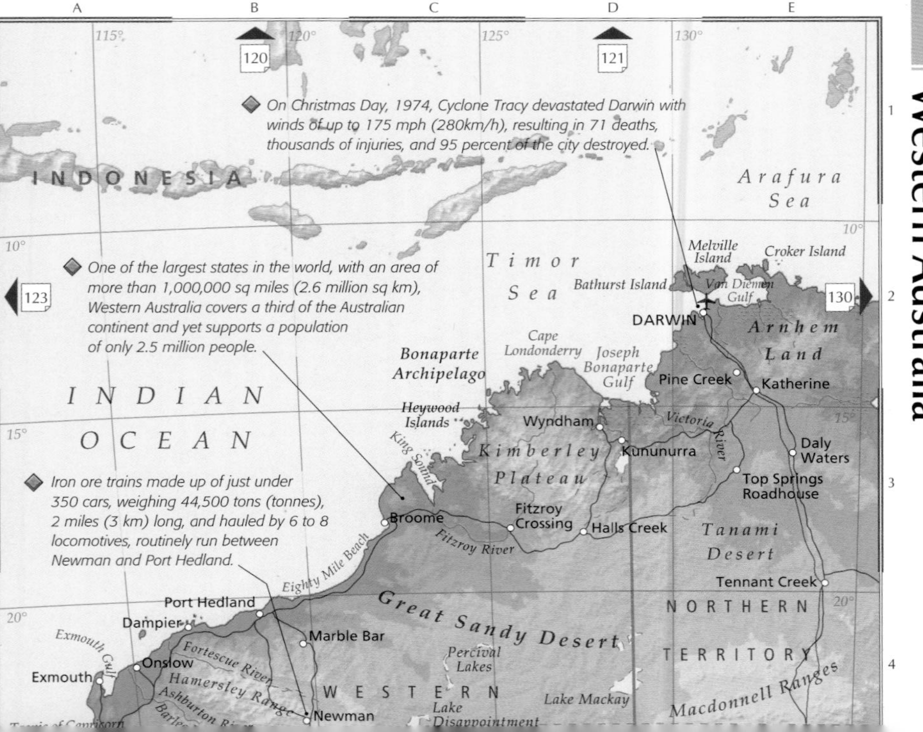
On Christmas Day, 1974, Cyclone Tracy devastated Darwin with winds of up to 175 mph (280km/h), resulting in 71 deaths, thousands of injuries, and 95 percent of the city destroyed.
One of the largest states in the world, with an area of more than 1,000,000 sq miles (2.6 million sq km), Western Australia covers a third of the Australian continent and yet supports a population of only 2.5 million people.
Iron ore trains made up of just under 350 cars, weighing 44,500 tons (tonnes), 2 miles (3 km) long, and hauled by 6 to 8 locomotives, routinely run between Newman and Port Hedland.
INDONESIA
Arafura Sea
Timor Sea
INDIAN OCEAN
Melville Island
Bathurst Island
Croker Island
Van Diemen Gulf
DARWIN
Arnhem Land
Cape Londonderry
Joseph Bonaparte Gulf
Bonaparte Archipelago
Heywood Islands
King Sound
Pine Creek
Katherine
Wyndham
Victoria River
Kununurra
Kimberley Plateau
Daly Waters
Top Springs Roadhouse
Broome
Fitzroy Crossing
Fitzroy River
Halls Creek
Tanami Desert
Tennant Creek
Eighty Mile Beach
Port Hedland
Dampier
Marble Bar
Great Sandy Desert
NORTHERN TERRITORY
Exmouth Gulf
Exmouth
Onslow
Fortescue River
Hamersley Range
Ashburton River
Percival Lakes
WESTERN
Lake Mackay
Macdonnell Ranges
Newman
Lake Disappointment
120
121
123
130

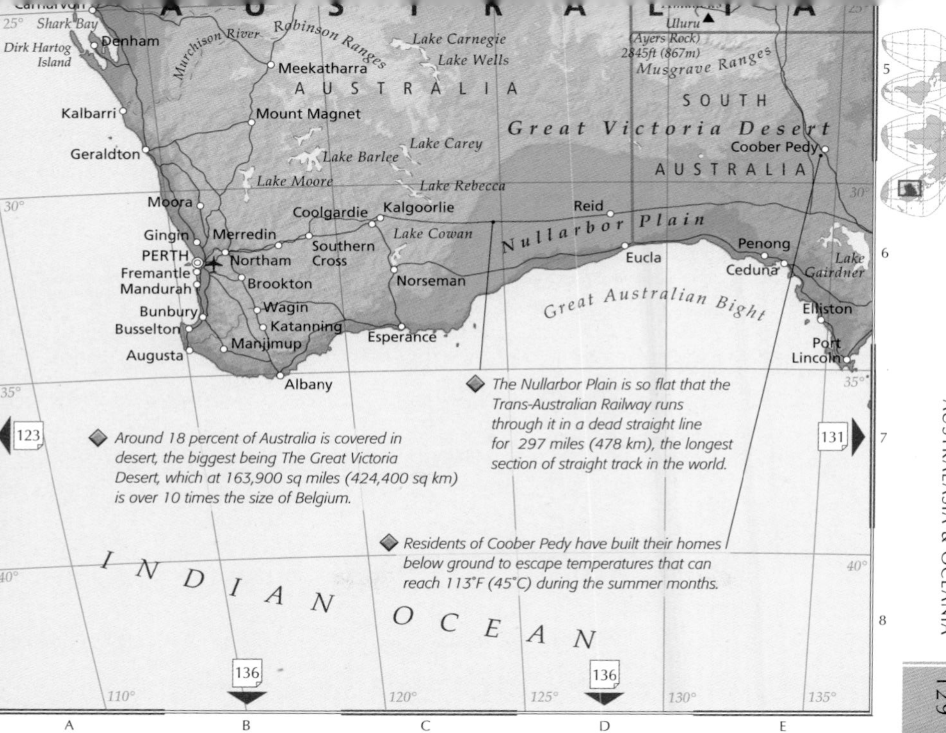
Shark Bay
Dirk Hartog Island
Denham
Murchison River
Robinson Ranges
Meekatharra
Lake Carnegie
Lake Wells
Uluru
(Ayers Rock)
2845ft (867m)
Musgrave Ranges
AUSTRALIA
SOUTH
Kalbarri
Mount Magnet
Great Victoria Desert
Geraldton
Lake Carey
Lake Barlee
Coober Pedy
AUSTRALIA
Lake Moore
Lake Rebecca
Moora
Coolgardie
Kalgoorlie
Reid
Nullarbor Plain
Gingin
Merredin
Lake Cowan
PERTH
Northam
Southern Cross
Penong
Eucla
Lake Gairdner
Ceduna
Fremantle
Mandurah
Brookton
Norseman
Great Australian Bight
Bunbury
Wagin
Elliston
Busselton
Katanning
Esperance
Port Lincoln
Augusta
Manjimup
Albany
INDIAN OCEAN
25°
30°
35°
40°
110°
120°
125°
130°
135°

◆ Around 18 percent of Australia is covered in desert, the biggest being The Great Victoria Desert, which at 163,900 sq miles (424,400 sq km) is over 10 times the size of Belgium.

◆ The Nullarbor Plain is so flat that the Trans-Australian Railway runs through it in a dead straight line for 297 miles (478 km), the longest section of straight track in the world.

◆ Residents of Coober Pedy have built their homes below ground to escape temperatures that can reach 113°F (45°C) during the summer months.

123
131
136
136

Eastern Australia

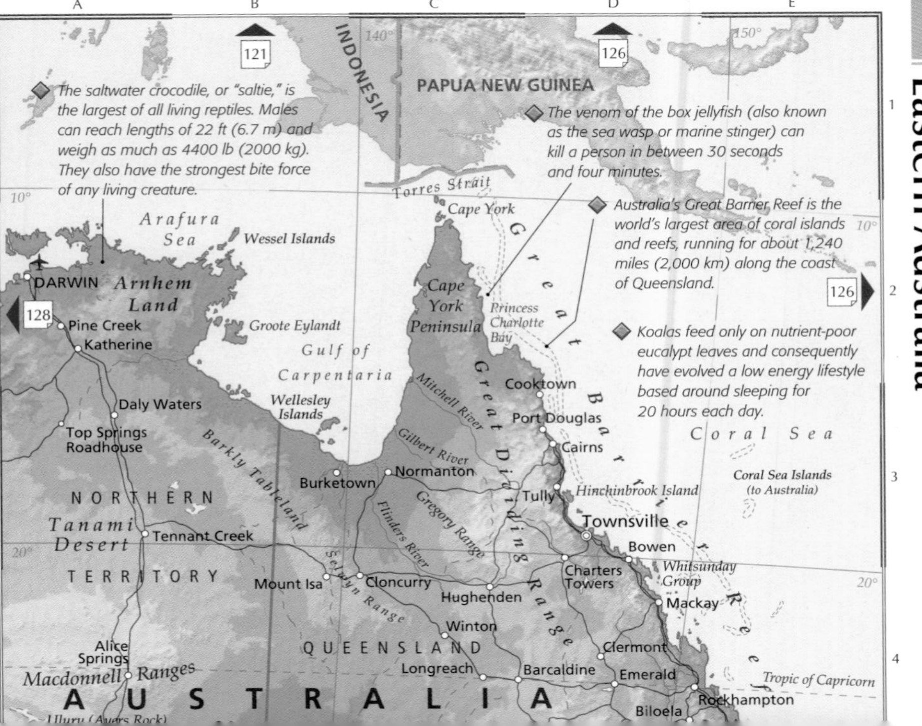

The saltwater crocodile, or "saltie," is the largest of all living reptiles. Males can reach lengths of 22 ft (6.7 m) and weigh as much as 4400 lb (2000 kg). They also have the strongest bite force of any living creature.
The venom of the box jellyfish (also known as the sea wasp or marine stinger) can kill a person in between 30 seconds and four minutes.
Australia's Great Barrier Reef is the world's largest area of coral islands and reefs, running for about 1,240 miles (2,000 km) along the coast of Queensland.
Koalas feed only on nutrient-poor eucalypt leaves and consequently have evolved a low energy lifestyle based around sleeping for 20 hours each day.
121
126
126
128
INDONESIA
PAPUA NEW GUINEA
Torres Strait
Cape York
Cape York Peninsula
Princess Charlotte Bay
Arafura Sea
Wessel Islands
Groote Eylandt
Gulf of Carpentaria
Wellesley Islands
Arnhem Land
DARWIN
Pine Creek
Katherine
Daly Waters
Top Springs Roadhouse
Tennant Creek
NORTHERN TERRITORY
Tanami Desert
Barkly Tableland
Burketown
Normanton
Mitchell River
Gilbert River
Flinders River
Gregory Range
Selwyn Range
Mount Isa
Cloncurry
Winton
Hughenden
Longreach
Barcaldine
QUEENSLAND
Great Dividing Range
Cooktown
Port Douglas
Cairns
Tully
Hinchinbrook Island
Townsville
Charters Towers
Bowen
Whitsunday Group
Mackay
Clermont
Emerald
Rockhampton
Biloela
Great Barrier Reef
Coral Sea
Coral Sea Islands (to Australia)
Tropic of Capricorn
Alice Springs
Macdonnell Ranges
AUSTRALIA
Uluru (Ayers Rock)
140°
150°
10°
20°

SOUTH AUSTRALIA
Great Victoria Desert
Coober Pedy
Lake Eyre North
-16m
Lake Blanche
Lake Eyre South
Marree
Lake Callabonna
Lake Torrens
Flinders Ranges
Lake Frome
Tarcoola
Penong
Ceduna
Lake Gairdner
Port Augusta
Broken Hill
Whyalla
Peterborough
Eyre Peninsula
Crystal Brook
Port Lincoln
Spencer Gulf
Gawler
ADELAIDE
Kangaroo Island
Grey Range
Barrier Range
Cunnamulla
St. George
Roma
Miles
Dalby
Toowoomba
BRISBANE
Surfer's Paradise
Gold Coast
Murwillumbah
Goondiwindi
Barwon River
Moree
Walgett
Grafton
Armidale
Coffs Harbour
Tamworth
Port Macquarie
Bourke
Wilcannia
Nyngan
NEW SOUTH WALES
Darling River
Ivanhoe
Dubbo
Lachlan River
Great Dividing Range
Newcastle
Gosford
Parramatta
SYDNEY
Murray River
Mildura
Cootamundra
Wollongong
Wagga Wagga
CANBERRA
AUSTRALIAN CAPITAL TERRITORY
Ouyen
Mount Kosciuszko 7310ft (2228m)
Australian Alps
Cooma
Horsham
Bendigo
VICTORIA
Mount Gambier
Ballarat
Geelong
MELBOURNE
Portland
Warrnambool
Traralgon
South East Point
King Island
Bass Strait
Flinders Island
Banks Strait
Tasman Sea
Marrawah
Burnie
Devonport
Launceston
TASMANIA
HOBART
30°
40°
150°
160°
5
6
7
8
A
B
C
D
E

129
134
136
136

Huge truck rigs known as Road Trains, which can reach up to 175 ft (53.5 m) in length, carry freight across the vast distances of the Australian interior. They have as many as four trailers, weighing more than 150 tons (tonnes) in total.

The platypus lives in an aquatic environment, suckles its young like a mammal, lays eggs, and has webbed feet and a bill resembling that of a duck.

New Zealand

The lizardlike tuatara is found on some of the islands and rocky stacks off New Zealand. It is the sole remaining representative of the reptilian order Sphenodontia, which first evolved before the dinosaurs. It has a third "eye" on the top of its head, which is sensitive to light.
Ninety Mile Beach is in fact only about 55 miles (88 km) long. Nevertheless, this still makes it one of the longest sandy beaches in the world.
Around 130 CE, something in the order of 33 billion tons (tonnes) of pumice was ejected in a massive volcanic eruption that left a 20,000 sq mile (51,800 sq km) debris field and created an enormous caldera that subsequently became Lake Taupo.
More than 39 million sheep thrive in New Zealand's mild climate, outnumbering the human population by eight to one.
Tasman Sea
North Island
NEW ZEALAND
Three Kings Islands
North Cape
Great Exhibition Bay
Te Kao
Kaitaia
Kaikohe
Paihia
Whangarei
Ruawai
Warkworth
Great Barrier Island
Hauraki Gulf
Takapuna
Auckland
Manurewa
Whitianga
Waiuku
Paeroa
Bay of Plenty
Tauranga
East Cape
Hamilton
Cambridge
Lake Rotorua
Whakatane
Ruatoria
Raukumara Ranges
Te Kuiti
Rotorua
North Taranaki Bight
Taupo
Lake Taupo
Gisborne
New Plymouth
Taumarunui
Wairoa
Stratford
Hawke Bay
Napier
Taihape
Hastings
South Taranaki Bight
Hawera
Rangitikei
Wanganui
Waipawa
Cape Farewell
Tasman
Palmerston North
Woodville
Levin
Cape Turnagain
127
131
135
168°
170°
172°
174°
176°
178°
34°
36°
38°
40°
A
B
C
D
E
1
2
3
4

Though still the highest peak in New Zealand, at 12,316 ft (3754 m), a massive rock fall in 1991 reduced the height of Aoraki (Mount Cook) by 33 ft (10 m).
New Zealand has always been a leader in progressive social legislation. In 1893, it was the first country to grant women the right to vote.
The royal albatross colony on Otago Peninsula is the only mainland nesting site for these birds in the world. Soaring on wings up to 9'6" (3 m) across, breeding pairs mate for life and have been known to live for over 60 years.
The Kakapo is a nocturnal flightless parrot that lives in burrows. When in danger, its main form of defense is to remain perfectly still, which made it an easy target for predators such as the dogs, cats, rats, and ferrets that were introduced in the 19th century. Consequently, it is in grave danger of extinction; in 2014 there were only 126 birds left in existence.
WELLINGTON
Cape Palliser
Cook Strait
Richmond
Seddonville
Westport
Blenheim
Richmond Range
Wairau
Reefton
Clarence
Greymouth
Kaikoura
Hokitika
Hurunui
Otira
Pegasus Bay
Rangiora
Christchurch
Southern Alps
Rakaia
Fox Glacier
Aoraki (Mt Cook) 12,283 (3744m)
Haast
Mayfield
Canterbury Plains
Ashburton
Banks Peninsula
Fairlie
Canterbury Bight
Milford Sound
Lake Wanaka
Timaru
South Island
Wanaka
Waitaki
Studholme
Lake Wakatipu
Queenstown
Oamaru
Lake Te Anau
Alexandra
Fiordland
Te Anau
Lumsden
Clutha
Taieri
Otago Peninsula
Mosgiel
Dunedin
Waiau
Gore
Balclutha
PACIFIC OCEAN
Riverton
Invercargill
Foveaux Strait
Halfmoon Bay
Stewart Island
South West Cape
0 km 100
0 miles 100
42° 44° 46° 48°
166° 168° 170° 172° 174° 176° 178°
131
135
136
136
A B C D E
5 6 7 8

The Pacific Ocean

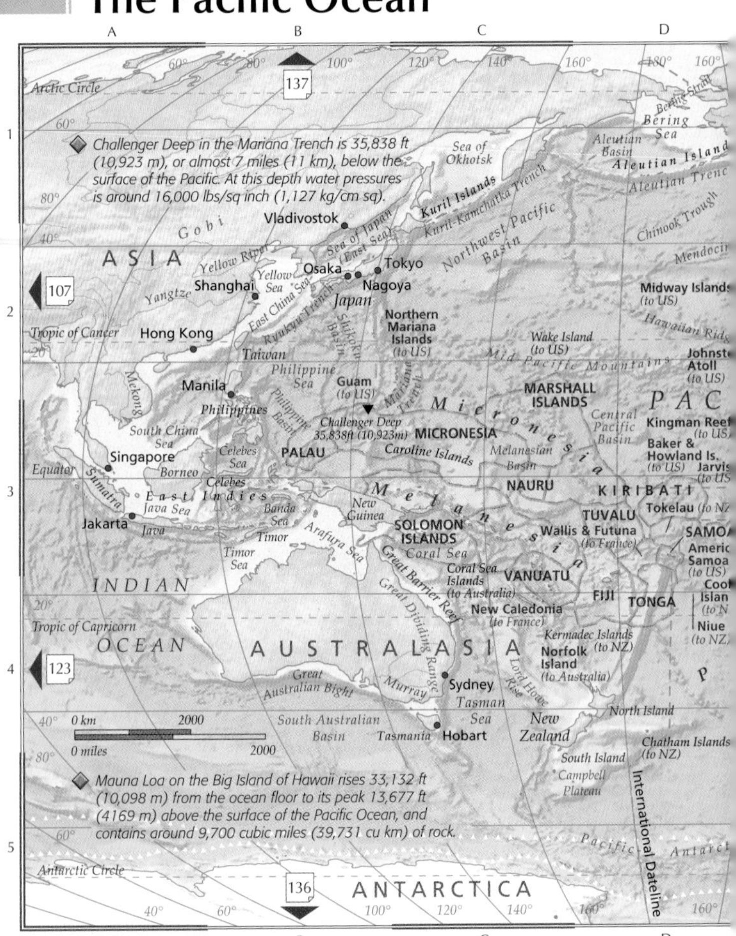
Challenger Deep in the Mariana Trench is 35,838 ft (10,923 m), or almost 7 miles (11 km), below the surface of the Pacific. At this depth water pressures is around 16,000 lbs/sq inch (1,127 kg/cm sq).
Mauna Loa on the Big Island of Hawaii rises 33,132 ft (10,098 m) from the ocean floor to its peak 13,677 ft (4169 m) above the surface of the Pacific Ocean, and contains around 9,700 cubic miles (39,731 cu km) of rock.
137
107
123
136
Arctic Circle
Tropic of Cancer
Equator
Tropic of Capricorn
Antarctic Circle
Bering Strait
Bering Sea
Aleutian Basin
Aleutian Islands
Aleutian Trench
Sea of Okhotsk
Kuril Islands
Kuril-Kamchatka Trench
Northwest Pacific Basin
Chinook Trough
Gobi
Vladivostok
Sea of Japan (East Sea)
ASIA
Yellow River
Yellow Sea
Osaka
Tokyo
Nagoya
Shanghai
Yangtze
East China Sea
Ryukyu Trench
Japan
Shikoku Basin
Northern Mariana Islands (to US)
Midway Islands (to US)
Hawaiian Ridge
Hong Kong
Taiwan
Philippine Sea
Guam (to US)
Mariana Trench
Wake Island (to US)
Mid Pacific Mountains
Johnston Atoll (to US)
Mekong
Manila
Philippines
Philippine Basin
Micronesia
MARSHALL ISLANDS
Central Pacific Basin
South China Sea
Challenger Deep 35,838ft (10,923m)
MICRONESIA
Kingman Reef (to US)
Baker & Howland Is. (to US)
Jarvis (to US)
Singapore
Celebes Sea
PALAU
Caroline Islands
Melanesian Basin
Borneo
Sumatra
Celebes
East Indies
NAURU
KIRIBATI
Java Sea
Banda Sea
New Guinea
Melanesia
Tokelau (to NZ)
Jakarta
Java
Timor
Arafura Sea
SOLOMON ISLANDS
TUVALU
Wallis & Futuna (to France)
Timor Sea
Coral Sea
Great Barrier Reef
Coral Sea Islands (to Australia)
VANUATU
American Samoa (to US)
INDIAN OCEAN
Great Dividing Range
FIJI
TONGA
New Caledonia (to France)
Niue (to NZ)
Kermadec Islands (to NZ)
AUSTRALASIA
Norfolk Island (to Australia)
Lord Howe Rise
Great Australian Bight
Murray
Sydney
Tasman Sea
North Island
0 km 2000
0 miles 2000
South Australian Basin
Tasmania
Hobart
New Zealand
Chatham Islands (to NZ)
South Island
Campbell Plateau
International Dateline
Pacific Antarctic
ANTARCTICA

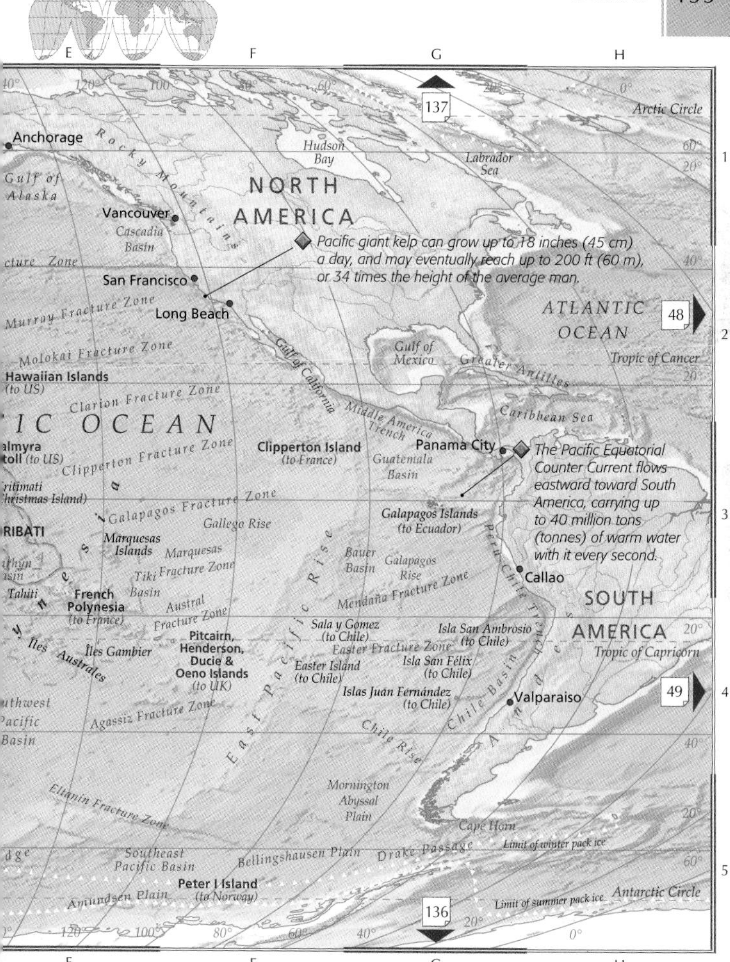
E
F
G
H
137
Arctic Circle
Anchorage
Rocky Mountains
Hudson Bay
Labrador Sea
Gulf of Alaska
NORTH AMERICA
Vancouver
Cascadia Basin
Pacific giant kelp can grow up to 18 inches (45 cm) a day, and may eventually reach up to 200 ft (60 m), or 34 times the height of the average man.
San Francisco
Murray Fracture Zone
Long Beach
ATLANTIC OCEAN
48
Molokai Fracture Zone
Gulf of Mexico
Greater Antilles
Tropic of Cancer
Hawaiian Islands (to US)
Gulf of California
Clarion Fracture Zone
Caribbean Sea
Middle America Trench
IC OCEAN
Clipperton Island (to France)
Panama City
The Pacific Equatorial Counter Current flows eastward toward South America, carrying up to 40 million tons (tonnes) of warm water with it every second.
Clipperton Fracture Zone
Guatemala Basin
Galapagos Fracture Zone
Galapagos Islands (to Ecuador)
Gallego Rise
RIBATI
Marquesas Islands
Marquesas
Bauer Basin
Galapagos Rise
Tiki Fracture Zone
Callao
Tahiti
French Polynesia (to France)
Basin
Mendaña Fracture Zone
SOUTH AMERICA
Austral Fracture Zone
Sala y Gomez (to Chile)
Isla San Ambrosio (to Chile)
Pitcairn, Henderson, Ducie & Oeno Islands (to UK)
Îles Gambier
Îles Australes
Easter Fracture Zone
Easter Island (to Chile)
Isla San Félix (to Chile)
Tropic of Capricorn
Islas Juan Fernández (to Chile)
Valparaiso
49
Agassiz Fracture Zone
East Pacific Rise
Chile Rise
Chile Basin
Peru-Chile Trench
Andes
Mornington Abyssal Plain
Eltanin Fracture Zone
Cape Horn
Limit of winter pack ice
Southeast Pacific Basin
Bellingshausen Plain
Drake Passage
Peter I Island (to Norway)
Amundsen Plain
Limit of summer pack ice
Antarctic Circle
136
1
2
3
4
5

Antarctica

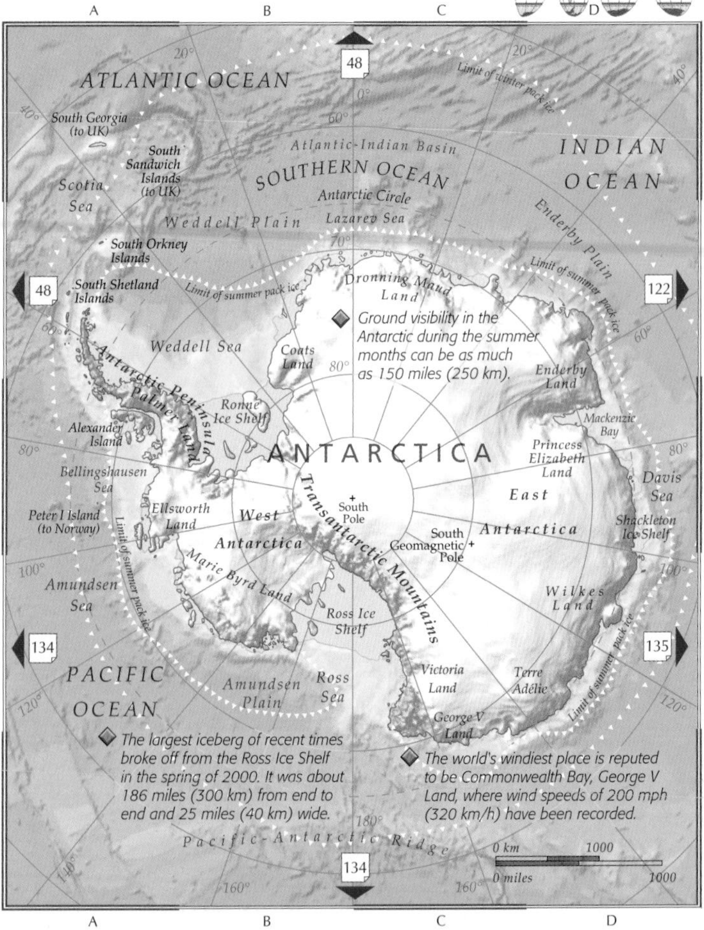

A B C D

48

ATLANTIC OCEAN

South Georgia (to UK)

South Sandwich Islands (to UK)

Scotia Sea

Atlantic-Indian Basin

SOUTHERN OCEAN

INDIAN OCEAN

Antarctic Circle

Lazarev Sea

Weddell Plain

Enderby Plain

Limit of winter pack ice

South Orkney Islands

South Shetland Islands

Limit of summer pack ice

Dronning Maud Land

48

122

◆ Ground visibility in the Antarctic during the summer months can be as much as 150 miles (250 km).

Weddell Sea

Coats Land

Enderby Land

Antarctic Peninsula

Palmer Land

Ronne Ice Shelf

Alexander Island

Mackenzie Bay

ANTARCTICA

Princess Elizabeth Land

Bellingshausen Sea

Davis Sea

Transantarctic Mountains

South Pole

East Antarctica

Peter I Island (to Norway)

Ellsworth Land

West Antarctica

South Geomagnetic Pole

Shackleton Ice Shelf

Marie Byrd Land

Amundsen Sea

Wilkes Land

Ross Ice Shelf

134

135

PACIFIC OCEAN

Amundsen Plain

Ross Sea

Victoria Land

Terre Adélie

George V Land

◆ The largest iceberg of recent times broke off from the Ross Ice Shelf in the spring of 2000. It was about 186 miles (300 km) from end to end and 25 miles (40 km) wide.

◆ The world's windiest place is reputed to be Commonwealth Bay, George V Land, where wind speeds of 200 mph (320 km/h) have been recorded.

Pacific-Antarctic Ridge

0 km 1000

0 miles 1000

134

A B C D

Arctic

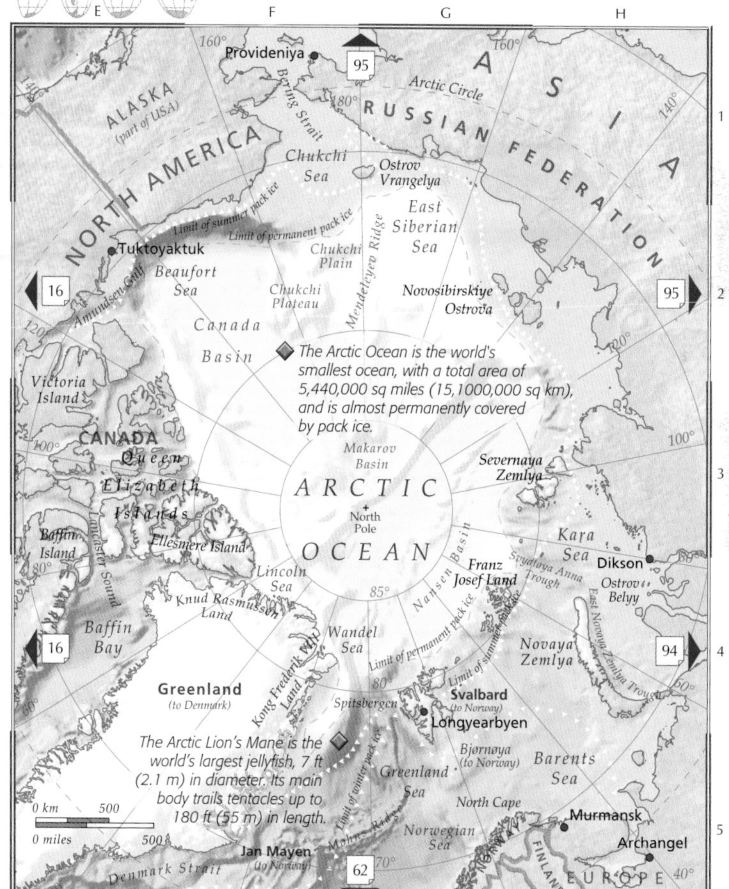
E
F
G
H
1
2
3
4
5
95
16
16
95
94
62
ASIA
RUSSIAN FEDERATION
Arctic Circle
ALASKA
(part of USA)
NORTH AMERICA
Providenіya
Bering Strait
Chukchi Sea
Ostrov Vrangelya
East Siberian Sea
Limit of summer pack ice
Limit of permanent pack ice
Tuktoyaktuk
Beaufort Sea
Chukchi Plain
Mendeleyev Ridge
Chukchi Plateau
Novosibirskiye Ostrova
Amundsen Gulf
Canada Basin
Victoria Island
CANADA
Queen Elizabeth Islands
Makarov Basin
ARCTIC OCEAN
North Pole
Severnaya Zemlya
Baffin Island
Lancaster Sound
Ellesmere Island
Kara Sea
Dikson
Ostrov Belyy
Franz Josef Land
Svyataya Anna Trough
Nansen Basin
Lincoln Sea
Knud Rasmussen Land
Baffin Bay
Wandel Sea
East Novaya Zemlya Trough
Novaya Zemlya
Greenland
(to Denmark)
Kong Frederik VIII Land
Spitsbergen
Svalbard
(to Norway)
Longyearbyen
Bjørnøya
(to Norway)
Barents Sea
Greenland Sea
Limit of winter pack ice
North Cape
Murmansk
Archangel
Mohns Ridge
Norwegian Sea
NORWAY
FINLAND
EUROPE
Jan Mayen
(to Norway)
Denmark Strait
0 km 500
0 miles 500
The Arctic Ocean is the world's smallest ocean, with a total area of 5,440,000 sq miles (15,1000,000 sq km), and is almost permanently covered by pack ice.
The Arctic Lion's Mane is the world's largest jellyfish, 7 ft (2.1 m) in diameter. Its main body trails tentacles up to 180 ft (55 m) in length.

The world factfiles

North & Central America

ASIA
ARCTIC
North Pole
OCEAN
Franz Josef Land
(to Russia)
Svalbard
(to Norway)
Jan Mayen
(to Norway)
Queen Elizabeth Islands
Yukon
ALASKA
Greenland
(Denmark)
Baffin Bay
Baffin Island
NUUK
Arctic Circle
Mackenzie
Great Bear Lake
Great Slave Lake
Lake Athabasca
Rocky Mount
PACIFIC
OCEAN
Reindeer Lake
Hudson Bay
CANADA
Labrador
Lake Winnipeg
Laurentian Mountains
Snake
Lake Superior
Great
Lake Huron
Gulf of St.Lawrence
St Pierre &
Miquelon

ATLANTIC
OCEAN
OF AMERICA
Lake Erie
Ohio
Arkansas
Mississippi
Appalachian Mountains
WASHINGTON, D.C.
Bermuda
(UK)
Sargasso Sea
Tropic of Cancer
Sierra Madre Occidental
Rio Grande
MEXICO
Gulf of Mexico
MEXICO CITY
HAVANA
CUBA
Cayman Islands (UK)
NASSAU
THE BAHAMAS
Turks & Caicos Islands (UK)
DOMINICAN REPUBLIC
Puerto Rico (US)
SANTO DOMINGO
HAITI
PORT-AU-PRINCE
JAMAICA
KINGSTON
Virgin Islands (US)
British Virgin Islands (UK)
Anguilla (UK)
ST KITTS & NEVIS
ANTIGUA & BARBUDA
Guadeloupe
(France)
Montserrat (UK)
DOMINICA
Martinique (France)
ST LUCIA
BARBADOS
ST VINCENT & THE GRENADINES
GRENADA
Aruba (Neth.)
Curaçao
(Neth.)
Bonaire
(Neth.)
TRINIDAD & TOBAGO
BELMOPAN
BELIZE
GUATEMALA
GUATEMALA CITY
HONDURAS
TEGUCIGALPA
SAN SALVADOR
EL SALVADOR
NICARAGUA
MANAGUA
COSTA RICA
SAN JOSÉ
PANAMA CITY
PANAMA
Clipperton Island
(French Polynesia)
Andes
SOUTH AMERICA
Equator
0 1000 km
0 1000 miles

POLITICAL FACTFILE

TOTAL AREA:
8,116,571 sq miles
(21,021,940 sq km)

TOTAL NUMBER OF COUNTRIES:
23

TOTAL POPULATION:
560 million

LARGEST CITY WITH POPULATION:
Mexico City, Mexico 22.2 million

COUNTRY WITH HIGHEST POPULATION DENSITY:
Barbados 1807 people per sq mile
(698 people per sq km)

LARGEST COUNTRY:
Canada 3,855,171 sq miles
(9,984,670 sq km)

SMALLEST COUNTRY:
St. Kitts & Nevis 101 sq miles
(261 sq km)

South America

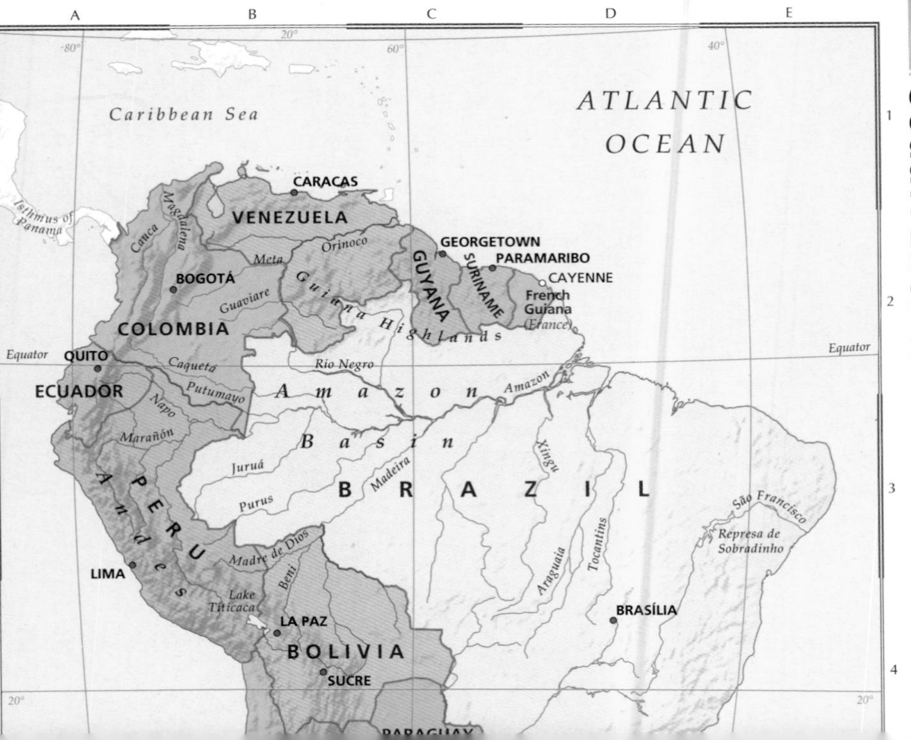
A
B
C
D
E
1
2
3
4
Caribbean Sea
ATLANTIC OCEAN
Isthmus of Panama
CARACAS
VENEZUELA
Magdalena
Cauca
Orinoco
Meta
BOGOTÁ
Guaviare
COLOMBIA
Guiana Highlands
GEORGETOWN
GUYANA
SURINAME
PARAMARIBO
CAYENNE
French Guiana (France)
Equator
QUITO
ECUADOR
Caquetá
Putumayo
Napo
Marañón
Rio Negro
Amazon Basin
Amazon
Juruá
Purus
Madeira
BRAZIL
Xingu
Araguaia
Tocantins
São Francisco
Represa de Sobradinho
BRASÍLIA
PERU
Andes
LIMA
Madre de Dios
Beni
Lake Titicaca
LA PAZ
BOLIVIA
SUCRE
PARAGUAY
80°
60°
40°
20°

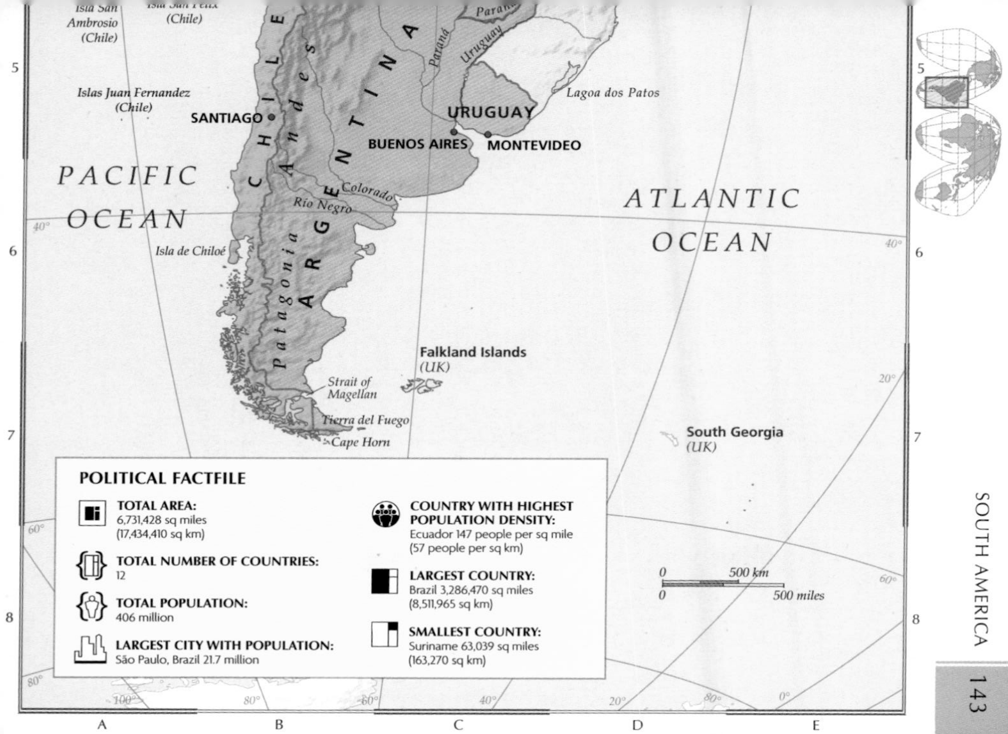
Ambrosio
(Chile)
(Chile)
Islas Juan Fernandez
(Chile)
SANTIAGO
CHILE
Andes
ARGENTINA
Paraná
Uruguay
URUGUAY
BUENOS AIRES
MONTEVIDEO
Lagoa dos Patos
PACIFIC
OCEAN
Colorado
Río Negro
Isla de Chiloé
Patagonia
Falkland Islands
(UK)
Strait of
Magellan
Tierra del Fuego
Cape Horn
ATLANTIC
OCEAN
South Georgia
(UK)
0 500 km
0 500 miles
POLITICAL FACTFILE
TOTAL AREA:
6,731,428 sq miles
(17,434,410 sq km)
TOTAL NUMBER OF COUNTRIES:
12
TOTAL POPULATION:
406 million
LARGEST CITY WITH POPULATION:
São Paulo, Brazil 21.7 million
COUNTRY WITH HIGHEST
POPULATION DENSITY:
Ecuador 147 people per sq mile
(57 people per sq km)
LARGEST COUNTRY:
Brazil 3,286,470 sq miles
(8,511,965 sq km)
SMALLEST COUNTRY:
Suriname 63,039 sq miles
(163,270 sq km)

Africa

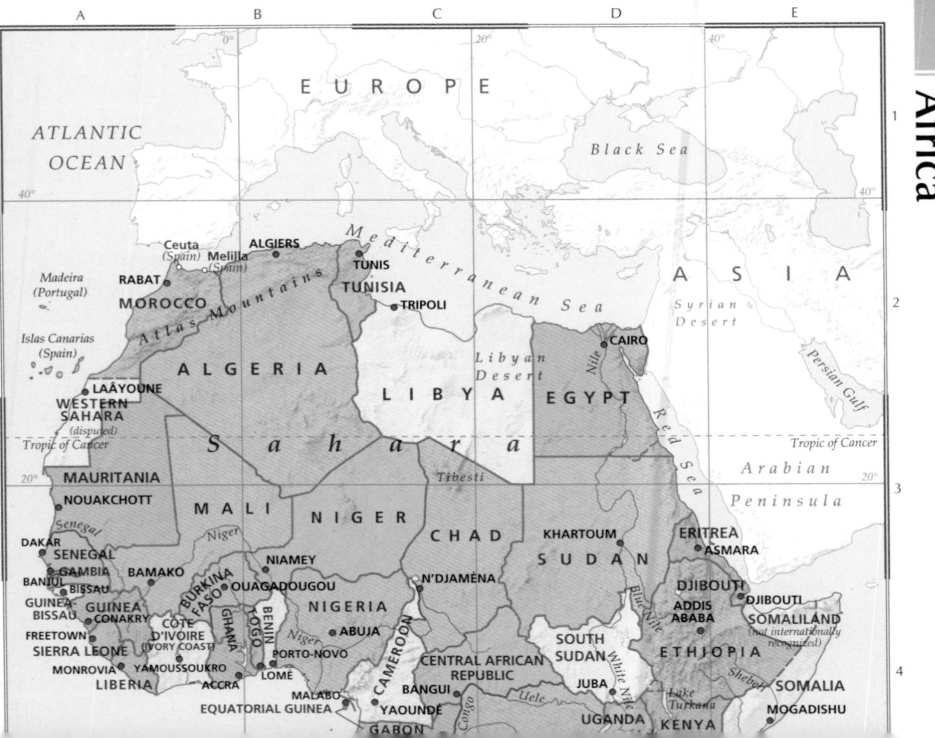
A
B
C
D
E
1
2
3
4
EUROPE
ATLANTIC
OCEAN
Black Sea
ASIA
Mediterranean Sea
Syrian Desert
Persian Gulf
Red Sea
Arabian Peninsula
Tropic of Cancer
Libyan Desert
Sahara
Tibesti
Atlas Mountains
Madeira
(Portugal)
Islas Canarias
(Spain)
Ceuta
(Spain)
Melilla
(Spain)
RABAT
MOROCCO
ALGIERS
ALGERIA
TUNIS
TUNISIA
TRIPOLI
LIBYA
CAIRO
Nile
EGYPT
LAÂYOUNE
WESTERN
SAHARA
(disputed)
MAURITANIA
NOUAKCHOTT
MALI
NIGER
CHAD
KHARTOUM
SUDAN
ERITREA
ASMARA
DJIBOUTI
DJIBOUTI
ADDIS
ABABA
SOMALILAND
(not internationally
recognized)
ETHIOPIA
Shebeli
SOMALIA
MOGADISHU
Blue Nile
White Nile
SOUTH
SUDAN
JUBA
Lake
Turkana
UGANDA
KENYA
CENTRAL AFRICAN
REPUBLIC
BANGUI
Uele
Congo
CAMEROON
YAOUNDÉ
GABON
MALABO
EQUATORIAL GUINEA
N'DJAMENA
NIGERIA
ABUJA
Niger
NIAMEY
PORTO-NOVO
BENIN
TOGO
LOMÉ
GHANA
ACCRA
OUAGADOUGOU
BURKINA
FASO
BAMAKO
CÔTE
D'IVOIRE
(IVORY COAST)
YAMOUSSOUKRO
Senegal
DAKAR
SENEGAL
GAMBIA
BANJUL
BISSAU
GUINEA-
BISSAU
GUINEA
CONAKRY
FREETOWN
SIERRA LEONE
MONROVIA
LIBERIA
0°
20°
40°

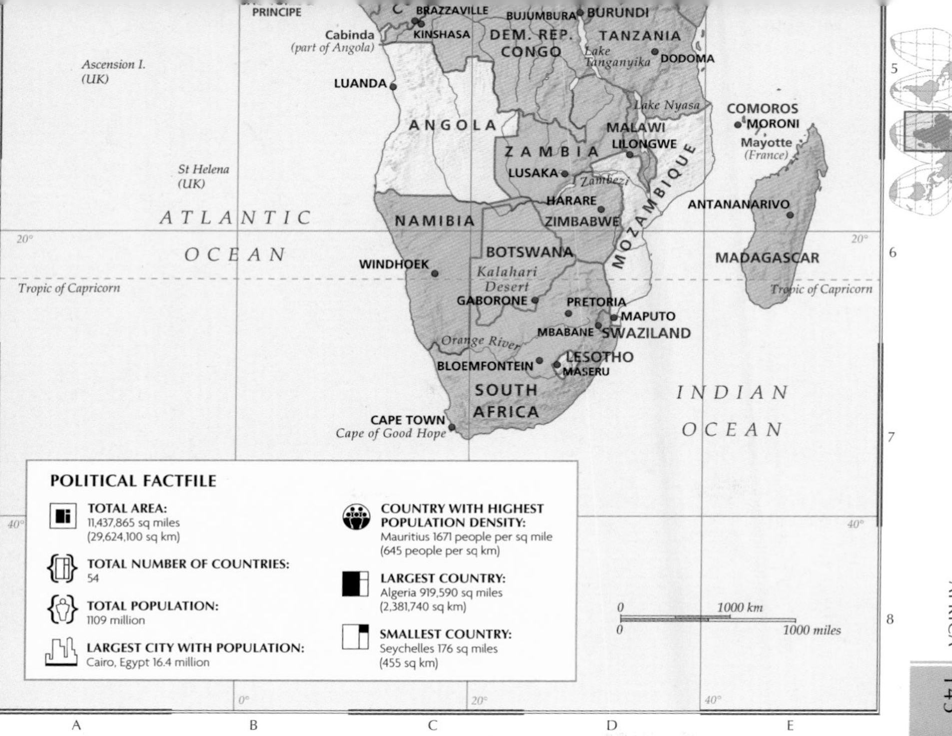
PRINCIPE
BRAZZAVILLE
KINSHASA
Cabinda
(part of Angola)
BUJUMBURA
BURUNDI
DEM. REP. CONGO
TANZANIA
Lake Tanganyika
DODOMA
Ascension I.
(UK)
LUANDA
Lake Nyasa
COMOROS
MORONI
Mayotte
(France)
ANGOLA
MALAWI
LILONGWE
ZAMBIA
LUSAKA
Zambezi
St Helena
(UK)
HARARE
ZIMBABWE
MOZAMBIQUE
ANTANANARIVO
ATLANTIC OCEAN
NAMIBIA
BOTSWANA
MADAGASCAR
WINDHOEK
Kalahari Desert
Tropic of Capricorn
GABORONE
PRETORIA
MAPUTO
MBABANE
SWAZILAND
Orange River
LESOTHO
BLOEMFONTEIN
MASERU
SOUTH AFRICA
INDIAN OCEAN
CAPE TOWN
Cape of Good Hope
20°
40°
0°
0 1000 km
0 1000 miles
A B C D E
5 6 7 8

POLITICAL FACTFILE

TOTAL AREA:
11,437,865 sq miles
(29,624,100 sq km)

TOTAL NUMBER OF COUNTRIES:
54

TOTAL POPULATION:
1109 million

LARGEST CITY WITH POPULATION:
Cairo, Egypt 16.4 million

COUNTRY WITH HIGHEST POPULATION DENSITY:
Mauritius 1671 people per sq mile
(645 people per sq km)

LARGEST COUNTRY:
Algeria 919,590 sq miles
(2,381,740 sq km)

SMALLEST COUNTRY:
Seychelles 176 sq miles
(455 sq km)

Europe

A
B
C
D
1
2
3
4
5
POLITICAL FACTFILE
TOTAL AREA:
3,739,678 sq miles
(9,685,756 sq km)
TOTAL NUMBER OF COUNTRIES:
46
TOTAL POPULATION:
721 million
LARGEST CITY WITH POPULATION:
Moscow, European Russia 16.7 million
COUNTRY WITH HIGHEST POPULATION DENSITY:
Monaco 48,181 people per sq mile
(18,531 people per sq km)
LARGEST COUNTRY:
European Russia 1,527,341 sq miles
(3,955,818 sq km)
SMALLEST COUNTRY:
Vatican City, Italy 0.17 sq miles
(0.44 sq km)
REYKJAVÍK
ICELAND
Arctic Circle
Norwegian Sea
Faroe Islands
(Denmark)
Shetland Islands
Outer Hebrides
Orkney Islands
British Isles
North Sea
NORWAY
OSLO
IRELAND
DUBLIN
UNITED KINGDOM
DENMARK
COPENHAGEN
AMSTERDAM
NETH.
Elbe
LONDON
THE HAGUE
BERLIN
BELGIUM
BRUSSELS
GERMANY
LUXEMBOURG
LUXEMBOURG
PARIS
Loire
PRAGU
CZECH REPUBL
Bay of Biscay
FRANCE
Rhine
LIECH.
BRATISLAV
BERN
VIENNA
SWITZERLAND
AUSTRIA
Garonne
SLOVENI
LJUBLJANA
ZAGREB
CROATIA
ATLANTIC OCEAN
PORTUGAL
Ebro
MONACO
Tagus
MADRID
ANDORRA
SAN MARINO
SARAJE
LISBON
SPAIN
Corsica
BOSN & HE
Madeira
(Portugal)
Guadalquivir
VATICAN CITY
ROME
ITALY
Balearic Islands
Gibraltar
(UK)
Sardinia
Ceuta
(Spain)
Mediterranean
Melilla
(Spain)
Canary Islands
(Spain)
Sicily
AFRICA
VALLETTA
MALTA
40°
20°
70°
0°
50°
60°
30°

E
F
G
H
1
2
3
4
5
FINLAND
HELSINKI
STOCKHOLM
TALLINN
ESTONIA
Baltic Sea
LATVIA
RIGA
LITHUANIA
VILNIUS
KALININGRAD
(Russ.Fed.)
MINSK
BELARUS
WARSAW
POLAND
KIEV
UKRAINE
SLOVAKIA
BUDAPEST
HUNGARY
MOLDOVA
CHIŞINĂU
ROMANIA
SERBIA
BELGRADE
BUCHAREST
MONTENEGRO
PODGORICA
Danube
PRISHTINË
SOFIA
BULGARIA
SKOPJE
MACED.
TURKEY
TIRANA
ALBANIA
GREECE
ATHENS
Crete
Cyprus
Black Sea
Dnieper
(the Ukrainian territory of Crimea was annexed by Russia in 2014)
Caucasus
Caspian Sea
Lake Onega
Lake Ladoga
Northern Dvina
MOSCOW
RUSSIAN FEDERATION
Ural Mountains
Volga
Ural
Don
Ob
Irtysh
Aral Sea
ASIA
0
1000 km
0
1000 miles

Asia

A
B
C
D
1
2
3
4
5
ARCTIC OCEAN
Franz Josef Land
Severnaya Zemlya
Laptev Sea
Kara Sea
RUSSIAN FEDERATION
EUROPE
Ob
Yenisey
Irtysh
Black Sea
Lake Baikal
ASTANA
ANKARA
TURKEY
GEORGIA
TBILISI
KAZAKHSTAN
ULAN BATOR
MONGOLIA
CYPRUS
NICOSIA
ARMENIA
YEREVAN
AZERBAIJAN
BAKU
UZBEKISTAN
BEIRUT
SYRIA
LEBANON
DAMASCUS
TURKMENISTAN
BISHKEK
KYRGYZSTAN
JERUSALEM
AMMAN
AŞGABAT
TASHKENT
TEHRĀN
ISRAEL
JORDAN
BAGHDAD
DUSHANBE
TAJIKISTAN
IRAQ
IRAN
KABUL
CHINA
KUWAIT
KUWAIT
AFGHANISTAN
ISLAMABAD
MANAMA
BAHRAIN
RIYADH
QATAR
DOHA
PAKISTAN
NEW DELHI
NEPAL
THIMPHU
BHUTAN
SAUDI ARABIA
ABU DHABI
U.A.E.
MUSCAT
Indus
KATHMANDU
Ganges
BANGLADESH
DHAKA
Red Sea
AFRICA
SANA
YEMEN
OMAN
INDIA
MYANMAR (BURMA)
VIETNA
HANOI
LAOS
Arabian Sea
NAY PYI TAW
VIENTIANE
THAILAND
BANGKOK
CAMBODIA
Socotra (Yemen)
Bay of Bengal
Laccadive Islands (India)
Andaman & Nicobar Islands (India)
COLOMBO
SRI JAYEWARDENAPURA KOTTE
MALE'
MALDIVES
SRI LANKA
KUALA LUMPUR
PUTRAJAYA
SINGAPORE
INDIAN OCEAN
Tropic of Cancer
Equator
JAKAR
40°
20°
60°
80°
140°
100°

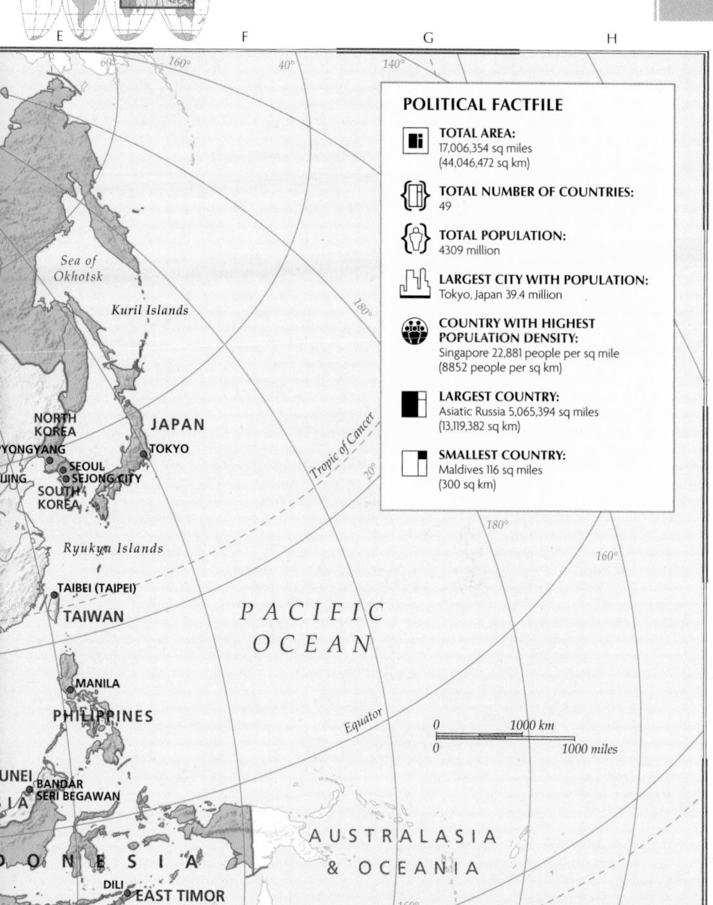

E
F
G
H
1
2
3
4
5
Sea of Okhotsk
Kuril Islands
NORTH KOREA
PYONGYANG
JAPAN
TOKYO
SEOUL
SEJONG CITY
SOUTH KOREA
Ryukyu Islands
TAIBEI (TAIPEI)
TAIWAN
PACIFIC OCEAN
Tropic of Cancer
Equator
MANILA
PHILIPPINES
BANDAR SERI BEGAWAN
DILI
EAST TIMOR
AUSTRALASIA & OCEANIA
0
1000 km
0
1000 miles

POLITICAL FACTFILE

TOTAL AREA:
17,006,354 sq miles
(44,046,472 sq km)

TOTAL NUMBER OF COUNTRIES:
49

TOTAL POPULATION:
4309 million

LARGEST CITY WITH POPULATION:
Tokyo, Japan 39.4 million

COUNTRY WITH HIGHEST POPULATION DENSITY:
Singapore 22,881 people per sq mile
(8852 people per sq km)

LARGEST COUNTRY:
Asiatic Russia 5,065,394 sq miles
(13,119,382 sq km)

SMALLEST COUNTRY:
Maldives 116 sq miles
(300 sq km)

Australasia & Oceania

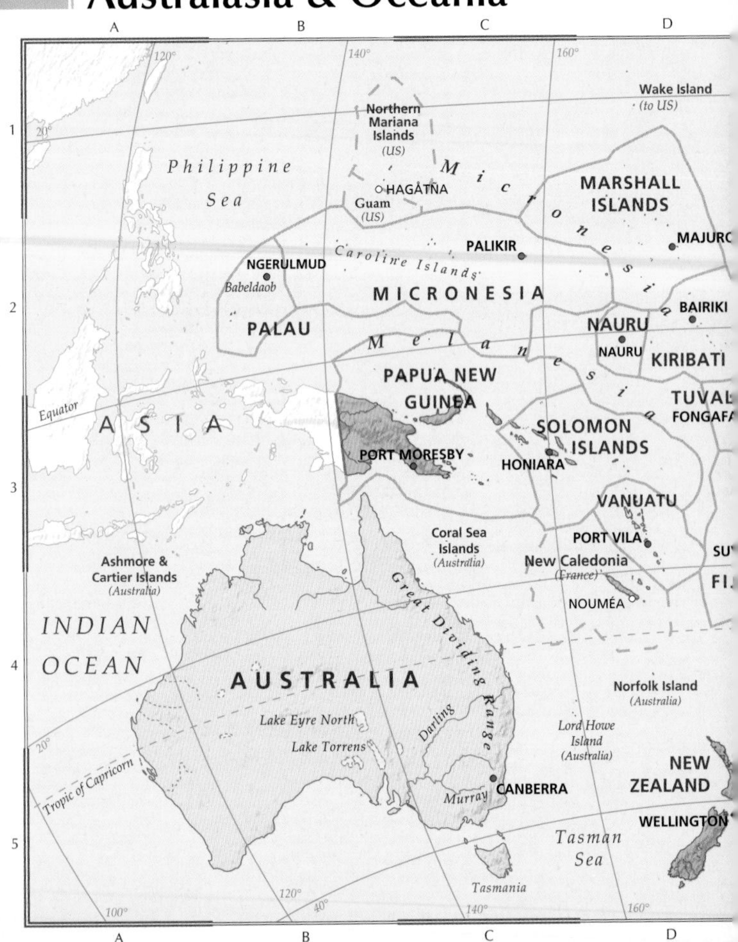

A
B
C
D
1
2
3
4
5
120°
140°
160°
20°
Wake Island
(to US)
Northern Mariana Islands
(US)
Philippine Sea
Micronesia
HAGÅTÑA
Guam
(US)
MARSHALL ISLANDS
MAJURO
PALIKIR
Caroline Islands
NGERULMUD
Babeldaob
MICRONESIA
BAIRIKI
PALAU
NAURU
NAURU
Melanesia
KIRIBATI
PAPUA NEW GUINEA
TUVALU
Equator
ASIA
SOLOMON ISLANDS
PORT MORESBY
HONIARA
VANUATU
Coral Sea Islands
(Australia)
PORT VILA
Ashmore & Cartier Islands
(Australia)
New Caledonia
(France)
Great Dividing Range
NOUMÉA
INDIAN OCEAN
AUSTRALIA
Norfolk Island
(Australia)
Lake Eyre North
Darling
Lord Howe Island
(Australia)
Lake Torrens
Tropic of Capricorn
NEW ZEALAND
Murray
CANBERRA
WELLINGTON
Tasman Sea
Tasmania
100°
120°
40°
140°
160°

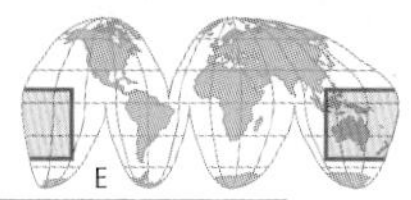

E F G H

POLITICAL FACTFILE

TOTAL AREA:
3,244,632 sq miles (8,403,608 sq km)

TOTAL NUMBER OF COUNTRIES:
14

TOTAL POPULATION:
37.5 million

LARGEST CITY WITH POPULATION:
Sydney, Australia 4.8 million

COUNTRY WITH HIGHEST POPULATION DENSITY:
Nauru 1165 people per sq mile (449 people per sq km)

LARGEST COUNTRY:
Australia 2,967,893 sq miles (7,686,850 sq km)

SMALLEST COUNTRY:
Nauru 8.1 sq miles (21 sq km)

Johnston Atoll
(US)
Baker & Howland Islands
(US)
Jarvis Island
(US)
KIRIBATI
Phoenix Islands
KIRIBATI
PACIFIC OCEAN
Equator
Tokelau
(NZ)
Wallis & Futuna
(Fr.)
MATĀ'UTU
SAMOA
ĀPIA
American Samoa
(US)
PAGO PAGO
Cook Islands
(NZ)
Marquesas Islands
TONGA
Niue
(NZ)
NUKU'ALOFA
Society Islands
PAPEETE
AVARUA
French Polynesia
(France)
Îles Australes
Pitcairn, Henderson, Ducie & Oeno Islands
(UK)
Kermadec Islands
(New Zealand)
Tropic of Capricorn
International Dateline
Polynesia
Chatham Islands
(New Zealand)
0 1000 km
0 1000 miles
160° 140° 120° 100° 180° 20° 40°
1 2 3 4 5
E F G H

Key to factfile maps

FOREWORD

This factfile is intended as a guide to a world that is continually changing as political fashions and personalities come and go. Nevertheless, all the material in these factfiles has been researched from the most up-to-date and authoritative sources to give an incisive portrait of the geographical, social, and economic characteristics that make each country unique.

KEY TO MAP SYMBOLS

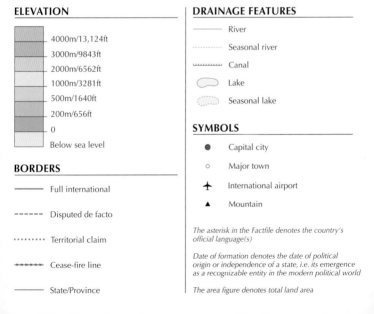

ELEVATION

- 4000m/13,124ft
- 3000m/9843ft
- 2000m/6562ft
- 1000m/3281ft
- 500m/1640ft
- 200m/656ft
- 0
- Below sea level

BORDERS

- Full international
- Disputed de facto
- Territorial claim
- Cease-fire line
- State/Province

DRAINAGE FEATURES

- River
- Seasonal river
- Canal
- Lake
- Seasonal lake

SYMBOLS

- Capital city
- Major town
- International airport
- Mountain

The asterisk in the Factfile denotes the country's official language(s)

Date of formation denotes the date of political origin or independence of a state, i.e. its emergence as a recognizable entity in the modern political world

The area figure denotes total land area

Afghanistan

About 75% of this landlocked Asian country is inaccessible. The Islamist *Taliban*, ousted in 2001, continue to fight a guerrilla war against Afghan and NATO-led forces.

GEOGRAPHY

Predominantly mountainous. Highest range is the Hindu Kush. Mountains are bordered by fertile plains. Desert plateau in the south.

CLIMATE

Harsh continental. Hot, dry summers. Cold winters with heavy snow, especially in the Hindu Kush.

PEOPLE & SOCIETY

Mujahideen factions fought first against Soviet invaders (from 1979), and then against each other (after 1989). *Taliban* insurgents won control in 1996 and imposed a strict Islamist regime: women were denied all rights and ethnic tensions were exacerbated. In 2001, a US-led intervention justified as a "war on terrorism" helped install an elected anti-*Taliban* regime. NATO troops led the anti-insurgency campaign, but aimed ultimately to hand over and withdraw.

THE ECONOMY

Mainly agricultural, severely disrupted by war. Illicit opium trade is big cash earner. Natural gas pipeline planned from the Caspian Sea to Pakistan.

INSIGHT: *The UN estimates that it could take 100 years to remove the 10 million landmines laid since 1979*

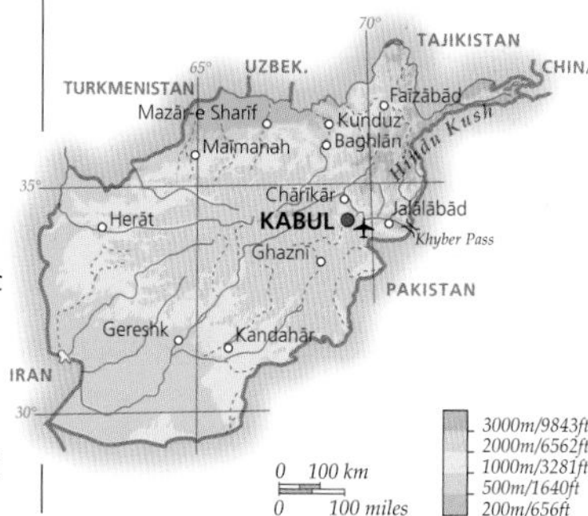
TAJIKISTAN
CHINA
UZBEK.
TURKMENISTAN
70°
65°
35°
30°
Mazār-e Sharīf
Fāīzābād
Kunduz
Baghlān
Maīmanah
Hindu Kush
Chārīkār
Herāt
KABUL
Jalālābād
Khyber Pass
Ghaznī
PAKISTAN
Gereshk
Kandahār
IRAN
0 100 km
0 100 miles
3000m/9843ft
2000m/6562ft
1000m/3281ft
500m/1640ft
200m/656ft

FACTFILE

OFFICIAL NAME: Islamic Republic of Afghanistan
DATE OF FORMATION: 1919
CAPITAL: Kabul
POPULATION: 30.6 million
TOTAL AREA: 250,000 sq. miles (647,500 sq. km)
DENSITY: 122 people per sq. mile
LANGUAGES: Pashtu*, Tajik, Dari*, other
RELIGIONS: Sunni Muslim 80%, Shi'a Muslim 19%, other 1%
ETHNIC MIX: Pashtun 38%, Tajik 25%, Hazara 19%, Uzbek and Turkmen 15%, other 3%
GOVERNMENT: Nonparty system
CURRENCY: Afghani = 100 puls

Albania

Lying at the southeastern end of the Adriatic Sea, Albania was the last east European country to liberalize its economy. The regional strife of the 1990s has left a difficult legacy.

GEOGRAPHY

Narrow coastal plain. Interior is mostly hills and mountains. Forest and scrub cover over 40% of the land.

CLIMATE

Mediterranean coastal climate, with warm summers and cool winters. Mountains receive heavy rains or snows in winter.

PEOPLE & SOCIETY

The pace of economic reform remains a major issue. Albania's application for EU membership reached candidate status in 2014. Mosques and churches have reopened in what was once the world's only officially atheist state. The Greek minority in the south suffers much discrimination.

INSIGHT: *The Albanians' name for their country, Shqipërisë, means "Land of the Eagles"*

THE ECONOMY

Oil and natural gas reserves have potential to offset rudimentary infrastructure and lack of foreign investment. Organized crime problem.

2000m/6562ft
1000m/3281ft
500m/1640ft
200m/656ft
Sea Level
MONTENEGRO
KOSOVO
(disputed)
Lake Scutari
Shkodër
Kukës
42°
Adriatic Sea
MACEDONIA
TIRANA
Durrës
Elbasan
Lake Ohrid
41°
Lushnjë
Fier
Berat
Lake Prespa
Vlorë
Korçë
40°
Delvinë
Ionian Sea
GREECE
20°
0 50 km
0 50 miles

FACTFILE

OFFICIAL NAME: Republic of Albania
DATE OF FORMATION: 1912
CAPITAL: Tirana
POPULATION: 3.2 million
TOTAL AREA: 11,100 sq. miles (28,748 sq. km)
DENSITY: 302 people per sq. mile
LANGUAGES: Albanian*, Greek
RELIGIONS: Sunni Muslim 70%, Albanian Orthodox 20%, Roman Catholic 10%
ETHNIC MIX: Albanian 98%, Greek 1%, other 1%
GOVERNMENT: Parliamentary system
CURRENCY: Lek = 100 qindarka (qintars)

Algeria

On the Mediterranean coast, and independent from France since 1962, Algeria is now Africa's largest country. Its regime used the army to keep Islamists from power in 1992.

GEOGRAPHY

85% of the country lies within the Sahara Desert. Fertile coastal region with plains and hills rises to meet the Atlas Mountains.

CLIMATE

Coastal areas are warm and temperate, with most rainfall during the mild winters. The south is very hot, with negligible rainfall.

PEOPLE & SOCIETY

Algerians are predominantly Arab, under 35 years of age, and urban. Berbers consider the mountainous Kabylia region in the northeast to be their homeland. They have been granted greater ethnic rights in recent years. The Sahara sustains just 500,000 people, mainly oil workers or Tuareg nomads herding goats and camels. A national reconciliation process has followed the suppression of the Islamist challenge to the regime.

THE ECONOMY

Oil and natural gas exports. Political turmoil has led to exodus of skilled foreign labor. Limited agriculture.

INSIGHT: *Some of the world's highest dunes are located in the deserts of east central Algeria*

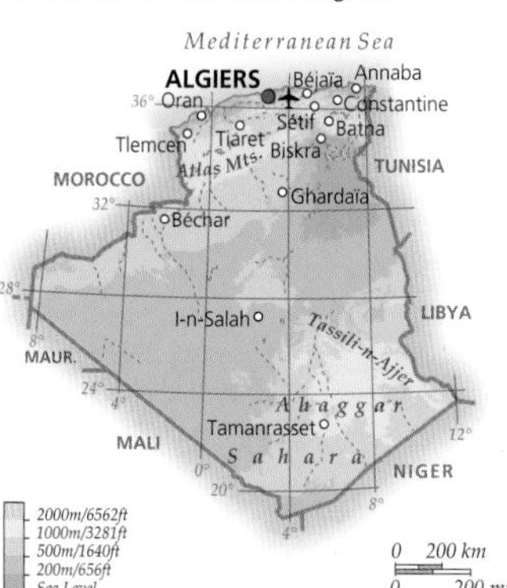
Mediterranean Sea
ALGIERS
Béjaïa
Annaba
36°
Oran
Constantine
Sétif
Batna
Tlemcen
Tiaret
Biskra
Atlas Mts.
TUNISIA
MOROCCO
Ghardaïa
32°
Béchar
28°
I-n-Salah
Tassili-n-Ajjer
LIBYA
8°
MAUR.
24°
4°
Ahaggar
Tamanrasset
12°
MALI
Sahara
0°
NIGER
20°
8°
4°
2000m/6562ft
1000m/3281ft
500m/1640ft
200m/656ft
Sea Level
0 200 km
0 200 miles

FACTFILE

OFFICIAL NAME: People's Democratic Republic of Algeria

DATE OF FORMATION: 1962

CAPITAL: Algiers

POPULATION: 39.2 million

TOTAL AREA: 919,590 sq. miles (2,381,740 sq. km)

DENSITY: 43 people per sq. mile

LANGUAGES: Arabic*, Tamazight, French

RELIGIONS: Sunni Muslim 99%, Christian and Jewish 1%

ETHNIC MIX: Arab 75%, Berber 24%, European and Jewish 1%

GOVERNMENT: Presidential system

CURRENCY: Algerian dinar = 100 centimes

Andorra

A tiny landlocked principality, Andorra lies high in the eastern Pyrenees between France and Spain. It held its first full elections in 1993. Tourism is the main source of income.

GEOGRAPHY

High mountains, with six deep, glaciated valleys that drain into the Valira River as it flows into Spain.

CLIMATE

Cool, wet springs followed by dry, warm summers. Mountain snows linger until March.

PEOPLE & SOCIETY

Immigration is strictly monitored and restricted by quota to French and Spanish nationals seeking employment in Andorra. Low taxes attract wealthy expatriates. A referendum in 1993 ended 715 years of semifeudal status, but Andorran society remains conservative.

INSIGHT: *Andorra's coprincipality status dates from the 13th century. The "princes" are the president of France and the bishop of Urgel in Spain.*

THE ECONOMY

Tourism and duty-free sales dominate the economy. Banking secrecy laws and low consumer taxes promote investment and commerce. France and Spain effectively decide economic policy. The country is dependent on imported food and raw materials.

2000m/6562ft
1000m/3281ft
500m/1640ft
FRANCE
Pyrenees
42°35′
Arinsal
Soldeu
Canillo
Ordino
Encamp
Port d'Envalira
Escaldes
42°30′
ANDORRA LA VELLA
Valira
Sant Julià de Lòria
1°40′
1°35′
1°25′
1°30′
SPAIN
0 5 km
0 5 miles

FACTFILE

OFFICIAL NAME: Principality of Andorra
DATE OF FORMATION: 1278
CAPITAL: Andorra la Vella
POPULATION: 85,293
TOTAL AREA: 181 sq. miles (468 sq. km)
DENSITY: 474 people per sq. mile
LANGUAGES: Spanish, Catalan*, French, Portuguese
RELIGIONS: Roman Catholic 94%, other 6%
ETHNIC MIX: Spanish 46%, Andorran 28%, other 18%, French 8%
GOVERNMENT: Parliamentary system
CURRENCY: Euro = 100 cents

Angola

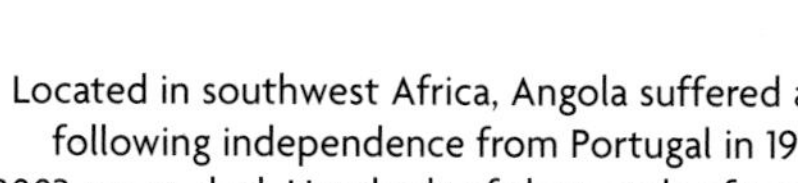

Located in southwest Africa, Angola suffered a civil war following independence from Portugal in 1975, until a 2002 peace deal. Hundreds of thousands of people died.

GEOGRAPHY

Most of the land is hilly and grass-covered. Desert in the south. Mountains in the center and north.

CLIMATE

Varies from temperate to tropical. Rainfall decreases north to south. Coast is cooler and dry.

PEOPLE & SOCIETY

Civil war pitched the ruling Kimbundu-dominated MPLA against UNITA, representing the Ovimbundu. Multiparty elections in 1991–1992, after the MPLA had abandoned Marxism, failed to stall the war for long. Power-sharing from 2002 ended when the MPLA won the 2008 election. In 2006, separatists in the Cabinda exclave agreed a peace deal.

INSIGHT: *Angola has the greatest number of amputees (caused by landmines) in the world*

THE ECONOMY

Potentially one of Africa's richest countries, but long civil war hampered economic development. Oil and diamonds are exported.

CONGO
CABINDA
(part of Angola)
Congo
DEM. REP. CONGO
M'Banza Congo
Uíge
LUANDA
Lucapa
Malanje
Saurimo
ATLANTIC
OCEAN
Cuanza
Luena
Zambezi
Lobito
Benguela
Huambo
Planalto do Bié
Lubango
Menongue
ZAMBIA
Namibe
Cunene
NAMIBIA
BOTSWANA
0 200 km
0 200 miles

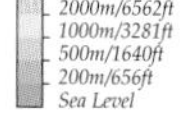

2000m/6562ft
1000m/3281ft
500m/1640ft
200m/656ft
Sea Level

FACTFILE

OFFICIAL NAME: Republic of Angola
DATE OF FORMATION: 1975
CAPITAL: Luanda
POPULATION: 21.5 million
TOTAL AREA: 481,351 sq. miles (1,246,700 sq. km)
DENSITY: 45 people per sq. mile
LANGUAGES: Portuguese*, Umbundu, Kimbundu, Kikongo
RELIGIONS: Roman Catholic 68%, Protestant 20%, indigenous beliefs 12%
ETHNIC MIX: Ovimbundu 37%, other 25%, Kimbundu 25%, Bakongo 13%
GOVERNMENT: Presidential system
CURRENCY: Readjusted kwanza = 100 lwei

Antarctica

The circumpolar continent of Antarctica is almost entirely covered by ice, some up to 1.2 miles (2 km) thick. It also contains 90% of the Earth's freshwater reserves.

GEOGRAPHY

The bulk of Antarctica's ice is contained in the Greater Antarctic Ice Sheet – a huge dome that rises steeply from the coast and flattens to a plateau in the interior.

CLIMATE

Powerful winds create a storm belt around the continent, which brings cloud, fog, and blizzards. Winter temperatures can fall to –112°F (–80°C).

PEOPLE & SOCIETY

No indigenous population. Scientists and logistical staff work at the 40 permanent, and as many as 100 temporary, research stations. A few Chilean settler families live on King George Island. Tourism is mostly by cruise ship to the Antarctic Peninsula. Annual tourist numbers are around 35,000.

Territorial Claims:

Chilean claim
Argentinian claim
Brazilian zone of interest
British claim
Norwegian undefined limit
Australian claim
French claim
New Zealand claim

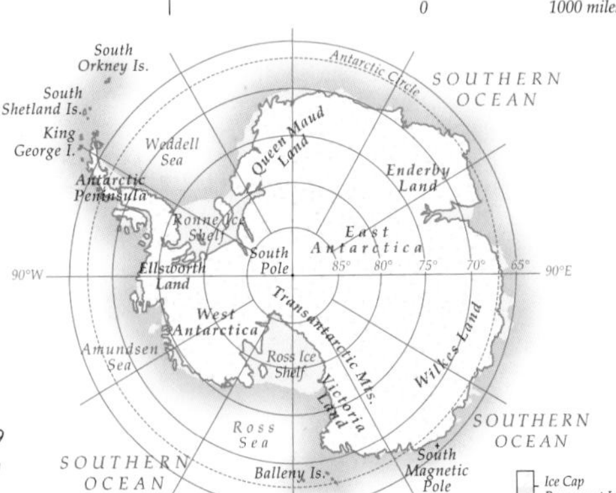
0 1000 km
0 1000 miles
South Orkney Is.
South Shetland Is.
King George I.
Antarctic Circle
SOUTHERN OCEAN
Weddell Sea
Queen Maud Land
Enderby Land
Antarctic Peninsula
Ronne Ice Shelf
South Pole
East Antarctica
85° 80° 75° 70° 65°
90°W
90°E
Ellsworth Land
West Antarctica
Transantarctic Mts.
Amundsen Sea
Ross Ice Shelf
Victoria Land
Wilkes Land
SOUTHERN OCEAN
Ross Sea
SOUTHERN OCEAN
Balleny Is.
South Magnetic Pole
Ice Cap Permanent Ice
180°

The Antarctic Treaty of 1959 holds all territorial claims in abeyance in the interest of international cooperation

FACTFILE

DATE OF FORMATION: 1961

TOTAL AREA: 5,405,000 sq. miles (14,000,000 sq. km)

INSIGHT: *If the ice sheets of Antarctica were to melt, the world's oceans would rise by as much as 200–210 ft (60–65 m)*

Antigua & Barbuda

A former colony of Spain, France, and the UK, Antigua and Barbuda lies at the outer edge of the Leeward Islands group in the Caribbean, and includes the uninhabited islet of Redonda.

GEOGRAPHY

Mainly low-lying limestone and coral islands with some higher volcanic areas. Antigua's coast is indented with bays and harbors.

CLIMATE

Tropical, moderated by trade winds and sea breezes. Humidity and rainfall are low for the region.

PEOPLE & SOCIETY

Population almost entirely of African origin, with small communities of Europeans and South Asians. Women's status has risen as a result of greater access to education. Wealth disparities are small. The Bird family dominated politics from 1960, but lost power to the United Progressive Party (UPP) from 2004.

INSIGHT: *In 1865, Redonda was "claimed" by an eccentric Englishman as a kingdom for his son*

THE ECONOMY

Tourism is the main source of revenue and the biggest provider of jobs. Financial services and Internet gambling are expanding. High debt.

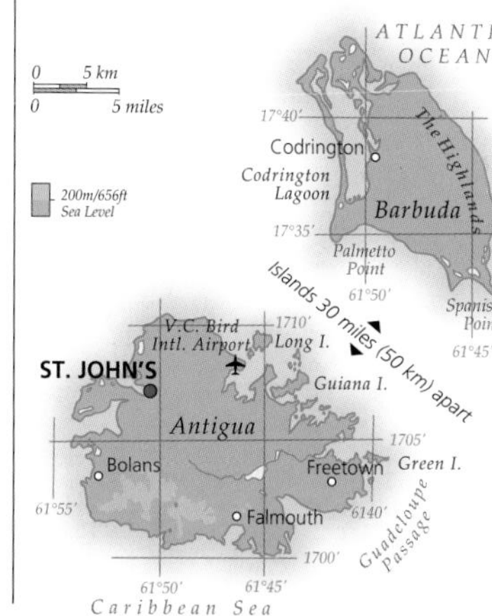
ATLANTIC OCEAN
0 5 km
0 5 miles
200m/656ft
Sea Level
17°40'
Codrington
Codrington Lagoon
The Highlands
Barbuda
17°35'
Palmetto Point
61°50'
Spanish Point
61°45'
Islands 30 miles (50 km) apart
V.C. Bird Intl. Airport
1710'
Long I.
ST. JOHN'S
Guiana I.
Antigua
1705'
Bolans
Freetown
Green I.
61°55'
Falmouth
6140'
Guadeloupe Passage
1700'
61°50'
61°45'
Caribbean Sea

FACTFILE

OFFICIAL NAME: Antigua and Barbuda
DATE OF FORMATION: 1981
CAPITAL: St. John's
POPULATION: 90,156
TOTAL AREA: 170 sq. miles (442 sq. km)
DENSITY: 530 people per sq. mile
LANGUAGES: English*, English patois
RELIGIONS: Anglican 45%, other Protestant 42%, Roman Catholic 10%, other 2%, Rastafarian 1%
ETHNIC MIX: Black African 95%, other 5%
GOVERNMENT: Parliamentary system
CURRENCY: E. Caribbean $ = 100 cents

Argentina

Argentina occupies most of southern South America. After 30 years of intermittent military rule, democracy returned in 1983. Economic crash in 2001 led to largest-ever debt default.

GEOGRAPHY

The Andes form a natural border with Chile in the west. East are the heavily wooded plains (Gran Chaco) and treeless but fertile Pampas plains. Bleak and arid Patagonia lies in the south.

CLIMATE

The Andes are semiarid in the north and snowy in the south. Pampas have a mild climate with summer rains.

PEOPLE & SOCIETY

People are largely of European descent; over one-third are of Italian origin. Indigenous peoples are now a tiny minority, living mainly in Andean regions or in the Gran Chaco. The middle classes were worst hit by the economic meltdown of 2001–2002.

INSIGHT: *The Tango originated in the poorer quarters of Buenos Aires at the end of the 19th century*

THE ECONOMY

Agricultural exports led recovery. Drought and global downturn in 2008. Recession again in 2014, another default.

BOLIVIA
60° PARAGUAY
50°
Salta
San Miguel de Tucumán
Gran Chaco
Salado
Posadas
Corrientes
BRAZIL
CHILE
30°
Santa Fe
Paraná
URUGUAY
San Juan
Córdoba
Rosario
BUENOS AIRES
Mendoza
La Plata
Pampas
Santa Rosa
Mar del Plata
Bahía Blanca
Neuquén
Negro
Bahía Blanca
40°
Viedma
ATLANTIC OCEAN
Patagonia
Golfo San Jorge
Falkland Islands (to UK)
Bahía Grande
50°
Río Gallegos
Strait of Magellan
Tierra del Fuego
0 400 km
0 400 miles
4000m/13124ft
3000m/9843ft
2000m/6562ft
1000m/3281ft
200m/656ft
Sea Level

FACTFILE

OFFICIAL NAME: Republic of Argentina
DATE OF FORMATION: 1816
CAPITAL: Buenos Aires
POPULATION: 41.4 million
TOTAL AREA: 1,068,296 sq. miles (2,766,890 sq. km)
DENSITY: 39 people per sq. mile
LANGUAGES: Spanish*, Italian, Amerindian languages
RELIGIONS: Roman Catholic 70%, other 18%, Protestant 9%, Muslim 2%, Jewish 1%
ETHNIC MIX: Indo-European 97%, *Mestizo* (European–Amerindian) 2%, Amerindian 1%
GOVERNMENT: Presidential system
CURRENCY: Argentine peso = 100 centavos

Armenia

The smallest of the former USSR's republics, Armenia lies landlocked in the Lesser Caucasus Mountains. After 1988, a confrontation with Azerbaijan dominated national life.

GEOGRAPHY

Rugged and mountainous, with expanses of semidesert and a large lake in the east: Sevana Lich.

CLIMATE

Continental climate, with little rainfall in the lowlands. The winters are often bitterly cold.

PEOPLE & SOCIETY

Christianity is the dominant religion, but minority groups are well integrated. War with Azerbaijan over the enclave of Nagorno Karabakh forced 350,000 Armenians living in Azerbaijan to return home, many to live in poverty. There are close and important ties to the 11-million-strong Armenian diaspora.

INSIGHT: *In the 4th century, Armenia became the first country to adopt Christianity as its state religion*

THE ECONOMY

Overseas remittances and agriculture each account for a sixth of GDP. Main products are wine, tobacco, potatoes, and fruit. Well-developed machine-building and manufacturing – includes textiles and bottling of mineral water.

3000m/9843ft
2000m/6562ft
1000m/3281ft
500m/1640ft
44°
GEORGIA
Alaverdi
Vanadzor
Gyumri
Sevan
AZERBAIJAN
46°
Lesser Caucasus
TURKEY
Hrazdan
Ashtarak
Sevana Lich
Vagharshapat
YEREVAN
40°
Armavir
Aras
Ararat
AZERBAIJAN
Kapan
Aras
IRAN
0 50 km
0 50 miles

FACTFILE

OFFICIAL NAME: Republic of Armenia
DATE OF FORMATION: 1991
CAPITAL: Yerevan
POPULATION: 3 million
TOTAL AREA: 11,506 sq. miles (29,800 sq. km)
DENSITY: 261 people per sq. mile
LANGUAGES: Armenian*, Azeri, Russian
RELIGIONS: Armenian Apostolic Church (Orthodox) 88%, Armenian Catholic Church 6%, other 6%
ETHNIC MIX: Armenian 98%, Yezidi 1%, other 1%
GOVERNMENT: Parliamentary system
CURRENCY: Dram = 100 luma

Australia

An island continent in its own right, Australia is the world's sixth-largest country. European settlement began over 200 years ago. Most Australians now live in cities along the coast.

GEOGRAPHY

Located between the Indian and Pacific oceans, Australia has a variety of landscapes, including tropical rainforests, the arid plateaus, ridges, and vast deserts of the "red center," the lowlands and river systems draining into Lake Eyre, rolling tracts of pastoral land, and magnificent beaches around much of the coastline. In the far east are the mountains of the Great Dividing Range. Famous natural features include Uluru (Ayers Rock) and the Great Barrier Reef.

CLIMATE

The west and south are semi-arid with hot summers. The arid interior can reach 120°F (50°C) in the central desert areas. The north is hot throughout the year, and humid during the summer monsoon. East, southeast, and southwest coastal areas are temperate.

PEOPLE & SOCIETY

The first settlers arrived in Australia at least 100,000 years ago. Today, the Aborigines make up around 2% of the population. European colonization began in 1788, and was dominated by British and Irish immigrants, some of whom were convicts. White-only immigration drives brought many Europeans to Australia, but since the 1960s multiculturalism has been encouraged and most new settlers are Asian; Cantonese has overtaken Italian as the second most widely spoken language. Wealth disparities are small, but Aborigines, the exception in an otherwise integrated society, are marginalized: their average life expectancy is around ten years less than other Australians. Illegal immigration is a key political divide; Liberal–National government policies aim to turn back asylum seekers or process and resettle them offshore.

FACTFILE

OFFICIAL NAME: Commonwealth of Australia
DATE OF FORMATION: 1901
CAPITAL: Canberra
POPULATION: 23.3 million
TOTAL AREA: 2,967,893 sq. miles (7,686,850 sq. km)
DENSITY: 8 people per sq. mile
LANGUAGES: English*, Cantonese, other
RELIGIONS: Various Protestant 38%, Roman Catholic 26%, nonreligious 19%, other 17%
ETHNIC MIX: European 90%, Asian 7%, Aboriginal 2%, other 1%
GOVERNMENT: Parliamentary system
CURRENCY: Australian dollar = 100 cents

THE ECONOMY

Efficient mining and agriculture: particular success in viticulture. Large resource base: coal, iron ore, bauxite, and most other minerals. Protectionism abandoned to open up Australian markets. Concentration on trade with Asia: China's rapidly expanding demand for minerals means it has now surpassed Japan as Australia's major trading partner. Upward trend in Asian visitor arrivals has strengthened tourism. The effects of droughts, floods, and cyclones have dented economic growth in recent years.

INSIGHT: *Australia has the most endemic mammals and reptiles in the world. Species include marsupials such as the kangaroo and wombat, the egg-laying platypus, and the freshwater crocodile*

Arafura Sea
Timor Sea
Darwin
Arnhem Land
Gulf of Carpentaria
Bamaga
Cape York
Great Barrier Reef
PACIFIC OCEAN
INDIAN OCEAN
Kimberley Plateau
Cairns
Coral Sea
NORTHERN TERRITORY
Townsville
Great Dividing Range
Port Hedland
Great Sandy Desert
Mount Isa
Mackay
Lake Disappointment
Lake Mackay
Macdonnell Ranges
Alice Springs
Hamersley Range
Gibson Desert
Rockhampton
QUEENSLAND
Bundaberg
Uluru (Ayers Rock) (867m)
Simpson Desert
Fraser I.
WESTERN AUSTRALIA
Carnarvon
Lake Carnegie
Gympie
Meekatharra
Brisbane
Toowoomba
Ipswich
Gold Coast
Great Victoria Desert
Lake Eyre
SOUTH AUSTRALIA
Surfers Paradise
Geraldton
Grafton
Darling
Kalgoorlie
Nullarbor Plain
Flinders Ranges
Coffs Harbour
Port Augusta
Broken Hill
NEW SOUTH WALES
Perth
Fremantle
Rockingham
Bunbury
Cape Leeuwin
Darling Range
Whyalla
Port Pirie
Newcastle
Sydney
Port Lincoln
Elizabeth
Adelaide
Wagga Wagga
Wollongong
Esperance
Murray
Albury
CANBERRA
AUSTRALIAN CAPITAL TERRITORY
Albany
Kangaroo I.
Bendigo
VICTORIA
Australian Alps
Great Australian Bight
Melbourne
Geelong
Tasman Sea
Bass Strait
Burnie
TASMANIA
Launceston
Hobart
South East Cape
10°
20°
30°
40°
120°
130°
140°
150°
1000m/3281ft
500m/1640ft
200m/656ft
Sea Level
Below Sea Level
0 400 km
0 400 miles

Austria

Bordering eight countries in the heart of Europe, Austria was created in 1918 after the collapse of the Habsburg Empire. Neutral after World War II, it joined the EU in 1995.

GEOGRAPHY

Mainly mountainous. Alps and foothills cover the west and south. Lowlands in the east are part of the Danube River basin.

CLIMATE

Temperate continental climate. The western Alpine regions have colder winters and more rainfall.

PEOPLE & SOCIETY

Though Austrians speak German, they like to stress their distinctive identity in relation to Germany. Vienna is a major cultural center. Minorities are few; there are some ethnic Croats, Slovenes, and Hungarians, plus refugees from conflict in former Yugoslavia. Though strongly Roman Catholic, Austrian society is less conservative than some southern German *Länder*. Class divisions remain strong.

THE ECONOMY

Large manufacturing base, despite lack of energy resources. The skilled labor force is key to high-tech exports. Eurozone member. Limited GDP growth has returned since 2009 recession.

INSIGHT: *Many of the world's great composers were Austrian, including Mozart, Haydn, Schubert, and Strauss*

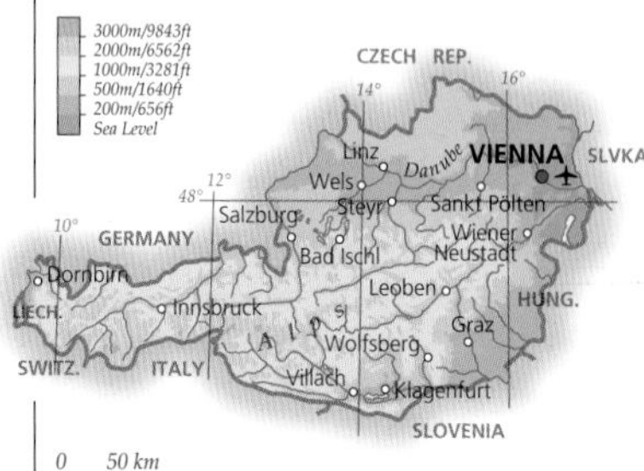

3000m/9843ft
2000m/6562ft
1000m/3281ft
500m/1640ft
200m/656ft
Sea Level
CZECH REP.
14°
16°
Linz
Danube
VIENNA
SLVKA
Wels
12°
48°
Steyr
Sankt Pölten
Salzburg
10°
GERMANY
Wiener Neustadt
Bad Ischl
Dornbirn
Leoben
LIECH.
Innsbruck
HUNG.
Graz
Wolfsberg
SWITZ.
ITALY
Villach
Klagenfurt
SLOVENIA
0 50 km
0 50 miles

FACTFILE

OFFICIAL NAME: Republic of Austria

DATE OF FORMATION: 1918

CAPITAL: Vienna

POPULATION: 8.5 million

TOTAL AREA: 32,378 sq. miles (83,858 sq. km)

DENSITY: 266 people per sq. mile

LANGUAGES: German*, Croatian, Slovenian, Hungarian (Magyar)

RELIGIONS: Roman Catholic 78%, nonreligious 9%, other 8%, Protestant 5%

ETHNIC MIX: Austrian 93%, Croat, Slovene, and Hungarian 6%, other 1%

GOVERNMENT: Parliamentary system

CURRENCY: Euro = 100 cents

Azerbaijan

Situated on the western coast of the Caspian Sea, it was the first Soviet republic to declare independence in 1991. Territorial disputes with Armenia have dominated politics since.

GEOGRAPHY

Caucasus Mountains in west, including Naxçivan exclave south of Armenia. Flat, low-lying terrain on the coast of the Caspian Sea.

CLIMATE

Low rainfall. Continental, with bitter winters, inland. Subtropical in coastal regions.

PEOPLE & SOCIETY

Azeris, a Muslim people with ethnic links to Turks, form a large majority. Thousands of Armenians, Russians, and Jews have left since independence. Influx of half a million Azeri refugees fleeing war with Armenia over the disputed enclave of Nagorno Karabakh. Armenians there operate with de facto independence. The status of women deteriorated after the fall of communism but they are slowly regaining their position.

THE ECONOMY

Oil and natural gas exports drive economic growth. Pipeline to Ceyhan, Turkey, has opened up European market. Severe pollution in Baku.

INSIGHT: *The fire-worshipping Zoroastrian faith originated in Azerbaijan in the 6th century BCE*

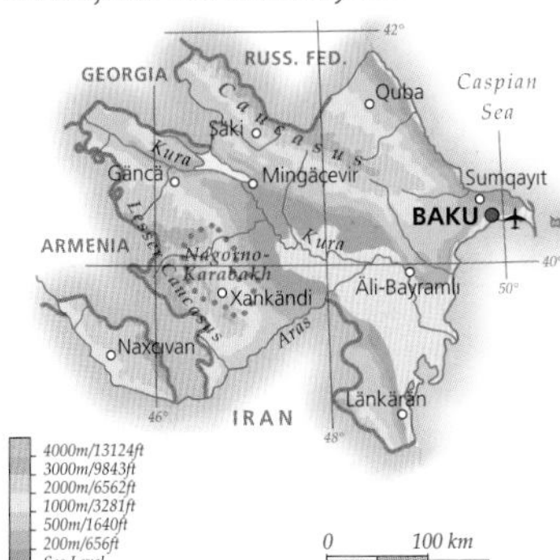
42°
RUSS. FED.
GEORGIA
Caspian Sea
Quba
Caucasus
Şäki
Kura
Gäncä
Mingäçevir
Sumqayıt
BAKU
ARMENIA
Kura
Lesser Caucasus
Nagorno-Karabakh
Xankändi
Äli-Bayramlı
40°
50°
Aras
Naxçivan
Länkärän
46°
IRAN
48°
4000m/13124ft
3000m/9843ft
2000m/6562ft
1000m/3281ft
500m/1640ft
200m/656ft
Sea Level
Below Sea Level
0
100 km
0
100 miles

FACTFILE

OFFICIAL NAME: Republic of Azerbaijan
DATE OF FORMATION: 1991
CAPITAL: Baku
POPULATION: 9.4 million
TOTAL AREA: 33,436 sq. miles (86,600 sq. km)
DENSITY: 281 people per sq. mile
LANGUAGES: Azeri*, Russian
RELIGIONS: Shi'a Muslim 68%, Sunni Muslim 26%, Russian Orthodox 3%, Armenian Apostolic Church (Orthodox) 2%, other 1%
ETHNIC MIX: Azeri 91%, other 3%, Lazs 2%, Russian 2%, Armenian 2%
GOVERNMENT: Presidential system
CURRENCY: New manat = 100 gopik

The Bahamas

Located off the Florida coast in the western Atlantic, the Bahamas comprises an archipelago of some 700 islands and 2400 cays, only around 30 of which are inhabited.

GEOGRAPHY

Long, mainly flat coral formations with a few low hills. Some islands have pine forests, lagoons, and mangrove swamps.

CLIMATE

Subtropical. Hot summers and mild winters. Heavy rainfall, especially in summer. Hurricanes can strike in July–December.

PEOPLE & SOCIETY

Over 60% of the population live on New Providence. Tourism employs over half of the labor force. There are marked wealth disparities, from urban professionals in the banking sector to traditional fishermen on outlying islands and illegal Haitian and Cuban immigrants. More women are now entering the professions. Government priorities are tackling narcotics trafficking and combating money laundering.

THE ECONOMY

Major tourist destination, especially for US visitors. Financial services: banking and insurance.

INSIGHT: *The country's extensive merchant fleet consists mainly of "flag-of-convenience" vessels registered by foreign owners*

Straits of Florida
Grand Bahama I.
Freeport
Great Abaco
Berry Is.
New Providence
Eleuthera I.
Nicholls Town
NASSAU
ATLANTIC OCEAN
Andros I.
Andros Town
Exuma Sound
Cat I.
San Salvador
Exuma Cays
Rum Cay
Long I.
Crooked I.
Mayaguana
Acklins I.
Caicos Passage
Great Inagua
200m/656ft
Sea Level
0 100 km
0 100 miles
26°
24°
22°
78°
76°
74°

FACTFILE

OFFICIAL NAME: Commonwealth of the Bahamas

DATE OF FORMATION: 1973

CAPITAL: Nassau

POPULATION: 400,000

TOTAL AREA: 5382 sq. miles (13,940 sq. km)

DENSITY: 103 people per sq. mile

LANGUAGES: English*, English Creole, French Creole

RELIGIONS: Baptist 32%, other 29%, Anglican 20%, Roman Catholic 19%

ETHNIC MIX: Black African 85%, other 15%

GOVERNMENT: Parliamentary system

CURRENCY: Bahamian dollar = 100 cents

Bahrain

Bahrain is an archipelago of 49 islands between the Qatar peninsula and the Saudi Arabian mainland. Only three of the islands are inhabited. It was the first Gulf emirate to export oil.

GEOGRAPHY

All islands are low-lying. The largest, Bahrain Island, is mainly sandy plains and salt marshes.

CLIMATE

Summers are hot and humid. Winters are mild. Low rainfall.

PEOPLE & SOCIETY

The key social division is between the Shi'a majority and Sunni minority. Sunnis hold the best jobs in bureaucracy and business while Shi'as tend to do menial work. Bahrain is socially liberal. The al-Khalifa family has ruled since 1783, but transformed Bahrain into a constitutional monarchy in 2002. Protests calling for greater democracy rocked the country since the 2011 "Arab Spring".

INSIGHT: *The 16 Hawar Islands were awarded to Bahrain in 2001 after a lengthy dispute with Qatar*

THE ECONOMY

Main exports are refined petroleum and aluminum products. As oil reserves run out, natural gas is of increasing importance. Major Middle East offshore banking center, hit by global banking crisis in 2008–2009.

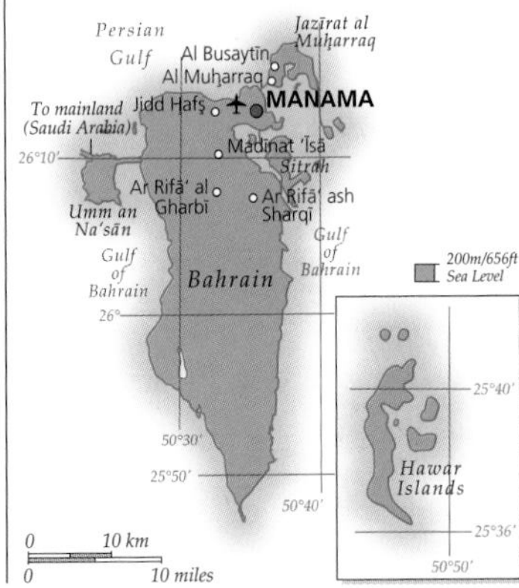
Persian Gulf
Jazīrat al Muḩarraq
Al Busaytīn
Al Muḩarraq
To mainland (Saudi Arabia)
Jidd Ḩafş
MANAMA
Madīnat 'Īsā
Sitrah
26°10'
Ar Rifā' al Gharbī
Ar Rifā' ash Sharqī
Umm an Na'sān
Gulf of Bahrain
Gulf of Bahrain
Bahrain
26°
200m/656ft
Sea Level
25°40'
Hawar Islands
50°30'
25°50'
50°40'
25°36'
0 10 km
0 10 miles
50°50'

FACTFILE

OFFICIAL NAME: Kingdom of Bahrain

DATE OF FORMATION: 1971

CAPITAL: Manama

POPULATION: 1.3 million

TOTAL AREA: 239 sq. miles (620 sq. km)

DENSITY: 4762 people per sq. mile

LANGUAGES: Arabic*

RELIGIONS: Muslim (mainly Shi'a) 99%, other 1%

ETHNIC MIX: Bahraini 63%, Asian 19%, other Arab 10%, Iranian 8%

GOVERNMENT: Mixed monarchical-parliamentary system

CURRENCY: Bahraini dinar = 1000 fils

Bangladesh

Bangladesh lies at the north end of the Bay of Bengal and frequently suffers devastating flood, cyclones, and famine. It seceded from Pakistan in 1971.

GEOGRAPHY

Mostly flat alluvial plains and deltas of the Brahmaputra and Ganges rivers. Southeast coasts are fringed with mangrove forests.

CLIMATE

Hot and humid. During the monsoon, water levels can rise 20 ft (6 m) above sea level.

PEOPLE & SOCIETY

After a period of military rule, Bangladesh returned to democracy in 1991; political instability has continued, however, and corruption is a major problem. A third of the population live in poverty, but living standards are improving. Women are prominent in politics, but their rights are neglected.

INSIGHT: *Torrential monsoon rains flood two-thirds of the country every year*

THE ECONOMY

Agriculture is vulnerable to unpredictable climate. Bangladesh accounts for 80% of world jute fiber exports. Poor infrastructure deters investment. Growing textile industry.

500m/1640ft
200m/656ft
Sea Level
88°
90°
92°
26°
24°
22°
Rangpur
Saidpur
Dinajpur
Brahmaputra
INDIA
Jamalpur
Sylhet
Mymensingh
Rajshahi
Shirajganj Ghat
Brahmanbaria
Pabna
Ganges (Padma)
DHAKA
INDIA
Comilla
Haringhat
Jessore
Khulna
Barisal
Mouths of the Ganges
Chittagong
Bay of Bengal
MYANMAR (BURMA)
0 100 km
0 100 miles

FACTFILE

OFFICIAL NAME: People's Republic of Bangladesh
DATE OF FORMATION: 1971
CAPITAL: Dhaka
POPULATION: 157 million
TOTAL AREA: 55,598 sq. miles (144,000 sq. km)
DENSITY: 3029 people per sq. mile
LANGUAGES: Bengali*, Urdu, Chakma, Marma, Garo, Khasi, Santhali, Tripuri, Mro
RELIGIONS: Muslim (mainly Sunni) 88%, Hindu 11%, other 1%
ETHNIC MIX: Bengali 98%, other 2%
GOVERNMENT: Parliamentary system
CURRENCY: Taka = 100 poisha

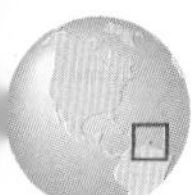

Barbados

Barbados is the most easterly of the Caribbean islands. Once solely inhabited by the native Arawak, Barbados was first colonized by British settlers in the 1620s.

GEOGRAPHY

Encircled by coral reefs. Fertile and predominantly flat, with a few gentle hills to the north.

CLIMATE

Moderate tropical climate. Sunnier and drier than its more mountainous neighbors.

PEOPLE & SOCIETY

Independent from the UK since 1966. Some latent tension between the economically dominant white community and the majority black population, but violence is rare. Increasing social mobility has enabled black Barbadians to enter the professions. Despite political stability, and good welfare and education services, pockets of abject poverty remain.

INSIGHT: *Barbados retains a strong British influence and is referred to by its neighbors as "Little England"*

THE ECONOMY

Well-developed tourism sector based on climate and accessibility. Financial services, offshore banking, and information processing are key industries. Sugar production has dwindled. High cost of living.

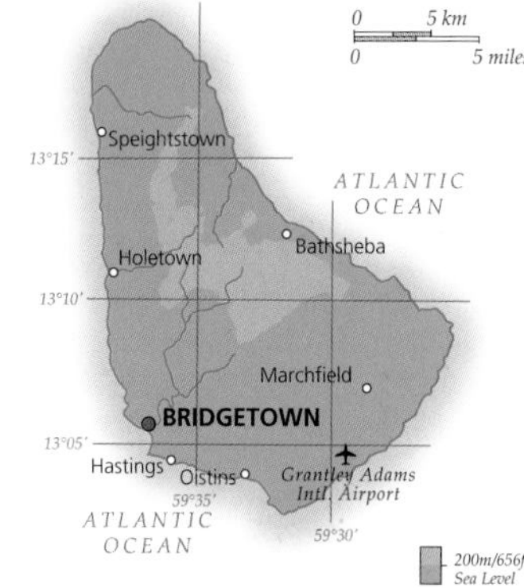
0 5 km
0 5 miles
Speightstown
13°15′
ATLANTIC OCEAN
Bathsheba
Holetown
13°10′
Marchfield
BRIDGETOWN
13°05′
Hastings
Oistins
Grantley Adams Intl. Airport
59°35′
59°30′
ATLANTIC OCEAN
200m/656ft
Sea Level

FACTFILE

OFFICIAL NAME: Barbados
DATE OF FORMATION: 1966
CAPITAL: Bridgetown
POPULATION: 300,000
TOTAL AREA: 166 sq. miles (430 sq. km)
DENSITY: 1807 people per sq. mile
LANGUAGES: Bajan (Barbadian English), English*
RELIGIONS: Anglican 40%, other 24%, nonreligious 17%, Pentecostal 8%, Methodist 7%, Roman Catholic 4%
ETHNIC MIX: Black African 92%, White 3%, other 3%, mixed race 2%
GOVERNMENT: Parliamentary system
CURRENCY: Barbados dollar = 100 cents

Belarus

Literally "White Russia," Belarus lies landlocked in eastern Europe. It reluctantly became independent when the USSR broke up in 1991. It has few resources other than agriculture.

GEOGRAPHY

Mainly plains and low hills. The Dnieper and Dvina rivers drain the eastern lowlands. Vast Pripet Marshes in the southwest.

CLIMATE

Extreme continental climate. Winters are long, sub-freezing, but mainly dry; summers are hot.

PEOPLE & SOCIETY

Only 2% of people are non-Slav, so ethnic tension is minimal. Russian culture dominates. Belarus was the slowest ex-Soviet state to implement political reform; President Lukashenka has been labeled as Europe's last dictator. Enthusiasm for a merger with Russia has waned. Wealth is held by a small ex-Communist elite. Fallout from the 1986 Chernobyl nuclear disaster in Ukraine still seriously affects health and the environment.

THE ECONOMY

Industry outmoded and mainly state-owned. Depends on Russia for energy and raw materials: tensions over natural gas prices.

INSIGHT: *The number of cancer and leukemia cases soared after the 1986 Chernobyl disaster*

200m/656ft
Sea Level
LATVIA
56°
Western Dvina
Vitsyebsk/Vitebsk
RUSS. FED.
LITHUANIA
Orsha
Barysaw/Borisov
54°
Lida
MINSK
POLAND
Hrodna/Grodno
Mahilyow/Mogilev
Slutsk
Babruysk/Bobruysk
Baranavichy/ Baranovichi
Dnieper
Homyel'/ Gomel'
Brest
Pinsk
Pripet Marshes
Rechytsa
52°
Mazyr
32°
26°
UKRAINE
24°
UKRAINE
28°
30°
0 100 km
0 100 miles

FACTFILE

OFFICIAL NAME: Republic of Belarus
DATE OF FORMATION: 1991
CAPITAL: Minsk
POPULATION: 9.4 million
TOTAL AREA: 80,154 sq. miles (207,600 sq. km)
DENSITY: 117 people per sq. mile
LANGUAGES: Belarussian*, Russian*
RELIGIONS: Orthodox Christian 80%, Roman Catholic 14%, other 4%, Protestant 2%
ETHNIC MIX: Belarussian 81%, Russian 11%, Polish 4%, Ukrainian 2%, other 2%
GOVERNMENT: Presidential system
CURRENCY: Belarussian rouble = 100 kopeks

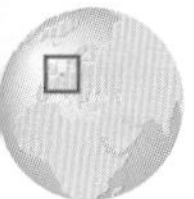

Belgium

Belgium lies in northwestern Europe. Its history has been marked by tensions between the majority Dutch-speaking (Flemish) and minority French-speaking (Walloon) communities.

GEOGRAPHY

Low-lying coastal plain covers two-thirds of the country. Land becomes hilly and forested in the southeast (Ardennes).

CLIMATE

Maritime climate with Gulf Stream influences. Mild temperatures, with heavy cloud cover and rain. More rainfall and weather fluctuations at the coast.

PEOPLE & SOCIETY

Since 1970, Flemish regions have become more prosperous than those of the minority Walloons, overturning traditional roles and increasing friction. Belgium moved to a federal system from 1980 in order to contain tensions, but recent fractious politics have raised doubts over the union's survival. The Flemish separatist N-VA heads the Flanders government and since 2010 has been the largest party at federal level. Brussels hosts key EU institutions.

THE ECONOMY

Variety of industrial exports, including steel, glassware, cut diamonds, and textiles. High levels of public debt. Bureaucracy larger than European average.

INSIGHT: *Belgium holds the world record for the country with the longest period without a government*

North Sea
NETHERLANDS
Oostende
Brugge
Antwerpen
Gent
Mechelen
Meuse
51°
Kortrijk
Aalst
Leuven
BRUSSELS
Tournai
Liège
3°
La Louvière
GER.
Mons
Namur
Charleroi
FRANCE
4°
50°
Ardennes
LUX.
5°
6°
500m/1640ft
200m/656ft
Sea Level
0 40 km
0 40 miles

FACTFILE

OFFICIAL NAME: Kingdom of Belgium
DATE OF FORMATION: 1830
CAPITAL: Brussels
POPULATION: 11.1 million
TOTAL AREA: 11,780 sq. miles (30,510 sq. km)
DENSITY: 876 people per sq. mile
LANGUAGES: Dutch*, French*, German*
RELIGIONS: Roman Catholic 88%, other 10%, Muslim 2%
ETHNIC MIX: Fleming 58%, Walloon 33%, other 6%, Italian 2%, Moroccan 1%
GOVERNMENT: Parliamentary system
CURRENCY: Euro = 100 cents

Belize

Belize lies on the eastern shore of the Yucatan Peninsula. Formerly called British Honduras, Belize was the last Central American country to gain its independence, in 1981.

GEOGRAPHY

Almost half the land area is forested. Low mountains in southeast. Flat swampy coastal plains.

CLIMATE

Tropical. Very hot and humid, with May–December rainy season.

PEOPLE & SOCIETY

English-speaking black Creoles are outnumbered by Spanish speakers, including native *mestizos* (European–Amerindian) and immigrants from neighboring states. The Creoles have traditionally dominated society, but high levels of emigration to the US have weakened their influence. The Afro-Carib *garifuna* have their own language. Corruption, and trafficking of people and narcotics, are major problems.

INSIGHT: *Belize's barrier reef is the second-largest in the world*

THE ECONOMY

Tourism, agriculture, and offshore banking. Oil extraction began in 2005. Sugar, textiles, lobsters, and shrimp are exported. Serious hurricane damage is a recurring problem.

0 50 km
0 50 miles
88°
Louisville
Corozal
MEXICO
18°
Hondo
Orange Walk
New River
Maskall
Crooked Tree
Belize City
Belize
Reef
BELMOPAN
San Ignacio
17°
Dangriga
GUATEMALA
Maya Mts.
Barrier
Monkey River Town
San Antonio
Punta Gorda
16°
Caribbean Sea
Sarstoon
89°
1000m/3281ft
500m/1640ft
200m/656ft
Sea Level

FACTFILE

OFFICIAL NAME: Belize
DATE OF FORMATION: 1981
CAPITAL: Belmopan
POPULATION: 300,000
TOTAL AREA: 8867 sq. miles (22,966 sq. km)
DENSITY: 34 people per sq. mile
LANGUAGES: English Creole, Spanish, English*, Mayan, Garifuna (Carib)
RELIGIONS: Roman Catholic 62%, other 20%, Anglican 12%, Methodist 6%
ETHNIC MIX: *Mestizo* 49%, Creole 25%, Maya 11%, other 9%, Garifuna 6%
GOVERNMENT: Parliamentary system
CURRENCY: Belizean dollar = 100 cents

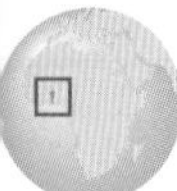

Benin

Benin stretches north from the west African coast. In 1990, Benin became one of the pioneers of African democratization, ending 17 years of one-party Marxist-Leninist rule.

GEOGRAPHY

Sandy coastal region. Numerous lagoons lie just behind the shoreline. Forested plateaus inland. Mountains in the northwest.

CLIMATE

Hot and humid in the south. Two rainy seasons. Hot, dusty *harmattan* winds blow during the December–February dry season.

PEOPLE & SOCIETY

There are 42 different ethnic groups. The southern Fon have tended to dominate politics. Other major groups are the Adja and Yoruba. The northern Fulani follow a nomadic lifestyle. North–south tension is mainly due to the south being more developed. French culture, centered on Cotonou, is highly prized. Substantial differences in wealth reflect a strongly hierarchical society.

THE ECONOMY

Strong agricultural sector: cash crops include cotton, oil palm, and cashew nuts. Large-scale smuggling is a serious problem. France is the main aid donor. Recent floods.

INSIGHT: *Voodoo is thought to have originated in Benin, and was taken to Haiti by slaves*

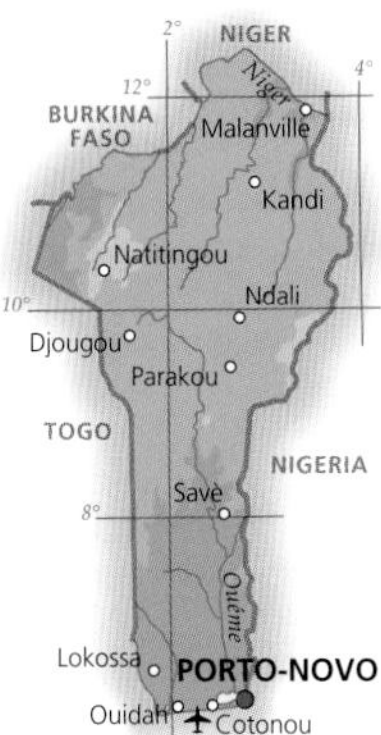
NIGER
Niger
BURKINA FASO
Malanville
Kandi
Natitingou
Ndali
Djougou
Parakou
TOGO
NIGERIA
Save
Ouémé
Lokossa
PORTO-NOVO
Ouidah
Cotonou
ATLANTIC OCEAN
2°
4°
12°
10°
8°

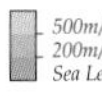
500m/1640ft
200m/656ft
Sea Level
0 100 km
0 100 miles

FACTFILE

OFFICIAL NAME: Republic of Benin
DATE OF FORMATION: 1960
CAPITAL: Porto-Novo
POPULATION: 10.3 million
TOTAL AREA: 43,483 sq. miles (112,620 sq. km)
DENSITY: 241 people per sq. mile
LANGUAGES: Fon, Bariba, Yoruba, Adja, Houeda, Somba, French*
RELIGIONS: Indigenous beliefs and Voodoo 50%, Christian 30%, Muslim 20%
ETHNIC MIX: Fon 41%, other 21%, Adja 16%, Yoruba 12%, Bariba 10%
GOVERNMENT: Presidential system
CURRENCY: CFA franc = 100 centimes

Bhutan

Perched in the eastern Himalayas between India and China lies the landlocked Kingdom of Bhutan. It is largely closed to the outside world to protect its culture; TV was banned until 1999.

GEOGRAPHY

Low, tropical southern strip rising through fertile central valleys to high Himalayas in the north. Around 70% of the land is forested.

CLIMATE

South is tropical, north is alpine, cold, and harsh. Central valleys warmer in east than west.

PEOPLE & SOCIETY

The king was absolute monarch until 1998, and the first democratic elections were held a decade later. Most people are devoutly Buddhist and originate from Tibet. The Hindu Nepalese settled in the south. Bhutan has 20 languages. In 1988, Dzongkha (a Tibetan dialect native to just 16% of the people) was made the official language. The Nepalese community regard this as "cultural imperialism," causing considerable ethnic tensions.

THE ECONOMY

Reliant on India for trade. Most people farm their own plots of land and herd cattle and yaks. Steep land unsuited for cultivation. Development of cash crops for Asian markets.

INSIGHT: *In 2004 Bhutan became the first country in the world to ban smoking and the sale of tobacco*

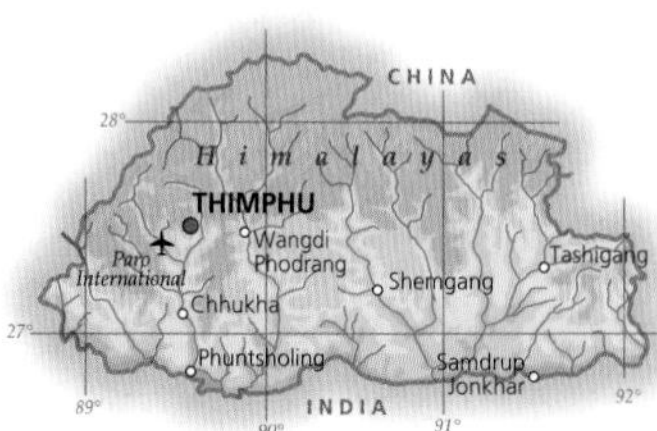
CHINA
Himalayas
THIMPHU
Paro International
Wangdi Phodrang
Shemgang
Tashigang
Chhukha
Phuntsholing
Samdrup Jonkhar
INDIA
28°
27°
89°
90°
91°
92°
0 50 km
0 50 miles

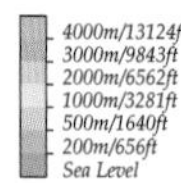
4000m/13124ft
3000m/9843ft
2000m/6562ft
1000m/3281ft
500m/1640ft
200m/656ft
Sea Level

FACTFILE

OFFICIAL NAME: Kingdom of Bhutan
DATE OF FORMATION: 1656
CAPITAL: Thimphu
POPULATION: 800,000
TOTAL AREA: 18,147 sq. miles (47,000 sq. km)
DENSITY: 44 people per sq. mile
LANGUAGES: Dzongkha*, Nepali, Assamese
RELIGIONS: Mahayana Buddhist 75%, Hindu 25%
ETHNIC MIX: Drukpa 50%, Nepalese 35%, other 15%
GOVERNMENT: Mixed monarchical–parliamentary system
CURRENCY: Ngultrum = 100 chetrum

Bolivia

Landlocked high in central South America, Bolivia is one of the region's poorest countries. La Paz is the world's highest capital city: 13,385 feet (3631 m) above sea level.

GEOGRAPHY

A high windswept plateau, the *altiplano*, lies between two Andean mountain ranges. Semiarid grasslands to the east; dense tropical forests to the north.

CLIMATE

Altiplano has extreme tropical climate, with night-frost in winter. North and east are hot and humid.

PEOPLE & SOCIETY

Wealthy Spanish-descended families have traditionally controlled the economy. The indigenous majority faces widespread discrimination. Amerindian Evo Morales, president from 2005, is cutting poverty, redistributing land, and pushing for international recognition of legal coca use.

INSIGHT: *Between 1825 and 1982 Bolivia averaged more than one armed coup a year*

THE ECONOMY

Gold, silver, zinc, tin, oil, natural gas: all vulnerable to world price fluctuations. Social issues and nationalization of natural gas sector deter investors. Major coca producer. Lack of manufacturing. Rich eastern provinces want autonomy.

3000m/9843ft
2000m/6562ft
1000m/3281ft
500m/1640ft
200m/656ft
Sea Level
68°
64°
60°
12°
16°
20°
Guayaramerín
Riberalta
PERU
Beni
Guaporé
Trinidad
Lake Titicaca
BRAZIL
LA PAZ
Cochabamba
Montero
Santa Cruz
Oruro
SUCRE
Puerto Suárez
Altiplano
Potosí
Gran Chaco
CHILE
Tupiza
Tarija
PARAGUAY
ARGENTINA
0 200 km
0 200 miles

FACTFILE

OFFICIAL NAME: Plurinational State of Bolivia
DATE OF FORMATION: 1825
CAPITALS: La Paz (administrative); Sucre (judicial)
POPULATION: 10.7 million
TOTAL AREA: 424,162 sq. miles (1,098,580 sq. km)
DENSITY: 26 people per sq. mile
LANGUAGES: Aymara*, Quechua*, Spanish*
RELIGIONS: Roman Catholic 93%, other 7%
ETHNIC MIX: Quechua 37%, Aymara 32%, *Mestizo* (mixed European–Amerindian) 13%, European 10%, other 8%
GOVERNMENT: Presidential system
CURRENCY: Boliviano = 100 centavos

Bosnia & Herzegovina

Perched in the highlands of southeast Europe, Bosnia and Herzegovina was the focus of the bitter ethnic conflict that accompanied the early 1990s dissolution of the Yugoslav state.

GEOGRAPHY

Hills and mountains, with narrow river valleys. Lowlands in the north. Mainly deciduous forest covers about half of the total area.

CLIMATE

Continental. Hot summers and cold, often snowy winters.

PEOPLE & SOCIETY

Despite sharing the same origin and spoken language, Bosnians have been divided by history between Orthodox Serbs, Roman Catholic Croats, and Muslim Bosniaks. Ethnic cleansing was practiced by all sides in the civil war, displacing about 60% of the population. Hopes for EU integration will require further ethnic reconciliation.

INSIGHT: *The murder of Archduke Ferdinand of Austria in Sarajevo in 1914 triggered the First World War*

THE ECONOMY

Potential to recover status as a thriving market economy with a strong manufacturing base, but still struggles with resettling refugees and the legacy of war. Little foreign investment.

CROATIA
Sava
Prijedor
Modriča
REPUBLICA SRPSKA
Bihać
Banja Luka
Doboj
Tuzla
SERBIA
Zvornik
Dinaric Alps
Bosna
Travnik
Zenica
Drina
Srebrenica
44°
Bugojno
16°
FEDERACIJA BOSNA I HERCEGOVINA
SARAJEVO
CROATIA
Mostar
MONTENEGRO
2000m/6562ft
1000m/3281ft
500m/1640ft
200m/656ft
Sea Level
18°
0 50 km
0 50 miles

FACTFILE

OFFICIAL NAME: Bosnia and Herzegovina

DATE OF FORMATION: 1992

CAPITAL: Sarajevo

POPULATION: 3.8 million

TOTAL AREA: 19,741 sq. miles (51,129 sq. km)

DENSITY: 192 people per sq. mile

LANGUAGES: Bosnian*, Serbian*, Croatian*

RELIGIONS: Muslim (mainly Sunni) 40%, Orthodox Christian 31%, Roman Catholic 15%, other 10%, Protestant 4%

ETHNIC MIX: Bosniak 48%, Serb 34%, Croat 16%, other 2%

GOVERNMENT: Parliamentary system

CURRENCY: Marka = 100 pfeninga

Botswana

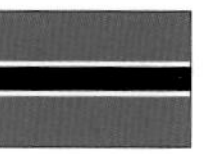

Landlocked in the heart of southern Africa, Botswana boasts the world's largest inland river delta. Diamonds provide potential wealth, but the country is crippled by HIV/AIDS.

GEOGRAPHY

Lies on vast plateau, high above sea level. Hills in the east. Kalahari Desert in center and southwest. Swamps and salt pans elsewhere and in Okavango Basin.

CLIMATE

Dry and prone to drought. Summer wet season, April–October. Winters are warm, with cold nights.

PEOPLE & SOCIETY

The nomadic San bushmen, the first inhabitants, are marginalized. One in five adults are living with HIV/AIDS: only Swaziland and Lesotho are worse affected. Life expectancy is around 64 years. Diamond revenue has widened wealth inequalities.

INSIGHT: *Water, Botswana's most precious resource, is honored in the name of the currency – pula*

THE ECONOMY

Overreliance on diamonds: vulnerable to world price fluctuations. Beef is exported to Europe. Tourism aimed at wealthy wildlife enthusiasts. AIDS is devastating the population.

1000m/3281ft
500m/1640ft
ZAMBIA
Kwando
Kasane
Okavango
Delta
NAMIBIA
ZIMBABWE
Maun
20°
Makgadikgadi
Francistown
Ghanzi
Selebi Phikwe
Serowe
Kalahari
Desert
Mahalapye
Limpopo
24°
28°
GABORONE
Mochudi
Kanye
Lobatse
SOUTH
AFRICA
24°
20°
0 200 km
0 200 miles

FACTFILE

OFFICIAL NAME: Republic of Botswana
DATE OF FORMATION: 1966
CAPITAL: Gaborone
POPULATION: 2 million
TOTAL AREA: 231,803 sq. miles (600,370 sq. km)
DENSITY: 9 people per sq. mile
LANGUAGES: Setswana, English*, Shona, San, Khoikhoi, isiNdebele
RELIGIONS: Christian 70%, nonreligious 20%, traditional beliefs 6%, other 4%
ETHNIC MIX: Tswana 79%, Kalanga 11%, other 10%
GOVERNMENT: Presidential system
CURRENCY: Pula = 100 thebe

Brazil

Covering almost half of South America, Brazil is the site of the world's largest and ecologically most important rainforest. The country has immense natural and economic resources.

GEOGRAPHY

Rainforest grows around the massive Amazon River and its delta, covering almost half of Brazil's total land area. Apart from the basin of the River Plate to the south, the rest of the country consists of highlands. The mountainous east is part-forested and part-desert. The coastal plain in the southeast has swampy areas. The Atlantic coastline is 1240 miles (2000 km) long.

CLIMATE

Brazil's share of the Amazon Basin has a model tropical equatorial climate, with high temperatures and rainfall all year round. The Brazilian plateau has far greater seasonal variation. The dry northeast suffers frequent droughts, though coastal regions are occasionally flooded by bouts of torrential rain. The south has hot summers and cool winters.

PEOPLE & SOCIETY

Diverse population includes Amerindians, black people of African descent, European immigrants, and those of mixed race. Amerindians suffer prejudice from most other groups. Shanty towns in the cities attract poor migrants from the northeast. Urban crime, violent land disputes, and unchecked development in Amazonia tarnish Brazil's image as a modern nation. Catholicism and the family unit remain strong.

THE ECONOMY

Dominant regional economy. Huge potential for growth based on abundant natural resources. A leading exporter of coffee, sugar, soybeans, and orange juice. Social tension threatens stability. Infrastructure needs investment. Downturn in 2014.

FACTFILE

OFFICIAL NAME: Federative Rep. of Brazil
DATE OF FORMATION: 1822
CAPITAL: Brasília
POPULATION: 200 million
TOTAL AREA: 3,286,470 sq. miles (8,511,965 sq. km)
DENSITY: 61 people per sq. mile
LANGUAGES: Portuguese*, German, Japanese, Italian, Spanish, Polish, Amerindian languages
RELIGIONS: Roman Catholic 74%, Protestant 15%, atheist 7%, other 4%
ETHNIC MIX: White 54%, mixed race 38%, Black 6%, other 2%
GOVERNMENT: Presidential system
CURRENCY: Real = 100 centavos

◆ **INSIGHT:** *Since 1900, a third of Brazil's indigenous Amerindian groups have become extinct due to disease, starvation, or the forceful taking of land by miners, loggers, and settlers*

VENEZUELA
French Guiana (France)
SURINAME
GUYANA
Boa Vista
Branco
Guiana Highlands
Macapá
Ilha de Marajó
Belém
Equator
ATLANTIC OCEAN
Rio Negro
Japurá
Amazon Basin
Manaus
Amazon
Santarém
Juruá
Madeira
Tapajós
Tocantins
São Luís
Parnaíba
Fortaleza
San Fernando de Noronha
Iriri
Xingu
Imperatriz
Teresina
Purus
Porto Velho
Rio Branco
Aripuanã
Juruena
São Manuel
Tocantins
Juazeiro do Norte
Natal
João Pessoa
Campina Grande
Olinda
Recife
Represa de Sobradinho
Maceió
Chapada dos Parecis
Guaporé
Planalto de Mato Grosso
Taguatinga
São Francisco
10°
Aracaju
Feira de Santana
BOLIVIA
Araguaia
Salvador
Cuiabá
Brazilian Highlands
BRASÍLIA
Itabuna
Vitória da Conquista
Goiânia
Montes Claros
60°
Pantanal
Paraguay
Uberlândia
Governador Valadares
Uberaba
Campo Grande
Belo Horizonte
Ribeirão Preto
Bauru
Vitória
20°
Nova Iguaçu
Campos
PARAGUAY
Campinas
Londrina
Duque de Caxias
São Paulo
Rio de Janeiro
Paraná
Santos
Curitiba
40°
Joinville
Florianópolis
ARGENTINA
ATLANTIC OCEAN
Caxias do Sul
Porto Alegre
30°
Lagoa dos Patos
Pelotas
50°
URUGUAY
Rio Grande
Mirim Lagoon
2000m/6562ft
1000m/3281ft
500m/1640ft
200m/656ft
Sea Level
0 500 km
0 500 miles

Brunei

Lying on the northern coast of the island of Borneo, Brunei is surrounded and divided in two by the Malaysian state of Sarawak. It has been independent since 1984.

GEOGRAPHY

Mostly dense lowland rainforest and mangrove swamps, with some mountains in the southeast.

CLIMATE

Tropical. Six-month rainy season with very high humidity.

PEOPLE & SOCIETY

Malays benefit from positive discrimination. Many in the Chinese community are stateless. Since a failed rebellion in 1962, Brunei has been ruled by decree of the sultan. In 1990, "Malay Muslim Monarchy" was introduced, promoting Islamic values as state ideology. Women, less restricted than in some Muslim states, usually wear headscarves but not the veil.

INSIGHT: *The sultan spent US$350 million building the world's largest palace at Bandar Seri Begawan*

THE ECONOMY

Oil and natural gas production has brought one of the world's highest standards of living. Massive overseas investments. Major consumer of high-tech hi-fi, video equipment, and Western designer clothes.

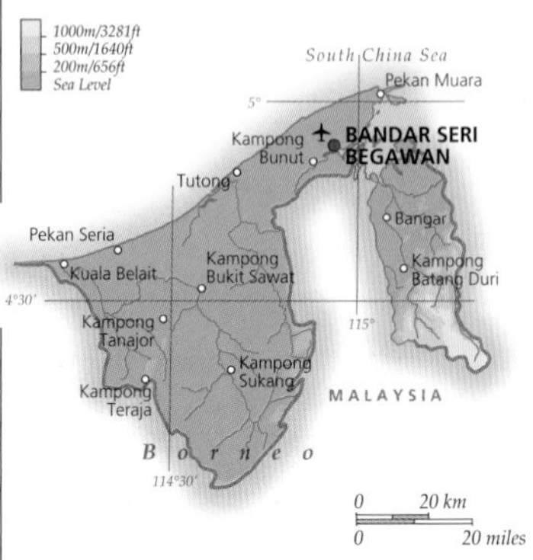
1000m/3281ft
500m/1640ft
200m/656ft
Sea Level
South China Sea
Pekan Muara
5°
Kampong Bunut
BANDAR SERI BEGAWAN
Tutong
Bangar
Pekan Seria
Kuala Belait
Kampong Bukit Sawat
Kampong Batang Duri
4°30′
115°
Kampong Tanajor
Kampong Sukang
Kampong Teraja
MALAYSIA
Borneo
114°30′
0 20 km
0 20 miles

FACTFILE

OFFICIAL NAME: Brunei Darussalam
DATE OF FORMATION: 1984
CAPITAL: Bandar Seri Begawan
POPULATION: 400,000
TOTAL AREA: 2228 sq. miles (5770 sq. km)
DENSITY: 197 people per sq. mile
LANGUAGES: Malay*, English, Chinese
RELIGIONS: Muslim (mainly Sunni) 66%, Buddhist 14%, Christian 10%, other 10%
ETHNIC MIX: Malay 67%, Chinese 16%, other 11%, indigenous 6%
GOVERNMENT: Monarchy
CURRENCY: Brunei dollar = 100 cents

Bulgaria

Located in southeastern Europe, Bulgaria was under communist rule from 1947 to 1989. Significant political and economic reform since then enabled it to join the EU in 2007.

GEOGRAPHY

Mountains run east–west across center and along southern border. Danube plain in north, Thracian plain in southeast. Black Sea to the east.

CLIMATE

Hot summers, cooler at the coast. Snowy winters, especially in mountains. East winds bring seasonal extremes.

PEOPLE & SOCIETY

The communists tried forcibly to suppress cultural identities; once free movement was allowed in 1989, there was a large exodus of Bulgarian Turks. Privatizations in the 1990s left many Turks landless, prompting further emigration. Roma suffer discrimination at all levels of society. Women have equal rights in theory, but society remains patriarchal. EU accession included caveats demanding further action against organized crime, human trafficking, and corruption.

THE ECONOMY

Good agricultural production, including grapes, for well-developed wine industry, and tobacco. Expertise in software development. Industry and infrastructure are outdated.

INSIGHT: *Archaeologists have found evidence of wine-making in Bulgaria dating back over 5000 years*

ROMANIA
44°
Danube
Ruse
Dobrich
Pleven
Vratsa
Shumen
Varna
SERBIA
Veliko Tŭrnovo
Balkan Mountains
SOFIA
Sliven
Burgas
Pernik
Kazanlŭk
Stara Zagora
Yambol
Black Sea
Pazardzhik
Plovdiv
42°
MAC.
Khaskovo
TURKEY
28°
24°
GREECE
26°
0 50 km
0 50 miles
2000m/6562ft
1000m/3281ft
500m/1640ft
200m/656ft
Sea Level

FACTFILE

OFFICIAL NAME: Republic of Bulgaria

DATE OF FORMATION: 1908

CAPITAL: Sofia

POPULATION: 7.2 million

TOTAL AREA: 42,822 sq. miles (110,910 sq. km)

DENSITY: 169 people per sq. mile

LANGUAGES: Bulgarian*, Turkish, Romani

RELIGIONS: Bulgarian Orthodox 83%, Muslim 12%, other 4%, Roman Catholic 1%

ETHNIC MIX: Bulgarian 84%, Turkish 9%, Roma 5%, other 2%

GOVERNMENT: Parliamentary system

CURRENCY: Lev = 100 stotinki

Burkina Faso

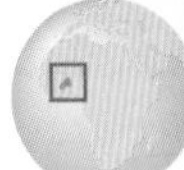

The west African state of Burkina Faso was known as Upper Volta until 1984. It became a multiparty state in 1991, though former military ruler Blaise Compaoré remains in power.

GEOGRAPHY

The Sahara covers the north of the country. The south is largely savanna. The three main rivers are the Black, White, and Red Voltas.

CLIMATE

Tropical. Dry, cool weather November–February. Erratic rain March–April, mostly in southeast.

PEOPLE & SOCIETY

No single ethnic group is dominant, but the Mossi, from around Ouagadougou, have always played an important part in government. The people from the west are much more ethnically mixed. Extreme poverty has led to a strong sense of egalitarianism. Most women are still denied access to education, though their absence from public life belies their real power and social influence.

THE ECONOMY

Cotton is the major cash crop, but the encroaching Sahara Desert is restricting agriculture. Beneficiary of foreign debt cancellation plans.

INSIGHT: *Droughts and poor soils mean that many Burkinabés seek work southward in Ghana and Côte d'Ivoire*

500m/1640ft
200m/656ft
Sea Level
MALI
NIGER
Ouahigouya
Kaya
OUAGADOUGOU
Koudougou
Fada-Ngourma
12°
Black Volta
White Volta
Red Volta
Tenkodogo
Bobo-Dioulasso
Léo
BENIN
Banfora
Black Volta
GHANA
TOGO
0°
CÔTE D'IVOIRE (IVORY COAST)
4°
0 100 km
0 100 miles

FACTFILE

OFFICIAL NAME: Burkina Faso

DATE OF FORMATION: 1960

CAPITAL: Ouagadougou

POPULATION: 16.9 million

TOTAL AREA: 105,869 sq. miles (274,200 sq. km)

DENSITY: 160 people per sq. mile

LANGUAGES: Mossi, Fulani, French*, Tuareg, Dyula, Songhai

RELIGIONS: Muslim 55%, Christian 25% traditional beliefs 20%

ETHNIC MIX: Mossi 48%, other 21%, Peul 10%, Lobi 7%, Bobo 7%, Mandé 7%

GOVERNMENT: Presidential system

CURRENCY: CFA franc = 100 centimes

Burundi

Small, densely populated and landlocked, Burundi lies just south of the equator, on the Nile–Congo watershed in central Africa. More than two-thirds of people live below the poverty line.

GEOGRAPHY

Hilly with high plateaus in center and savanna in the east. Great Rift Valley on western side.

CLIMATE

Temperate, with high humidity. Heavy and frequent rainfall, mostly October–May. Highlands have frost.

PEOPLE & SOCIETY

Burundi has been riven by ethnic conflict between majority Hutu and the Tutsi, who controlled the army – with repeated large-scale massacres: hundreds of thousands of people died between 1993 and 2004. The constitution now guarantees an ethnic balance in the government and army. Twa pygmies were not involved in the conflict.

INSIGHT: *Burundi's fertility rate is one of the highest in Africa. On average, women have six children*

THE ECONOMY

Overwhelmingly agricultural economy, mostly subsistence. Small quantities of gold and tungsten. Potential of oil in Lake Tanganyika. Ongoing political fragility.

RWANDA
Kirundo
Ngozi
Muyinga
Kayanza
3°
Bubanza
Cankuzo
Karuzi
BUJUMBURA
Ruyigi
Gitega
DEM. REP. CONGO
TANZANIA
Bururi
Rutana
4°
Lake Tanganyika
29°
Makamba
Nyanza-Lac
30°
0 50 km
0 50 miles
2000m/6562ft
1000m/3281ft
500m/1640ft

FACTFILE

OFFICIAL NAME: Republic of Burundi
DATE OF FORMATION: 1962
CAPITAL: Bujumbura
POPULATION: 10.2 million
TOTAL AREA: 10,745 sq. miles (27,830 sq. km)
DENSITY: 1030 people per sq. mile
LANGUAGES: Kirundi*, French*, Kiswahili
RELIGIONS: Roman Catholic 62%, traditional beliefs 23%, Muslim 10%, Protestant 5%
ETHNIC MIX: Hutu 85%, Tutsi 14%, Twa 1%
GOVERNMENT: Presidential system
CURRENCY: Burundi franc = 100 centimes

Cambodia

Located on the Indochinese peninsula in southeast Asia, Cambodia has emerged from genocide, civil war, and invasion from Vietnam. Tourism has rebounded, and is a key income earner.

GEOGRAPHY

Mostly low-lying basin. Tônlé Sap (Great Lake) drains into the Mekong River. Forested mountains and plateau east of the Mekong.

CLIMATE

Tropical. High temperatures throughout the year. Heavy rainfall during May–October monsoon.

PEOPLE & SOCIETY

Devastated by US bombing, then by the Khmer Rouge regime, whose extreme Marxist program killed over a million between 1975 and 1979, Cambodia then endured further civil conflict and Vietnamese occupation. The effects are still felt, reflected in the high rates of orphans, widows, and land-mine victims. A fragile stability has lasted since elections in 1993. King Norodom Sihanouk, a key figure in politics, abdicated in 2004.

THE ECONOMY

Economy is heavily aid-reliant, still recovering from civil war. Rubber and timber are exported. Self-sufficient in rice. Garment industry is growing. Land disputes and corruption issues.

INSIGHT: *Cambodia has many impressive temples (including Angkor Wat), which date from when the country was the center of the Khmer Empire*

THAILAND
LAOS
Phumĭ Sâmraông
Choăm Khsant
Vĭrôchey
14°
Sisŏphŏn
Phumĭ Kâmpóng Trâbêk
Bătdâmbâng
Tônlé Sap
Mekong
Poŭthĭsăt
Kâmpóng Chhnăng
Krâchéh
12°
Kâmpóng Cham
Krŏng Kaôh Kŏng
PHNOM PENH
Prey Vêng
Gulf of Thailand
Sihanoukville (Kâmpóng Saôm)
VIETNAM
104°
106°
1000m/3281ft
500m/1640ft
200m/656ft
Sea Level
0 100 km
0 100 miles

FACTFILE

OFFICIAL NAME: Kingdom of Cambodia

DATE OF FORMATION: 1953

CAPITAL: Phnom Penh

POPULATION: 15.1 million

TOTAL AREA: 69,900 sq. miles (181,040 sq. km)

DENSITY: 222 people per sq. mile

LANGUAGES: Khmer*, French, Chinese, Vietnamese, Cham

RELIGIONS: Buddhist 93%, Muslim 6%, Christian 1%

ETHNIC MIX: Khmer 90%, Vietnamese 5%, other 4%, Chinese 1%

GOVERNMENT: Parliamentary system

CURRENCY: Riel = 100 sen

Cameroon

Situated in the corner of the Gulf of Guinea, Cameroon was effectively a one-party state for 30 years. Multiparty elections, since 1992, regularly return that same party to power.

GEOGRAPHY

Over half the land is forested: equatorial rainforest in north, evergreen forest and wooded savanna in south. Mountains in the west.

CLIMATE

South is equatorial, with plentiful rainfall, declining inland. Far north is beset by drought.

PEOPLE & SOCIETY

Around 230 ethnic groups; no single group is dominant. The Bamileke is the largest, though it has never held political power. North–south tensions are diminished by the ethnic diversity. There is more rivalry between majority French- and minority English-speakers.

INSIGHT: *Cameroon's name derives from the Portuguese word* camarões, *after the shrimp fished by the early European explorers*

THE ECONOMY

Oil reserves. Very diversified agricultural economy – timber, cocoa, bananas, coffee. Fuel smuggling from Nigeria undermines refinery profits. Corruption. Port for Chad and CAR.

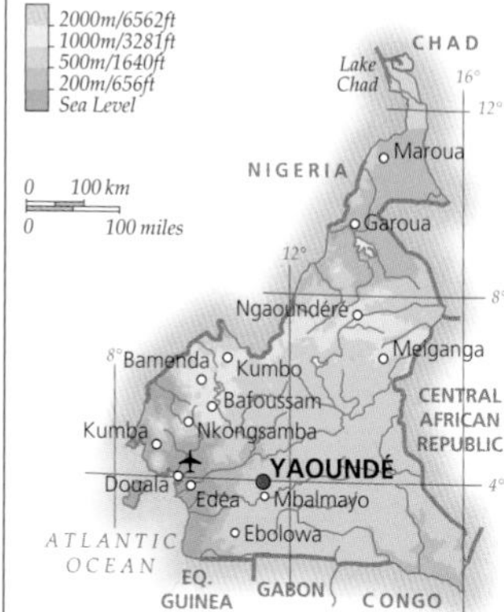
2000m/6562ft
1000m/3281ft
500m/1640ft
200m/656ft
Sea Level
0 100 km
0 100 miles
CHAD
Lake Chad
16°
12°
NIGERIA
Maroua
Garoua
12°
8°
Ngaoundéré
8°
Bamenda
Kumbo
Meiganga
Bafoussam
CENTRAL AFRICAN REPUBLIC
Kumba
Nkongsamba
YAOUNDÉ
Douala
4°
Edéa
Mbalmayo
Ebolowa
ATLANTIC OCEAN
EQ. GUINEA
GABON
CONGO

FACTFILE

OFFICIAL NAME: Republic of Cameroon
DATE OF FORMATION: 1960
CAPITAL: Yaoundé
POPULATION: 22.3 million
TOTAL AREA: 183,567 sq. miles (475,400 sq. km)
DENSITY: 124 people per sq. mile
LANGUAGES: Bamileke, Fang, Fulani, French*, English*
RELIGIONS: Roman Catholic 35%, traditional beliefs 25%, Muslim 22%, Protestant 18%
ETHNIC MIX: Cameroon highlanders 31%, Bantu 27%, other 21%, Kirdi 11%, Fulani 10%
GOVERNMENT: Presidential system
CURRENCY: CFA franc = 100 centimes

Canada

Canada extends from the Arctic to its US border along the 49th parallel. Unified under British rule from 1763, its development and expansion attracted large-scale immigration.

GEOGRAPHY

The world's second-largest country, stretching north to Cape Colombia on Ellesmere Island, south to Lake Erie, and across five time zones from the Pacific seaboard to Newfoundland. Arctic tundra and islands in the far north give way southward to forests, interspersed with lakes and rivers, and then the vast Canadian Shield, which covers over half the area of Canada. Rocky Mountains in west, beyond which are the Coast Mountains, islands, and fjords. Fertile lowlands in the east.

CLIMATE

Ranges from polar and subpolar in the north, to continental in the south. Winters in the interior are colder and longer than on the coast, with temperatures well below freezing and deep snow; summers are hotter. Pacific coast has the mildest winters.

PEOPLE & SOCIETY

Two-thirds of the population live in the Great Lakes–St. Lawrence lowlands, fostering some shared cultural values with the neighboring US. Important differences, however, include wider welfare provision and Commonwealth membership. The French-speaking Québécois wish to preserve their culture and language from further Anglicization, and demand to be recognized as a "distinct society." The government welcomes ethnic diversity among immigrants, promoting a policy that encourages each group to maintain its own culture. Other sizable immigrant groups include Chinese, Italians, Germans. Ukrainians, and Portuguese. Land claims made by the indigenous peoples are being redressed. Nunavut, an Inuit-governed territory that covers nearly a quarter of Canada's land area, was created from a portion of the Northwest Territories in 1999. Women are well represented at most levels of business and government.

FACTFILE

OFFICIAL NAME: Canada
DATE OF FORMATION: 1867
CAPITAL: Ottawa
POPULATION: 35.2 million
TOTAL AREA: 3,855,171 sq. miles (9,984,670 sq. km)
DENSITY: 10 people per sq. mile
LANGUAGES: English*, French*, Chinese, other
RELIGIONS: Roman Catholic 44%, Protestant 29%, other and nonreligious 27%
ETHNIC ORIGIN: British, French, and other European 87%, Asian 9%, Amerindian, Métis, and Inuit 4%
GOVERNMENT: Parliamentary system
CURRENCY: Canadian dollar = 100 cents

THE ECONOMY

Wide-ranging resources, providing exports, cheap energy, and raw materials for manufacturing, underpin a high standard of living, with smaller wealth disparities than in the US. Prices for primary exports fluctuate, but the high oil price has encouraged development of Alberta's vast oil fields. Manufactured exports have flourished under growing global competition, especially since the creation in 1994 of the NAFTA free trade area, but reliance on the US market makes the Canadian economy vulnerable to US slowdowns. Unemployment rose during the 2009 recession, but the economy rebounded quickly.

INSIGHT: *The Magnetic North Pole, where the dipping needle of a compass stands still, migrates across northern Canada*

ARCTIC OCEAN
+Magnetic North Pole
Ellesmere I.
Queen Elizabeth Islands
Parry Islands
Bathurst I.
Baffin Bay
Devon I.
Beaufort Sea
Banks I.
UNITED STATES OF AMERICA (ALASKA)
Victoria Island
Baffin Island
Davis Strait
Mackenzie Mountains
Great Bear Lake
Melville Peninsula
YUKON TERRITORY
Whitehorse
NUNAVUT
Iqaluit (Frobisher Bay)
NORTHWEST TERRITORIES
Southampton I.
Rocky Mountains
Yellowknife
Great Slave Lake
Labrador Sea
Péninsule d'Ungava
BRITISH COLUMBIA
PACIFIC OCEAN
Peace
Athabasca
Lake Athabasca
Hudson Bay
NEWFOUNDLAND & LABRADOR
Labrador
Queen Charlotte Island
Coast Mountains
MANITOBA
St John's
ALBERTA
SASKATCHEWAN
James Bay
QUÉBEC
Gulf of St Lawrence
Newfoundland
Edmonton
St Lawrence
Lake Winnipeg
PRINCE EDWARD I.
Vancouver Island
Calgary
Saskatoon
ONTARIO
NEW BRUNSWICK
Victoria
Vancouver
Lethbridge
Regina
Winnipeg
Québec
Halifax
NOVA SCOTIA
Thunder Bay
Laval
Montréal
Lake Huron
OTTAWA
Lake Superior
Toronto
Oshawa
UNITED STATES OF AMERICA
Lake Michigan
Hamilton
Lake Ontario
Niagara Falls
ATLANTIC OCEAN
Windsor
Lake Erie
3000m/9843ft
2000m/6562ft
1000m/3281ft
500m/1640ft
200m/656ft
Sea Level
0 400 km
0 400 miles

Cape Verde

Off the west coast of Africa, in the Atlantic Ocean, lies the group of islands that make up Cape Verde, a Portuguese colony until it gained independence in 1975.

GEOGRAPHY

Ten main islands and eight smaller islets, all of volcanic origin. Mostly mountainous, with steep cliffs and rocky headlands.

CLIMATE

Warm, and very dry. Subject to droughts that can sometimes last for years at a time.

PEOPLE & SOCIETY

Most people are of mixed Portuguese–African origin (*Mestiço*); the rest are descendants of African slaves or more recent immigrants. Creolization of the culture negates ethnic tensions. Over half of the population live on Santiago. Around 700,000 Cape Verdeans live abroad, mostly in the US.

INSIGHT: *Poor soils and lack of surface water mean that Cape Verde is dependent on food aid*

THE ECONOMY

Most people are subsistence farmers. Clothing is the main export. No natural resources. Mid-Atlantic location ensures work maintaining ships and planes.

0
50 km
0
50 miles
2000m/6562ft
1000m/3281ft
500m/1640ft
200m/656ft
Sea Level
Santo Antão
17°
Mindelo
São Vicente
Santa Luzia
São Nicolau
Sal
Boa Vista
Sal Rei
25°
Ilhas de Barlavento
16°
ATLANTIC
OCEAN
Ilhas de Sotavento
Maio
Tarrafil
15°
São Filipe
PRAIA
Brava
Santiago (São Tiago)
Fogo
23°
24°

FACTFILE

OFFICIAL NAME: Republic of Cape Verde
DATE OF FORMATION: 1975
CAPITAL: Praia
POPULATION: 500,000
TOTAL AREA: 1557 sq. miles (4033 sq. km)
DENSITY: 321 people per sq. mile
LANGUAGES: Portuguese Creole, Portuguese*
RELIGIONS: Roman Catholic 97%, other 2%, Protestant (Church of the Nazarene) 1%
ETHNIC MIX: *Mestiço* 71%, African 28%, European 1%
GOVERNMENT: Mixed presidential-parliamentary system
CURRENCY: Escudo = 100 centavos

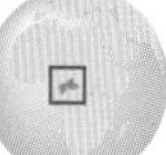

Central African Republic

The Central African Republic (CAR) is a landlocked country lying between the basins of the Chad and Congo Rivers. Politics suffers frequent interruption by coups and rebellions.

GEOGRAPHY

Comprises a low plateau, covered by scrub or savanna. North is arid. Equatorial rainforests in the south. The Ubangi River forms the border with the Democratic Republic of the Congo.

CLIMATE

The south is equatorial; the north is hot and dry. Rain occurs all year round, with heaviest falls between July and October.

PEOPLE & SOCIETY

The Baya and Banda are the largest ethnic groups, but the lingua franca is Sango, a trading creole spoken by the minorities in the south who have traditionally provided most political leaders. Less than 2% of the population live in the north. Recent rebellions by northern militias have displaced thousands of people.

THE ECONOMY

Dominated by subsistence farming. Exports include diamonds, cotton, timber, and coffee. Aid needed to support refugees. Instability and poor infrastructure hinder progress.

INSIGHT: *"Emperor" Bokassa's eccentric rule from 1965 to 1979 was followed by military dictatorship until democracy was restored in 1993*

1000m/3281ft
500m/1640ft
200m/656ft
Sea Level
Birao
24°
SUDAN
20°
Ouanda Djallé
16°
CHAD
Ndélé
8°
SOUTH SUDAN
Batangafo
Kaga Bandoro
Bozoum
Bambari
Bouar
Sibut
Carnot
BANGUI
Bangassou
CAMEROON
Berbérati
Mobaye
Ubangi
4°
CONGO
DEM. REP. CONGO
0 200 km
0 200 miles

FACTFILE

OFFICIAL NAME: Central African Republic
DATE OF FORMATION: 1960
CAPITAL: Bangui
POPULATION: 4.6 million
TOTAL AREA: 240,534 sq. miles (622,984 sq. km)
DENSITY: 19 people per sq. mile
LANGUAGES: Sango, Banda, Gbaya, French*
RELIGIONS: Traditional beliefs 35%, Roman Catholic 25%, Protestant 25%, Muslim 15%
ETHNIC MIX: Baya 33%, Banda 27%, other 17%, Mandjia 13%, Sara 10%,
GOVERNMENT: Transitional regime
CURRENCY: CFA franc = 100 centimes

Chad

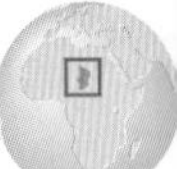

Landlocked in north-central Africa, Chad has had a turbulent history since independence from France in 1960. Intermittent periods of civil war followed a military coup in 1975.

GEOGRAPHY

Mostly plateaus sloping westward to Lake Chad. Northern third is Sahara. Tibesti Mountains in north rise to 10,826 ft (3300 m).

CLIMATE

Three distinct zones: desert in north, semiarid region in center, and tropics in south.

PEOPLE & SOCIETY

Half the population live in Chad's southern fifth. The northern third has only 100,000 people, mainly Muslim Toubou nomads. Democracy was restored in 1996 by ex-coup leader Idriss Déby, who has won all elections since. Instability has continued, first with tension between Muslims and southern Christians and, more recently, with rebellions in the east.

INSIGHT: *Lake Chad is slowly drying up – it is now estimated to be just 3% of the size it was in 1963*

THE ECONOMY

The discovery of oil, and the opening of a pipeline to the coast via Cameroon, are transforming Chad's economy, though the new wealth is unlikely to reach most people.

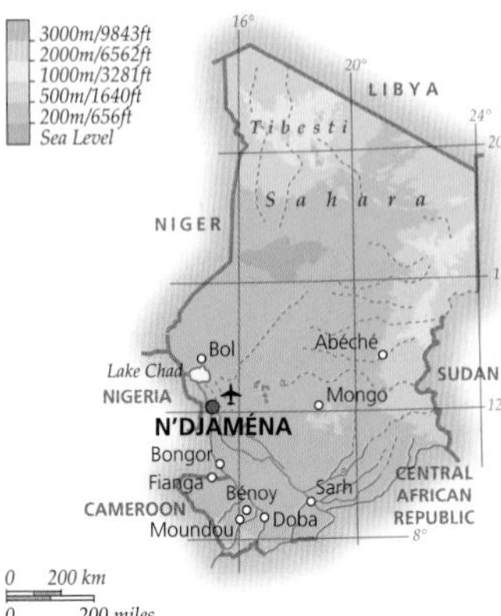
3000m/9843ft
2000m/6562ft
1000m/3281ft
500m/1640ft
200m/656ft
Sea Level
16°
20°
24°
20°
16°
12°
8°
LIBYA
Tibesti
Sahara
NIGER
Bol
Abéché
Lake Chad
NIGERIA
Mongo
SUDAN
N'DJAMÉNA
Bongor
Fianga
Bénoy
Sarh
CENTRAL AFRICAN REPUBLIC
CAMEROON
Moundou
Doba
0 200 km
0 200 miles

FACTFILE

OFFICIAL NAME: Republic of Chad
DATE OF FORMATION: 1960
CAPITAL: N'Djaména
POPULATION: 12.8 million
TOTAL AREA: 495,752 sq. miles (1,284,000 sq. km)
DENSITY: 26 people per sq. mile
LANGUAGES: French*, Sara, Arabic*, Maba
RELIGIONS: Muslim 51%, Christian 35%, traditional beliefs 7%, animist 7%
ETHNIC MIX: Other 30%, Sara 28%, Mayo-Kebbi 12%, Arab 12%, Ouaddai 9%, Kanem-Bornou 9%
GOVERNMENT: Presidential system
CURRENCY: CFA franc = 100 centimes

Chile

Chile extends in a ribbon down the west coast of South America. It returned to elected civilian rule in 1989 after a referendum forced out military dictator General Pinochet.

GEOGRAPHY

Fertile valleys in the center between the coast and the Andes. Atacama Desert in north. Deep-sea channels, lakes, and fjords in south.

CLIMATE

Arid in the north. Hot, dry summers and mild winters in the center. Higher Andean peaks have glaciers and year-round snow. Very wet and stormy in the south.

PEOPLE & SOCIETY

Most people are *mestizo* (mixed Spanish–Amerindian descent), and are highly urbanized. General Pinochet's dictatorship was brutally repressive, but the business and middle classes prospered. Over a third of the population live in Santiago, many in large slums. There are three main indigenous groups, including the Rapa Nui of Easter Island.

THE ECONOMY

World's biggest copper producer. Growth in foreign investment due to political stability. Exports include wine, fishmeal, fruits, and salmon. Serious earthquake damage in 2010.

INSIGHT:

Chile's Atacama Desert is the driest place on Earth, making it the perfect location for hi-tech space observatories

70°
PERU
BOLIVIA
Arica
20°
Iquique
Atacama Desert
Antofagasta
Andes
PACIFIC OCEAN
30°
Viña del Mar
Valparaíso
SANTIAGO
Rancagua

Talcahuano
Talca
Concepción
Chillán
Temuco
Valdivia
40°
Puerto Montt
Isla de Chiloé
Andes
ARGENTINA
50°
Punta Arenas
Strait of Magellan
Cape Horn
4000m/13124ft
3000m/9843ft
2000m/6562ft
1000m/3281ft
Sea Level
0 300 km
0 300 miles

FACTFILE

OFFICIAL NAME: Republic of Chile

DATE OF FORMATION: 1818

CAPITAL: Santiago

POPULATION: 17.6 million

TOTAL AREA: 292,258 sq. miles (756,950 sq. km)

DENSITY: 61 people per sq. mile

LANGUAGES: Spanish*, Amerindian languages

RELIGIONS: Roman Catholic 89%, other and nonreligious 11%

ETHNIC MIX: *Mestizo* and European 90%, other Amerindian 9%, Mapuche 1%

GOVERNMENT: Presidential system

CURRENCY: Chilean peso = 100 centavos

China

Covering a vast area of eastern Asia, China is bordered by 14 countries. A one-party Communist state since 1949, it has recently become a dominant force in global manufacturing.

GEOGRAPHY

A land of huge physical diversity, China has a long Pacific coastline to the east. Two-thirds of the country is uplands. The southwestern mountains include Tibet, the world's highest plateau; in the northwest, the Tien Shan Mountains separate the arid Tarim and Dzungarian basins. The rolling hills and plains of the low-lying east are home to two-thirds of the population.

CLIMATE

China is divided into two main climatic regions. The north and west are semiarid or arid, with extreme temperature variations. The south and east are warmer and more humid, with year-round rainfall. Winter temperatures vary with latitude, but are warmest on the subtropical southeast coast. Summer temperatures are more uniform, rising above 70°F (21°C).

PEOPLE & SOCIETY

Most people are Han Chinese. The rest of the population belong to one of 55 minority nationalities, or recognized ethnic groups. Many of these groups have a disproportionate political significance as they live in strategic border areas. A policy of resettling Han Chinese in remote regions is deeply resented and has led to uprisings in Xinjiang and Tibet. The government has relaxed the one-child family policy, particularly for minorities, after some small groups were brought close to extinction. Chinese society is patriarchal in practice, and generations tend to live together. However, economic change is breaking down the social controls of the Mao Zedong era. Divorce and unemployment are rising. A resurgence of religious belief has occurred in recent years. Materialism has replaced the puritanism of the past; there are now more cell phones in China than in the US.

FACTFILE

OFFICIAL NAME: People's Republic of China
DATE OF FORMATION: 960
CAPITAL: Beijing
POPULATION: 1.39 billion
TOTAL AREA: 3,705,386 sq. miles (9,596,960 sq. km)
DENSITY: 385 people per sq. mile
LANGUAGES: Mandarin*, Cantonese, other
RELIGIONS: Nonreligious 59%, traditional beliefs 20%, other 13%, Buddhist 6%, Muslim 2%
ETHNIC MIX: Han 92%, other 4%, Hui 1%, Miao 1%, Manchu 1%, Zhuang 1%
GOVERNMENT: One-party state
CURRENCY: Yuan = 10 jiao = 100 fen

THE ECONOMY

China has shifted from a centrally planned to a market-oriented economy; liberalization has gone furthest in the south where the emerging business class is based. Exports led annual GDP growth of over 10% in 2003–2007. Faced with a global downturn from 2008, Chinese stimulus packages boosted domestic spending. The buying power of China's huge market for raw materials and consumer goods helped drive global recovery. China is now the world's largest exporter and second-largest economy. The Twelfth Five-Year Plan (2011–2015) seeks to limit population growth and improve social infrastructure.

INSIGHT: *China has the world's oldest continuous civilization. Its recorded history began 4000 years ago, with the Shang dynasty*

Amur
RUSSIAN FEDERATION
50°
Heihe
Manzhouli
Qiqihar
Manchurian Plain
Harbin
Jixi
Changchun
Jilin
Shenyang
Fushun
Anshan
NORTH KOREA
40°
Dandong
130°
Dalian
Bo Hai
KAZAKHSTAN
Altay
Karamay
Yining
Ürümqi
Tien Shan
KYRGYZSTAN
Hami
MONGOLIA
Gobi
Xilinhot
Fuxin
Jinzhou
INNER MONGOLIA
BEIJING
Tangshan
Tianjin
Korla
Lop Nur
TAJIKISTAN
Kashi
Taklimakan Shamo
AFGHANISTAN
Altun Shan
Yumen
Datong
Shijiazhuang
PAKISTAN
Golmud
Qinghai Hu
Huang He
Jinan
Zibo
Qingdao
Aksai Chin-administered by China, claimed by India
Kunlun Shan
Xining
Lanzhou
Luoyang
Zhengzhou
Yellow Sea
Plateau of Tibet
Xuzhou
Demchok/Dêmqog-administered by China, claimed by India
XIZANG ZIZHIQU (TIBET)
Baoji
Xi'an
Huainan
Nanjing
Nanyang
Shanghai
Guangyuan
Salween
Wuhan
Yangtze
Himalayas
Lhasa
Chengdu
Shashi
Hangzhou
30°
80°
Mekong
NEPAL
Zigong
Chongqing
Poyang Hu
BHUTAN
Changsha
Nanchang
East China Sea
90°
INDIA
Guiyang
Hengyang
Fuzhou
Kunming
Liuzhou
Wuzhou
Shantou
MYANMAR (BURMA)
Nanning
Guangzhou
120°
Macao
Hong Kong
VIETNAM
LAOS
Gulf of Tonkin
20°
100°
Hainan Dao
South China Sea
110°
4000m/13124ft
3000m/9843ft
2000m/6562ft
1000m/3281ft
500m/1640ft
200m/656ft
Sea Level
0 400 km
0 400 miles

Colombia

Lying in northwest South America, Colombia has coastlines on both the Caribbean and the Pacific. It is primarily noted for its coffee, emeralds, gold, and cocaine trafficking.

GEOGRAPHY

The densely forested and almost uninhabited east is separated from the western coastal plains by the Andes, which divide into three ranges *(cordilleras)* with intervening valleys.

CLIMATE

Coastal plains are hot and wet. The highlands are much cooler. The equatorial east has two wet seasons.

PEOPLE & SOCIETY

Most Colombians are of mixed blood. Blacks and Amerindians have the least political representation. Civil conflict since the 1960s has killed over 220,000 people and displaced more than five million. The fighting is deeply entwined with the narcotics trade. Violent crime is common.

INSIGHT: *Colombia is the world's main source of emeralds*

THE ECONOMY

Healthy and diversified export sector – includes coffee and coal. Considerable growth potential, but narcotics-related violence and corruption deter foreign investors.

Caribbean Sea
12°
Santa Marta
Barranquilla
Valledupar
Cartagena
Sincelejo
Montería
PANAMA
Cúcuta
VENEZUELA
8°
Bucaramanga
Medellín
Meta
Manizales
Armenia
BOGOTÁ
Villavicencio
Orinoco
PACIFIC OCEAN
4°
Cali
Neiva
Negro
Popayán
Pasto
Andes
68°
Equator
ECUADOR
Putumayo
Caquetá
BRAZIL
76°
PERU
72°
3000m/9843ft
2000m/6562ft
1000m/3281ft
500m/1640ft
Sea Level
0 200 km
0 200 miles

FACTFILE

OFFICIAL NAME: Republic of Colombia

DATE OF FORMATION: 1819

CAPITAL: Bogotá

POPULATION: 48.3 million

TOTAL AREA: 439,733 sq. miles (1,138,910 sq. km)

DENSITY: 120 people per sq. mile

LANGUAGES: Spanish*, Wayuu, Páez, other Amerindian languages

RELIGIONS: Roman Catholic 95%, other 5%

ETHNIC MIX: *Mestizo* (European–Amerindian) 58%, White 20%, European–African 14%, African 4%, African–Amerindian 3%, Amerindian 1%

GOVERNMENT: Presidential system

CURRENCY: Colombian peso = 100 centavos

Comoros

Off the east African coast, between Mozambique and Madagascar, lies the archipelago republic of the Comoros, comprising three main islands and a number of smaller islets.

GEOGRAPHY

Main islands are of volcanic origin and are heavily forested. The remainder are coral atolls.

CLIMATE

Hot and humid all year round, especially on the coasts. November to May is hottest and wettest period.

PEOPLE & SOCIETY

The Comoros has absorbed a diversity of people over the years, including Africans, Arabs, Polynesians,and Persians. There have also been Portuguese, Dutch, French, and Indian immigrants. Ethnic discord is rare, but regional tensions between islands are marked. The country is politically unstable and there have been frequent coups. A fragile new federal system was introduced in 2002, though in 2009 the island presidents were reduced to governors. A political and business elite controls most of the wealth.

THE ECONOMY

One of the world's poorest countries. Subsistence-level farming. Vanilla and cloves are main cash crops. Lack of basic infrastructure.

INSIGHT: *The Comoros is the world's largest producer of ylang-ylang – an extract from tree blossom used in manufacturing perfumes*

Grande Comore
(Njazidja)
1000m/3281f
500m/1640ft
200m/656ft
Sea Level
12°30′
Koimbani
MORONI
Foumbouni
Dembéni
INDIAN OCEAN
12°
43°30′
Mohéli
(Mwali)
Ouani
Moutsamudou
Mozambique
Channel
Fomboni
Moya
Anjouan
(Nzwani)
0 20 km
0 20 miles
11°30′
44°
44°30′

FACTFILE

OFFICIAL NAME: Union of the Comoros

DATE OF FORMATION: 1975

CAPITAL: Moroni

POPULATION: 700,000

TOTAL AREA: 838 sq. miles (2170 sq. km)

DENSITY: 813 people per sq. mile

LANGUAGES: Arabic*, Comoran*, French*

RELIGIONS: Muslim (mainly Sunni) 98%, Roman Catholic 1%, other 1%

ETHNIC MIX: Comoran 97%, other 3%

GOVERNMENT: Presidential system

CURRENCY: Comoros franc = 100 centimes

Congo

Astride the equator in west-central Africa, this former French colony emerged from 20 years of Marxist-Leninist rule in 1990. Democracy was soon overshadowed by years of violence.

GEOGRAPHY

Mostly forest- or savanna-covered plateaus, drained by the Ubangi and Congo river systems. Narrow coastal plain is lined with sand dunes and lagoons.

CLIMATE

Hot, tropical. Temperatures rarely fall below 86°F (30°C). Two wet and two dry seasons. Rainfall is heaviest south of the equator.

PEOPLE & SOCIETY

One of the most tribally conscious and heavily urbanized countries in Africa, with most people living in the Brazzaville–Pointe-Noire region. Main tensions are between the Bakongo in the north and the Mbochi in the south. Relative peace was secured in 1999, and "ninja" rebels in the Pool region, around Brazzaville, signed a peace deal in 2003.

THE ECONOMY

Oil provides over 85% of export revenue. Timber is extracted. Foreign debt cut by two-thirds in 2010. Industrial base around Brazzaville and Pointe-Noire.

INSIGHT: *In 1970, Congo became the first African country to declare itself a communist state*

0 200 km
0 200 miles
500m/1640ft
200m/656ft
Sea Level
C. A. R.
CAMEROON
Ouésso
Sangha
Ubangi
Equator
Owando
GABON
Congo
Djambala
Mossendjo
DEM. REP. CONGO
Loudima
Nkayi
4°
BRAZZAVILLE
ATLANTIC OCEAN
Kinkala
Pointe-Noire
ANGOLA
(Cabinda)
12°
16°

FACTFILE

OFFICIAL NAME: Republic of the Congo
DATE OF FORMATION: 1960
CAPITAL: Brazzaville
POPULATION: 4.4 million
TOTAL AREA: 132,046 sq. miles (342,000 sq. km)
DENSITY: 33 people per sq. mile
LANGUAGES: Kongo, Teke, Lingala, French*
RELIGIONS: Traditional beliefs 50%, Roman Catholic 35%, Protestant 13%, Muslim 2%
ETHNIC MIX: Bakongo 51%, Teke 17%, other 16%, Mbochi 11%, Mbédé 5%
GOVERNMENT: Presidential system
CURRENCY: CFA franc = 100 centimes

Congo, Dem. Rep. (DRC)

A former Belgian colony in east-central Africa, the Democratic Republic of the Congo (DRC) is Africa's second-largest country and the scene of one of its worst regional wars.

GEOGRAPHY

Rainforested basin of Congo River occupies 60% of the land area. High mountain ranges and lakes stretch down the eastern border.

CLIMATE

Tropical and humid. Distinct wet and dry seasons south of the equator. The north is mainly wet.

PEOPLE & SOCIETY

There are 12 main ethnic groups and around 190 smaller ones. Civil war from 1996 drew neighboring countries into a bloody conflict. The indigenous forest pygmies, victimized in the war, are now a marginalized group. A tentative peace deal in 2003 has been undermined by intercommunal violence in the east.

INSIGHT: *The DRC's rainforests comprise 6% of the world's, and 50% of Africa's, remaining woodlands*

THE ECONOMY

Rich resource base: minerals (copper, coltan, cobalt, diamonds) dominate export earnings. War and decades of corruption have caused economic collapse. Food aid is needed to ease humanitarian crisis.

20°
28°
CENTRAL AFRICAN REPUBLIC
SOUTH SUDAN
Ubangi
Bumba
Isiro
Lake Albert
Equator
Mbandaka
Kisangani
UGANDA
CONGO
Congo
Congo Basin
Lualaba
Goma
RWANDA
12°
KINSHASA
Bukavu
BURUNDI
ANGOLA (Cabinda)
Ilebo
Kikwit
Kananga
Kalemie
TANZANIA
Matadi
Mbuji-Mayi
Lake Tanganyika
ATLANTIC OCEAN
8°
Kamina
ANGOLA
Kasai
Likasi
ZAMBIA
Lubumbashi
ZAMBIA
2000m/6562ft
1000m/3281ft
500m/1640ft
200m/656ft
Sea Level
0 200 km
0 200 miles

FACTFILE

OFFICIAL NAME: Democratic Republic of the Congo

DATE OF FORMATION: 1960

CAPITAL: Kinshasa

POPULATION: 67.5 million

TOTAL AREA: 905,563 sq. miles (2,345,410 sq. km)

DENSITY: 77 people per sq. mile

LANGUAGES: Kiswahili, Tshiluba, French*

RELIGIONS: Christian 70%, Kimbanguist 10%, Muslim 10%, traditional beliefs and other 10%

ETHNIC MIX: Other 55%, Mongo, Luba, Kongo, and Mangbetu-Azande 45%

GOVERNMENT: Presidential system

CURRENCY: Congolese franc = 100 centimes

Costa Rica

Costa Rica, Central America's most stable country, is rich in pristine scenery and exotic wildlife. Its neutrality in foreign affairs is long-standing, but it has strong ties with the US.

GEOGRAPHY

Coastal plains of swamp and savanna rise to a fertile central plateau, which leads to a mountain range with active volcanic peaks.

CLIMATE

Hot and humid in coastal regions. Temperate central uplands. High annual rainfall.

PEOPLE & SOCIETY

Most people are *mestizo,* of partly Spanish–partly Amerindian origin. There is a black, English-speaking minority and around 35,000 indigenous Amerindians. Plantation owners are the wealthiest group, while one in five people live in poverty. Nonetheless, living standards are high for the region, and education and healthcare provision is good.

INSIGHT: *Costa Rica's 1949 constitution bans a national army*

THE ECONOMY

Main exports are bananas, coffee, pineapples, and beef, but all vulnerable to fluctuating world prices. Stability has attracted multinationals. History of high inflation. Pioneer of eco-tourism. Plans to be the world's first carbon neutral country (by 2025).

0 50 km
0 50 miles
85°
84°
83°
11°
10°
9°
8°
NICARAGUA
San Juan
Liberia
Cañas
Quesada
San Ramón
Heredia
Puntarenas
SAN JOSÉ
Turrialba
Limón
Cartago
Caribbean Sea
Cordillera de Talamanca
San Isidro
PACIFIC OCEAN
PANAMA
Península de Osa
3000m/9843ft
2000m/6562ft
1000m/3281ft
500m/1640ft
200m/656ft
Sea Level

FACTFILE

OFFICIAL NAME: Republic of Costa Rica
DATE OF FORMATION: 1838
CAPITAL: San José
POPULATION: 4.9 million
TOTAL AREA: 19,730 sq. miles (51,100 sq. km)
DENSITY: 249 people per sq. mile
LANGUAGES: Spanish*, English Creole, Bribri, Cabecar
RELIGIONS: Roman Catholic 71%, Evangelical 14%, nonreligious 11%, other 4%
ETHNIC MIX: *Mestizo* and European 94%, Black 3%, Chinese 1%, Amerindian 1%, other 1%
GOVERNMENT: Presidential system
CURRENCY: C.R. colón = 100 céntimos

Côte d'Ivoire (Ivory Coast)

One of the larger nations along the coast of west Africa, Côte d'Ivoire is the world's biggest cocoa producer. Since 2002 its image of stability has been rocked by civil war and electoral chaos.

GEOGRAPHY

Sandy coastal strip and rainforested interior, with savanna plateau in north.

CLIMATE

Hot all year. Two wet seasons in south; north has one, with lower rainfall.

PEOPLE & SOCIETY

Over 60 tribes; largest is the Baoulé (an Akan group). Southern Christians harbor resentment against non-Ivorian Muslims in the north. Plantations employ millions of migrant workers (including children), though thousands fled back to Burkina during the 2002–2005 civil war. Rebels joined a transitional government in 2007. President Gbagbo delayed elections until 2010 and then refused to step down; civil conflict led to his ouster.

INSIGHT: *The Basilica of Our Lady of Peace in Yamoussoukro is the largest church in the world*

THE ECONOMY

Main crops are cocoa and coffee. Oil is now major export. Good infrastructure. Lack of professional training. Instability deters investment.

MALI
BURKINA FASO
GUINEA
GHANA
LIBERIA
Odienné
Korhogo
Lac de Kossou
Bouaké
Man
Daloa
Abengourou
Guiglo
YAMOUSSOUKRO
Dimbokro
Gagnoa
Divo
Abidjan
Grand-Bassam
San Pédro
Ivory Coast
Gulf of Guinea
ATLANTIC OCEAN
10°
8°
6°
4°

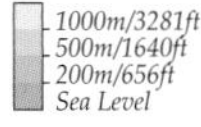
1000m/3281ft
500m/1640ft
200m/656ft
Sea Level

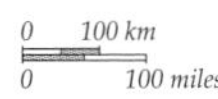
0 100 km
0 100 miles

FACTFILE

OFFICIAL NAME: Republic of Côte d'Ivoire
DATE OF FORMATION: 1960
CAPITAL: Yamoussoukro
POPULATION: 20.3 million
TOTAL AREA: 124,502 sq. miles (322,460 sq. km)
DENSITY: 165 people per sq. mile
LANGUAGES: Akan, French*, Krou, Voltaïque
RELIGIONS: Muslim 38%, Roman Catholic 25%, traditional beliefs 25% , Protestant 6%, other 6%
ETHNIC MIX: Akan 42%, Voltaïque 18%, Mandé du Nord 17%, Krou 11%, Mandé du Sud 10% other 2%
GOVERNMENT: Presidential system
CURRENCY: CFA franc = 100 centimes

Croatia

Though it was controlled by Hungary from medieval times and was a part of the Yugoslav state for much of the 20th century, Croatia has a very strong national identity.

GEOGRAPHY

Rocky, mountainous Adriatic coastline is dotted with islands. Interior is a mixture of wooded mountains and broad valleys.

CLIMATE

The interior has a temperate continental climate. Mediterranean climate along the Adriatic coast.

PEOPLE & SOCIETY

Croats are distinguished from Bosniaks and Serbs by their Roman Catholic faith and use of the Latin alphabet. Many Serbs fled Croatia during the early 1990s conflict that accompanied Yugoslavia's breakup. Croatia's entry into the EU, delayed by border disputes with Slovenia, finally occurred in 2013.

INSIGHT: *Croatia only regained control of Serb-occupied Eastern Slavonia, around Vukovar, in 1998*

THE ECONOMY

The war cost the economy an estimated $50 billion. Unemployment has been persistently high. Corruption deters foreign investment. Tourism is mainly on the Dalmatian coast. EU membership.

0 50 km
0 50 miles
Varaždin
Čakovec
Koprivnica
HUNGARY
Drava
46°
SLOVENIA
Virovitica
Danube
SERBIA
ZAGREB
Karlovac
Osijek
Kupa
Rijeka
Slavonia
Sava
Vukovar
Istra
Slavonski Brod
Pula
BOSNIA & HERZEGOVINA
14°
Zadar
44°
Dinaric Alps
Dalmatia
Split
Adriatic Sea
16°
Dubrovnik
MON.
18°
1000m/3281ft
500m/1640ft
200m/656ft
Sea Level

FACTFILE

OFFICIAL NAME: Republic of Croatia
DATE OF FORMATION: 1991
CAPITAL: Zagreb
POPULATION: 4.3 million
TOTAL AREA: 21,831 sq. miles (56,542 sq. km)
DENSITY: 197 people per sq. mile
LANGUAGES: Croatian*
RELIGIONS: Roman Catholic 88%, other 7%, Orthodox Christian 4%, Muslim 1%
ETHNIC MIX: Croat 90%, Serb 5%, other 5%
GOVERNMENT: Parliamentary system
CURRENCY: Kuna = 100 lipa

Cuba

A former Spanish colony, Cuba is the largest island in the Caribbean. It became the only communist country in the Americas after Fidel Castro seized power in 1959.

GEOGRAPHY

Mostly fertile plains and basins. Three mountainous areas. Forests of pine and mahogany cover one-quarter of the country.

CLIMATE

Subtropical. Hot all year round, and very hot in summer. Heaviest rainfall in the mountains. Hurricanes can strike in the fall.

PEOPLE & SOCIETY

The Castro regime has reduced formerly extreme wealth disparities, given education a high priority, and established an efficient health service. Political dissent, however, is not tolerated. A dramatic fall in living standards since the late 1980s has led thousands of Cubans to flee to the US, to seek asylum. About 70% of Cubans are of Spanish descent. There is little ethnic tension.

THE ECONOMY

Sugar industry now superseded by tourism and nickel. US trade embargo, since 1961. Shortages drive black market. Parallel use of US dollar (1993–2004), and then convertible peso, boosted investment but created a "dollarized" elite: dual peso system to be scrapped.

INSIGHT: *Fidel Castro had become the world's longest-serving non-hereditary ruler before handing power to his brother Raúl in 2006*

Straits of Florida
HAVANA
Marianao
Matanzas
ATLANTIC
OCEAN
Santa Clara
Pinar del Río
Cienfuegos
22°
Ciego de Avila
Camagüey
84°
Archipiélago de los Canarreos
80°
82°
Holguín
Bayamo
Guantánamo
Caribbean Sea
Santiago de Cuba
20°
78°
76°
GUANTÁNAMO BAY
(to USA)
1000m/3281ft
500m/1640ft
200m/656ft
Sea Level
0 100 km
0 100 miles

FACTFILE

OFFICIAL NAME: Republic of Cuba
DATE OF FORMATION: 1902
CAPITAL: Havana
POPULATION: 11.3 million
TOTAL AREA: 42,803 sq. miles (110,860 sq. km)
DENSITY: 264 people per sq. mile
LANGUAGES: Spanish*
RELIGIONS: Nonreligious 49%, Roman Catholic 40%, atheist 6%, other 4%, Protestant 1%
ETHNIC MIX: Mulatto (mixed race) 51%, White 37%, Black 11%, Chinese 1%
GOVERNMENT: One-party state
CURRENCY: Cuban peso = 100 centavos

Cyprus

Cyprus lies south of Turkey in the eastern Mediterranean. Since 1974, it has been partitioned between the Turkish-occupied north and the Greek-Cypriot south.

GEOGRAPHY

Mountains in the center-west give way to a fertile plain in the east, flanked by hills to the northeast.

CLIMATE

Mediterranean. Summers are hot and dry. Winters are mild, with snow in the mountains.

PEOPLE & SOCIETY

The Greek majority practice Orthodox Christianity. Since the 16th century, a minority community of Turkish Muslims has lived in the north of the island. In 1974 Turkish troops occupied the north and proclaimed the Turkish Republic of Northern Cyprus (TRNC), but it is recognized only by Turkey. Over 100,000 mainland Turks have settled there since. UN-led mediation failed to reunite the island ahead of EU accession in 2004, so the north was left out of membership; peace talks continue.

THE ECONOMY

Tourism. Eurozone member. Weathered 2009 downturn, but banks crashed in 2013: Cypriots lost savings under IMF/EU bailout terms. North lacks investment and wages are lower.

INSIGHT: *The Green Line, which separates north from south, was opened for the first time in 2003*

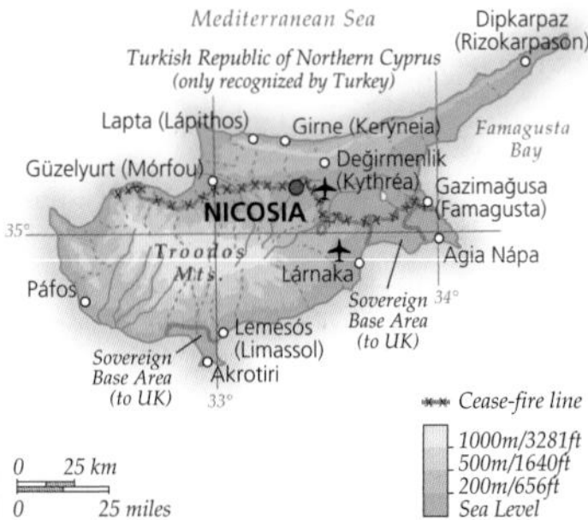
Mediterranean Sea
Turkish Republic of Northern Cyprus
(only recognized by Turkey)
Dipkarpaz
(Rizokarpason)
Lapta (Lápithos)
Girne (Keryneia)
Famagusta Bay
Güzelyurt (Mórfou)
Değirmenlik
(Kythréa)
Gazimağusa
(Famagusta)
NICOSIA
35°
Troodos Mts.
Lárnaka
Agia Nápa
Páfos
Sovereign Base Area
(to UK)
34°
Lemesós
(Limassol)
Sovereign Base Area
(to UK)
Akrotiri
33°
Cease-fire line
1000m/3281ft
500m/1640ft
200m/656ft
Sea Level
0 25 km
0 25 miles

FACTFILE

OFFICIAL NAME: Republic of Cyprus
DATE OF FORMATION: 1960
CAPITAL: Nicosia
POPULATION: 1.1 million
TOTAL AREA: 3571 sq. miles (9250 sq. km)
DENSITY: 308 people per sq. mile
LANGUAGES: Greek*, Turkish*
RELIGIONS: Orthodox Christian 78%, Muslim 18%, other 4%
ETHNIC MIX: Greek 81%, Turkish 11%, other 8%
GOVERNMENT: Presidential systems
CURRENCY: Euro = 100 cents (new Turkish lira in TRNC = 100 kurus)

Czech Republic

Once part of Czechoslovakia, a central European communist state in 1948–1989, the Czech Republic peacefully dissolved its union with Slovakia in 1993. It joined the EU in 2004.

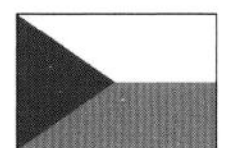

GEOGRAPHY

Landlocked in central Europe. Bohemia, the western territory, is a plateau surrounded by mountains. Moravia, in the east, is characterized by hills and lowlands.

CLIMATE

Cool, sometimes cold winters and warm summer months, which bring most of the annual rainfall.

PEOPLE & SOCIETY

Secular and urban society, with high divorce rates. Czechs make up the vast majority of the population, while the next largest group are Moravians. The 300,000 Slovaks left after partition are now permitted dual citizenship. Ethnic tensions are few, but there is widespread hostility toward the Roma minority. A new commercial elite is emerging alongside postcommunist entrepreneurs.

THE ECONOMY

Traditional heavy industries (machinery, iron, car-making) have been successfully privatized. Prague attracts tourists. Skilled workforce. Will join euro in 2017 at earliest.

INSIGHT: *Charles University in Prague was founded in the 13th century*

GERMANY
Liberec
Ústí nad Labem
Karlovy Vary
Elbe
50°
POLAND
Kladno
PRAGUE
Hradec Králové
Plzeň
Pardubice
Bohemia
Ostrava
Olomouc
Havířov
České Budějovice
Moravia
Zlín
Brno
AUSTRIA
SLOVAKIA
14°
16°
18°

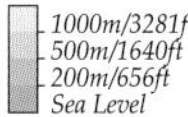
1000m/3281ft
500m/1640ft
200m/656ft
Sea Level

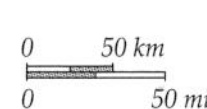
0 50 km
0 50 miles

FACTFILE

OFFICIAL NAME: Czech Republic
DATE OF FORMATION: 1993
CAPITAL: Prague
POPULATION: 10.7 million
TOTAL AREA: 30,450 sq. miles (78,866 sq. km)
DENSITY: 351 people per sq. mile
LANGUAGES: Czech*, Slovak, Hungarian (Magyar)
RELIGIONS: Roman Catholic 39%, atheist 38%, other 18%, Protestant 3%, Hussite 2%
ETHNIC MIX: Czech 90%, other 4%, Moravian 4%, Slovak 2%
GOVERNMENT: Parliamentary system
CURRENCY: Czech koruna = 100 haleru

Denmark

Denmark occupies the Jutland peninsula and over 400 islands in southern Scandinavia. Greenland and the Faeroe Islands are self-governing associated territories.

GEOGRAPHY

Fertile farmland covers two-thirds of the terrain, which is among the flattest in the world. About 100 islands are inhabited.

CLIMATE

Damp, temperate climate with mild summers and cold, wet winters. Rainfall is moderate.

PEOPLE & SOCIETY

Income distribution is the most even in the West. Danish liberalism is challenged over immigration: cultural clashes have arisen with immigrant minorities. Almost all women now work; Denmark is a world leader in childcare provision. Marriage is becoming less common, even for couples with children.

INSIGHT: *Denmark is Europe's oldest kingdom – the monarchy dates back to the 10th century*

THE ECONOMY

Natural gas and oil reserves. Skilled workforce key to high-tech industrial success. Pork, bacon, dairy products are exported. Opted not to join the euro, though its currency is pegged.

200m/656ft
Sea Level
Bornholm
15°
Rønne
55°
Skagerrak
Aalborg
Kattegat
Jylland
Viborg
Randers
Silkeborg
Herning
Århus
56°
Helsingør
Horsens
COPENHAGEN
Vejle
Roskilde
Esbjerg
Odense
Kolding
Fyn
Sjælland
North Sea
Svendborg
Næstved
Sønderborg
Baltic Sea
8°
GERMANY
Lolland
Nykøbing
Falster
10°
12°
0 50 km
0 50 miles

FACTFILE

OFFICIAL NAME: Kingdom of Denmark
DATE OF FORMATION: 950
CAPITAL: Copenhagen
POPULATION: 5.6 million
TOTAL AREA: 16,639 sq. miles (43,094 sq. km)
DENSITY: 342 people per sq. mile
LANGUAGES: Danish*
RELIGIONS: Evangelical Lutheran 95%, Roman Catholic 3%, Muslim 2%
ETHNIC MIX: Danish 96%, other (including Scandinavian and Turkish) 3%, Faeroese and Inuit 1%
GOVERNMENT: Parliamentary system
CURRENCY: Danish krone = 100 øre

Djibouti

A city-state with a desert hinterland, Djibouti lies in northeast Africa on the Red Sea. Once known as the French Territory of the Afars and Issas, independence came in 1977.

GEOGRAPHY

Mainly low-lying desert and semidesert, with a volcanic mountain range in the north.

CLIMATE

Almost no rain, though the monsoon is very humid. The 109°F (45°C) heat of summer is unbearable.

PEOPLE & SOCIETY

The main ethnic groups are the Issas in the south, and the nomadic Afars in the north. Tensions between them developed into a guerrilla war in 1991–1994. Smaller tribal groups make up the rest of the population, and the rural peoples are mostly nomadic. Wealth is concentrated in Djibouti city. France exerts considerable influence in Djibouti, supporting it financially and maintaining a naval base and a military garrison.

THE ECONOMY

Djibouti's major assets are its ports in a key Red Sea location.

INSIGHT: *Chewing the leaves of the mildly narcotic qat shrub is an age-old social ritual in Djibouti*

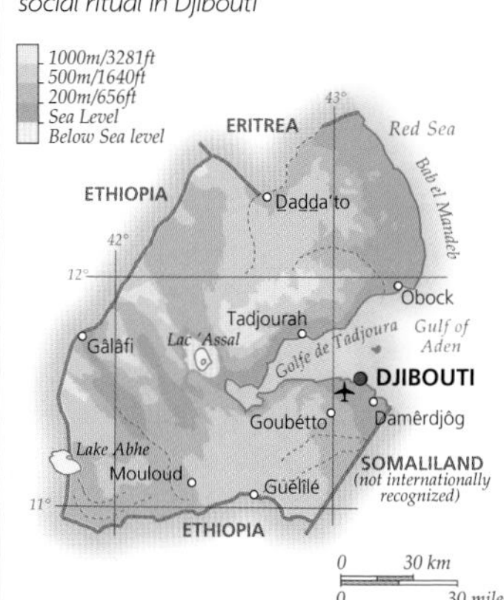
1000m/3281ft
500m/1640ft
200m/656ft
Sea Level
Below Sea level
43°
ERITREA
Red Sea
Bab el Mandeb
ETHIOPIA
Dadda'to
42°
12°
Obock
Tadjourah
Gulf of Aden
Gâlâfi
Lac 'Assal
Golfe de Tadjoura
DJIBOUTI
Goubétto
Damêrdjôg
Lake Abhe
Mouloud
Guêlilé
SOMALILAND
(not internationally recognized)
11°
ETHIOPIA
0 30 km
0 30 miles

FACTFILE

OFFICIAL NAME: Republic of Djibouti
DATE OF FORMATION: 1977
CAPITAL: Djibouti
POPULATION: 900,000
TOTAL AREA: 8494 sq. miles (22,000 sq. km)
DENSITY: 101 people per sq. mile
LANGUAGES: Somali, Afar, French*, Arabic*
RELIGIONS: Muslim (mainly Sunni) 94%, Christian 6%
ETHNIC MIX: Issa 60%, Afar 35%, other 5%
GOVERNMENT: Presidential system
CURRENCY: Djibouti franc = 100 centimes

Dominica

Dominica is renowned as the Caribbean island that resisted European colonization until the 18th century. It achieved independence from the UK in 1978.

GEOGRAPHY

Mountainous and densely forested. Volcanic activity has given the land very fertile soils, hot springs, geysers, and black sand beaches.

CLIMATE

Tropical, cooled by constant trade winds. Heavy annual rainfall. Tropical depressions and hurricanes are likely June–November.

PEOPLE & SOCIETY

The majority of Dominicans are descendants of African slaves brought over to work on banana plantations. The Carib Territory on the northeast of the island is home to the only surviving indigenous community in the Caribbean. Wealth disparities are not as marked as elsewhere in the region, but the alleviation of poverty has become a major plank of government policy.

THE ECONOMY

Based on bananas, but has lost preferential access to EU market. Some diversification: flowers, coffee, fruit. Agriculture vulnerable to hurricanes. Eco-tourism. Some offshore banking.

INSIGHT: *Dominica is known as "Nature Island," due to its spectacular flora and fauna*

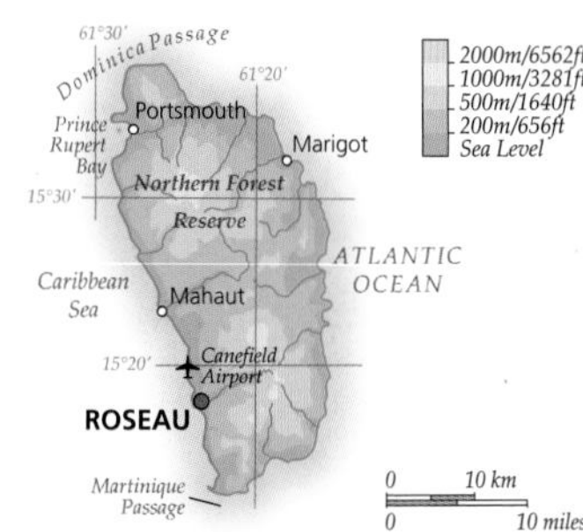
61°30'
Dominica Passage
61°20'
Prince Rupert Bay
Portsmouth
Marigot
15°30'
Northern Forest Reserve
ATLANTIC OCEAN
Caribbean Sea
Mahaut
15°20'
Canefield Airport
ROSEAU
Martinique Passage
2000m/6562ft
1000m/3281ft
500m/1640ft
200m/656ft
Sea Level
0
10 km
0
10 miles

FACTFILE

OFFICIAL NAME: Commonwealth of Dominica
DATE OF FORMATION: 1978
CAPITAL: Roseau
POPULATION: 73,286
TOTAL AREA: 291 sq. miles (754 sq. km)
DENSITY: 253 people per sq. mile
LANGUAGES: French Creole, English*
RELIGIONS: Roman Catholic 77%, Protestant 15%, other 8%
ETHNIC MIX: Black 87%, mixed race 9%, Carib 3%, other 1%
GOVERNMENT: Parliamentary system
CURRENCY: East Caribbean dollar = 100 cents

Dominican Republic

The Dominican Republic occupies the eastern two-thirds of the island of Hispaniola in the Caribbean. Spanish-speaking, it seeks closer ties to the anglophone West Indies.

GEOGRAPHY

Highlands and rainforested mountains – including the highest peak in the Caribbean, Pico Duarte – interspersed with fertile valleys. Extensive coastal plain in the east.

CLIMATE

Hot and humid close to sea level, cooler at altitude. Heavy rainfall, especially in the northeast.

PEOPLE & SOCIETY

White landowners – especially those descended from the original Spanish settlers – form the wealthy elite. The mixed-race majority controls commerce and forms the bulk of the professional middle classes. White and mixed-race women are entering the professions. Great disparities of wealth exist; the black and Haitian-immigrant populations occupy the bottom of the social ladder.

THE ECONOMY

Mining (nickel and gold), sugar, and textiles. Tourism, remittances, and exports all rely heavily on US market. Hidden economy based on trans-shipment of narcotics to the US.

INSIGHT: *Santo Domingo is the oldest city in the Americas. It was founded in 1496 by the brother of Christopher Columbus*

20°
Monte Cristi
Puerto Plata
ATLANTIC OCEAN
Mao
Santiago
San Francisco de Macorís
Pico Duarte 10,417ft(3175m)
HAITI
La Vega
19°
Cordillera Central
San Juan
SANTO DOMINGO
El Seibo
Lago Enriquillo
San Cristóbal
La Romana
San Pedro de Macorís
Barahona
70°
69°
18°
71°
Caribbean Sea
2000m/6562ft
1000m/3281ft
500m/1640ft
200m/656ft
Sea Level
0 50 km
0 50 miles

FACTFILE

OFFICIAL NAME: Dominican Republic
DATE OF FORMATION: 1865
CAPITAL: Santo Domingo
POPULATION: 10.4 million
TOTAL AREA: 18,679 sq. miles (48,380 sq. km)
DENSITY: 557 people per sq. mile
LANGUAGES: Spanish*, French Creole
RELIGIONS: Roman Catholic 95%, other and nonreligious 5%
ETHNIC MIX: Mixed race 73%, European 16%, Black African 11%
GOVERNMENT: Presidential system
CURRENCY: Dominican Republic peso = 100 centavos

East Timor

East Timor occupies the once Portuguese-owned eastern half of the island of Timor. Invaded by Indonesia in 1975, it became independent in 2002 following a long struggle.

GEOGRAPHY

A narrow coastal plain gives way to forested highlands. The mountain backbone rises to 9715 ft (2963 m).

CLIMATE

Tropical. Heavy rain in wet season (December–March), then dry and hot, particularly in the north.

PEOPLE & SOCIETY

The population is almost entirely Roman Catholic. The Timorese are a mix of Malay and Papuan peoples, and many indigenous Papuan tribes survive. There is an urban Chinese minority, and ethnic Indonesian settlers became numerous after annexation in 1975. Preindependence violence in 1999 was politically rather than ethnically motivated. Women do not have access to the professions and levels of domestic violence are notably high. Living standards are low.

THE ECONOMY

Widespread poverty. Violence in 1999 damaged infrastructure. Riots in 2006 undermined stability, further deterring foreign investment. Agreement with Australia on division of oil revenue from the Timor Sea.

INSIGHT: *Once dependent on sandalwood, the economy is being transformed by oil under the Timor Sea*

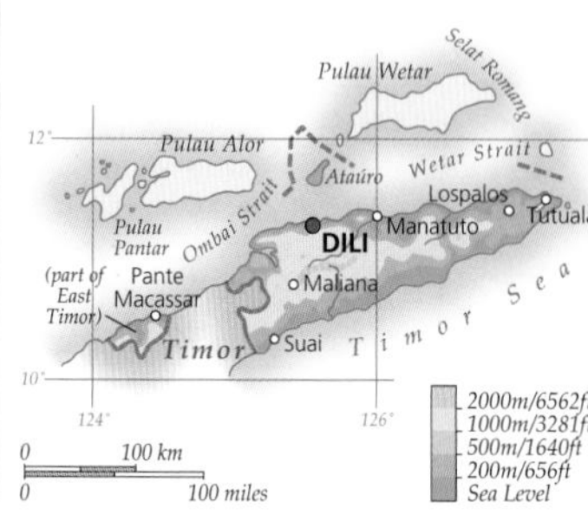
Selat Romang
Pulau Wetar
12°
Pulau Alor
Wetar Strait
Ataúro
Lospalos
Tutuala
Manatuto
Pulau Pantar
Ombai Strait
DILI
(part of East Timor)
Pante Macassar
Maliana
Sea
Timor
Suai
Timor
10°
124°
126°
0
100 km
0
100 miles
2000m/6562ft
1000m/3281ft
500m/1640ft
200m/656ft
Sea Level

FACTFILE

OFFICIAL NAME: Democratic Republic of Timor-Leste
DATE OF FORMATION: 2002
CAPITAL: Dili
POPULATION: 1.1 million
TOTAL AREA: 5756 sq. miles (14,874 sq. km)
DENSITY: 195 people per sq. mile
LANGUAGES: Tetum* (Portuguese/Austronesian), Bahasa Indonesia, Portuguese*
RELIGIONS: Roman Catholic 95%, other (including Muslim and Protestant) 5%
ETHNIC MIX: Malay/Papuan groups c. 85%, Indonesian c. 13%, Chinese 2%
GOVERNMENT: Parliamentary system
CURRENCY: US dollar = 100 cents

Ecuador

Once part of the Inca heartland, Ecuador lies on the western coast of South America. Its territory includes the fascinating Galápagos Islands, 610 miles (970 km) to the west.

GEOGRAPHY

Broad coastal plain, inter-Andean central highlands, dense jungle in upper Amazon basin.

CLIMATE

The climate is hot and moist on the coast, cool in the Andes, and hot equatorial in the Amazon basin.

PEOPLE & SOCIETY

Most people are of Amerindian–Spanish extraction (*mestizo*). Black communities exist on the coast. The strong and largely unified Amerindian movement leads the pressure for social reform. Recent left-wing policies have given greater rights to women, the poor, and Amerindians. Extreme poverty has fallen from 17% in 2006 to 8.6% in 2013.

INSIGHT: *Darwin's study on the Galápagos Islands in 1856 played a major part in his theory of evolution*

THE ECONOMY

Oil provides around half of export earnings. World's biggest banana exporter. Use of US dollar offers stability, but less control. Defaulted on debt in 2008, prioritizing social spending.

0 100 km
0 100 miles
PACIFIC OCEAN
COLOMBIA
76°
Esmeraldas
San Miguel
Ibarra
Equator
QUITO
Napo
Santo Domingo de los Colorados
Manta
Portoviejo
Ambato
Riobamba
Milagro
Guayaquil
Gulf of Guayaquil
Cuenca
Machala
Andes
4°
Loja
PERU
80°
4000m/13124ft
3000m/9843ft
2000m/6562ft
1000m/3281ft
500m/1640ft
200m/656ft
Sea Level

FACTFILE

OFFICIAL NAME: Republic of Ecuador
DATE OF FORMATION: 1830
CAPITAL: Quito
POPULATION: 15.7 million
TOTAL AREA: 109,483 sq. miles (283,560 sq. km)
DENSITY: 147 people per sq. mile
LANGUAGES: Spanish*, Quechua, other Amerindian languages
RELIGIONS: Roman Catholic 95%; Protestant, Jewish, and other 5%
ETHNIC MIX: *Mestizo* 77%, White 11%, Amerindian 7%, Black African 5%
GOVERNMENT: Presidential system
CURRENCY: US dollar = 100 cents

Egypt

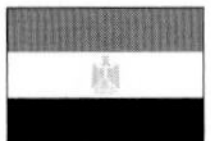

Occupying the northeast corner of Africa, Egypt is divided by the highly fertile Nile Valley. A long tradition of ethnic and religious tolerance has been shaken by the rise in Islamism.

GEOGRAPHY

Fertile Nile Valley separates arid Libyan Desert from smaller semiarid eastern desert. Sinai peninsula has mountains in south.

CLIMATE

Summers are very hot, but winters are cooler. Rainfall is negligible, except on the coast.

PEOPLE & SOCIETY

Mubarak's military-backed regime was ousted in a popular uprising in the "Arab Spring" of 2011, but the subsequent elected Muslim Brotherhood government was in turn ousted. Clashes between Muslims and Copts are rising. Women's access to education and economic status are threatened by Islamism. Rapidly growing population. Poverty in the south.

INSIGHT: *In 450 BCE Herodotus visited the already-ancient pyramids*

THE ECONOMY

Oil and gas. Cotton. Tolls from the Suez Canal. Tourist industry and foreign investment affected by terrorist attacks and ongoing political instability.

Mediterranean Sea
Nile Delta
Al Iskandarīyah
Bur Sā'īd
ISRAEL
Al Ismā'īlīya
Suez Canal
CAIRO
As Suways
JORDAN
Munkhafad al Qaţţāra
Al Jīzah
Al Minyā
Sinai
LIBYA
Nile
28°
Asyūţ
Hurghada
Sawhāj
Qinā
Red Sea
Al Uqşur
Libyan Desert
Aswān
24°
Administrative border
Lake Nasser
SUDAN
Political border
28°
32°
36°
2000m/6562ft
1000m/3281ft
500m/1640ft
200m/656ft
Sea Level
Below Sea Level
0 200 km
0 200 miles

FACTFILE

OFFICIAL NAME: Arab Republic of Egypt

DATE OF FORMATION: 1936

CAPITAL: Cairo

POPULATION: 82.1 million

TOTAL AREA: 386,660 sq. miles (1,001,450 sq. km)

DENSITY: 214 people per sq. mile

LANGUAGES: Arabic*, French, English, Berber

RELIGIONS: Muslim (mainly Sunni) 90%, Coptic Christian and other 10%

ETHNIC MIX: Egyptian 99%, other (Nubian, Armenian, Greek, Berber) 1%

GOVERNMENT: Transitional regime

CURRENCY: Egyptian pound = 100 piastres

El Salvador

El Salvador is Central America's smallest and most densely populated country. Already struggling to recover from a civil war in the 1980s, it was badly struck by earthquakes in 2001.

GEOGRAPHY

El Salvador is a narrow coastal belt backed by two mountain ranges. There is a central plateau. The country is located within a seismic zone, and there are more than 20 volcanic peaks.

CLIMATE

Tropical coastal belt is very hot, with seasonal rains. Cooler, temperate climate in highlands.

PEOPLE & SOCIETY

Ethnic tensions are few. Economic disparities sparked the 1981–1991 civil war between the US-backed government and left-wing FMLN guerrillas; 75,000 people died, many of them unarmed civilians, and human rights abuses were widespread. In 2009 the FMLN won the presidency, but wealth disparities still exist despite some reform. Gangs now control much of daily life; the murder rate is rising again despite a 2012 truce.

THE ECONOMY

Coffee, sugar. Garment industry. Overseas remittances. Frequent natural disasters damage infrastructure and deepen country's reliance on aid. Most businesses suffer extortion by gangs. Violence deters investors and tourism.

INSIGHT: *Independent since 1841, El Salvador is named after Jesus Christ, "the savior" of Christians*

GUATEMALA
Metapán
HONDURAS
89°
90°
Santa Ana
Lempa
Chalatenango
Lempa
14°
88°
Embalse Cerrón Grande
Ahuachapán
Sensuntepeque
Sonsonate
SAN SALVADOR
San Vicente
Zacatecoluca
Lempa
San Miguel
La Unión
Usulután
PACIFIC OCEAN
13°
2000m/6562ft
1000m/3281ft
500m/1640ft
200m/656ft
Sea Level
0 25 km
0 25 miles

FACTFILE

OFFICIAL NAME: Republic of El Salvador
DATE OF FORMATION: 1841
CAPITAL: San Salvador
POPULATION: 6.3 million
TOTAL AREA: 8124 sq. miles (21,040 sq. km)
DENSITY: 788 people per sq. mile
LANGUAGES: Spanish*
RELIGIONS: Roman Catholic 80%, Evangelical 18%, other 2%
ETHNIC MIX: *Mestizo* (European–Amerindian) 90%, White 9%, Amerindian 1%
GOVERNMENT: Presidential system
CURRENCY: Salvadorean colón = 100 centavos; US dollar = 100 cents

Equatorial Guinea

Comprising the mainland territory of Río Muni and five islands on the west coast of central Africa, Equatorial Guinea, despite its name, lies just north of the equator.

GEOGRAPHY

The islands are mountainous and volcanic. The mainland is lower, with mangrove swamps along the coast.

CLIMATE

The island of Bioco is extremely wet and humid. The mainland is only marginally drier and cooler.

PEOPLE & SOCIETY

Equatorial Guinea is the only Spanish-speaking country in Africa. Río Muni is sparsely populated and most people there are Fang, an ethnic group also found in Cameroon and northern Gabon. Bioco is populated by Bubi and a minority of Creoles known as Fernandinos. Tensions between the two territories have been reignited by the discovery of oil off Bioco. Wealth is concentrated in the ruling clan; oil revenue since 1995 has made little impact on most people.

THE ECONOMY

Oil and gas now account for almost all of exports; the government has promised to reinvest oil funds in development. Timber, cocoa, coffee.

INSIGHT: *In 2003, state radio declared President Obiang Nguema to be "like God in Heaven"*

2000m/6562ft
1000m/3281ft
500m/1640ft
200m/656ft
Sea Level
MALABO
3°30'N
Isla da Bioco
Bight of Biafra
9°
ATLANTIC OCEAN
CAMEROON
Micomeseng
2°
Gulf of Guinea
Bata
Niefang
Mongomo
Uolo
Mbini
Río Muni
Cabo San Juan
Etembue
Cogo
Nsoc
Isla de Corisco
GABON
10°
0
40 km
0
40 miles

FACTFILE

OFFICIAL NAME: Republic of Equatorial Guinea

DATE OF FORMATION: 1968

CAPITAL: Malabo

POPULATION: 800,000

TOTAL AREA: 10,830 sq. miles (28,051 sq. km)

DENSITY: 74 people per sq. mile

LANGUAGES: Spanish*, Fang, Bubi, French*

RELIGIONS: Roman Catholic 90%, other 10%

ETHNIC MIX: Fang 85%, other 11%, Bubi 4%

GOVERNMENT: Presidential system

CURRENCY: CFA franc = 100 centimes

Eritrea

Lying along the southwest shore of the Red Sea, Eritrea won a long war for independence from Ethiopia in 1993. The two neighbors fought a bitter border war in 1998–2000.

GEOGRAPHY

Mostly consists of rugged mountains, bush, and the Danakil Desert, which falls below sea level.

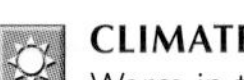

CLIMATE

Warm in the mountains; desert areas are hot. Droughts from July onward are common.

PEOPLE & SOCIETY

Tigrinya-speakers, mainly Orthodox Christians, are the most numerous of nine main ethnic groups. A strong sense of nationhood has been forged by war. Women played a vital role in combat. Around two-thirds of people are subsistence farmers. Multiparty elections, due under the 1997 constitution, are yet to be held.

INSIGHT: *Eritrea was modern Italy's first African colony. It's named for the ancient Greek for Red Sea: Erythra Thalassa*

THE ECONOMY

Legacy of disruption and destruction from wars; resettlement of refugees. Susceptible to drought and famine: dependent on food aid. Most of the population live at subsistence level. Potential for extraction of gold, copper, and oil. Red Sea location: port at Massawa.

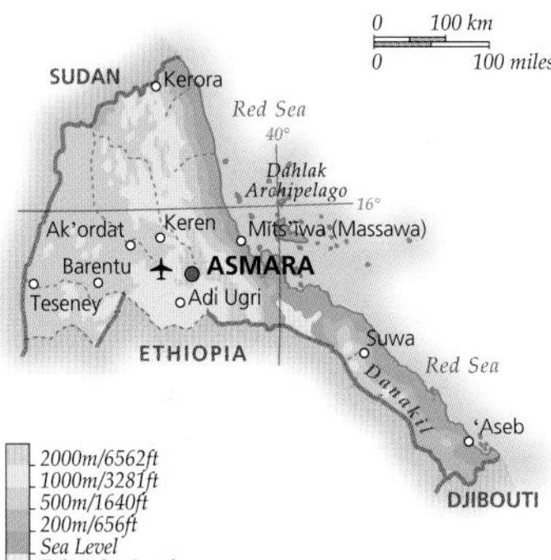
0 100 km
0 100 miles
SUDAN
Kerora
Red Sea
40°
Dahlak Archipelago
16°
Ak'ordat
Keren
Mits'iwa (Massawa)
Barentu
ASMARA
Teseney
Adi Ugri
ETHIOPIA
Suwa
Danakil
Red Sea
'Aseb
DJIBOUTI
2000m/6562ft
1000m/3281ft
500m/1640ft
200m/656ft
Sea Level
Below Sea Level

FACTFILE

OFFICIAL NAME: State of Eritrea
DATE OF FORMATION: 1993
CAPITAL: Asmara
POPULATION: 6.3 million
TOTAL AREA: 46,842 sq. miles (121,320 sq. km)
DENSITY: 139 people per sq. mile
LANGUAGES: Tigrinya*, English*, Tigre, Afar, Arabic*, Saho, Bilen, Kunama, Nara, Hadareb
RELIGIONS: Christian 50%, Muslim 48%, other 2%
ETHNIC MIX: Tigray 50%, Tigre 31%, other 9%, Saho 5%, Afar 5%
GOVERNMENT: Mixed presidential–parliamentary system
CURRENCY: Nakfa = 100 cents

Estonia

The smallest and most Western-oriented of the former Soviet-ruled Baltic states, Estonia is also the most developed, but its standard of living is well below the EU average.

GEOGRAPHY

Estonia's terrain is flat, boggy, and partly forested, with over 1500 islands. Lake Peipus forms much of the eastern border with Russia.

CLIMATE

Maritime, with some continental extremes. Harsh winters, with cool summers and damp springs.

PEOPLE & SOCIETY

Estonians are related ethnically and linguistically to the Finns. Friction between ethnic Estonians and the large Russian minority led to a reassertion of Estonian culture and language. Outright discrimination against the Russian language was only ended in 2000. Estonians are predominantly Lutheran. Families are small. The divorce rate has reduced since the 1980s peak. Market reforms have increased prosperity; a few people have become very rich.

THE ECONOMY

Timber and oil shale. Good productivity. Strong growth accompanied EU accession in 2004, but first EU country to enter recession in 2008. Drastic spending cuts aided quick revival. Joined eurozone in 2011. Low debt burden.

INSIGHT: *Estonia pioneered online voting in 2007, and voting by cell phone in 2011*

Gulf of Finland
26°
28°
TALLINN
Rakvere
Kohtla-Järve
Narva
Baltic Sea
Tapa
59°
Haapsalu
Paide
Lake Peipus
RUSS. FED.
Hiiumaa
Tartu
Viljandi
Pärnu
Saaremaa
Võrtsjärv
Lake Pskov
Gulf of Riga
58°
Valga
Võru
LATVIA
22°
24°
200m/656ft
Sea Level
0 50 km
0 50 miles

FACTFILE

OFFICIAL NAME: Republic of Estonia
DATE OF FORMATION: 1991
CAPITAL: Tallinn
POPULATION: 1.3 million
TOTAL AREA: 17,462 sq. miles (45,226 sq. km)
DENSITY: 75 people per sq. mile
LANGUAGES: Estonian*, Russian
RELIGIONS: Evangelical Lutheran 56%, Orthodox Christian 25%, other 19%
ETHNIC MIX: Estonian 69%, Russian 25%, other 4%, Ukrainian 2%
GOVERNMENT: Parliamentary system
CURRENCY: Euro = 100 cents

Ethiopia

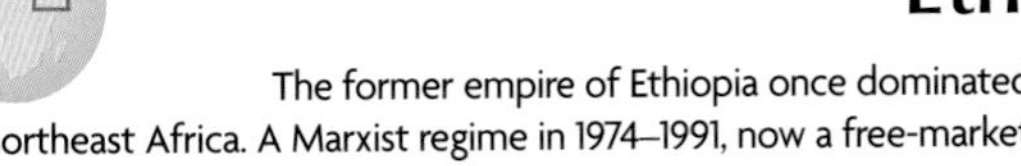

The former empire of Ethiopia once dominated northeast Africa. A Marxist regime in 1974–1991, now a free-market democracy, it has suffered economic, civil, and natural crises.

GEOGRAPHY

Great Rift Valley divides mountainous northwest region from desert lowlands in northeast and southeast. Ethiopian Plateau is drained mainly by the Blue Nile.

CLIMATE

Moderate, with summer rains. Highlands are warm, with night frost and snowfalls on the mountains.

PEOPLE & SOCIETY

76 Ethiopian nationalities speak 286 languages. Oromo (or Gallas) are the largest group. Ethnic representation is a major political issue. Orthodox Christianity has a very ancient history in Ethiopia. Former emperor Haile Selassie inspired Rastafarianism.

INSIGHT: *King Solomon and the Queen of Sheba are said to have founded the Kingdom of Abyssinia (Ethiopia) c. 1000 BCE*

THE ECONOMY

Overwhelmingly dependent on agriculture; coffee is main export crop. War-damaged infrastructure and periodic serious droughts and famines undermine growth. There is a heavy reliance on food aid. Landlocked since secession of Eritrea.

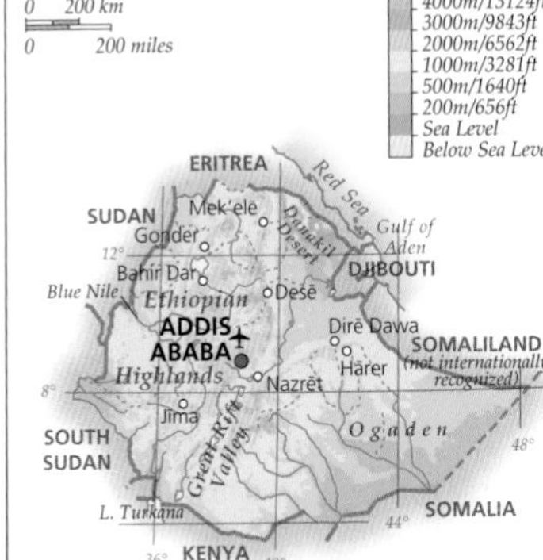
0 200 km
0 200 miles
4000m/13124ft
3000m/9843ft
2000m/6562ft
1000m/3281ft
500m/1640ft
200m/656ft
Sea Level
Below Sea Level
ERITREA
Red Sea
SUDAN
Mek'ele
Gonder
Danakil Desert
Gulf of Aden
12°
Bahir Dar
DJIBOUTI
Blue Nile
Ethiopian
Desē
ADDIS ABABA
Dirē Dawa
SOMALILAND
(not internationally recognized)
Harer
Highlands
Nazrēt
8°
Jīma
SOUTH SUDAN
Ogaden
Great Rift Valley
48°
L. Turkana
44°
SOMALIA
36°
KENYA
40°

FACTFILE

OFFICIAL NAME: Federal Democratic Republic of Ethiopia

DATE OF FORMATION: 1896

CAPITAL: Addis Ababa

POPULATION: 94.1 million

TOTAL AREA: 435,184 sq. miles (1,127,127 sq. km)

DENSITY: 220 people per sq. mile

LANGUAGES: Amharic*, Tigrinya, other

RELIGIONS: Orthodox Christian 40%, Muslim 40%, traditional beliefs 15%, other 5%

ETHNIC MIX: Oromo 40%, Amhara 25%, other 13%, Sidama 9%, Tigray 7%, Somali 6%

GOVERNMENT: Parliamentary system

CURRENCY: Birr = 100 cents

Fiji

A volcanic archipelago in the South Pacific, with two large islands and 880 islets. Tensions between native Fijians and the Indian minority have sparked a succession of coups.

GEOGRAPHY

Main islands are mountainous, fringed by coral reefs. Remainder are limestone and coral formations.

CLIMATE

Tropical. High temperatures all year round. Cyclones are a hazard.

PEOPLE & SOCIETY

The British introduced workers from India in the late 19th century, and by 1946 their descendants outnumbered the ethnic Fijians. Ethnic-Fijian nationalism is strong. Many Indo-Fijians left after the 1987 coup, restoring ethnic Fijians to a majority. The first Indo-Fijian-dominated government was ousted in 2000. The army led another coup in 2006: elections were held in 2014. Women are lobbying for more rights.

INSIGHT: *Both Fijians and Indians practice fire-walking; Indians walk on hot embers, Fijians on heated stones*

THE ECONOMY

Tourism was main sector, though damaged by instability. Coups have also caused international isolation. All sectors struggling: sugar production, gold mining, textiles, timber, and commercial fishing.

1000m/3281ft
500m/1640ft
Sea Level
PACIFIC OCEAN
16°
Vanua Levu
Labasa
Nabavatu
Yasawa Group
Nabouwalu
Bligh Water
Taveuni
Koro
Rakiraki
Lautoka
Ovalau
Viti Levu
Koro Sea
Lakeba Passage
18°
Gau
Sigatoka
SUVA
Lau Group
Kadavu Passage
Moala
Kadavu
178°E
180°
PACIFIC OCEAN
0 100 km
0 100 miles

FACTFILE

OFFICIAL NAME: Republic of Fiji
DATE OF FORMATION: 1970
CAPITAL: Suva
POPULATION: 900,000
TOTAL AREA: 7054 sq. miles (18,270 sq. km)
DENSITY: 128 people per sq. mile
LANGUAGES: Fijian, English*, Hindi, Urdu, Tamil, Telugu
RELIGIONS: Hindu 38%, Methodist 37%, Roman Catholic 9%, Muslim 8%, other 8%
ETHNIC MIX: Melanesian (Fijian) 51%, Indian 44%, other 5%
GOVERNMENT: Parliamentary system
CURRENCY: Fiji dollar = 100 cents

Finland

Finland's language and national identity have been influenced by both its Scandinavian and Russian neighbors. Once aligned with the USSR, Finland is now a member of the EU.

GEOGRAPHY

South and center are flat, with low hills and many lakes. Uplands and low mountains in the north. 60% of the land area is forested.

CLIMATE

Long, harsh winters with frequent snowfalls. Short, warmer summers. Rainfall is low, and decreases northward.

PEOPLE & SOCIETY

One in four of the population lives in the Greater Helsinki region. Swedish-speakers live mainly in the Åland Islands in the southwest. The Sámi (Lapps) lead a seminomadic existence inside the Arctic Circle. Women make up 48% of the labor force, continuing a long tradition of equality between the sexes. Finnish women were the first in Europe to get the vote, in 1906, and the first in the world able to stand for parliament. Families tend to be close-knit.

THE ECONOMY

Strong engineering and electronics sectors: home of Nokia. Wood, pulp, and paper production.

INSIGHT: *Finland has Europe's largest inland waterway system*

500m/1640ft
200m/656ft
Sea Level
0 100 km
0 100 miles
70°
NORWAY
Inarijärvi
Lapland
SWEDEN
RUSS. FED.
Arctic Circle
Rovaniemi
65°
Oulu
Gulf of Bothnia
Vaasa
Kuopio
Joensuu
Jyväskylä
Haukivesi
Pori
Tampere
Saimaa
Lahti
Turku
30°
Åland
Kotka
60°
Espoo
HELSINKI
20°
Baltic Sea
25°

FACTFILE

OFFICIAL NAME: Republic of Finland
DATE OF FORMATION: 1917
CAPITAL: Helsinki
POPULATION: 5.4 million
TOTAL AREA: 130,127 sq. miles (337,030 sq. km)
DENSITY: 46 people per sq. mile
LANGUAGES: Finnish*, Swedish*, Sámi
RELIGIONS: Evangelical Lutheran 83%, other 15%, Orthodox Christian 1%, Roman Catholic 1%
ETHNIC MIX: Finnish 93%, other (including Sámi) 7%
GOVERNMENT: Parliamentary system
CURRENCY: Euro = 100 cents

France

Stretching across western Europe, from the English Channel (la Manche) to the Mediterranean Sea, France was Europe's first modern republic, and is still a leading industrial power.

GEOGRAPHY

Broad plain covers northern half of the country. High mountain ranges in the east and southwest, with a mountainous plateau in the center.

CLIMATE

Three main climates: temperate and damp northwest; continental east; and Mediterranean south.

PEOPLE & SOCIETY

Strong national identity coexists with pronounced regional differences, including local languages. Immigration laws have been tightened since the 1970s, but ethnic minorities growing up in city suburbs feel increasingly alienated. Wearing the veil is banned in public. New equality laws are under debate.

INSIGHT: *France is the most popular tourist destination in the world, with over 80 million visitors a year*

THE ECONOMY

Chemicals, electronics, heavy engineering, cars, and aircraft typify a strong and diversified export sector. World leader in cosmetics, perfumes, and quality wines. Modernized agriculture.

Calais
Lille
English Channel
BELGIUM
Channel Is. (to UK)
Le Havre
Amiens
LUX.
Rouen
Reims
GERMANY
Caen
PARIS
Strasbourg
Brest
Versailles
Le Mans
Nancy
Rennes
Orléans
Mulhouse
Rhine
Loire
Tours
Dijon
Nantes
Besançon
SWITZ.
L. Geneva
Bay of Biscay
Clermont-Ferrand
Mâcon
Limoges
Lyon
Cognac
Massif Central
St.-Étienne
Grenoble
Bordeaux
ITALY
Rhône
Alps
Avignon
Aix-en-Provence
Montpellier
MONACO
Biarritz
Toulouse
Nice
Marseille
Cannes
Pyrenees
Toulon
SPAIN
ANDORRA
Perpignan
Corse (Corsica)
Mediterranean Sea
3000m/9843ft
2000m/6562ft
1000m/3281ft
500m/1640ft
200m/656ft
Sea Level
0 100 km
0 100 miles

FACTFILE

OFFICIAL NAME: French Republic
DATE OF FORMATION: 987
CAPITAL: Paris
POPULATION: 64.3 million
TOTAL AREA: 211,208 sq. miles (547,030 sq. km)
DENSITY: 303 people per sq. mile
LANGUAGES: French*, Provençal, German, Breton, Catalan, Basque
RELIGIONS: Roman Catholic 88%, Muslim 8%, Protestant 2%, Jewish 1%, Buddhist 1%
ETHNIC MIX: French 90%, North African 6%, German (Alsace) 2%, Breton 1%, other 1%
GOVERNMENT: Mixed presidential–parliamentary system
CURRENCY: Euro = 100 cents

Gabon

Gabon is a former French colony straddling the equator on Africa's west coast. Independent since 1960, it returned to multiparty politics in 1990, after 22 years of one-party rule.

GEOGRAPHY

Low plateaus and mountains lie beyond the coastal strip. Two-thirds of the land is covered by rainforest.

CLIMATE

Hot and tropical, with little distinction between seasons. Cold Benguela current cools the coast.

PEOPLE & SOCIETY

Some 40 different languages are spoken. The Fang, who live mainly in the north, are the largest ethnic group, but have yet to gain control of the government. Oil wealth has led to the growth of an affluent middle class, but one in three people still live in poverty. Menial jobs are done by immigrant workers. Education follows the French system. With 87% of people living in towns, Gabon is one of Africa's most urbanized countries. The government is encouraging population growth.

THE ECONOMY

Oil accounts for 75% of exports, but reserves are dwindling: not much post-oil planning. High debt problem. Tropical hardwoods and manganese.

INSIGHT: *Libreville was founded as a settlement for freed French slaves in 1849*

CAMEROON
EQUATORIAL GUINEA
Oyem
CONGO
Makokou
LIBREVILLE
Equator
Port-Gentil
Ogooué
Lambaréné
Koulamoutou
Moanda
Franceville
Mouila
Tchibanga
CONGO
ATLANTIC OCEAN
12°
0 100 km
0 100 miles
500m/1640ft
200m/656ft
Sea Level

FACTFILE

OFFICIAL NAME: Gabonese Republic
DATE OF FORMATION: 1960
CAPITAL: Libreville
POPULATION: 1.7 million
TOTAL AREA: 103,346 sq. miles (267,667 sq. km)
DENSITY: 17 people per sq. mile
LANGUAGES: Fang, French*, Punu, Sira, Nzebi, Mpongwe
RELIGIONS: Christian (mainly Roman Catholic) 55%, traditional beliefs 40%, other 4%, Muslim 1%
ETHNIC MIX: Fang 26%, Shira-punu 24%, other 24%, foreign residents 15%, Nzabi-duma 11%
GOVERNMENT: Presidential system
CURRENCY: CFA franc = 100 centimes

Gambia

Gambia is a riverbank state on the west coast of Africa, almost entirely surrounded by Senegal. It was renowned for its stability until its government was overthrown in a coup in 1994.

GEOGRAPHY

Located on the narrow strip of land bordering the Gambia River. Long, sandy beaches are backed by mangrove swamps along the river. Savanna and tropical forests higher up.

CLIMATE

Subtropical, with wet, humid months July–October, and warm, dry season November–May.

PEOPLE & SOCIETY

Little tension between various ethnic groups. The largest group, the Mandinka, has traditionally held power. Islam is a strong social influence, though there is no official state religion. A small expatriate community from the UK lives on the coast. Seasonal migrants come from neighboring states to harvest groundnuts each year. Women are active as traders. Yahya Jammeh, who led the 1994 coup, is still the elected president.

THE ECONOMY

Around 75% of the labor force is involved in agriculture. Groundnuts are the principal crop. Fish stocks are declining. Eco-tourism is promoted, though most visitors come for the beaches. Banjul is one of west Africa's finest deepwater ports: significant re-export trade. Smuggling problems.

INSIGHT: *Overfishing in the waters off Gambia and Senegal, mainly by foreign vessels, is a growing problem*

SENEGAL
16°
15°
14°
Bakau
BANJUL
Serekunda
Brikama
Gunjur
Farafenni
Gambia
Georgetown
Basse
Santa Su
SENEGAL
ATLANTIC OCEAN
0 50 km
0 50 miles
200m/656ft
Sea Level

FACTFILE

OFFICIAL NAME: Republic of the Gambia

DATE OF FORMATION: 1965

CAPITAL: Banjul

POPULATION: 1.8 million

TOTAL AREA: 4363 sq. miles (11,300 sq. km)

DENSITY: 466 people per sq. mile

LANGUAGES: Mandinka, Fulani, Wolof, Jola, Soninke, English*

RELIGIONS: Sunni Muslim 90%, Christian 8%, traditional beliefs 2%

ETHNIC MIX: Mandinka 42%, Fulani 18%, Wolof 16%, Jola 10%, Serahuli 9%, other 5%

GOVERNMENT: Presidential system

CURRENCY: Dalasi = 100 butut

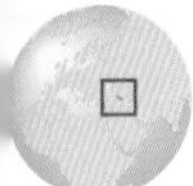

Georgia

Located on the eastern shore of the Black Sea, Georgia has been torn by civil war and ethnic disputes since achieving independence from the Soviet Union in 1991.

GEOGRAPHY

Kura Valley lies between Caucasus Mountains in the north and Lesser Caucasus range in south. Lowlands along the Black Sea coast.

CLIMATE

Subtropical along the coast, changing to continental extremes at high altitudes. Rainfall is moderate.

PEOPLE & SOCIETY

Paternalistic society, with strong family, cultural, and literary traditions. Georgia was converted to Christianity in 326 CE. Armenians in the south are the poorest group. Civil conflicts in the early 1990s against Abkhaz and Osset separatists displaced 300,000 people. Abkhazia and South Ossetia now effectively operate as separate states, backed up by Russian forces since the 2008 war. Russia opposes Georgian hopes of joining the EU and NATO.

THE ECONOMY

Transit revenues from pipelines taking oil to the West. Long-established and booming wine industry. Political instability. Fast pace of reforms in late 2000s, at cost of high unemployment.

INSIGHT: *Western Georgia was the land of the legendary Golden Fleece of Greek mythology*

RUSSIAN FEDERATION
Caucasus
Sokhumi
Zugdidi
Black Sea
Poti
Kutaisi
Samt'redia
Tskhinvali
Gori
Telavi
Batumi
Kura
Akhaltsikhe
TBILISI
Rustavi
Lesser Caucasus
TURKEY
ARMENIA
AZERBAIJAN
40°
42°
44°
46°
3000m/9843ft
2000m/6562ft
1000m/3281ft
500m/1640ft
200m/656ft
Sea Level
0 100 km
0 100 miles

FACTFILE

OFFICIAL NAME: Georgia
DATE OF FORMATION: 1991
CAPITAL: Tbilisi
POPULATION: 4.3 million
TOTAL AREA: 26,911 sq. miles (69,700 sq. km)
DENSITY: 160 people per sq. mile
LANGUAGES: Georgian*, Russian, Azeri, Armenian, Mingrelian, Ossetian, Abkhazian
RELIGIONS: Georgian Orthodox 74%, Muslim 10%, Russian Orthodox 10%, Armenian Apostolic Church (Orthodox) 4%, other 2%
ETHNIC MIX: Georgian 84%, Armenian 6%, Azeri 6%, Russian 2%, Ossetian 1%, other 1%
GOVERNMENT: Presidential system
CURRENCY: Lari = 100 tetri

Germany

Europe's strongest industrial power and its most populous nation, Germany was divided after military defeat in 1945 into a free-market west and a communist east, but reunified in 1990.

GEOGRAPHY

Central European coastal plains in the north, rising to rolling hills of central region and Alps in far south.

CLIMATE

Damp, temperate in northern and central regions. Continental extremes in mountainous south.

PEOPLE & SOCIETY

Regionalism is strong. The north is mainly Protestant, while the south is staunchly Roman Catholic. Social and economic differences still exist between east and west. Turks are the largest single ethnic minority; many came as guest workers in the 1950s–1970s. Immigration rules now favor skilled workers. Feminism is strong.

INSIGHT: *Germany's rivers and canals carry as much freight as its busy highways*

THE ECONOMY

Major exporter of electronics, heavy engineering, chemicals, and cars. Worst recession for 60 years in 2008–2009. Aging population.

DENMARK
Baltic Sea
Kiel
Rostock
North Sea
54°
Hamburg
Lübeck
POLAND
Bremen
Elbe
Oder
NETHER-
LANDS
Hannover
BERLIN
52°
Magdeburg
Duisburg
Dortmund
Essen
Kassel
Leipzig
Düsseldorf
Köln
Erfurt
Dresden
Bonn
Chemnitz
BELGIUM
Rhine
Frankfurt am Main
14°
50°
CZECH REPUBLIC
LUX.
Mannheim
Nürnberg
6°
Danube
FRANCE
Stuttgart
Rhine
München
14°
48°
SWITZ.
Bavarian Alps
AUSTRIA
8°
10°
12°
2000m/6562ft
1000m/3281ft
500m/1640ft
200m/656ft
Sea Level
0 100 km
0 100 miles

FACTFILE

OFFICIAL NAME: Federal Republic of Germany

DATE OF FORMATION: 1871

CAPITAL: Berlin

POPULATION: 82.7 million

TOTAL AREA: 137,846 sq. miles (357,021 sq. km)

DENSITY: 613 people per sq. mile

LANGUAGES: German*, Turkish

RELIGIONS: Protestant 34%, Roman Catholic 33%, other 30%, Muslim 3%

ETHNIC MIX: German 92%, other 3%, other European 3%, Turkish 2%

GOVERNMENT: Parliamentary system

CURRENCY: Euro = 100 cents

Ghana

The heartland of the ancient Ashanti kingdom, Ghana in west Africa was once known as the Gold Coast. It has experienced intermittent periods of military rule since independence in 1957.

GEOGRAPHY

Mostly low-lying. The west is covered by rainforest. One of the world's largest artificial lakes – Lake Volta – was created by damming the White Volta River.

CLIMATE

Tropical. There are two wet seasons in the south, but the north is drier, and has just one.

PEOPLE & SOCIETY

Around 75 cultural-linguistic groups. The largest is the Akan, who include the Ashanti and Fanti peoples. Southern peoples are richer and more urban than those of the north. There are few tribal tensions. Family ties are strong. Women play a major role in market trading. The 2000 election saw Ghana's first peaceful handover of power. Poverty levels have been significantly reduced.

THE ECONOMY

World's second-largest cocoa producer. Oil discovered in 2007: on stream from 2010. Hardwood trees such as maple and sapele. Gold mining.

INSIGHT: *Ghana was the first colony in west Africa to gain independence*

BURKINA FASO
2°
0°
0 100 km
0 100 miles
Bolgatanga
Wa
10°
White Volta
Black Volta
Tamale
CÔTE D'IVOIRE (IVORY COAST)
8°
Lake Volta
Sunyani
TOGO
Kumasi
Koforidua
Volta
6°
Asamankese
Nsawam
Tema
Cape Coast
ACCRA
Sekondi-Takoradi
Gold Coast
Gulf of Guinea
ATLANTIC OCEAN
500m/1640ft
200m/656ft
Sea Level

FACTFILE

OFFICIAL NAME: Republic of Ghana
DATE OF FORMATION: 1957
CAPITAL: Accra
POPULATION: 25.9 million
TOTAL AREA: 92,100 sq. miles (238,540 sq. km)
DENSITY: 292 people per sq. mile
LANGUAGES: Twi, Fanti, Ewe, Ga, Adangbe, Gurma, Dagomba (Dagbani), English*
RELIGIONS: Christian 69%, Muslim 16%, traditional beliefs 9%, other 6%
ETHNIC MIX: Akan 49%, Mole-Dagbani 17%, Ewe 13%, other 13%, Ga and Ga-Adangbe 8%
GOVERNMENT: Presidential system
CURRENCY: Cedi = 100 pesewas

Greece

The Balkan state of Greece is bounded on three sides by the Mediterranean, Aegean, and Ionian seas. It has a strong seafaring tradition, with some of the world's richest shipowners.

GEOGRAPHY

Mountainous peninsula and over 2000 islands. Large plain along the mainland's Aegean coast.

CLIMATE

Mainly Mediterranean, with dry, hot summers. Alpine climate in northern mountain areas.

PEOPLE & SOCIETY

Postwar industrial development altered the dominance of agriculture and seafaring. Rural exodus to cities has been stemmed but a third of the population lives in Athens. Age-old culture and Greek Orthodox Church balance social mobility. Civil marriage and divorce only legalized in 1982. There has been much recent civil unrest against severe austerity measures.

INSIGHT: *The modern Olympics, first held in Athens in 1896, evolved from Olympia's ancient Greek games*

THE ECONOMY

Public debt and budget deficit very high: EU bailouts to avoid bankruptcy. World's largest shipping fleet. One of Europe's top tourist destinations. Fruit, vegetables, olives. Large black economy.

BULGARIA
MACEDONIA
TURKEY
ALBANIA
Dráma
Xánthi
Sérres
Thessaloníki
Alexandroúpoli
Kateríni
Thracian Sea
Límnos
Ioánnina
Lárisa
Kérkyra (Corfu)
Kérkyra
Vólos
Vóreies Sporádes
Lésvos
Pindos
Lamía
Aegean Sea
Kefalloniá
Pátra
Peiraías
ATHENS
Chíos
Kórinthos
Sámos
Zákynthos
Isthmós Korinthou
Ionian Sea
Pelopónnisos
Náxos
Kalámata
Kos
Sea of Crete
Ródos
Mediterranean Sea
Chaniá
Irákleio
Kárpathos
Kríti (Crete)
40°
20°
38°
22°
36°
24°
26°
28°
2000m/6562ft
1000m/3281ft
500m/1640ft
200m/656ft
Sea Level
0 100 km
0 100 miles

FACTFILE

OFFICIAL NAME: Hellenic Republic
DATE OF FORMATION: 1829
CAPITAL: Athens
POPULATION: 11.1 million
TOTAL AREA: 50,942 sq. miles (131,940 sq. km)
DENSITY: 220 people per sq. mile
LANGUAGES: Greek*, Turkish, Macedonian, Albanian
RELIGIONS: Orthodox Christian 98%, Muslim 1%, other 1%
ETHNIC MIX: Greek 98%, other 2%
GOVERNMENT: Parliamentary system
CURRENCY: Euro = 100 cents

Grenada

The southernmost of the Windward Islands, Grenada made world headlines in 1983 when the US and Caribbean allies mounted an invasion to sever links with Castro's Cuba.

GEOGRAPHY

Volcanic in origin, with densely forested central mountains. Its territory also includes the islands of Carriacou and Petite Martinique.

CLIMATE

Tropical, tempered by trade winds. Hurricanes are a hazard in the July–November wet season.

PEOPLE & SOCIETY

Grenadians are mainly of African origin; their traditions remain strong, especially on Carriacou. Inter-ethnic marriage has reduced tensions between the groups. Extended families, often headed by women, are the norm. Wealth disparities are not marked, but levels of poverty are growing.

INSIGHT: *Known as "the spice island of the Caribbean," it is the world's second-largest nutmeg producer*

THE ECONOMY

Severe damage from Hurricane Ivan in 2004 to crops and 90% of buildings; reconstruction taking years. Nutmeg, cocoa, bananas, and mace. Smuggling is a serious problem.

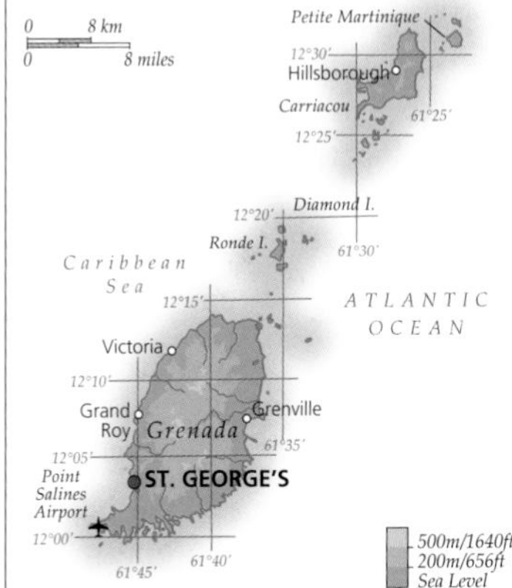
0 8 km
0 8 miles
Petite Martinique
12°30'
Hillsborough
Carriacou
61°25'
12°25'
Diamond I.
12°20'
Ronde I.
61°30'
Caribbean Sea
ATLANTIC OCEAN
12°15'
Victoria
12°10'
Grand Roy
Grenada
Grenville
61°35'
12°05'
ST. GEORGE'S
Point Salines Airport
12°00'
61°45'
61°40'
500m/1640ft
200m/656ft
Sea Level

FACTFILE

OFFICIAL NAME: Grenada
DATE OF FORMATION: 1974
CAPITAL: St. George's
POPULATION: 109,590
TOTAL AREA: 131 sq. miles (340 sq. km)
DENSITY: 837 people per sq. mile
LANGUAGES: English*, English Creole
RELIGIONS: Roman Catholic 68%, Anglican 17%, other 15%
ETHNIC MIX: Black African 82%, *Mulatto* (mixed race) 13%, East Indian 3%, other 2%
GOVERNMENT: Parliamentary system
CURRENCY: East Caribbean dollar = 100 cents

Guatemala

The largest and most populous nation on the Central American isthmus, Guatemala returned to civilian rule in 1986 after 32 years of violent and repressive military rule.

GEOGRAPHY

Narrow Pacific coastal plain. Central highlands with volcanoes. Short coast on the Caribbean Sea. Tropical rainforests in the north.

CLIMATE

Tropical: hot and humid in coastal regions and north. More temperate in central highlands.

PEOPLE & SOCIETY

Amerindians, concentrated in the highlands, form a majority. Power, wealth, and land are controlled by *ladinos* (Westernized Amerindians and *mestizos*). Catholicism is predominant, mixed with Amerindian beliefs. Literacy is low. A quarter of the population live on less than $2 a day. Violent crime is a problem.

INSIGHT: *Guatemala, which means "land of trees," was the center of the ancient Mayan civilization*

THE ECONOMY

Coffee, sugar, and bananas are top exports. Tourism. Damage from natural disasters. Marked wealth inequalities inhibit domestic market.

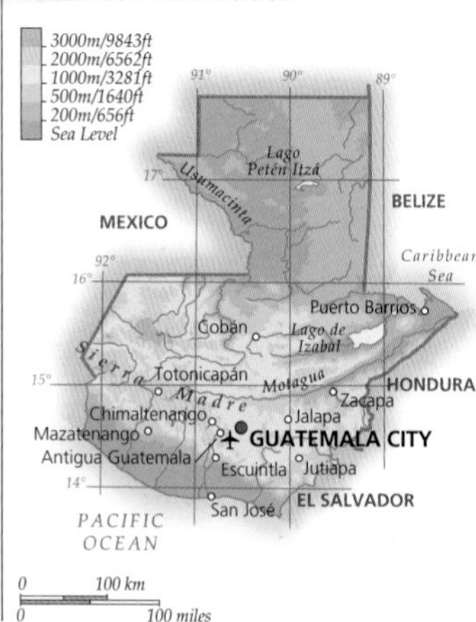
3000m/9843ft
2000m/6562ft
1000m/3281ft
500m/1640ft
200m/656ft
Sea Level
91°
90°
89°
17°
92°
16°
15°
14°
Lago Petén Itzá
Usumacinta
MEXICO
BELIZE
Caribbean Sea
Puerto Barrios
Cobán
Lago de Izabal
Sierra Madre
Totonicapán
Motagua
Zacapa
HONDURAS
Chimaltenango
Jalapa
Mazatenango
GUATEMALA CITY
Antigua Guatemala
Escuintla
Jutiapa
San José
EL SALVADOR
PACIFIC OCEAN
0
100 km
0
100 miles

FACTFILE

OFFICIAL NAME: Republic of Guatemala
DATE OF FORMATION: 1838
CAPITAL: Guatemala City
POPULATION: 15.5 million
TOTAL AREA: 42,042 sq. miles (108,890 sq. km)
DENSITY: 370 people per sq. mile
LANGUAGES: Quiché, Mam, Cakchiquel, Kekchí, Spanish*
RELIGIONS: Roman Catholic 65%, Protestant 33%, other and nonreligious 2%
ETHNIC MIX: Amerindian 60%, *Mestizo* (European–Amerindian) 30%, other 10%
GOVERNMENT: Presidential system
CURRENCY: Quetzal = 100 centavos

Guinea

Located on the west coast of Africa, Guinea was the first French colony in Africa to gain independence, in 1958. The country was under military rule in 1984–1995 and 2008–2010.

GEOGRAPHY

Coastal plains and mangrove swamps in west rise to forested or savanna highlands in the south. Semidesert in the north.

CLIMATE

Tropical, with a wet season April–October. Conakry is especially rainy. Hot, dry *harmattan* wind blows from Sahara during dry season.

PEOPLE & SOCIETY

Peul and Malinké make up most of the population, but rivalries between them have allowed coastal peoples such as the Soussou to dominate politics. Daily life revolves around the extended family. Women acquired influence under Marxist party rule between 1958 and 1984, but the Muslim revival since then has reversed the trend. Private enterprise has created a business class. A deadly Ebola outbreak hit the country in 2014.

THE ECONOMY

Substantial gold, diamond, and especially bauxite reserves. Cash crops: bananas, coffee, pineapples, palm oil. Poor infrastructure. Instability.

INSIGHT: *The colors of Guinea's flag represent the three words of the country's motto: work (red), justice (yellow), and solidarity (green)*

SENEGAL
MALI
GUINEA-BISSAU
Fouta Djallon
Labé
Siguiri
Niger
Niger
Boké
Kindia
Kankan
10°
CONAKRY
CÔTE D'IVOIRE (IVORY COAST)
ATLANTIC OCEAN
12°
SIERRA LEONE
Kissidougou
Nzérékoré
LIBERIA
8°
1000m/3281ft
500m/1640ft
200m/656ft
Sea Level
0 100 km
0 100 miles

FACTFILE

OFFICIAL NAME: Republic of Guinea
DATE OF FORMATION: 1958
CAPITAL: Conakry
POPULATION: 11.7 million
TOTAL AREA: 94,925 sq. miles (245,857 sq. km)
DENSITY: 123 people per sq. mile
LANGUAGES: Pulaar, Malinké, Soussou, French*
RELIGIONS: Muslim 85%, Christian 8% traditional beliefs 7%
ETHNIC MIX: Peul 40%, Malinké 30%, Soussou 20%, other 10%
GOVERNMENT: Presidential system
CURRENCY: Guinea franc = 100 centimes

Guinea-Bissau

Known as Portuguese Guinea while a colony, Guinea-Bissau lies on Africa's west coast. Since 1994, its nascent democracy has been plagued by coups and rebellions.

GEOGRAPHY

Low-lying, apart from savanna highlands in northeast. Rainforests and swamps are found along coastal areas.

CLIMATE

Tropical, with wet season May-November and dry season December-April. Hot, dry *harmattan* desert wind blows during dry season.

PEOPLE & SOCIETY

The largest ethnic group is the Balante, who live in the south. Though only around 1% of the population, the mixed race Portuguese–African *mestiços* dominate the top ranks of government and bureaucracy. Most people live and work on small family farms, grouped in self-contained villages. The bulk of the urban population live in Bissau, where they face economic hardship. Narcotics traffickers are taking advantage of the ongoing instability.

THE ECONOMY

Mostly subsistence farming. Lack of sufficiency in rice staple. Main cash crop is cashew nuts. Major cocaine transit route from South America to Europe. Offshore oil as yet untapped. Fisheries and timber potential.

INSIGHT: *In 1974, Guinea-Bissau became the first Portuguese colony to gain independence*

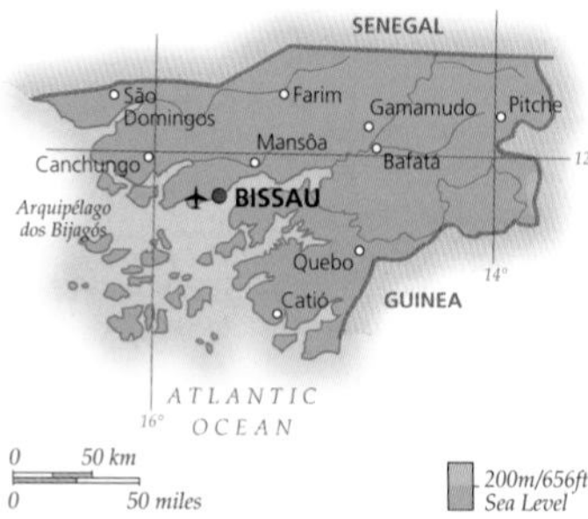

SENEGAL
São Domingos
Farim
Gamamudo
Pitche
Mansôa
Canchungo
Bafatá
12°
Arquipélago dos Bijagós
BISSAU
Quebo
14°
Catió
GUINEA
ATLANTIC OCEAN
16°
0 50 km
0 50 miles
200m/656ft
Sea Level

FACTFILE

OFFICIAL NAME: Republic of Guinea-Bissau

DATE OF FORMATION: 1974

CAPITAL: Bissau

POPULATION: 1.7 million

TOTAL AREA: 13,946 sq. miles (36,120 sq. km)

DENSITY: 157 people per sq. mile

LANGUAGES: Portuguese Creole, Balante, Fulani, Malinké, Portuguese*

RELIGIONS: Traditional beliefs 50%, Muslim 40%, Christian 10%

ETHNIC MIX: Balante 30%, Fulani 20%, other 16%, Mandyako 14%, Mandinka 13%, Papel 7%

GOVERNMENT: Presidential system

CURRENCY: CFA franc = 100 centimes

Guyana

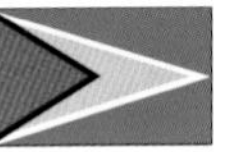

On the northeast coast of South America, Guyana is the continent's only English-speaking country. Independent since 1966, it has close ties with the anglophone Caribbean.

GEOGRAPHY

Mainly artificial coast, reclaimed by dikes and dams from swamps and tidal marshes. Forests cover 85% of the interior, rising to savanna uplands and mountains.

CLIMATE

Tropical. Coast cooled by sea breezes. Lowlands are hot, wet, and humid. Highlands are a little cooler.

PEOPLE & SOCIETY

Guyana is a complex multiracial society. Tension exists between the Afro-Guyanese, descended from slaves, and the Indo-Guyanese, descendants of laborers brought over after slavery was abolished. Politics is highly polarized around this split and has often spilled over into violence on the streets. Amerindian subsistence farmers are the poorest people in society and have little representation.

THE ECONOMY

Diverse exports: gold, sugar, fish, bauxite, rice, timber, diamonds. Debt relief granted. Narcotics transit zone.

INSIGHT: *Guyana means "land of many waters," reflecting its dense network of rivers*

ATLANTIC OCEAN
VENEZUELA
Spring Garden
GEORGETOWN
Bartica
New Amsterdam
Linden
Corriverton
Guiana Highlands
Courantyne
BRAZIL
SURINAME
Essequibo
(claimed by Suriname)
(claimed by Venezuela)
8°
6°
4°
2°
60°
58°
1000m/3281ft
500m/1640ft
200m/656ft
Sea Level
0 100 km
0 100 miles

FACTFILE

OFFICIAL NAME: Cooperative Republic of Guyana

DATE OF FORMATION: 1966

CAPITAL: Georgetown

POPULATION: 800,000

TOTAL AREA: 83,000 sq. miles (214,970 sq. km)

DENSITY: 11 people per sq. mile

LANGUAGES: English Creole, Hindi, Tamil, Amerindian languages, English*

RELIGIONS: Christian 57%, Hindu 28%, Muslim 10%, other 5%

ETHNIC MIX: East Indian 43%, Black African 30%, mixed race 17%, Amerindian 9%, other 1%

GOVERNMENT: Presidential system

CURRENCY: Guyanese dollar = 100 cents

Haiti

Formerly a French colony, Haiti shares the Caribbean island of Hispaniola with the Dominican Republic. At independence in 1804, it became the world's first black republic.

GEOGRAPHY

Predominantly mountainous, with forests and fertile plains.

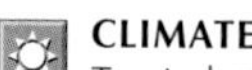

CLIMATE

Tropical, with rain throughout the year. Humid in coastal areas, much cooler in the mountains.

PEOPLE & SOCIETY

Most Haitians are of African descent. A few have European roots, primarily French. The rigid class structure maintains vast disparities of wealth. The majority of the population live in extreme poverty; Haiti is one of the poorest countries in the Americas. A combination of political oppression and a collapsing economy led thousands to seek asylum in the US or the Dominican Republic. Though most are Christians, many Haitians practice Voodoo, which was recognized as an official religion in 2003.

THE ECONOMY

Fragile economy completely shattered by 2010 earthquake. Ongoing problems of instability, hurricane damage, high unemployment, narcotics trafficking.

INSIGHT: *A slave rebellion headed by Toussaint Louverture in 1791 led to Haiti's independence*

Île de la Tortue
ATLANTIC OCEAN
20°
Port-de-Paix
Cap-Haïtien
Limbé
Fort-Liberté
1000m/3281ft
500m/1640ft
200m/656ft
Sea Level
Massif du Nord
Gonaïves
Golfe de la Gonâve
Desdunes
St-Marc
Hinche
Petite-Rivière-de-l'Artibonite
19°
Île de la Gonâve
DOMINICAN REP.
Jérémie
PORT-AU-PRINCE
Pétionville
Massif de la Hotte
Cayes
Jacmel
18°
Caribbean Sea
74°
72°
0 50 km
0 50 miles

FACTFILE

OFFICIAL NAME: Republic of Haiti
DATE OF FORMATION: 1804
CAPITAL: Port-au-Prince
POPULATION: 10.3 million
TOTAL AREA: 10,714 sq. miles (27,750 sq. km)
DENSITY: 968 people per sq. mile
LANGUAGES: French Creole*, French*
RELIGIONS: Roman Catholic 55%, Protestant 28%, other (including Voodoo) 16%, nonreligious 1%
ETHNIC MIX: Black African 95%, *Mulatto* (mixed race) and European 5%
GOVERNMENT: Presidential system
CURRENCY: Gourde = 100 centimes

Honduras

Straddling the Central American isthmus, Honduras returned to democratic rule in 1984, after a period of military government. Hurricane Mitch devastated the country in 1998.

GEOGRAPHY

Narrow plains along both coasts, with a mountainous interior, cut by river valleys. Tropical forests, swamps, and lagoons in the east.

CLIMATE

Tropical coastal lowlands are hot and humid, with May–October rains. Interior is cooler and drier.

PEOPLE & SOCIETY

The majority of the population is *mestizo* (mixed European–Amerindian). An English-speaking *garífuna* (black) community and Miskito Amerindians struggle to preserve their rights to land along the remote Caribbean coast. Women's status remains low. Wealth inequalities are large and poverty is at the root of social tension. Two-thirds of the population live in poverty. The army ousted the president in 2009. Violent crime is a major issue.

THE ECONOMY

Garments, coffee, bananas, and shellfish are exported. Remittances account for a fifth of GDP. Debt relief from 2005. Mineral potential. High underemployment and corruption.

INSIGHT: *The Honduran currency is named after a Lenca Indian chief who was the main leader of resistance to the Spanish conquest in the 16th century*

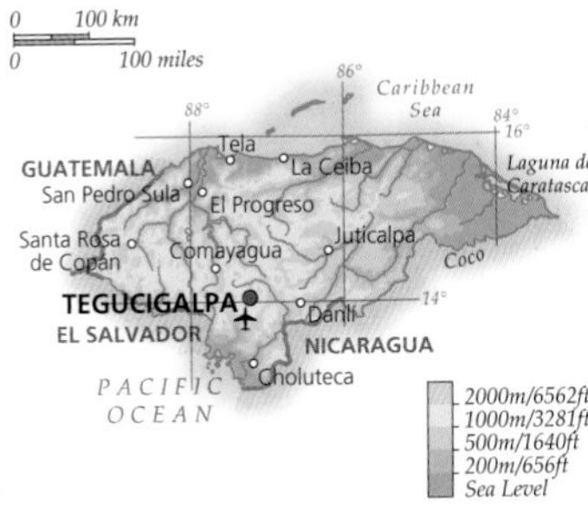
0 100 km
0 100 miles
Caribbean Sea
88°
86°
84°
16°
14°
Tela
La Ceiba
Laguna de Caratasca
GUATEMALA
San Pedro Sula
El Progreso
Santa Rosa de Copán
Comayagua
Juticalpa
Coco
TEGUCIGALPA
Danlí
EL SALVADOR
NICARAGUA
Choluteca
PACIFIC OCEAN
2000m/6562ft
1000m/3281ft
500m/1640ft
200m/656ft
Sea Level

FACTFILE

OFFICIAL NAME: Republic of Honduras
DATE OF FORMATION: 1838
CAPITAL: Tegucigalpa
POPULATION: 8.1 million
TOTAL AREA: 43,278 sq. miles (112,090 sq. km)
DENSITY: 187 people per sq. mile
LANGUAGES: Spanish*, Garífuna (Carib), English Creole
RELIGIONS: Roman Catholic 97%, Protestant 3%
ETHNIC MIX: *Mestizo* 90%, Black African 5%, Amerindian 4%, White 1%
GOVERNMENT: Presidential system
CURRENCY: Lempira = 100 centavos

Hungary

Landlocked in central Europe, Hungary was one of the twin centers of the once-great Habsburg Empire. It lost two-thirds of its historical territory for supporting Germany in WW I.

GEOGRAPHY

Landlocked. Fertile plains in east and northwest; west and north are hilly. The Danube River cuts through the country and the capital.

CLIMATE

Continental, with wet springs, late but very hot summers, and cold, cloudy winters. The transition between seasons tends to be sudden.

PEOPLE & SOCIETY

Hungary's population has been shrinking since the 1980s. Mostly ethnic Hungarian (Magyar), there are small minorities of Germans, Jews, and neighboring peoples. Roma face particular discrimination. The government is greatly concerned about the fate of ethnic Hungarians in Romania, Serbia, and Slovakia. Hungary joined the EU in 2004. Working hours are longer than in western Europe.

THE ECONOMY

Strong industrial base. Hard-hit by 2007–2009 global downturn: currency plummeted. IMF bailout to avoid meltdown. Spending cuts. Fast growth in 2014. No date set for joining euro.

INSIGHT: *The Hungarian language is Asian in origin and is most closely related to Finnish*

SLOVAKIA
UKRAINE
AUST.
SLOVENIA
CROATIA
SERBIA
ROMANIA
Miskolc
Nyíregyháza
Debrecen
Győr
Danube
Tatabánya
BUDAPEST
Szombathely
Szolnok
Székesfehérvár
Balaton
Kecskemét
Békéscsaba
Nagykanizsa
Szeged
Pécs
18°
20°
22°
48°
46°
0 50 km
0 50 miles
500m/1640ft
200m/656ft
Sea Level

FACTFILE

OFFICIAL NAME: Hungary
DATE OF FORMATION: 1918
CAPITAL: Budapest
POPULATION: 10 million
TOTAL AREA: 35,919 sq. miles (93,030 sq. km)
DENSITY: 280 people per sq. mile
LANGUAGES: Hungarian (Magyar)*
RELIGIONS: Roman Catholic 52%, Calvinist 16%, other 15%, nonreligious 14%, Lutheran 3%
ETHNIC MIX: Magyar 90%, Roma 4%, German 3%, Serb 2%, other 1%
GOVERNMENT: Parliamentary system
CURRENCY: Forint = 100 fillér

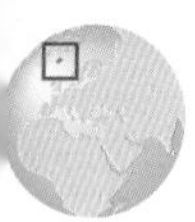

Iceland

Europe's westernmost country, Iceland's strategic ocean location straddles the Mid-Atlantic Ridge. Its spectacular landscape is largely uninhabited, aside from coastal towns.

GEOGRAPHY

Grassy coastal lowlands, with fjords in the north. Central plateau of cold lava desert, geothermal springs, and glaciers. Around 200 volcanoes, with numerous geysers and solfataras.

CLIMATE

Its location in the middle of the Gulf Stream moderates the climate. Mild winters and brief, cool summers.

PEOPLE & SOCIETY

Icelanders share a strong national identity, with few foreign residents. Their language has changed little in 700 years, in part due to the country's isolation. There is high social mobility, free health care, and low-cost heating (geothermal and hydropower). Iceland's recent banking collapse and near financial ruin has swung the long-running debate over EU membership in favor of joining.

THE ECONOMY

Once reliant on fish. Aluminum smelting. Tourism. Banks overexposed in 2007–2009 global downturn. Nation bankrupt, króna depreciated 90%.

INSIGHT: *The word geyser is taken from Geysir (the "gusher") in southwest Iceland*

Denmark Strait
Arctic Circle
0 50 km
0 50 miles
Norwegian Sea
24°
Akureyri
Húsavík
Akranes
Keflavík
REYKJAVÍK
Kópavogur
Hafnarfjörður
Selfoss
66°
Egilsstaðir
22°
Vestmannaeyjar
Vatnajökull
20°
18°
16°
64°
14°
ATLANTIC OCEAN
1000m/3281ft
500m/1640ft
200m/656ft
Sea Level
Ice Cap

FACTFILE

OFFICIAL NAME: Republic of Iceland
DATE OF FORMATION: 1944
CAPITAL: Reykjavík
POPULATION: 300,000
TOTAL AREA: 39,768 sq. miles (103,000 sq. km)
DENSITY: 8 people per sq. mile
LANGUAGES: Icelandic*
RELIGIONS: Evangelical Lutheran 84%, nonreligious 3%, Roman Catholic 3%, other (mostly Christian) 10%
ETHNIC MIX: Icelandic 94%, other 5%, Danish 1%
GOVERNMENT: Parliamentary system
CURRENCY: Icelandic króna = 100 aurar

India

India is the world's second most populous country and largest democracy. Despite some success in reducing the birth rate, its population will probably overtake China's by 2028.

GEOGRAPHY

Separated from northern Asia by the Himalaya mountain range, India forms a subcontinent. As well as the Himalayas, there are two other main geographical regions, the Indo-Gangetic plain, which lies between the foothills of the Himalayas and the Vindhya Mountains, and the central-southern Deccan plateau. The Ghats are smaller mountain ranges located on the east and west coasts.

CLIMATE

Varies greatly according to latitude, altitude, and season. Most of India has three seasons: hot, wet, and cool. Summer temperatures in the north can reach 104°F (40°C). Monsoon rains normally break in June, petering out in September to October. In the cool season, the weather is mainly dry. The climate in the warmer south is less variable than in the north.

PEOPLE & SOCIETY

India's planners, overseeing an economic revolution, see its growing population rather than environmental constraints as the main brake on development. Nationwide awareness campaigns promote birth control but cultural and religious pressures encourage large families. Rural deprivation spurs urban migration, to live in sprawling slums. Over 70% of people survive on less than $2 a day. The majority of Indians are Hindu. Various attempts to reform the Hindu caste system, which determines social standing and even marriage, have met with violent opposition. Severe tensions exist between Hindus and the Muslim minority, especially in Kashmir and Gujarat. Smaller ethnic groups exist in the northeast, and many struggle for greater autonomy. Over two million people are living with HIV/AIDS.

FACTFILE

OFFICIAL NAME: Republic of India
DATE OF FORMATION: 1947
CAPITAL: New Delhi
POPULATION: 1.25 billion
TOTAL AREA: 1,269,338 sq. miles (3,287,590 sq. km)
DENSITY: 1091 people per sq. mile
LANGUAGES: Hindi*, English*, Urdu, Bengali, Marathi, Telugu, Tamil, Bihari, Gujarati, Kanarese
RELIGIONS: Hindu 81%, Muslim 13%, Christian 2%, Sikh 2%, Buddhist 1%, other 1%
ETHNIC MIX: Indo-Aryan 72%, Dravidian 25%, Mongoloid and other 3%
GOVERNMENT: Parliamentary system
CURRENCY: Indian rupee = 100 paise

THE ECONOMY

One of the world's fastest-growing economies. Protectionism has given way to free-market economics. Tea, gems, textiles exported. High-tech industries, outsourcing center. Success of "Bollywood" films. Cheap labor. Huge market, held back by poverty.

INSIGHT: *India's national animal, the tiger, was depicted as early as 4000 years ago by the Mohenjo-Daro civilization*

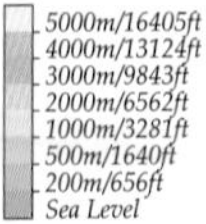

Indonesia

Formerly called the Dutch East Indies, Indonesia is the world's largest archipelago, with 18,108 islands scattered across 3000 miles (5000 km). It is the world's fourth most populous nation.

GEOGRAPHY

Indonesia is highly mountainous, with numerous tropical swamps. The land is covered with dense rainforest, especially on New Guinea, where it remains largely unexplored. There are more than 200 volcanoes, many of which are still active. Earthquakes, eruptions, and tsunamis are hazards. The islands of Java, Bali, Lombok, Sumatra, and Borneo were once joined together by dry land, which has since been submerged by rising sea levels. Coastal lowland development distinguishes some of the large islands.

CLIMATE

The climate is predominantly tropical monsoon. Variations relate mainly to differences in latitude and altitude; hilly areas are cooler overall. Rain falls throughout the year, often in thunderstorms, but there is a relatively dry season from June to September.

PEOPLE & SOCIETY

The basic Melanesian–Malay ethnic division disguises a diverse society. Bahasa Indonesia, the national language, coexists with at least 250 other spoken languages or dialects. Attempts by the Javanese

Bandaaceh
Strait of Malacca
100°
Langsa
Aceh
Medan
Kepulauan Natuna
Pematangsiantar
Pulau Nias
Pakanbaru
Singkawang
Pontianak
Padang
Sumatra
Kepulauan Mentawai
Pegunungan Barisan
Jambi
Bangka
Pangkalpinang
Ketapang
Palembang
Pulau Belitung
Bengkulu
Bandar Lampung
JAKARTA
INDIAN OCEAN
Bogor
Semara
Bandung
Jav
Yogyakar
Surakarta

FACTFILE

OFFICIAL NAME: Republic of Indonesia
DATE OF FORMATION: 1949
CAPITAL: Jakarta
POPULATION: 250 million
TOTAL AREA: 741,096 sq. miles (1,919,440 sq. km)
DENSITY: 360 people per sq. mile
LANGUAGES: Javanese, Sundanese, Madurese, Bahasa Indonesia*, Dutch
RELIGIONS: Sunni Muslim 86%, Christian 9%, Hindu 2%, other 2%, Buddhist 1%
ETHNIC MIX: Javanese 41%, other 32%, Sundanese 15%, coastal Malays 12%
GOVERNMENT: Presidential system
CURRENCY: Rupiah = 100 sen

political elite to suppress local cultures have been vigorously opposed, especially by the Aceh of northern Sumatra, and the Papuans. Religious and interethnic hostility is a problem, with clashes between Christians and Muslims in many areas, and discrimination against ethnic Chinese leading to mob attacks on their businesses. Gender equality is enshrined in law; women are active in public life.

THE ECONOMY

Varied resources, especially natural gas. Cheap and plentiful labor pool. Sizable state-owned sector, and state control of prices of basic goods. Large foreign debt rescheduled. The 2004 tsunami, which killed over 130,000 people, devastated northern Sumatra. Bureaucracy and corruption damage business confidence. Regional conflicts and terrorist attacks deter tourists and investors. Piracy is rife.

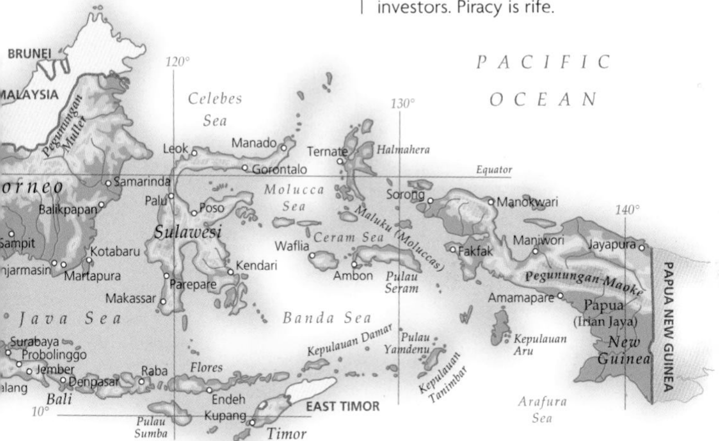
BRUNEI
MALAYSIA
Pegunungan Muller
120°
130°
140°
PACIFIC
OCEAN
Celebes Sea
Manado
Leok
Ternate
Halmahera
Gorontalo
Equator
Samarinda
Molucca Sea
Sorong
Manokwari
Palu
Balikpapan
Poso
Maluku (Moluccas)
Sulawesi
Ceram Sea
Sampit
Waflia
Fakfak
Maniwori
Jayapura
Kotabaru
Kendari
Ambon
Pulau Seram
Martapura
Pegunungan Maoke
PAPUA NEW GUINEA
Parepare
Makassar
Amamapare
Papua (Irian Jaya)
Java Sea
Banda Sea
Surabaya
Probolinggo
Jember
Kepulauan Damar
Pulau Yamdenu
Kepulauan Aru
New Guinea
Denpasar
Raba
Flores
Kepulauan Tanimbar
Bali
Endeh
EAST TIMOR
Arafura Sea
10°
Kupang
Pulau Sumba
Timor
4000m/13124ft
3000m/9843ft
2000m/6562ft
1000m/3281ft
500m/1640ft
Sea Level
0
500 km
0
500 miles

◆ **INSIGHT:** *Indonesia has a very youthful population: almost 30% of its people are under 15 years of age*

Iran

Since the 1979 Islamic fundamentalist revolution led by Ayatollah Khomeini, the Middle Eastern country of Iran has been the world's largest theocracy.

GEOGRAPHY

High desert plateau with large salt pans in the east. West and north are mountainous. Coastal land bordering Caspian Sea is rainy and forested.

CLIMATE

Desert climate. Hot summers, and bitterly cold winters. Area around the Caspian Sea is more temperate.

PEOPLE & SOCIETY

Many ethnic groups, including Persians, Azaris (ethnically related to Azeris), and Kurds. Militant Shi'a Islamism has dominated since the 1979 revolution. The mullahs' belief that adherence to religious values is more important than economic welfare has led to fall in living standards. Female emancipation has been reversed. Student-backed demonstrations favoring greater liberalism have been suppressed. International sanctions press for end of uranium enrichment program.

THE ECONOMY

A leading oil producer, though sanctions limit exports. Government restricts contact with the West, blocking acquisition of vital technology. High unemployment, inflation. Black market.

INSIGHT: *More than a hundred offenses carry the death penalty*

AZERBAIJAN
TURKMENISTAN
TURKEY
Tabrīz
Ardabīl
Caspian Sea
Orūmīyeh
Mashhad
TEHRĀN
Zagros Mountains
Qom
Kermānshāh
Arāk
Iranian Plateau
AFGHANISTAN
Eşfahān
IRAQ
Ahvāz
Khorramshahr
Kermān
Ābādān
KUWAIT
Shīrāz
Zāhedān
PAKISTAN
Persian Gulf
Bandar-e 'Abbās
40°
35°
45°
30°
50°
55°
60°
3000m/9843ft
2000m/6562ft
1000m/3281ft
500m/1640ft
200m/656ft
Sea Level
0 200 km
0 200 miles

FACTFILE

OFFICIAL NAME: Islamic Republic of Iran
DATE OF FORMATION: 1502
CAPITAL: Tehran
POPULATION: 77.4 million
TOTAL AREA: 636,293 sq. miles (1,648,000 sq. km)
DENSITY: 123 people per sq. mile
LANGUAGES: Farsi*, Azeri, Luri, Gilaki, Arabic, Mazanderani, Kurdish, Turkmen, Baluchi
RELIGIONS: Shi'a Muslim 89%, Sunni Muslim 9%, other 2%
ETHNIC MIX: Persian 51%, Azari 24%, other 10%, Lur and Bakhtiari 8%, Kurdish 7%
GOVERNMENT: Islamic theocracy
CURRENCY: Iranian rial = 100 dinars

Iraq

Oil-rich Iraq is situated in the central Middle East. The last five decades have been dominated by dictatorship, war, and civil strife. A US-led Coalition ousted Saddam Hussein in 2003.

GEOGRAPHY

Mainly desert. The Tigris and Euphrates rivers water fertile regions and create the southern marshland. Mountains along northeast border.

CLIMATE

Southern deserts have hot, dry summers and mild winters. North has dry summers, but winters can be harsh in the mountains. Rainfall is low.

PEOPLE & SOCIETY

Carved out of remnants of the Ottoman Empire, Iraq is home to Arab Muslims (mainly Shi'a, some Sunni), northern Kurds (persecuted under Saddam), and smaller minorities. Since Saddam's removal, sectarian violence has overshadowed efforts to build democracy. US forces withdrew in 2011. By 2014 Islamic State jihadists controlled part of the country. After years of war and sanctions, poverty is widespread.

THE ECONOMY

Economy and infrastructure have been destroyed. Given stability and aid for reconstruction, hopes of recovery would rest on massive oil reserves.

INSIGHT: *As Mesopotamia, Iraq was the site where the Sumerians established the world's first civilization*

0 100 km
0 100 miles
TURKEY
Al Mawşil
Arbil
As Sulaymānīyah
Kirkūk
SYRIA
IRAN
Euphrates
Tigris
Buhayrat ath Tharthār
Ba'qūbah
Ar Ramādī
BAGHDAD
Syrian Desert
JORDAN
Karbalā'
Al 'Amārah
An Najaf
Euphrates
Tigris
SAUDI ARABIA
An Nāşirīyah
Al Başrah
KUWAIT
36°
40°
32°
30°
44°
48°
3000m/9843ft
2000m/6562ft
1000m/3281ft
500m/1640ft
200m/656ft
Sea Level

FACTFILE

OFFICIAL NAME: Republic of Iraq
DATE OF FORMATION: 1932
CAPITAL: Baghdad
POPULATION: 33.8 million
TOTAL AREA: 168,753 sq. miles (437,072 sq. km)
DENSITY: 200 people per sq. mile
LANGUAGES: Arabic*, Kurdish*, Turkic languages, Armenian, Assyrian
RELIGIONS: Shi'a Muslim 60%, Sunni Muslim 35%, other (including Christian) 5%
ETHNIC MIX: Arab 80%, Kurdish 15%, Turkmen 3%, other 2%
GOVERNMENT: Parliamentary system
CURRENCY: New Iraqi dinar = 1000 fils

Ireland

In the Atlantic Ocean off the west coast of Britain, the Irish Republic governs about 85% of the island of Ireland, with the remainder (Northern Ireland) being part of the UK.

GEOGRAPHY

Low mountain ranges along an irregular coastline surround an inland plain punctuated by lakes, undulating hills, and peat bogs.

CLIMATE

The Gulf Stream accounts for the mild and wet climate. Snow is rare, except in the mountains.

PEOPLE & SOCIETY

Though homogeneous in ethnicity and Roman Catholic by religion, society has undergone a major generational change, liberalizing birth control, divorce, abortion, and general attitudes. Traditionally an emigrant nation, except for a decade of net immigration in the 2000s. Ireland and the UK signed a peace deal over Northern Ireland in 1998.

INSIGHT: *About 40% of Irish people can speak Irish Gaelic*

THE ECONOMY

Efficient agriculture, electronics, and food-processing industries. Rapid growth until 2008: housing bubble burst, banks faltered. Large EU bailouts to avoid bankruptcy. Struggling with budget deficit.

1000m/3281ft
500m/1640ft
200m/656ft
Sea Level
Donegal
Donegal Bay
UNITED KINGDOM (Northern Ireland)
Sligo
54°
Dundalk
Irish Sea
Westport
Mullingar
Athlone
Galway
DUBLIN
Dún Laoghaire
Shannon
Shannon Airport
Lough Derg
ATLANTIC OCEAN
Wicklow Mts.
Limerick
Kilkenny
Tralee
Tipperary
Wexford
Clonmel
Waterford
52°
Killarney
Cork
Celtic Sea
6°
8°
10°
0 50 km
0 50 miles

FACTFILE

OFFICIAL NAME: Ireland
DATE OF FORMATION: 1922
CAPITAL: Dublin
POPULATION: 4.6 million
TOTAL AREA: 27,135 sq. miles (70,280 sq. km)
DENSITY: 173 people per sq. mile
LANGUAGES: English*, Irish Gaelic*
RELIGIONS: Roman Catholic 87%, other and nonreligious 10%, Anglican 3%
ETHNIC MIX: Irish 99%, other 1%
GOVERNMENT: Parliamentary system
CURRENCY: Euro = 100 cents

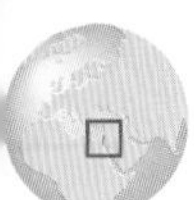

Israel

Created as a new state in 1948, Israel lies on the eastern shore of the Mediterranean. Palestinian resistance to Israeli occupation has led to years of fierce violence.

GEOGRAPHY

Coastal plain. Desert in the south. In the east lie the Great Rift Valley and the Dead Sea – the lowest point on the Earth's land surface.

CLIMATE

Summers are hot and dry. Wet season, March–November, is mild.

PEOPLE & SOCIETY

Large numbers of Jews settled in Palestine before Israel was founded in 1948. After World War II, there was a massive increase in immigration. Sephardi Jews from the Middle East and Mediterranean are now in the majority, but Ashkenazi Jews from central Europe still dominate business and politics. Palestinians in Gaza and Jericho gained limited autonomy in 1994 but Israeli–Palestinian talks on a two-state solution, backed by most of the world, have repeatedly foundered.

THE ECONOMY

High-tech industries, modern infrastructure, and educated workforce, but hampered by conflict and boycotts.

INSIGHT: *All Jews worldwide have the right to Israeli citizenship*

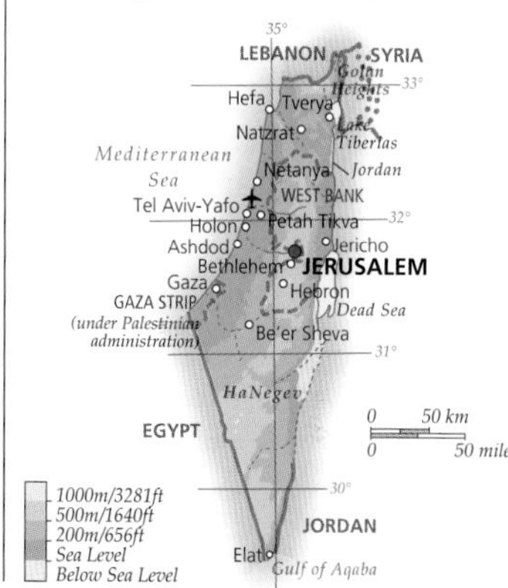
35°
LEBANON
SYRIA
Golan Heights
33°
Hefa
Tverya
Natzrat
Lake Tiberias
Mediterranean Sea
Netanya
Jordan
WEST BANK
Tel Aviv-Yafo
Holon
Petah Tikva
32°
Ashdod
Jericho
Bethlehem
JERUSALEM
Gaza
Hebron
GAZA STRIP
(under Palestinian administration)
Dead Sea
Be'er Sheva
31°
HaNegev
0 50 km
0 50 miles
EGYPT
30°
1000m/3281ft
500m/1640ft
200m/656ft
Sea Level
Below Sea Level
JORDAN
Elat
Gulf of Aqaba

FACTFILE

OFFICIAL NAME: State of Israel
DATE OF FORMATION: 1948
CAPITAL: Jerusalem (not internationally recognized)
POPULATION: 7.7 million
TOTAL AREA: 8019 sq. miles (20,770 sq. km)
DENSITY: 981 people per sq. mile
LANGUAGES: Hebrew*, Arabic*, Yiddish, German, Russian, Polish, Romanian, Persian
RELIGIONS: Jewish 76%, Muslim (mainly Sunni) 16%, other 4%, Christian 2%, Druze 2%
ETHNIC MIX: Jewish 76%, Arab 20%, other 4%
GOVERNMENT: Parliamentary system
CURRENCY: Shekel = 100 agorot

Italy

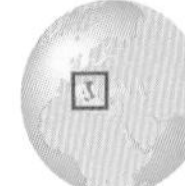

The Italian peninsula was home to the Roman Empire, one of the greatest ancient civilizations. The south has two famous volcanoes, Vesuvius and Etna.

GEOGRAPHY

The Appennines form the backbone of a rugged peninsula, extending from the Alps into the Mediterranean Sea. Alluvial plain in the north.

CLIMATE

Mediterranean in the south. Seasonal extremes in the mountains and on the northern alluvial plain.

PEOPLE & SOCIETY

Ethnically homogeneous, but with a gulf between the prosperous, industrial north and the poorer, agricultural south. Strong regional identities persist, especially on Sicily and Sardinia. Family ties remain strong, though the influence of the Roman Catholic Church has lessened.

INSIGHT: *Italy was a collection of dukedoms, monarchies, and city-states before unification in the 1860s*

THE ECONOMY

World leader in industrial and product design, fashion, textiles. Strong tourism and agriculture. Large public sector debt: austerity packages. Reforms have failed to restore GDP growth. Lack of jobs.

3000m/9843ft
2000m/6562ft
1000m/3281ft
500m/1640ft
200m/656ft
Sea Level
SWITZERLAND
AUSTRIA
SLOVENIA
FRANCE
Bolzano
Milano
Verona
Trieste
Torino
Po
Venezia
Genova
Parma
Golfo di Venezia
Bologna
Rimini
SAN MARINO
Pisa
Firenze
Ancona
Perugia
Adriatic Sea
ROME
VATICAN CITY
Appennino
Bari
Sassari
Napoli
Taranto
Lecce
Salerno
Sardegna (Sardinia)
Tyrrhenian Sea
Cagliari
Cosenza
Ionian Sea
Messina
Mediterranean Sea
Palermo
Sicilia (Sicily)
Siracusa
45°
40°
15°
0 100 km
0 100 miles

FACTFILE

OFFICIAL NAME: Italian Republic
DATE OF FORMATION: 1861
CAPITAL: Rome
POPULATION: 61 million
TOTAL AREA: 116,305 sq. miles (301,230 sq. km)
DENSITY: 537 people per sq. mile
LANGUAGES: Italian*, German, French, Rhaeto-Romanic, Sardinian
RELIGIONS: Roman Catholic 85%, other and nonreligious 13%, Muslim 2%
ETHNIC MIX: Italian 94%, other 4%, Sardinian 2%
GOVERNMENT: Parliamentary system
CURRENCY: Euro = 100 cents

Jamaica

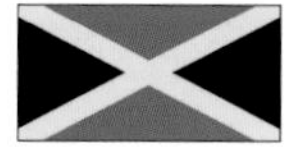

First colonized by the Spanish and then by the English, the Caribbean island of Jamaica achieved independence in 1962. It remains an influential force in Caribbean politics.

GEOGRAPHY

Mainly mountainous, with lush tropical vegetation. Inaccessible limestone area in the northwest. Low, irregular coastal plains are broken by hills and plateaus.

CLIMATE

Tropical. Hot and humid at sea level, with temperate mountain areas. Hurricanes are likely June–November.

PEOPLE & SOCIETY

Social tensions result from vast disparities in wealth, rather than race. Economic and political life is dominated by a few wealthy, long-established families. Many women hold senior positions in public life. Armed crime, much of it narcotics-related, is a problem. Large areas of Kingston, which have their own patois, are ruled by violent gangs. Jamaican music styles are influential worldwide.

THE ECONOMY

Major bauxite producer, though sector vulnerable to changes in world prices. Tourism and light industry. Sugar, bananas, coffee, and rum are exported. Debt burden dominates budget. High underemployment.

INSIGHT: *Jamaica's Rastafarians revere the late emperor of Ethiopia, Haile Selassie, as their spiritual leader, and see Africa as their spiritual home*

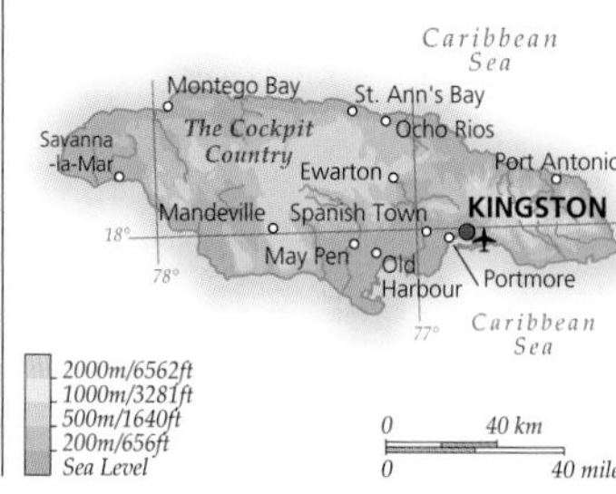
Caribbean Sea
Montego Bay
St. Ann's Bay
Ocho Rios
Savanna -la-Mar
The Cockpit Country
Ewarton
Port Antonio
Mandeville
Spanish Town
KINGSTON
18°
May Pen
Old Harbour
Portmore
78°
77°
Caribbean Sea
2000m/6562ft
1000m/3281ft
500m/1640ft
200m/656ft
Sea Level
0 40 km
0 40 miles

FACTFILE

OFFICIAL NAME: Jamaica
DATE OF FORMATION: 1962
CAPITAL: Kingston
POPULATION: 2.8 million
TOTAL AREA: 4243 sq. miles (10,990 sq. km)
DENSITY: 670 people per sq. mile
LANGUAGES: English Creole, English*
RELIGIONS: Other and nonreligious 45%, other Protestant 20%, Church of God 18%, Baptist 10%, Anglican 7%
ETHNIC MIX: Black African 91%, *Mulatto* (mixed race) 7%, European and Chinese 1%, East Indian 1%
GOVERNMENT: Parliamentary system
CURRENCY: Jamaican dollar = 100 cents

Japan

Japan is located off the east Asian coast and comprises four principal islands and over 3000 smaller ones. A powerful economy, it has an emperor as ceremonial head of state.

GEOGRAPHY

The terrain is predominantly mountainous, with fertile coastal plains; over two-thirds is woodland. There is no single continuous mountain range; the mountains divide into many small land blocks separated by lowlands and dissected by numerous river valleys. The islands lie on the Pacific "Ring of Fire," and earthquakes and volcanic eruptions are frequent. The Pacific coast is vunerable to tsunamis. There are numerous hot springs.

CLIMATE

Generally temperate–oceanic. Spring is warm and sunny, while summer is hot and humid, with high rainfall. In western Hokkaido and northwest Honshu, winters are very cold, with heavy snowfall. Freak storms and damaging floods in recent years have raised concern over global climate changes.

PEOPLE & SOCIETY

One of the most racially homogeneous societies in the world. A sense of order and social structure was founded on a strongly ingrained respect for elders and social superiors. In business, this underpinned the now much-diluted "lifetime employer" concept, where company allegiance determined social life as well as career. There is little tradition of generational rebellion, but the youth market is powerful and current fashions focus on teenagers. The education system is highly pressurized. Nongraduates have difficulty reaching management-level jobs, so competition for university places is intense. Long-term jobs for women are now the norm. One of the world's best healthcare systems and increased longevity have led to an aging population, with one in four people already over 65. The cost of living is high, especially in Tokyo.

FACTFILE

OFFICIAL NAME: Japan
DATE OF FORMATION: 1590
CAPITAL: Tokyo
POPULATION: 127 million
TOTAL AREA: 145,882 sq. miles (377,835 sq. km)
DENSITY: 874 people per sq. mile
LANGUAGES: Japanese*, Korean, Chinese
RELIGIONS: Shinto and Buddhist 76%, Buddhist 16%, other (including Christian) 8%
ETHNIC MIX: Japanese 99%, other (mainly Korean) 1%
GOVERNMENT: Parliamentary system
CURRENCY: Yen = 100 sen

THE ECONOMY

World's third-largest economy. A market leader in high-tech electronics and cars. Global spread of business. Once-revolutionary management and production methods. Long-term research and development. Talent for developing ideas from abroad. Protectionism in domestic economy. Reform of financial sector delayed by traditional economic power brokers. Major coal importer. Retreat from nuclear power after massive damage caused by 2011 earthquake and tsunami: resulting energy imports bill ended 30 years of trade surpluses.

INSIGHT: *The Japanese are still among the world's most avid newspaper readers, with daily sales around 47 million copies*

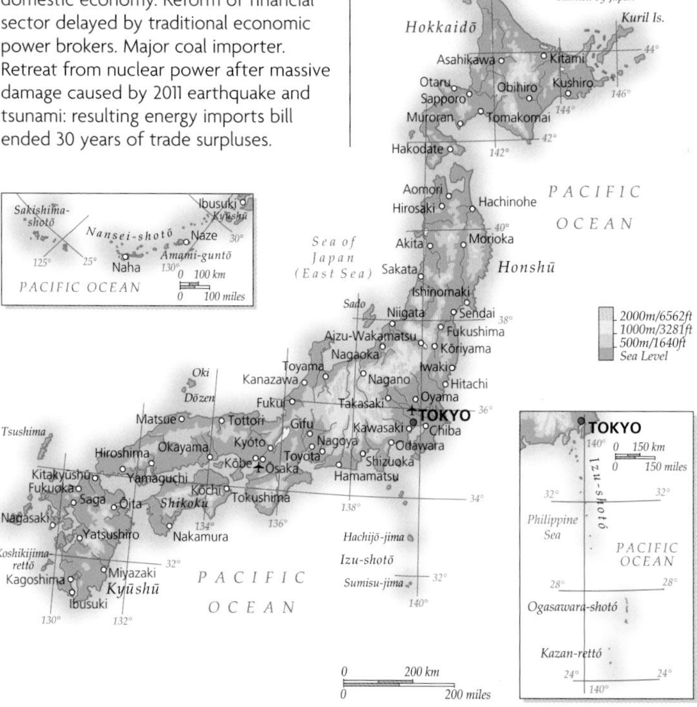

La Pérouse Strait
Kuril Islands Administered by the Russ. Fed., claimed by Japan
Kuril Is.
Hokkaidō
Asahikawa
Kitami
Otaru
Sapporo
Obihiro
Kushiro
Muroran
Tomakomai
Hakodate
Aomori
Hirosaki
Hachinohe
PACIFIC OCEAN
Akita
Morioka
Honshū
Sea of Japan (East Sea)
Sakata
Ishinomaki
Sado
Niigata
Sendai
Fukushima
Aizu-Wakamatsu
Kōriyama
Nagaoka
Toyama
Kanazawa
Nagano
Iwaki
Hitachi
Oki
Dōzen
Fukui
Takasaki
Oyama
TOKYO
Matsue
Tottori
Gifu
Kawasaki
Chiba
Tsushima
Kyōto
Nagoya
Odawara
Hiroshima
Okayama
Kōbe
Ōsaka
Toyota
Shizuoka
Kitakyūshū
Yamaguchi
Hamamatsu
Fukuoka
Saga
Ōita
Kōchi
Tokushima
Shikoku
Nagasaki
Yatsushiro
Nakamura
Hachijō-jima
Koshikijima-rettō
Izu-shotō
Miyazaki
Kagoshima
Kyūshū
Sumisu-jima
Ibusuki
PACIFIC OCEAN
Sakishima-shotō
Ibusuki
Kyūshū
Nansei-shotō
Naze
Amami-guntō
Naha
0 100 km
0 100 miles
PACIFIC OCEAN
2000m/6562ft
1000m/3281ft
500m/1640ft
Sea Level
TOKYO
0 150 km
0 150 miles
Izu-shotō
Philippine Sea
PACIFIC OCEAN
Ogasawara-shotō
Kazan-rettō
0 200 km
0 200 miles

Jordan

The Kingdom of Jordan lies east of Israel, and borders the Palestinian West Bank. Usually pro-Western in outlook, Jordan fears the rise of Islamists in Syria and Iraq.

GEOGRAPHY

Mostly desert plateaus, with occasional salt pans. Lowest parts lie along the eastern shores of the Dead Sea and the Jordan River.

CLIMATE

Hot, dry summers. Cool, wet winters. Areas below sea level very hot in summer, and warm in winter.

PEOPLE & SOCIETY

Jordanians are mainly Muslim with a strong national identity, but with Bedouin roots. The monarchy's power base lies among the rural tribes, which also provide the backbone of the army. Protests since 2011 have elicited gradual political reform, with greater powers for parliament. Jordan ceded its claim to the West Bank to the aspiring Palestinian state in 1988. Palestinian refugees make up over a third of the population. Recent influx of over 600,000 Syrian refugees.

THE ECONOMY

Lack of water. Exports garments, potash, fertilizers, and phosphates. Tourism hit by regional instability.

INSIGHT: *The Nabataean ruins of the ancient city of Petra attract thousands of tourists every year*

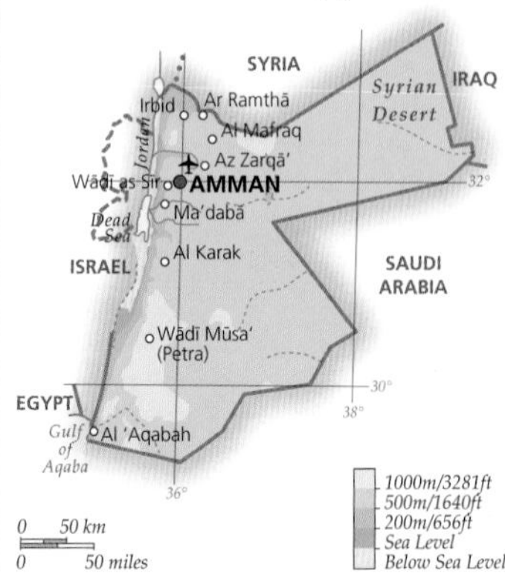
SYRIA
IRAQ
Syrian Desert
Irbid
Ar Ramthā
Al Mafraq
Az Zarqā'
Wādī as Sīr
AMMAN
Jordan
Ma'dabā
Dead Sea
Al Karak
ISRAEL
SAUDI ARABIA
Wādī Mūsā' (Petra)
EGYPT
Gulf of Aqaba
Al 'Aqabah
32°
30°
38°
36°
0 50 km
0 50 miles
1000m/3281ft
500m/1640ft
200m/656ft
Sea Level
Below Sea Level

FACTFILE

OFFICIAL NAME: Hashemite Kingdom of Jordan
DATE OF FORMATION: 1946
CAPITAL: Amman
POPULATION: 7.3 million
TOTAL AREA: 35,637 sq. miles (92,300 sq. km)
DENSITY: 213 people per sq. mile
LANGUAGES: Arabic*
RELIGIONS: Sunni Muslim 92%, Christian 6%, other 2%
ETHNIC MIX: Arab 98%, Circassian 1%, Armenian 1%
GOVERNMENT: Monarchy
CURRENCY: Jordanian dinar = 1000 fils

Kazakhstan

Kazakhstan was the last of the former Soviet republics to declare independence. Foreign investment in the oil and natural gas sector is strengthening its regional power.

GEOGRAPHY

Mainly steppe. Volga Delta and Caspian Sea in the west. Central plateau. Inhospitable Altai Mountains in the east. Semidesert in the south.

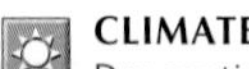

CLIMATE

Dry continental. Temperature variations between desert south and northern steppes are large. Winters are mildest near the Caspian Sea.

PEOPLE & SOCIETY

Kazakhstan's ethnic diversity arose mainly from forced settlements there during Soviet times. Since independence, the proportion of ethnic Russians has dropped. Many emigrated, while ethnic Kazakhs arrived from neighboring states. Very few Kazakhs maintain a traditional nomadic lifestyle, but Islam and loyalty to clans remain strong. There are significant disparities of wealth.

THE ECONOMY

Vast mineral resources: natural gas, oil, bismuth, uranium, and cadmium. Oil pipelines to China and Black Sea. Many Western investors. Wheat exported. Sale of farmland legal only since 2003.

INSIGHT: *The Soviet-built Baykonyr space center is still an important launch site for international missions*

RUSS. FED.
RUSS. FED.
Kostanay
Rudnyy
Ural'sk
Irtysh
ASTANA
Kirghiz Steppe
Karagandy
Ust'-Kamenogorsk
Ozero Balkhash
Zhezkazgan
Caspian Sea
Baykonyr
Taldykorgan
Aktau
Syr Darya
Kyzylorda
Almaty
CHINA
Aral Sea
Taraz
UZBEK.
Shymkent
TURKMEN.
KYRGYZSTAN
3000m/9843ft
2000m/6562ft
1000m/3281ft
500m/1640ft
200m/656ft
Sea Level
Below Sea level
0 400 km
0 400 miles

FACTFILE

OFFICIAL NAME: Republic of Kazakhstan
DATE OF FORMATION: 1991
CAPITAL: Astana
POPULATION: **16.4** million
TOTAL AREA: 1,049,150 sq. miles (2,717,300 sq. km)
DENSITY: 16 people per sq. mile
LANGUAGES: Kazakh*, Russian, Ukrainian, German, Uzbek, Tatar, Uighur
RELIGIONS: Muslim (mainly Sunni) 47%, Orthodox Christian 44%, other 9%
ETHNIC MIX: Kazakh 57%, Russian 27%, other 8%, Ukrainian 3%, Uzbek 3%, German 2%
GOVERNMENT: Presidential system
CURRENCY: Tenge = 100 tiyn

Kenya

Kenya straddles the equator on Africa's east coast. After nearly 40 years in power, the KANU party was soundly defeated in elections in 2002. Corruption is a serious issue.

GEOGRAPHY

A central plateau is divided by the Great Rift Valley. North of the equator is mainly semidesert. To the east lies a fertile coastal belt.

CLIMATE

The coast and the Great Rift Valley are hot and humid. The plateau interior is temperate. The northeastern desert is hot and dry. Rain usually falls April–May and October–November.

PEOPLE & SOCIETY

70 ethnic groups share about 40 languages. Strong clan and family links in rural areas are being weakened by urban migration. Poverty, severe drought, and years of high population growth exacerbate ethnic tensions.

INSIGHT: *Kenya has more than 60 game reserves, national parks, and marine reservations*

THE ECONOMY

Tourism, hurt by sporadic violence. Flowers, tea, and coffee. Sizable informal economy. Diversified manufacturing sector. Needs food aid, especially to cope with 2011 famine. Oil exploration.

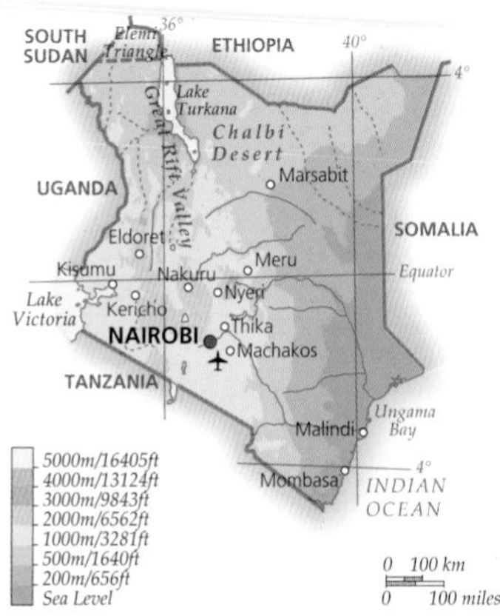
SOUTH SUDAN
Elemi Triangle
36°
ETHIOPIA
40°
4°
Lake Turkana
Chalbi Desert
Great Rift Valley
Marsabit
UGANDA
SOMALIA
Eldoret
Kisumu
Nakuru
Meru
Equator
Lake Victoria
Kericho
Nyeri
Thika
NAIROBI
Machakos
TANZANIA
Ungama Bay
Malindi
Mombasa
4°
INDIAN OCEAN
5000m/16405ft
4000m/13124ft
3000m/9843ft
2000m/6562ft
1000m/3281ft
500m/1640ft
200m/656ft
Sea Level
0 100 km
0 100 miles

FACTFILE

OFFICIAL NAME: Republic of Kenya

DATE OF FORMATION: 1963

CAPITAL: Nairobi

POPULATION: 44.4 million

TOTAL AREA: 224,961 sq. miles (582,650 sq. km)

DENSITY: 203 people per sq. mile

LANGUAGES: Kiswahili*, English*, Kikuyu, Luo, Kalenjin, Kamba

RELIGIONS: Christian 80%, Muslim 10% traditional beliefs 9%, other 1%

ETHNIC MIX: Other 28%, Kikuyu 22%, Luhya 14%, Luo 14%, Kalenjin 11%, Kamba 11%

GOVERNMENT: Presidential system

CURRENCY: Kenya shilling = 100 cents

Kiribati

Situated in the mid-Pacific, the islands adopted the name Kiribati (pronounced "Keer-ee-bus," a corruption of their former name "Gilberts") upon independence from Britain in 1979.

GEOGRAPHY

Kiribati consists of three groups of tiny, very low-lying coral atolls scattered across 1,930,000 sq. miles (5 million sq. km) of ocean. Most of the 33 atolls have central lagoons.

CLIMATE

Central islands have a maritime equatorial climate. Those to north and south are tropical, with constant high temperatures. There is little rainfall.

PEOPLE & SOCIETY

Officially I-Kiribati, many local people still refer to themselves as Gilbertese. Almost all are Micronesian, apart from the inhabitants of the island of Banaba, who employed anthropologists to establish their racial distinction. Most people are poor subsistence farmers and many travel abroad to work. The islands are effectively ruled by traditional chiefs.

THE ECONOMY

Since exhaustion of Banaba's phosphate deposits in 1980, copra (dried coconut) and fish have become the main exports. Foreign aid and remittances are vital to compensate for Kiribati's isolation and lack of resources.

INSIGHT: *In 1981, the UK paid A$10 million to Banabans to compensate for the destruction of their island by mining*

All land under 200m/656ft

PACIFIC OCEAN
Tungaru
Tarawa
Equator
Kiritimati
Line Islands
Banaba
170°
Phoenix Islands
180°
170°
160°
Millennium Island
10°
150°
Tarawa 173°
1°30'N
Bonriki
Betio
BAIRIKI
0 600 km
0 600 miles

FACTFILE

OFFICIAL NAME: Republic of Kiribati
DATE OF FORMATION: 1979
CAPITAL: Bairiki (Tarawa Atoll)
POPULATION: 103,248
TOTAL AREA: 277 sq. miles (717 sq. km)
DENSITY: 377 people per sq. mile
LANGUAGES: English*, Kiribati
RELIGIONS: Roman Catholic 55%, Kiribati Protestant Church 36%, other 9%
ETHNIC MIX: Micronesian 99%, other 1%
GOVERNMENT: Presidential system
CURRENCY: Australian dollar = 100 cents

North Korea

Separated from the democratic South by the world's most heavily defended border, the Stalinist North Korean state has been isolated from the outside world since 1948.

GEOGRAPHY

Mostly mountainous, with fertile plains in the southwest.

CLIMATE

Continental. Warm summers and cold winters, especially in the north, where snow is common.

PEOPLE & SOCIETY

Life is heavily regulated. Cult of personality is more powerful than the state-controlled religions, which include Korea's own Chondogyo. Women are expected to work and to run the home. Children are looked after in state-run crèches. The Korean Worker's Party is the sole party. Its elite have a privileged lifestyle. Globally condemned for its nuclear weapons tests, the regime's grip on power perpetuates its pariah status.

INSIGHT: *Internet access is limited, and restricted to the political elite*

THE ECONOMY

Minerals are only resource. Vital aid streams lost with global collapse of communism after 1989. Decades of economic mismanagement have led to chronic food shortages. Lack of fuel. Disproportionate defense budget.

2000m/6562ft
1000m/3281ft
500m/1640ft
200m/656ft
Sea Level
RUSS. FED.
CHINA
Ch'ŏngjin
Kanggye
Kimch'aek
Hŭich'ŏn
Iwŏn
Sinŭiju
Hamhŭng
Hŭngnam
Korea Bay
Wŏnsan
Sea of Japan (East Sea)
PYONGYANG
Namp'o
Haeju
SOUTH KOREA
Kaesŏng
Yellow Sea
42°
130°
40°
124°
38°
126°
128°
0 50 km
0 50 miles

FACTFILE

OFFICIAL NAME: Democratic People's Republic of Korea

DATE OF FORMATION: 1948

CAPITAL: Pyongyang

POPULATION: 24.9 million

TOTAL AREA: 46,540 sq. miles (120,540 sq. km)

DENSITY: 536 people per sq. mile

LANGUAGES: Korean*

RELIGIONS: Government-controlled religions include Chondogyo, Buddhism, and Christianity

ETHNIC MIX: Korean 100%

GOVERNMENT: One-party state

CURRENCY: North Korean won = 100 chon

South Korea

South Korea occupies the southern half of the Korean peninsula. Under US sponsorship, it was separated from the communist North in 1948 and is now a capitalist economy.

GEOGRAPHY

Over 80% is mountainous and two-thirds is forested. The flattest and most populous parts lie along the west coast and in the extreme south.

CLIMATE

There are four distinct seasons. Winters are dry, and bitterly cold. Summers are hot and humid.

PEOPLE & SOCIETY

Inhabited for the last 2000 years by a single ethnic group. The nuclear family is replacing traditional extended households. Since the 1953 armistice, the Koreas have remained technically at war. Reunification is the ultimate goal, but the two sides fluctuate between harsh rhetoric or belligerence and conciliation, allowing cross-border family reunions.

INSIGHT: *Half of all Koreans are named Kim, Lee, Park, or Choi*

THE ECONOMY

World's biggest shipbuilder. High-tech goods and cars: rising demand from China. Strong regional competition. Aging population.

0 50 km
0 50 miles
NORTH KOREA
Sea of Japan (East Sea)
128°
126°
38°
Gangneung
Donghae
SEOUL
Incheon
Seongnam
Suwon
SEJONG CITY
Yellow Sea
Daejeon
36°
Gunsan
Daegu
Ulsan
Gwangju
Masan
Busan
Korea Strait
Mokpo
Yeosu
34°
Jeju Strait
Jeju
Jeju-do
1000m/3281ft
500m/1640ft
200m/656ft
Sea Level

FACTFILE

OFFICIAL NAME: Republic of Korea
DATE OF FORMATION: 1948
CAPITALS: Seoul; Sejong City (administrative)
POPULATION: 49.3 million
TOTAL AREA: 38,023 sq. miles (98,480 sq. km)
DENSITY: 1293 people per sq. mile
LANGUAGES: Korean*
RELIGIONS: Mahayana Buddhist 47%, Protestant 38%, Roman Catholic 11%, Confucianist 3%, other 1%
ETHNIC MIX: Korean 100%
GOVERNMENT: Presidential system
CURRENCY: South Korean won = 100 chon

Kosovo

Once part of the former Yugoslav state, Kosovo seceded from Serbia in 2008. International recognition, mainly from Western countries, is strongly opposed by Serbia and Russia.

GEOGRAPHY

Landlocked and mountainous, with two plains in the east and west.

CLIMATE

Continental, with warm, sunny summers and cold, snowy winters.

PEOPLE & SOCIETY

The balance of Albanians to Serbs in Kosovo has changed dramatically over centuries, both groups suffering interethnic violence at various times. Attacks against Albanians in the late 1990s caused a million to flee. After NATO stepped in, many Serbs left: Albanians now form a 92% majority. Most Albanians are Muslim. Serbs dominate three northern provinces, which have threatened to secede.

INSIGHT: *The UN administered Kosovo in 1999–2008 after NATO intervention to stop Serb ethnic cleansing*

THE ECONOMY

One of the poorest countries in Europe. Aid and remittances cover a large trade deficit. Organized crime: smuggling of fuel, cigarettes, and cement. Uncertain status deters foreign investors. High unemployment. Use of euro has helped fight inflation. Lignite deposits. Inefficient agriculture.

SERBIA
21°
20°
22°
43°
42°
MONT.
Mokra Gora
Mitrovicë/Mitrovica
Vushtrri/Vučitrn
Pejë/Peć
Kamenicë/Kamenica
PRISHTINË
Deçan/Dečane
Klinë/Klina
Gjilan/Gnjilane
Gjakovë/Đakovica
Ferizaj/Uroševac
Prizren
ALBANIA
MACEDONIA
1000m/3281ft
500m/1640ft
200m/656ft
0 50 km
0 50 miles

FACTFILE

OFFICIAL NAME: Republic of Kosovo
DATE OF FORMATION: 2008
CAPITAL: Prishtinë
POPULATION: 1.8 million
TOTAL AREA: 4212 sq. miles (10,908 sq. km)
DENSITY: 427 people per sq. mile
LANGUAGES: Albanian*, Serbian*, Bosniak, Gorani, Roma, Turkish
RELIGIONS: Muslim 92%, Roman Catholic 4%, Orthodox Christian 4%
ETHNIC MIX: Albanian 92%, Serb 4%, Bosniak and Gorani 2%, Turkish 1%, Roma 1%
GOVERNMENT: Parliamentary system
CURRENCY: Euro = 100 cents

Kuwait

Kuwait lies at the northwest tip of the Gulf, dwarfed by its neighbors Iraq, Iran, and Saudi Arabia. It was a British protectorate until 1961, when full independence was granted.

GEOGRAPHY

Terrain is low-lying desert. The lowest land is in the north. Cultivation is only possible along the coast.

CLIMATE

Summers are very hot and dry. Winters are cooler, with some rain and occasional frost at night.

PEOPLE & SOCIETY

Oil-rich monarchy, ruled by the al-Sabah family. It is a conservative Sunni Muslim society, but women are relatively free. Nonetheless, a 1999 decree giving women the vote was blocked for six years in parliament by Islamic traditionalists. Immigrant workers, from other Arab states, India, and Pakistan, now outnumber native citizens. US-led forces rescued Kuwait after the 1990 Iraqi invasion, and later used it as a launchpad for the 2003 invasion to oust Saddam Hussein.

THE ECONOMY

Oil and natural gas dominate the economy. Skilled workforce, raw materials, and food are imported. High standard of living. Financial services: stock market lost 40% of value in 2008.

INSIGHT: *During the 1991 Gulf War, Iraq deliberately set fire to 800 of Kuwait's 950 oil wells*

0 25 km
0 25 miles
IRAQ
30°
48°
Jazīrat Būbīyān
Jāl al-Liyāḩ
Shiqqat al Qalīb
Al Bahrah
Persian Gulf
KUWAIT CITY
Al Jahrā'
As Salīmīyah
As Salimī
Qalīb ash Shuyūkh
Al Fuḩayḩīl
Al Aḩmadī
Aş Şubayḩīyah
SAUDI ARABIA
Ash Shuqayq
200m/656ft
Sea Level
Al Wafrā'

FACTFILE

OFFICIAL NAME: State of Kuwait
DATE OF FORMATION: 1961
CAPITAL: Kuwait City
POPULATION: 3.4 million
TOTAL AREA: 6880 sq. miles (17,820 sq. km)
DENSITY: 494 people per sq. mile
LANGUAGES: Arabic*, English
RELIGIONS: Sunni Muslim 45%, Shi'a Muslim 40%, Christian, Hindu, and other 15%
ETHNIC MIX: Kuwaiti 45%, other Arab 35%, South Asian 9%, other 7%, Iranian 4%
GOVERNMENT: Monarchy
CURRENCY: Kuwaiti dinar = 1000 fils

Kyrgyzstan

A small and mountainous landlocked state in central Asia, Kyrgyzstan is one of the least urbanized ex-Soviet republics, and was slow to develop its own sense of cultural identity.

GEOGRAPHY

The mountainous spurs of the Tien Shan range contain glaciers, alpine meadows, forests, and narrow valleys. Semidesert in the west.

CLIMATE

Varies from permanent snow and cold deserts at high altitudes, to hot deserts in low regions.

PEOPLE & SOCIETY

Ethnic Kyrgyz have only been in the majority since the late 1980s – due to a high birth rate and the emigration of ethnic Russians. Wary of losing skills vital to the economy, the government has attempted to deter Russians from leaving; concessions include making Russian an official language. There are some tensions between Kyrgyz and Uzbeks, and a trend toward greater Islamization, particularly in the poorer south.

THE ECONOMY

Mainly still under state control; corruption issues. Agriculture employs a third of the labor force. Cotton, wool, meat, and tobacco exports. Mercury, gold, and antimony are mined. Great potential for hydroelectric power.

INSIGHT: *Kyrgyz folklore is based around the 1000-year-old poem, Manas, which takes a week to recite*

KAZAKHSTAN
76°
80°
72°
BISHKEK
Tokmak
Ozero
Karakol
Issyk-Kul'
Talas
Kara-Balta
Issyk-Kul'
Tien Shan
42°
Naryn
Dzhalal-Abad
UZBEKISTAN
Osh
CHINA
40°
Sulyukta
TAJIKISTAN
0 100 km
0 100 miles
4000m/13124ft
3000m/9843ft
2000m/6562ft
1000m/3281ft
500m/1640ft

FACTFILE

OFFICIAL NAME: Kyrgyz Republic
DATE OF FORMATION: 1991
CAPITAL: Bishkek
POPULATION: 5.5 million
TOTAL AREA: 76,641 sq. miles (198,500 sq. km)
DENSITY: 72 people per sq. mile
LANGUAGES: Kyrgyz*, Russian*, Uzbek, Tatar, Ukrainian
RELIGIONS: Muslim (mainly Sunni) 70%, Orthodox Christian 30%
ETHNIC MIX: Kyrgyz 69%, Uzbek 14%, Russian 9%, other 6%, Dungan 1%, Uighur 1%
GOVERNMENT: Presidential system
CURRENCY: Som = 100 tyiyn

Laos

A French colony prior to 1953, Laos lies landlocked in southeast Asia. Heavily bombed during the Vietnam War, it fell in 1975 to communist insurgents, whose regime remains in power.

GEOGRAPHY

Largely forested mountains, broadening in the north to a plateau. Lowlands along the Mekong Valley.

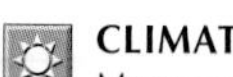

CLIMATE

Monsoon rains September–May. The rest of the year is hot and dry.

PEOPLE & SOCIETY

There are over 60 ethnic groups. Lowland Laotians (Lao Loum) live along the Mekong River and are rice farmers. Upland and highland Laotians (Lao Theung and Lao Soung) traditionally employ environmentally damaging slash-and-burn farming, and grow illegal cash crops (notably opium). Government efforts to reform these practices are resisted.

INSIGHT: *Three small Laotian kingdoms were unified under French control in 1899*

THE ECONOMY

One of world's least developed nations. Poor infrastructure. Gold, copper, electricity, timber, garments, and coffee are exported. Levels of foreign investment are rising.

CHINA
0 100 km
0 100 miles
22°
Phôngsali
MYANMAR (BURMA)
VIETNAM
Houayxay
Xam Nua
20°
Mekong
Louangphabang
Xaignabouli
Xiangkhoang
100°
THAILAND
Ban Naxon
Pakxan
VIENTIANE
Mekong
18°
102°
Thakhek
THAILAND
Khanthabouli
16°
Muang Khôngxédôn
Salavan
104°
Pakxé
2000m/6562ft
1000m/3281ft
500m/1640ft
200m/656ft
Sea Level
14°
CAMBODIA
106°

FACTFILE

OFFICIAL NAME: Lao People's Democratic Republic

DATE OF FORMATION: 1953

CAPITAL: Vientiane

POPULATION: 6.8 million

TOTAL AREA: 91,428 sq. miles (236,800 sq. km)

DENSITY: 76 people per sq. mile

LANGUAGES: Lao*, Mon-Khmer, Yao, Vietnamese, Chinese, French

RELIGIONS: Buddhist 65%, other (including animist) 34%, Christian 1%

ETHNIC MIX: Lao Loum 66%, Lao Theung 30%, Lao Soung 2%, other 2%

GOVERNMENT: One-party state

CURRENCY: New kip = 100 at

Latvia

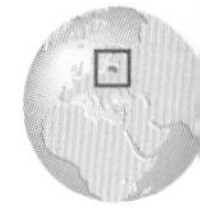

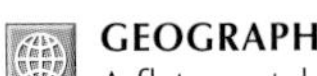

Latvia lies on the east coast of the Baltic Sea. Like its Baltic neighbors, it regained independence from Moscow in 1991, and joined the EU and NATO in 2004.

GEOGRAPHY

A flat coastal plain which is deeply indented by the Gulf of Riga. Poor drainage creates many bogs and swamps in the forested interior.

CLIMATE

Temperate, with warm summers and cold winters. There is steady rainfall throughout the year.

PEOPLE & SOCIETY

Latvians make up just under two-thirds of the population and are mostly Lutheran. They have been officially favored by the state since 1991 over the largely Orthodox Christian Russian minority. Latvian was declared the only official language in 2000 and has been used exclusively in schools since 2004. This discrimination has strained relations with neighboring Russia. Women enjoy full equality. The divorce rate is high.

THE ECONOMY

Service-led economy. After fast growth, global credit crunch brought Latvia to verge of bankruptcy in 2008: banks were bailed out, stringent austerity measures imposed. Worst recession in EU ensued. Back to fastest growth in EU in 2012–2013. Adopted euro in 2014.

INSIGHT: *In Latvia, life expectancy for men is ten years less than for women*

ESTONIA
Baltic Sea
Gulf of Riga
RUSS. FED.
Valmiera
Ventspils
Cēsis
RIGA
Jūrmala
Western Dvina
Saldus
Dobele
Jelgava
Jēkabpils
Liepāja
Daugavpils
LITHUANIA
BELARUS
58°
56°
22°
24°
26°
28°
200m/656ft
Sea Level
0 50 km
0 50 miles

FACTFILE

OFFICIAL NAME: Republic of Latvia
DATE OF FORMATION: 1991
CAPITAL: Riga
POPULATION: 2.1 million
TOTAL AREA: 24,938 sq. miles (64,589 sq. km)
DENSITY: 84 people per sq. mile
LANGUAGES: Latvian*, Russian
RELIGIONS: Other 43%, Lutheran 24%, Roman Catholic 18%, Orthodox Christian 15%
ETHNIC MIX: Latvian 62%, Russian 27%, Belarussian 3%, other 4%, Ukrainian 2%, Polish 2%
GOVERNMENT: Parliamentary system
CURRENCY: Euro = 100 cents

Lebanon

Once a vibrant cultural hotspot, Lebanon suffered 14 years of civil war and occupation until a 1989 peace deal. It now fears spillover from neighboring Syria's own civil war.

GEOGRAPHY

Behind a narrow Mediterranean coastal plain, two parallel mountain ranges run the length of the country, separated by the fertile Beqaa Valley.

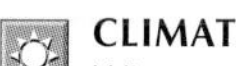

CLIMATE

Winters are mild and summers are hot, with high coastal humidity. Snow falls on high ground in winter.

PEOPLE & SOCIETY

Huge gulf exists between the poor and a small, rich elite. Politics reflects divisions between the traditional ruling Maronite Christians and Sunni and Shi'a Muslims. A 1989 power-sharing deal ended civil war. Syria acted as power broker until made to withdraw in 2005. Political crises add to instability. Israel attacked in 2006 in a botched bid to crush Iran-backed Hezbollah militants. Lebanon hosts over a million Syrian refugees and 450,000 from Palestine.

THE ECONOMY

Wine and fruit. Much infrastructure destroyed. Instability undermines Beirut's role as regional financial center. High public debt. Refugee influx.

INSIGHT: *The Cedar of Lebanon has been the nation's symbol for more than 2000 years*

Mediterranean Sea
SYRIA
Tripoli
Zgharta
0 20 km
0 20 miles
Jabal Lubnan
Anti-Lebanon
Joûnié
BEIRUT
Baabda
Baalbek
Zahlé
El Beqaa
34°
SYRIA
Saïda
Nabatîyé
36°
Soûr
Golan Heights
ISRAEL
33°
3000m/9843ft
2000m/6562ft
1000m/3281ft
500m/1640ft
200m/656ft
Sea Level

FACTFILE

OFFICIAL NAME: Lebanese Republic

DATE OF FORMATION: 1941

CAPITAL: Beirut

POPULATION: 4.8 million

TOTAL AREA: 4015 sq. miles (10,400 sq. km)

DENSITY: 1215 people per sq. mile

LANGUAGES: Arabic*, French, Armenian, Assyrian

RELIGIONS: Muslim 60%, Christian 39%, other 1%

ETHNIC MIX: Arab 95%, Armenian 4%, other 1%

GOVERNMENT: Parliamentary system

CURRENCY: Lebanese pound = 100 piastres

Lesotho

The landlocked Kingdom of Lesotho is entirely surrounded by – and economically dependent on – South Africa, which even sent in troops to restore calm after rioting in 1998.

GEOGRAPHY

A high mountainous plateau, cut by valleys and ravines. The Maluti Range runs through the center. The Drakensberg Range lies to the east.

CLIMATE

Temperate. Summers are hot with torrential rain storms. Snow is frequent in the mountains in winter.

PEOPLE & SOCIETY

The overwhelming majority of people are Sotho, though there are some South Asians, Europeans, and Chinese. A strong sense of national identity has tended to minimize ethnic tensions. Many men work as migrant laborers in South Africa, leaving women to run households.

INSIGHT: *Lesotho has one of the highest literacy rates in Africa – but one of the highest rates of HIV/AIDS too*

THE ECONOMY

Dependent on South Africa. Water and energy exported from Highlands Water Scheme. Subsistence farming. Garment exports struggle to compete. HIV/AIDS is depleting workforce.

Caledon
SOUTH AFRICA
Hlotse
29°
Teyateyaneng
MASERU
Maluti
Mokhotlong
Mantsonyane
Morija
Mafeteng
Drakensberg
30°
Orange River
Mohales Hoek
SOUTH AFRICA
29°
28°
3000m/9843ft
2000m/6562ft
1000m/3281ft
0 50 km
0 50 miles

FACTFILE

OFFICIAL NAME: Kingdom of Lesotho
DATE OF FORMATION: 1966
CAPITAL: Maseru
POPULATION: 2.1 million
TOTAL AREA: 11,720 sq. miles (30,355 sq. km)
DENSITY: 179 people per sq. mile
LANGUAGES: English*, Sesotho*, isiZulu
RELIGIONS: Christian 90%, traditional beliefs 10%
ETHNIC MIX: Sotho 99%, European and Asian 1%
GOVERNMENT: Parliamentary system
CURRENCY: Loti = 100 lisente

Liberia

Liberia, on Africa's Atlantic coast, was founded as a republic of freed slaves. A brutal coup in 1980 and years of civil war have left a legacy of gang violence and looting.

GEOGRAPHY

A coastline of beaches and mangrove swamps rises to forested plateaus and highlands inland.

CLIMATE

High temperatures. There is only one wet season, from May to October, except in the extreme southeast.

PEOPLE & SOCIETY

The key social distinction used to be between Americo-Liberians – descendants of freed slaves – and the indigenous tribal peoples. However, political assimilation and intermarriage have eased tensions. Intertribal tension is now a much more serious problem, fueling the 1990–2003 civil war. A deadly Ebola outbreak hit the country in 2014.

INSIGHT: *Liberia is named after the people liberated from slavery who arrived from the US in the 1800s*

THE ECONOMY

War caused economic collapse. Rubber is key export. Bans now lifted on timber and diamond exports. Revenue from merchant shipping licenses. Debt burden. Vast iron ore reserves. Shutdown in 2014 due to Ebola.

1000m/3281ft
500m/1640ft
200m/656ft
Sea Level
SIERRA LEONE
Voinjama
8°
GUINEA
Tubmanburg
Robertsport
Gbanga
CÔTE D'IVOIRE (IVORY COAST)
MONROVIA
Harbel
Zwedru
6°
Buchanan
ATLANTIC OCEAN
Greenville
10°
Harper
8°
0 50 km
0 50 miles

FACTFILE

OFFICIAL NAME: Republic of Liberia
DATE OF FORMATION: 1847
CAPITAL: Monrovia
POPULATION: 4.3 million
TOTAL AREA: 43,000 sq. miles (111,370 sq. km)
DENSITY: 116 people per sq. mile
LANGUAGES: Kpelle, Vai, Bassa, Kru, Grebo, Kissi, Gola, Loma, English*
RELIGIONS: Christian 40%, traditional beliefs 40%, Muslim 20%
ETHNIC MIX: Indigenous tribes (12 groups) 49%, Kpellé 20%, Bassa 16%, Gio 8%, Krou 7%
GOVERNMENT: Presidential system
CURRENCY: Liberian dollar = 100 cents

Libya

Situated on north Africa's Mediterranean coast, Libya was declared a revolutionary state in 1969 by Colonel Gaddafi. Civil war, launched in the 2011 "Arab Spring," ousted his regime.

GEOGRAPHY

Apart from the coastal strip and a mountain range in the south, Libya is desert or semidesert.

CLIMATE

Hot and arid. The coastal area has a temperate climate, with mild, wet winters and hot, dry summers.

PEOPLE & SOCIETY

Once a nation of nomads and livestock herders, it is almost 80% urban. Gaddafi's revolution wiped out private enterprise and the middle classes, and promoted Islam and African unity. Sanctions were lifted after Libya offered compensation for terrorist bombings and ended its Weapons of Mass Destruction (WMD) program. In 2011, rebels from the east took power with international help, but failed to unite the country. Tripoli is in the sway of Islamist militias, while rival parliaments vie for political control.

THE ECONOMY

Oil is key export. Dates, olives, and fruit grow in oases, but most food is imported. Recent instability. Corruption and mismanagement.

INSIGHT: *90% of Libya is still desert, despite grand irrigation projects*

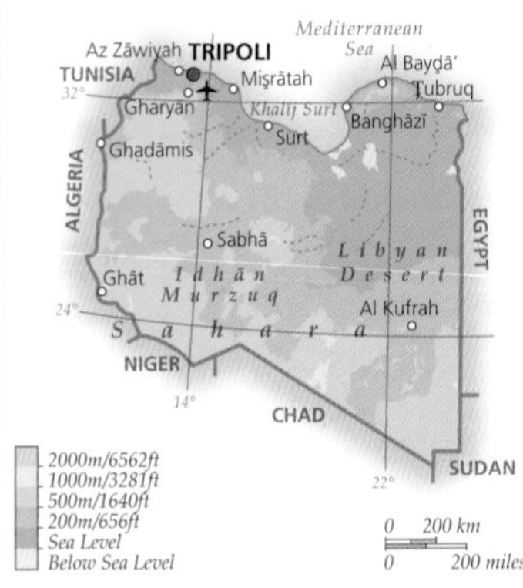
Mediterranean Sea
Az Zāwiyah
TRIPOLI
TUNISIA
Mişrātah
Al Bayḍā'
Tubruq
Gharyān
Khalīj Surt
Banghāzī
Surt
Ghadāmis
ALGERIA
EGYPT
Sabhā
Libyan Desert
Ghāt
Idhān Murzuq
Al Kufrah
Sahara
NIGER
CHAD
SUDAN
32°
24°
14°
22°
2000m/6562ft
1000m/3281ft
500m/1640ft
200m/656ft
Sea Level
Below Sea Level
0 200 km
0 200 miles

FACTFILE

OFFICIAL NAME: State of Libya
DATE OF FORMATION: 1951
CAPITAL: Tripoli
POPULATION: 6.2 million
TOTAL AREA: 679,358 sq. miles (1,759,540 sq. km)
DENSITY: 9 people per sq. mile
LANGUAGES: Arabic*, Tuareg
RELIGIONS: Muslim (mainly Sunni) 97%, other 3%
ETHNIC MIX: Arab and Berber 97%, other 3%
GOVERNMENT: Transitional regime
CURRENCY: Libyan dinar = 1000 dirhams

Liechtenstein

Perched in the Alps between Switzerland and Austria, the state of Liechtenstein became an independent principality of the Holy Roman Empire in 1719. It has close links with Switzerland.

GEOGRAPHY

The upper Rhine Valley covers the western third of the country. The mountains and narrow valleys of the eastern Alps make up the remainder.

CLIMATE

Warm, dry summers. Winters are cold, with heavy snow in the mountains from December to March.

PEOPLE & SOCIETY

The principality's role as a financial center accounts for its many foreign residents (a third of the population). Half of the workforce are cross-border commuters. Living standards are high, with few social tensions. Linked by a customs union since 1924, Switzerland handles Liechtenstein's foreign affairs and defense issues.

INSIGHT: *Women in Liechtenstein obtained the vote only in 1984*

THE ECONOMY

Banking secrecy (now modified) and low taxes help attract foreign investment. Anti-money-laundering rules are recent. Diversified exports include precision instruments, dental products, and chemicals.

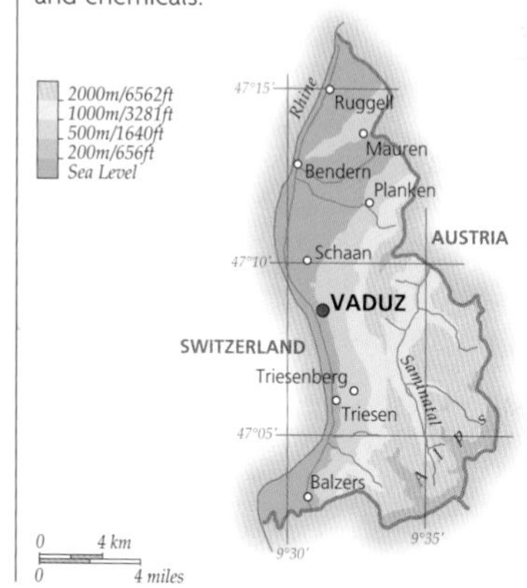
2000m/6562ft
1000m/3281ft
500m/1640ft
200m/656ft
Sea Level
47°15'
Rhine
Ruggell
Mauren
Bendern
Planken
AUSTRIA
47°10'
Schaan
VADUZ
SWITZERLAND
Triesenberg
Samina tal
Triesen
47°05'
Balzers
9°30'
9°35'
0 4 km
0 4 miles

FACTFILE

OFFICIAL NAME: Principality of Liechtenstein

DATE OF FORMATION: 1719

CAPITAL: Vaduz

POPULATION: 37,000

TOTAL AREA: 62 sq. miles (160 sq. km)

DENSITY: 597 people per sq. mile

LANGUAGES: German*, Alemannish dialect, Italian

RELIGIONS: Roman Catholic 79%, other 13%, Protestant 8%

ETHNIC MIX: Liechtensteiner 66%, other 12%, Swiss 10%, Austrian 6%, German 3%, Italian 3%

GOVERNMENT: Parliamentary system

CURRENCY: Swiss franc = 100 rappen/centimes

Lithuania

Lying on the eastern coast of the Baltic Sea, Lithuania is the largest of the Baltic states. The first Soviet republic to declare independence from Moscow in 1991, it joined the EU in 2004.

GEOGRAPHY

Mostly flat with moors, bogs, and an intensively farmed central lowland. Numerous lakes and forested sandy ridges in the east.

CLIMATE

Coastal location moderates continental extremes. Cold winters, cool summers, and steady rainfall.

PEOPLE & SOCIETY

Homogeneous population, with Lithuanians forming a large majority. Only 1200 Jews, known as Litvaks, remain in Lithuania. Strong Roman Catholic tradition and historic links with Poland. There are better relations among ethnic groups than in other Baltic states and interethnic marriages are fairly common. However, ethnic Russians and Poles see a threat from "Lithuanianization." A large income gap has grown since independence.

THE ECONOMY

High-tech and heavy industries: engineering, shipbuilding, food processing. Bounced back from deep recession in 2009. Litas pegged to euro; adoption of euro set for 2015.

INSIGHT: *The "amber coast" of Lithuania produces most of the world's amber – fossilized resin*

LATVIA
22°
24°
26°
56°
Viekšniai
Telšiai
Plungė
Šiauliai
Panevėžys
Baltic Sea
Klaipėda
Skaudvilė
Ukmergė
Neman
Kaunas
RUSSIAN FEDERATION
VILNIUS
BELARUS
Alytus
POLAND
Druskininkai
54°
200m/656ft
Sea Level
0 50 km
0 50 miles

FACTFILE

OFFICIAL NAME: Republic of Lithuania
DATE OF FORMATION: 1991
CAPITAL: Vilnius
POPULATION: 3 million
TOTAL AREA: 25,174 sq. miles (65,200 sq. km)
DENSITY: 119 people per sq. mile
LANGUAGES: Lithuanian*, Russian
RELIGIONS: Roman Catholic 77%, other and nonreligious 17%, Russian Orthodox 4%, Protestant 1%, Old Believers 1%
ETHNIC MIX: Lithuanian 85%, Polish 7%, Russian 6%, Belarussian 1%, other 1%
GOVERNMENT: Parliamentary system
CURRENCY: Litas = 100 centu

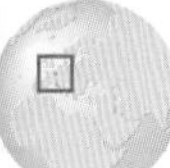

Luxembourg

Part of the plateau of the Ardennes in western Europe, Luxembourg is one of Europe's richest states. A tax haven and banking center, it is also home to key EU institutions.

GEOGRAPHY

Dense Ardennes forests in the north, with a low, open plateau to the south. Undulating terrain throughout.

CLIMATE

The climate is moist, with warm summers and mild winters. Snow is common only in the Ardennes.

PEOPLE & SOCIETY

Ethnic tensions are rare, despite a large proportion of foreigners (over a third of residents). Integration has been straightforward; most are fellow western Europeans and Catholics, mainly from Italy and Portugal. Low unemployment and high salaries promote stability. Divorce rates are rising and marriage is becoming less common.

INSIGHT: *Luxembourg's capital is home to around 2000 investment funds and 150 banks*

THE ECONOMY

Traditional industries such as steelmaking have given way to the banking and service sectors. Low taxes and banking secrecy laws attract foreign investors.

500m/1640ft
200m/656ft
Sea Level
Clervaux
Ardennes
50°
GERMANY
Ettelbrück
Echternach
Mersch
Moselle
BELGIUM
LUXEMBOURG
Pétange
Differdange
49°30′
Esch-sur -Alzette
Dudelange
FRANCE
6°
6°30′
0 10 km
0 10 miles

FACTFILE

OFFICIAL NAME: Grand Duchy of Luxembourg

DATE OF FORMATION: 1867

CAPITAL: Luxembourg-Ville

POPULATION: 500,000

TOTAL AREA: 998 sq. miles (2586 sq. km)

DENSITY: 501 people per sq. mile

LANGUAGES: Luxembourgish*, German*, French*

RELIGIONS: Roman Catholic 97%, Protestant, Orthodox Christian, and Jewish 3%

ETHNIC MIX: Luxembourger 62%, foreign residents 38%

GOVERNMENT: Parliamentary system

CURRENCY: Euro = 100 cents

Macedonia

Landlocked Macedonia, formerly part of Yugoslavia, was hit hard in the 1990s by sanctions on its northern trading partners, and in 2001 by conflict with its Albanian minority.

GEOGRAPHY

Mainly mountainous or hilly, with deep river basins in the center. Plains in the northeast and southwest.

CLIMATE

Continental climate with wet springs and dry autumns. Heavy snowfalls in northern mountains.

PEOPLE & SOCIETY

Slav Macedonians are mostly Orthodox Christians, with some Muslims. Officially, Muslim Albanians account for 25% of the population, but they claim to number a third. Albanian militants fought a bitter war against the state in 2001. A peace deal promised greater equality, but is yet to be fully implemented. A major stumbling block to EU and NATO accession is Greece's objection to the name Macedonia, in order to prevent any possibility of claims to historic "Macedonian" lands in north Greece.

THE ECONOMY

Steel, minerals, clothing, shoes, and tobacco exported. High unemployment. Organized crime and large gray economy. Progress with reforms. Investment boosted by EU candidate status.

INSIGHT: *Ohrid is the deepest lake in Europe at 964 ft (294 m)*

0 50 km
0 50 miles
SERBIA
BULGARIA
KOSOVO
(disputed)
Kumanovo
SKOPJE
Tetovo
42°
Kočani
Veles
Štip
Gostivar
ALBANIA
Kičevo
Strumica
Vardar
Prilep
Ohrid
Bitola
Lake Ohrid
41°
Lake Prespa
22°
GREECE
1000m/3281ft
500m/1640ft
200m/656ft
Sea Level

FACTFILE

OFFICIAL NAME: Republic of Macedonia
DATE OF FORMATION: 1991
CAPITAL: Skopje
POPULATION: 2.1 million
TOTAL AREA: 9781 sq. miles (25,333 sq. km)
DENSITY: 212 people per sq. mile
LANGUAGES: Macedonian*, Albanian*, Turkish, Romani, Serbian
RELIGIONS: Orthodox Christian 65%, Muslim 29%, Roman Catholic 4%, other 2%
ETHNIC MIX: Macedonian 64%, Albanian 25%, Turkish 4%, Roma 3%, Serb 2%, other 2%
GOVERNMENT: Mixed presidential–parliamentary system
CURRENCY: Macedonian denar = 100 deni

Madagascar

Lying off east Africa in the Indian Ocean, the former French colony of Madagascar is the world's fourth-largest island. Power struggles erupted onto the streets in 2002 and 2009.

GEOGRAPHY

More than two-thirds is a savanna-covered plateau, which drops in the east through rainforests to the coast.

CLIMATE

Tropical and often hit by cyclones. Monsoons affect the east coast. The southwest is much drier.

PEOPLE & SOCIETY

People are Malay-Indonesian in origin, intermixed with later migrants from Africa. The main ethnic division is between the Merina of the central plateau and the poorer *côtier* (coastal) peoples. The Merina were the country's historic rulers, and remain the social elite. The 2009 unrest led to four years of political transition.

INSIGHT: *80% of Madagascar's plants and many of its animal species are found nowhere else*

THE ECONOMY

Most people are farmers. Cash crops are vanilla, coffee, and cloves. Garments and shrimp also exported. Political crises deter investors.

0 200 km
0 200 miles
2000m/6562ft
1000m/3281ft
500m/1640ft
200m/656ft
Sea Level
12°
16°
20°
24°
44°
48°
Antsirañana
Sambava
Analalava
Mahajanga
Marovoay
Toamasina
ANTANANARIVO
Antsirabe
Morondava
Ambositra
Fianarantsoa
Mozambique Channel
INDIAN OCEAN
Toliara
Farafangana
Amboasary

FACTFILE

OFFICIAL NAME: Republic of Madagascar
DATE OF FORMATION: 1960
CAPITAL: Antananarivo
POPULATION: 22.9 million
TOTAL AREA: 226,656 sq. miles (587,040 sq. km)
DENSITY: 102 people per sq. mile
LANGUAGES: Malagasy*, French*, English*
RELIGIONS: Traditional beliefs 52%, Christian (mainly Roman Catholic) 41%, Muslim 7%
ETHNIC MIX: Other Malay 46%, Merina 26%, Betsimisaraka 15%, Betsileo 12%, other 1%
GOVERNMENT: Mixed presidential–parliamentary system
CURRENCY: Ariary = 5 iraimbilanja

Malawi

A former colony of the UK, Malawi lies landlocked in southeast Africa, following the Great Rift Valley. Its name means "the land where the sun is reflected in the water like fire."

GEOGRAPHY

Lake Nyasa takes up one-fifth of the landscape. Highlands lie west of the lake. Much of the land is covered by forests and savanna.

CLIMATE

Mainly subtropical. The south is hot and humid. Highlands are cooler.

PEOPLE & SOCIETY

Most Malawians share a common Bantu origin. Protestant Chewa live in central regions, while Muslim Yao live along the lake and in the south. Unlike neighboring states, ethnicity has not been exploited for political ends. Multiparty elections in 1994 ended the 30-year dictatorship of Dr. Banda. Half of the population lives in poverty.

INSIGHT: *Lake Nyasa is 353 miles (568 km) in length and contains at least 500 species of fish*

THE ECONOMY

Mainly subsistence farming. Tobacco accounts for over half of export earnings. Tea and sugar are grown. Drought and corruption are problems.

0 100 km
0 100 miles
34°
Karonga
10°
TANZANIA
Mzuzu
Euthini
12°
ZAMBIA
Chisumulti Likoma
(to Malawi)
Lake
Nyasa
MOZAMBIQUE
Great Rift Valley
LILONGWE
Salima
36°
14°
Dedza
Mangochi
MOZAMBIQUE
Zomba
Blantyre
16°
Nsanje
2000m/6562ft
1000m/3281ft
500m/1640ft
200m/656ft
Sea Level

FACTFILE

OFFICIAL NAME: Republic of Malawi
DATE OF FORMATION: 1964
CAPITAL: Lilongwe
POPULATION: 16.4 million
TOTAL AREA: 45,745 sq. miles (118,480 sq. km)
DENSITY: 451 people per sq. mile
LANGUAGES: Chewa, Lomwe, Yao, Ngoni, English*
RELIGIONS: Protestant 55%, Muslim 20%, Roman Catholic 20%, traditional beliefs 5%
ETHNIC MIX: Bantu 99%, other 1%
GOVERNMENT: Presidential system
CURRENCY: Malawi kwacha = 100 tambala

Malaysia

Malaysia stretches 1240 miles (2000 km) across southeast Asia from the Malay peninsula to Sabah in eastern Borneo. Federated in 1963, it included Singapore for two years.

GEOGRAPHY

The Malay Peninsula has central mountains, an eastern coastal belt, and fertile western plains. Swampy coastal plains rise to mountains on Borneo.

CLIMATE

Warm equatorial. Rainfall always heavy, but with distinct rainy seasons.

INSIGHT: *Malaysia is southeast Asia's major tourist destination, with over 25 million visitors a year*

PEOPLE & SOCIETY

The key distinction is between Malays (Bumiputras, literally "sons of the soil") and the Chinese, who traditionally controlled most economic activity. Since the 1970s, Malays have been favored for education and jobs, in order to address this imbalance.

THE ECONOMY

Successful industrial base includes electronics, manufacturing, and heavy industry. Tourism is a major earner. Leading producer of palm oil, tin, and tropical hardwoods.

THAILAND
Kangar
Kota Bharu
George Town
Kuala Terengganu
Taiping
Malay Peninsula
KUALA LUMPUR
PUTRAJAYA
Klang
Mersing
SINGAPORE
INDONESIA
South China Sea
Kepulauan Natuna
Natuna Sea
Kuching
Sri Aman
Sibu
Sarawak
Bintulu
Miri
BRUNEI
Borneo
Kota Kinabalu
Kudat
Sandakan
Keningau
Sabah
Sulu Sea
INDONESIA
INDONESIA
2000m/6562ft
1000m/3281ft
500m/1640ft
200m/656ft
Sea Level
0 100 km
0 100 miles

FACTFILE

OFFICIAL NAME: Malaysia
DATE OF FORMATION: 1963
CAPITALS: Kuala Lumpur; Putrajaya (administrative)
POPULATION: 29.7 million
TOTAL AREA: 127,316 sq. miles (329,750 sq. km)
DENSITY: 234 people per sq. mile
LANGUAGES: Bahasa Malaysia*, Malay, Chinese, Tamil, English
RELIGIONS: Muslim 61%, Buddhist 19%, Christian 9%, Hindu 6%, other 5%
ETHNIC MIX: Malay 53%, Chinese 26%, indigenous tribes 12%, Indian 8%, other 1%
GOVERNMENT: Parliamentary system
CURRENCY: Ringgit = 100 sen

Maldives

Set in the Indian Ocean, southwest of Sri Lanka, the Maldives is an archipelago of 1191 small coral islands, or atolls. 200 are inhabited. The word atoll comes from the Dhivehi word "atolu."

GEOGRAPHY

Consists of low-lying islands and coral atolls. The larger ones are covered in lush, tropical vegetation.

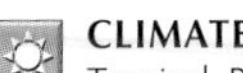

CLIMATE

Tropical. Rain falls throughout the year, but is heaviest June–November, during the monsoon. Violent storms occasionally hit the northern islands.

PEOPLE & SOCIETY

Maldivians, who are all Sunni Muslim, are descended from Sinhalese, Dravidian, Arab, and black ancestors. A third of the population live on Male'. Tourism has grown on separate resort islands away from residents. Politics was controlled by a group of influential families until young reformers pushed for parties to be legalized in 2005. However, legislative stalemate followed, and a controversial presidential election in 2013 returned the former elite to power.

THE ECONOMY

Fluctuating tourist industry is the economic mainstay. Fish, especially tuna, are the main export. Upgraded to a "middle income" country, despite 2004 tsunami damage.

INSIGHT:

The islands, which all lie below 4 ft (1.2 m), are threatened by rising sea levels, brought about by global warming and climatic changes

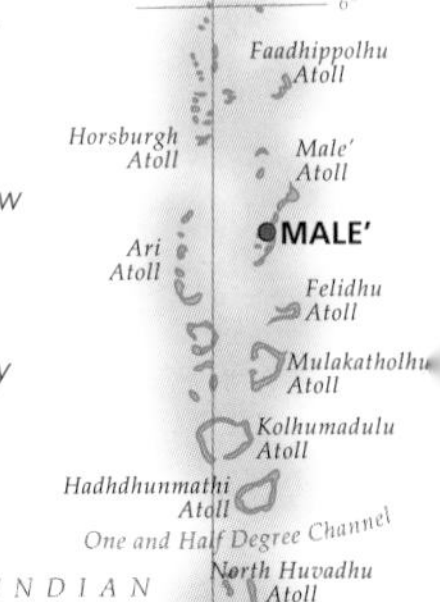
Ihavandippolhu Atoll
6°
Faadhippolhu Atoll
Horsburgh Atoll
Male' Atoll
MALE'
Ari Atoll
Felidhu Atoll
Mulakatholhu Atoll
Kolhumadulu Atoll
Hadhdhunmathi Atoll
One and Half Degree Channel
North Huvadhu Atoll
South Huvadhu Atoll
INDIAN OCEAN
Sea Level
0 100 km
0 100 miles

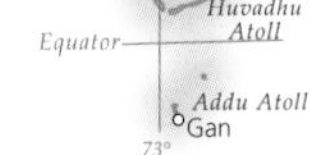
Equator
Addu Atoll
Gan
73°

FACTFILE

OFFICIAL NAME: Republic of Maldives
DATE OF FORMATION: 1965
CAPITAL: Male'
POPULATION: 300,000
TOTAL AREA: 116 sq. miles (300 sq. km)
DENSITY: 2586 people per sq. mile
LANGUAGES: Dhivehi* (Maldivian), Sinhala, Tamil, Arabic
RELIGIONS: Sunni Muslim 100%
ETHNIC MIX: All Maldivians are of Arab–Sinhalese–Malay descent
GOVERNMENT: Presidential system
CURRENCY: Rufiyaa = 100 laari

Mali

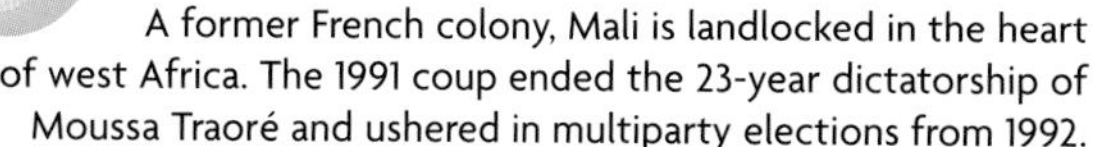

A former French colony, Mali is landlocked in the heart of west Africa. The 1991 coup ended the 23-year dictatorship of Moussa Traoré and ushered in multiparty elections from 1992.

GEOGRAPHY

The northern half lies in the Sahara. The inland delta of the Niger River flows through grassy savanna in the south.

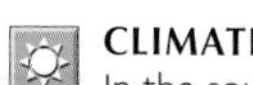

CLIMATE

In the south, intensely hot, dry weather precedes the westerly rains. The north is almost rainless.

PEOPLE & SOCIETY

Most people live in the south and are farmers, herders, or river fishermen. Nomadic Fulani and Tuareg herders travel the northern plains. Rebellion broke out there in 2012, initially Tuareg-led, but Islamist insurgents soon seized key towns. They were pushed back with international help, but low-level conflict continues. Women have little status.

INSIGHT: *Tombouctou (Timbuktu) was the center of the 14th-century Malinké trading empire*

THE ECONOMY

Widespread poverty. Less than 2% of land can be cultivated. Vulnerable to drought. Gold, high-quality cotton, and livestock account for 90% of exports. Tourism held back by instability and kidnappings by Al-Qaeda in the Maghreb.

24°
ALGERIA
MAURITANIA
Sahara
20°
Adrar des Ifôghas
Niger
Tombouctou
Gao
16°
Senegal
SENEGAL
Kayes
Mopti
NIGER
4°
Ségou
0°
BAMAKO
Koulikoro
12°
BURKINA FASO
Sikasso
12°
GUINEA
8°
CÔTE D'IVOIRE (IVORY COAST)
4°
0 200 km
0 200 miles
500m/1640ft
200m/656ft
Sea Level

FACTFILE

OFFICIAL NAME: Republic of Mali
DATE OF FORMATION: 1960
CAPITAL: Bamako
POPULATION: 15.3 million
TOTAL AREA: 478,764 sq. miles (1,240,000 sq. km)
DENSITY: 32 people per sq. mile
LANGUAGES: Bambara, Fulani, Senufo, Soninke, French*
RELIGIONS: Muslim (mainly Sunni) 90%, traditional beliefs 6%, Christian 4%
ETHNIC MIX: Bambara 52%, other 18%, Fulani 11%, Saracolé 7%, Soninka 7%, Tuareg 5%
GOVERNMENT: Presidential system
CURRENCY: CFA franc = 100 centimes

Malta

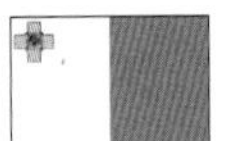

The densely populated Maltese archipelago lies between Africa and Europe. Controlled throughout its history by successive colonial powers, it gained independence from the UK in 1964.

GEOGRAPHY

The main island of Malta has low hills and a ragged coastline with numerous harbors, bays, sandy beaches, and rocky coves. The island of Gozo is more densely vegetated.

CLIMATE

Mediterranean climate. There are many hours of sunshine all year round, with very little rainfall.

PEOPLE & SOCIETY

Over the centuries, the Maltese have been subject to Arab, Sicilian, Spanish, French, and British influences. Today, the population is socially conservative and devoutly Roman Catholic – Malta only legalized divorce in 2011, the last European country except the Vatican to do so. Population density is among the highest in the world. Illegal migration from Africa has increased since Malta joined the EU in 2004.

THE ECONOMY

Tourism provides 30% of GDP. Joined eurozone in 2008. Developing offshore banking, high-tech industry. Semiconductors exported. Most goods have to be imported.

INSIGHT: *Malta is the only country to receive the George Cross for gallantry, in 1942 for national resilience to relentless German bombardment*

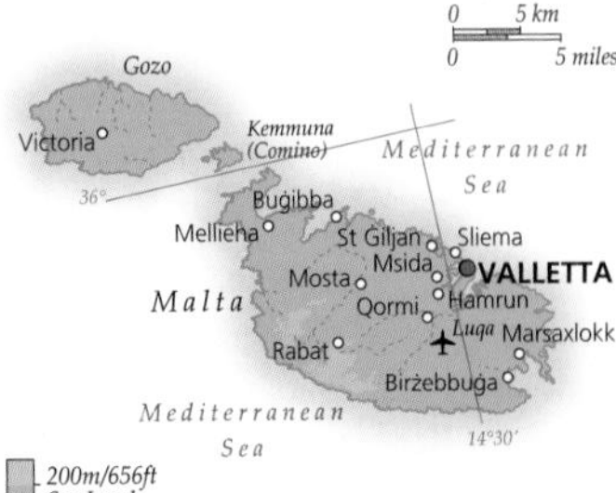

0 5 km
0 5 miles
Gozo
Victoria
Kemmuna
(Comino)
Mediterranean Sea
36°
Bugibba
Mellieha
St Giljan
Sliema
Msida
VALLETTA
Mosta
Malta
Qormi
Hamrun
Luqa
Marsaxlokk
Rabat
Birżebbuġa
Mediterranean Sea
14°30'
200m/656ft
Sea Level

FACTFILE

OFFICIAL NAME: Republic of Malta
DATE OF FORMATION: 1964
CAPITAL: Valletta
POPULATION: 400,000
TOTAL AREA: 122 sq. miles (316 sq. km)
DENSITY: 3226 people per sq. mile
LANGUAGES: Maltese*, English*
RELIGIONS: Roman Catholic 98%, other and nonreligious 2%
ETHNIC MIX: Maltese 96%, other 4%
GOVERNMENT: Parliamentary system
CURRENCY: Euro = 100 cents

Marshall Islands

Under US rule as part of the UN Trust Territory of the Pacific Islands until independence in 1986, the Marshall Islands comprises a group of 34 widely scattered atolls.

GEOGRAPHY

Narrow coral rings with sandy beaches enclosing lagoons. Those in the south have thicker vegetation. Kwajalein is the world's largest atoll.

CLIMATE

Tropical oceanic, cooled year round by northeast trade winds.

PEOPLE & SOCIETY

Over half the popluation live in Majuro, the capital and commercial center. Life on the outlying islands is still traditional, based around subsistence agriculture and fishing. Tensions are high due to poor living conditions, especially in periods of drought or flooding. Society is matrilineal, with land and titles handed down through the mother's clan.

INSIGHT: *In 1954, Bikini Atoll was the site for the testing of the largest US H-bomb – the 18–22 megaton Bravo*

THE ECONOMY

Almost totally dependent on US aid and the rent paid by the US for its missile base on Kwajalein Atoll. High unemployment. Revenue from licenses to fish in Marshallese waters for tuna. Copra and coconut oil are the only significant agricultural exports.

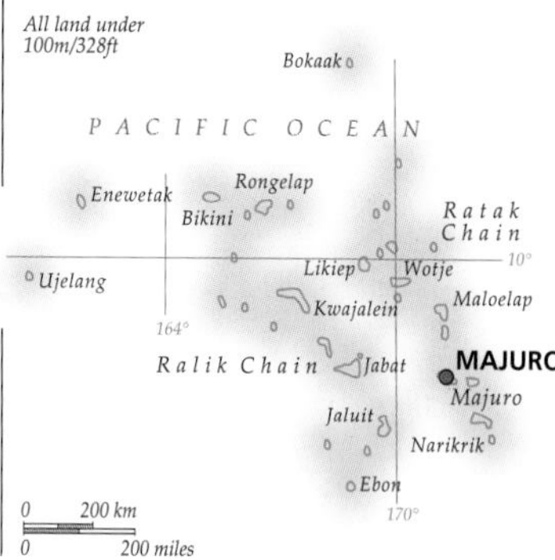
All land under 100m/328ft
Bokaak
PACIFIC OCEAN
Enewetak
Rongelap
Bikini
Ratak Chain
Ujelang
Likiep
Wotje
10°
Kwajalein
Maloelap
164°
Ralik Chain
Jabat
MAJURO
Majuro
Jaluit
Narikrik
Ebon
170°
0 200 km
0 200 miles

FACTFILE

OFFICIAL NAME: Republic of the Marshall Islands

DATE OF FORMATION: 1986

CAPITAL: Majuro

POPULATION: 69,747

TOTAL AREA: 70 sq. miles (181 sq. km)

DENSITY: 996 people per sq. mile

LANGUAGES: Marshallese*, English*, Japanese, German

RELIGIONS: Protestant 90%, Roman Catholic 8%, other 2%

ETHNIC MIX: Micronesian 90%, other 10%

GOVERNMENT: Presidential system

CURRENCY: US dollar = 100 cents

Mauritania

Two-thirds of Mauritania's territory is desert – the only productive land is that drained by the Senegal River. The country has taken a strongly Arab direction since 1964.

GEOGRAPHY

The Sahara, barren except for some scattered oases, covers the north. Savanna lands lie to the south.

CLIMATE

The climate is generally hot and dry, aggravated by the dusty *harmattan* wind. Summer rain in the south, virtually none in the north.

PEOPLE & SOCIETY

The Maures control political and economic life. Family solidarity among nomadic peoples is particularly strong. Ethnic tension centers on the oppression of the black minority. Tens of thousands of blacks are estimated to be in illegal slavery. Coups have interrupted civilian rule in recent years.

INSIGHT: *Slavery officially became illegal in Mauritania in 1980, but de facto slavery still persists*

THE ECONOMY

Agriculture and herding. Iron, copper, and gold mining. World's largest gypsum deposits. Offshore oil from 2006. Rich fishing grounds.

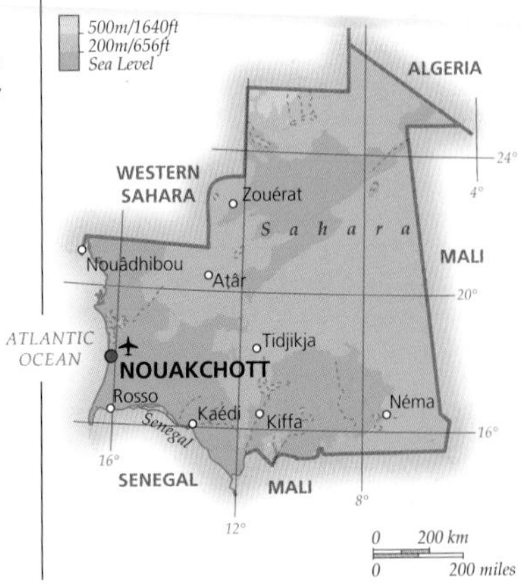
500m/1640ft
200m/656ft
Sea Level
ALGERIA
WESTERN SAHARA
Zouérat
Sahara
MALI
Nouâdhibou
Atâr
ATLANTIC OCEAN
Tidjikja
NOUAKCHOTT
Rosso
Kaédi
Kiffa
Néma
Senegal
SENEGAL
MALI
24°
20°
16°
4°
8°
12°
16°
0 200 km
0 200 miles

FACTFILE

OFFICIAL NAME: Islamic Republic of Mauritania

DATE OF FORMATION: 1960

CAPITAL: Nouakchott

POPULATION: 3.9 million

TOTAL AREA: 397,953 sq. miles (1,030,700 sq. km)

DENSITY: 10 people per sq. mile

LANGUAGES: Arabic*, Hassaniyah Arabic, Wolof, French

RELIGIONS: Sunni Muslim 100%

ETHNIC MIX: Maure 81%, Wolof 7%, Tukolor 5%, other 4%, Soninka 3%

GOVERNMENT: Presidential system

CURRENCY: Ouguiya = 5 khoums

Mauritius

The islands that make up Mauritius lie in the Indian Ocean east of Madagascar. They have enjoyed considerable economic success following recent industrial diversification and expansion.

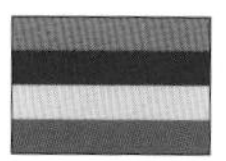

GEOGRAPHY

The volcanic main island of Mauritius is ringed by coral reefs, and rises from the coast to a fertile central plateau. The outer islands – Rodrigues, the Agalega Islands, and the Cargados Carajos Shoals – lie some 300 miles (500 km) to the north.

CLIMATE

Warm and humid. Tropical storms are frequent December–March, the hottest and wettest months.

PEOPLE & SOCIETY

Most people are descendants of laborers brought over from India in the 19th century. A small minority of French descent form the wealthiest group. Creoles (descendants of African slaves) complain of discrimination. Literacy is high. Health care is free. Crime rates are low. Less-developed Rodrigues has been self-governing since 2001.

THE ECONOMY

Clothing manufacture, tourism, and sugar. Loss of preferential trade terms for sugar and textiles. Offshore financial center. Growing outsourcing and ICT industries. Most food is imported.

INSIGHT: *The islands form part of the Mascarene Archipelago – once a land bridge between Asia and Africa*

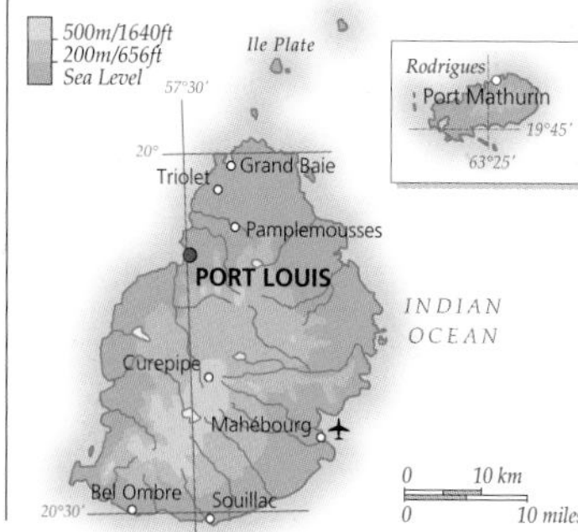
500m/1640ft
200m/656ft
Sea Level
57°30'
Ile Plate
Rodrigues
Port Mathurin
19°45'
63°25'
20°
Triolet
Grand Baie
Pamplemousses
PORT LOUIS
INDIAN OCEAN
Curepipe
Mahébourg
Bel Ombre
Souillac
20°30'
0 10 km
0 10 miles

FACTFILE

OFFICIAL NAME: Republic of Mauritius
DATE OF FORMATION: 1968
CAPITAL: Port Louis
POPULATION: 1.2 million
TOTAL AREA: 718 sq. miles (1860 sq. km)
DENSITY: 1671 people per sq. mile
LANGUAGES: French Creole, Hindi, Urdu, Tamil, Chinese, English*, French
RELIGIONS: Hindu 48%, Roman Catholic 24%, Muslim 17%, Protestant 9%, other 2%
ETHNIC MIX: Indo-Mauritian 68%, Creole 27%, Sino-Mauritian 3%, Franco-Mauritian 2%
GOVERNMENT: Parliamentary system
CURRENCY: Mauritian rupee = 100 cents

Mexico

Mexico stretches from the US border southward into the ancient Aztec and Mayan heartlands. Independence from Spain came in 1836. One in five Mexicans lives in the sprawling capital.

GEOGRAPHY

Coastal plains along the Pacific and Atlantic seaboards rise to a high arid central plateau. To the east and west are the Sierra Madre mountain ranges. Limestone lowlands form the projecting Yucatan peninsula.

CLIMATE

The plateau and high mountains are warm for much of the year. Pacific coast is tropical: storms occur mostly March–December. Northwest is dry.

PEOPLE & SOCIETY

Most Mexicans are *mestizos* of Spanish–Amerindian descent. Rural Amerindians are largely segregated from Hispanic society and most live in poverty, though the state promotes their culture. The Zapatista movement backs indigenous rights. Few women in male-dominated politics and business. Narcotics-related violent crime is rising.

THE ECONOMY

One of world's largest oil producers. Corn, fruit, vegetables, sugar are cash crops. NAFTA has boosted exports, but exposes farmers to subsidized US competition. Wealth disparity. Hit hard by 2008–2009 global downturn and swine flu crisis.

INSIGHT: *More people cross the US–Mexican border each year – illegally or legally – than any other border in the world*

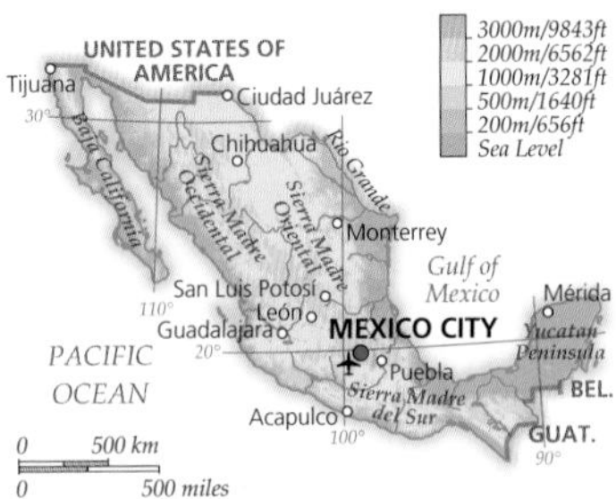
UNITED STATES OF AMERICA
Tijuana
Ciudad Juárez
Baja California
Chihuahua
Rio Grande
Sierra Madre Occidental
Sierra Madre Oriental
Monterrey
Gulf of Mexico
San Luis Potosí
Mérida
León
Guadalajara
MEXICO CITY
Yucatan Peninsula
PACIFIC OCEAN
Puebla
Sierra Madre del Sur
BEL.
Acapulco
GUAT.
30°
110°
20°
100°
90°
0 500 km
0 500 miles
3000m/9843ft
2000m/6562ft
1000m/3281ft
500m/1640ft
200m/656ft
Sea Level

FACTFILE

OFFICIAL NAME: United Mexican States
DATE OF FORMATION: 1836
CAPITAL: Mexico City
POPULATION: 122 million
TOTAL AREA: 761,602 sq. miles (1,972,550 sq. km
DENSITY: 166 people per sq. mile
LANGUAGES: Spanish*, Nahuatl, Mayan, Zapotec, Mixtec, Otomi, Totonac, Tzotzil
RELIGIONS: Roman Catholic 77%, other 14%, Protestant 6%, nonreligious 3%
ETHNIC MIX: *Mestizo* 60%, Amerindian 30%, European 9%, other 1%
GOVERNMENT: Presidential system
CURRENCY: Mexican peso = 100 centavos

Micronesia

The Federated States of Micronesia (FSM), situated in the western Pacific, comprise 607 islands and atolls grouped into four main island states: Pohnpei, Kosrae, Chuuk, and Yap.

GEOGRAPHY

Mixture of high volcanic islands with forested interiors, and low-lying coral atolls. Some of the islands have coastal mangrove swamps.

CLIMATE

Tropical, with high humidity. There is very heavy rainfall outside the January–March dry season.

INSIGHT: *Chuuk's lagoon contains the sunken wrecks of over 100 Japanese ships and 270 planes from World War II*

PEOPLE & SOCIETY

Micronesians are physically, culturally, and linguistically diverse. Melanesians live on Yap, Polynesians in Pohnpei. The supply of electricity and running water is limited. Society is based on matrilineal clans.

THE ECONOMY

Dependent on US aid. Fishing licenses are a key source of foreign revenue. Tourism, fishing, betel nuts, copra are economic mainstays. Trust fund created to reduce aid reliance.

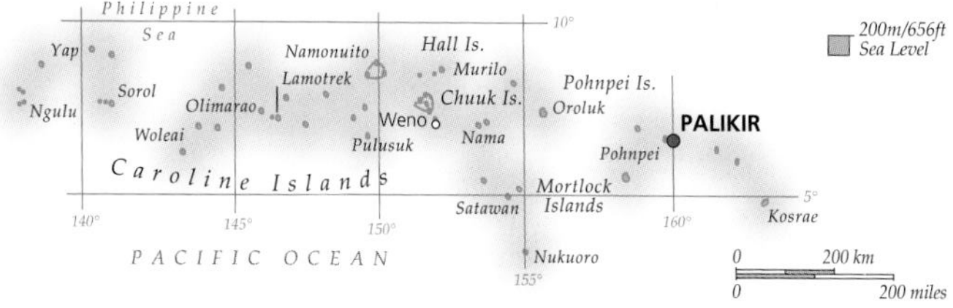
Philippine Sea
Yap
Ngulu
Sorol
Woleai
Olimarao
Namonuito
Lamotrek
Hall Is.
Murilo
Chuuk Is.
Weno
Pulusuk
Nama
Pohnpei Is.
Oroluk
PALIKIR
Pohnpei
Caroline Islands
Mortlock Islands
Satawan
Kosrae
Nukuoro
PACIFIC OCEAN
10°
5°
140°
145°
150°
155°
160°
200m/656ft
Sea Level
0
200 km
0
200 miles

FACTFILE

OFFICIAL NAME: Federated States of Micronesia
DATE OF FORMATION: 1986
CAPITAL: Palikir (Pohnpei Island)
POPULATION: 106,104
TOTAL AREA: 271 sq. miles (702 sq. km)
DENSITY: 392 people per sq. mile
LANGUAGES: Trukese, Pohnpeian, Kosraean, Yapese, English*
RELIGIONS: Roman Catholic 50%, Protestant 47%, other 3%
ETHNIC MIX: Chuukese 49%, Pohnpeian 24%, other 14%, Kosraean 6%, Yapese 5%, Asian 2%
GOVERNMENT: Nonparty system
CURRENCY: US dollar = 100 cents

Moldova

The most densely populated of the former Soviet republics, Moldova has strong ethnic, linguistic, and cultural links with Romania, but relations with Russia remain paramount.

GEOGRAPHY

Steppes and hilly plains are drained by the Dniester and Prut rivers.

CLIMATE

Warm summers and relatively mild winters. Moderate rainfall is evenly spread throughout the year.

PEOPLE & SOCIETY

A shared heritage with Romania defines national identity, though in 1994 Moldovans voted against possible reunification with Romania. Most of the population is engaged in intensive agriculture. Transnistria is a breakaway state along the east bank of the Dniester, home to a largely ethnic Slav population. The Gagauz, in the south, have accepted autonomy.

INSIGHT: *Vast underground wine vaults contain entire "streets" of bottles built into rock quarries*

THE ECONOMY

Poorest country in Europe. Mainly agricultural: produces wine, tobacco, fruit. Food processing and textiles. Depends on Russia for raw materials, fuel, exports. Political instability.

UKRAINE
Dniester
Edineț
Rîșcani
48°
Soroca
Florești
Bălți
Prut
Rîbnița
Dniester
Dubăsari Reservoir
Orhei
TRANSNISTRIA (disputed)
CHIȘINĂU
Tiraspol
ROMANIA
Tighina (Bendery)
Comrat
46°
Cahul
28°
0 50 km
0 50 miles
200m/656ft
Sea Level

FACTFILE

OFFICIAL NAME: Republic of Moldova

DATE OF FORMATION: 1991

CAPITAL: Chisinau

POPULATION: 3.5 million

TOTAL AREA: 13,067 sq. miles (33,843 sq. km)

DENSITY: 269 people per sq. mile

LANGUAGES: Moldovan*, Ukrainian, Russian

RELIGIONS: Orthodox Christian 93%, other 6%, Baptist 1%

ETHNIC MIX: Moldovan 84%, Ukrainian 7%, Gagauz 5%, Russian 2%, Bulgarian 1%, other 1%

GOVERNMENT: Parliamentary system

CURRENCY: Moldovan leu = 100 bani

Monaco

Monaco is a tiny principality on the Côte d'Azur. Its destiny changed radically when the casino was opened in 1863. Today, it promotes its image as an upmarket, glamorous destination.

GEOGRAPHY

A rocky promontory overlooking a narrow coastal strip that has been enlarged through land reclamation.

CLIMATE

Mediterranean. Summers are hot and dry; days with 12 hours of sunshine are not uncommon. Winters are mild and sunny.

PEOPLE & SOCIETY

Less than 20% of residents are Monégasques. Almost half are French, the rest Italian, American, British, Belgian, and others. Nationals enjoy considerable privileges, including housing subsidies to protect them from Monaco's high property prices, and the right of first refusal before a job can be offered to a foreigner. Women have equal status, but only acquired the vote in 1962. Prince Albert married South African swimmer Charlene Wittstock in 2011.

THE ECONOMY

Tourism, gambling, financial services. Banking secrecy laws and tax-haven conditions attract foreign investment. Close links and customs union with France (but not in EU). No resources: depends on imports.

INSIGHT: *High-profile social and sporting events attract large crowds each spring, including the Rose Ball, Tennis Open, and Grand Prix*

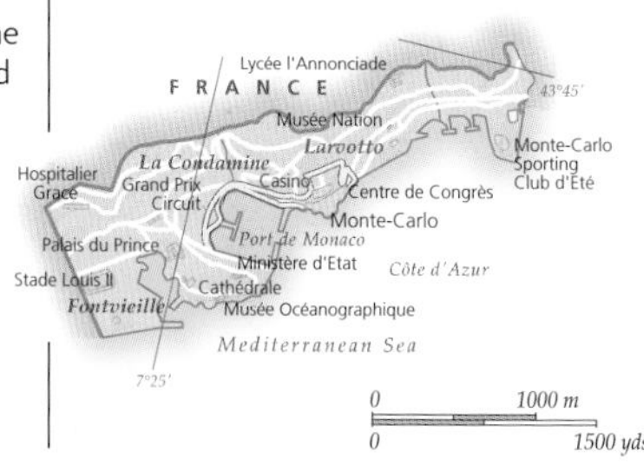
Lycée l'Annonciade
FRANCE
43°45'
Musée Nation
Larvotto
Monte-Carlo Sporting Club d'Été
Hospitalier Grace
La Condamine
Grand Prix Circuit
Casino
Centre de Congrès
Monte-Carlo
Palais du Prince
Port de Monaco
Ministère d'Etat
Côte d'Azur
Stade Louis II
Cathédrale
Fontvieille
Musée Océanographique
Mediterranean Sea
7°25'
0
1000 m
0
1500 yds

FACTFILE

OFFICIAL NAME: Principality of Monaco
DATE OF FORMATION: 1861
CAPITAL: Monaco-Ville
POPULATION: 36,136
TOTAL AREA: 0.75 sq. miles (1.95 sq. km)
DENSITY: 48,181 people per sq. mile
LANGUAGES: French*, Italian, Monégasque, English
RELIGIONS: Roman Catholic 89%, Protestant 6%, other 5%
ETHNIC MIX: French 47%, other 21%, Italian 16%, Monégasque 16%
GOVERNMENT: Mixed monarchical–parliamentary system
CURRENCY: Euro = 100 cents

Mongolia

Landlocked between Russia and China, Mongolia is a huge, isolated, and sparsely populated nation. Over two-thirds of the country is part of the Gobi Desert.

GEOGRAPHY

A mountainous steppe plateau in the north, with lakes in the north and west. The desert region of the Gobi dominates the south.

CLIMATE

Continental. Mild summers and long, dry, very cold winters, with heavy snowfall. Temperatures can drop as low as –22°F (–30°C).

PEOPLE & SOCIETY

Mongolia was unified by Genghis Khan in 1206 and was later absorbed into Manchu China. A majority of ethnic Mongolians live within China in Inner Mongolia. Tibetan Buddhism dominates. The traditional, nomadic way of life has been eroded as urban migration continues, spurred by ferocious winters, known as *zud*, which can devastate the rural economy.

THE ECONOMY

Rich deposits of oil, coal, copper, uranium, and other minerals remain largely untapped. Cashmere exports. Democracy, from 1990, brought a shift toward a market economy, but also rising poverty. State involvement in mining is an issue. Agriculture uses a third of the workforce, mainly as herders.

INSIGHT: *Horseracing, wrestling, and archery are the national sports*

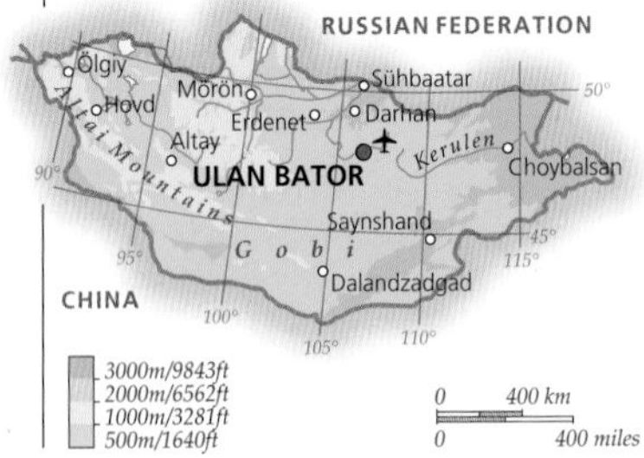
RUSSIAN FEDERATION
Ölgiy
Hovd
Mörön
Sühbaatar
Erdenet
Darhan
Altay
Altai Mountains
ULAN BATOR
Kerulen
Choybalsan
Saynshand
Gobi
Dalandzadgad
CHINA
50°
45°
90°
95°
100°
105°
110°
115°
3000m/9843ft
2000m/6562ft
1000m/3281ft
500m/1640ft
0 400 km
0 400 miles

FACTFILE

OFFICIAL NAME: Mongolia
DATE OF FORMATION: 1924
CAPITAL: Ulan Bator
POPULATION: 2.8 million
TOTAL AREA: 604,247 sq. miles (1,565,000 sq. km)
DENSITY: 5 people per sq. mile
LANGUAGES: Khalkha Mongolian*, Kazakh
RELIGIONS: Tibetan Buddhist 50%, nonreligious 40%, Shamanist and Christian 6%, Muslim 4%
ETHNIC MIX: Khalkh 95%, Kazakh 4%, other 1%
GOVERNMENT: Mixed presidential–parliamentary system
CURRENCY: Tugrik (tögrög) = 100 möngö

Montenegro

Perched on the Adriatic coast, this tiny republic became a separate state in 2006, after 88 years of federation with its neighbors in various forms of the state of Yugoslavia.

GEOGRAPHY

A narrow coastal strip on the Adriatic. Fertile lowland plains around Lake Scutari. Mountainous interior with deep canyons.

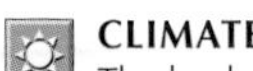

CLIMATE

The lowlands have hot, dry summers and mild winters. Heavy snow in winter in the mountains.

PEOPLE & SOCIETY

Most Montenegrins are Orthodox Christians. They speak a language closely related to Serbian, that also uses Cyrillic script. Muslim Albanians, who make up 70% of the population of the southern Ulcinj region, supported independence. Foreigners, particularly Russians, British, and Serbs, are buying Adriatic real estate.

INSIGHT: *Dark forests once cloaked Montenegro's mountains; its name means "Black Mountain"*

THE ECONOMY

Tourism (along Adriatic) drives growth. Bauxite reserves, aluminum industry. Return of investment, foreign aid. Crackdown on cigarette smuggling, black market, corruption led to approval in 2010 as candidate for EU membership. Uses euro, though not part of eurozone.

BOSNIA & HERZEGOVINA
Pljevlja
SERBIA
20°
Pivsko Jezero
Bijelo Polje
43°
Piva
Sinjavina
Tara
Berane
Hajla
Rožaje
Dinaric Alps
Lim
KOSOVO
(disputed)
Nikšić
CRO.
Herceg-Novi
Cetinje
PODGORICA
Tivat
ALBANIA
Budva
Adriatic Sea
Lake Scutari
Bar
42°
0 20 km
0 20 miles
Ulcinj
2000m/6562ft
1000m/3281ft
500m/1640ft
200m/656ft
Sea Level

FACTFILE

OFFICIAL NAME: Montenegro
DATE OF FORMATION: 2006
CAPITAL: Podgorica
POPULATION: 600,000
TOTAL AREA: 5332 sq. miles (13,812 sq. km)
DENSITY: 113 people per sq. mile
LANGUAGES: Montenegrin*, Serbian, Albanian, Bosniak, Croatian
RELIGIONS: Orthodox Christian 74%, Muslim 18%, Roman Catholic 4%, other 4%
ETHNIC MIX: Montenegrin 43%, Serb 32%, other 12%, Bosniak 8%, Albanian 5%
GOVERNMENT: Parliamentary system
CURRENCY: Euro = 100 cents

Morocco

Morocco is a former French colony in northwest Africa. Since 1975, it has occupied the territory of Western Sahara, the future of which is yet to be determined by UN-supervised referendum.

GEOGRAPHY

Fertile coastal plain is interrupted in the east by the Rif Mountains. Atlas Mountain ranges to the south. Beyond lies the outer fringe of the Sahara.

CLIMATE

Ranges from temperate and warm in the north, to semiarid in the south. Cooler in the mountains.

PEOPLE & SOCIETY

The Berber minority descend from north Africa's original inhabitants, and live mainly in mountain villages. The Arab majority inhabits the lowlands. Morocco is unusual among Arab states in granting Jews religious freedom and civil rights. The king is spiritual leader and head of state. During the 2011 "Arab Spring" protesters called for more democracy. Islamists have gained influence in politics. Islamist militancy and the emergence of terrorist cells are of concern.

THE ECONOMY

Major exporter of phosphates. Investment in tourism and agriculture. Fishing. Relations with EU strained over illegal immigrants and cannabis trade.

INSIGHT: *Karueein University in Fès, founded in 859 CE, is the world's oldest existing educational institution*

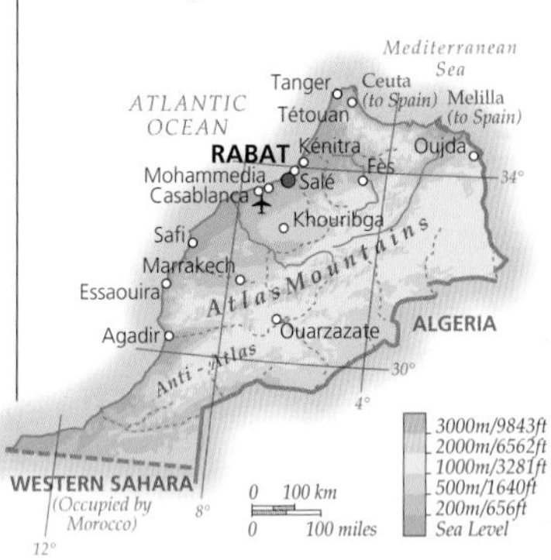
Mediterranean Sea
ATLANTIC OCEAN
Tanger
Ceuta (to Spain)
Melilla (to Spain)
Tétouan
RABAT
Kénitra
Oujda
Fès
Mohammedia
Salé
Casablanca
Khouribga
Safi
Marrakech
Essaouira
Atlas Mountains
Agadir
Ouarzazate
ALGERIA
Anti - Atlas
34°
30°
4°
8°
12°
WESTERN SAHARA (Occupied by Morocco)
0 100 km
0 100 miles
3000m/9843ft
2000m/6562ft
1000m/3281ft
500m/1640ft
200m/656ft
Sea Level

FACTFILE

OFFICIAL NAME: Kingdom of Morocco
DATE OF FORMATION: 1956
CAPITAL: Rabat
POPULATION: 33 million
TOTAL AREA: 172,316 sq. miles (446,300 sq. km)
DENSITY: 192 people per sq. mile
LANGUAGES: Arabic*, Tamazight (Berber), French, Spanish
RELIGIONS: Muslim (mainly Sunni) 99%, other (mostly Christian) 1%
ETHNIC MIX: Arab 70%, Berber 29%, European 1%
GOVERNMENT: Mixed monarchical–parliamentary system
CURRENCY: Mor. dirham = 100 centimes

Mozambique

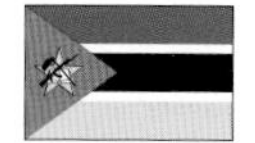

Mozambique lies on the southeast African coast. It was torn apart by a savage and devastating civil war between the Marxist government and a rebel faction between 1977 and 1992.

GEOGRAPHY

Largely a savanna-covered plateau. The coast is fringed by coral reefs and lagoons. The Zambezi River bisects the country.

CLIMATE

Tropical. Temperatures are hottest on the coast. Extremes of rainfall: drought and flood.

PEOPLE & SOCIETY

Tensions exist between north and south, rather than between ethnic groups. Life is centered on the extended family. Polygamy is fairly common. The country is struggling with the legacy of a war that killed around a million people, and the effects of frequent floods and droughts. Half the population lives in abject poverty.

INSIGHT: *Maputo's busy port serves Zimbabwe and South Africa*

THE ECONOMY

Extremely dependent on aid. Mineral potential. Cashew nuts, shrimp, cotton exported. Debt relief.

0 200 km
0 200 miles
TANZANIA
Rovuma
12°
Lake Nyasa
MALAWI
Lichinga
Pemba
Lúrio
Nacala
ZAMBIA
Lake Cahora Bassa
Lumbo
Nampula
16°
Tete
Zambezi
Quelimane
40°
ZIMBABWE
Beira
Mozambique Channel
20°
INDIAN OCEAN
Limpopo
Funhalouro
Inhambane
24°
SOUTH AFRICA
Xai-Xai
36°
MAPUTO
SWAZILAND
SOUTH AFRICA
32°
2000m/6562ft
1000m/3281ft
500m/1640ft
200m/656ft
Sea Level

FACTFILE

OFFICIAL NAME: Republic of Mozambique

DATE OF FORMATION: 1975

CAPITAL: Maputo

POPULATION: 25.8 million

TOTAL AREA: 309,494 sq. miles (801,590 sq. km)

DENSITY: 85 people per sq. mile

LANGUAGES: Makua, Xitsonga, Sena, Lomwe, Portuguese*

RELIGIONS: Traditional beliefs 56%, Christian 30%, Muslim 14%

ETHNIC MIX: Makua Lomwe 47%, Tsonga 23%, Malawi 12%, Shona 11%, Yao 4%, other 3%

GOVERNMENT: Presidential system

CURRENCY: New metical = 100 centavos

Myanmar (Burma)

Forming the eastern shores of the Bay of Bengal and the Andaman Sea in southeast Asia, Myanmar has suffered from isolation, political repression, and ethnic conflict.

GEOGRAPHY

The fertile Irrawaddy basin lies at the center. Mountains to the west, Shan plateau to the east. Tropical rainforest covers much of the land.

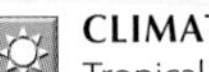

CLIMATE

Tropical. Hot summers, with high humidity, and warm winters.

PEOPLE & SOCIETY

The military, in power from 1962, paid little regard to human rights, and didn't tolerate opposition. The National League for Democracy won elections in 1990, but was kept from power. Elections in 2010, nominally restoring civilian rule, were dominated by the new military-backed party. Ethnic minorities are fighting for independence.

INSIGHT: *Myanmar is one of the world's biggest teak exporters, though reserves are diminishing rapidly*

THE ECONOMY

Corrupt, mismanaged, subject to sanctions – but gas, teak, and gems are exported. One of world's largest illegal opium producers. Goods sold on black market carry high prices.

INDIA
CHINA
LAOS
THAILAND
Myitkyina
Irrawaddy
Monywa
Mandalay
Pakokku
Sagaing
Shan Plateau
Mekong
Sittwe
Taunggyi
NAY PYI TAW
Taungoo
Thandwe
Pyay
Hinthada
Bago
Insein
Pathein
Thaton
Yangon (Rangoon)
Mawlamyine
Kyaikkami
Mouths of the Irrawaddy
Bay of Bengal
Dawei
Andaman Sea
Myeik
Mergui Archipelago
Isthmus of Kra
0 200 km
0 200 miles
4000m/13124ft
2000m/6562ft
1000m/3281ft
500m/1640ft
200m/656ft
Sea Level

FACTFILE

OFFICIAL NAME: Republic of the Union of Myanmar
DATE OF FORMATION: 1948
CAPITAL: Nay Pyi Taw
POPULATION: 53.3 million
TOTAL AREA: 261,969 sq. miles (678,500 sq. km)
DENSITY: 210 people per sq. mile
LANGUAGES: Burmese (Myanmar)*, Shan, Karen, Rakhine, Chin, Yangbye, Kachin, Mon
RELIGIONS: Buddhist 89%, Christian 4%, Muslim 4%, other 2%, Animist 1%
ETHNIC MIX: Burman (Bamah) 68%, other 12%, Shan 9%, Karen 7%, Rakhine 4%
GOVERNMENT: Presidential system
CURRENCY: Kyat = 100 pyas

Namibia

Located in southwestern Africa, Namibia gained independence from South Africa in 1990, after 24 years of armed struggle. It regained the territory of Walvis Bay in 1994.

GEOGRAPHY

The Namib Desert stretches along the coastal strip. Inland, a ridge of mountains rises to 8000 ft (2500 m). The Kalahari Desert lies in the east.

CLIMATE

Almost rainless. The coast is usually shrouded in thick fog, unless the hot, dry *berg* wind is blowing.

PEOPLE & SOCIETY

The Ovambo, the main ethnic group, live mainly in the more populous north. Some 100,000 whites, many of German descent, are centered around Windhoek and still control the economy. The minority San and Khoi bushmen are among the oldest human communities in the world. Homosexual rights are restricted.

INSIGHT: *The Namib is the Earth's oldest, and one of its driest, deserts*

THE ECONOMY

Varied mineral resources, notably uranium and diamonds. Rich offshore fishing grounds. High unemployment. HIV/AIDS epidemic. One of Africa's most skewed distributions of wealth.

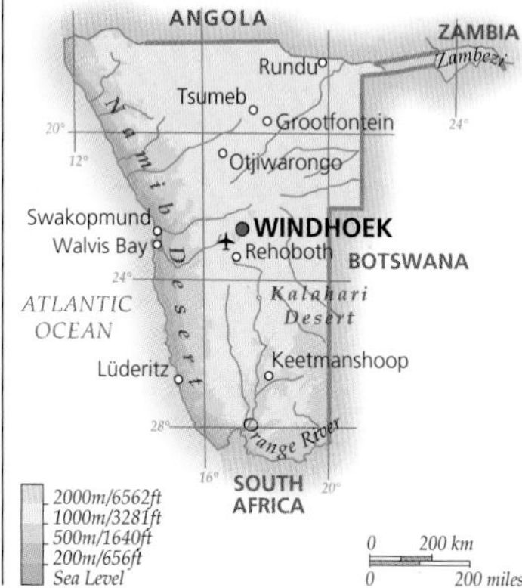
ANGOLA
ZAMBIA
Zambezi
Rundu
Tsumeb
Grootfontein
Otjiwarongo
Namib Desert
Swakopmund
Walvis Bay
WINDHOEK
Rehoboth
BOTSWANA
ATLANTIC OCEAN
Kalahari Desert
Lüderitz
Keetmanshoop
Orange River
SOUTH AFRICA
20°
12°
24°
28°
16°
20°
24°
2000m/6562ft
1000m/3281ft
500m/1640ft
200m/656ft
Sea Level
0 200 km
0 200 miles

FACTFILE

OFFICIAL NAME: Republic of Namibia
DATE OF FORMATION: 1990
CAPITAL: Windhoek
POPULATION: 2.3 million
TOTAL AREA: 318,694 sq. miles (825,418 sq. km)
DENSITY: 7 people per sq. mile
LANGUAGES: Ovambo, Kavango, English*, Bergdama, German, Afrikaans
RELIGIONS: Christian 90%, traditional beliefs 10%
ETHNIC MIX: Ovambo 50%, other tribes 22%, Kavango 9%, Damara 7%, Herero 7%, other 5%
GOVERNMENT: Presidential system
CURRENCY: Namibian dollar = 100 cents

Nauru

Nauru lies in the Pacific, northeast of Australia. Phosphate deposits gave its inhabitants huge temporary wealth, but economic mismanagement has left them facing ruin.

GEOGRAPHY

A single low-lying coral atoll, with a fertile coastal belt. Coral cliffs encircle an elevated interior plateau.

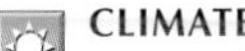

CLIMATE

Equatorial, moderated by sea breezes. Occasional long droughts.

PEOPLE & SOCIETY

Native Nauruans are of mixed Micronesian and Polynesian origin. Most live in simple, traditional houses and spend their money on luxury cars and consumer goods. Welfare and education are free. A diet of imported processed foods has caused widespread obesity and diabetes. Mining was left to imported laborers, mainly from Kiribati, who lived in enclaves of male-only barracks and had few rights. Many young Nauruans leave to seek a better life in Australia or New Zealand.

THE ECONOMY

Phosphate revenues diminished. Sale of fishing rights only other resource. State trust fund invested badly overseas. Offshore banking facilities closed after international pressure.

INSIGHT: *Phosphate mining has left 80% of the island uninhabitable*

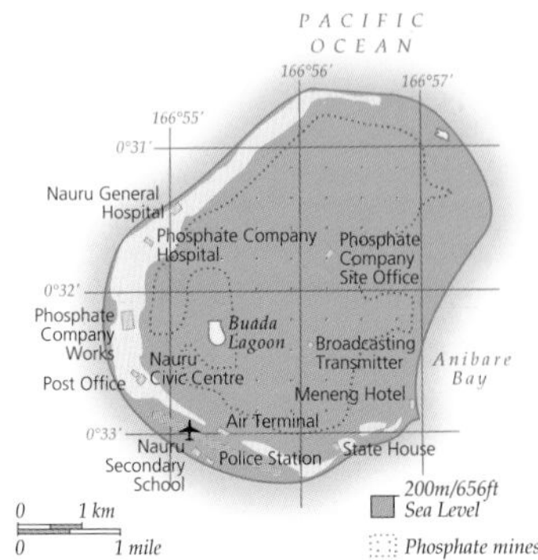
PACIFIC OCEAN
166°56′
166°57′
166°55′
0°31′
0°32′
0°33′
Nauru General Hospital
Phosphate Company Hospital
Phosphate Company Site Office
Phosphate Company Works
Buada Lagoon
Broadcasting Transmitter
Anibare Bay
Nauru Civic Centre
Post Office
Meneng Hotel
Air Terminal
Nauru Secondary School
Police Station
State House
0 1 km
0 1 mile
200m/656ft
Sea Level
Phosphate mines

FACTFILE

OFFICIAL NAME: Republic of Nauru
DATE OF FORMATION: 1968
CAPITAL: None
POPULATION: 9434
TOTAL AREA: 8.1 sq. miles (21 sq. km)
DENSITY: 1165 people per sq. mile
LANGUAGES: Nauruan*, Kiribati, Chinese, Tuvaluan, English
RELIGIONS: Nauruan Congregational Church 60%, Roman Catholic 35%, other 5%
ETHNIC MIX: Nauruan 93%, Chinese 5%, other Pacific islanders 1%, European 1%
GOVERNMENT: Nonparty system
CURRENCY: Australian dollar = 100 cents

Nepal

Nepal, lying between India and China on the southern shoulder of the Himalayas, is one of the world's poorest countries. Its agricultural economy is heavily dependent on the monsoon.

GEOGRAPHY

Mainly mountainous. The area includes some of the highest mountains in the world, including Mount Everest. Flat, fertile river plains form the south.

CLIMATE

Warm monsoon season from July to October. The rest of the year is dry, sunny, and mild. Winter temperatures in the Himalayas average 14°F (–10°C).

PEOPLE & SOCIETY

Tensions are few between the diverse ethnic groups. Buddhist women, including Sherpas, face fewer social restrictions than Hindus. Trafficking of women and child labor are problems. Human rights violations rose during the 1999–2006 Maoist insurgency. The peace deal led to the abolition of the monarchy and the Maoists joining the political mainstream, but fractious coalitions mean instability continues.

THE ECONOMY

Agriculture employs two-thirds of workforce. Crops include rice and wheat. Tourism and investment affected by instability. Reliant on aid and overseas remittances. Hydropower potential.

INSIGHT: *Southern Nepal was the birthplace of Buddha (Prince Siddhartha Gautama) in 563 BCE*

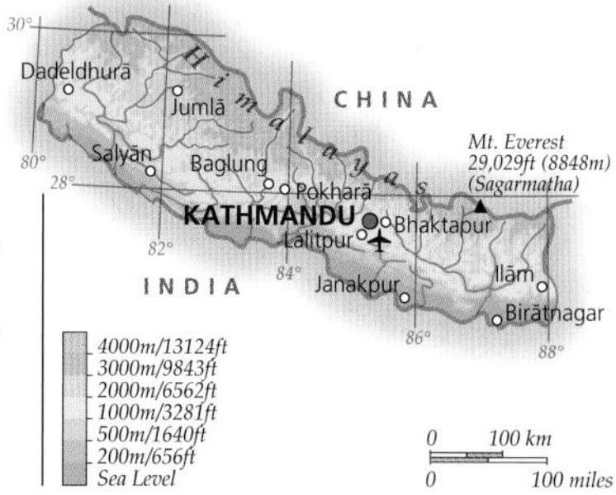

30°
Dadeldhura
Jumlā
Himalayas
CHINA
Mt. Everest
29,029ft (8848m)
(Sagarmatha)
80°
28°
Salyān
Baglung
Pokharā
KATHMANDU
Bhaktapur
Lalitpur
82°
84°
INDIA
Janakpur
Ilām
Birātnagar
86°
88°
4000m/13124ft
3000m/9843ft
2000m/6562ft
1000m/3281ft
500m/1640ft
200m/656ft
Sea Level
0 100 km
0 100 miles

FACTFILE

OFFICIAL NAME: Federal Democratic Republic of Nepal
DATE OF FORMATION: 1769
CAPITAL: Kathmandu
POPULATION: 27.8 million
TOTAL AREA: 54,363 sq. miles (140,800 sq. km)
DENSITY: 526 people per sq. mile
LANGUAGES: Nepali*, Maithili, Bhojpuri
RELIGIONS: Hindu 81%, Buddhist 11%, Muslim 4%, other (including Christian) 4%
ETHNIC MIX: Other 52%, Chhetri 16%, Hill Brahman 13%, Tharu 7%, Magar 7%, Tamang 5%
GOVERNMENT: Transitional regime
CURRENCY: Nepalese rupee = 100 paisa

Netherlands

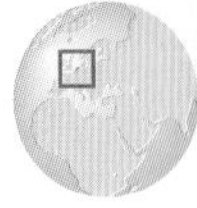

Astride the delta of five major rivers in northwest Europe, the Netherlands built its historic wealth on maritime trade. Rotterdam is Europe's largest port.

GEOGRAPHY

Mainly flat, with 27% of the land below sea level and protected by dunes, dikes, and canals. There are a few low hills in the south and east.

CLIMATE

Mild, rainy winters and cool summers. Gales from the North Sea are common in fall and winter.

PEOPLE & SOCIETY

The Dutch have a long history of welcoming immigrants from former colonies and refugees seeking asylum. However, lack of integration is now raising fears about the failing asylum system, immigrant crime, and militant Islam. Population is mostly urban and the density is high. The state does not try to impose a particular morality on its citizens. Laws concerning sexuality, narcotics-taking, and euthanasia are among the world's most liberal.

THE ECONOMY

Major trading hub. High-profile multinationals. Diverse industrial base: chemicals, machinery, electronics, and metals. Costly social welfare system.

INSIGHT: *In 2002, the Netherlands became the first country in the world to legalize euthanasia*

Sea Level
Below Sea Level
Waddeneilanden
Waddenzee
Groningen
Leeuwarden
53°
North Sea
IJsselmeer
AMSTERDAM
Haarlem
'S-GRAVENHAGE
(THE HAGUE)
Leiden
Utrecht
Apeldoorn
Enschede
52°
Delft
Neder Rijn
Arnhem
Rotterdam
Nijmegen
7°
GERMANY
Maas
Breda
Tilburg
Eindhoven
Maas
5°
4°
BELGIUM
51°
0 40 km
0 40 miles
Maastricht
6°

FACTFILE

OFFICIAL NAME: Kingdom of the Netherlands

DATE OF FORMATION: 1648

CAPITALS: Amsterdam and The Hague

POPULATION: 16.8 million

TOTAL AREA: 16,033 sq. miles (41,526 sq. km)

DENSITY: 1283 people per sq. mile

LANGUAGES: Dutch*, Frisian

RELIGIONS: Roman Catholic 36%, other 34%, Protestant 27%, Muslim 3%

ETHNIC MIX: Dutch 82%, other 12%, Turkish 2%, Surinamese 2%, Moroccan 2%

GOVERNMENT: Parliamentary system

CURRENCY: Euro = 100 cents

New Zealand

Lying in the South Pacific, 990 miles (1600 km) southeast of Australia, New Zealand comprises North and South Islands, separated by the Cook Strait, and many smaller islands.

GEOGRAPHY

North Island, noted for hot springs and geysers, has the bulk of the population. South Island is mostly mountainous, with eastern lowlands.

CLIMATE

Generally temperate and damp. The far north is almost subtropical, whereas southern winters are cold.

PEOPLE & SOCIETY

Maoris were the first settlers, 1200 years ago. Today's majority European population is descended mainly from British migrants who settled after 1840. Maoris' living and education standards are generally lower than average. The government is continuing to negotiate the settlement of Maori land claims.

INSIGHT: *New Zealand was the first country to give women the vote (1893)*

THE ECONOMY

Modern agricultural sector; world's top exporter of dairy products. Dairy vies with tourism as the biggest foreign-exchange earner. Hi-tech manufacturing. Open economy. Strong trade links.

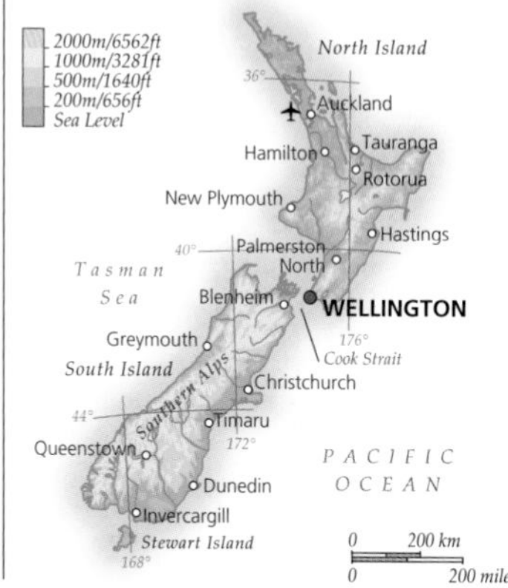
2000m/6562ft
1000m/3281ft
500m/1640ft
200m/656ft
Sea Level
North Island
36°
Auckland
Hamilton
Tauranga
Rotorua
New Plymouth
Hastings
40°
Palmerston North
Tasman Sea
Blenheim
WELLINGTON
Greymouth
176°
Cook Strait
South Island
Southern Alps
Christchurch
44°
Timaru
172°
Queenstown
PACIFIC OCEAN
Dunedin
Invercargill
Stewart Island
168°
0 200 km
0 200 miles

FACTFILE

OFFICIAL NAME: New Zealand
DATE OF FORMATION: 1947
CAPITAL: Wellington
POPULATION: 4.5 million
TOTAL AREA: 103,737 sq. miles (268,680 sq. km)
DENSITY: 43 people per sq. mile
LANGUAGES: English*, Maori*
RELIGIONS: Anglican 24%, other 22%, Presbyterian 18%, nonreligious 16%, Roman Catholic 15%, Methodist 5%
ETHNIC MIX: European 75%, Maori 15%, other 7%, Samoan 3%
GOVERNMENT: Parliamentary system
CURRENCY: New Zealand dollar = 100 cents

Nicaragua

Nicaragua lies at the heart of Central America. The Sandinista revolution of 1978 led to 11 years of civil war between the left-wing Sandinistas and the right-wing US-backed Contras.

GEOGRAPHY

Extensive forested plains in the east. Central mountain region with many active volcanoes. The Pacific coastlands are dominated by lakes.

CLIMATE

Tropical. The lowlands are hot all year round. The mountains are cooler. Prone to occasional hurricanes.

PEOPLE & SOCIETY

Most people are *mestizo* (mixed Spanish–Amerindian), and there is a large white elite. Caribbean regions are home to communities of Miskito Amerindians and blacks, who gained autonomy in 1987. The revolution improved the status of women, but these gains have been undone by rampant poverty.

INSIGHT: *Lake Nicaragua is the only freshwater lake in the world to contain marine animals*

THE ECONOMY

Textiles, coffee, meat, tobacco are main exports: affected by world price fluctuations. Remittances from abroad. Substantial debt relief has cut debt to around 50% of GDP. Corruption.

1000m/3281ft
500m/1640ft
200m/656ft
Sea Level
Coco
HONDURAS
14°
Ocotal
Mosquito Coast
Caribbean Sea
Estelí
Matagalpa
Chinandega
Matiguas
León
MANAGUA
Juigalpa
12°
San Rafael del Sur
Granada
Bluefields
Rivas
Lago de Nicaragua (Lake Nicaragua)
86°
COSTA RICA
San Juan
84°
0 100 km
0 100 miles

FACTFILE

OFFICIAL NAME: Republic of Nicaragua
DATE OF FORMATION: 1838
CAPITAL: Managua
POPULATION: 6.1 million
TOTAL AREA: 49,998 sq. miles (129,494 sq. km)
DENSITY: 133 people per sq. mile)
LANGUAGES: Spanish*, English Creole, Miskito
RELIGIONS: Roman Catholic 80%, Protestant Evangelical 17%, other 3%
ETHNIC MIX: *Mestizo* 69%, White 17%, Black 9%, Amerindian 5%
GOVERNMENT: Presidential system
CURRENCY: Córdoba oro = 100 centavos

Niger

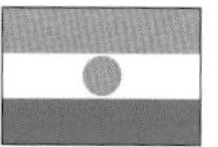

Niger lies in west Africa, upstream from Nigeria on the Niger River. One of the world's poorest states, it was ruled by one-party or military regimes until multipartyism was allowed in 1992.

GEOGRAPHY

The north and northeast regions are part of the Sahara. The Aïr Mountains in the center rise high above the desert. Savanna lies to the south.

CLIMATE

High temperatures persist for most of the year at around 95°F (35°C). The north is virtually rainless.

PEOPLE & SOCIETY

Tuareg nomads in the north feel excluded from politics and the benefits of their area's uranium resources. An early 1990s rebellion reignited briefly in 2007–2009. In the south, egalitarianism and a sense of community help to combat economic difficulties. Almost the entire urban population lives in slum conditions. Two-thirds of the population is under 25. Women have limited rights and restricted access to education. The army seized power briefly in 2010.

THE ECONOMY

Vast uranium deposits. Frequent droughts and food shortages. Banditry. Expansion of Sahara. Oil potential.

INSIGHT: *The name Niger comes from the Tuareg word* n'eghirren, *which means "flowing water"*

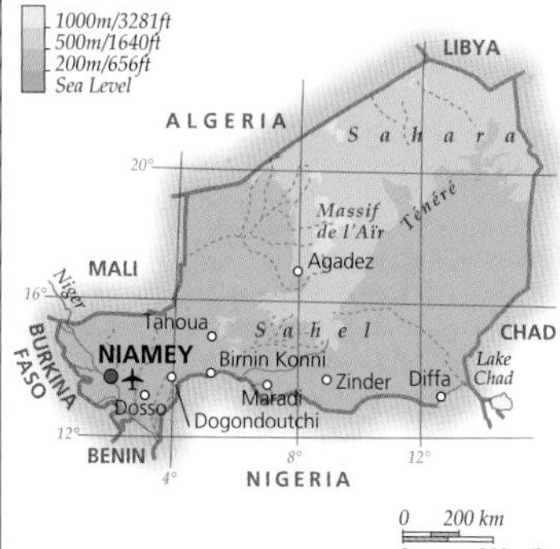

1000m/3281ft
500m/1640ft
200m/656ft
Sea Level
LIBYA
ALGERIA
Sahara
Ténéré
Massif de l'Aïr
Agadez
MALI
Niger
BURKINA FASO
Tahoua
Sahel
CHAD
NIAMEY
Birnin Konni
Zinder
Diffa
Lake Chad
Maradi
Dosso
Dogondoutchi
BENIN
NIGERIA
20°
16°
12°
4°
8°
12°
0 200 km
0 200 miles

FACTFILE

OFFICIAL NAME: Republic of Niger
DATE OF FORMATION: 1960
CAPITAL: Niamey
POPULATION: 17.8 million
TOTAL AREA: 489,188 sq. miles (1,267,000 sq. km)
DENSITY: 36 people per sq. mile
LANGUAGES: Hausa, Djerma, Fulani, Tuareg, Teda, French*
RELIGIONS: Muslim 99%, other (including Christian) 1%
ETHNIC MIX: Hausa 53%, Djerma and Songhai 21%, Tuareg 11%, Fulani 7%, Kanuri 6%, other 2%
GOVERNMENT: Presidential system
CURRENCY: CFA franc = 100 centimes

Nigeria

West Africa's biggest nation, Nigeria is a federation of 36 states and the capital, Abuja. Dominated by military governments since 1966, democracy returned in 1999.

GEOGRAPHY

Coastal area of beaches, swamps, and lagoons gives way to rainforest, and then to savanna on the high plateaus. Semidesert to the north.

CLIMATE

The south is hot, rainy and humid for most of the year. The arid north has one very humid wet season. The Jos Plateau and highlands are cooler.

PEOPLE & SOCIETY

Some 250 ethnic groups: tensions threaten national unity, with sporadic intercommunal violence. The mainly Muslim north has introduced *sharia* (Islamic law); Boko Haram militants use bombings, assassinations, and abductions to fight for an Islamic state. Women have more economic independence in the south. Militants in the oil-rich Niger Delta demand a share in the oil wealth for the region's impoverished population.

THE ECONOMY

Overdependent on oil, principal export since 1970s. Mismanagement and corruption. Debt reduced. Instability.

INSIGHT: *Nigeria is Africa's most populous state – one in every six Africans is Nigerian*

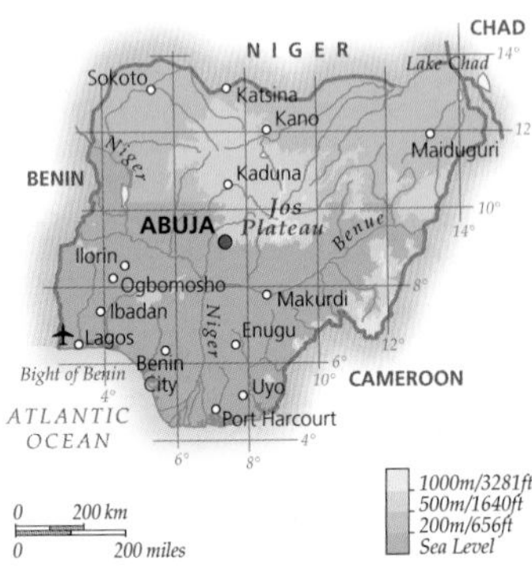
CHAD
NIGER
Lake Chad
Sokoto
Katsina
Kano
Maiduguri
Niger
BENIN
Kaduna
Jos Plateau
ABUJA
Benue
Ilorin
Ogbomosho
Makurdi
Ibadan
Niger
Lagos
Enugu
Benin City
Bight of Benin
CAMEROON
Uyo
ATLANTIC OCEAN
Port Harcourt
0 200 km
0 200 miles
1000m/3281ft
500m/1640ft
200m/656ft
Sea Level

FACTFILE

OFFICIAL NAME: Federal Republic of Nigeria
DATE OF FORMATION: 1960
CAPITAL: Abuja
POPULATION: 174 million
TOTAL AREA: 356,667 sq. miles (923,768 sq. km)
DENSITY: 494 people per sq. mile
LANGUAGES: Hausa, English*, Yoruba, Ibo
RELIGIONS: Muslim 50%, Christian 40%, traditional beliefs 10%
ETHNIC MIX: Other 29%, Hausa 21%, Yoruba 21%, Ibo 18%, Fulani 11%
GOVERNMENT: Presidential system
CURRENCY: Naira = 100 kobo

Norway

The Kingdom of Norway traces the rugged western coast of Scandinavia. Settlements are largely restricted to southern and coastal areas. Vast oil and natural gas revenues bring prosperity.

GEOGRAPHY

The western coast is indented with numerous fjords and features tens of thousands of islands. Mountains and plateaus cover most of the country.

CLIMATE

Mild coastal climate. Inland, the weather is more extreme, with warmer summers and cold, snowy winters.

PEOPLE & SOCIETY

Fairly homogeneous, but has welcomed refugees from Iraq, Somalia, Bosnia, Sri Lanka, and elsewhere. Strong family tradition, but divorce is common. Fair-minded consensus promotes female equality, boosted by the generous childcare provision. Wealth is more evenly distributed than in most countries. Voted against joining the EU in 1994.

INSIGHT: *Near Narvik, mainland Norway is only 4 miles (7 km) wide*

THE ECONOMY

Western Europe's top oil and natural gas producer: trust fund saves for post-oil future. Metal, chemical, and engineering industries. Generous aid donor. High cost of living.

Hammerfest
Tromsø
RUSS. FED.
FINLAND
Narvik
Bodø
Arctic Circle
Norwegian Sea
SWEDEN
Trondheim
Ålesund
Lillehammer
Bergen
Hønefoss
North Sea
OSLO
Moss
Stavanger
Kristiansand
Skagerrak
2000m/6562ft
1000m/3281ft
500m/1640ft
200m/656ft
Sea Level
0 200 km
0 200 miles
70°
32°
68°
28°
24°
20°
66°
16°
64°
62°
60°
12°
58°
8°

FACTFILE

OFFICIAL NAME: Kingdom of Norway
DATE OF FORMATION: 1905
CAPITAL: Oslo
POPULATION: 5 million
TOTAL AREA: 125,181 sq. miles (324,220 sq. km)
DENSITY: 42 people per sq. mile
LANGUAGES: Norwegian* (*Bokmål* "book language" and *Nynorsk* "new Norsk"), Sámi
RELIGIONS: Evangelical Lutheran 88%, other and nonreligious 8%, Muslim 2%, Pentecostal 1%, Roman Catholic 1%
ETHNIC MIX: Norwegian 93%, other 6%, Sámi 1%
GOVERNMENT: Parliamentary system
CURRENCY: Norwegian krone = 100 øre

Oman

Oman occupies a strategic position on the Arabian Peninsula, at the entrance to the Persian Gulf. It is the least developed Gulf state, despite modest oil exports.

GEOGRAPHY

Mostly gravelly desert, with mountains in the north and south. Some narrow fertile coastal strips.

CLIMATE

Blistering heat in the west. Summer temperatures often climb above 113°F (45°C). Southern uplands receive rains June–September.

PEOPLE & SOCIETY

Urban drift has seen most Omanis move to northern towns. The majority are Ibadi Muslims who follow an appointed leader, the imam. Ibadism is not opposed to freedom for women, and a few women hold positions of authority. Baluchi from Pakistan are the largest group of foreign workers.

INSIGHT: *Until the late 1980s, Oman was closed to all but business or official visitors*

THE ECONOMY

Oil and natural gas account for almost all export revenue. Commercially extractable reserves are limited. Other exports include fish, animals, and dates. Foreigners work in all sectors.

2000m/6562ft
1000m/3281ft
500m/1640ft
200m/656ft
Sea Level
Strait of Hormuz
Al Khaşab
Musandam Peninsula
Gulf of Oman
UAE
Şuḩār
MUSCAT
Al Qābil
Ar Rustāq
Bahlah
Şamad
Şūr
24°
60°
Arabian Sea
SAUDI ARABIA
20°
Duqm
Ar Rub' al Khālī
INDIAN OCEAN
Şawqirah
YEMEN
Şalālah
52°
56°
0 100 km
0 100 miles

FACTFILE

OFFICIAL NAME: Sultanate of Oman
DATE OF FORMATION: 1951
CAPITAL: Muscat
POPULATION: 3.6 million
TOTAL AREA: 82,031 sq. miles (212,460 sq. km)
DENSITY: 44 people per sq. mile
LANGUAGES: Arabic*, Baluchi, Farsi, Hindi, Punjabi
RELIGIONS: Ibadi Muslim 75%, other Muslim and Hindu 25%
ETHNIC MIX: Arab 88%, Baluchi 4%, Persian 3%, Indian and Pakistani 3%, African 2%
GOVERNMENT: Monarchy
CURRENCY: Omani rial = 1000 baisa

Pakistan

Once a part of British India, Pakistan was created in 1947 in response to demands for an independent Muslim state. In 1971, Bangladesh (former East Pakistan) became a separate state.

GEOGRAPHY

Indus floodplain across east and south. Hindu Kush mountains in north. Semidesert plateau, mountains in west.

CLIMATE

Temperatures can soar to 122°F (50°C) in south and west, and fall to –4°F (–20°C) in the Hindu Kush.

PEOPLE & SOCIETY

Punjabis dominate government and the army. Tensions with minority groups, exacerbated by the vast gap between rich and poor. Strong family ties permeate politics and business. Relations with India are tense over Kashmir and terrorism. Islamist *taliban* insurgency in tribal areas on Afghan border: fighting has displaced millions.

INSIGHT: *In 1988, Pakistan elected Benazir Bhutto as the first female prime minister in the Muslim world*

THE ECONOMY

Major cotton and rice producer, but unpredictable weather conditions often affect crop. Textiles. Instability. Corruption. Aid to fight terrorism and for earthquake reconstruction.

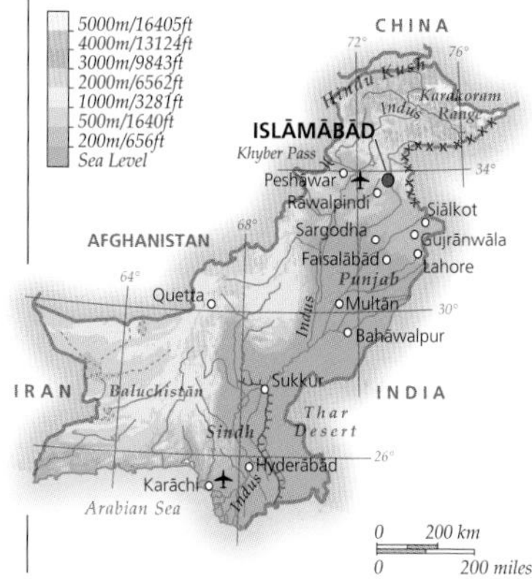
5000m/16405ft
4000m/13124ft
3000m/9843ft
2000m/6562ft
1000m/3281ft
500m/1640ft
200m/656ft
Sea Level
CHINA
72°
76°
Hindu Kush
Karakoram Range
Indus
ISLĀMĀBĀD
Khyber Pass
34°
Peshawar
Rawalpindi
Siālkot
68°
Sargodha
Gujrānwāla
AFGHANISTAN
Faisalābād
Lahore
64°
Punjab
Quetta
Indus
Multān
30°
Bahāwalpur
IRAN
Baluchistān
Sukkur
INDIA
Thar Desert
Sindh
26°
Hyderābād
Karāchi
Indus
Arabian Sea
0 200 km
0 200 miles

FACTFILE

OFFICIAL NAME: Islamic Republic of Pakistan
DATE OF FORMATION: 1947
CAPITAL: Islamabad
POPULATION: 182 million
TOTAL AREA: 310,401 sq. miles (803,940 sq. km)
DENSITY: 612 people per sq. mile
LANGUAGES: Punjabi, Sindhi, Pashtu, Urdu*, Baluchi, Brahui
RELIGIONS: Sunni Muslim 77%, Shi'a Muslim 20%, Hindu 2%, Christian 1%
ETHNIC MIX: Punjabi 56%, Pathan (Pashtun) 15%, Sindhi 14%, Mohajir 7%, Baluchi 4%, other 4%
GOVERNMENT: Parliamentary system
CURRENCY: Pakistani rupee = 100 paisa

Palau

The 300-island Palau archipelago (known locally as Belau) lies in the western Pacific Ocean. It achieved independence in 1994, and is gradually reducing its aid dependence.

GEOGRAPHY

Terrain varies from thickly forested mountains to limestone and coral reefs. Babeldaob, the largest island, is volcanic, with many rivers and waterfalls.

CLIMATE

Hot and wet. Little variation in daily and seasonal temperatures. February–April is the dry season.

PEOPLE & SOCIETY

Native Palauans are a mix of the original Southeast Asian migrants and Pacific settlers. A modern influx from Asia, particularly the Philippines, China, and Bangladesh, has led to tension. As 70% of the population live on the island-city of Koror, a new capital was constructed recently on Babeldaob. Native culture is preserved on outer islands despite strong influence from the US and Japan. Modekngei is a blend of Christianity and local beliefs.

THE ECONOMY

Tourism and fishing licenses are main earners. Coconuts, bananas, and taro. New 15-year US aid plan to 2024.

INSIGHT: *Palau's reefs contain 1500 species of fish and 700 types of coral*

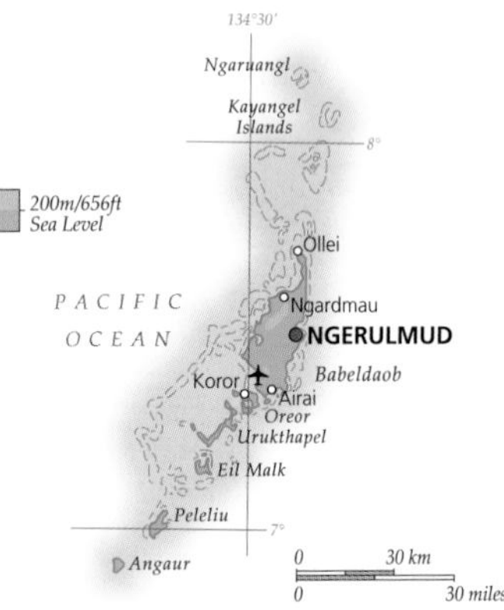
134°30'
Ngaruangl
Kayangel Islands
8°
200m/656ft
Sea Level
Ollei
PACIFIC OCEAN
Ngardmau
NGERULMUD
Babeldaob
Koror
Airai
Oreor
Urukthapel
Eil Malk
Peleliu
7°
Angaur
0 30 km
0 30 miles

FACTFILE

OFFICIAL NAME: Republic of Palau
DATE OF FORMATION: 1994
CAPITAL: Ngerulmud
POPULATION: 21,108
TOTAL AREA: 177 sq. miles (458 sq. km)
DENSITY: 108 people per sq. mile
LANGUAGES: Palauan*, English*, Japanese, Angaur, Tobi, Sonsorolese
RELIGIONS: Christian 66%, Modekngei 34%
ETHNIC MIX: Palauan 74%, Filipino 16%, other 6%, Chinese and other Asian 4%
GOVERNMENT: Nonparty system
CURRENCY: US dollar = 100 cents

Panama

A Spanish colony until 1821, Panama is the southernmost country in Central America. The colossal Panama Canal (which was under US control until 2000) links the Pacific and Atlantic oceans.

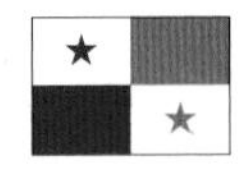

GEOGRAPHY

Lowlands along both coasts, with savanna-covered plains and rolling hills. Mountainous interior. Swamps and rainforests in the east.

CLIMATE

Hot and humid, with heavy rainfall in the May–December wet season. Cooler at high altitudes.

PEOPLE & SOCIETY

A multiethnic society, dominated by people of mixed Spanish–Amerindian origin (*mestizo*). Amerindians live in remote areas. The Panama Canal and former US military bases (the last of which closed in 1999) have given society a cosmopolitan outlook, but Catholicism and the extended family remain strong. Wealth is unevenly divided. Money-laundering, narcotics trafficking, and corruption are rife.

THE ECONOMY

Colón Free Trade Zone: world's second-largest. Income from the canal (expansion project underway) and merchant ships sailing under flag of Panama. Banana and shrimp exports.

INSIGHT: *The Panama Canal shortens the sea route between the east coast of the US and Japan by 3000 miles (4800 km)*

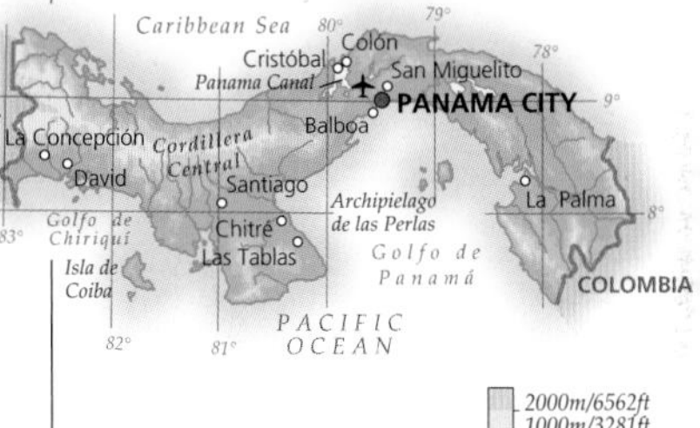
Caribbean Sea
Colón
Cristóbal
Panama Canal
San Miguelito
PANAMA CITY
Balboa
COSTA RICA
La Concepción
David
Cordillera Central
Santiago
Archipiélago de las Perlas
La Palma
Golfo de Chiriquí
Chitré
Las Tablas
Golfo de Panamá
Isla de Coiba
COLOMBIA
PACIFIC OCEAN
80°
79°
78°
9°
8°
83°
82°
81°
0 100 km
0 100 miles
2000m/6562ft
1000m/3281ft
500m/1640ft
200m/656ft
Sea Level

FACTFILE

OFFICIAL NAME: Republic of Panama
DATE OF FORMATION: 1903
CAPITAL: Panama City
POPULATION: 3.9 million
TOTAL AREA: 30,193 sq. miles (78,200 sq. km)
DENSITY: 133 people per sq. mile
LANGUAGES: English Creole, Spanish*, Amerindian languages, Chibchan languages
RELIGIONS: Roman Catholic 84%, Protestant 15%, other 1%
ETHNIC MIX: *Mestizo* 70%, Black 14%, White 10%, Amerindian 6%
GOVERNMENT: Presidential system
CURRENCY: Balboa = 100 centésimos; US dollar is also legal tender

Papua New Guinea

A former Australian colony, Papua New Guinea (PNG) occupies the eastern section of the island of New Guinea and several other island groups. Much of the country is isolated.

GEOGRAPHY

Mountainous and forested mainland, with broad, swampy river valleys. 40 active volcanoes in the north. Around 600 outer islands.

CLIMATE

Hot and humid in lowlands, cooling toward highlands, where snow can fall on highest peaks.

PEOPLE & SOCIETY

Around 800 language groups and even more tribes. The main social distinction is between lowlanders, who have frequent contact with the outside world, and the very isolated, but increasingly threatened, highlanders. Great tensions exist between highland tribes, and vendettas can often last several generations. The island of Bougainville has been granted autonomy and promised a referendum on independence by 2020.

THE ECONOMY

Minerals: gold, copper, oil, and natural gas. High government spending almost led to national bankruptcy in 2002. Strong GDP growth since 2007.

INSIGHT: *PNG is home to the only known poisonous birds; contact with the feathers of some species of pitohui produces skin blisters*

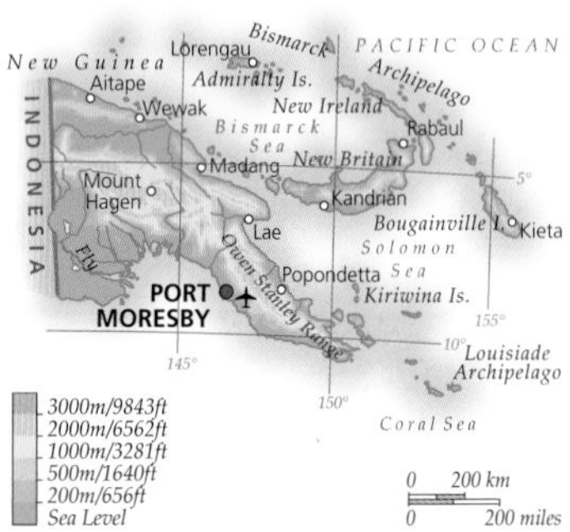
Bismarck Archipelago
PACIFIC OCEAN
New Guinea
Lorengau
Admiralty Is.
Aitape
Wewak
New Ireland
Bismarck Sea
Rabaul
INDONESIA
Madang
New Britain
5°
Mount Hagen
Kandrian
Lae
Bougainville
Kieta
Solomon Sea
Fly
Owen Stanley Range
Popondetta
PORT MORESBY
Kiriwina Is.
155°
10°
Louisiade Archipelago
145°
150°
Coral Sea
3000m/9843ft
2000m/6562ft
1000m/3281ft
500m/1640ft
200m/656ft
Sea Level
0 200 km
0 200 miles

FACTFILE

OFFICIAL NAME: Independent State of Papua New Guinea
DATE OF FORMATION: 1975
CAPITAL: Port Moresby
POPULATION: 7.3 million
TOTAL AREA: 178,703 sq. miles (462,840 sq. km)
DENSITY: 42 people per sq. mile
LANGUAGES: Pidgin English, Papuan, English*, Motu, c.800 native languages
RELIGIONS: Protestant 60%, Roman Catholic 37%, other 3%
ETHNIC MIX: Melanesian or mixed race 100%
GOVERNMENT: Parliamentary system
CURRENCY: Kina = 100 toea

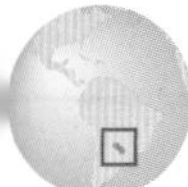

Paraguay

Landlocked in central South America, and once a Spanish colony, Paraguay's post independence history has included periods of military rule. Free elections held since 1993.

GEOGRAPHY

The Paraguay River divides the hilly and forested east from a flat alluvial plain, with marsh and semidesert scrub land in the west.

CLIMATE

Subtropical. The Gran Chaco is generally hotter and drier. All areas experience floods and droughts.

PEOPLE & SOCIETY

The population is mainly *mestizo* (mixed Spanish and native Guaraní origin). Most people are bilingual, though in rural areas Guaraní is more widely used. Cattle ranchers populate the Chaco, along with communities of the German-origin Mennonite Church. Right-wing Colorados in power for decades, except 2008–2012.

INSIGHT: *The War of the Triple Alliance (1864–1870) killed almost 90% of Paraguay's male population*

THE ECONOMY

Agriculture: soybeans are the main export. Electricity exported from massive hydroelectric dams, including Itaipú (world's second-largest, jointly run with Brazil). Large informal economy. Corruption and smuggling.

BOLIVIA
60°
20°
Paraguay
Gran Chaco
BRAZIL
0 100 km
0 100 miles
Pedro Juan Caballero
Concepción
ARGENTINA
25°
Represa de Itaipú
ASUNCIÓN
Coronel Oviedo
Lambaré
Villarrica
Ciudad del Este
Pilar
Paraná
Encarnación
55°
1000m/3281ft
500m/1640ft
200m/656ft
Sea Level

FACTFILE

OFFICIAL NAME: Republic of Paraguay
DATE OF FORMATION: 1811
CAPITAL: Asunción
POPULATION: 6.8 million
TOTAL AREA: 157,046 sq. miles (406,750 sq. km)
DENSITY: 44 people per sq. mile
LANGUAGES: Guaraní*, Spanish*, German
RELIGIONS: Roman Catholic 90%, Protestant (including Mennonite) 10%
ETHNIC MIX: *Mestizo* 91%, other 7%, Amerindian 2%
GOVERNMENT: Presidential system
CURRENCY: Guaraní = 100 céntimos

Peru

Once the heart of the Inca Empire, before the Spanish conquest in the 16th century, Peru lies on the Pacific coast of South America, just south of the equator.

GEOGRAPHY

Coastal plain rises to Andes Mountains. Uplands, dissected by fertile valleys, lie east of the Andes. Tropical forest in extreme east.

CLIMATE

Coast is mainly arid. Middle slopes of the Andes are temperate; higher peaks are snow-covered. East is hot, humid, and very wet.

PEOPLE & SOCIETY

Though most people are Amerindians or mixed-race *mestizos*, society is dominated by a small group of Spanish descendants. Amerindians, and the small black community, suffer discrimination in towns, but access to information and political power are growing; the first Amerindian president was elected in 2001–2006. Clashes with left-wing militants killed almost 70,000 people between 1980 and 2000.

THE ECONOMY

Abundant mineral resources: notably copper and gold. Rich Pacific fish stocks. World's largest cocaine producer.

INSIGHT: *Lake Titicaca is the world's highest navigable lake*

Equator
COLOMBIA
ECUADOR
Putumayo
Amazon
Iquitos
Marañón
Piura
Chiclayo
Ucayali
BRAZIL
Trujillo
Chimbote
Pucallpa
Huánuco
Andes
LIMA
Huancayo
Callao
Cusco
PACIFIC OCEAN
Ayacucho
Ica
Juliaca
Lake Titicaca
Arequipa
BOLIVIA
Tacna
CHILE
4°
8°
12°
16°
80°
76°
72°
4000m/13124ft
2000m/6562ft
500m/1640ft
Sea Level
0 200 km
0 200 miles

FACTFILE

OFFICIAL NAME: Republic of Peru
DATE OF FORMATION: 1824
CAPITAL: Lima
POPULATION: 30.4 million
TOTAL AREA: 496,223 sq. miles (1,285,200 sq. km)
DENSITY: 62 people per sq. mile
LANGUAGES: Spanish*, Quechua*, Aymara
RELIGIONS: Roman Catholic 81%, other 19%
ETHNIC MIX: Amerindian 45%, *Mestizo* (European–Amerindian) 37%, White 15%, other 3%
GOVERNMENT: Presidential system
CURRENCY: New sol = 100 céntimos

Philippines

Lying in the western Pacific Ocean, the Philippines is the world's second-largest archipelago, with 7107 islands, of which 4600 are named but only around 1000 inhabited.

GEOGRAPHY

Larger islands are forested and mountainous. Over 20 active volcanoes. Frequent earthquakes.

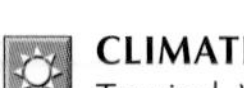

CLIMATE

Tropical. Warm and humid all year round. Typhoons occur in the rainy season: June–October.

PEOPLE & SOCIETY

Over 100 ethnic groups, most of which are of Malay origin. The Catholic Church is a dominant cultural force; it opposes family-planning, despite high population growth. The Chinese minority has been established for 400 years. Women play a prominent part in society. High literacy levels. Islamist separatists and communist insurgents undermine stability.

INSIGHT: *Mass "People Power" demonstrations have brought down two presidents, in 1986 and 2001*

THE ECONOMY

Coconuts, bananas, pineapples exported. Growing outsourcing center. Remittances from abroad. Corruption and poor infrastructure limit growth.

2000m/6562ft
1000m/3281ft
500m/1640ft
200m/656ft
Sea Level
Babuyan Is.
PACIFIC OCEAN
Luzon
Philippine Sea
Cabanatuan
Angeles
MANILA
Batangas
Legazpi City
South China Sea
Mindoro
Calbayog
Samar
Panay
Iloilo
Bacolod City
Cebu
Palawan
Puerto Princesa
Negros
Butuan
Sulu Sea
Iligan
Balabac Strait
Davao
Zamboanga
General Santos
Sulu Archipelago
Mindanao
Celebes Sea
20°
16°
12°
8°
4°
116°
120°
124°
0 200 km
0 200 miles

FACTFILE

OFFICIAL NAME: Republic of the Philippines

DATE OF FORMATION: 1946

CAPITAL: Manila

POPULATION: 98.4 million

TOTAL AREA: 115,830 sq. miles (300,000 sq. km)

DENSITY: 855 people per sq. mile

LANGUAGES: Filipino*, English*, Tagalog, Cebuano, Ilocano, Hiligaynon, many others

RELIGIONS: Roman Catholic 81%, Protestant 9%, Muslim 5%, other (including Buddhist) 5%

ETHNIC MIX: Other 34%, Tagalog 28%, Cebuano 13%, Ilocano 9%, Hiligaynon 8%, Bisaya 8%

GOVERNMENT: Presidential system

CURRENCY: Philippine peso = 100 centavos

Poland

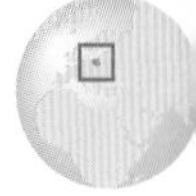

Located in the heart of Europe, Poland has undergone massive social, economic, and political change since the collapse of communism in 1989. It joined the EU in 2004.

GEOGRAPHY

Lowlands, part of the North European Plain, cover most of the country. The Tatra Mountains run along the southern border.

CLIMATE

Rainfall peaks during the hot summers. Cold winters with snow, especially in mountains.

PEOPLE & SOCIETY

Ethnic homogeneity masks social tensions. Secular liberals criticize the semiofficial status of the Roman Catholic Church, though its influence is now waning. Abortion is banned, except for special cases. Growing wealth disparities are resented. The German minority in the west is becoming more assertive.

INSIGHT: *Wild wisent (European bison) live in the Bialowieza Forest straddling the Poland–Belarus border*

THE ECONOMY

Heavy industries dominate; services growing. Foreign investment reflects large potential market. Rapid privatization. Only EU state to avoid recession in 2007–2009 global downturn. Not adopting euro yet.

Baltic Sea
RUSSIAN FEDERATION
LITHUANIA
BELARUS
UKRAINE
SLOVAKIA
CZECH REP.
GERMANY
Gdynia
Gdańsk
Olsztyn
Szczecin
Bydgoszcz
Białystok
Oder
Włocławek
Poznań
WARSAW
Wisła
Zielona Góra
Łódź
Radom
Lublin
Wrocław
Częstochowa
Gliwice
Katowice
Rzeszów
Kraków
Tatra Mts.
14°
16°
18°
20°
22°
24°
54°
52°
50°

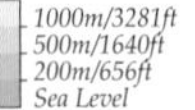

1000m/3281ft
500m/1640ft
200m/656ft
Sea Level
0 100 km
0 100 miles

FACTFILE

OFFICIAL NAME: Republic of Poland
DATE OF FORMATION: 1918
CAPITAL: Warsaw
POPULATION: 38.2 million
TOTAL AREA: 120,728 sq. miles (312,685 sq. km)
DENSITY: 325 people per sq. mile
LANGUAGES: Polish*
RELIGIONS: Roman Catholic 93%, other and nonreligious 5%, Orthodox Christian 2%
ETHNIC MIX: Polish 98%, other 2%
GOVERNMENT: Parliamentary system
CURRENCY: Zloty = 100 groszy

Portugal

Portugal, with its long Atlantic coast, lies on the western side of the Iberian Peninsula, which it shares with Spain. It is the most westerly country on the European mainland.

GEOGRAPHY

The Tagus River bisects the country roughly east to west, dividing mountainous north from lower and more undulating south.

CLIMATE

North is cool and moist. South is warmer, with dry, mild winters.

PEOPLE & SOCIETY

A homogeneous and stable society, which is losing some of its conservative traditions. History of immigration from former colonies, and recently from eastern Europe. Urban areas and the south are more socially liberal. The north is more responsive to traditional Roman Catholic values. Family ties remain important.

INSIGHT: *Portugal is the world's leading producer of cork, which comes from the bark of the cork oak*

THE ECONOMY

Tourism. Exports of vegetables, fruit, wine, cars, and clothing. Mounting debt forced EU bailout in 2011 and tough cuts to reduce the budget deficit.

42°
Viana do Castelo
Porto
Vila Real
Douro
Vila Nova de Gaia
ATLANTIC OCEAN
Coimbra
40°
Santarém
SPAIN
Estoril
LISBON
Barreiro
Évora
Setúbal
38°
Beja
Algarve
Portimão
Faro
8°
0 100 km
0 100 miles
33°
Madeira
17°
Madeira Is.
0 50 km
0 50 miles
São Miguel
38°
30°
Azores
26°
0 200 km
0 200 miles
1000m/3281ft
500m/1640ft
200m/656ft
Sea Level

FACTFILE

OFFICIAL NAME: Portuguese Republic
DATE OF FORMATION: 1139
CAPITAL: Lisbon
POPULATION: 10.6 million
TOTAL AREA: 35,672 sq. miles (92,391 sq. km)
DENSITY: 299 people per sq. mile
LANGUAGES: Portuguese*
RELIGIONS: Roman Catholic 92%, Protestant 4%, nonreligious 3%, other 1%,
ETHNIC MIX: Portuguese 98%, African and other 2%
GOVERNMENT: Parliamentary system
CURRENCY: Euro = 100 cents

Qatar

Qatar projects from the Arabian Peninsula into the Persian Gulf. A founding member of OPEC, it is one of the region's wealthiest states due to oil and natural gas exports.

GEOGRAPHY

Flat, semiarid desert with dunes and salt pans. Vegetation is limited to small patches of scrub.

CLIMATE

Hot and humid. Temperatures in summer can soar to over 104°F (40°C). Rainfall is rare.

PEOPLE & SOCIETY

Only one in five residents is native-born; the rest are guest workers from across the Middle East, the Indian subcontinent, Southeast Asia, and north Africa. Qataris were once nomadic Bedouins, but since the advent of oil wealth, most now live in Doha and its suburbs, leaving the north dotted with abandoned villages. Women enjoy relative freedom; most wear the veil.

INSIGHT: *There are three times as many men as women in Qatar*

THE ECONOMY

Steady supply of crude oil and huge natural gas reserves, plus related industries. All other raw materials and most foods are imported. Strong GDP growth in 2004–2011. Economy is heavily dependent on foreign workforce.

51
Ar Ru'ays
Al Khuwayr
26
Gulf of Bahrain
Madīnat al Ka'bān
Al Khawr
Ash Shahanīyah
Ar Rayyān
DOHA
Umm Bāb
Al Wakrah
25
As Salwā
Persian Gulf
SAUDI ARABIA
UAE
0 30 km
0 30 miles
200m/656ft
Sea Level

FACTFILE

OFFICIAL NAME: State of Qatar

DATE OF FORMATION: 1971

CAPITAL: Doha

POPULATION: 2.2 million

TOTAL AREA: 4416 sq. miles (11,437 sq. km)

DENSITY: 518 people per sq. mile

LANGUAGES: Arabic*

RELIGIONS: Muslim (mainly Sunni) 95%, other 5%

ETHNIC MIX: Qatari 20%, other Arab 20%, Indian 20%, Nepalese 13%, Filipino 10%, other 10%, Pakistani 7%

GOVERNMENT: Monarchy

CURRENCY: Qatar riyal = 100 dirhams

Romania

Once dominated by Poles, Hungarians, and Ottomans, Romania has been slowly converting to a market economy since the 1989 overthrow of its communist regime. It joined the EU in 2007.

GEOGRAPHY

Carpathian Mountains encircle the Transylvanian plateau. Wide plains to the south and east. Danube River forms southern border.

CLIMATE

Continental. Summers are hot and humid, winters are cold and snowy. Very heavy spring rains.

PEOPLE & SOCIETY

Romanians are ethnically distinct from their Slav and Hungarian (Magyar) neighbors. Hungarians are the largest minority, living mainly in Transylvania. They are protected by the influence of Hungary, unlike the Roma, who suffer discrimination. Net emigration (since EU membership) is slowing. Low birth rate.

INSIGHT: *In 2001, Romania became the last country in Europe to lift its ban on homosexuality*

THE ECONOMY

Polluting, outdated heavy industry. Unmechanized agricultural sector. Textile and metal exports led growth in 2000s. High budget deficits exposed economy in 2007–2009 global downturn: IMF bailout, austerity measures. Plans to join euro in 2019. Privatization continues.

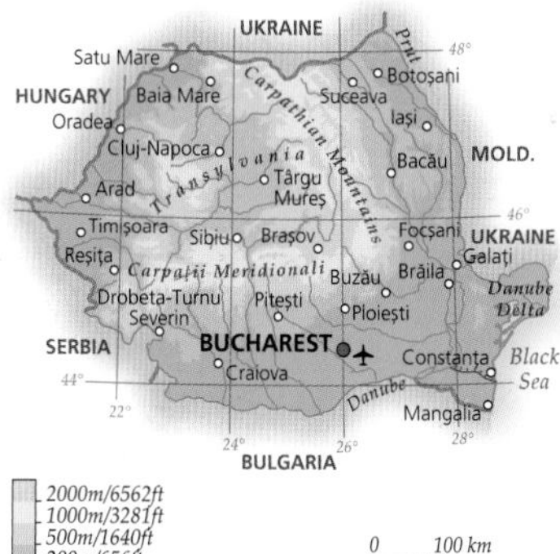
UKRAINE
Prut
48°
Satu Mare
Botoșani
HUNGARY
Baia Mare
Carpathian Mountains
Suceava
Oradea
Iași
Cluj-Napoca
Transylvania
Bacău
MOLD.
Târgu Mureș
Arad
46°
Timișoara
Sibiu
Brașov
Focșani
UKRAINE
Galați
Reșița
Carpații Meridionali
Buzău
Brăila
Danube Delta
Drobeta-Turnu Severin
Pitești
Ploiești
SERBIA
BUCHAREST
Constanța
Black Sea
Craiova
44°
Danube
Mangalia
22°
24°
26°
28°
BULGARIA
2000m/6562ft
1000m/3281ft
500m/1640ft
200m/656ft
Sea Level
0 100 km
0 100 miles

FACTFILE

OFFICIAL NAME: Romania

DATE OF FORMATION: 1878

CAPITAL: Bucharest

POPULATION: 21.7 million

TOTAL AREA: 91,699 sq. miles (237,500 sq. km)

DENSITY: 244 people per sq. mile

LANGUAGES: Romanian*, Hungarian (Magyar), Romani, German

RELIGIONS: Romanian Orthodox 87%, Roman Catholic 5%, Protestant 5%, Greek Orthodox 1%, Uniate 1%, other 1%

ETHNIC MIX: Romanian 89%, Magyar 7%, Roma 3%, other 1%

GOVERNMENT: Presidential system

CURRENCY: New Romanian leu = 100 bani

Russian Federation

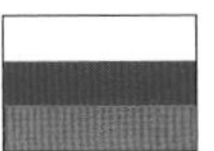

The Russian Federation was the core of the old Soviet Union, which broke up in 1991. Russia is still the world's largest state. Its diversity is a source of both strength and problems.

GEOGRAPHY

The Ural Mountains divide the European steppes and forests from the tundra and forests of Siberia. South-central deserts and mountains.

PEOPLE & SOCIETY

57 "nationalities" and 95 minorities in addition to ethnic Russians. Separatism suppressed. Population predicted to fall to 107 million by 2050. HIV/AIDS rising.

CLIMATE

Continental in European Russia, with warm summers and freezing winters. Elsewhere climate ranges from sub-arctic to Mediterranean and hot desert.

THE ECONOMY

Vast resources (oil, gas, metals, timber). Inefficient industry, agriculture. Tax evasion. Black market and organized crime. Wealth disparities. 2009 recession.

ARCTIC OCEAN
Barents Sea
Severnaya Zemlya
Bering Sea
180°
FINLAND
Murmansk
Kaliningrad (Russ. Fed.)
60°
Sankt Peterburg (St Petersburg)
BELARUS
30°
MOSCOW
Nizhniy Novgorod
UKRAINE
Ural Mts
Perm'
Yenisey
Noril'sk
Magadan
Kamchatka
Yakutsk
Sea of Okhotsk
Siberia
Ob'
Lena
Sakhalin
150°
Caucasus
Volgograd
GEORGIA
Omsk
Tomsk
Grozny
AZERB.
KAZAKHSTAN
Irkutsk
Chita
Sea of Japan (East Sea)
Vladivostok
CHINA
60°
Trans-Siberian Railroad
MONGOLIA
90°
120°
3000m/9843ft
2000m/6562ft
1000m/3281ft
500m/1640ft
200m/656ft
Sea Level
Below Sea Level
0 1000 km
0 1000 miles

INSIGHT: *The Trans-Siberian Railroad, running 5578 miles (9297 km) from Moscow to Vladivostok, is the longest in the world, traversing eight time zones*

FACTFILE

OFFICIAL NAME: Russian Federation

DATE OF FORMATION: 1480

CAPITAL: Moscow

POPULATION: 143 million

TOTAL AREA: 6,592,735 sq. miles (17,075,200 sq. km)

DENSITY: 22 people per sq. mile

LANGUAGES: Russian*, Tatar, Ukrainian, other

RELIGIONS: Orthodox Christian 75%, Muslim 14%, other 11%

ETHNIC MIX: Russian 80%, other 12%, Tatar 4%, Ukrainian 2%, Chavash 1%, Bashkir 1%

GOVERNMENT: Mixed presidential–parliamentary system

CURRENCY: Russian rouble = 100 kopeks

Rwanda

Rwanda lies just south of the equator in east central Africa, far from the nearest sea port. Since independence from France in 1962, ethnic tensions have dominated politics.

GEOGRAPHY

A series of plateaus descend from the ridge of volcanic peaks in the west to the Akagera River on the eastern border. The Great Rift Valley also passes through this region.

CLIMATE

Tropical, though tempered by the altitude. Two wet seasons are separated by a dry season, from June to August. Heaviest rain in the west.

PEOPLE & SOCIETY

For over 500 years the cattle-owning Tutsi minority were politically dominant over the land-owning Hutu. In 1959, violent revolt led to a reversal of the roles. Ethnic tensions are fierce; in the most recent violence, in 1994, over 800,000 people, mostly Tutsi, were massacred in an act of state-backed genocide; trials are ongoing. Most people live at subsistence level.

THE ECONOMY

Reliant on aid. Production of tea and speciality coffee is booming. Decade of strong GDP growth. Exports tin, coltan, and iron ore. Ecotourism is growing. Possible oil and gas reserves. Landlocked: high transportation costs.

INSIGHT: *Rwanda's parliament in 2008 was the first in the world to have more women members than men*

0
50 km
0
50 miles
UGANDA
TANZANIA
Akagera
DEM. REP. CONGO
Ruhengeri
Byumba
Gisenyi
Lake Kivu
KIGALI
2°
Kibuye
Gitarama
Kibungo
Cyangugu
Butare
30°
29°
BURUNDI
2000m/6562ft
1000m/3281ft
500m/1640ft

FACTFILE

OFFICIAL NAME: Republic of Rwanda

DATE OF FORMATION: 1962

CAPITAL: Kigali

POPULATION: 11.8 million

TOTAL AREA: 10,169 sq. miles (26,338 sq. km)

DENSITY: 1225 people per sq. mile

LANGUAGES: Kinyarwanda*, French*, Kiswahili, English*

RELIGIONS: Christian 94%, Muslim 5% traditional beliefs 1%

ETHNIC MIX: Hutu 85%, Tutsi 14%, other (including Twa) 1%

GOVERNMENT: Presidential system

CURRENCY: Rwanda franc = 100 centimes

St. Kitts & Nevis

A popular Caribbean tourist destination, St. Kitts and Nevis lies in the northern part of the Leeward Island chain. Nevis is the smaller and less developed of the two islands.

GEOGRAPHY

Volcanic in origin, with forested, mountainous interiors. Nevis has hot and cold springs.

CLIMATE

Tropical, tempered by trade winds. Little seasonal variation in temperature. Moderate rainfall.

PEOPLE & SOCIETY

The majority of the population are descended from former African slaves. There are small numbers of Europeans, and South Asians, and a community of Lebanese. Levels of emigration are high, and overseas remittances are an important source of national income. The government has pledged to retrain sugar workers. Native professionals and civil servants have largely replaced the former expatriate elite. The secessionist movement on Nevis remains an issue.

THE ECONOMY

Successful tourist industry is vulnerable to downturns in US market. Financial services. Once-key sugar industry closed down in 2005.

INSIGHT: *Nevis has been renowned as a spa since the 18th century, and is known as the "Queen of the Caribbean"*

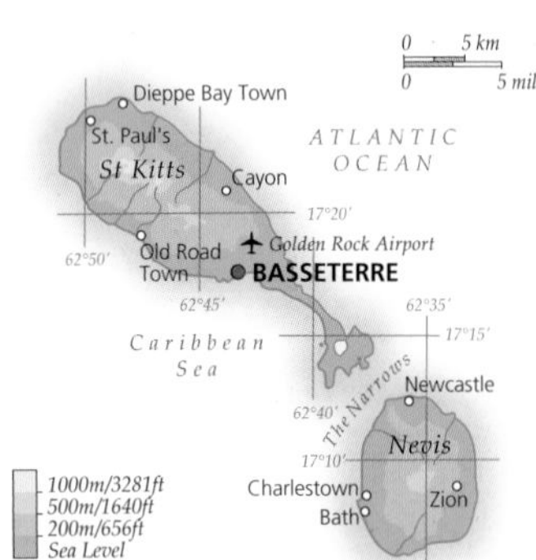
0 5 km
0 5 miles
Dieppe Bay Town
St. Paul's
St Kitts
Cayon
ATLANTIC OCEAN
17°20'
Old Road Town
Golden Rock Airport
BASSETERRE
62°50'
62°45'
62°35'
17°15'
Caribbean Sea
The Narrows
Newcastle
62°40'
Nevis
17°10'
Charlestown
Bath
Zion
1000m/3281ft
500m/1640ft
200m/656ft
Sea Level

FACTFILE

OFFICIAL NAME: Federation of Saint Christopher and Nevis

DATE OF FORMATION: 1983

CAPITAL: Basseterre

POPULATION: 51,134

TOTAL AREA: 101 sq. miles (261 sq. km)

DENSITY: 368 people per sq. mile

LANGUAGES: English*, English Creole

RELIGIONS: Anglican 33%, Methodist 29%, other 22%, Moravian 9%, Roman Catholic 7%

ETHNIC MIX: Black 95%, mixed race 3%, White 1%, other and Amerindian 1%

GOVERNMENT: Parliamentary system

CURRENCY: East Caribbean dollar = 100 cents

St. Lucia

St. Lucia is one of the most beautiful of the Caribbean Windward Islands. Ruled by France and the UK at different times in its past, the island retains the influences of both.

GEOGRAPHY

Volcanic and mountainous, with some broad fertile valleys. The Pitons, ancient lava cones, rise from the sea on the forested west coast.

CLIMATE

Tropical, moderated by trade winds. May–October wet season brings daily warm showers. Rainfall is highest in the mountains.

PEOPLE & SOCIETY

The population is a tension-free mixture of descendants of Africans, Caribs, and Europeans. Family life and the Roman Catholic Church are important to most St. Lucians. In rural areas, women often head the households and run much of the farming. Plantation and hotel owners are the richest group. There is growing local resistance to overdevelopment of the island for tourism.

THE ECONOMY

Bananas are still biggest export, but struggling to compete since loss of preferential access to EU market. Successful tourism. Offshore banking.

INSIGHT: *St. Lucia has two Nobel laureates, the most per capita in the world*

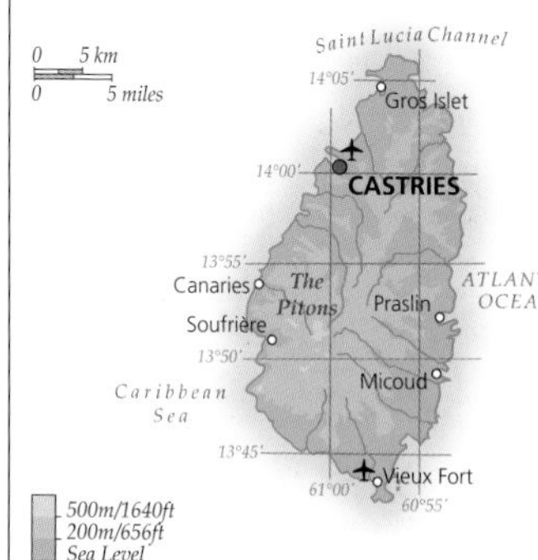

Saint Lucia Channel
0 5 km
0 5 miles
14°05′
Gros Islet
14°00′
CASTRIES
13°55′
Canaries
The Pitons
Praslin
ATLANTIC OCEAN
Soufrière
13°50′
Micoud
Caribbean Sea
13°45′
61°00′
Vieux Fort
60°55′
500m/1640ft
200m/656ft
Sea Level

FACTFILE

OFFICIAL NAME: Saint Lucia
DATE OF FORMATION: 1979
CAPITAL: Castries
POPULATION: 162,781
TOTAL AREA: 239 sq. miles (620 sq. km)
DENSITY: 690 people per sq. mile
LANGUAGES: English*, French Creole
RELIGIONS: Roman Catholic 90%, other 10%
ETHNIC MIX: Black 83%, *Mulatto* (mixed race) 13%, Asian 3%, other 1%
GOVERNMENT: Parliamentary system
CURRENCY: East Caribbean dollar = 100 cents

St. Vincent & the Grenadines

The islands of St. Vincent and the Grenadines form part of the Windward group in the Caribbean. St. Vincent is mostly volcanic, while the Grenadines are flat, mainly bare, coral reefs.

GEOGRAPHY

St. Vincent is mountainous and forested, with one of two active volcanoes in the Caribbean, La Soufrière. The Grenadines are 32 islands and cays, fringed by beaches.

CLIMATE

Tropical, with constant trade winds. Hurricanes are likely during the wet season in July–November.

PEOPLE & SOCIETY

Population is racially diverse; intermarriage has reduced tensions. Society is informal and relaxed, but family life is strongly influenced by the Christian Church. Locals fear that their traditional lifestyle is being threatened by the expanding tourist industry.

INSIGHT: *The islands' precolonial inhabitants, the Carib, named them "Harioun" – home of the blessed*

THE ECONOMY

Dependent on agriculture and tourism. Bananas are the main cash crop. Tourism, targeted at the jet-set and cruise-ship markets, is concentrated on the Grenadines.

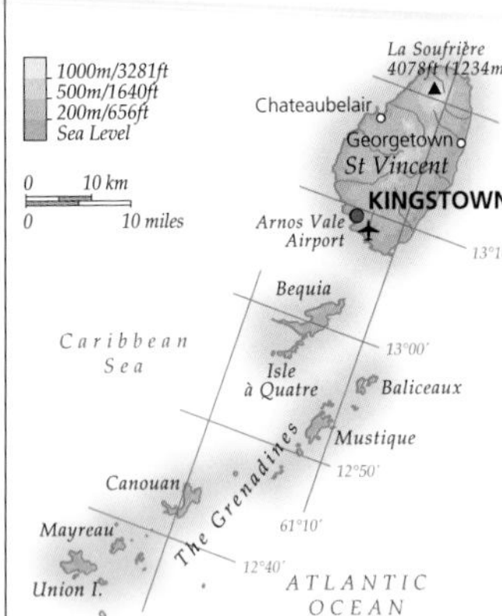
1000m/3281ft
500m/1640ft
200m/656ft
Sea Level
0 10 km
0 10 miles
La Soufrière 4078ft (1234m)
Chateaubelair
Georgetown
St Vincent
KINGSTOWN
Arnos Vale Airport
13°20′
13°10′
Bequia
13°00′
Caribbean Sea
Isle à Quatre
Baliceaux
Mustique
12°50′
The Grenadines
Canouan
Mayreau
Union I.
61°10′
12°40′
61°20′
ATLANTIC OCEAN

FACTFILE

OFFICIAL NAME: Saint Vincent and the Grenadines

DATE OF FORMATION: 1979

CAPITAL: Kingstown

POPULATION: 103,220

TOTAL AREA: 150 sq. miles (389 sq. km)

DENSITY: 788 people per sq. mile

LANGUAGES: English*, English Creole

RELIGIONS: Anglican 47%, Methodist 28%, Roman Catholic 13%, other 12%

ETHNIC MIX: Black 66%, *Mulatto* (mixed race) 19%, other 12%, Carib 2%, Asian 1%

GOVERNMENT: Parliamentary system

CURRENCY: East Caribbean dollar = 100 cents

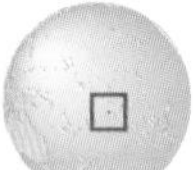

Samoa

The Pacific islands of Samoa gained independence from New Zealand in 1962. Four of the nine volcanic islands are inhabited – Apolima, Manono, Savai'i, and Upolu.

GEOGRAPHY

Comprises two large islands and seven smaller ones. The two largest islands have rainforested, mountainous interiors surrounded by coastal lowlands and coral reefs.

CLIMATE

Tropical, with high humidity. Cooler in May–November. Cyclone season is December–March.

PEOPLE & SOCIETY

Ethnic Samoans are the world's second-largest Polynesian group, after the Maoris. Their way of life is communal and formalized. Extended family groups own 80% of the land. Each family has an elected chief, who looks after its political and social interests. Large-scale migration to the US and New Zealand reflects the country's lack of jobs and the attractions of a Western lifestyle.

THE ECONOMY

Exports fish, coconut products (oil, cream, copra), and nonu fruit. Growth of tourism, offshore banking, and light manufacturing (Japanese car parts). Dependent on aid and expatriate remittances. Rainforests are increasingly exploited for timber.

INSIGHT: *Samoa was named for the sacred (sa) chickens (moa) of Lu, son of Tagaloa, the god of creation*

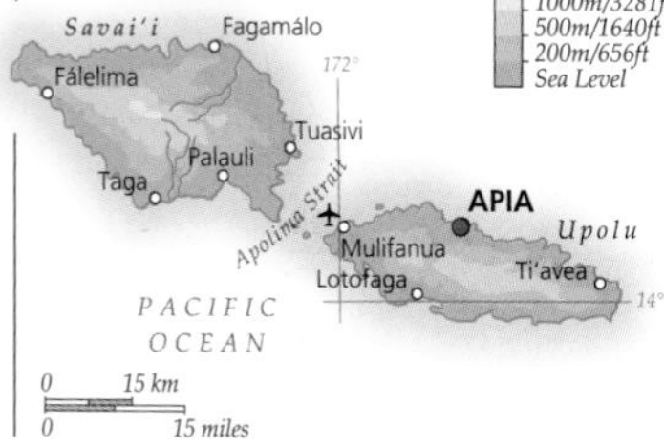
1000m/3281ft
500m/1640ft
200m/656ft
Sea Level
Savai'i
Fagamálo
Fálelima
172°
Tuasivi
Palauli
Taga
Apolima Strait
APIA
Upolu
Mulifanua
Lotofaga
Ti'avea
14°
PACIFIC OCEAN
0 15 km
0 15 miles

FACTFILE

OFFICIAL NAME: Independent State of Samoa

DATE OF FORMATION: 1962

CAPITAL: Apia

POPULATION: 200,000

TOTAL AREA: 1104 sq. miles (2860 sq. km)

DENSITY: 183 people per sq. mile

LANGUAGES: Samoan*, English*

RELIGIONS: Christian 99%, other 1%

ETHNIC MIX: Polynesian 91%, Euronesian (mixed European and Polynesian) 7%, other 2%

GOVERNMENT: Parliamentary system

CURRENCY: Tala = 100 sene

San Marino

Perched on the slopes of Monte Titano in the Italian Appennines, San Marino has maintained its independence since the 4th century CE, but Italy effectively controls most of its affairs.

GEOGRAPHY

Distinctive limestone outcrop of Monte Titano dominates wooded hills and pastures near Italy's Adriatic coast.

CLIMATE

High altitude and sea breezes moderate a Mediterranean climate. Hot summers and cool, wet winters.

PEOPLE & SOCIETY

Territory is divided into nine "castles," or districts. Tightly knit society, with 16 centuries of tradition. Strict immigration rules require 30-year residence before applying for citizenship. Living standards are similar to those in northern Italy. About 12,000 Sammarinesi live abroad, most in Italy.

INSIGHT: *Sales of postage stamps and coins contribute around 10% of the national income*

THE ECONOMY

Tourism, banking, manufacturing, and investment all hit by 2008–2009 global downturn. Banking transparency has improved. Lower tax rates than Italy. Wine, cheese, olive oil, textiles, and ceramics are exported. Also relies on Italian subsidy and infrastructure.

44°
Dogana
Serravalle
Fiorina
Cailungo
Gualdicciolo
Borgo Maggiore
SAN MARINO
ITALY
Monte Titano
2424ft (739m)
Faetano
Murata
ITALY
Appennino
Chiesanuova
Montegiardino
12°30'

500m/1640ft
200m/656ft
Sea Level

0
4 km
0
4 miles

FACTFILE

OFFICIAL NAME: Republic of San Marino
DATE OF FORMATION: 1631
CAPITAL: San Marino
POPULATION: 32,448
TOTAL AREA: 23.6 sq. miles (61 sq. km)
DENSITY: 1352 people per sq. mile
LANGUAGES: Italian*
RELIGIONS: Roman Catholic 93%, other and nonreligious 7%
ETHNIC MIX: Sammarinese 88%, Italian 10%, other 2%
GOVERNMENT: Parliamentary system
CURRENCY: Euro = 100 cents

Sao Tome & Principe

A former Portuguese colony, Sao Tome and Principe comprises two main islands and surrounding islets, off the west coast of Africa. Elections in 1991 ended 15 years of Marxism.

GEOGRAPHY

Islands scattered across the equator. Sao Tome and Principe are heavily forested and mountainous.

CLIMATE

Hot and humid, but cooled by the Benguela Current. Plentiful rainfall.

PEOPLE & SOCIETY

Population is mostly black, though Portuguese culture predominates. Blacks run the political parties. Society is well integrated and free from racial prejudice. Príncipe assumed autonomous status in 1995. There is a growing business class. The extended family offers the main form of social security. One of Africa's highest aid-to-population ratios.

INSIGHT: *The population is entirely of immigrant descent: the islands were uninhabited when colonized in 1470*

THE ECONOMY

Cocoa provides 90% of export earnings. Coconuts, pepper, coffee also farmed. Tourism. Reliant on aid. Offshore oil expected to come onstream shortly.

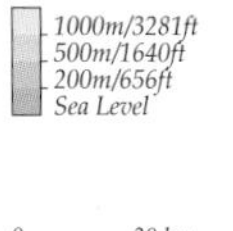
1000m/3281ft
500m/1640ft
200m/656ft
Sea Level

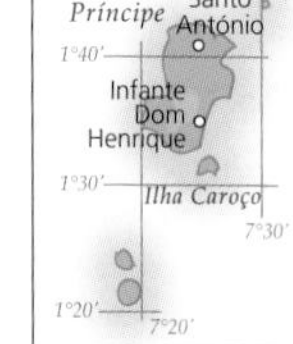
Príncipe
Santo António
1°40'
Infante Dom Henrique
1°30'
Ilha Caroço
7°30'
1°20'
7°20'

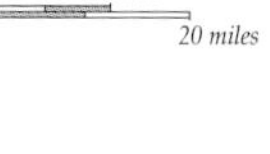
0
20 km
0
20 miles

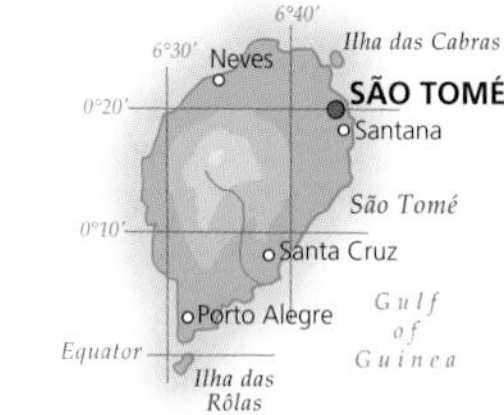
6°40'
6°30'
Neves
Ilha das Cabras
SÃO TOMÉ
0°20'
Santana
São Tomé
0°10'
Santa Cruz
Porto Alegre
Gulf of Guinea
Equator
Ilha das Rôlas

FACTFILE

OFFICIAL NAME: Democratic Republic of Sao Tome and Principe

DATE OF FORMATION: 1975

CAPITAL: São Tomé

POPULATION: 200,000

TOTAL AREA: 386 sq. miles (1001 sq. km)

DENSITY: 539 people per sq. mile

LANGUAGES: Portuguese Creole, Portuguese*

RELIGIONS: Roman Catholic 84%, other 16%

ETHNIC MIX: Black 90%, Portuguese and Creole 10%

GOVERNMENT: Presidential system

CURRENCY: Dobra = 100 céntimos

Saudi Arabia

Occupying most of the Arabian Peninsula, Saudi Arabia covers an area the size of western Europe. It is the world's largest oil producer and has a major petrochemicals industry.

GEOGRAPHY

Mostly desert or semidesert plateau. Mountain ranges in the west run parallel to the Red Sea and drop steeply to a coastal plain.

CLIMATE

In summer, temperatures often soar above 118°F (48°C), but in winter they may fall below freezing. Rainfall is rare.

PEOPLE & SOCIETY

Most Saudis are Sunni Muslims who embrace *sharia* (Islamic law) and follow the strictly orthodox Wahhabi interpretation of Islam in their daily lives. Women are obliged to wear the veil, cannot hold a driver's license, and have no role in public life. The al-Sa'ud family rules with absolute power. Supported by the religious establishment, it controls all political life and makes few concessions to any calls for wider public participation.

THE ECONOMY

Vast oil and natural gas reserves. A third of workers are foreign. Attractive jobs for young Saudis are scarce, however.

INSIGHT: *Three million Muslims a year make the hajj (pilgrimage) to the holy city of Mecca. Only practicing Muslims are allowed inside the city*

JORDAN
IRAQ
EGYPT
An Nafud
KUWAIT
Tabūk
Persian Gulf
Buraydah
Ad Dammān
BAHRAIN
Al Hufūf
QATAR
Al Madīnah (Medina)
RIYADH
Haraḑ
UAE
Jiddah (Jedda)
Makkah (Mecca)
Aṭ Ṭā'if
Red Sea
Ar Rub' al Khālī
OMAN
Abhā
YEMEN
2000m/6562ft
1000m/3281ft
500m/1640ft
200m/656ft
Sea Level
0 200 km
0 200 miles

FACTFILE

OFFICIAL NAME: Kingdom of Saudi Arabia
DATE OF FORMATION: 1932
CAPITAL: Riyadh
POPULATION: 28.8 million
TOTAL AREA: 756,981 sq. miles (1,960,582 sq. km)
DENSITY: 35 people per sq. mile
LANGUAGES: Arabic*
RELIGIONS: (Native population) Sunni Muslim 85%, Shi'a Muslim 15%
ETHNIC MIX: Arab 72%, foreign residents (mostly south or southeast Asian) 20%, Afro-Asian 8%
GOVERNMENT: Monarchy
CURRENCY: Saudi riyal = 100 halalat

Senegal

Senegal's capital, Dakar, stands on the westernmost cape of Africa. After independence from France, Senegal became a single-party state, but it has had multiparty elections since 1981.

GEOGRAPHY

Arid semidesert in the north. The south is mainly savanna bushland. Plains in the southeast.

CLIMATE

Tropical, with humid rainy conditions June–October, and a drier season December–May. The coast is cooled by northern trade winds.

PEOPLE & SOCIETY

Interethnic marriage has reduced ethnic tensions. Groups can be identified regionally. Dakar is a Wolof area, with the Serer concentrated to the east and southeast of Dakar. The Senegal River is dominated by the Peul and Toucouleur. The Diola (Jola) in Casamance have felt politically excluded, prompting a long-running secessionist struggle; a cease-fire in 2014 may signal the conflict's end. A large diaspora raises global awareness of Senegalese culture and music.

THE ECONOMY

Good infrastructure, particularly port at Dakar. Fishing (though stocks diminishing). Remittances. Phosphate mining. Groundnuts. Development of tourism. Oil potential off Casamance.

INSIGHT: *Senegal's name derives from the Muslim Zenega Berbers who invaded in the 1300s*

Senegal
Saint-Louis
MAURITANIA
ATLANTIC OCEAN
Louga
Matam
Senegal
DAKAR
Thiès
Diourbel
Mbour
14°
Kaolack
Kaffrine
Tambacounda
MALI
GAMBIA
Casamance
Kolda
Gambia
Ziguinchor
GUINEA-BISSAU
GUINEA
16°
12°

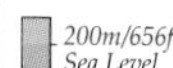
200m/656ft
Sea Level

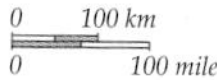
0 100 km
0 100 miles

FACTFILE

OFFICIAL NAME: Republic of Senegal
DATE OF FORMATION: 1960
CAPITAL: Dakar
POPULATION: 14.1 million
TOTAL AREA: 75,749 sq. miles (196,190 sq. km)
DENSITY: 190 people per sq. mile
LANGUAGES: Wolof, Serer, Pulaar, Diola, Mandinka, Malinké, Soninké, French*
RELIGIONS: Sunni Muslim 95%, Christian (mainly Catholic) 4%, traditional beliefs 1%
ETHNIC MIX: Wolof 43%, Serer 15%, other 14%, Peul 14%, Toucouleur 9%, Diola 5%
GOVERNMENT: Presidential system
CURRENCY: CFA franc = 100 centimes

Serbia

The central and eastern region of what was once Yugoslavia, Serbia was a pariah state until Slobodan Milosevic was ousted in 2000. Montenegro broke away in 2006, and Kosovo in 2008.

GEOGRAPHY

Landlocked since secession of Montenegro. Fertile Danube plain in the north, rolling uplands in the center and southeast. Mountains in southwest.

CLIMATE

Continental in north, with wet springs and warm summers. Colder winters with heavy snow in south.

PEOPLE & SOCIETY

Serbs are Orthodox Christian and use the Cyrillic script. Catholic Magyars (Hungarians) in Vojvodina have some autonomy. Society was severely shaken in the 1990s by interethnic conflict. After Serbia's cooperation in apprehending suspected war criminals, it was granted EU candidate status, but the issue of Kosovo is a major obstacle to accession.

INSIGHT: *The medieval Serbian Empire reached into northern Greece*

THE ECONOMY

Recovery from sanctions and 1999 NATO bombing: GDP only returned to pre-1990 level by 2006. Reserves of coal, oil. Strong industrial base. Privatization ongoing. Foreign investment growing. Danube is a key transportation link.

HUNGARY
20°
0 50 km
0 50 miles
Subotica
46°
Vojvodina
Zrenjanin
Danube
CROATIA
Novi Sad
ROMANIA
Pančevo
Šabac
22°
BELGRADE
Smederevo
Danube
BOSNIA & HERZEGOVINA
Kragujevac
44°
Čačak
Kraljevo
Kruševac
Niš
Leskovac
MONTENEGRO
KOSOVO
(disputed)
BULG.
2000m/6562ft
1000m/3281ft
500m/1640ft
200m/656ft
Sea Level
MACEDONIA

FACTFILE

OFFICIAL NAME: Republic of Serbia
DATE OF FORMATION: 2006
CAPITAL: Belgrade
POPULATION: 9.5 million
TOTAL AREA: 29,905 sq. miles (77,453 sq. km)
DENSITY: 318 people per sq. mile
LANGUAGES: Serbian*, Hungarian (Magyar)
RELIGIONS: Orthodox Christian 85%, other 6%, Roman Catholic 6%, Muslim 3%
ETHNIC MIX: Serb 83%, other 10%, Magyar 4%, Bosniak 2%, Roma 1%
GOVERNMENT: Parliamentary system
CURRENCY: Serbian dinar = 100 para

Seychelles

Formerly a UK colony, the Seychelles comprises 115 islands in the Indian Ocean. After 14 years as a one-party state, multiparty elections were introduced in 1993.

GEOGRAPHY

Mostly low-lying coral atolls, but 40, including the largest, Mahé, are mountainous and are the only granitic midocean islands in the world.

CLIMATE

Tropical oceanic climate. Hot and humid. Rainy season December–May.

PEOPLE & SOCIETY

The islands were uninhabited when French settlers arrived in the 18th century. Today, the population is homogeneous – a result of intermarriage between ethnic groups. Almost 90% of people live on Mahé. Living standards are among Africa's highest. Poverty is rare and the welfare system caters to all.

INSIGHT: *The Seychelles' unique species include the coco-de-mer palm, which produces the world's largest seeds*

THE ECONOMY

Tourism is main sector, based on appeal of beaches and exotic wildlife. Tuna is fished and canned for export. Re-export trade. All domestic requirements are imported. Virtually no mineral resources. High debt-servicing burden. Lack of foreign exchange.

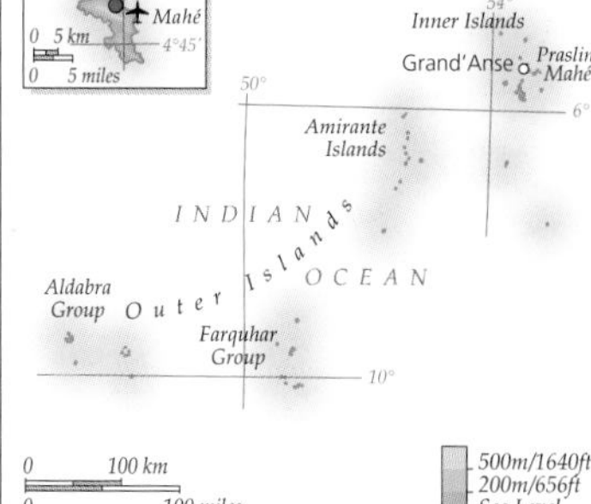
55°30'
VICTORIA
Mahé
0 5 km
4°45'
0 5 miles
54°
Inner Islands
Grand'Anse
Praslin
Mahé
50°
6°
Amirante Islands
INDIAN OCEAN
Outer Islands
Aldabra Group
Farquhar Group
10°
0 100 km
0 100 miles
500m/1640ft
200m/656ft
Sea Level

FACTFILE

OFFICIAL NAME: Republic of Seychelles
DATE OF FORMATION: 1976
CAPITAL: Victoria
POPULATION: 90,846
TOTAL AREA: 176 sq. miles (455 sq. km)
DENSITY: 874 people per sq. mile
LANGUAGES: French Creole*, English*, French*
RELIGIONS: Roman Catholic 82%, Anglican 6%, other (including Muslim) 6%, other Christian 4%, Hindu 2%
ETHNIC MIX: Creole 89%, Indian 5%, other 4%, Chinese 2%
GOVERNMENT: Presidential system
CURRENCY: Seychelles rupee = 100 cents

Sierra Leone

The west African state of Sierra Leone achieved independence from the UK in 1961. Today, trying to recover from ten years of devastating civil war, it is one of the world's poorest nations.

GEOGRAPHY

Flat plain, running the length of the coast, stretches inland for 83 miles (133 km). Beyond, forests rise to highlands near neighboring Guinea in the northeast.

CLIMATE

Hot tropical weather, with very high rainfall and humidity. The dusty, northeastern *harmattan* wind blows November–April.

PEOPLE & SOCIETY

Mende and Temne are the major ethnic groups. Freetown's citizens are largely descended from slaves freed from Britain and the US, resulting in a strongly Anglicized Creole culture in the capital. The countryside is less developed. A brutal civil war broke out in 1991 and was not properly resolved until a 2001 peace agreement. Two million people were displaced during the conflict. A deadly Ebola outbreak hit the country in 2014.

THE ECONOMY

Aid is vital: reconstruction will take years. Diamond exports, though smuggling is rife. Rutile and bauxite also mined. Coffee and cocoa are cash crops, but most farming is subsistence.

INSIGHT: *The British philanthropist Granville Sharp set up a settlement for freed slaves in Freetown in 1787*

1000m/3281ft
500m/1640ft
200m/656ft
Sea Level
10°
GUINEA
Kabala
Makeni
Lunsar
FREETOWN
Koidu
Boajibu
8
Bo
Kenema
Sherbro I.
Zimmi
LIBERIA
ATLANTIC
OCEAN
12°
0 50 km
0 50 miles

FACTFILE

OFFICIAL NAME: Republic of Sierra Leone
DATE OF FORMATION: 1961
CAPITAL: Freetown
POPULATION: 6.1 million
TOTAL AREA: 27,698 sq. miles (71,740 sq. km)
DENSITY: 221 people per sq. mile
LANGUAGES: Mende, Temne, Krio, English*
RELIGIONS: Muslim 60%, Christian 30%, traditional beliefs 10%
ETHNIC MIX: Mende 35%, Temne 32%, other 21%, Limba 8%, Kuranko 4%
GOVERNMENT: Presidential system
CURRENCY: Leone = 100 cents

Singapore

Linked to the southernmost tip of the Malay peninsula by a causeway, Singapore was established as a trading settlement in 1819. It is now one of Asia's most important commercial centers.

GEOGRAPHY

Little remains of the original vegetation on Singapore Island. The other 54 much smaller islands are little more than swampy jungle.

CLIMATE

Equatorial. Hot and humid, with heavy rainfall all year round.

PEOPLE & SOCIETY

Chinese majority includes old-established English-speaking Straits Chinese and more recent immigrants. Median income is highest in Indian households and lowest in Malay households. Significant expatriate workforce. Aging population: cash incentives, longer maternity leave aim to boost birth rate. Society is highly regulated; official campaigns aim to improve public behavior. Crime is low; punishment can be severe. Living standards are among world's highest.

THE ECONOMY

Wealth from success as entrepôt and center of high-tech industries, such as electronics and pharmaceuticals. Leads research in new biotechnologies. All food, energy, and water imported. Worst-ever recession in 2008–2009.

INSIGHT: *Chewing gum was banned outright from 1992 to 2004*

0 5 km
0 5 miles
Causeway
MALAYSIA
Pulau Ubin
Lim Chu Kang
Bukit Panjang
Pulau Tekong
Choa Chu Kang
Houngang New Town
Bukit Timah
Jurong
Changi International Airport
1°20′
Jurong Industrial Estate
Bedok New Town
Queenstown
City
Telok Blangah
South China Sea
Sedat Pandan
Sentosa
Pulau Brani
103°40′
103°50′
Strait of Singapore
Urban areas
Open areas
Nature reserves

FACTFILE

OFFICIAL NAME: Republic of Singapore

DATE OF FORMATION: 1965

CAPITAL: Singapore

POPULATION: 5.4 million

TOTAL AREA: 250 sq. miles (648 sq. km)

DENSITY: 22,881 people per sq. mile

LANGUAGES: Mandarin*, Malay*, Tamil*, English*

RELIGIONS: Buddhist 55%, Taoist 22%, Muslim 16%, Hindu, Christian, and Sikh 7%

ETHNIC MIX: Chinese 74%, Malay 14%, Indian 9%, other 3%

GOVERNMENT: Parliamentary system

CURRENCY: Singapore dollar = 100 cents

Slovakia

Landlocked in central Europe, Slovakia became a separate state in 1993, splitting ex-communist Czechoslovakia in two. It joined the EU in 2004 and the eurozone five years later.

GEOGRAPHY

The Tatra Mountains stretch along the northern border with Poland. Southern lowlands include the fertile Danube plain.

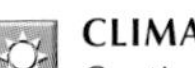

CLIMATE

Continental. Moderately warm summers and steady rainfall. Cold winters with heavy snowfalls.

PEOPLE & SOCIETY

The majority Slovaks are the dominant group. The Magyars (Hungarians) seek protection of their language and culture, backed by Hungary. Magyar parties exist in the political mainstream, and on occasion form part of the ruling coalition. Ethnic Czechs have dual citizenship. Roma are unrepresented and face significant discrimination. Rural eastern regions are least developed.

THE ECONOMY

Heavy industry, especially cars. Exports hit by 2007–2009 global downturn. Inexpensive workforce. Rising foreign investment. High unemployment, budget deficits. Successful privatizations.

INSIGHT: *From 1526 to 1784 Bratislava, then known as Pozsony, served as the capital of Hungary*

POLAND
20°
22°
18°
Carpathian Mts.
Bardejov
Žilina
CZECH REPUBLIC
Martin
Prešov
Trenčín
Košice
UKRAINE
Banská Bystrica
AUS.
Trnava
Nitra
Lučenec
BRATISLAVA
48°
Danube
HUNGARY
0 50 km
0 50 miles
2000m/6562ft
1000m/3281ft
500m/1640ft
200m/656ft
Sea Level

FACTFILE

OFFICIAL NAME: Slovak Republic
DATE OF FORMATION: 1993
CAPITAL: Bratislava
POPULATION: 5.5 million
TOTAL AREA: 18,859 sq. miles (48,845 sq. km)
DENSITY: 290 people per sq. mile
LANGUAGES: Slovak*, Hungarian (Magyar), Czech
RELIGIONS: Roman Catholic 69%, other 13%, nonreligious 13%, Greek Catholic (Uniate) 4%, Orthodox Christian 1%
ETHNIC MIX: Slovak 86%, Magyar 10%, Roma 2%, Czech 1%, other 1%
GOVERNMENT: Parliamentary system
CURRENCY: Euro = 100 cents

Slovenia

Lying at the junction of central Europe and the Balkans, Slovenia seceded from socialist Yugoslavia in 1991. In 2004, it became the first former Yugoslav state to join the EU.

GEOGRAPHY

Alpine terrain with hills and mountains. Forests cover almost half the country's area. There is a short coastline on the Adriatic Sea.

CLIMATE

Mediterranean climate on the small coastal strip. The alpine interior has continental extremes.

PEOPLE & SOCIETY

Long historical association with western Europe, accounts for the "Alpine" rather than "Balkan" outlook of Slovenia's people, despite close similarities to other former Yugoslavs. The absence of sizable Serb or Croat minorities made for a relatively peaceful secession from Yugoslavia. There are small communities of Italians and Magyars (Hungarians) in the southwest and east respectively.

THE ECONOMY

First new EU member to join eurozone (in 2007). Export-oriented, so vulnerable to global economic trends. Competitive manufacturing industry. Sizable state-owned sector remains.

INSIGHT: *A wheel found in a marsh in 2003 is claimed to be the world's oldest, pre-dating 3000 BCE*

1000m/3281ft
500m/1640ft
200m/656ft
Sea Level
AUSTRIA
HUNGARY
Murska Sobota
Mura
Maribor
Drava
Ptuj
Jesenice
Kranj
Celje
LJUBLJANA
Sava
ITALY
16°
46°
Nova Gorica
Krško
Brežice
Postojna
Adriatic Sea
CROATIA
Kolpa
0 25 km
0 25 miles
14°

FACTFILE

OFFICIAL NAME: Republic of Slovenia
DATE OF FORMATION: 1991
CAPITAL: Ljubljana
POPULATION: 2.1 million
TOTAL AREA: 7820 sq. miles (20,253 sq. km)
DENSITY: 269 people per sq. mile
LANGUAGES: Slovenian*
RELIGIONS: Roman Catholic 58%, other 28%, Atheist 10%, Orthodox Christian 2%, Muslim 2%
ETHNIC MIX: Slovene 83%, other 12%, Serb 2%, Croat 2%, Bosniak 1%
GOVERNMENT: Parliamentary system
CURRENCY: Euro = 100 cents

Solomon Islands

The Solomons archipelago comprises several hundred coral reef islands scattered in the southwestern Pacific. Most of the population live on the six largest islands.

GEOGRAPHY

The six largest islands are volcanic, mountainous, and thickly forested. Flat coastal plains provide the only cultivable land.

CLIMATE

Northern islands are hot and humid all year round; farther south a cool season develops. November–April wet season brings cyclones.

PEOPLE & SOCIETY

Almost all Solomon Islanders are Melanesian. Animist beliefs exist alongside Christianity. Tensions are regional; Guadalcanal natives (Isatabu) fought against immigrant Malaitan workers in the 1998–2000 conflict, displacing thousands and ruining the economy. In 2003, Australian-led peacekeepers arrived. A new devolved "state system" has granted outlying islands more autonomy and brought a semblance of stability.

THE ECONOMY

Subsistence farming and fishing sustain 75% of people. Cash crops are copra and cocoa. Gold deposits. Civil conflict bankrupted the government, closed the main gold mine, and cut trade links. Forests have been depleted.

INSIGHT: *The battle for Japanese-held Guadalcanal was the first major US offensive in the Pacific War during World War II*

PACIFIC OCEAN
Choiseul
Santa Isabel
New Georgia
Gizo
Munda
New Georgia Is.
Malaita
HONIARA
Guadalcanal
Santa Cruz Islands
Kirakira
San Cristobal
Lata
Rennell
Solomon Sea
5°
10°
155°
160°
165°
170°
500m/1640ft
Sea Level
0 200 km
0 200 miles

FACTFILE

OFFICIAL NAME: Solomon Islands
DATE OF FORMATION: 1978
CAPITAL: Honiara
POPULATION: 600,000
TOTAL AREA: 10,985 sq. miles (28,450 sq. km)
DENSITY: 56 people per sq. mile
LANGUAGES: English*, Pidgin English, Melanesian Pidgin, c. 120 others
RELIGIONS: Church of Melanesia (Anglican) 34%, Roman Catholic 19%, other 19%, South Seas Evangelical Church 17%, Methodist 11%
ETHNIC MIX: Melanesian 93%, Polynesian 4%, Micronesian 2%, other 1%
GOVERNMENT: Parliamentary system
CURRENCY: Solomon Is. dollar = 100 cents

Somalia

A semiarid state occupying the Horn of Africa, Somalia was formed from the Italian and British colonies of Somaliland. Conflict has left it without effective government since 1991.

GEOGRAPHY

Highlands in the north, flatter scrub-covered land to the south. Coastal areas are more fertile.

CLIMATE

Very dry, except for the north coast, which is hot and humid. The interior has among the world's highest average annual temperatures.

PEOPLE & SOCIETY

The clan system forms the basis of commercial, political, and social life. The minority Bantu are traditionally seen as socially inferior to Somalis. Since the 1991 coup, Somalia has lacked strong central authority. Somaliland claims independence, and Puntland autonomy. Islamist militias controlled rump Somalia by 2009, and al-Shabab still holds sway in the south. A new federal structure was formulated in 2012 ahead of the latest attempt to form a national government.

THE ECONOMY

Ongoing war. All goods, except arms, are in short supply. Piracy, banditry. Few natural resources. Prone to drought; latest famine in 2011–2012 killed 260,000. Somaliland is more stable, but its trade is hampered by lack of global recognition.

INSIGHT: *Until 1973, Somali was an unwritten language*

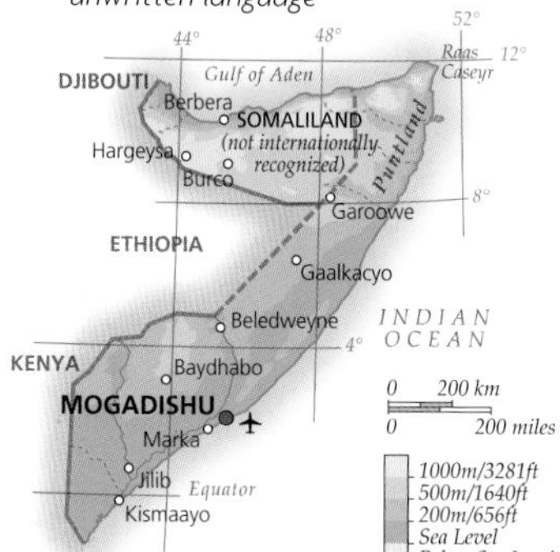

44°
48°
52°
12°
8°
4°
Raas Caseyr
DJIBOUTI
Gulf of Aden
Berbera
SOMALILAND
(not internationally recognized)
Hargeysa
Burco
Puntland
Garoowe
ETHIOPIA
Gaalkacyo
Beledweyne
INDIAN OCEAN
KENYA
Baydhabo
MOGADISHU
Marka
Jilib
Equator
Kismaayo
0 200 km
0 200 miles
1000m/3281ft
500m/1640ft
200m/656ft
Sea Level
Below Sea Level

FACTFILE

OFFICIAL NAME: Federal Republic of Somalia
DATE OF FORMATION: 1960
CAPITAL: Mogadishu
POPULATION: 10.5 million
TOTAL AREA: 246,199 sq. miles (637,657 sq. km)
DENSITY: 43 people per sq. mile
LANGUAGES: Somali*, Arabic*, English, Italian
RELIGIONS: Sunni Muslim 99%, Christian 1%
ETHNIC MIX: Somali 85%, other 15%
GOVERNMENT: Nonparty system
CURRENCY: Somali shilin = 100 senti

South Africa

After 80 years of white minority rule, South Africa held its first multiracial, multiparty elections in 1994. Victory for the blacks marked the symbolic overturning of long years of apartheid.

GEOGRAPHY

Much of the interior is grassy *veld*. Desert in the west and far north. Mountains east, south, and west.

CLIMATE

Warm, temperate, and dry. Cape Town has a Mediterranean climate. Semiarid in the west.

PEOPLE & SOCIETY

The majority black population now dominates politically, but the minority white community still controls the economy. A small black middle class is growing, but unemployment among blacks remains high. Over five million people are HIV-positive, but the fight against AIDS is hampered by social attitudes. Violent crime is a problem.

INSIGHT: *Over the last century, South Africa has produced over half of the world's gold*

THE ECONOMY

Africa's largest, most developed economy. Leading mineral producer, notably metals, diamonds, coal. Tourism is also key. Wealth gap has widened: jobs, housing, and better access to basic services are needed to fight poverty.

2000m/6562ft
1000m/3281ft
500m/1640ft
Sea Level
ZIMBABWE
MOZAMBIQUE
BOTSWANA
Limpopo
PRETORIA
Middelburg
Johannesburg
SWAZILAND
Soweto
Kalahari
Desert
Vryburg
NAMIBIA
Vaal
Piet Retief
Upington
Kroonstad
Orange
Kimberley
BLOEMFONTEIN
Pietermaritzburg
Northern Karoo
LESOTHO
Durban
Middelburg
Drakensberg
INDIAN
OCEAN
CAPE
TOWN
Great Karoo
Beaufort West
East London
George
Port Elizabeth
Cape of
Good Hope
0 400 km
0 400 miles
20°
24°
28°
32°

FACTFILE

OFFICIAL NAME: Republic of South Africa
DATE OF FORMATION: 1934
CAPITALS: Pretoria; Cape Town; Bloemfontein
POPULATION: 52.8 million
TOTAL AREA: 471,008 sq. miles (1,219,912 sq. km)
DENSITY: 112 people per sq. mile
LANGUAGES: English*, isiZulu*, isiXhosa*, Afrikaans*, 7 other official languages*
RELIGIONS: Christian 68%, animist and traditional beliefs 29%, Muslim 2%, Hindu 1%
ETHNIC MIX: Black 80%, White 9%, Colored 9%, Asian 2%
GOVERNMENT: Presidential system
CURRENCY: Rand = 100 cents

South Sudan

A long civil war in Sudan led to independence in 2011 for the mainly Christian southern part. The landlocked new state is poor and lacks vital infrastructure, despite its oil reserves.

GEOGRAPHY

The White Nile flows through South Sudan, from remote forest areas into the world's largest swamp, the Sudd.

CLIMATE

Tropical South Sudan's long, heavy rains result in some areas getting cut off. January to March is drier.

PEOPLE & SOCIETY

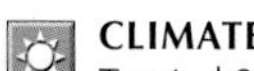

Most people are subsistence farmers. Village life is based on extended families; arranged marriages involve the payment of bride-price. There are over 60 language groups. The common cause of independence engendered ethnic unity. The Sudanese People's Liberation Movement, whose armed wing led the fighting, holds power in the new country, but in 2013 a fallout between president and vice president spiraled into civil war, exposing ethnic divisions between Dinka and Nuer.

THE ECONOMY

Needs foreign aid for humanitarian crisis and development. Issues over oil revenue and borders remain unresolved with Sudan, which controls sole oil export pipeline. Inherited foreign debt.

INSIGHT: *Decades of fighting from 1983 left over four million internally displaced*

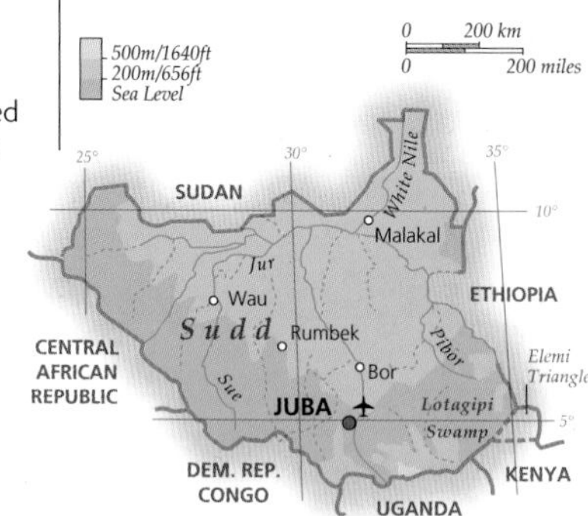
500m/1640ft
200m/656ft
Sea Level
0 200 km
0 200 miles
25°
30°
35°
10°
5°
SUDAN
White Nile
Malakal
Jur
Wau
ETHIOPIA
Sudd
Rumbek
Pibor
CENTRAL AFRICAN REPUBLIC
Bor
Elemi Triangle
Sue
JUBA
Lotagipi Swamp
DEM. REP. CONGO
KENYA
UGANDA

FACTFILE

OFFICIAL NAME: Republic of South Sudan
DATE OF FORMATION: 2011
CAPITAL: Juba
POPULATION: 11.3 million
TOTAL AREA: 248,777 sq. miles (644,329 sq. km)
DENSITY: 45 people per sq. mile
LANGUAGES: English*, Arabic, Dinka, Nuer, Zande, Bari, Shilluk, Lotuko
RELIGIONS: Over half of the population follow Christian or traditional beliefs
ETHNIC MIX: Dinka 40%, Nuer 15%, Bari 10%, Azande 10%, Shilluk 10%, Arab 10%, other 5%
GOVERNMENT: Transitional regime
CURRENCY: South Sudan pound = 100 piastres

Spain

At its unification under Ferdinand and Isabella in 1492, Spain occupied a pivotal position between Europe, Africa, the North Atlantic, and the Mediterranean.

GEOGRAPHY

Mountain ranges in the north, center, and south, with a huge central plateau. Mediterranean lowlands. Verdant valleys in the northwest.

CLIMATE

Maritime in north. Hotter and drier in south. The central plateau has an extreme climate.

PEOPLE & SOCIETY

A vigorous ethnic regionalism, suppressed under Franco's fascist regime, now flourishes. There are 17 autonomous regions. People remain churchgoing, though Roman Catholic teachings on social issues are often flouted. Spanish women are increasingly emancipated, with strong political representation.

INSIGHT: *Over 3000 festivals and feasts take place each year in Spain*

THE ECONOMY

Exports food, wine. Few natural resources. Large fishing fleet. Tourism, motor industry hit by global downturn; soaring unemployment since abrupt end of construction boom. Austerity program aim to cut debt and deficits. A target for economic migrants from Africa.

0 100 km
0 100 miles
Bay of Biscay
A Coruña
Gijón
Santander
Bilbao
Donostia/
San Sebastián
FRANCE
ANDORRA
Pyrenees
Vigo
León
Burgos
Ourense
Logroño
Lleida
Valladolid
Soria
Zaragoza
Barcelona
Tarragona
Ávila
PORTUGAL
Tagus
MADRID
Menorca
Getafe
Mallorca
Palma
Valencia
Badajoz
Albacete
Ibiza
Islas Baleares
Córdoba
Murcia
Alicante
Huelva
Sevilla
Granada
Cartagena
Málaga
Almería
Cádiz
Mediterranean Sea
2000m/6562ft
1000m/3281ft
500m/1640ft
200m/656ft
Sea Level

FACTFILE

OFFICIAL NAME: Kingdom of Spain

DATE OF FORMATION: 1492

CAPITAL: Madrid

POPULATION: 46.9 million

TOTAL AREA: 194,896 sq. miles (504,782 sq. km)

DENSITY: 243 people per sq. mile

LANGUAGES: Spanish*, Catalan*, Galician*, Basque*

RELIGIONS: Roman Catholic 96%, other 4%

ETHNIC MIX: Castilian Spanish 72%, Catalan 17%, Galician 6%, Basque 2%, Roma 1%, other 2%

GOVERNMENT: Parliamentary system

CURRENCY: Euro = 100 cents

Sri Lanka

The teardrop-shaped island of Sri Lanka is separated from India by the Palk Strait. Ethnic Tamil rebels – the Tamil Tigers – were defeated in 2009, after a brutal 26-year civil war.

GEOGRAPHY

The main island is dominated by rugged central highlands. Fertile northern plains are dissected by rivers. Much of the land is tropical jungle.

CLIMATE

Tropical, with breezes on the coast and cooler air in highlands. Northeast is driest and hottest.

PEOPLE & SOCIETY

The Sinhalese are mostly Buddhist, while Tamils are mostly Hindu. Moors are the Muslim descendants of Arab traders. Tamils were the minority group favored by the British colonists. Majority-Sinhalese power since independence in 1948 fueled tensions, erupting into civil war in 1983. The eventual government victory in 2009 made this the only rebel insurgency ever defeated in modern times.

THE ECONOMY

Garment industry. Remittances. Major tea exporter. End of costly civil war; return of foreign investment and tourists. Decade of strong GDP growth.

INSIGHT: *Sri Lanka elected the world's first woman prime minister, Sirimavo Bandaranaike, in 1960*

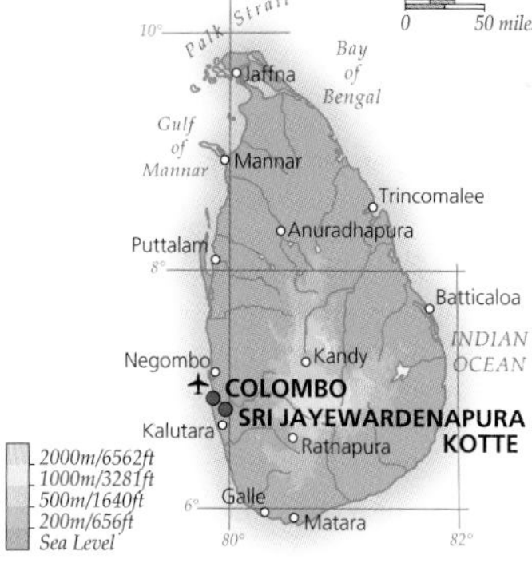
0 50 km
0 50 miles
Palk Strait
10°
Bay of Bengal
Jaffna
Gulf of Mannar
Mannar
Trincomalee
Anuradhapura
Puttalam
8°
Batticaloa
INDIAN OCEAN
Negombo
Kandy
COLOMBO
SRI JAYEWARDENAPURA KOTTE
Kalutara
Ratnapura
2000m/6562ft
1000m/3281ft
500m/1640ft
200m/656ft
Sea Level
6°
Galle
Matara
80°
82°

FACTFILE

OFFICIAL NAME: Democratic Socialist Republic of Sri Lanka

DATE OF FORMATION: 1948

CAPITAL: Colombo / Sri Jayewardenapura Kotte

POPULATION: 21.3 million

TOTAL AREA: 25,332 sq. miles (65,610 sq. km)

DENSITY: 852 people per sq. mile

LANGUAGES: Sinhala*, Tamil*, English

RELIGIONS: Buddhist 69%, Hindu 15%, Muslim 8%, Christian 8%

ETHNIC MIX: Sinhalese 74%, Tamil 18%, Moor 7%, other 1%

GOVERNMENT: Mixed presidential–parliamentary system

CURRENCY: Sri Lanka rupee = 100 cents

Sudan

The secession of the black African south in 2011 left Sudan as Africa's third-largest country. Darfur in the west is suffering a terrible humanitarian crisis.

GEOGRAPHY

Lies within the upper Nile basin. Mostly arid plains. Highlands border the Red Sea in the northeast.

CLIMATE

North is hot, arid desert with constant dry winds. Rainy season lasting a few months in the south.

PEOPLE & SOCIETY

About two million people are nomads. There are many ethnic groups. Islamic law, imposed by the Arab majority, restricts women's freedoms and alienated the non-Muslim south, which finally seceded in 2011 after prolonged conflict. Ethnic violence by Arab militias in Darfur since 2003 has killed 300,000 people and created a huge refugee crisis within Sudan and in neighboring Chad and CAR. President Bashir faces an international arrest warrant for crimes against humanity.

THE ECONOMY

Oil reserves reduced by secession of South. Cotton, sesame, gum arabic. Violence and drought hamper farming. Millions of people displaced. Large debt.

INSIGHT: *Sudan has more pyramids than Egypt: over 200 structures remain from ancient Nubian kingdoms on the Nile*

25°
30°
35°
EGYPT
LIBYA
Nubian Desert
Red Sea
20°
Nile
Port Sudan
Atbara
CHAD
Darfur
Omdurman
ERITREA
KHARTOUM
Kassala
15°
El Geneina
Sodiri
Wad Medani
El Obeid
Kosti
White Nile
Blue Nile
ETHIOPIA
10°
C.A.R.
SOUTH SUDAN

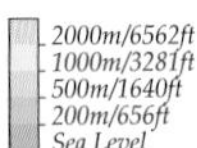
2000m/6562ft
1000m/3281ft
500m/1640ft
200m/656ft
Sea Level

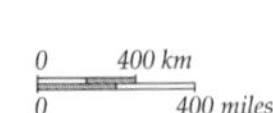
0
400 km
0
400 miles

FACTFILE

OFFICIAL NAME: Republic of the Sudan
DATE OF FORMATION: 1956
CAPITAL: Khartoum
POPULATION: 38 million
TOTAL AREA: 718,722 sq. miles (1,861,481 sq. km)
DENSITY: 53 people per sq. mile
LANGUAGES: Arabic*, Nubian, Beja, Fur
RELIGIONS: Nearly the whole population is Muslim (mainly Sunni)
ETHNIC MIX: Arab 60%, other 18%, Nubian 10%, Beja 8%, Fur 3%, Zaghawa 1%
GOVERNMENT: Presidential system
CURRENCY: New Sudanese pound = 100 piastres

Suriname

Suriname is a former Dutch colony on the north coast of South America. Democracy was restored in 1991, after almost 11 years of military rule. The Netherlands is still a major donor of aid.

GEOGRAPHY

Mostly covered by tropical rainforest. Coastal plain rises to central plateaus and the Guiana Highlands.

CLIMATE

Tropical. Hot and humid, but cooled by trade winds. High rainfall, especially in the interior.

PEOPLE & SOCIETY

The Dutch brought laborers from South Asia and Java. Independence saw mass emigration: around 350,000 Surinamese live in the Netherlands. Of those left, over 85% live near the coast, the rest in scattered rainforest communities. Indigenous Amerindians only number a few thousand. *Bosnegers* – descended from runaway African slaves – fought the military government in the late 1980s. Under civilian rule, each group has had a political party representing its interests.

THE ECONOMY

Alumina and gold are the key exports. Rice and bananas are main cash crops. Oil production and tourism are growing. Excessive bureaucracy.

INSIGHT: *In a 1667 Anglo-Dutch deal, Holland gained Suriname but lost New Amsterdam (now New York)*

ATLANTIC OCEAN
56°
54°
58°
6°
4°
2°
Nieuw Nickerie
PARAMARIBO
Nieuw Amsterdam
Kwakoegron
Brokopondo
Courantyne
Maroni
W.J. van Blommesteinmeer
FRENCH GUIANA
GUYANA
Guiana Highlands
BRAZIL
1000m/3281ft
500m/1640ft
200m/656ft
Sea Level
0 200 km
0 200 miles

FACTFILE

OFFICIAL NAME: Republic of Suriname
DATE OF FORMATION: 1975
CAPITAL: Paramaribo
POPULATION: 500,000
TOTAL AREA: 63,039 sq. miles (163,270 sq. km)
DENSITY: 8 people per sq. mile
LANGUAGES: Sranan (Creole), Dutch*, Hindi, Javanese, Sarnami, Saramaccan, Chinese, Carib
RELIGIONS: Christian 48%, Hindu 27%, Muslim 20%, traditional beliefs 5%
ETHNIC MIX: E Indian 27%, Creole 18%, Black 15%, Javanese 15%, mixed race 13%, other 12%
GOVERNMENT: Mixed presidential–parliamentary system
CURRENCY: Surinamese dollar = 100 cents

Swaziland

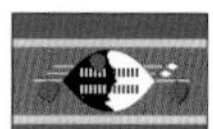

The tiny southern African kingdom of Swaziland is crippled with HIV/AIDS and economically dependent on South Africa. Vocal demands for multiparty democracy have been ignored.

GEOGRAPHY

Mainly high plateaus and mountains. Rolling grasslands and low scrub plains to the east. Pine forests on western border.

CLIMATE

Temperatures rise and rainfall declines as the land descends eastward, from high to low grassy *veld*.

PEOPLE & SOCIETY

One of Africa's most conservative states, though there is pressure from urban-based modernizers. Political system promotes Swazi tradition and is dominated by powerful monarchy. Women face discrimination. Swaziland has the world's highest prevalence of HIV/AIDS: chastity is urged to combat its spread.

INSIGHT: *Polygamy is practiced in Swaziland – when King Sobhuza died in 1982, he left 100 widows*

THE ECONOMY

Sugarcane is the main cash crop. Wood pulp and soft drink concentrates are also exported. Loss of workforce to HIV/AIDS, and high cost of health care.

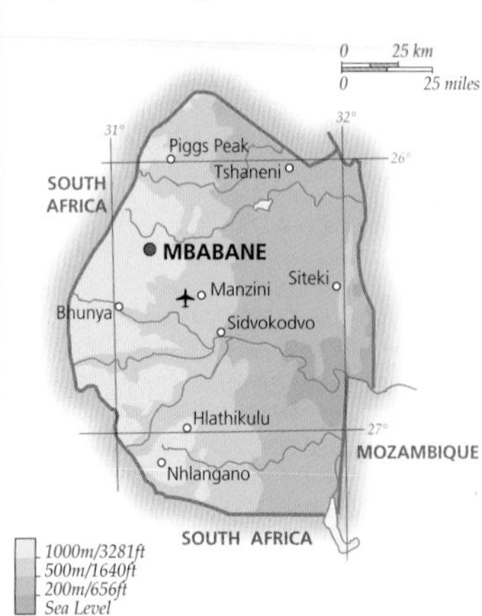
0 25 km
0 25 miles
31°
32°
26°
27°
Piggs Peak
Tshaneni
SOUTH AFRICA
MBABANE
Manzini
Siteki
Bhunya
Sidvokodvo
Hlathikulu
MOZAMBIQUE
Nhlangano
SOUTH AFRICA
1000m/3281ft
500m/1640ft
200m/656ft
Sea Level

FACTFILE

OFFICIAL NAME: Kingdom of Swaziland
DATE OF FORMATION: 1968
CAPITAL: Mbabane
POPULATION: 1.2 million
TOTAL AREA: 6704 sq. miles (17,363 sq. km)
DENSITY: 181 people per sq. mile
LANGUAGES: English*, siSwati*, isiZulu, Xitsonga
RELIGIONS: Traditional beliefs 40%, other 30%, Roman Catholic 20%, Muslim 10%
ETHNIC MIX: Swazi 97%, other 3%
GOVERNMENT: Monarchy
CURRENCY: Lilangeni = 100 cents

Sweden

The largest Scandinavian country by both population and area, Sweden has one of the world's most extensive welfare systems and is among the leading proponents of equal rights for women.

GEOGRAPHY

Heavily forested, with many lakes. Northern plateau extends beyond the Arctic Circle. Southern lowlands are widely cultivated.

CLIMATE

Southern coasts warmed by Gulf Stream. Northern areas have more extreme continental climate.

PEOPLE & SOCIETY

The nuclear family forms the basis of society, but the marriage rate is one of the lowest in the world, and cohabitation is now common. The model welfare system is paid for by a high tax burden. Women are well represented at all levels. A minority of 30,000 Sámi lives in the far north. Most industries and the bulk of population are based in and around the southern cities. An EU member since 1995, Sweden has voted not to join the euro.

THE ECONOMY

Companies of global importance, including Volvo, Saab, SFK, Ericsson. Highly developed infrastructure. Up-to-date technology. Skilled workforce.

INSIGHT: *Sweden has maintained a position of armed neutrality since 1815*

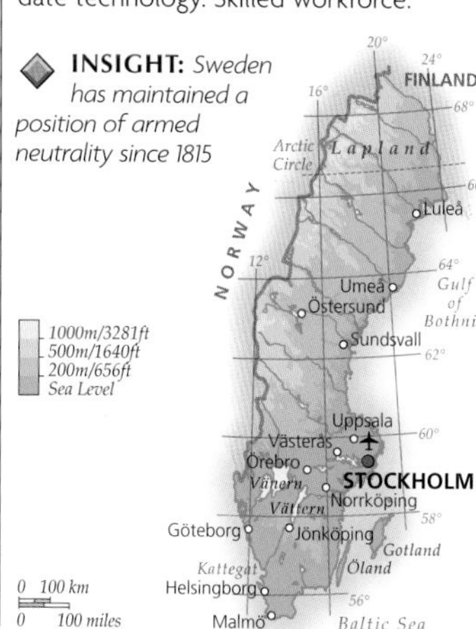
20°
24°
16°
FINLAND
68°
Arctic Circle
Lapland
66°
NORWAY
Luleå
12°
64°
Gulf of Bothnia
Umeå
Östersund
1000m/3281ft
500m/1640ft
200m/656ft
Sea Level
Sundsvall
62°
Uppsala
60°
Västerås
Örebro
STOCKHOLM
Vänern
Norrköping
Vättern
58°
Göteborg
Jönköping
Gotland
Kattegat
Öland
0 100 km
Helsingborg
56°
0 100 miles
Malmö
Baltic Sea

FACTFILE

OFFICIAL NAME: Kingdom of Sweden
DATE OF FORMATION: 1523
CAPITAL: Stockholm
POPULATION: 9.6 million
TOTAL AREA: 173,731 sq. miles (449,964 sq. km)
DENSITY: 60 people per sq. mile
LANGUAGES: Swedish*, Finnish, Sámi
RELIGIONS: Evangelical Lutheran 75%, other 13%, other Protestant 5%, Muslim 5%, Roman Catholic 2%
ETHNIC MIX: Swedish 86%, foreign-born or first-generation immigrant 12%, Finnish and Sámi 2%
GOVERNMENT: Parliamentary system
CURRENCY: Swedish krona = 100 öre

Switzerland

One of the world's most prosperous countries, Switzerland sits at the center of Europe. It has retained its neutral status through every major European conflict since 1815.

GEOGRAPHY

Mostly mountainous, with river valleys. The Alps cover 60% of its area; the Jura in the west cover 10%. Lowlands lie along the east–west axis.

CLIMATE

Most rain falls in the warm summer months. Winters are snowy, but milder and foggy away from the mountains. Avalanches are a problem.

PEOPLE & SOCIETY

Switzerland is composed of distinct German-Swiss, French-Swiss, and Italian-Swiss linguistic groups. In the east, a 60,000-strong minority speaks Romansch. The country is divided into 26 autonomous cantons (states), each with control over health care, education, housing, and taxation. Public referenda are widely used to decide policy. Society is conservative; marriage is common but divorce is above the EU average rate.

THE ECONOMY

Diversified economy relies on services – the banking sector manages over a quarter of the world's offshore private wealth – and specialized industries (engineering, watches, etc).

INSIGHT: *Famed for its neutrality, Switzerland only joined the UN in 2002, and remains outside the EU*

GERMANY
Schaffhausen
Rhine
Lake Constance
Basel
Winterthur
Sankt Gallen
FRANCE
Jura
Zürich
AUSTRIA
Biel
Neuchâtel
Luzern
LIECHTENSTEIN
Lac de Neuchâtel
BERN
Chur
Rhine
Interlaken
Davos
Alps
Lausanne
Lake Geneva
Montreux
Rhône
Brig
Locarno
Sion
Genève
ITALY
FRANCE
Lake Maggiore
Lugano
ITALY
47°
46°
6°
8°
10°

0 50 km
0 50 miles
3000m/9843ft
2000m/6562ft
1000m/3281ft
500m/1640ft
200m/656ft

FACTFILE

OFFICIAL NAME: Swiss Confederation
DATE OF FORMATION: 1291
CAPITAL: Bern
POPULATION: 8.1 million
TOTAL AREA: 15,942 sq. miles (41,290 sq. km)
DENSITY: 528 people per sq. mile
LANGUAGES: German*, Swiss-German, French*, Italian*, Romansch*
RELIGIONS: Roman Catholic 42%, Protestant 35%, other and nonreligious 19%, Muslim 4%
ETHNIC MIX: German 64%, French 20%, other 9%, Italian 6%, Romansch 1%
GOVERNMENT: Parliamentary system
CURRENCY: Swiss franc = 100 rappen/centimes

Syria

Stretching from the eastern Mediterranean to the Tigris River, Syria's borders are regarded as an artificial creation of French colonial rule by many Syrians. Civil war erupted in 2011.

GEOGRAPHY

A short stretch of coastal plain is backed by a low range of hills. The Euphrates River cuts through a vast interior desert plateau.

CLIMATE

Mediterranean coastal climate. Inland areas are arid. In winter, snow is common on the mountains.

PEOPLE & SOCIETY

Towns tend to lie within 60 miles (100 km) of the coast. Most Syrians are Sunni Muslim, but the Shi'a Alawis control politics. The authoritarian Assad regime, in power since 1970, fiercely repressed pro-democracy "Arab Spring" protests in 2011, and brutal conflict soon broke out. 200,000 have been killed and ten million are displaced, including many Palestinians and Iraqis formerly sheltering in Syrian refugee camps. Islamic State (IS) jihadists control the Euphrates valley.

THE ECONOMY

Conflict has destroyed economy. Oil fields held by rebels, production down. Sanctions limit exports. Lack of food, medicines. Infrastructure bombed.

INSIGHT: *Syria is an ancient land; there are at least 3500 as yet unexcavated archaeological sites*

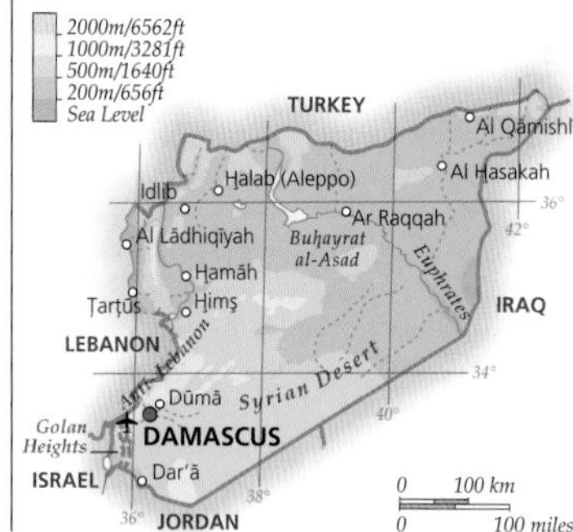
2000m/6562ft
1000m/3281ft
500m/1640ft
200m/656ft
Sea Level
TURKEY
Al Qāmishlī
Al Ḩasakah
Idlib
Ḩalab (Aleppo)
Ar Raqqah
Al Lādhiqīyah
Buḩayrat al-Asad
Euphrates
Ḩamāh
Ţarţūs
Ḩimş
IRAQ
LEBANON
Anti-Lebanon
Syrian Desert
Dūmā
Golan Heights
DAMASCUS
ISRAEL
Dar'ā
JORDAN
36°
34°
42°
40°
38°
0 100 km
0 100 miles

FACTFILE

OFFICIAL NAME: Syrian Arab Republic

DATE OF FORMATION: 1941

CAPITAL: Damascus

POPULATION: 21.9 million

TOTAL AREA: 71,498 sq. miles (184,180 sq. km)

DENSITY: 308 people per sq. mile

LANGUAGES: Arabic*, French, Kurdish, Armenian, Circassian, Assyrian, Aramaic

RELIGIONS: Sunni Muslim 74%, Alawi (Shi'a sect) 12%, Christian 10%, Druze 3%, other 1%

ETHNIC MIX: Arab 90%, Kurdish 9%, Armenian, Turkmen, and Circassian 1%

GOVERNMENT: Presidential system

CURRENCY: Syrian pound = 100 piastres

Taiwan

The republic of Taiwan (formerly Formosa) is on an island 80 miles (130 km) off the southeast coast of mainland China, which still considers it to be a renegade province.

GEOGRAPHY

Mountain region covers two-thirds of the island. Highly fertile lowlands and coastal plains.

CLIMATE

Tropical monsoon. Hot and humid. Typhoons July–September. Snow falls in mountains in winter.

PEOPLE & SOCIETY

Most Taiwanese are Han Chinese, descendants of the 1644 migration of the Ming dynasty from the mainland. The modern republic was created in 1949, when the nationalist Kuomintang was expelled from the mainland following Communist victory in the civil war. 100,000 emigrés established themselves as a ruling class. Initial resentment has subsided as a new Taiwan-born generation has taken over the reins of power. The aboriginal minority suffers discrimination.

THE ECONOMY

Successful economy of small, adaptable companies. High-tech goods: TVs, computers, and semiconductors. Rising trade, investment with China.

INSIGHT: *Taiwan lost its seat at the UN to Beijing in 1971: both claim to represent "China"*

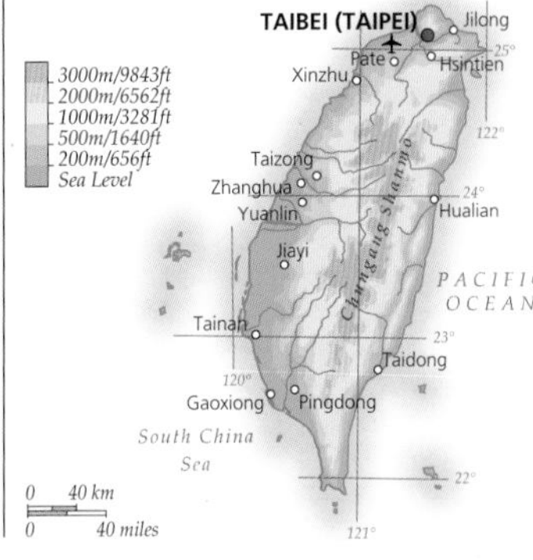
TAIBEI (TAIPEI)
Jilong
Pate
Hsintien
Xinzhu
3000m/9843ft
2000m/6562ft
1000m/3281ft
500m/1640ft
200m/656ft
Sea Level
Taizong
Zhanghua
Yuanlin
Hualian
Jiayi
Chungang Shanmo
PACIFIC OCEAN
Tainan
Taidong
Gaoxiong
Pingdong
South China Sea
0 40 km
0 40 miles
25°
122°
24°
23°
120°
22°
121°

FACTFILE

OFFICIAL NAME: Republic of China (ROC)
DATE OF FORMATION: 1949
CAPITAL: Taibei (Taipei)
POPULATION: 23.3 million
TOTAL AREA: 13,892 sq. miles (35,980 sq. km)
DENSITY: 1871 people per sq. mile
LANGUAGES: Amoy Chinese, Mandarin Chinese*, Hakka Chinese
RELIGIONS: Buddhist, Confucianist, and Taoist 93%, Christian 5%, other 2%
ETHNIC MIX: Han Chinese (pre-20th-century migration) 84%, Han Chinese (20th-century migration) 14%, Aboriginal 2%
GOVERNMENT: Presidential system
CURRENCY: Taiwan dollar = 100 cents

Tajikistan

Tajikistan lies landlocked on the western slopes of the Pamirs in central Asia. Soon after the breakup of the USSR in 1991, civil war erupted between ruling communists and Islamists.

GEOGRAPHY

Mainly mountainous: bare slopes of the Pamir ranges, with fast-flowing rivers, cover most of the country. Small but fertile Fergana Valley in northwest.

CLIMATE

Continental extremes in the valleys. Bitterly cold winters in the mountains. Rainfall is low.

PEOPLE & SOCIETY

Unlike the other former Soviet republics of central Asia, Tajikistan is dominated by a people of Persian (Iranian) rather than Turkic origin. The main ethnic conflict is with the Turkic Uzbek minority. Russians are discriminated against; most fled in the 1992–1997 civil war, and standards of living fell dramatically. Islamist militants are active. Two million people work abroad, primarily in Russia.

THE ECONOMY

Mass poverty. Declining cotton revenue. Also exports aluminum. Uranium deposits. Transit route for illicit Afghan opium. Corruption. Needs reforms to attract foreign investment.

INSIGHT: *Carpet-making, an ancient tradition learned from Persia, is still a major source of revenue*

0 100 km
0 100 miles
4000m/13124ft
3000m/9843ft
2000m/6562ft
1000m/3281ft
500m/1640ft
200m/656ft
70°
72°
74°
68°
40°
38°
UZBEKISTAN
Fergana Valley
Khujand
Isfara
Ŭroteppa
KYRGYZSTAN
CHINA
Panjakent
DUSHANBE
Norak
Pamirs
Qŭrghonteppa
Kŭlob
Khorugh
Farkhor
Amu Darya
AFGHANISTAN
PAKISTAN

FACTFILE

OFFICIAL NAME: Republic of Tajikistan
DATE OF FORMATION: 1991
CAPITAL: Dushanbe
POPULATION: 8.2 million
TOTAL AREA: 55,251 sq. miles (143,100 sq. km)
DENSITY: 148 people per sq. mile
LANGUAGES: Tajik*, Uzbek, Russian
RELIGIONS: Sunni Muslim 95%, Shi'a Muslim 3%, other 2%
ETHNIC MIX: Tajik 80%, Uzbek 15%, other 3%, Kyrgyz 1%, Russian 1%
GOVERNMENT: Presidential system
CURRENCY: Somoni = 100 diram

Tanzania

The east African state of Tanzania was formed in 1964 by the union of Tanganyika and the Zanzibar islands. A third of its area is game reserve or national park.

GEOGRAPHY

The mainland is mostly a high plateau lying to the east of the Great Rift Valley. Forested coastal plain. Highlands in the north and south.

CLIMATE

Tropical on the coast and Zanzibar. Semiarid on central plateau, semitemperate in the highlands. March–May rains.

PEOPLE & SOCIETY

99% of people belong to one of 120 small ethnic Bantu groups. Arabs, Asians, and Europeans make up the remaining population. Use of Kiswahili as the lingua franca has eliminated ethnic rivalries. The majority of Tanzanians are subsistence famers.

INSIGHT: *At 19,340 ft (5895 m), Kilimanjaro in northeast Tanzania is Africa's highest mountain*

THE ECONOMY

Reliant on agriculture, including forestry and cattle. Coffee, cotton, tea, cashew nuts, sisal, and cloves are cash crops. Gold, diamonds, and gems mined. Safari and beach tourism. Debt relief.

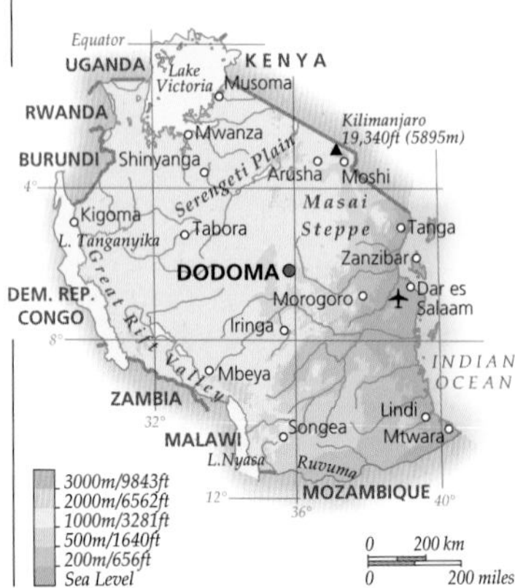
Equator
UGANDA
Lake Victoria
KENYA
Musoma
RWANDA
Mwanza
Kilimanjaro 19,340ft (5895m)
BURUNDI
Shinyanga
Serengeti Plain
Arusha
Moshi
4°
Masai Steppe
Kigoma
L. Tanganyika
Tabora
Tanga
Zanzibar
DODOMA
Great Rift Valley
DEM. REP. CONGO
Morogoro
Dar es Salaam
Iringa
8°
INDIAN OCEAN
Mbeya
ZAMBIA
32°
Lindi
Mtwara
Songea
MALAWI
L.Nyasa
Ruvuma
MOZAMBIQUE
12°
36°
40°
3000m/9843ft
2000m/6562ft
1000m/3281ft
500m/1640ft
200m/656ft
Sea Level
0 200 km
0 200 miles

FACTFILE

OFFICIAL NAME: United Republic of Tanzania
DATE OF FORMATION: 1964
CAPITAL: Dodoma
POPULATION: 49.3 million
TOTAL AREA: 364,898 sq. miles (945,087 sq. km)
DENSITY: 144 people per sq. mile
LANGUAGES: Kiswahili*, Sukuma, Chagga, Nyamwezi, Hehe, Makonde, Yao, English*
RELIGIONS: Christian 63%, Muslim 35%, other 2%
ETHNIC MIX: Native African (over 120 tribes) 99%, European, Asian, and Arab 1%
GOVERNMENT: Presidential system
CURRENCY: Tanzanian shilling = 100 cents

Thailand

Thailand lies at the heart of mainland southeast Asia. Continuing rapid industrialization has resulted in massive congestion in the capital and a serious depletion of natural resources.

GEOGRAPHY

One-third is low plateau, drained by tributaries of the Mekong River. Central plain is the most fertile area.

CLIMATE

Tropical. Hot, humid March–May; monsoon rains May–October; cooler season November–March.

PEOPLE & SOCIETY

Buddhism is a national binding force. 600,000 hill tribes-people live in the north and northeast. The Chinese minority is the most assimilated in the region. In the undeveloped far south, Malay Islamists are fighting for secession. Politics has been unstable since the 2006 fall of populist Prime Minister Thaksin; the military intervened again in 2014.

INSIGHT: *Thailand, meaning "land of the free," is the only SE Asian nation never to have been colonized*

THE ECONOMY

Successful manufacturing. Natural gas reserves. Leading exporter of rice, rubber. Political turmoil. Tourism, though sex industry harms image. Damage from natural disasters.

0 200 km
0 200 miles
MYANMAR (BURMA)
LAOS
Mekong
Chiang Mai
Udon Thani
Salween
Khon Kaen
Phitsanulok
Nakhon Sawan
Ubon Ratchathani
Nakhon Ratchasima
BANGKOK
CAMBODIA
Ratchaburi
Pattaya
Gulf of Thailand
Chumphon
Isthmus of Kra
Nakhon Si Thammarat
Phuket
Songkhla
Hat Yai
Malay Peninsula
Andaman Sea
MALAYSIA
20°
16°
12°
8°
104°
100°
2000m/6562ft
1000m/3281ft
500m/1640ft
200m/656ft
Sea Level

FACTFILE

OFFICIAL NAME: Kingdom of Thailand
DATE OF FORMATION: 1238
CAPITAL: Bangkok
POPULATION: 67 million
TOTAL AREA: 198,455 sq. miles (514,000 sq. km)
DENSITY: 340 people per sq. mile
LANGUAGES: Thai*, Chinese, Malay, Khmer, Mon, Karen, Miao
RELIGIONS: Buddhist 95%, Muslim 4%, other (including Christian) 1%
ETHNIC MIX: Thai 83%, Chinese 12%, Malay 3%, Khmer and other 2%
GOVERNMENT: Transitional regime
CURRENCY: Baht = 100 satang

Togo

Togo lies sandwiched between Ghana and Benin in west Africa. General Eyadema ruled from 1967–2005; his son succeeded him. Lomé port is an important entrepôt for regional trade.

GEOGRAPHY

Central forested region bounded by savanna lands to the north and south. Mountain range stretches southwest to northeast.

CLIMATE

Coast hot and humid; drier inland. Rainy season March–July, with heaviest falls in the west.

PEOPLE & SOCIETY

Harsh resentment between Ewe in the south and Kabye in the north. Kabye control the military, but the north is less developed than the south. Extended family is important. Tribalism and nepotism are key factors in everyday life. Some ethnic groups, such as the Mina, have matriarchal societies.

INSIGHT: *The "Nana Benz," the entrepreneurial market-women of Lomé, control Togo's retail trade*

THE ECONOMY

Most people are farmers. Self-sufficient in staple foods. Togo's main cash crops are coffee and cocoa: cotton has declined. Its phosphate deposits are the most mineral-rich in the world, but easily extractable reserves are depleted and the sector needs investment.

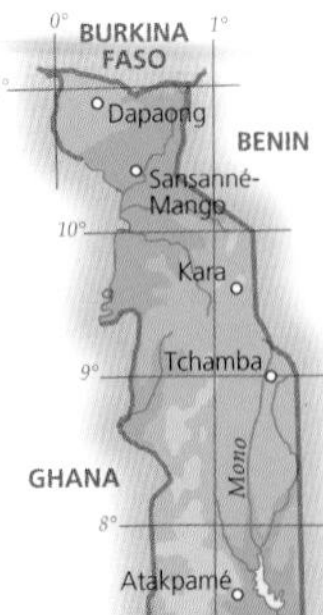
BURKINA FASO
0°
1°
11°
Dapaong
BENIN
Sansanné-Mango
10°
Kara
9°
Tchamba
Mono
GHANA
8°
Atakpamé
Mono
7°
Kpalimé
Tsévié
Aného
LOMÉ
6°
ATLANTIC OCEAN
500m/1640ft
200m/656ft
Sea Level
0 50 km
0 50 miles

FACTFILE

OFFICIAL NAME: Togolese Republic
DATE OF FORMATION: 1960
CAPITAL: Lomé
POPULATION: 6.8 million
TOTAL AREA: 21,924 sq. miles (56,785 sq. km)
DENSITY: 324 people per sq. mile
LANGUAGES: Ewe, Kabye, Gurma, French*
RELIGIONS: Christian 47%, traditional beliefs 33%, Muslim 14%, other 6%
ETHNIC MIX: Ewe 46%, other African 41%, Kabye 12%, European 1%
GOVERNMENT: Presidential system
CURRENCY: CFA franc = 100 centimes

Tonga

Tonga is a South Pacific archipelago of 170 islands; only 45 of these islands are inhabited. The king retains significant powers though some democratic reforms were introduced in 2011.

GEOGRAPHY

Easterly islands are generally low and fertile. Those in the west are higher and volcanic in origin.

CLIMATE

Tropical oceanic. Temperatures range between 68°F (20°C) and 86°F (30°C) all year round. Heavy rainfall, especially February–March.

PEOPLE & SOCIETY

Tonga is the last remaining Polynesian monarchy. All land belongs to the crown, but is administered by nobles who allot it to the common people. Respect for traditional values is high, though younger, Westernized Tongans are starting to question some attitudes. The first elected commoner became prime minister in 2006.

INSIGHT: *Unique in the Pacific, Tonga was never brought under foreign rule*

THE ECONOMY

Squashes and vanilla exported. Remittances. Potential for tourism and fisheries. Large debt owed to China for rebuilding of capital's business district, destroyed in 2006 prodemocracy riots.

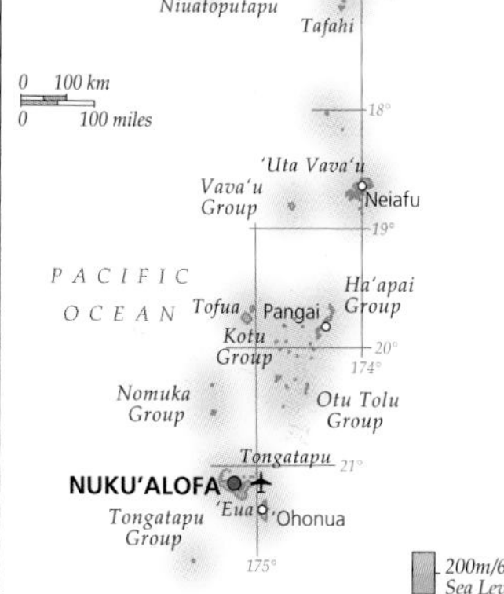
17°
Niuatoputapu
Tafahi
0 100 km
0 100 miles
18°
'Uta Vava'u
Vava'u Group
Neiafu
19°
PACIFIC OCEAN
Ha'apai Group
Tofua
Pangai
Kotu Group
20°
174°
Nomuka Group
Otu Tolu Group
Tongatapu
21°
NUKU'ALOFA
'Eua
'Ohonua
Tongatapu Group
175°
200m/656ft
Sea Level

FACTFILE

OFFICIAL NAME: Kingdom of Tonga
DATE OF FORMATION: 1970
CAPITAL: Nuku'alofa
POPULATION: 106,322
TOTAL AREA: 289 sq. miles (748 sq. km)
DENSITY: 382 people per sq. mile
LANGUAGES: English*, Tongan*
RELIGIONS: Free Wesleyan 41%, other 17%, Roman Catholic 16%, Church of Jesus Christ of Latter-Day Saints 14%, Free Church of Tonga 12%
ETHNIC MIX: Tongan 98%, other 2%
GOVERNMENT: Monarchy
CURRENCY: Pa'anga (Tongan dollar) = 100 seniti

Trinidad & Tobago

The two islands of the former UK colony of Trinidad and Tobago are the most southerly of the Caribbean Windward Islands, lying just 9 miles (15 km) off the coast of Venezuela.

GEOGRAPHY

Both islands are hilly and wooded. Trinidad has a rugged mountain range in the north, and swamps on its east and west coasts.

CLIMATE

Tropical, with July–December wet season. Escapes the region's hurricanes, which pass to the north.

PEOPLE & SOCIETY

Trinidad's East Indian community is the Caribbean's largest and holds onto its Muslim and Hindu heritage. There are tensions with the mainly Christian blacks; political parties are divided along race lines. Blacks form the majority on Tobago. High rates of kidnapping and murder are an issue.

INSIGHT: *Trinidad and Tobago is the birthplace of steel bands and Calypso music*

THE ECONOMY

Oil and natural gas: major provider of liquefied natural gas to US, but reserves are declining fast. Associated industries: second-largest producer of methanol. Tourism on wildlife-rich Tobago.

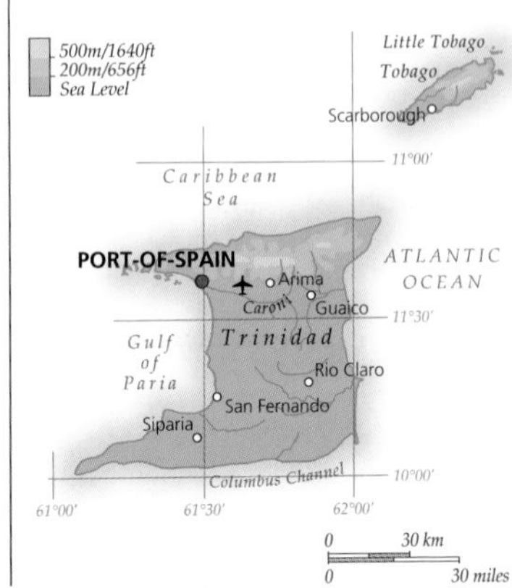
500m/1640ft
200m/656ft
Sea Level
Little Tobago
Tobago
Scarborough
11°00'
Caribbean Sea
ATLANTIC OCEAN
PORT-OF-SPAIN
Arima
Caroni
Guaico
11°30'
Gulf of Paria
Trinidad
Rio Claro
San Fernando
Siparia
Columbus Channel
10°00'
61°00'
61°30'
62°00'
0
30 km
0
30 miles

FACTFILE

OFFICIAL NAME: Republic of Trinidad and Tobago
DATE OF FORMATION: 1962
CAPITAL: Port-of-Spain
POPULATION: 1.3 million
TOTAL AREA: 1980 sq. miles (5128 sq. km)
DENSITY: 656 people per sq. mile
LANGUAGES: English Creole, English*, Hindi, French, Spanish
RELIGIONS: Roman Catholic 26%, Hindu 23%, other 23%, Protestant 22%, Muslim 6%
ETHNIC MIX: East Indian 40%, Black 38%, mixed race 20%, White, Chinese, other 2%
GOVERNMENT: Parliamentary system
CURRENCY: Trin. & Tob. dollar = 100 cents

Tunisia

A French north African colony until 1956, Tunisia was relatively liberal in social terms, but in 2011 protesters ousted the dictatorial president, triggering the "Arab Spring" across the region.

GEOGRAPHY

Mountains in the north are surrounded by plains. Vast, low-lying salt pans in the center. To the south lies the Sahara Desert.

CLIMATE

Summer temperatures are high. The north is often wet and windy in winter. Far south is arid.

PEOPLE & SOCIETY

The population is almost entirely of Arab-Berber descent, with Jewish and Christian minorities. Many still live in extended family groups of three or four generations. Women have better rights than in most other Arab countries and make up a quarter of the workforce. The low birth rate is a result of a long-standing family planning policy. The Islamist-led transitional government elected in 2011 was replaced by a consensus government in 2014.

THE ECONOMY

Competitive and diversified. Expanding manufacturing. Exports olives, dates, citrus fruit, phosphates. Instability, affecting tourism. Free trade with EU.

INSIGHT: *Tunisia was the center of trading empires from the 9th century BCE*

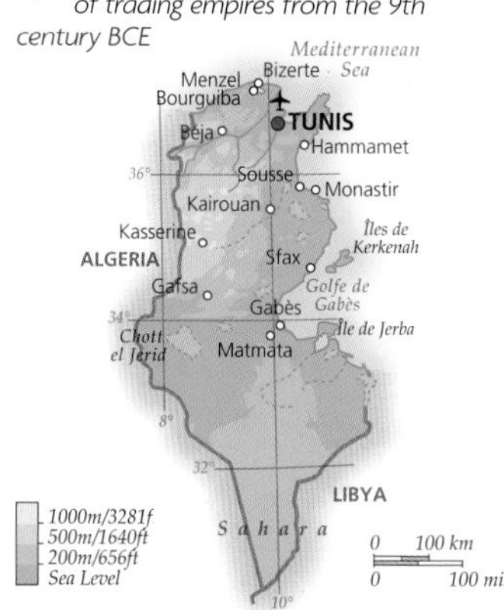
Mediterranean Sea
Bizerte
Menzel Bourguiba
TUNIS
Hammamet
Béja
Sousse
Monastir
Kairouan
Kasserine
Îles de Kerkenah
ALGERIA
Sfax
Gafsa
Golfe de Gabès
Gabès
Île de Jerba
Chott el Jerid
Matmata
LIBYA
Sahara
36°
34°
32°
8°
10°
1000m/3281ft
500m/1640ft
200m/656ft
Sea Level
0 100 km
0 100 miles

FACTFILE

OFFICIAL NAME: Tunisian Republic
DATE OF FORMATION: 1956
CAPITAL: Tunis
POPULATION: 11 million
TOTAL AREA: 63,169 sq. miles (163,610 sq. km)
DENSITY: 183 people per sq. mile
LANGUAGES: Arabic*, French
RELIGIONS: Muslim (mainly Sunni) 98%, Christian 1%, Jewish 1%
ETHNIC MIX: Arab and Berber 98%, Jewish 1%, European 1%
GOVERNMENT: Transitional regime
CURRENCY: Tunisian dinar = 1000 millimes

Turkey

Lying partly in the region of eastern Thrace in Europe, but mostly in Asia, Turkey's position gives it significant influence in the Mediterranean, the Black Sea, and the Middle East.

GEOGRAPHY

Asian Turkey (Anatolia) is dominated by two mountain ranges, separated by a high, semidesert plateau. Coastal regions are fertile.

CLIMATE

Coast has a Mediterranean climate. Interior has cold, snowy winters and hot, dry summers.

PEOPLE & SOCIETY

Despite racial diversity, Turkey has a strong sense of national identity, and close links with other Turkic states. Kurds, the largest minority, based in the southeast, have waged a violent campaign for greater autonomy intermittently since 1984. The current political dominance of Islamists challenges Turkey's cherished identity as a secular state. It has applied to join the EU, but progress will be slow.

THE ECONOMY

Liberalized economy, boosted by self-sufficient agriculture, and textiles, tourism, and manufacturing sectors. Route of Asian oil pipelines to Europe.

INSIGHT: *Turkey had two of the seven wonders of the ancient world: the tomb of King Mausolus at Halicarnassus (now Bodrum), and the temple of Artemis at Ephesus*

FACTFILE

OFFICIAL NAME: Republic of Turkey
DATE OF FORMATION: 1923
CAPITAL: Ankara
POPULATION: 74.9 million
TOTAL AREA: 301,382 sq. miles (780,580 sq. km)
DENSITY: 252 people per sq. mile
LANGUAGES: Turkish*, Kurdish, Arabic, Circassian, Armenian, Greek, Georgian, Ladino
RELIGIONS: Muslim (mainly Sunni) 99%, other 1%
ETHNIC MIX: Turkish 70%, Kurdish 20%, other 8%, Arab 2%
GOVERNMENT: Parliamentary system
CURRENCY: Turkish lira = 100 kurus

Turkmenistan

Stretching from the Caspian Sea into the central Asian desert, Turkmenistan has had less upheaval than most ex-Soviet states, under President Niyazov's dictatorial rule (1991–2006).

GEOGRAPHY

Low Garagum Desert covers 80% of the country. Mountains on southern border with Iran. Fertile Amu Darya Valley in north.

CLIMATE

Arid desert climate with extreme summer heat, but sub-freezing winter temperatures.

PEOPLE & SOCIETY

The Turkmen were once largely nomadic, and the tribal unit remains strong, with population clustered around desert oases. "Turkmenization" of government, education, and religion has strained relations with Uzbek and Russian minorities. Political reform since Niyazov's sudden death in 2006 led to multiparty elections in 2013, though all seats were won by the former sole party and Niyazov's successor runs a similarly authoritarian regime.

THE ECONOMY

State-controlled, though there is some private investment. Natural gas and oil are main resources. Overintensive farming of cotton. Black market.

INSIGHT: *President Niyazov created an elaborate personality cult, styling himself as Turkmenbashi – "head" of all Turkmen*

0 200 km
0 200 miles
KAZAKHSTAN
Garabogaz Aylagy
Köneürgenç
Daşoguz
UZBEKISTAN
Türkmenbaşy
Turan Lowland
Balkanabat
Gumdag
Serdar
Amu Darya
40°
Caspian Sea
Garagum
Türkmenabat
AŞGABAT
IRAN
Tejen
Atamyrat
Mary
55°
Garagum Kanaly
65°
1000m/3281ft
500m/1640ft
200m/656ft
Sea Level
Below Sea Level
60°
Serhetabat
AFGHANISTAN

FACTFILE

OFFICIAL NAME: Turkmenistan
DATE OF FORMATION: 1991
CAPITAL: Asgabat
POPULATION: 5.2 million
TOTAL AREA: 188,455 sq. miles (488,100 sq. km)
DENSITY: 28 people per sq. mile
LANGUAGES: Turkmen*, Uzbek, Russian, Kazakh, Tatar
RELIGIONS: Sunni Muslim 89%, Orthodox Christian 9%, other 2%
ETHNIC MIX: Turkmen 85%, other 6%, Uzbek 5%, Russian 4%
GOVERNMENT: Presidential system
CURRENCY: New manat = 100 tenge

Tuvalu

One of the world's smallest, most isolated states, Tuvalu lies in the central Pacific. The nine islands were linked to the Gilbert Islands (Kiribati) as a UK colony until independence.

GEOGRAPHY

A series of coral atolls, none more than 15 ft (4.6 m) above sea level. Poor soils restrict vegetation to bush, coconut palms, and breadfruit trees.

CLIMATE

Hot all year round. Heavy annual rainfall. Hurricane season brings many violent storms.

PEOPLE & SOCIETY

People are mostly Polynesian. Around half the population lives on Funafuti, where government jobs are based. Life is communal and traditional. Most people live by subsistence farming, digging pits out of the coral to grow crops. Fresh water is precious, due to frequent droughts.

INSIGHT: *Low-lying Tuvalu, like the Maldives, is set to disappear with rising sea levels*

THE ECONOMY

World's smallest economy. Remittances from Tuvaluan seafarers. Sale of fishing licenses. Copra, stamps, and coins exported. Income from trust fund and the lease of .tv Internet suffix.

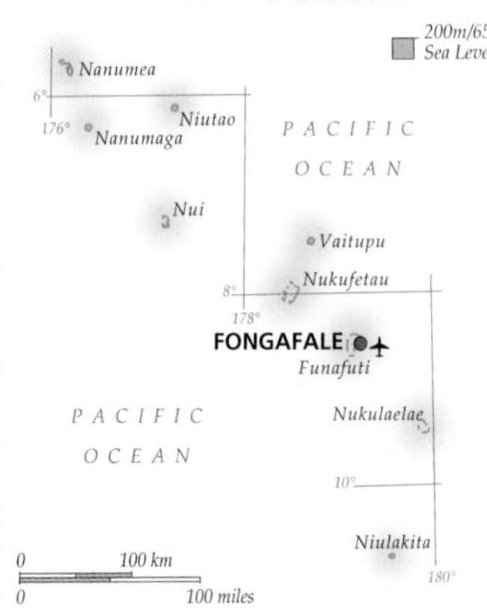
200m/656ft
Sea Level
Nanumea
6°
176°
Niutao
Nanumaga
PACIFIC
OCEAN
Nui
Vaitupu
Nukufetau
8°
178°
FONGAFALE
Funafuti
PACIFIC
OCEAN
Nukulaelae
10°
Niulakita
180°
0
100 km
0
100 miles

FACTFILE

OFFICIAL NAME: Tuvalu
DATE OF FORMATION: 1978
CAPITAL: Fongafale, on Funafuti Atoll
POPULATION: 10,698
TOTAL AREA: 10 sq. miles (26 sq. km)
DENSITY: 1070 people per sq. mile
LANGUAGES: Tuvaluan, Kiribati, English*
RELIGIONS: Church of Tuvalu 97%, Baha'i 1%, Seventh-day Adventist 1%, other 1%
ETHNIC MIX: Polynesian 96%, Micronesian 4%
GOVERNMENT: Nonparty system
CURRENCY: Australian dollar and Tuvaluan dollar = 100 cents each

Uganda

Landlocked in east Africa, Uganda has a history of ethnic strife. Under President Museveni, steps have been taken to restore peace and to rebuild the economy and democracy.

GEOGRAPHY

Predominantly a large plateau with the Ruwenzori mountain range and the Great Rift Valley in the west. Lake Victoria lies to the southeast. Vegetation is of savanna type.

CLIMATE

Altitude and the influence of the lakes modify the equatorial climate. Rain falls throughout the year; spring is the wettest period.

PEOPLE & SOCIETY

Mostly rural population comprising 13 main ethnic groups. President Museveni has worked hard to break down ethnic animosities, but a noticeable north–south divide persists, with most development in the south. After two decades of brutal clashes (1987–2008), the Ugandan army is still pursuing remnants of the Lord's Resistance Army across the DRC, South Sudan, and the CAR.

THE ECONOMY

Resource-rich, but undeveloped and poor. Exports coffee, fish, tea, and flowers. Oil exploration. Hydroelectric power is reducing oil imports. Great potential from mining. Debt relief.

INSIGHT: *Lake Victoria is the world's third-largest lake*

3000m/9843ft
2000m/6562ft
1000m/3281ft
500m/1640ft
SOUTH SUDAN
KENYA
DEM. REP. CONGO
RWANDA
TANZANIA
Arua
Gulu
Albert Nile
Lake Albert
Great Rift Valley
Lake Kyoga
Victoria Nile
Mbale
Tororo
Jinja
Kabarole
Kasese
Mubende
KAMPALA
Entebbe
Equator
Masaka
Sese Is.
Lake Edward
Mbarara
Lake Victoria
Kabale
4°
2°
32°
34°
0 100 km
0 100 miles

FACTFILE

OFFICIAL NAME: Republic of Uganda
DATE OF FORMATION: 1962
CAPITAL: Kampala
POPULATION: 37.6 million
TOTAL AREA: 91,135 sq. miles (236,040 sq. km)
DENSITY: 488 people per sq. mile
LANGUAGES: Luganda, Nkole, Chiga, Lango, Acholi, Teso, Lugbara, English*
RELIGIONS: Christian 85%, Muslim (mainly Sunni) 12%, other 3%
ETHNIC MIX: Other 50%, Baganda 17%, Banyakole 10%, Basoga 9%, Iteso 7%, Bakiga 7%
GOVERNMENT: Presidential system
CURRENCY: Uganda shilling = 100 cents

Ukraine

The former "breadbasket of the Soviet Union," Ukraine lies on the Black Sea. Divisions between pro-Russian sentiments and pro-European nationalism erupted into civil war in 2014.

GEOGRAPHY

Mainly fertile steppes and forests. Carpathian Mountains in west, Crimean chain in south. Pripet Marshes in northwest.

CLIMATE

Mainly continental climate, with distinct seasons. Southern Crimea has Mediterranean climate.

PEOPLE & SOCIETY

Over 90% of people in the west are Ukrainian, but in cities in the east and south, and in Crimea, Russians form a majority. Tatars returned to Crimea after the Soviet Union's collapse and comprise around 12% of the population there. Pro-Russian president Yanukovych's refusal to sign an EU deal provoked protests that ousted him from power in 2014. Russia responded by backing eastern rebels and annexing Crimea.

THE ECONOMY

Minerals: 5% of global reserves. Political instability, and conflict in the east. Slow reform of land laws, holding back agriculture. Oil/natural gas transit from Russia and the Caspian to Europe: natural gas price disputes with Russia.

INSIGHT: *Ukraine means "on the border," referring to its position on the edge of the old Russian Empire*

FACTFILE

OFFICIAL NAME: Ukraine
DATE OF FORMATION: 1991
CAPITAL: Kiev
POPULATION: 45.2 million
TOTAL AREA: 223,089 sq. miles (603,700 sq. km)
DENSITY: 194 people per sq. mile
LANGUAGES: Ukrainian*, Russian, Tatar
RELIGIONS: Christian (mainly Orthodox) 95%, other 5%
ETHNIC MIX: Ukrainian 78%, Russian 17%, other 5%
GOVERNMENT: Presidential system
CURRENCY: Hryvna = 100 kopiykas

United Arab Emirates

Bordering the Gulf on the northern coast of the Arabian Peninsula, the seven states of the UAE are Abu Dhabi, Dubai, Sharjah, Ajman, Umm al Qaywayn, Ras al Khaymah, and Fujayrah.

GEOGRAPHY

Mostly flat, semiarid desert with dunes, salt pans, and occasional oases. Cities are watered by extensive irrigation systems.

CLIMATE

Summers are humid, despite minimal rainfall. Sand-laden *shamal* winds blow in winter and spring.

PEOPLE & SOCIETY

Emirians, who make up just a quarter of the population, are mostly Sunni Muslims of Bedouin descent, and largely city dwellers. In theory, women enjoy equal rights with men. Poverty is rare and there is no income tax. The 1970s oil boom encouraged the immigration of workers, mostly from Asia. Western expatriates are permitted a virtually unrestricted lifestyle. Islamism, however, is a growing force among the young.

THE ECONOMY

Major oil and natural gas exporter; plentiful reserves. Dynamic Dubai: free trade zone, financial center (but 2008 global downturn caught overextended banks). Water is scarce. Imports most food. Some emirates are less developed.

INSIGHT: *Mina Jabal Ali, in Dubai, is the largest man-made port in the world*

500m/1640ft
200m/656ft
Sea Level
56°
OMAN
26°
Ras al Khaymah
Umm al Qaywayn
Ash Shāriqah (Sharjah)
Ajmān
Dubai
Fujayrah
52°
Persian Gulf
54°
QATAR
ABU DHABI
Al Maqta'
Ghuwayfāt
Tarif
Al 'Ayn
24°
Ḥabshān
OMAN
SAUDI ARABIA
0 50 km
0 50 miles

FACTFILE

OFFICIAL NAME: United Arab Emirates
DATE OF FORMATION: 1971
CAPITAL: Abu Dhabi
POPULATION: 9.3 million
TOTAL AREA: 32,000 sq. miles (82,880 sq. km)
DENSITY: 288 people per sq. mile
LANGUAGES: Arabic*, Farsi, Indian and Pakistani languages, English
RELIGIONS: Muslim (mainly Sunni) 96%, Christian, Hindu, and other 4%
ETHNIC MIX: Asian 60%, Emirian 25%, other Arab 12%, European 3%
GOVERNMENT: Monarchy
CURRENCY: UAE dirham = 100 fils

United Kingdom

Separated from continental Europe by the English Channel, the UK consists of Great Britain (England, Wales, and Scotland), several smaller islands, and Northern Ireland.

GEOGRAPHY

Rugged uplands dominate the landscape of Scotland, Wales, and northern England. All of the peaks in the United Kingdom over 4000 ft (1219 m) are in highland Scotland. The Pennine mountains, known as the "backbone of England," run the length of northern England. Lowland England rises into several ranges of rolling hills, and there is an interconnected system of rivers and canals. Over 600 islands, many uninhabited, lie west and north of the Scottish mainland.

CLIMATE

Generally mild, temperate, and highly changeable. Rain is fairly well distributed throughout the year. The west is generally wetter than the east, and the south warmer than the north. Winter snow is common in upland areas.

PEOPLE & SOCIETY

Scottish and Welsh people have a stronger sense of separate identity than the English; both Scotland and Wales have some self-government, as does Northern Ireland. In 2014 Scotland rejected independence in a referendum. Other ethnic minorities account for 5% of the population; more than half of them were born in the UK. Asian women in particular can be socially isolated. Asians and West Indians in most cities face deprivation and social stress, but white working-class youths were also evident when innercity rioting erupted in 2011. Income inequality is greater now than in 1884, when records began. In key areas such as policing, multiethnic recruitment has made little progress. Marriage is in decline. Over 40% of all births occur outside marriage, but most of them to cohabiting couples. Single-parent households account for just over a quarter of all families.

FACTFILE

OFFICIAL NAME: United Kingdom of Great Britain and Northern Ireland
DATE OF FORMATION: 1707
CAPITAL: London
POPULATION: 63.1 million
TOTAL AREA: 94,525 sq. miles (244,820 sq. km)
DENSITY: 676 people per sq. mile
LANGUAGES: English*, Welsh, Scottish Gaelic
RELIGIONS: Anglican 45%, other and nonreligious 37%, Roman Catholic 9%, Presbyterian 4%, Muslim 3%, Methodist 2%
ETHNIC MIX: English 80%, Scottish 9%, other 5%, Welsh 3%, Northern Irish 3%
GOVERNMENT: Parliamentary system
CURRENCY: Pound sterling = 100 pence

THE ECONOMY

World leader in financial services, pharmaceuticals, and defense industries. Strong multinationals. Precision engineering and high-tech industries, including biotechnology and telecommunications. Energy sector based on declining North Sea oil and natural gas reserves. Innovative in computer software development. Flexible working practices. Long-term decline of manufacturing sector, particularly heavy industries and car manufacture, partially offset by rise in financial and other services. Nonparticipant in euro. High levels of government, corporate, and consumer debt: banks made major losses in 2007–2009 global downturn. Bailouts and stimulus packages pushed the government's finances further into the red. Tackling the deficit by cuts in spending puts pressure on growth strategy and social programs, with rising unemployment.

INSIGHT: *The UK has no formal written constitution, but a stable government system based on Parliament, which originated as a check on royal power in the 13th century*

Orkney Is.
Shetlands Is.
Lerwick
Outer Hebrides
Stornoway
Inverness
Aberdeen
Scotland
Inner Hebrides
Oban
Dundee
Glasgow
Edinburgh
Londonderry
Northern Ireland
Belfast
Newcastle upon Tyne
Carlisle
Isle of Man
North Sea
Blackpool
Leeds
Liverpool
Blackburn
Sheffield
Manchester
IRELAND
England
Derby
Norwich
Birmingham
Leicester
Cambridge
Wales
Swansea
Oxford
Thames
LONDON
Cardiff
Bristol
Reading
Celtic Sea
Southampton
Dover
Exeter
ATLANTIC OCEAN
Plymouth
English Channel
1000m/3281ft
500m/1640ft
200m/656ft
Sea Level
100 km
100 miles

United States of America

Stretching across the most temperate part of North America, and with many natural resources, the US is the world's leading economic power and third-largest country.

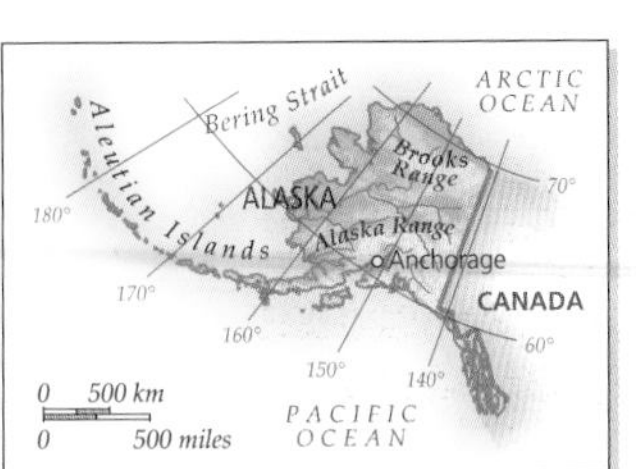
ARCTIC OCEAN
Bering Strait
Aleutian Islands
Brooks Range
ALASKA
Alaska Range
Anchorage
CANADA
PACIFIC OCEAN
180°
170°
160°
150°
140°
70°
60°
0 500 km
0 500 miles

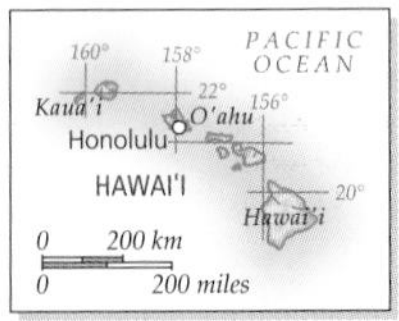
PACIFIC OCEAN
160°
158°
156°
22°
20°
Kaua'i
O'ahu
Honolulu
HAWAI'I
Hawai'i

0 200 km
0 200 miles

CANADA
PACIFIC OCEAN
Seattle
WASHINGTON
Spokane
Portland
MONTANA
Helena
OREGON
IDAHO
Boise
Coast Ranges
Rocky Mountains
Great Salt Lake
WYOMING
Great Basin
Reno
Sacramento
Oakland
San Francisco
Salt Lake City
NEVADA
UTAH
Sierra Nevada
Fresno
CALIFORNIA
Death Valley
Bakersfield
Las Vegas
Grand Canyon
Colorado
Los Angeles
ARIZONA
Albuquerque
120°
San Diego
Phoenix
NEW MEXICO
Tucson
El Paso
MEXICO
110°

GEOGRAPHY

The US has a varied topography. Forested mountains stretch from New England in the far northeast, giving way to lowlands and swamps in the extreme south. The central plains are dominated by the Mississippi–Missouri River system and the Great Lakes on the Canadian border. The Rocky Mountains in the west contain active volcanoes and drop to the coast across the earthquake-prone San Andreas Fault. The southwest is arid desert. Mountainous Alaska is mostly Arctic tundra.

CLIMATE

There are four main climatic zones. The north and east are continental and temperate, with heavy rainfall, warm summers, and cold winters. Florida and the Deep South are tropical and prone to hurricanes. The southwest is arid desert, with searing summer heat and low rainfall. Southern California is Mediterranean, with hot summers and mild winters.

◆ **INSIGHT:** *The United States of America has the world's oldest constitution. Drafted in 1787, it has operated continuously ever since, albeit with numerous amendments*

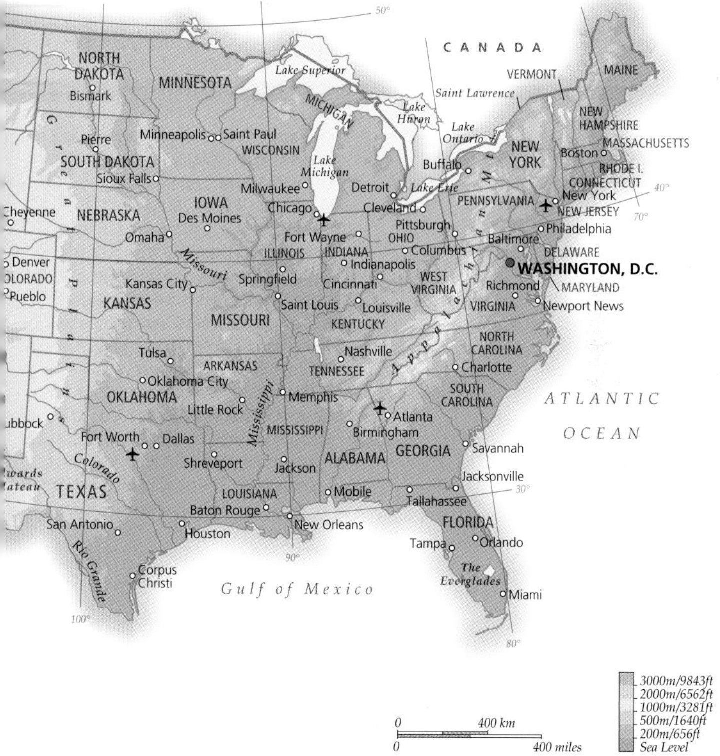

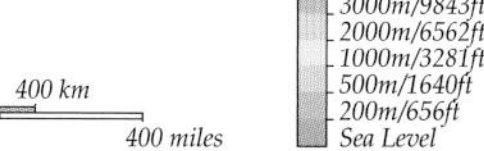
0
400 km
0
400 miles
3000m/9843ft
2000m/6562ft
1000m/3281ft
500m/1640ft
200m/656ft
Sea Level

United States of America

INSIGHT: *By law, the actual records collected in a United States census must remain confidential for 72 years*

PEOPLE & SOCIETY

Although the demographic, economic, and cultural dominance of White Americans is firmly entrenched after over 400 years of settlement, the ethnic balance of the country is shifting. Barack Obama, whose father was African, became the first non-White US president in 2009. The African-American community, originally uprooted by the slave trade, has a strong consciousness. Less well organized socially but more numerous, and faster-growing, the Hispanic community is predicted to number over 30% of the population by 2050. Native Americans, dispossessed in the 19th century, are now among the poorest people. Constitutionally, state and religion are clearly separated. Conservative Christianity, however, is increasingly dominant politically. Living standards are high, but bad diet and insufficient exercise have left over a third of Americans obese.

THE ECONOMY

World's largest economy: huge resource base; well-established high-tech, engineering, and entertainment industries; global spread of US culture. Decline of manufacturing as jobs lost to low-wage economies. The combination of the "war on terrorism" launched after 9/11, military involvement in Afghanistan and Iraq, and a drive to cut taxes sent government debt spiraling. Hurricane Katrina hit oil production in 2005. Then a "bubble" of excessive risky mortgage lending burst and the financial and stock market crisis went global after the Lehman Brothers bank crashed in 2008. An economic incentive programme, combining tax cuts with more public spending, helped lift the economy out of recession, but widened the gaping budget deficit. Obama's government has struggled with this ever since. Pressures to cut spending hurt its social agenda, while conservative opponents denounce tax increases as a threat to growth.

FACTFILE

OFFICIAL NAME: United States of America
DATE OF FORMATION: 1776
CAPITAL: Washington, D.C.
POPULATION: 320 million
TOTAL AREA: 3,717,792 sq. miles (9,626,091 sq. km)
DENSITY: 90 people per sq. mile
LANGUAGES: English*, Spanish, other
RELIGIONS: Protestant 52%, Roman Catholic 25%, other 20%, Jewish 2%, Muslim 1%
ETHNIC MIX: White 60%, Hispanic 17%, African American 14%, Asian 6%, Native American 2%, Hawaiian or Pacific Islander 1%
GOVERNMENT: Presidential system
CURRENCY: US dollar = 100 cents

Uruguay

Situated in southeastern South America, Uruguay returned to civilian government in 1985, after 12 years of military rule. Most land is used for farming: Uruguay is a major wool exporter.

GEOGRAPHY

Low, rolling grasslands cover 80% of the country. Narrow coastal plain. Alluvial floodplain in southwest. Five rivers flow westward and drain into the Uruguay River.

CLIMATE

Temperate throughout the country. Warm summers, mild winters, and moderate rainfall.

PEOPLE & SOCIETY

Uruguayans are largely second-or third-generation Italians or Spaniards. Wealth derived from cattle ranching enabled the country to establish the first welfare state in South America. Waves of emigration occurred during the economic decline of the 1960s, the period of military rule, and the 1999–2002 economic crisis. Though a Roman Catholic country, Uruguay is liberal in its attitude to religion and all forms are tolerated.

THE ECONOMY

Exports wool, meat, hides, rice, wood, soy. Well-educated workforce. Banking services. Mineral potential.

INSIGHT: *Uruguay's rich pastures are ideal for raising livestock; animal products bring in over 40% of export earnings*

200m/656ft
Sea Level
0 100 km
0 100 miles
56°
30°
Uruguay
Rivera
BRAZIL
Salto
Tacuarembó
54°
ARGENTINA
32°
Embalse del Río Negro
Paysandú
Melo
Mirim Lagoon
Fray Bentos
Paso de los Toros
Mercedes
Treinta y Tres
Trinidad
Colonia del Sacramento
San José de Mayo
34°
River Plate
Las Piedras
Rocha
58°
Punta del Este
MONTEVIDEO
ATLANTIC OCEAN

FACTFILE

OFFICIAL NAME: Eastern Republic of Uruguay
DATE OF FORMATION: 1828
CAPITAL: Montevideo
POPULATION: 3.4 million
TOTAL AREA: 68,039 sq. miles (176,220 sq. km)
DENSITY: 50 people per sq. mile
LANGUAGES: Spanish*
RELIGIONS: Roman Catholic 66%, other and nonreligious 30%, Jewish 2%, Protestant 2%
ETHNIC MIX: White 90%, *Mestizo* (European–Amerindian) 6%, Black 4%
GOVERNMENT: Presidential system
CURRENCY: Uruguayan peso = 100 centésimos

Uzbekistan

Sharing what is left of the Aral Sea with neighboring Kazakhstan, Uzbekistan lies on the ancient Silk Road between Asia and Europe. It is the most populous central Asian republic.

GEOGRAPHY

Arid and semiarid plains in much of the west. Fertile, irrigated farmland in the east lies below the peaks of the western Pamirs.

CLIMATE

Harsh continental climate. Summers can be extremely hot and dry; winters are cold.

PEOPLE & SOCIETY

Complex ethnic makeup. Ex-Communists are in firm control, but traditional social patterns based on clan, religion, and region have reemerged. Constitutional measures aim to control the influence of Islam: activities against Islamists have drawn international condemnation. Most people live in the fertile east. Birth rates are high, and the status of women continues to be low.

THE ECONOMY

Highly regulated. Reserves of natural gas, oil, coal, gold (has one of the world's largest gold mines), and other minerals. Cash crop is cotton: requires much irrigation. Grain imports necessary.

INSIGHT: *The Aral Sea holds just a tenth of its former volume of water, due to diversion of rivers for irrigation*

3000m/9843ft
2000m/6562ft
1000m/3281ft
500m/1640ft
200m/656ft
Sea Level
Aral Sea
KAZAKHSTAN
44°
Nukus
Kyzyl Kum
Turan Lowland
KYRGY.
Urganch
Chirchiq
56°
60°
Amu Darya
TASHKENT
Angren
Aydarko'l Ko'li
Olmaliq
Namangan
TURKMENISTAN
40°
Navoiy
Farg'ona
KYRGY.
Buxoro
Samarqand
72°
Qarshi
TAJIKISTAN
64°
0 100 km
0 100 miles
AFGHANISTAN
68°

FACTFILE

OFFICIAL NAME: Republic of Uzbekistan
DATE OF FORMATION: 1991
CAPITAL: Tashkent
POPULATION: 28.9 million
TOTAL AREA: 172,741 sq. miles (447,400 sq. km)
DENSITY: 167 people per sq. mile
LANGUAGES: Uzbek*, Russian, Tajik, Kazakh
RELIGIONS: Sunni Muslim 88%, Orthodox Christian 9%, other 3%
ETHNIC MIX: Uzbek 80%, other 6%, Russian 6%, Tajik 5%, Kazakh 3%
GOVERNMENT: Presidential system
CURRENCY: Som = 100 tiyin

Vanuatu

An archipelago of 82 islands and islets in the South Pacific, Vanuatu was ruled jointly by the UK and France from 1906 until independence in 1980. Politics is democratic but volatile.

GEOGRAPHY

Mountainous and volcanic, with coral beaches and dense rainforest. Cultivated land along the coasts.

CLIMATE

Tropical. Temperatures and rainfall decline from north to south.

PEOPLE & SOCIETY

Indigenous Melanesians form a majority. Ni-Vanuatu culture is traditional; local social and religious customs are strong, despite centuries of missionary influence. Subsistence farming and fishing are the main activities. 80% of the population lives on the 12 main islands. Women have lower social status than men and payment of bride-price is common.

INSIGHT: *With 112 indigenous tongues, Vanuatu has the world's highest per capita density of languages*

THE ECONOMY

Reliant on aid. Main exports are copra (dried coconut), kava, cocoa, and beef. Tourism. Offshore banking: rules tightened after international pressure.

Torres Islands
0 100 km
0 100 miles
14°
Banks Islands
Espiritu Santo
PACIFIC OCEAN
Aoba
Maéwo
Luganville
Pentecost
16°
Norsup
Ambrym
Malekula
Epi
Coral Sea
Shepherd Islands
PORT VILA
18°
Efate
168°
Erromango
Tanna
Isangel
20°
Aneityum
170°
1000m/3281ft
500m/1640ft
200m/656ft
Sea Level

FACTFILE

OFFICIAL NAME: Republic of Vanuatu
DATE OF FORMATION: 1980
CAPITAL: Port Vila
POPULATION: 300,000
TOTAL AREA: 4710 sq. miles (12,200 sq. km)
DENSITY: 64 people per sq. mile
LANGUAGES: Bislama (Melanesian pidgin)*, English*, French*, other indigenous languages
RELIGIONS: Presbyterian 37%, other 19%, Anglican 15%, Roman Catholic 15%, traditional beliefs 8%, Seventh-day Adventist 6%
ETHNIC MIX: ni-Vanuatu 94%, European 4%, other 2%
GOVERNMENT: Parliamentary system
CURRENCY: Vatu = 100 centimes

Vatican City

The Vatican City, or Holy See, the seat of the Roman Catholic Church, is a walled enclave in the Italian city of Rome. It is the world's smallest fully independent state.

GEOGRAPHY

The Vatican's territory includes 10 other buildings in Rome, plus the papal residence. The Vatican Gardens cover half the City's area.

CLIMATE

Mild winters with regular rainfall. Hot, dry summers with occasional thunderstorms.

PEOPLE & SOCIETY

The Vatican has about 800 permanent inhabitants, including over 100 lay persons. Thousands of lay staff are also employed. Citizenship can be acquired through long-term residence and holding a position within the City. The reigning pope has supreme legislative and judicial powers, and holds office for life. Though the Vatican City is officially neutral, papal opinion has a great influence on the world's 1.2 billion Roman Catholics.

THE ECONOMY

Investments and voluntary contributions made by Catholics worldwide (known as Peter's Pence) are backed up by tourist revenue and the issue of Vatican stamps and coins.

INSIGHT: *The Vatican City is the spiritual center for one in six of the world's population*

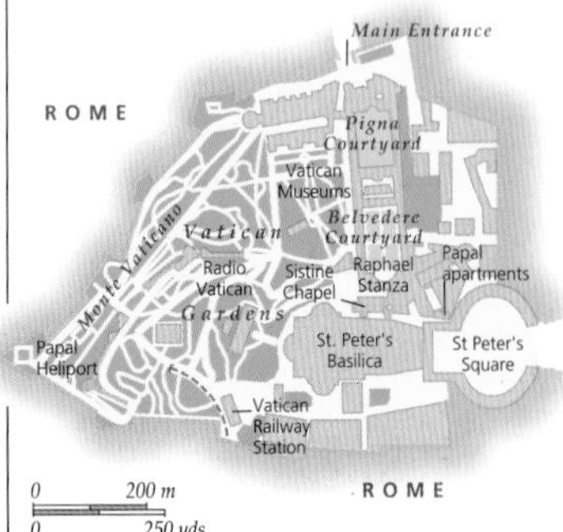
Main Entrance
ROME
Pigna Courtyard
Vatican Museums
Belvedere Courtyard
Vatican
Monte Vaticano
Radio Vatican
Sistine Chapel
Raphael Stanza
Papal apartments
Gardens
Papal Heliport
St. Peter's Basilica
St Peter's Square
Vatican Railway Station
0 200 m
0 250 yds
ROME

FACTFILE

OFFICIAL NAME: State of the Vatican City
DATE OF FORMATION: 1929
CAPITAL: Vatican City
POPULATION: 839
TOTAL AREA: 0.17 sq. miles (0.44 sq. km)
DENSITY: 4935 people per sq. mile
LANGUAGES: Italian*, Latin*
RELIGIONS: Roman Catholic 100%
ETHNIC MIX: Cardinals are from many nationalities, but Italians form the largest group. Most resident lay persons are Italian. The current pope is from Argentina.
GOVERNMENT: Papal state
CURRENCY: Euro = 100 cents

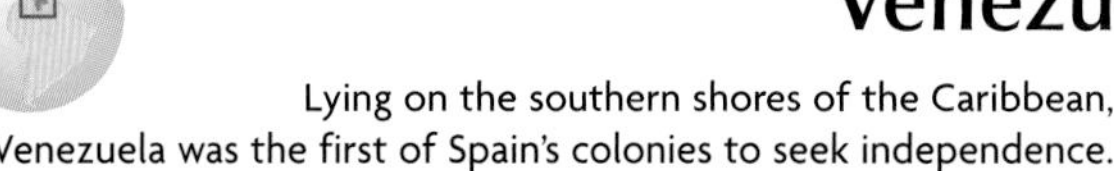

Venezuela

Lying on the southern shores of the Caribbean, Venezuela was the first of Spain's colonies to seek independence. Despite large oil revenues, many Venezuelans still live in poverty.

GEOGRAPHY

Andes Mountains and the Maracaibo lowlands in the northwest. Central grassy plains are drained by the Orinoco River system. Forested Guiana Highlands in the southeast.

CLIMATE

Tropical. Hot and humid. Uplands are cooler. Orinoco plains are alternately parched or flooded.

PEOPLE & SOCIETY

Venezuela is historically a "melting pot," with immigrants from Europe and all over Latin America. The few indigenous Amerindians live in remote areas. Venezuela has one of the most urbanized societies in the region, with most of its population living in the northern cities. The left-wing rhetoric of President Hugo Chávez (1999–2013) raised opposition within Venezuela from urban society, and from the US.

THE ECONOMY

Oil accounts for 95% of exports; world's largest reserves. Coal, gold, other minerals. Nationalizations are enlarging the inefficient, corruption-prone state sector and deterring foreign investors.

INSIGHT: *Venezuela's Angel Falls is the world's tallest waterfall, with a total drop of 3210 ft (979 m)*

0 200 km
0 200 miles
Caribbean Sea
Maracay
Valencia
CARACAS
Maracaibo
Cabimas
Lago de Maracaibo
Barquisimeto
Cumaná
Barcelona
ATLANTIC OCEAN
Barinas
Llanos
Ciudad Guayana
San Cristóbal
Orinoco
Ciudad Bolívar
Meta
Angel Falls
GUYANA
COLOMBIA
Guiana Highlands
Orinoco
BRAZIL
Equator
12°
8°
4°
72°
68°
64°
60°
2000m/6562ft
1000m/3281ft
500m/1640ft
200m/656ft
Sea Level

FACTFILE

OFFICIAL NAME: Bolivarian Republic of Venezuela

DATE OF FORMATION: 1830

CAPITAL: Caracas

POPULATION: 30.4 million

TOTAL AREA: 352,143 sq. miles (912,050 sq. km)

DENSITY: 89 people per sq. mile

LANGUAGES: Spanish*, Amerindian languages

RELIGIONS: Roman Catholic 96%, Protestant 2%, other 2%

ETHNIC MIX: *Mestizo* (European–Amerindian) 69%, White 20%, Black 9%, Amerindian 2%

GOVERNMENT: Presidential system

CURRENCY: Bolívar fuerte = 100 céntimos

Vietnam

French rule of Vietnam ended in 1954. Divided at 17°N, the US-backed South fought the Communist North. Reunified after the North's 1975 victory, it is run as a single-party state.

GEOGRAPHY

A heavily forested mountain range separates the northern Red River delta lowlands from the Mekong Delta in the south.

CLIMATE

Cool winters in north; south is tropical, with even temperatures.

PEOPLE & SOCIETY

Ethnic Vietnamese dominate; the Chinese minority was viewed as a corrupt bourgeoisie by the victorious Communists after the war. Mountain-based minorities *(montagnards)* were also sidelined; tensions persist over the settling of highlands by lowlanders. Women play an active role in society. There is no political or press freedom.

INSIGHT: *Intense US bombing and defoliant spraying in the 1962–1975 Vietnam War has scarred the landscape*

THE ECONOMY

Liberal economic policy *(doi moi)* from 1986: now one of fastest-growing economies. Major rice exporter. Cheap labor. Strong manufacturing: textiles, electrical goods. Diverse resource base.

CHINA
Red River
22°
LAOS
HANOI
Ha Long
Nam Dinh
Hai Phong
Gulf of Tonkin
Vinh
18°
0 100 km
0 100 miles
2000m/6562ft
1000m/3281ft
500m/1640ft
200m/656ft
Sea Level
Huê
Đa Nang
South China Sea
14°
CAMBODIA
Quy Nhon
Mekong
Nha Trang
Đa Lat
Long Xuyên
Hô Chi Minh
Vung Tau
Gulf of Thailand
Cân Tho
Mekong Delta
10°
104°
108°

FACTFILE

OFFICIAL NAME: Socialist Republic of Vietnam
DATE OF FORMATION: 1976
CAPITAL: Hanoi
POPULATION: 91.7 million
TOTAL AREA: 127,243 sq. miles (329,560 sq. km)
DENSITY: 730 people per sq. mile
LANGUAGES: Vietnamese*, Chinese, Thai, Khmer, Muong, Nung, Miao, Yao, Jarai
RELIGIONS: Other 74%, Buddhist 14%, Roman Catholic 7%, Cao Dai 3%, Protestant 2%
ETHNIC MIX: Vietnamese 86%, other 8%, Tay 2%, Thai 2%, Muong 2%
GOVERNMENT: One-party state
CURRENCY: Dông = 10 hao = 100 xu

Yemen

Located in southern Arabia, Yemen was formerly two countries: the People's Democratic Republic of Yemen (south and east) and the Yemen Arab Republic (northwest) were united in 1990.

GEOGRAPHY

Mountainous west with a fertile strip along the Red Sea. Arid desert and mountains elsewhere.

CLIMATE

Desert climate, modified by altitude, which affects temperatures by as much as 54°F (30°C).

PEOPLE & SOCIETY

Almost entirely of Arab and Bedouin descent, most Yemenis are Sunni Muslims, of the Shafi sect. In rural and northern areas, tribalism and Islamic orthodoxy are strong and most women wear the veil. Tension continues between cosmopolitan Aden and the more conservative north. Islamists have a growing political role. Popular protests that began in the 2011 "Arab Spring" ended President Saleh's 33-year rule. Foreigners are subject to attacks and kidnappings.

THE ECONOMY

Instability deters investment. Considerable oil and natural gas reserves. Agriculture is the largest employer: qat (mild narcotic), coffee, and cotton.

INSIGHT: *Mokha, on the Red Sea, gave its name to the first coffee beans exported to Europe in the 1600s*

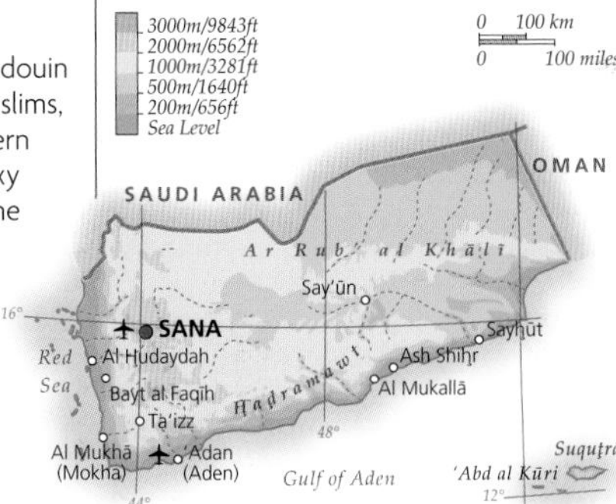
3000m/9843ft
2000m/6562ft
1000m/3281ft
500m/1640ft
200m/656ft
Sea Level
0 100 km
0 100 miles
SAUDI ARABIA
OMAN
Ar Rub' al Khālī
Say'ūn
SANA
Sayhūt
Red Sea
Al Hudaydah
Ash Shihr
Al Mukallā
Bayt al Faqīh
Hadramawt
Ta'izz
Al Mukhā (Mokha)
'Adan (Aden)
Gulf of Aden
Suquṭrā
'Abd al Kūri
16°
12°
44°
48°
52°

FACTFILE

OFFICIAL NAME: Republic of Yemen

DATE OF FORMATION: 1990

CAPITAL: Sana

POPULATION: 24.4 million

TOTAL AREA: 203,849 sq. miles (527,970 sq. km)

DENSITY: 112 people per sq. mile

LANGUAGES: Arabic*

RELIGIONS: Sunni Muslim 55%, Shi'a Muslim 42%, Christian, Hindu, and Jewish 3%

ETHNIC MIX: Arab 99%, Afro-Arab, Indian, Somali, and European 1%

GOVERNMENT: Transitional regime

CURRENCY: Yemeni rial = 100 fils

Zambia

Bordered to the south by the Zambezi River, Zambia lies at the heart of southern Africa. In 1991, it made a peaceful transition from single-party rule to multiparty democracy.

GEOGRAPHY

A high savanna plateau, broken by mountains in northeast. Vegetation mainly trees and scrub.

CLIMATE

Tropical, with three seasons: cool and dry, hot and dry, and wet. Southwest is prone to drought.

PEOPLE & SOCIETY

There are more than 70 different ethnic groups, but there are fewer tensions than in many African states. Major groups are the Bemba (in the northeast), Tonga (south), Nyanja (east), and Lozi (west). There are also thousands of refugees, mostly from the DRC and Angola. A National Gender Policy was issued in 2000 to redress inequalities between the sexes. The standard of living has fallen in real terms since independence. One in seven adults is infected with HIV/AIDS.

THE ECONOMY

Copper: output has risen since 2000, when decades of falling global prices ended. New agricultural exports, notably flowers. Debt relief.

INSIGHT: *Spray from Musi-o-Tunya (Victoria Falls) can be seen up to 20 miles (35 km) away*

1000m/3281ft
500m/1640ft
200m/656ft
L. Tanganyika
TANZANIA
32°
L. Mweru
DEM. REP. CONGO
24°
28°
Kasama
Mansa
MALAWI
12°
ANGOLA
Chingola
Mufulira
Kitwe
Ndola
Luanshya
Chipata
Kabwe
Mongu
LUSAKA
MOZAMBIQUE
16°
Zambezi
Monze
Choma
Lake Kariba
ZIMBABWE
NAMIBIA
Livingstone
BOTSWANA
Victoria Falls
0
200 km
0
200 miles

FACTFILE

OFFICIAL NAME: Republic of Zambia
DATE OF FORMATION: 1964
CAPITAL: Lusaka
POPULATION: 14.5 million
TOTAL AREA: 290,584 sq. miles (752,614 sq. km)
DENSITY: 51 people per sq. mile
LANGUAGES: Bemba, Tonga, Nyanja, Lozi, Lala-Bisa, Nsenga, English*
RELIGIONS: Christian 63%, traditional beliefs 36%, Muslim and Hindu 1%
ETHNIC MIX: Bemba 34%, other African 26%, Tonga 16%, Nyanja 14%, Lozi 9%, European 1%
GOVERNMENT: Presidential system
CURRENCY: New Zamb. kwacha = 100 ngwee

Zimbabwe

Situated in southern Africa, Zimbabwe achieved independence from the UK in 1980. President Robert Mugabe, in power since then, has become increasingly authoritarian.

GEOGRAPHY

High plateaus in center bordered by Zambezi River in the north and Limpopo in the south. Rivers crisscross central area.

CLIMATE

Tropical, though moderated by the high altitude. Wet season November–March. Drought is common in the eastern highlands.

PEOPLE & SOCIETY

Two main ethnic groups: Shona in the north and east, and Ndebele in the south. Shona outnumber Ndebele by four to one. Whites are generally far more affluent than blacks. Official efforts to redress this imbalance (such as land redistribution) have become increasingly aggressive. The political opposition to Mugabe joined him in a fractious unity government from 2009 to 2013 in an attempt to rebuild the country.

THE ECONOMY

Undermined by mismanagement, corruption, and international isolation. High unemployment. Abandoned own currency in 2009 after hyperinflation.

INSIGHT: *The ruins of the 1000-year-old city of Great Zimbabwe, after which the country is named, are near modern-day Masvingo*

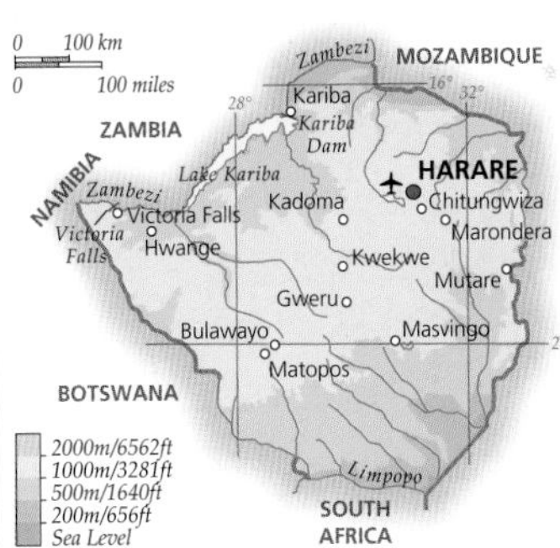
0 100 km
0 100 miles
Zambezi
MOZAMBIQUE
16°
32°
28°
Kariba
Kariba Dam
ZAMBIA
NAMIBIA
Lake Kariba
HARARE
Chitungwiza
Marondera
Zambezi
Victoria Falls
Victoria Falls
Hwange
Kadoma
Kwekwe
Mutare
Gweru
Bulawayo
Masvingo
20°
Matopos
BOTSWANA
2000m/6562ft
1000m/3281ft
500m/1640ft
200m/656ft
Sea Level
Limpopo
SOUTH AFRICA

FACTFILE

OFFICIAL NAME: Republic of Zimbabwe
DATE OF FORMATION: 1980
CAPITAL: Harare
POPULATION: 14.1 million
TOTAL AREA: 150,803 sq. miles (390,580 sq. km)
DENSITY: 94 people per sq. mile
LANGUAGES: Shona, isiNdebele, English*
RELIGIONS: Syncretic 50%, Christian 25%, traditional beliefs 24%, other 1%
ETHNIC MIX: Shona 71%, Ndebele 16%, other African 11%, White 1%, Asian 1%
GOVERNMENT: Presidential system
CURRENCY: US $, S African rand, euro, UK £, Botswanan pula, Australian $, Chinese yuan, Indian rupee, Japanese yen all legal tender

Overseas territories

Despite the rapid process of global decolonization since World War II, around eight million people in more than 50 territories around the world continue to live under the protection of Australia, Denmark, France, the Netherlands, New Zealand, Norway, the UK, or the USA. These remnants of former colonial empires may have persisted for economic, strategic, or political reasons and are administered by the protecting country in a variety of ways.

AUSTRALIA

Australia's overseas territories have not been an issue since Papua New Guinea became independent in 1975. Consequently, there is no overriding policy toward them.

Ashmore & Cartier Is. *Ref: 124 A3*

STATUS: External territory
CLAIMED: 1931
POPULATION: None
AREA: 2 sq miles (5.2 sq km)

Christmas Island *Ref: 123 E5*

STATUS: External territory
CLAIMED: 1958
CAPITAL: The Settlement
POPULATION: 1530
AREA: 52 sq miles (135 sq km)

Cocos Islands *Ref: 123 D5*

STATUS: External territory
CLAIMED: 1955
CAPITAL: West Island
POPULATION: 596
AREA: 5.5 sq miles (14 sq km)

Coral Sea Islands *Ref: 126 B4*

STATUS: External territory
CLAIMED: 1969
POPULATION: 8 (Meteorologists)
AREA: 1.2 sq miles (3 sq km)

Heard & McDonald Is. *Ref: 123 C7*

STATUS: External territory
CLAIMED: 1947
POPULATION: None
AREA: 161 sq miles (417 sq km)

Norfolk Island *Ref: 124 D4*

STATUS: External territory
CLAIMED: 1774
CAPITAL: Kingston
POPULATION: 2210
AREA: 13 sq miles (34 sq km)

DENMARK

The Faroes and Greenland have had home rule since 1948 and 1979 respectively.

Faroe Islands *Ref: 65 F5*

STATUS: External territory
CLAIMED: 1380
CAPITAL: Tórshavn
POPULATION: 49,469
AREA: 540 sq miles (1399 sq km)

Greenland *Ref: 64 D3*

STATUS: External territory
CLAIMED: 1380
CAPITAL: Nuuk
POPULATION: 56,483
AREA: 836,109 sq miles (2,166,086 sq km)

Overseas territories

FRANCE

France's relations with *L'Outre-Mer* stress interdependence rather than independence. *Départements* have their own governments. *Collectivités* have some autonomy.

Clipperton Island *Ref: 135 F3*
STATUS: Dependency of French Polynesia
CLAIMED: 1935
POPULATION: None
AREA: 3.4 sq miles (9 sq km)

French Guiana *Ref: 41 H3*
STATUS: Overseas department
CLAIMED: 1817
CAPITAL: Cayenne
POPULATION: 250,109
AREA: 35,135 sq miles (91,000 sq km)

French Polynesia *Ref: 127 H4*
STATUS: Overseas collectivity
CLAIMED: 1843
CAPITAL: Papeete
POPULATION: 276,831
AREA: 1608 sq miles (4165 sq km)

French Southern & Antarctic Lands
Ref: 123 B6
STATUS: Overseas territory
CLAIMED: 1772, 1840, 1843, 1924
CAPITAL: Port-aux-Français
POPULATION: 140
AREA: 169,800 sq miles (439,781 sq km)

Guadeloupe *Ref: 37 G4*
STATUS: Overseas department
CLAIMED: 1635
CAPITAL: Basse-Terre
POPULATION: 405,739
AREA: 629 sq miles (1628 sq km)

Martinique *Ref: 37 G4*
STATUS: Overseas department
CLAIMED: 1635
CAPITAL: Fort-de-France
POPULATION: 386,486
AREA: 425 sq miles (1100 sq km)

Mayotte *Ref: 61 G2*
STATUS: Overseas department
CLAIMED: 1843
CAPITAL: Mamoudzou
POPULATION: 212,645
AREA: 144 sq miles (374 sq km)

New Caledonia *Ref: 126 D5*
STATUS: Special collectivity
CLAIMED: 1853
CAPITAL: Nouméa
POPULATION: 262,000
AREA: 7347 sq miles (19,100 sq km)

Réunion *Ref: 61 H4*
STATUS: Overseas department
CLAIMED: 1638
CAPITAL: Saint-Denis
POPULATION: 840,974
AREA: 970 sq miles (2500 sq km)

St Barthélemy *Ref: 37 G3*
STATUS: Overseas collectivity
CLAIMED: 1878
CAPITAL: Gustavia
POPULATION: 7267
AREA: 8 sq miles (21 sq km)

St Martin *Ref: 37 E5*
STATUS: Overseas collectivity
CLAIMED: 1648
CAPITAL: Marigot
POPULATION: 31,264
AREA: 20 sq miles (53 sq km)

Overseas territories

St Pierre & Miquelon *Ref: 21 G4*
STATUS: Overseas collectivity
CLAIMED: 1604
CAPITAL: Saint-Pierre
POPULATION: 5716
AREA: 93 sq miles (242 sq km)

Wallis & Futuna *Ref: 127 E4*
STATUS: Overseas collectivity
CLAIMED: 1842
CAPITAL: Mata'Utu
POPULATION: 15,561
AREA: 106 sq miles (274 sq km)

NETHERLANDS

These islands were once part of the Dutch West Indies. They are now self-governing,

Aruba *Ref: 37 E5*
STATUS: Constituent country
CLAIMED: 1636
CAPITAL: Oranjestad
POPULATION: 102,911
AREA: 75 sq miles (194 sq km)

Bonaire *Ref: 37 E5*

STATUS: Special municipality
CLAIMED: 1816
CAPITAL: Kralendijk
POPULATION: 18,413
AREA: 113 sq miles (294 sq km)

Curaçao *Ref: 37 E5*

STATUS: Constituent country
CLAIMED: 1815
CAPITAL: Willemstad
POPULATION: 153,500
AREA: 171 sq miles (444 sq km)

Saba *Ref: 37 G3*
STATUS: Special municipality
CLAIMED: 1816
CAPITAL: The Bottom
POPULATION: 1846
AREA: 5 sq miles (13 sq km)

Sint-Eustatius *Ref: 37 G3*
STATUS: Special municipality
CLAIMED: 1784
CAPITAL: Oranjestad
POPULATION: 4020
AREA: 8 sq miles (21 sq km)

Sint-Maarten *Ref: 37 G3*
STATUS: Constituent country
CLAIMED: 1648
CAPITAL: Phillipsburg
POPULATION: 39,689
AREA: 13 sq miles (34 sq km)

NEW ZEALAND

New Zealand remains responsible for its territories' foreign policy and defense.

Cook Islands *Ref: 127 G4*

STATUS: Associated territory
CLAIMED: 1901
CAPITAL: Avarua
POPULATION: 13,700
AREA: 91 sq miles (235 sq km)

Niue *Ref: 127 F5*

STATUS: Associated territory
CLAIMED: 1901
CAPITAL: Alofi
POPULATION: 1190
AREA: 102 sq miles (264 sq km)

Overseas territories

Tokelau *Ref: 127 F3*
STATUS: Dependent territory
CLAIMED: 1926
CAPITAL: None
POPULATION: 1337
AREA: 4 sq miles (10 sq km)

NORWAY

There is a NATO base on Jan Mayen. Bouvet Island is a nature reserve.

Bouvet Island *Ref: 49 D7*
STATUS: Dependency
CLAIMED: 1928
POPULATION: None
AREA: 22 sq miles (58 sq km)

Jan Mayen *Ref: 65 F3*
STATUS: Dependency
CLAIMED: 1929
POPULATION: 18 (Meteorologists)
AREA: 147 sq miles (381 sq km)

Peter I. Island *Ref: 136 A3*
STATUS: Dependency
CLAIMED: 1931
POPULATION: None
AREA: 69 sq miles (180 sq km)

Svalbard *Ref: 65 F2*
STATUS: Dependency
CLAIMED: 1920
CAPITAL: Longyearbyen
POPULATION: 1872
AREA: 24,289 sq miles (62,906 sq km)

UNITED KINGDOM

The UK's dependencies are locally governed by a mix of elected and appointed officials.

Anguilla *Ref: 37 G3*

STATUS: Overseas territory
CLAIMED: 1650
CAPITAL: The Valley
POPULATION: 16,086
AREA: 37 sq miles (96 sq km)

Ascension Island *Ref: 49 C5*
STATUS: Overseas territory
CLAIMED: 1673
CAPITAL: Georgetown
POPULATION: 880
AREA: 34 sq miles (88 sq km)

Bermuda *Ref: 17 E6*

STATUS: Overseas territory
CLAIMED: 1612
CAPITAL: Hamilton
POPULATION: 65,024
AREA: 20 sq miles (53 sq km)

British Indian Ocean Territory
Ref: 122 C4 STATUS: Overseas territory

CLAIMED: 1814
CAPITAL: Diego Garcia
POPULATION: 4000
AREA: 23 sq miles (60 sq km)

British Virgin Islands *Ref: 37 F3*

STATUS: Overseas territory
CLAIMED: 1672
CAPITAL: Road Town
POPULATION: 32,680
AREA: 59 sq miles (153 sq km)

Cayman Islands *Ref: 36 B3*

STATUS: Overseas territory
CLAIMED: 1670
CAPITAL: George Town
POPULATION: 58,435
AREA: 100 sq miles (259 sq km)

Overseas territories

Falkland Islands *Ref: 47 D7*

STATUS: Overseas territory
CLAIMED: 1832
CAPITAL: Stanley
POPULATION: 2840
AREA: 4699 sq miles (12,173 sq km)

Gibraltar *Ref: 74 D5*

STATUS: Overseas territory
CLAIMED: 1713
CAPITAL: Gibraltar
POPULATION: 29,185
AREA: 2.5 sq miles (6.5 sq km)

Guernsey *Ref: 71 D8*

STATUS: Crown Dependency
CLAIMED: 1066
CAPITAL: St. Peter Port
POPULATION: 65,849
AREA: 25 sq miles (65 sq km)

Isle of Man *Ref: 71 C5*

STATUS: Crown Dependency
CLAIMED: 1765
CAPITAL: Douglas
POPULATION: 85,888
AREA: 221 sq miles (572 sq km)

Jersey *Ref: 71 D8*

STATUS: Crown Dependency
CLAIMED: 1066
CAPITAL: St. Helier
POPULATION: 96,513
AREA: 45 sq miles (116 sq km)

Montserrat *Ref: 37 G4*

STATUS: Overseas territory
CLAIMED: 1632
CAPITAL: Brades *(de facto)*
POPULATION: 5215
AREA: 40 sq miles (102 sq km)

Pitcairn Group of Is. *Ref: 125 G4*

STATUS: Overseas territory
CLAIMED: 1887
CAPITAL: Adamstown
POPULATION: 48
AREA: 18 sq miles (47 sq km)

Saint Helena *Ref: 49 D5*

STATUS: Overseas territory
CLAIMED: 1673
CAPITAL: Jamestown
POPULATION: 7776
AREA: 47 sq miles (122 sq km)

South Georgia & the South Sandwich Islands *Ref: 49 C7*

STATUS: Overseas territory
CLAIMED: 1775
POPULATION: None
AREA: 1387 sq miles (3592 sq km)

Tristan da Cunha *Ref: 49 D6*

STATUS: Overseas territory
CLAIMED: 1612
CAPITAL: Edinburgh
POPULATION: 264
AREA: 38 sq miles (98 sq km)

Turks & Caicos Islands *Ref: 37 E2*

STATUS: Overseas territory
CLAIMED: 1766
CAPITAL: Cockburn Town
POPULATION: 33,098
AREA: 166 sq miles (430 sq km)

UNITED STATES

Commonwealth territories are self-governing and an integral part of the US. Unincorporated territories have varying degrees of autonomy.

Overseas territories

American Samoa *Ref: 127 F4*

STATUS: Unincorp. territory
CLAIMED: 1900
CAPITAL: Pago Pago
POPULATION: 55,165
AREA: 75 sq miles (195 sq km)

Baker & Howland Islands *Ref: 127 E2*

STATUS: Unincorporated territory
CLAIMED: 1856
POPULATION: None
AREA: 0.5 sq miles (1.4 sq km)

Guam *Ref: 126 B1*

STATUS: Unincorp. territory
CLAIMED: 1898
CAPITAL: Hagåtña
POPULATION: 165,124
AREA: 212 sq miles (549 sq km)

Jarvis Island *Ref: 127 G2*

STATUS: Unincorporated territory
CLAIMED: 1856
POPULATION: None
AREA: 1.7 sq miles (4.5 sq km)

Johnston Atoll *Ref: 125 E1*

STATUS: Unincorporated territory
CLAIMED: 1858
POPULATION: None
AREA: 1 sq mile (2.8 sq km)

Kingman Reef *Ref: 127 F2*

STATUS: Unincorporated territory
CLAIMED: 1856
POPULATION: None
AREA: 0.4 sq miles (1 sq km)

Midway Islands *Ref: 134 D2*

STATUS: Unincorporated territory
CLAIMED: 1867
CAPITAL: None
POPULATION: 40
AREA: 2 sq miles (5.2 sq km)

Navassa Island *Ref: 36 D3*

STATUS: Unincorporated territory
CLAIMED: 1856
POPULATION: None
AREA: 2 sq miles (5.2 sq km)

Northern Mariana Islands *Ref: 124 C1*

STATUS: Comm. territory
CLAIMED: 1947
CAPITAL: Saipan
POPULATION: 53,855
AREA: 177 sq miles (457 sq km)

Palmyra Atoll *Ref: 127 G2*

STATUS: Incorporated territory
CLAIMED: 1898
POPULATION: None
AREA: 5 sq miles (12 sq km)

Puerto Rico *Ref: 37 F3*

STATUS: Comm. territory
CLAIMED: 1898
CAPITAL: San Juan
POPULATION: 3.62 million
AREA: 3515 sq miles (9104 sq km)

Virgin Islands *Ref: 37 F3*

V
I

STATUS: Unincorp. territory
CLAIMED: 1917
CAPITAL: Charlotte Amalie
POPULATION: 104,737
AREA: 137 sq miles (355 sq km)

Wake Island *Ref: 124 D1*

STATUS: Unincorporated territory
CLAIMED: 1898
CAPITAL: None
POPULATION: 150 (US air base)
AREA: 2.5 sq miles (6.5 sq km)

International organizations

This listing provides acronym definitions for the main international organizations concerned with worldwide economics, trade, and defense, plus an indication of membership.

ASEAN
Association of Southeast Asian Nations
ESTABLISHED: 1967
MEMBERS: Brunei, Cambodia, Indonesia, Laos, Malaysia, Myanmar, Philippines, Singapore, Thailand, Vietnam

CIS
Commonwealth of Independent States
ESTABLISHED: 1991
MEMBERS: Arm., Az., Belarus, Kaz., Kyrgy., Mold., Russia, Tajik., Turkmen.*, Ukraine*, Uzbek. **Unofficial members*

COMM *The Commonwealth of Nations*
ESTABLISHED: 1931; evolved out of the British Empire. Formerly known as the British Commonwealth of Nations.
MEMBERS: 53 *(Fiji currently suspended)*

EU *European Union*
ESTABLISHED: 1965; formerly known as EEC (European Economic Community) and EC (Economic Community)
MEMBERS: Austria, Belg., Bulg., Croatia, Cyprus, Czech Rep., Denmark, Est., Fin., Fr., Ger., Greece, Hung., Ireland, Italy, Lat., Lith., Lux., Malta, Neth., Pol., Port., Rom., Slvka., Slvna., Spain, Swed., UK

G8 *Group of 8*
ESTABLISHED: 1994
MEMBERS: Canada, France, Germany, Italy, Japan, Russia, UK, US

IMF *International Monetary Fund* (UN agency)
ESTABLISHED: 1945
MEMBERS: 188

NAFTA
North American Free Trade Agreement
ESTABLISHED: 1994
MEMBERS: Canada, Mexico, US

NATO
North Atlantic Treaty Organization
ESTABLISHED: 1949
MEMBERS: Albania, Belg., Bulg., Canada, Croatia, Czech Rep., Denmark, Est., France, Ger., Greece, Hung., Iceland, Italy, Lat., Lith., Lux., Neth., Norway, Poland, Port., Rom., Slovakia, Slovenia, Spain, Turkey, UK, US

OPEC *Organization of Petroleum Exporting Countries*
ESTABLISHED: 1960
MEMBERS: Algeria, Angola, Ecuador, Iran, Iraq, Kuwait, Libya, Nigeria, Qatar, Saudi Arabia, United Arab Emirates, Venezuela

UN *United Nations*
ESTABLISHED: 1945
MEMBERS: 193; all nations are represented, except Taiwan and Kosovo. The Vatican City has "observer status" only. In 2012, a UN resolution granted Palestine the status of "non-member observer state."

WTO *World Trade Organization*
ESTABLISHED: 1995
MEMBERS: 160 *(including EU, Hong Kong, Macao)*

Abbreviations

This glossary provides a comprehensive guide to the abbreviations used in this atlas.

abbrev. abbreviation
Afgh. Afghanistan
Amh. Amharic
anc. ancient
Ar. Arabic
Arm. Armenia/Armenian
Aus. Austria
Aust. Australia
Az. Azerbaijan

Bas. Basque
Bel. Belorussian
Belg. Belgium/Belgian
Bos. & Herz. Bosnia & Herzegovina
Bul. Bulgarian
Bulg. Bulgaria
Bur. Burmese

C Central
C. Cape
Cam. Cambodian
Cast. Castilian
Chin. Chinese
Comm. Commonwealth
Cord. Cordillera (Sp. mts.)
Cz. Czech
Czech Rep. Czech Republic

D.C. District of Columbia
Dan. Danish
Dominican Rep. Dominican Republic

E East
Emb. Embalse
Eng. English
Eq. Guinea Equatorial Guinea
Est. Estonia/Estonian

Faer. Faeroese
Fin. Finland/Finnish
Flem. Flemish
Fr. France/French
Geo. Georgia
Geor. Georgian
Ger. Germany/German
Gk. Greek

Heb. Hebrew
Hung. Hungary/Hungarian

I. Island
Ind. Indonesia, Indonesian
Is. Islands
It. Italian

Kaz. Kazakhstan/Kazakh
Kep. Kepulauan (Ind. island group)
Kir. Kirghiz
Kor. Korean
Kos. Kosovo
Kurd. Kurdish
Kyrgy. Kyrgyzstan

L. Lake, Lago
Lat. Latvia
Latv. Latvian
Leb. Lebanon
Liech. Liechtenstein
Lith. Lithuania/Lithuanian
Lux. Luxembourg

Mac. Macedonia
Med. Sea Mediterranean Sea
Mon. Montenegro
Mold. Moldova
Mt. Mount/Mountain
Mts. Mountains

N North
N. Korea North Korea
Neth. Netherlands
NW Northwest
NZ New Zealand

P. Pulau (Ind. island)
Peg. Pegunungan (Ind. mountain range)
Per. Persian
Pol. Poland/Polish
Port. Portugal, Portuguese
prev. previously
R. River, Rio, Río
Res. Reservoir
Rom. Romania/Romanian
Rus. Russian
Russ. Fed. Russian Federation

S South
S. Korea South Korea
SA South Africa
SCr. Serbian and Croatian
Serb. Serbia
Slvka. Slovakia
Slvna. Slovenia
Som. Somali
Sp. Spanish
St, St. Saint
Str. Strait
Swed. Swedish
Switz. Switzerland

Tajik. Tajikistan
Th. Thai
Turk. Turkish
Turkm. Turkmen
Turkmen. Turkmenistan

U.A.E. United Arab Emirates
UK United Kingdom
Ukr. Ukrainian
Uninhab. Uninhabitable
Unincorp. Unincorporated
Urug. Uruguayan
US United States of America
Uzb. Uzbek
Uzbek. Uzbekistan

var. variant
Vdkhr. Vodokhranilishche (Rus. reservoir)
Vdskh. Vodoskhovyshche (Ukr. reservoir)
Ven. Venezuela

W West
W. Sahara Western Sahara
Wel. Welsh

Yugo. Yugoslavia

Zamb. Zambian

A

Aabenraa Denmark 67 A8
Aachen Germany 76 A4
Aalborg Denmark 67 B7
Aalst Belgium 69 B5
Aba Nigeria 57 G5
Ābādān Iran 102 C4
Abadan Turkmenistan *prev.* Bezmein, Büzmeýin 104 B3
Abashiri Japan 112 D2
Abéché Chad 58 D3
Aberdeen Scotland, UK 70 D3
Aberdeen South Dakota, USA 25 E2
Aberdeen Washington, USA 26 A2
Aberystwyth Wales, UK 71 C6
Abhā Saudi Arabia 103 B6
Abidjan Côte d'Ivoire 56 D5
Abilene Texas, USA 29 F3
Abomey Benin 57 F4
Abu Dhabi *capital of* United Arab Emirates *var.* Abū Ẓaby 103 D5
Abuja *capital of* Nigeria 57 G4
Abū Ẓaby *see* Abu Dhabi
Acapulco Mexico 33 E5
Acarai Mountains *mountain range* Brazil/Guyana 41 F3
Acarigua Venezuela 40 D1
Accra *capital of* Ghana 57 E5
Acklins Island *island* The Bahamas 36 D2
Aconcagua, Cerro *peak* Argentina 46 B4
A Coruña Spain *Cast.* La Coruña 74 C1
ACT *see* Australian Capital Territory
Adalia *see* Antalya
Adalia, Gulf of *see* Antalya Körfezi
'Adan Yemen *Eng.* Aden 103 B7
Adana Turkey *var.* Seyhan 98 D4
Adapazarı Turkey *var.* Sakarya 98 B2
Ad Dahnā' *desert* Saudi Arabia *103 C5*
Ad Dakhla Western Sahara 52 A4
Ad Dawḩah *see* Doha
Addis Ababa *capital of* Ethiopia *Amh.* Ādīs Ābeba 55 C5
Adelaide Australia 131 B6
Adélie, Terre d' *territory* Antarctica 136 C4
Aden *see* 'Adan
Aden, Gulf of *sea feature* Indian Ocean 122 A3
Adige *river* Italy 78 C2
Ādīs Ābeba *see* Addis Ababa
Adıyaman Turkey 99 E4
Adriatic Sea Mediterranean Sea 78 D4
Aegean Sea Mediterranean Sea *Gk.* Aigaío Pélagos, *Turk.* Ege Denizi 87 D5
Aeolian Islands *see* Isole Eolie
Afghanistan *country* C Asia 104-105
Africa 50-51
Africa, Horn of *physical region* Ethiopia/Somalia 122 A3
Afyon Turkey *prev.* Afyonkarahisar 98 B3
Afyonkarahisar *see* Afyon
Agadez Niger 57 G3
Agadir Morocco 52 B2
Agassiz Fracture Zone *tectonic feature* Pacific Ocean 135 E4
Agen France 73 B6
Āgra India 116 D3
Agrigento Italy 79 C7
Agrínio Greece 87 B5
Aguarico *river* Ecuador/Peru 40 B4
Aguascalientes Mexico 32 D4
Ahaggar *mountains* Algeria *var.* Hoggar 53 E4
Ahmadābād India 116 C4
Ahvāz Iran 102 C4
Ahvenanmaa see Åland
Aigaío Pélagos *see* Aegean Sea
Aintab *see* Gaziantep
Aïr, Massif de l' *region* Niger 57 G2
Aix-en-Provence France 73 D6
Ajaccio Corse, France 73 E7
Ajdābiyā Libya 53 G2
Ajmer India 116 D3
Akaba *see* Al 'Aqabah
Akchâr *desert* Mauritania 56 C2
Akimiski Island *island* Canada 20 C3
Akita Japan 112 D3
Akjoujt Mauritania 56 C2
Akmola *see* Astana
Akmolinsk *see* Astana
Akpatok Island *island* Canada 21 E1
Akra Kanestron *see* Palioúri, Akrotírio
Akron Ohio, USA 22 D3
Aksai Chin *disputed region* China/India 108 B4
Aktau Kazakhstan *prev.* Shevchenko 96 A4
Akureyri Iceland 65 E4
Akyab *see* Sittwe
Alabama *state* USA 30 D3
Alacant *see* Alicante
Alajuela Costa Rica 34 D4
Alamogordo New Mexico, USA 28 D3
Åland *island group* Finland *Fin.* Ahvenanmaa 67 D6
Al 'Aqabah Jordan *var.* Akaba 101 B7
Alaska *state* USA 18
Alaska, Gulf of *sea feature* Pacific Ocean 16 C3
Alaska Range *mountain range* Alaska, USA 18 C3
Albacete Spain 75 E3
Alba Iulia Romania 90 B4
Albania *country* SE Europe 83
Albany Australia 129 B7
Albany Georgia, USA 31 E3
Albany New York, USA 23 F3
Albany Oregon, USA 26 A3
Albany *river* Canada 20 B3

Al Başrah Iraq *var.* Basra 102 C4
Al Bayḑā' Libya 53 G2
Albert, Lake *lake* Uganda/Dem. Rep. Congo 59 E5
Alberta *province* Canada 19 E4
Albi France 73 C6
Albuquerque New Mexico, USA 28 D2
Alcácer do Sal Portugal 74 C4
Aldabra Group *island group* Seychelles 61 G2
Aleg Mauritania 56 C3
Aleksandriya *see* Oleksandriya
Aleksandropol' *see* Gyumri
Aleksinac Serbia 82 E4
Alençon France 72 B3
Alessandria Italy 78 B2
Ålesund Norway 67 A5
Aleutian Basin *undersea feature* Bering Sea 134 D1
Aleutian Islands *islands* Alaska, USA 18 A3
Aleutian Trench *undersea feature* Pacific Ocean 134 D1
Alexander Island *island* Antarctica 136 A3
Alexandra New Zealand133 B7
Alexandretta *see* İskenderun
Alexandria *see* Al Iskandarīyah
Alexandria Louisiana, USA 30 B3
Alexandroúpoli Greece 86 D3
Al Fāshir *see* El Fasher
Alföld *see* Great Hungarian Plain
Algarve *region* Portugal 74 C4
Algeciras Spain 74 D5
Algeria *country* N Africa 52-53
Alghero Italy 79 A5
Algiers *capital of* Algeria 52 D1
Al Ḩasakah Syria 100 D2
Al Ḩudaydah Yemen 103 B7
Al Hufūf Saudi Arabia 103 C5
Alicante Spain *Cat.* Alacant 75 F4
Alice Springs Australia 130 A4
Al Iskandarīyah Egypt *Eng.* Alexandria 54 B1
Al Ismā'īlīya Egypt *Eng.* Ismalia 54 B1
Al Jawf Saudi Arabia 102 B4
Al Jazīrah *region* Iraq/Syria 100 E2
Al Jīzah Egypt *var.* El Gîza 54 B1
Al Karak Jordan 101 B6
Al Khalīl *see* Hebron
Al Khārijah Egypt *var.* El Khârga 54 B2
Al Khums Libya 53 F2
Al Khurţūm *see* Khartoum
Alkmaar Netherlands 68 C2
Al Kufrah Libya 53 H4
Al Lādhiqīyah Syria *Eng.* Latakia 100 B3
Allahābād India 117 E4
Allenstein *see* Olsztyn
Allentown Pennsylvania, USA 23 F4
Alma-Ata *capital of* Kazakhstan *Rus./Kaz.* Almaty 96 C5
Al Madīnah Saudi Arabia *Eng.* Medina 102 A5
Al Mafraq Jordan 101 B5
Almalyk Uzbekistan *Uzb.* Olmaliq 105 E2
Al Manāmah *see* Manama
Al Marj Libya 53 G2
Almaty *see* Alma-Ata
Al Mawşil Iraq *Eng.* Mosul 102 B3
Almelo Netherlands 68 E3
Almería Spain 75 E5
Al Minyā Egypt 54 B2
Al Mukallā Yemen 103 C7
Alofi *capital of* Niue 127 F5
Alor, Kepulauan *island group* Indonesia 121 E5
Alps *mountain range* C Europe 62 D4
Al Qāhirah *see* Cairo
Al Qāmishlī Syria *var.* Kamishli 100 E1
Al Qunayţirah Syria 100 B4
Altai Mountains *mountain range* C Asia 108 C2
Altamura Italy 79 E5
Altar, Desierto de *Desert* Mexico/USA *var.* Sonoran Desert 32 A1
Altay China 108 C2
Altay Mongolia 108 D2
Altun Shan *mountain range* China 108 C3
Alturas California, USA 26 B4
Al Uqşur Egypt *Eng.* Luxor 54 B2
Alytus Lithuania *Pol.* Olita 89 B5
Amadeus, Lake *seasonal lake* Australia 129 E5
Amakusa-nada *island group* Japan 113 A6
Amami-Ō-shima *island* Japan 113 A8
Amarillo Texas, USA 29 E2
Amazon *river* South America 38 C3
Amazon Basin *region* C South America 42 D2
Ambanja Madagascar 61 G2
Ambarchik Russian Federation 97 G2
Ambato Ecuador 40 A4
Amboasary Madagascar 61 F4
Ambon Indonesia 121 F4
Ambositra Madagascar 61 G3
Ambriz Angola 60 B1
Amdo China 108 C4
Ameland *island* Netherlands 68 D1
American Falls Reservoir *Reservoir* Idaho, USA 26 E4
American Samoa *unincorporated territory* USA, Pacific Ocean 127 F4
Amersfoort Netherlands 68 D3
Amga *river* Russian Federation 95 F2
Amiens France 72 C3
Amīndīvi Islands *island group* India 114 C2
Amirante Islands *island group* Seychelles 61 H1
Amman *capital of* Jordan 101 B5
Ammassalik Greenland *var.* Angmagssalik 64 D4

Ammochostos *see* Gazimağusa
Āmol Iran 102 C3
Amorgós *island* Greece 87 D6
Amritsar India 116 D2
Amsterdam *capital of* Netherlands 68 C3
Amsterdam Island *island* French Southern and Antarctic Lands 123 C6
Am Timan Chad 58 C3
Amu Darya *river* C Asia 104 D3
Amundsen Gulf *sea feature* Canada 19 E2
Amundsen Plain *undersea feature* Pacific Ocean 136 B4
Amundsen Sea Antarctica 97 G4
Amur *river* E Asia 97 G4 107 E1
Anabar *river* Russian Federation 95 E2
Anadolu Dağları *see* Doğu Karadeniz Dağlarıı
Anadyr' Russian Federation 97 H1
Anápolis Brazil 43 F4
Anatolia *region* SE Europe 85 G3
Anchorage Alaska, USA 18 C3
Ancona Italy 78 C3
Andalucía *region* Spain 74 D4
Andaman Islands *island group* India 115 H2 119 A5
Andaman Sea Indian Ocean 122 D3
Andes *mountain range* South America 39 B6
Andijon Uzbekistan *Rus.* Andizhan 105 F2
Andhra Pradesh *state* India 115 E1
Andizhan *see* Andijon
Andorra *country* SW Europe 73 B6
Andorra la Vella *capital of* Andorra 73 B6
Ándros *island* Greece 87 D5
Andros Island *island* The Bahamas 36 C1
Angara *river* C Asia 95 D3
Ángel de la Guarda, Isla *island* Mexico 32 B2
Angel Falls *see* Salto Ángel
Angeles Philippines 121 E1
Ángel, Salto *waterfall* Venezuela *Eng.* Angel Falls 41 F2
Ångermanälven *river* Sweden 66 C4
Angers France 72 B4
Anglesey *island* Wales, UK 71 C5
Angmagssalik *see* Ammassalik
Angola *country* C Africa 60
Angola Basin *undersea feature* Atlantic Ocean 49 D6
Angora *see* Ankara
Angoulême France 73 B5
Angren Uzbekistan 105 E2
Anguilla *overseas territory* UK, West Indies 37
Anhui *province* China *var.* Anhwei, Wan 111 C5
Anhwei *see* Anhui
Anjouan *island* Comoros 61 F2
Ankara *capital of* Turkey *prev.* Angora 98 C3
Annaba Algeria 53 E1
An Nafūd *desert region* Saudi Arabia 102 B4
An Najaf Iraq *var.* Najaf 102 B4
Annapolis Maryland, USA 23 F4
Ann Arbor Michigan, USA 22 C3
Annecy France 73 D5
Anshan China 110 D4
Ansongo Mali 57 E3
Antakya Turkey *var.* Hatay 98 D4
Antalaha Madagascar 61 G2
Antalya Turkey *prev.* Adalia 98 B4
Antalya, Gulf of *see* Antalya Körfezi
Antalya Körfezi *sea feature* Mediterranean Sea *Eng.* Gulf of Antalya, *var.* Gulf of Adalia 98 B4
Antananarivo *capital of* Madagascar *prev.* Tananarive 61 G3
Antarctica 136
Antarctic Peninsula *peninsula* Antarctica 136 A2
Antequera Spain 74 D5
Anticosti, Île d' *island* Canada 21 F3
Antigua *island* Antigua & Barbuda 37 G3
Antigua & Barbuda *country* West Indies 37
Anti-Lebanon *mountains* Lebanon/Syria 100 B4
Antipodes Islands *island group* New Zealand124 D5
Antofagasta Chile 46 B2
Antsirañana Madagascar 61 G2
Antsohihy Madagascar 61 G2
Antwerp *see* Antwerpen
Antwerpen Belgium *Eng.* Antwerp 69 C5
Anyang China 110 C4
Aoga-shima *island* Japan 113 D6
Aomori Japan 112 D3
Aoraki *peak* New Zealand *var.* Cook, Mount 133 B6
Aosta Italy 78 A2
Aoukâr *Plateau* Mauritania 56 D3
Apeldoorn Netherlands 68 D3
Apennines *see* Appennino
Apia *capital of* Samoa 127 F4
Appalachian Mountains *mountain range* E USA 17 D5
Appennino *mountain range* Italy *Eng.* Apennines 78 C4
Apure *river* Venezuela 40 D2
Aqaba *see* Al 'Aqabah
Aqaba, Gulf of *sea feature* Red Sea *Ar.* Khalīj al 'Aqabah 101 A8
'Aqabah, Khalīj al *see* Aqaba, Gulf of
Āqchah Afghanistan *var.* Āqcheh 104 D3
Āqcheh *see* Āqchah
Arabian Basin *undersea feature* Indian Ocean 122 B3
Arabian Peninsula *peninsula* Asia 85 H5 94 B5 103 C5
Arabian Sea Indian Ocean 122 B3
Aracaju Brazil 43 H3
Arad Romania 90 B4

Arafura Sea Asia/Australasia 126 A4
Araguaia *river* Brazil 43 F3
Arāk Iran 102 C3
Araks *see* Aras
Arak's *see* Aras
Aral Sea *inland sea* Kazakhstan/Uzbekistan 94 C3
Araouane Mali 57 E2
Ararat, Mount *peak* Turkey *var.* Great Ararat, *Turk.* Büyükağrı Dağı 94 F3
Aras *river* SW Asia *Arm.* Arak's, *Per.* Rūd-e Aras, *Rus.* Araks, *Turk.* Aras Nehri 99 G3
Aras Nehri *see* Aras
Arauca Colombia 40 C2
Arauca *river* Colombia/ Venezuela 40 C2
Arbīl Iraq *Kurd.* Hawlēr 102 B3
Arctic Ocean 18-19 137
Arda *river* Bulgaria/Greece 86 C3
Ardabīl Iran 102 C3
Ardennes *region* W Europe 69 D7
Arendal Norway 67 A6
Arensburg *see* Kuressaare
Arequipa Peru 42 B4
Arezzo Italy 78 C3
Argentina *country* S South America 46-47
Argentine Basin *undersea feature* Atlantic Ocean 49 B7
Argun *river* China/Russian Federation 95 E3
Århus Denmark 67 A7
Arica Chile 46 B1
Arizona *state* USA 28 B2
Arkansas *state* USA 30 B1
Arkansas *river* C USA 17 C5
Arkhangel'sk Russian Federation 92 C3 96 C2
Arles France 73 D6
Arlington Texas, USA 29 G3
Arlington Virginia, USA 23 E4
Arlon Belgium 69 D8
Armenia *country* SW Asia 99 G2
Armenia Colombia 40 B3
Armidale Australia 131 D5
Arnhem Netherlands 68 D4
Arnhem Land *region* Australia 128 E2
Arno *river* Italy 78 B3
Arran *island* Scotland, UK 70 C4
Ar Raqqah Syria 100 C2
Arras France 72 C3
Ar Riyāḑ *see* Riyadh
Ar Rub 'al Khālī *desert* Asia *Eng.* Empty Quarter, Great Sandy Desert 103 C6
Ar Rustāq Oman *var.* Rostak 103 D5
Artesia New Mexico, USA 28 D3
Artigas Uruguay 44 B4
Aru, Kepulauan *island group* Indonesia 121 G5
Arua Uganda 55 B6
Aruba *constituent country* Netherlands, West Indies 37 E5
Arusha Tanzania 55 C7
Asad, Buḩayrat al *Lake* Syria *Eng.* Lake Assad 100 C2
Asadābād Afghanistan 105 E4
Asahikawa Japan 112 D2
Asamankese Ghana 57 E5
Ascension Island *overseas territory* UK, Atlantic Ocean 49 C5
Ascoli Piceno Italy 78 C4
'Aseb Eritrea *var.* Assab 54 D4
Ashburton New Zealand 133 C6
Asheville North Carolina, USA 31 E1
Aşgabat *capital of* Turkmenistan *prev.* Ashkhabad, Poltoratsk 104 C3
Ashkhabad *see* Aşgabat
Ashmore and Cartier Islands *Australian external territory* Indian Ocean 124 A3
Ash Shāriqah United Arab Emirates *Eng.* Sharjah 103 D5
Asia 94-95 106-107
Asmara *capital of* Eritrea *Amh.* Asmera 54 C4
Asmera *see* Asmara
Assab *see* 'Aseb
As Salţ Jordan *var.* Salt 101 B5
Assamakka Niger 57 F2
Assen Netherlands 68 E2
Assad, Lake *see* Asad, Buḩayrat al
As Sulayyil Saudi Arabia 103 B6
As Suwaydā' Syria 101 B5
As Suways Egypt *Eng.* Suez 54 B1
Astana *country capital* Kazakhstan *prev.* Akmola, Akmolinsk, Tselinograd, Kaz. Aqmola. 96 C4
Astoria Oregon, USA 26 A2
Astrakhan' Russian Federation 93 B7
Astypálaia *island* Greece 87 D6
Asunción *capital of* Paraguay 44 B3
Aswān Egypt 54 B2
Asyūţ Egypt 54 B2
Atacama Desert *desert* Chile 46 B2
Atamyrat *prev.* Kerki. Turkmenistan 104 D3
Aţâr Mauritania 56 C2
Atbara Sudan 54 C3
Athabasca, Lake *lake* Canada 19 F4
Athens *capital of* Greece *Gk.* Athína, *prev.* Athínai 87 C5
Athens Georgia, USA 31 E2
Athína *see* Athens
Athínai *see* Athens
Athlone Ireland 71 B5
Ati Chad 58 C3
Atlanta Georgia, USA 30 D2
Atlantic City New Jersey, USA 23 F4
Atlantic Ocean 48-49
Atlantic-Indian Basin *undersea feature* Indian Ocean 136 B1
Atlantic-Indian Ridge *undersea feature* Atlantic Ocean 49 D7
Atlas Mountains *mountain range* Morocco 52 C2
Aţ Ţalfīlah Jordan 101 B6

Aţ Ţā'if Saudi Arabia 102 B6
Attapu Laos 119 E5
Attawapiskat Canada 20 C3
Attawapiskat *river* Canada 20 B3
Attu Island *island* Alaska, USA 18 A2
Auch France 73 B6
Auckland New Zealand 132 D3
Auckland Islands *island group* New Zealand124 D5
Augsburg Germany 77 C6
Augusta Australia 129 B7
Augusta Georgia, USA 31 E2
Augusta Maine, USA 23 G2
Aurillac France 73 C5
Aurora Colorado, USA 24 D4
Aurora Illinois, USA 22 B3
Aussig *see* Ústí nad Labem
Austin Texas, USA 29 G4
Australasia 124-125
Australes, Îles *island group* French Polynesia 125 F4
Austral Fracture Zone *tectonic feature* Pacific Ocean 125 H4
Australia *country* Pacific Ocean 124
Australian Alps Australia 131 D7
Australian Capital Territory *territory* Australia *abbrev.* A.C.T. *131* D6
Austria *country* C Europe 77
Auxerre France 72 C4
Avarua *capital of* Cook Islands 127 G5
Aveiro Portugal 74 C2
Avignon France 73 D6
Ávila Spain 74 D2
Avilés Spain 74 D1
Awbārī Libya 53 F3
Axel Heiberg Island *island* Canada 19 F1
Axios *see* Vardar
Ayacucho Peru 42 B4
Aydarko'l Ko'li *lake* Uzbekistan *var.* Aydarkŭl 104 D2
Aydarkŭl *see* Aydarko'l Ko'li
Aydın Turkey 98 A3
Ayer's Rock *see* Uluru
Ayr Scotland, UK 70 C4
Ayutthaya Thailand 119 C5
Ayvalık Turkey 98 A3
Azaouâd *desert* Mali 57 E2
A'zāz Syria 100 B2
Azerbaijan *country* SW Asia 99 G2
Azores *islands* Portugal, Atlantic Ocean 48 C3
Azov, Sea of Black Sea *Ukr.* Azovs'ke More, *Rus.* Azovskoye More 93 A6 91 G4
Azovs'ke More *see* Azov, Sea of
Azovskoye More *see* Azov, Sea of
Azul Argentina 46 D4
Azur, Côte d' *coastal region* France 73 E6
Az Zarqā' Jordan 101 B5
Az Zāwiyah Libya 53 F2

B

Baalbek Lebanon *var.* Ba'labakk 100 B4
Babeldaob *Island* Palau 124 B2
Babruysk/Bobruysk Belarus *Rus.* Bobruysk 89 D6
Babuyan Channel *channel* Philippines 121 E1
Bacan, Pulau *island* Indonesia 121 F4
Bačka Topola Serbia 82 D3
Bacău Romania 90 C4
Badajoz Spain 74 C4
Baden Switzerland 77 E6
Bādiyat ash Shām *see* Syrian Desert
Baffin Bay *sea feature* Atlantic Ocean 48 B1
Baffin Island *island* Canada 19 G2
Bafing *river* Africa 56 C3
Bafoussam Cameroon 58 B4
Bagdad *see* Baghdad
Bagé Brazil 44 C4
Baghdad *capital of* Iraq *var.* Bagdad, *Ar.* Baghdād 102 B3
Baghdād *see* Baghdad
Baghlān Afghanistan 105 E3
Bago Myanmar *prev.* Pegu 118 B4
Bagoé *river* Côte d'Ivoire/Mali 56 D4
Baguio Philippines 121 E1
Bahamas, The *country* West Indies, Atlantic Ocean 36
Baharden *see* Baharly
Baharly Turkmenistan *prev.* Baharden, Bäherden, Bakharden, Bakherden 104 B3
Bahāwalpur Pakistan 116 C3
Bäherden *see* Baharly
Bahía Blanca Argentina 47 C5
Bahía, Islas de la *islands* Honduras 34 D2
Bahir Dar Ethiopia 54 C4
Bahrain *country* SW Asia 103 C5
Baia Mare Romania 90 B3
Baikal, Lake *see* Baykal, Ozero
Bairiki *capital of* Kiribati 127 E2
Baishan China 110 E3
Baja Hungary 81 C7
Baja California *peninsula* Mexico *Eng.* Lower California 32 B2
Bajo Nuevo *island* Colombia 35 F2
Baker Oregon, USA 26 C3
Baker & Howland Islands *unincorporated territory* USA, Pacific Ocean 125 E2
Bakersfield California, USA 27 C7
Bakharden *see* Baharly
Bakherden *see* Baharly
Bākhtarān *see* Kermānshāh
Bakı *see* Baku
Baku *capital of* Azerbaijan *Az.* Bakı, *var.* Baky 99 H2
Baky *see* Baku
Balabac Strait *sea feature* South China Sea/Sulu Sea 120 D2

Ba‘labakk *see* Baalbek
Balakovo Russian Federation 93 C6
Bālā Murghāb Afghanistan 104 D4
Balaton *lake* Hungary *var.* Lake Balaton, *Ger.* Plattensee 81 C7
Balaton, Lake *see* Balaton
Balbina, Represa *Reservoir* Brazil 42 D2
Baleares, Islas *island group* Spain *Eng.* Balearic Islands 75 H3
Balearic Islands *see* Baleares, Islas
Bali *island* Indonesia 120 D5
Balıkesir Turkey 98 A3
Balikpapan Indonesia 120 D4
Balkanabat Turkmenistan *prev.* Nebitdag 104 B2
Balkan Mountains *mountain range* Bulgaria *Bul.* Stara Planina 86 C2
Balkhash Kazakhstan 96 C5
Balkhash, Lake *see* Balkhash, Ozero
Balkhash, Ozero *lake* Kazakhstan *Eng.* Lake Balkhash 94 C3
Ballarat Australia 131 C7
Balsas *river* Mexico 33 E5
Bălţi Moldova 90 D3
Baltic Port *see* Paldiski
Baltic Sea Atlantic Ocean 67 C7
Baltimore Maryland, USA 23 F4
Baltischport *see* Paldiski
Baltiski *see* Paldiski
Bamako *capital of* Mali 56 D3
Bambari Central African Republic 58 D4
Bamenda Cameroon 58 B4
Banaba *island* Kiribati *prev.* Ocean Island 127 E2
Bandaaceh Indonesia 120 A3
Banda, Laut *see* Banda Sea
Banda Sea *sea feature* Pacific Ocean *Ind.* Laut Banda 121 F4
Bandar-e ‘Abbās Iran 102 D4
Bandar-e Būshehr Iran 102 C4
Bandar Lampung Indonesia *prev.* Tanjungkarang 120 C4
Bandar Seri Begawan *capital of* Brunei 120 D3
Bandon Oregon, USA 26 A3
Bandundu Dem. Rep. Congo 59 C6
Bandung Indonesia 120 C5
Bangalore India 114 D2
Banggai, Kepulauan *island group* Indonesia 121 E4
Banghāzī Libya *Eng.* Benghazi 53 G2
Bangka, Palau *island* Indonesia 120 C4
Bangkok *capital of* Thailand *Th.* Krung Thep 119 C5
Bangladesh *country* S Asia 117
Bangor Northern Ireland, UK 71 B5
Bangor Maine, USA 23 G2
Bangui *capital of* Central African Republic 59 C5
Bani *river* Mali 56 D3
Banī Suwayf Egypt *var.* Beni Suef 54 B1
Banja Luka Bosnia & Herzegovina 82 B3
Banjarmasin Indonesia 120 D4
Banjul *capital of* Gambia 56 B3
Banks Island *island* Canada 19 E2
Banks Islands *island group* Vanuatu, Pacific Ocean 126 D4
Banks Peninsula *peninsula* New Zealand133 C6
Banks Strait *sea feature* Tasman Sea 131 C7
Banská Bystrica Slovakia *Ger.* Neusohl, *Hung.* Besztercebánya 81 C6
Bantry Bay *sea feature* Ireland 71 A6
Banyo Cameroon 58 B4
Banzare Seamounts *undersea feature* Indian Ocean 123 C7
Baotou China 109 F3
Baranavichy/Baranovichi Belarus *Rus.* Baranovichi, *Pol.* Baranowicze 89 C6
Baranovichi *see* Baranavichy/ Baranovichi
Baranowicze *see* Baranavichy/ Baranovichi
Barbados *country* West Indies 37 H4
Barbuda *island* Antigua & Barbuda 37 G3
Barcaldine Australia 130 C4
Barcelona Spain 75 G2
Barcelona Venezuela 41 E1
Barcolod City Philippines 121 E2
Bareilly India 117 E3
Barentsburg Svalbard 65 F2
Barentsøya *island* Svalbard 65 G2
Barents Sea Arctic Ocean 137 H5
Bari Italy 79 E5
Barinas Venezuela 40 D2
Barisan, Pegunungan *mountains* Indonesia 120 B4
Barkly Tableland *plateau* Australia 130 B3
Barlavento, Ilhas de *island group* Cape Verde *var.* Windward Islands 56 A2
Bar-le-Duc France 72 D3
Barlee, Lake *lake* Australia 129 B 5
Barlee Range *mountain range* Australia 128 B4
Barnaul Russian Federation 96 D4
Barnstaple England, UK 71 C7
Barquisimeto Venezuela 40 D1
Barra *island* Scotland, UK 70 B3
Barranquilla Colombia 40 B1
Barrier Range *mountain range* Australia 131 C5
Barrow *river* Ireland 71 B6
Barstow California, USA 27 C7
Bartang *river* Tajikistan 105 F3
Bartica Guyana 41 G2
Baruun-Urt Mongolia 109 F2
Barwon River *river* Australia 131 D5
Barysaw Belarus *Rus.* Borisov 89 D5
Basarabeasca Moldova 90 D4
Basel Switzerland 77 B6

Basra *see* Al Başrah
Bassein *see* Pathein
Basse-Terre *capital of* Guadeloupe 37 G4
Basseterre *capital of* St Kitts & Nevis 37 G3
Bass Strait *sea feature* Australia 131 C7
Bastia Corse, France 73 E7
Bastogne Belgium 69 D7
Bata Equatorial Guinea 58 A5
Batangas Philippines 121 E2
Bătdâmbâng Cambodia 119 D5
Bath England, UK 71 D6
Bathurst Canada 21 F4
Bathurst Island *island* Australia 128 D2
Bathurst Island *island* Canada 19 F2
Bāţin, Wādī al *dry watercourse* Asia 102 C4
Batman Turkey *var.* İluh 99 E4
Batna Algeria 53 E1
Baton Rouge Louisiana, USA 30 B3
Batticaloa Sri Lanka 115 E3
Batumi Georgia 99 F2
Bauru Brazil 44 D2
Bavarian Alps *mountains* Austria/Germany 77 C6
Bayamo Cuba 36 C2
Bayan Har Shan *mountain range* China 108 D4
Bayanhongor Mongolia 108 D2
Bay City Michigan, USA 22 C3
Baydhabo Somalia 55 D6
Baykal, Ozero *lake* Russian Federation *Eng.* Lake Baikal 95 E3
Bayonne France 73 A6
Baýramaly Turkmenistan 104 C3
Bayrūt *see* Beirut
Beaufort Sea Arctic Ocean 137 F2
Beaufort West South Africa 60 D5
Beaumont Texas, USA 29 H4
Beauvais France 72 C3
Béchar Algeria 52 C2
Be'er Sheva' Israel 101 A6
Beijing *capital of* China *var.* Peking 110 C4
Beira Mozambique 61 E3
Beirut *capital of* Lebanon *var.* Beyrouth, Bayrūt 100 B4
Beja Portugal 74 C4
Béjaïa Algeria 53 E1
Bek-Budi *see* Karshi
Békéscsaba Hungary 81 D7
Belarus *country* E Europe *var.* Belorusia 89
Belau see Palau
Belcher Islands *islands* Canada 20 C2
Beledweyne Somalia 55 D5
Belém Brazil 43 F2
Belfast Northern Ireland, UK 71 B5
Belfort France 72 E4
Belgaum India 114 C1
Belgium *country* W Europe 69
Belgorod Russian Federation 93 A5
Belgrade *capital of* Serbia *SCr.* Beograd 82 D3
Belitung, Pulau *island* Indonesia 120 C4
Belize *country* Central America 34
Belize City Belize 34 C1
Belle Île *island* France 72 A4
Belle Isle, Strait of *sea feature* Canada 21 G3
Bellevue Washington, USA 26 B2
Bellingham Washington, USA 26 B1
Bellingshausen Sea Antarctica 136 A3
Bello Colombia 40 B2
Bellville South Africa 60 C5
Belmopan *capital of* Belize 34 C1
Belo Horizonte Brazil 45 F1
Belorussia *see* Belarus
Belostok *see* Białystok
Beloye More Arctic Ocean *Eng.* White Sea 63 F1
Belyy, Ostrov *island* Russian Federation 137 H4
Bend Oregon, USA 26 B3
Bendery *see* Tighina
Bendigo Australia 131 C7
Benevento Italy 79 D5
Bengal, Bay of *sea feature* Indian Ocean 122 D3
Bengbu China 111 D5
Benghazi *see* Banghāzī
Bengkulu Indonesia 120 B4
Benguela Angola 60 B2
Beni *river* Bolivia 42 C4
Benidorm Spain 75 F4
Beni-Mellel Morocco 52 C2
Benin *country* N Africa *prev.* Dahomey 57
Benin, Bight of *sea feature* W Africa 57 F5
Benin City Nigeria 57 F5
Beni Suef *see* Banī Suwayf
Ben Nevis *mountain* Scotland, UK 70 C3
Benue *river* Cameroon/Nigeria 57 G4
Beograd *see* Belgrade
Berat Albania 83 D6
Berbera Somalia 54 D4
Berbérati Central African Republic 58 C5
Berdyans'k Ukraine 91 G4
Bereket Turkmenistan *prev.* *Gazandzhyk, var.* Kazandzhik, *Turkm.* Gazanjyk 104 B2
Berezina *see* Byerazino
Bergamo Italy 78 B2
Bergen Norway 67 A5
Bergse Maas *river* Netherlands 68 D4
Bering Sea Pacific Ocean 134 D1
Bering Strait *sea feature* Bering Sea/Chukchi Sea 134 D1
Berkeley California, USA 27 B6
Berlin *capital of* Germany 76 D3
Bermejo *river* Argentina 46 D2
Bermuda *overseas territory* UK, Atlantic Ocean 48 B3
Bern *capital of* Switzerland *Fr.* Berne 77 B7

Berne *see* Bern
Berner Alpen *mountain range* Switzerland 77 B7
Bertoua Cameroon 59 B5
Besançon France 72 D4
Besztercebánya *see* Banská Bystrica
Bethlehem West Bank 101 A5
Beyrouth *see* Beirut
Béziers France 73 C6
Bezmein *see* Abadan
Bhamo Myanmar 118 B2
Bhāvnagar India 116 C4
Bhōpal India 116 D4
Bhutan *country* S Asia 117
Biak, Pulau *island* Indonesia 121 G4
Białystok Poland *Rus.* Belostok 80 E3
Biel Switzerland 77 B7
Bielefeld Germany 76 B4
Bielitz-Biala *see* Bielsko-Biała
Bielsko-Biała Poland *Ger.* Bielitz-Biala 81 C5
Bié Plateau *upland* Angola 51 C6
Bighorn Mountains *mountains* C USA 24 C2
Bignona Senegal 56 B3
Big Spring Texas, USA 29 E3
Bihać Bosnia & Herzegovina 82 B3
Bihār *state* India 117 F3
Bijelo Polje Montenegro 82 D4
Bikāner India 116 C3
Bila Tserkva Ukraine 91 E2
Bilbao Spain 75 E1
Billings Montana, USA 24 C2
Bilma, Grand Erg de *desert* Niger 57 G3
Biloela Australia 130 D4
Biloxi Mississippi, USA 30 C3
Biltine Chad 58 D3
Binghamton New York, USA 23 F3
Birāk Libya 53 F3
Birātnagar Nepal 117 F3
Birmingham England, UK 71 D6
Birmingham Alabama, USA 30 D2
Bîr Mogreïn Mauritania 56 C1
Birsen *see* Biržai
Biržai Lithuania *Ger.* Birsen 88 C4
Biscay, Bay of *sea feature* Atlantic Ocean 62 C4
Bishkek *capital of* Kyrgyzstan *prev.* Frunze, Pishpek 105 F2
Bishop California, USA 27 C6
Biskra Algeria 53 E2
Bismarck North Dakota, USA 25 E2
Bismarck Archipelago *island group* Papua New Guinea 126 B3
Bismarck Sea *sea* Pacific Ocean 124 B2
Bissau *capital of* Guinea-Bissau 56 B4
Bitola Macedonia 83 E6
Bitterroot Range *mountains* NW USA 26 D2
Biwa-ko *lake* Japan 113 C5
Bizerte Tunisia 53 E1
Bjelovar Croatia 82 B2
Bjørnøya *Island* N Norway *Eng.* Bear Island 65 G3
Black Drin *river* Albania/ Macedonia 83 D5
Black Forest *see* Schwarzwald
Black Hills *mountains* C USA 24 D3
Blackpool England, UK 71 D5
Black River *river* China/Vietnam 118 D3
Black Sea Asia/Europe 63 F4
Black Volta *river* Ghana/Côte d'Ivoire 57 E4
Blackwater *river* Ireland 71 A6
Blagoevgrad Bulgaria 86 C3
Blagoveshchensk Russian Federation 97 G4
Blanca, Bahía *sea feature* Argentina 39 D5
Blanche, Lake *lake* Australia 131 B5
Blantyre Malawi 61 E2
Blenheim New Zealand 133 D5
Blida Algeria 52 D1
Bloemfontein *financial capital of* South Africa 60 D4
Blois France 72 C4
Bloomington Indiana, USA 22 C4
Bluefields Nicaragua 35 E3
Blue Mountains *mountains* W USA 26 C2
Blue Nile *river* Ethiopia/Sudan 54 C4
Blumenau Brazil 44 D3
Bo Sierra Leone 56 C4
Boa Vista Brazil 42 D1
Boa Vista *island* Cape Verde 56 A3
Bobo-Dioulasso Burkina Faso 56 D4
Bobruysk *see* Babruysk/ Bobruysk
Boca de la Serpiente *see* Serpent's Mouth, The
Bochum Germany 76 B4
Bodø Norway 66 C3
Bodrum Turkey 98 A4
Bogor Indonesia 120 C5
Bogotá *capital of* Colombia 40 B3
Bo Hai *sea feature* Yellow Sea 110 D4
Bohemian Forest *region* Germany 77 D5
Bohol Sea *Sea* Philippines 121 E2
Boise Idaho, USA 26 D3
Boké Guinea 56 C4
Bokhara *see* Buxoro
Bol Chad 58 B3
Bolivia *country* C South America 42-43
Bologna Italy 78 C3
Bolton England, UK 71 D5
Bolzano Italy *Ger.* Bozen 78 C2
Boma Dem. Rep. Congo 59 B7
Bombay *see* Mumbai
Bomu *river* Central African Republic/Dem. Rep. Congo 59 D5
Bonaire *special municipality* Netherlands, West Indies 37 E5

Bongo, Massif des *upland* Central African Republic 58 D4
Bongor Chad 58 C3
Bonn Germany 76 B4
Boosaaso Somalia 54 E4
Borås Sweden 67 B7
Bordeaux France 73 B5
Borger Texas, USA 29 E2
Borisov *see* Barysaw
Borlänge Sweden 67 C6
Borneo *island* SE Asia 120-121
Bornholm *island* Denmark 67 C8
Bosanski Šamac Bosnia & Herzegovina 82 C3
Bosna *river* Bosnia & Herzegovina 82 C3
Bosna I Hercegovina, Federacija Admin. region *republic* Bosnia and Herzegovina 82 C4
Bosnia & Herzegovina *country* SE Europe 82-83
Bosporus *sea feature* Turkey *Turk.* İstanbul Boğazi 98 B2
Bossangoa Central African Republic 58 C4
Bosten Hu *Lake* China 108 C3
Boston Massachusetts, USA 23 G3
Bothnia, Gulf of *sea feature* Baltic Sea 67 C5
Botoşani Romania 90 C3
Botswana *country* southern Africa 60
Bouar Central African Republic 58 C4
Bougainville Island *island* Papua New Guinea 126 C3
Bougouni Mali 56 D4
Boulder Colorado, USA 24 C4
Boulogne-sur-Mer France 72 C2
Bourges France 72 C4
Bourgogne *region* France *Eng.* Burgundy 72 D4
Bourke Australia 131 C5
Bournemouth England, UK 71 D7
Bouvet Island *external territory* Norway, Atlantic Ocean 49 D7
Bowen Australia 130 D3
Bowling Green Kentucky, USA 22 C5
Bozeman Montana, USA 24 B2
Bozen *see* Bolzano
Brač *island* Croatia 82 B4
Bradford England, UK 71 D5
Braga Portugal 74 C2
Bragança Portugal 74 C2
Brahmaputra *river* Asia 117 G3
Brăila Romania 90 D4
Brainerd Minnesota, USA 25 F2
Brandon Canada 19 F5
Brasília *capital of* Brazil 43 F4
Braşov Romania 90 C4
Bratislava *capital of* Slovakia *Ger.* Pressburg, *Hung.* Pozsony 81 C6
Bratsk Russian Federation 97 E4
Braunau am Inn Austria 77 D6
Braunschweig Germany *Eng.* Brunswick 76 C4
Brazil *country* South America 42-43
Brazil Basin *undersea feature* Atlantic Ocean 49 C5
Brazilian Highlands *upland* Brazil 43 G4
Brazos *river* SW USA 29 G3
Brazzaville *capital of* Congo 59 B6
Brecon Beacons *hills* Wales, UK 71 C6
Breda Netherlands 68 C4
Bregenz Austria 77 B7
Bremen Germany 76 B3
Bremerhaven Germany 76 B3
Brescia Italy 78 B2
Breslau *see* Wrocław
Brest Belarus *Pol.* Brześć nad Bugiem, *prev.* Brześć Litewski, *Rus.* Brest-Litovsk 89 B6
Brest France 72 A3
Brest-Litovsk *see* Brest
Bretagne *region* France *Eng.* Brittany 72 A3
Brezhnev *see* Naberezhnyye Chelny
Bria Central African Republic 58 D4
Bridgetown *capital of* Barbados 37 H4
Brig Switzerland 77 B5
Brighton England, UK 71 E7
Brindisi Italy 79 E5
Brisbane Australia 131 E5
Bristol England, UK 71 D6
British Columbia *province* Canada 18-19
British Indian Ocean Territory *overseas territory* UK, Indian Ocean 122 C4
British Isles *islands* W Europe 70-71
British Virgin Islands *overseas territory* UK, West Indies 37
Brittany *see* Bretagne
Brno Czech Republic *Ger.* Brünn 81 B5
Broken Arrow Oklahoma, USA 29 G1
Broken Hill Australia 131 B6
Broken Ridge *undersea feature* Indian Ocean 123 D6
Bromberg *see* Bydgoszcz
Brooks Range *mountains* Alaska, USA 18 D2
Brookton Australia 129 B6
Broome Australia 128 C3
Brownfield Texas, USA 29 E2
Brownsville Texas, USA 29 G5
Bruges *see* Brugge
Brugge Belgium *Fr.* Bruges 69 A5
Brunei *country* E Asia 120 D3
Brünn *see* Brno
Brunswick Georgia, USA 31 E3
Brunswick *see* Braunschweig
Brusa *see* Bursa
Brussel *see* Brussels
Brussels *capital of* Belgium *Fr.* Bruxelles, *Flem.* Brussel 69 C6
Brüx *see* Most
Bruxelles *see* Brussels
Bryan Texas, USA 29 G3

Bryansk Russian Federation 93 A5 96 A2
Brześć Litewski *see* Brest
Brześć nad Bugiem *see* Brest
Bucaramanga Colombia 40 C2
Buchanan Liberia 56 C5
Bucharest *capital of* Romania 90 C5
Budapest *capital of* Hungary 81 C6
Budweis *see* České Budějovice
Buenaventura Colombia 40 B3
Buenos Aires *capital of* Argentina 46 D4
Buenos Aires, Lago *lake* Argentina/Chile 47 B6
Buffalo New York, USA 23 E3
Bug *river* E Europe 90 C1
Bujumbura *capital of* Burundi *prev.* Usumbura 55 B7
Bukavu Dem. Rep. Congo 59 E6
Bukhara *see* Buxoro
Bulawayo Zimbabwe 60 D3
Bulgan Mongolia 109 E2
Bulgaria *country* E Europe 86
Bumba Dem. Rep. Congo 59 D5
Bunbury Australia 129 B6
Bundaberg Australia 130 E4
Bunia Dem. Rep. Congo 59 E5
Buraydah Saudi Arabia 103 B5
Burē Ethiopia 54 C4
Burgas Bulgaria 86 E2
Burgos Spain 75 E2
Burgundy *see* Bourgogne
Burketown Australia 130 B3
Burkina Faso *country* W Africa 57
Burlington Iowa, USA 25 G4
Burlington Vermont, USA 23 F2
Burma *see* Myanmar
Burnie Tasmania 131 C8
Burns Oregon, USA 26 C3
Bursa Turkey *prev.* Brusa 98 B3
BūrSa'īd Egypt *Eng.* Port Said 54 B1
Burtnieku Ezers *lake* Latvia 88 C3
Buru, Pulau *island* Indonesia 121 E4
Burundi *country* C Africa 55
Busan South Korea *prev.* Pusan110 E4
Busselton Australia 129 B7
Butembo Dem. Rep. Congo 59 E5
Buton, Pulau *Island* Indonesia 121 E4
Butte Montana, USA 24 B2
Butuan Philippines 121 F2
Buxoro Uzbekistan *var.* Bokhara, *Rus.* Bukhara 104 D2
Büyükağrı Dağı *see* Ararat, Mount
Buzău Romania 90 C4
Büzmeýin *see* Abadan
Byarezina *river* Belarus *Rus.* Berezina 89 D6
Bydgoszcz Poland *Ger.* Bromberg 80 C3
Byzantium *see* İstanbul

C

Caazapá Paraguay 44 C3
Cabanatuan Philippines 121 E1
Cabimas Venezuela 40 C1
Cabinda *exclave* Angola 60 B1
Cabot Strait *sea feature* Atlantic Ocean 21 G4
Čačak Serbia 82 D4
Cáceres Spain 74 D3
Cachoeiro de Itapemirim Brazil 45 F1
Cadiz Philippines 121 E2
Cádiz Spain 74 D5
Caen France 72 B3
Cagayan de Oro Philippines 121 F2
Cagliari Italy 79 A5
Cahors France 73 B5
Cairns Australia 130 D3
Cairo *capital of* Egypt *Ar.* Al Qāhirah, *var.* El Qâhira 54 B1
Čakovec Croatia 82 B2
Calabar Nigeria 57 G5
Calabria *region* Italy 79 D6
Calafate *see* El Calafate
Calais France 72 C2
Calais Maine, USA 23 H1
Calama Chile 46 B2
Calbayog Philippines 121 F2
Calcutta *see* Kolkata
Caldas da Rainha Portugal 74 B3
Caldwell Idaho, USA 27 C3
Caleta Olivia Argentina 47 C6
Calgary Canada 19 E5
Cali Colombia 40 A3
Calicut India *see* Kozhikode 114 D2
California *state* USA 26-27
California, Golfo de *sea feature* Pacific Ocean *Eng.* California, Gulf of 32 B2 123 F2
Callabonna, Lake *lake* Australia131 B5
Callao Peru 42 A3
Caltanissetta Italy 79 C7
Camagüey Cuba 36 C2
Cambodia *country* SE Asia *Cam.* Kampuchea 119
Cambridge England, UK 71 E6
Cambridge New Zealand132 D2
Cameroon *country* W Africa 58-59
Campbell Plateau *undersea feature* Pacific Ocean 134 C5
Campeche Mexico 33 G4
Campeche, Bahía de *sea feature* Mexico *Eng.* Gulf of Campeche 33 G4
Campina Grande Brazil 43 H3
Campinas Brazil 45 E2
Campo Grande Brazil 44 C1
Campos Brazil 45 F2
Canada *country* North America 16-17
Canada Basin *undersea feature* Arctic Ocean *var.* Laurentian Basin 137 F2
Canadian River *river* SW USA 29 E2
Çanakkale Turkey 98 A3
Çanakkale Boğazı *see* Dardanelles
Canarias, Islas *islands* Spain *Eng.* Canary Islands 50 A2

Canary Basin *undersea feature* Atlantic Ocean 48 C4
Canary Islands *see* Canarias, Islas
Canaveral, Cape *coastal feature* Florida, USA 31 F4
Canberra *capital of* Australia 131 D6
Cancún Mexico 33 H3
Caniapiscau *river* Canada 21 E2
Caniapiscau, Réservoir *Reservoir* Canada 21 E3
Canik Dağları *mountains* Turkey 98 D2
Çankırı Turkey 98 C2
Cannes France 73 D6
Canoas Brazil 44 D4
Canterbury England, UK 71 E6
Canterbury Bight *sea feature* Pacific Ocean 133 C6
Canterbury Plains *plain* New Zealand 133 B6
Cân Thơ Vietnam 119 D6
Canton Ohio, USA 22 D4
Canton *see* Guangzhou
Cape Basin *undersea feature* Atlantic Ocean 49 D6
Cape Town *legislative capital of* South Africa 60 C5
Cape Verde *country* Atlantic Ocean 56 A2
Cape Verde Basin *undersea feature* Atlantic Ocean 48 C4
Cape York Peninsula *peninsula* Australia 124 B3
Cap-Haïtien Haiti 36 D3
Capri, Isola di *island* Italy 79 D5
Caquetá *river* Colombia 40 C4
CAR *see* Central African Republic
Caracas *capital of* Venezuela 40 D1
Carazinho Brazil 44 C3
Carbondale Illinois, USA 22 B5
Carcassonne France 73 C6
Cardiff Wales, UK 71 C6
Cardigan Bay *sea feature* Wales, UK 71 C6
Carey, Lake *lake* Australia 129 C5
Caribbean Sea Atlantic Ocean 36-37
Carlisle England, UK 70 D4
Carlsbad New Mexico, USA 28 D3
Carlsberg Ridge *undersea feature* Indian Ocean 122 B4
Carnavon Australia 128 A5
Carnegie, Lake *lake* Australia 129 C5
Carolina Brazil 43 F3
Caroline Island *see* Millennium Island
Caroline Islands *island group* Micronesia 126 B1
Caroní *river* Venezuela 41 F2
Carpathian Mountains *mountain range* E Europe *var.* Carpathians 63 E4
Carpathians *see* Carpathian Mountains
Carpaţii Meridionali *mountain range* Romania *Eng.* South Carpathians, Transylvanian Alps 90 B4
Carpentaria, Gulf of *sea feature* Australia 130 B2
Carson City Nevada, USA 27 B5
Cartagena Colombia 40 B1
Cartagena Spain 75 F4
Cartago Costa Rica 35 E4
Cartwright Canada 21 G2
Carúpano Venezuela 41 E1
Casablanca Morocco 52 C2
Casa Grande Arizona, USA 28 B3
Cascade Range *mountain range* Canada/USA 26 B2
Cascais Portugal 74 B3
Casper Wyoming, USA 24 C3
Caspian Sea *inland sea* Asia/ Europe 94 B4
Castellón de la Plana Spain 75 F3
Castelo Branco Portugal 74 C3
Castries *capital of* St Lucia 37 G4
Castro Chile 47 B6
Cat Island *island* The Bahamas 36 D1
Catania Italy 79 D7
Catanzaro Italy 79 D6
Cauca *river* Colombia 40 B2
Caucasus *mountains* Asia/ Europe 93 A7
Caura *river* Venezuela 41 E2
Caviana, Ilha *island* Brazil 43 F1
Cawnpore *see* Kānpur
Caxias do Sul Brazil 44 D4
Cayenne *capital of* French Guiana 41 H3
Cayman Islands *overseas territory* UK, West Indies 36
Cebu Philippines 121 E2
Cedar Rapids Iowa, USA 25 G3
Cedros, Isla *island* Mexico 32 A2
Ceduna Australia131 A6
Cefalù Italy 79 C6
Celebes *see* Sulawesi
Celebes Sea Pacific Ocean *Ind.* Laut Sulawesi 134 B3
Celje Slovenia 77 E7
Central African Republic *country* C Africa *abbrev.* CAR 58-59
Central, Cordillera *mountain range* Philippines 121 E1
Central Makrān Range *mountains* Pakistan 116 A3
Central Pacific Basin *undersea feature* Pacific Ocean 125 E1
Central Russian Upland *upland* Russian Federation 94 B3
Central Siberian Plateau *see* Srednesibirskoye Ploskogor'ye
Central Siberian Uplands *see* Srednesibirskoye Ploskogor'ye
Central, Sistema *mountain range* Spain 74 D3
Cephalonia *see* Kefalloniá
Ceram Sea *Sea* Indonesia 121 F4
Cernăuţi *see* Chernivtsi
Cēsis Latvia *Ger.* Wenden 88 C3
České Budějovice Czech Republic *Ger.* Budweis 81 B5
Ceuta *external territory* Spain, N Africa 52 C1

Cévennes *mountains* France 73 C6
Ceylon *see* Sri Lanka
Ceylon Plain *undersea feature* Indian Ocean 122 C4
Chad *country* C Africa 58
Chad, Lake *lake* C Africa 58 B3
Chāgai Hills *mountains* Pakistan 116 A2
Chagos-Laccadive Plateau *undersea feature* Indian Ocean 122 C4
Chagos Trench *undersea feature* Indian Ocean 122 C4
Chalkída Greece 87 C5
Challenger Deep *undersea feature* Pacific Ocean 134 B3
Châlons-en-Champagne France 72 D3
Chambéry France 73 D5
Champaign Illinois, USA 22 B4
Chañaral Chile 46 B2
Chandīgarh India 116 D2
Chang, Ko *island* Thailand 119 C5
Changchun China 110 D3
Chang Jiang *river* China *var.* Yangtze 111 B6
Changsha China 111 C6
Chaniá Greece 87 C7
Channel Islands *island group* California, USA 27 B8
Channel Islands *island group* UK 71 D8
Channel-Port-aux-Basques Canada 21 G4
Channel Tunnel France/UK 71 E7
Chapala, Lago de *lake* Mexico 32 D4
Chardzhev *see* Türkmenabat
Chardzhou *see* Türkmenabat
Chari *river* C Africa 58 C3
Chārīkār Afghanistan 105 E4
Chärjew *see* Türkmenabat
Charleroi Belgium 69 C6
Charleston South Carolina, USA 31 F2
Charleston West Virginia, USA 22 D5
Charleville Australia 130 C4
Charlotte North Carolina, USA 31 F1
Charlotte Amalie *capital of* Virgin Islands 37 F3
Charlottesville Virginia, USA 23 E5
Charlottetown Canada 21 G4
Charters Towers Australia 130 D3
Chartres France 72 C3
Châteauroux France 72 C4
Chatham Islands *islands* New Zealand 134 D4
Chattanooga Tennessee, USA 30 D1
Chauk Myanmar 118 A3
Chaves Portugal 74 C2
Cheboksary Russian Federation 93 C5
Cheboygan Michigan, USA 22 C2
Chech, Erg *desert* Algeria/ Mali 56 D1
Che-chiang *see* Zhejiang
Cheju-do *see* Jeju-do
Cheju Strait *see* Jeju Strait
Chekiang *see* Zhejiang
Cheleken *see* Hazar
Chelyabinsk Russian Federation 96 C3
Chemnitz Germany *prev.* Karl-Marx-Stadt 76 D4
Chenāb *river* Pakistan 116 C2
Chengdu China 111 B5
Chennai India *prev.* Madras 115 E2
Cherbourg France 72 B3
Cherepovets Russian Federation 92 B4
Cherkasy Ukraine 91 E2
Cherkessk Russian Federation 93 A7
Chernigov see Chernihiv
Chernihiv Ukraine *Rus.* Chernigov 91 E1
Chernivtsi Ukraine *Rus.* Chernovtsy, *Rom.* Cernăuți 90 C3
Chernobyl' *see* Chornobyl'
Chernovtsy *see* Chernivtsi
Chernyakhovsk Kaliningrad, Russian Federation 88 B4
Chesapeake Bay *sea feature* USA 23 F5
Chester England, UK 71 D5
Cheyenne Wyoming, USA 24 D4
Chiang-hsi *see* Jiangxi
Chiang Mai Thailand 118 B4
Chiang-su *see* Jiangsu
Chiba Japan 113 D5
Chicago Illinois, USA 22 B3
Chiclayo Peru 42 A3
Chico California, USA 27 B5
Chicoutimi Canada 21 E4
Chifeng China *var.* Ulanhad 109 F2
Chihli *see* Hebei
Chihuahua Mexico 32 C2
Chile *country* S South America 46-47
Chile Basin *undersea feature* Pacific Ocean 135 G4
Chile Chico Chile 47 B6
Chile Rise *undersea feature* Pacific Ocean 135 G4
Chi-lin *see* Jilin
Chillán Chile 46 B4
Chiloé, Isla de *island* Chile 47 B6
Chimborazo *peak* Ecuador 38 A3
Chimbote Peru 42 A3
Chimkent *see* Shymkent
Chimoio Mozambique 61 E3
China *country* E Asia 108-109
Chinandega Nicaragua 34 C3
Chindwinn *river* Myanmar 118 A2
Chinghai *see* Qinghai
Chingola Zambia 60 D2
Chinook Trough *undersea feature* Pacific Ocean 134 D1
Chíos Greece 87 D5
Chíos *island* Greece *prev.* Khíos 87 D5
Chirchik Uzbekistan *Uzb.* Chirchiq 105 E2
Chirchiq *see* Chirchik
Chiriquí, Golfo de *sea feature* Panama 35 E5

Chişinău *capital of* Moldova, *var.* Kishinev 90 D3
Chita Russian Federation 97 F4
Chitré Panama 35 F5
Chittagong Bangladesh 117 G4
Chitungwiza Zimbabwe 60 D3
Choluteca Honduras 34 C3
Choma Zambia 60 D3
Chona *river* Russian Federation 95 E2
Chon Buri Thailand 119 C5
Ch'ŏngjin North Korea 110 E3
Chongqing *province* China *var.* Chungking 111 B5
Chonos, Archipiélago de los *island group* Chile 47 B6
Chornobyl' Ukraine *Rus.* Chernobyl' 91 E1
Choûm Mauritania 56 C2
Choybalsan Mongolia 109 F2
Christchurch New Zealand 133 C6
Christmas Island *external territory* Australia, Indian Ocean 122 D5
Christmas Island *see* Kiritimati
Christmas Ridge *undersea feature* Pacific Ocean 125 F1
Chuan *see* Sichuan
Chubut *river* Argentina 47 B6
Chudskoye Ozero *see* Peipus, Lake
Chuí *see* Chuy
Chukchi Plain *undersea feature* Arctic Ocean 137 G2
Chukchi Sea Arctic Ocean *Rus.* Chukotskoye More 137 F1
Chukotskoye More *see* Chukchi Sea
Chula Vista California, USA 27 C8
Chulym *river* Russian Federation 94 D3
Chumphon Thailand 119 C6
Chungking *see* Chongqing
Chuquicamata Chile 46 B2
Chur Switzerland 77 B7
Churchill Canada 19 G4
Chuuk Islands *island group* Micronesia 126 B1
Chuy Brazil *var.* Chuí 44 C5
Cienfuegos Cuba 36 B2
Cieza Spain 75 F4
Cilacap Indonesia 120 C5
Cincinnati Ohio, USA 22 C4
Ciudad Bolívar Venezuela 41 E2
Ciudad del Este Paraguay 44 C3
Ciudad de México *see* Mexico City
Ciudad Guayana Venezuela 41 E2
Ciudad Juárez Mexico 32 C1
Ciudad Obregón Mexico 32 B2
Ciudad Ojeda Venezuela 40 C1
Ciudad Real Spain 75 E3
Ciudad Valles Mexico 33 E3
Ciudad Victoria Mexico 33 E3
Clarence *river* New Zealand 133 C5
Clarion Fracture Zone *tectonic feature* Pacific Ocean 125 G1
Clarksville Tennessee, USA 30 D1
Clearwater Florida, USA 31 E4
Clermont Australia 130 D4
Clermont-Ferrand France 73 C5
Cleveland Ohio, USA 22 D3
Clipperton Fracture Zone *tectonic feature* Pacific Ocean 125 G2
Clipperton Island *external territory* France, Pacific Ocean 135 F3
Cloncurry Australia 130 C3
Clovis New Mexico, USA 29 E2
Cluj-Napoca Romania 90 B3
Clutha *river* New Zealand 133 B7
Coast Ranges *mountain range* W USA 26 A5
Coats Island *island* Canada 20 C1
Coats Land *physical region* Antarctica 136 B2
Coatzacoalcos Mexico 33 G4
Cobán Guatemala 34 B2
Cochabamba Bolivia 42 C4
Cochin India *see* Kochi 114 D3
Cochrane Canada 20 C4
Cochrane Chile 47 B6
Coco *river* Honduras/Nicaragua 34 D2
Cocos Basin *undersea feature* Indian Ocean 122 D4
Cocos Islands *external territory* Australia, Indian Ocean 122 D5
Cod, Cape *coastal feature* NE USA 23 G3
Coeur d'Alene Idaho, USA 26 C2
Coffs Harbour Australia 131 E6
Coihaique Chile 47 B6
Coimbatore India 114 D3
Coimbra Portugal 74 C3
Colchester England, UK 71 E6
Colmar France 72 E4
Cologne *see* Köln
Colombia *country* N South America 40-41
Colombo *administrative capital of* Sri Lanka 115 E4
Colón Panama 35 F4
Colón, Archipiélago de *see* Galapagos Islands
Colorado *state* USA 24 C4
Colorado *river* USA 16 B5
Colorado *river* Argentina 47 C5
Colorado Plateau *upland region* S USA 28 B1
Colorado Springs Colorado, USA 24 D4
Columbia South Carolina, USA 31 F2
Columbia *river* NW USA 26 C1
Columbus Georgia, USA 30 D3
Columbus Mississippi, USA 30 C2
Columbus Nebraska, USA 25 E4
Columbus Ohio, USA 22 D4
Comayagua Honduras 34 C2

Comilla Bangladesh 117 G4
Communism Peak *peak* Tajikistan *Rus.* Pik Kommunizma, *prev.* Stalin Peak, Garmo Peak 105 F3
Como, Lago di *lake* Italy 78 B2
Comodoro Rivadavia Argentina 47 C6
Comoros *country* Indian Ocean 61
Conakry *capital of* Guinea 56 C4
Concepción Chile 47 B5
Concepción Paraguay 44 B2
Conchos *river* Mexico 32 C2
Concord New Hampshire, USA 22 G2
Concordia E Argentina 46 D3
Congo *country* C Africa 59
Congo *river* C Africa *var.* Zaire 51 C5
Congo Basin *drainage basin* C Africa 59 C5
Congo, Democratic Republic of *country* C Africa 59
Connecticut *state* USA 23 G3
Constance, Lake *river* C Europe 77 B6
Constantine Algeria 53 E1
Constantinople *see* İstanbul
Constanţa Romania 90 D5
Coober Pedy Australia 131 A5
Cook, Mount *see* Aoraki
Cook Islands *associated territory* New Zealand, Pacific Ocean 127 G4
Cook Strait *sea feature* New Zealand 133 D5
Cooktown Australia 130 D2
Cooma Australia 131 D7
Coos Bay Oregon, USA 26 A3
Cootamundra Australia 131 D6
Copenhagen *capital of* Denmark 67 B7
Copiapó Chile 46 B3
Coppermine *see* Kuglukutuk
Coquimbo Chile 46 B3
Corabia Romania 90 B5
Coral Sea Pacific Ocean 130 E3
Coral Sea Islands *external territory* Australia, Coral Sea 130 E3
Corantijn *see* Courantyne
Cordillera Cantábrica *mountain range* Spain 74 D1
Córdoba Argentina 46 C3
Córdoba Spain 74 D4
Cordova Alaska, USA 18 D3
Corfu *see* Kérkyra
Corinth *see* Kórinthos
Corinth, Gulf of *see* Korinthiakós Kólpos
Corinto Nicaragua 34 C3
Cork Ireland 71 B6
Corner Brook Canada 21 G3
Coro Venezuela 40 D1
Coronel Oviedo Paraguay 44 C2
Corpus Christi Texas, USA 29 G5
Corrib, Lough *lake* Ireland 71 A5
Corrientes Argentina 46 D3
Corse *island* France *Eng.* Corsica 73 E7 84 D2
Corsica *see* Corse
Çorum Turkey 98 D2
Corvallis Oregon, USA 26 A3
Cosenza Italy 79 D6
Costa Blanca *coastal region* Spain 75 F4
Costa Brava *coastal region* Spain 75 H2
Costa Rica *country* Central America 34-35
Côte d'Ivoire *country* W Africa *Eng.* Ivory Coast 56 D4
Cottbus Germany 76 D4
Council Bluffs Iowa, USA 25 F4
Courantyne *river* Guyana / Suriname *var.* Corantijn 41 G3
Courland Lagoon *sea feature* Baltic Sea 88 B4
Coventry England, UK 71 D6
Covilhã Portugal 74 C3
Cowan, Lake *lake* Australia 129 C6
Cozumel, Isla de *island* Mexico 33 H3
Cracow *see* Kraków
Craiova Romania 90 B5
Cremona Italy 78 B2
Cres *island* Croatia 82 A3
Crescent City California, USA 26 A4
Crete *see* Kríti
Crete, Sea of Mediterranean Sea *Gk.* Kritikó Pélagos 87 D7
Crimea *see* Krym
Cristóbal Panama 48 A4
Croatia *country* SE Europe 82
Croker Island *island* Australia 128 E2
Crotone Italy 79 E6
Crozet Basin *undersea feature* Indian Ocean 123 B6
Crozet Islands *island group* Indian Ocean 123 B7
Crystal Brook Australia 131 B6
Cuanza *river* Angola 60 B2
Cuba *country* West Indies 36
Cubango *see* Okavango
Cúcuta Colombia 40 C2
Cuenca Ecuador 40 A5
Cuenca Spain 75 E3
Cuernavaca Mexico 33 E4
Cuiabá Brazil 43 E4
Culiacán Mexico 32 C3
Cumaná Venezuela 41 E1
Cumberland Maryland, USA 23 E4
Cunene *river* Angola/Namibia 60 B3
Cunnamulla Australia 131 C5
Curaçao *constituent country* Netherlands, West Indies 37 E5
Curicó Chile 46 B4
Curitiba Brazil 44 D3
Cusco Peru *prev.* Cuzco 42 B4
Cuttack India 117 F5
Cuxhaven Germany 76 B3
Cuyuni *river* Guyana/Venezuela 41 F2
Cuzco *see* Cusco

Cyclades *see* Kykládes
Cymru *see* Wales
Cyprus *country* Mediterranean Sea 98 C5
Czechoslovakia *see* Czech Republic *or* Slovakia
Czech Republic *country* C Europe 80-81
Częstochowa Poland *Ger.* Tschenstochau 80 C4
Człuchów Poland 80 C3

Dacca *see* Dhaka
Daegu South Korea *prev.* Taegu 110 E4
Daejeon South Korea *prev.* Taejŏn 110 E4
Dagden *see* Hiiumaa
Dagö *see* Hiiumaa
Dagupan Philippines 121 E1
Da Hinggan Ling *mountain range* China *Eng.* Great Khingan Range 109 G1
Dahomey *see* Benin
Dakar *capital of* Senegal 56 B3
Đakovo Croatia 82 C3
Dalain Hob China 108 D3
Dalaman Turkey 98 B4
Dalandzadgad Mongolia 109 E3
Đa Lat Vietnam 119 E5
Dalby Australia 131 D5
Dalian China 110 D4
Dallas Texas, USA 29 G3
Dalmacija *region* Croatia 82 B4
Daly Waters Australia 128 E3
Damān India 116 C5
Damas *see* Damascus
Damascus Syria *var.* Esh Sham, *Fr.* Damas, *Ar.* Dimashq 100 B4
Dampier Australia 128 B4
Damxung China 108 C5
Đa Nâng Vietnam 119 E4
Dandong China 110 D4
Daneborg Greenland 65 E3
Danghara Tajikistan 105 E3
Danmarksstraedet *see* Denmark Strait
Danube *river* C Europe 63 E4
Danville Virginia, USA 23 E5
Danzig *see* Gdańsk
Danzig, Gulf of *76 C2 Gulf* Poland 80 C2
Dar'ā Syria 101 B5
Dardanelles *sea feature* Turkey *Turk.* Çanakkale Boğazı 98 A2
Dar es Salaam Tanzania 55 C7
Darfur *Cultural region* Sudan 54 A4
Darhan Mongolia 109 E2
Darien, Gulf of *sea feature* Caribbean Sea 35 G5
Darling *river* Australia 131 C6
Darmstadt Germany 77 B5
Darnah Libya 53 H2
Dartmoor *region* England, UK 71 C7
Dartmouth Canada 21 F4
Darwin Australia 128 D2
Dashhowuz *see* Daşoguz
Daşoguz Turkmenistan *prev.* Tashauz, *Turkm.* Dashhowuz 104 C2
Datong China 110 C4
Daugava *see* Western Dvina
Daugavpils Latvia *Ger.* Dünaburg, *Rus.* Dvinsk 88 D4
Dāvangere India 114 D2
Davao Philippines 121 F3
Davao Gulf *gulf* Philippines 121 F3
Davenport Iowa, USA 25 G3
David Panama 35 E5
Davie Ridge *undersea feature* Indian Ocean 123 A5
Davis Sea Indian Ocean 136 D3
Davis Strait *sea feature* Atlantic Ocean 64 C3
Dawei Myanmar *prev.* Tavoy 119 B5
Dayr az Zawr Syria 100 D3
Dayton Ohio, USA 22 C4
Daytona Beach Florida, USA 31 F4
Dead Sea *salt lake* SW Asia *Ar.* Al Baḩr al Mayyit, Baḩrat Lūt, *Heb.* Yam HaMelaḥ 101 B5
Death Valley *valley* W USA 27 C6
Deatnu *river* Finland/Norway 66 D2
Debrecen Hungary *prev.* Debreczen, *Ger.* Debreczin 81 D6
Debreczen *see* Debrecen
Debreczin *see* Debrecen
Decatur Illinois, USA 22 B4
Deccan *plateau* India 106 B3 115 D1
Děčín Czech Republic *Ger.* Tetschen 80 B4
Dej Romania 90 B3
Delaware *state* USA 23 F4
Delémont Switzerland 77 A7
Delft Netherlands 68 C4
Delfzijl Netherlands 68 E1
Delhi India 116 D3
Del Rio Texas, USA 29 F4
Demchok *disputed region* China/India *var.* Dêmqog 108 B4
Demopolis Alabama, USA *30 C2*
Dêmqog *see* Demchok
Denali *see* Mount McKinley
Denham Australia 129 A5
Den Helder Netherlands 68 C2
Denizli Turkey 98 B4
Denmark *country* NW Europe 67
Denmark Strait *sea feature* Greenland/Iceland *var.* Danmarksstraedet 65 D4
Denpasar Indonesia 120 D5
Denton Texas, USA 29 G2
Denver Colorado, USA 24 D4
Dera Ghāzi Khān Pakistan 116 C2
Derby England, UK 71 D6
Derg, Lough *lake* Ireland 71 B6
Desē Ethiopia 54 C4
Deseado *river* Argentina 47 C6
Des Moines Iowa, USA 25 F3

Despoto Planina *see* Rhodope Mountains
Dessau Germany 76 D4
Detroit Michigan, USA 22 D3
Deutschendorf *see* Poprad
Deva Romania 90 B4
Deventer Netherlands 68 D3
Devollit, Lumi i *river* Albania 83 D6
Devon Island *island* Canada 19 F2
Devonport Tasmania, Australia 131 C8
Dezfūl Iran 102 C3
Dhaka *capital of* Bangladesh *var.* Dacca 117 G4
Dhanbād India 117 F4
Dhrepanon, Ákra *see* Drépano, Akrotírio
Diamantina Fracture Zone *tectonic feature* Indian Ocean 123 E6
Dickinson North Dakota, USA 24 D2
Diekirch Luxembourg 69 D7
Dieppe France 72 C3
Digul *River* Indonesia 121 H5
Dijon France 72 D4
Dikson Taymyrskiy (Dolgano-Nenetskiy) Russian Federation 137 H4
Dili *capital of* East Timor 121 F5
Dilling Sudan 54 B4
Dilolo Dem. Rep. Congo 59 D8
Dimashq *see* Damascus
Dimitrovo *see* Pernik
Dinant Belgium 69 C7
Dinaric Alps *mountains* Bosnia & Herzegovina/Croatia 82 B4
Diourbel Senegal 56 B3
Dirē Dawa Ethiopia 55 D5
Dirk Hartog Island *island* Australia 129 A5
Disappointment, Lake *salt lake* Australia 128 C4
Dispur India 117 G3
Divinópolis Brazil 45 F1
Diyarbakır Turkey 99 E4
Dkaraganda *see* Zhezkazgan
Djambala Congo 59 B6
Djibouti *country* E Africa 54
Djibouti *capital of* Djibouti *var.* Jibuti 54 D4
Dnepr *see* Dnieper
Dnieper *river* E Europe *Bel.* Dynapro, *Rus.* Dnepr 63 F4
Dniester *river* Moldova/Ukraine 90 D3
Dnipropetrovs'k Ukraine 91 F3
Dobele Latvia *Ger.* Doblen 88 C3
Doberai, Jazirah *Peninsula* Indonesia 121 G4
Doblen *see* Dobele
Doboj Bosnia & Herzegovina 82 C3
Dobrich Bulgaria 86 E1
Dodecanese *see* Dodekánisa
Dodekánisa *islands* Greece *Eng.* Dodecanese 87 E6
Dodge City Kansas, USA 25 E5
Dodoma *capital of* Tanzania 55 C7
Doğu Karadeniz Dağlarıı *mountains* Turkey *var.* Anadolu Dağları 99 E2
Doha *capital of* Qatar *Ar.* Ad Dawḩah 103 C5
Dolisie Congo 59 B6
Dolomites *see* Dolomitiche, Alpi
Dolomitiche, Alpi *mountains* Italy *Eng.* Dolomites 78 C2
Dolores Argentina 46 D4
Dolores Hidalgo Mexico 33 E4
Dominica *country* West Indies 37
Dominican Republic *country* West Indies 37
Don *river* Russian Federation 93 B6 96 A3
Donegal Bay *sea feature* Ireland 71 A5
Donets *river* Russian Federation/Ukraine 93 A6
Donets'k Ukraine 91 G3
Dongguan China 111 C6
Dongola Sudan 54 B3
Donostia/San Sebastián Spain *Sp.* San Sebastián 75 E1
Dordogne *river* France 73 B5
Dordrecht Netherlands 68 C4
Dorpat *see* Tartu
Dortmund Germany 76 B4
Dothan Alabama, USA 30 D3
Douai France 72 D3
Douala Cameroon 59 A5
Douglas UK 71 C5
Douglas Arizona, USA 28 C3
Dourados Brazil 44 C2
Douro *river* Portugal/Spain *Sp.* Duero 74 C2
Dover England, UK 71 E7
Dover Delaware, USA 23 F4
Drakensberg *mountain range* Lesotho/South Africa 60 D5
Drake Passage *sea feature* Atlantic Ocean/Pacific Ocean 39 C8
Dráma Greece 86 C3
Drammen Norway 67 B6
Drau *river* C Europe *var.* Drava 77 D7 82 C3
Drava *river* C Europe *var.* Drau 81 C7
Drépano, Akrotírio *coastal feature* Greece *var.* Dhrepanon Ákra 86 C4
Dresden Germany 76 D4
Drina *river* Bosnia & Herzegovina/Serbia 82 D4
Drobeta-Turnu Severin Romania *prev.* Turnu Severin 90 B4
Dronning Maud Land *region* Antarctica 137 B1
Druskieniki *see* Druskininkai
Druskininkai Lithuania *Pol.* Druskieniki 89 B5
Dubayy United Arab Emirates 103 D5
Dubăsari Moldova 90 D3
Dubawnt *river* Canada 19 F4
Dubbo Australia 131 D6
Dublin *capital of* Ireland 71 B5
Dubrovnik Croatia 83 C5
Dubuque Iowa, USA 25 G3
Duero *river* Portugal/Spain *Port.* Douro 74 D2
Dugi Otok *island* Croatia 82 A4
Duisburg Germany 76 A4
Dulan China 108 D4
Duluth Minnesota, USA 25 F2

Dumfries Scotland, UK 70 C4
Düna *see* Western Dvina
Dünaburg *see* Daugavpils
Dundalk Ireland 71 B5
Dundee Scotland, UK 70 D3
Dunedin New Zealand 133 B7
Dunkerque France *Eng.* Dunkirk 72 C2
Dunkirk *see* Dunkerque
Duqm Oman 103 E6
Durango Mexico 32 D3
Durango Colorado, USA 24 C5
Durazno Uruguay 44 C5
Durban South Africa 60 E4
Durham North Carolina, USA 31 F1
Durrës Albania 83 C5
Dushanbe *capital of* Tajikistan *var.* Dyushambe, *prev.* Stalinabad 105 E3
Düsseldorf Germany 76 A4
Dutch Harbor Alaska, USA 18 B3
Dvinsk *see* Daugavpils
Dynapro *see* Dnieper
Dyushambe *see* Dushanbe
Dzaudzhikau *see* Vladikavkaz
Dzhalal-Abad Kyrgyzstan *Kir.* Jalal-Abad 105 F2
Dzhambul *see* Taraz
Dzhezkazgan see Zhezkazgan
Dzvina *see* Western Dvina

E

Eagle Pass Texas, USA 29 F4
East Antarctica *region* Antarctica 136 C3
East Cape *coastal feature* New Zealand 132 E2
East China Sea Pacific Ocean 111 E5
Easter Fracture Zone *tectonic feature* Pacific Ocean 135 G4
Easter Island *island* Pacific Ocean 135 F4
Eastern Ghats *mountain range* India 117 B5
Eastern Sierra Madre *see* Sierra Madre Oriental
East Falkland *island* Falkland Islands 47 D7
East Indiaman Ridge *undersea feature* Indian Ocean 23 D5
East Indies *island group* Asia 122 E4
East London South Africa 60 D5
Eastmain *river* Canada 20 D3
East Pacific Rise *undersea feature* Pacific Ocean 135 F4
East Siberian Sea *see* Vostochno-Sibirskoye More
East St Louis Illinois, USA 22 B4
East Timor *country* SE Asia 121
East Novaya Zemlya Trench *var.* Novaya Zemlya Trench. *Undersea feature* Kara Sea 137 H4
Eau Claire Wisconsin, USA 22 A2
Ebolowa Cameroon 59 B5
Ebro *river* Spain 75 F2
Ecuador *country* NW South America 40
Ede Netherlands 68 D3
Ede Nigeria 57 F4
Edgeøya *island* Svalbard 65 G2
Edinburgh Scotland, UK 70 C4
Edirne Turkey 98 A2
Edmonton Canada 19 E5
Edward, Lake *lake* Uganda/ Dem. Rep. Congo 59 E6
Edwards Plateau *upland* S USA 29 F4
Efate *Island* Vanuatu *prev.* Sandwich Island 124 D4
Effingham Illinois, USA 22 B4
Eforie-Sud Romania 90 D5
Egadi, Isole *island group* Italy 79 B6
Ege Denizi *see* Aegean Sea
Eger *see* Ohře
Egypt *country* NE Africa 54
Eighty Mile Beach *beach* Australia 128 C3
Eindhoven Netherlands 69 D5
Eisenstadt Austria 77 E6
Eivissa *see* Ibiza
Elat Israel 101 A7
Elazig Turkey 99 E3
Elba, Isola d' *island* Italy 78 B4
Elbasan Albania 83 D6
Elbe *river* Czech Republic/ Germany 81 B5
Elbing *see* Elbląg
Elbląg Poland *Ger.* Elbing 80 D2
El'brus *peak* Russian Federation 93 A7
El Calafate Argentina *var.* Calafate 47 B7
Elche Spain *Cat.* Elx 75 F4
Elda Spain 75 F4
Eldoret Kenya 55 C6
Eleuthera *island* The Bahamas 36 C1
El Fasher Sudan *var.* Al Fāshir 54 A4
El Geneina Sudan 54 A4
Elgin Scotland, UK 70 C3
El Gîza *see* Al Jízah
El Ḫank *cliff* Mauritania 56 D1
Elista Russian Federation 93 B6
El Khalīl *see* Hebron
El Khârga *see* Al Khārijah
Elko Nevada, USA 27 D5
Ellensburg Washington, USA 26 B2
Ellesmere Island *island* Canada 19 F1
Ellsworth Land *region* Antarctica 136 A3
Elmira New York, USA 23 E3
El Mreyyé *desert* Mauritania 56 D2
El Obeid Sudan 54 B4
El Paso Texas, USA 28 D3
El Puerto de Santa María Spain 74 D5
El Qâhira *see* Cairo
El Salvador *country* Central America 34
Eltanin Fracture Zone *tectonic feature* Pacific Ocean 135 E5
El Tigre Venezuela 41 E2

Elx *see* Elche
Ely Nevada USA 27 D5
Emden Germany 76 B3
Emerald Australia 130 D4
Emmen Netherlands 68 E2
Empty Quarter *see* Ar Rub' al Khali
Ems *river* Germany/Netherlands 76 B3
Encarnación Paraguay 44 C3
Enderbury Island *atoll* Kiribati 136 C2
Enderby Land *region* Antarctica 136 C2
Enderby Plain *undersea feature* Indian Ocean 123 B7
England *national region* UK 70-71
English Channel *sea feature* Atlantic Ocean 71 D7
Enguri *river* Georgia *Rus.* Inguri 99 F1
Enid Oklahoma, USA 29 F1
Ennedi *plateau* Chad 58 D2
Enns *river* Austria 77 D6
Enschede Netherlands 68 E3
Ensenada Mexico 32 A1
Entebbe Uganda 55 B6
Enugu Nigeria 57 G5
Eolie, Isole *island group* Italy *Eng.* Lipari Islands, *var.* Aeolian Islands 79 D6
Eperies *see* Prešov
Eperjes *see* Prešov
Épinal France 72 E4
Equatorial Guinea *country* W Africa 59
Erdenet Mongolia 109 E2
Erechim Brazil 44 D3
Erenhot China 109 F2
Erevan *see* Yerevan
Ereğli Turkey 98 C4
Erfurt Germany 76 C4
Erie Pennsylvania, USA 22 D3
Erie, Lake *lake* Canada/USA 17 D5
Eritrea *country* E Africa 54
Erivan *see* Yerevan
Erlangen Germany 77 C5
Ernākulam India 114 D3
Er Rachidia Morocco 52 C2
Erzerum *see* Erzurum
Erzgebirge *mountain range* Czech Republic/Germany *var* Krušné Hory 77 D5
Erzincan Turkey 99 E3
Erzurum Turkey *prev.* Erzerum 99 F3
Esbjerg Denmark 67 A7
Esch-sur-Alzette Luxembourg 69 D8
Escuintla Guatemala 34 B2
Eşfahān Iran 102 C3
Esh Sham *see* Damascus
Eskişehir Turkey 98 B3
Esmeraldas Ecuador 40 A4
Esperance Australia 129 C6
Espiritu Santo *Island* Vanuatu 124 D3
Espoo Finland 67 D6
Esquel Argentina 47 B6
Essaouira Morocco 52 B2
Essen Germany 76 A4
Essequibo *river* Guyana 41 G3
Estelí Nicaragua 34 D3
Estevan Canada 19 F5
Estonia *country* E Europe 88 D2
Ethiopia *country* E Africa 54-55
Ethiopian Highlands *upland* E Africa 50 D4
Etna, Mount *peak* Sicily, Italy 79 D7
Etosha Pan *salt basin* Namibia 60 C3
Eucla Australia 129 D6
Eugene Oregon, USA 26 A3
Eugene Washington, USA 26 B1
Euphrates *river* SW Asia 102 C4
Europe 62-63
Evansville Indiana, USA 22 B5
Everest, Mount *peak* China/ Nepal 108 B5
Everett Washington, USA 26 B1
Everglades, The *wetlands* Florida, USA 31 F5
Évvoia *island* Greece 87 C5
Exeter England, UK 71 C7
Exmoor *region* England, UK 71 C7
Exmouth Australia 128 A4
Exmouth Gulf *gulf* Australia 128 A4
Exmouth Plateau *undersea feature* Indian Ocean 123 E5
Eyre North, Lake *salt lake* Australia131 B5
Eyre Peninsula *peninsula* Australia131 A6
Eyre South, Lake *salt lake* Australia131 B5

F

Fada-N'gourma Burkina Faso 57 E4
Faroe Islands *external territory* Denmark, Atlantic Ocean *Far.* Fóroyar, *Dan.* Færøerne, *var.* Faeroe Islands 65 F5
Færøerne *see* Faroe Islands
Faguibine, Lac *lake* Mali 57 E3
Fairbanks Alaska, USA 18 D3
Fairlie New Zealand 133 B6
Faisalābād Pakistan 116 C2
Faīzābād Afghanistan *prev.* Feyzābād 105 E3
Falkland Islands *overseas territory* UK, Atlantic Ocean 47 D7
Fallon Nevada, USA 27 C5
Falun Sweden 67 C6
Famagusta *see* Gazimağusa
Farafangana Madagascar 61 G4
Farāh Afghanistan 104 C5
Farasān, Jazā'ir *island group* Saudi Arabia 103 B6
Farewell, Cape *headland* New Zealand 132 C4
Farewell, Cape *see* Nunap Isua
Farghona *see* Farg'ona
Farg'ona Uzbekistan *prev.* Novyy Margilan, *Uzb.* Farghona 105 F2
Fargo North Dakota, USA 25 E2
Farkhor Tajikistan 105 E3
Farmington New Mexico, USA 28 C1

Faro Portugal 74 C4
Farquhar Group *island group* Seychelles 61 G2
Farvel, Cap see Nunap Isua
Faxaflói *bay* Iceland 64 D5
Faya Chad 58 C2
Fayetteville Arkansas, USA 30 A1
Fayetteville North Carolina, USA 31 F1
Fdérik Mauritania 56 C1
Fear, Cape *coastal feature* North Carolina, USA 31 G2
Fehmarn *island* Germany 76 C2
Fehmarn Belt *sea feature* Germany 76 C2
Feira de Santana Brazil 43 G3
Fellin *see* Viljandi
Fengtien *see* Liaoning
Fenoarivo *see* Fenoarivo Atsinanana
Fenoarivo Atsinanana Madagascar *prev.* Fenoarivo 61 G3
Fens, The *wetland* England, UK 71 E6
Fergana *see* Farg'ona
Ferizaj/Uroševac Kosovo *Serb.* Uroševac 83 D5
Ferrara Italy 78 C3
Ferrol Spain 74 C1
Fès Morocco *Eng.* Fez 52 C2
Feyzābād *see* Faīzābād
Fez *see* Fès
Fianarantsoa Madagascar 61 G3
Fier Albania 83 D6
Figueira da Foz Portugal 74 C3
Figueres Spain 75 G2
Figuig Morocco 52 D2
Fiji *country* Pacific Ocean 127
Finland *country* N Europe 66-67
Finland, Gulf of *sea feature* Baltic Sea 67 E6
Fiordland *physical region* New Zealand 133 A7
Firenze Italy *Eng.* Florence 78 C3
Fishguard Wales, UK 71 C6
Fitzroy *river* Australia 128 C3
Fitzroy Crossing Australia 128 D3
Fiume see Rijeka
Flagstaff Arizona, USA 28 B2
Flanders *region* Belgium 69 A5
Flensburg Germany 76 B2
Flinders Island *island* Australia 131 C7
Flinders Ranges *mountain range* Australia 131 B6
Flinders River *river* Australia 130 C3
Flin Flon Canada 19 F5
Flint Michigan, USA 22 C3
Flint Island *island* Kiribati 127 H4
Florence Alabama, USA 30 C2
Florence South Carolina, USA 31 F2
Florence *see* Firenze
Florencia Colombia 40 B3
Flores Guatemala 34 B1
Flores *island* Indonesia 121 E5
Flores, Laut *see* Flores Sea
Flores Sea Pacific Ocean *Ind.* Laut Flores 121 E5
Florianópolis Brazil 44 D3
Florida *state* USA 31 E4
Florida, Straits of *sea feature* The Bahamas/USA 31 F5 36 B1
Florida Keys *island chain* Florida, USA 31 F5
Flórina Greece 86 B3
Flushing *see* Vlissingen
Foča Bosnia & Herzegovina 82 C4
Focşani Romania 90 C4
Foggia Italy 79 D5
Fogo *island* Cape Verde 56 A3
Foligno Italy 78 C4
Fongafale *capital of* Tuvalu 127 E3
Fonseca, Gulf of *sea feature* El Salvador/Honduras 34 C3
Forlì Italy 78 C3
Formentera *island* Spain 75 G4
Former Yugoslav Republic of Macedonia *see* Macedonia
Formosa Argentina 46 D2
Formosa *see* Taiwan
Formosa Strait *see* Taiwan Strait
Fóroyar *see* Faroe Islands
Fortaleza Brazil 43 H2
Fortescue River *river* Australia 128 B4
Fort Collins Colorado, USA 24 D4
Fort-de-France *capital of* Martinique 37 G4
Forth *river* Scotland, UK 70 C4
Forth, Firth of *inlet* Scotland, UK 70 D4
Fort Lauderdale Florida, USA 31 F5
Fort McMurray Canada 19 F4
Fort Myers Florida, USA 31 E4
Fort Peck Lake *lake* Montana, USA 24 C1
Fort Saint John Canada 19 E4
Fort Smith Canada 19 E4
Fort Smith Arkansas, USA 30 A1
Fort Wayne Indiana, USA 22 C4
Fort William Scotland, UK 70 C3
Fort Worth Texas, USA 29 G3
Foveaux Strait *sea feature* New Zealand 133 A7
Fox Glacier New Zealand 133 B6
Franca Brazil 45 E1
France *country* W Europe 72-73
Francistown Botswana 60 D3
Frankfort Kentucky, USA 22 C5
Frankfurt *see* Frankfurt am Main
Frankfurt am Main Germany *Eng.* Frankfurt 77 B5
Frankfurt an der Oder Germany 76 D5
Fränkische Alb *mountains* Germany 77 C6
Frantsa-Iosifa, Zemlya *islands* Russian Federation *Eng.* Franz Josef Land 137 G4
Franz Josef Land *see* Frantsa-Iosifa, Zemlya

Fraser Island *island* Australia 130 E4
Frauenburg *see* Saldus
Fray Bentos Uruguay 44 B5
Fredericksburg Virginia, USA 23 E4
Fredericton Canada 21 F4
Frederikshavn Denmark 67 B7
Fredrikstad Norway 67 B6
Freeport The Bahamas 36 C1
Freeport Texas, USA 29 G4
Freetown *capital of* Sierra Leone 56 C4
Freiburg im Breisgau Germany 77 B6
Fremantle Australia 129 B6
French Guiana *overseas department* France, N South America 41
French Polynesia *overseas collectivity* France, Pacific Ocean 135 E3
French Southern and Antarctic Lands *French overseas territory* Indian Ocean *Fr.* Terres Australes et Antarctiques Françaises 123 C7
Fresnillo Mexico 32 D1
Fresno California, USA 27 B6
Fobisher Bay *see* Iqaluit
Frome, Lake *salt lake* Australia 131 B5
Frunze *see* Bishkek
Fu-chien *see* Fujian
Fuerte Olimpo Paraguay 44 B1
Fuerteventura *island* Spain 52 A3
Fuhkien *see* Fujian
Fujian *province* China *var.* Fu-chien, Fuhkien, Fukien, Min 111 D6
Fukien *see* Fujian
Fukui Japan 113 C5
Fukuoka Japan 113 A6
Fukushima Japan 112 D4
Fulda Germany 77 C5
Fünfkirchen *see* Pécs
Fushun China 110 D3
Furnas, Represa de *Reservoir* Brazil 45 E1
Fuxin China 110 D3
Fujian China *prev.* Linchuan 111 D6
FYR Macedonia *see* Macedonia

Gaalkacyo Somalia 55 E5
Gabès Tunisia 53 E2
Gabon *country* W Africa 59
Gaborone *capital of* Botswana 60 D4
Gabrovo Bulgaria 86 D2
Gadsden Alabama, USA 30 D2
Gaeta, Golfo di *sea feature* Italy 79 C5
Gafsa Tunisia 53 E2
Gagnoa Côte d'Ivoire 56 D5
Gagra Georgia 99 E1
Gairdner, Lake *lake* Australia 131 B6
Galapagos Fracture Zone *tectonic feature* Pacific Ocean 135 F3
Galapagos Islands *islands* Ecuador, Pacific Ocean *var.* Tortoise Islands, *Sp.* Archipiélago de Colón 135 G3
Galapagos Rise *undersea feature* Pacific Ocean 135 G3
Galaţi Romania 90 D4
Galesburg Illinois, USA 22 B4
Galicia *region* Spain 74 C1
Galilee, Sea of *see* Tiberias, Lake
Galle Sri Lanka 115 E4
Gallego Rise *undersea feature* Pacific Ocean 135 F3
Gallipoli Italy 79 E5
Gällivare Sweden 66 D3
Gallup New Mexico, USA 28 C2
Galveston Texas, USA 29 G4
Galway Ireland 71 A5
Gambia *country* W Africa 56
Gambia *River* Africa 56 C3
Gambier, Îles *island group* French Polynesia 135 E4
Gan *see* Gansu
Gan *see* Jiangxi
Gäncä Azerbaijan *Rus.* Gyandzha, *prev.* Kirovabad, Yelisavetpol 99 G2
Gand see Gent
Gander Canada 21 H3
Gandia Spain 75 F3
Ganges *river* S Asia 116 F4
Ganges Fan *Undersea feature* Bay of Bengal 122 D3
Ganges, Mouths of the *wetlands* Bangladesh/India 117 G4
Gangtok India 117 G3
Gansu *province* China *var.* Gan, Kansu 111 B5
Gao Mali 57 E3
Gaoual Guinea 56 C4
Gaoxiong Taiwan *prev.* Kaohsiung 111 D7
Gar China *var.* Shiquanhe 108 A4
Garagum Kanaly *canal* Turkmenistan *prev.* Karakumskiy Kanal 104 C3
Garagum *desert* Turkmenistan *var.* Kara Kum, Karakumy 104 C2
Garda, Lago di *lake* Italy 78 B2
Gardēz Afghanistan *prev.* Gardīz105 E4
Gardīz *see* Gardēz
Garissa Kenya 55 C6
Garmo Peak see Communism Peak
Garonne *river* France 73 B5
Garoowe Somalia 55 E5
Garoua Cameroon 58 B4
Gary Indiana, USA 22 B3
Gaspé Canada 21 F4
Gastonia North Carolina, USA 31 E1
Gävle Sweden 67 C5
Gaya India 117 F4
Gaza Gaza Strip 101 A6
Gazandzhyk *see* Bereket
Gazanjyk *see* Bereket
Gaza Strip *disputed territory* SW Asia 101 A6

Gaziantep Turkey *prev.* Aintab 98 D4
Gazimağusa Cyprus *var.* Famagusta *Gk.* Ammochostos 98 C5
Gdańsk Poland *Ger.* Danzig 80 C2
Gdingen *see* Gdynia
Gdynia Poland *Ger.* Gdingen 80 C2
Gedaref Sudan 54 C4
Geelong Australia 131 C7
Gëkdepe *see* Gökdepe
Gemena Dem. Rep. Congo 59 C5
General Eugenio A. Garay Paraguay 44 A1
General Santos Philippines 121 F3
Geneva *see* Genève
Geneva, Lake *lake* France/ Switzerland *Fr.* Lac Léman, *var.* Le Léman, *Ger.* Genfer See 77 A7
Genève Switzerland *Eng.* Geneva 77 A7
Genfer See *see* Geneva, Lake
Gengen Gol China 109 F1
Genk Belgium 69 D5
Genoa *see* Genova
Genova Italy *see* Genoa 78 B3
Genova, Golfo di *sea feature* Italy 78 B3
Gent Belgium *Fr.* Gand, *Eng.* Ghent 69 B5
Geok-Tepe *see* Gökdepe
George South Africa 60 D5
George V Land *physical region* Antarctica 136 C4
Georgenburg *see* Jurbarkas
George Town *capital of* Cayman Islands 36 B3
Georgetown *capital of* Guyana 41 G2
George Town Malaysia 120 B3
Georgia *country* SW Asia 99 F2
Georgia *state* USA 31 E3
Gera Germany 76 C4
Geraldton Australia 129 A5
Gereshk Afghanistan 104 D5
Germany *country* W Europe 76-77
Gerona *see* Girona
Getafe Spain 75 E3
Gettysburg Pennsylvania, USA 23 E4
Gevgelija Macedonia 83 E6
Ghana *country* W Africa 57
Ghanzi Botswana 60 C3
Ghardaïa Algeria 52 D2
Gharyān Libya 53 F2
Ghaznī Afghanistan 105 E4
Ghent *see* Gent
Gibraltar *overseas territory* UK, SW Europe 74 D5
Gibson Desert *desert region* Australia 128 C4
Gijón Spain *var.* Xixón 74 D1
Gilbert Islands see Tungaru
Gilbert River *river* Australia 130 C3
Gillette Wyoming, USA 24 C3
Gingin Australia 129 B6
Girin *see* Jilin
Girne Cyprus *var.* Kyrenia 98 C5
Girona Spain *var.* Gerona 75 G2
Gisborne New Zealand 132 E3
Giurgiu Romania 90 C5
Gjirokastër Albania 83 D6
Gjøvik Norway 67 B5
Glasgow Scotland, UK 70 C4
Gleiwitz *see* Gliwice
Glendale Arizona, USA 28 B2
Glendive Montana, USA 24 D2
Gliwice Poland *Ger.* Gleiwitz 81 C5
Gloucester England, UK 71 D6
Glubokoye *see* Hlybokaye
Gobi *desert* China/Mongolia 108 D3
Godāveri *river* India 106 B3 115 E1
Godoy Cruz Argentina 46 B4
Godthåb *see* Nuuk
Godwin Austin, Mount *see* K2
Goiânia Brazil 43 F4
Gökdepe Turkmenistan *prev.* Geok-Tepe, *prev.* Gëkdepe 104 B3
Golan Heights *disputed territory* SW Asia 100 B4
Gold Coast *coastal region* Australia 131 E5
Goldingen *see* Kuldīga
Golmud China 108 D4
Goma Dem. Rep. Congo 59 E6
Gomel' *see* Homyel'/Gomel'
Gómez Palacio Mexico 32 D2
Gonaïves Haiti 36 D3
Gonder Ethiopia 54 C4
Gongola *river* Nigeria 57 G4
Good Hope, Cape of *coastal feature* South Africa 60 C5
Goondiwindi Australia 131 D5
Goose Lake *lake* W USA 26 B4
Goré Chad 58 C4
Gorē Ethiopia 55 C5
Gore New Zealand 133 B7
Gorgān Iran 102 D3
Gorki *see* Horki
Gor'kiy *see* Nizhniy Novgorod
Gorlovka *see* Horlivka
Gorontalo Indonesia 121 E4
Gorzów Wielkopolski Poland *Ger.* Landsberg 80 B3
Gospić Croatia 82 B3
Gosford Australia 131 D6
Gostivar Macedonia 83 D5
Göteborg Sweden 67 B7
Gotel Mountains *mountain range* Nigeria 57 G4
Gotland *island* Sweden 67 C7
Gotō-rettō *island group* Japan 113 A6
Göttingen Germany 76 C4
Gouda Netherlands 68 C4
Gough Island *overseas territory* UK, Atlantic Ocean 49 D7
Gouin, Réservoir *Reservoir* Canada 20 D4
Gouré Niger 57 G3
Governador Valadares Brazil 43 G4 45 F1
Govĭ Altayn Nuruu *mountain range* Mongolia 109 E3
Gozo *island* Malta 79 C7
Grafton Australia 131 E5
Grampian Mountains *mountains* Scotland, UK 70 C3

Granada Nicaragua 34 D3
Granada Spain 75 E4
Gran Canaria *island* Spain 52 A3
Gran Chaco *region* C South America 38 C4 44 A2 46 D2
Grand Bahama *island* The Bahamas 36 C1
Grand Banks *undersea feature* Atlantic Ocean 48 B3
Grand Canyon *valley* SW USA 28 B1
Grande, Rio *river* Brazil 45 E1
Grande, Rio *River* Mexico/ USA 17 B6
Grande Comore *island* Comoros 61 F2
Grande Prairie Canada 19 E4
Grand Erg Occidental *desert region* Algeria 52 D2
Grand Erg Oriental *desert region* Algeria/Tunisia 53 E3
Grand Falls Canada 21 G3
Grand Forks North Dakota, USA 25 E1
Grand Junction Colorado, USA 24 C4
Grand Rapids Michigan, USA 22 C3
Graudenz *see* Grudziądz
Graz Austria 77 E7
Great Abaco *island* The Bahamas 36 C1
Great Ararat *see* Ararat, Mount
Great Australian Bight *sea feature* Australia 129 D6
Great Barrier Island *island* N NZ 132 D2
Great Barrier Reef *coral reef* Coral Sea 130 C4
Great Basin *region* USA 26 D4
Great Bear Lake *lake* Canada 19 E3
Great Dividing Range *mountain range* Australia 130-131
Great Exhibition Bay *inlet* New Zealand132 C1
Great Wall of China *ancient monument* China 110 C4
Greater Antilles *island group* West Indies 36 C3
Great Exuma Island *island* The Bahamas 36 C2
Great Falls Montana, USA 24 B1
Great Hungarian Plain *plain* SE Europe *Hung.* Alföld 81 D7
Great Inagua *island* The Bahamas 36 D2
Great Khingan Range *see* Da Hinggan Ling
Great Lakes, The *lakes* N America *see* Erie, Huron, Michigan, Ontario, Superior 17 C5
Great Nicobar *island* India 115 H3
Great Plain of China *region* China 106 E2
Great Plains *region* N America 16-17 C5
Great Rift Valley *valley* E Africa/SW Asia 55 C6
Great Salt Desert *see* Kavīr, Dasht-e
Great Salt Lake *salt lake* Utah, USA 24 B3
Great Sand Sea *desert region* Egypt/Libya 53 H3
Great Sandy Desert *desert* Australia 128 C4
Great Sandy Desert *see* Ar Rubʻ al Khali
Great Slave Lake *lake* Canada 19 E4
Great Victoria Desert *desert* Australia 129 C5
Greece *country* SE Europe 86-87
Green Bay Wisconsin, USA 22 B2
Greenland *external territory* Denmark, Atlantic Ocean *var.* Grønland 64
Greenland Sea Atlantic Ocean 65 F2
Greenock Scotland, UK 70 C4
Greensboro North Carolina, USA 31 F1
Greenville South Carolina, USA 31 E2
Greifswald Germany 76 D2
Gregory Range *mountain range* Australia 130 C3
Grenada *country* West Indies 37 G5
Grenoble France 73 D5
Greymouth New Zealand 133 B5
Grey Range *mountain range* Australia 124 B4
Grimsby England, UK 71 E5
Grodno *see* Hrodna/Grodno
Groningen Netherlands 68 E1
Grønland *see* Greenland
Groote Eylandt *island* Australia 130 B2
Grootfontein Namibia 60 C3
Grosseto Italy 78 B4
Grosskanizsa *see* Nagykanizsa
Groznyy Russian Federation 93 B7 96 A4
Grudziądz Poland *Ger.* Graudenz 80 C3
Grünberg in Schlesien *see* Zielona Góra
Guadalajara Mexico 32 D4
Guadalcanal *island* Solomon Islands 124 C3
Guadalquivir *river* Spain 74 D4
Guadeloupe *overseas department* France, West Indies 37 G4
Guadiana *river* Portugal/Spain 74 C4
Gualeguaychú Argentina 46 D4
Guam *unincorporated territory* USA, Pacific Ocean 126 B1
Guanare Venezuela 40 D1
Guanare *river* Venezuela 40 D2
Guangdong *province* China *var.* Kuang-tung, Kwangtung, Yue 111 C6
Guangxi *autonomous region* China *var.* Kwangsi 111 B6
Guangzhou China *Eng.* Canton 111 C6
Guantánamo Cuba 36 D3
Guaporé *River* Bolivia/Brazil 32 D3
Guarapuava Brazil 44 D3
Guatemala *country* Central America 34
Guatemala Basin *undersea feature* Pacific Ocean 135 G3
Guatemala City *capital of* Guatemala 34 B2

Guaviare *river* Colombia 40 D3
Guayaquil Ecuador 40 A4
Guayaquil, Golfo do *sea feature* Ecuador/Peru 40 A5
Guernsey *British Crown Dependency* Channel Islands 71 D8
Güney Dogu Toroslar *mountain range* SE Turkey 99 F3
Guiana Highlands *upland* N South America 38 C2
Guider Cameroon 58 B4
Guimarães Portugal 74 C2
Guinea *country* W Africa 56
Guinea, Gulf of *sea feature* Atlantic Ocean 49 D5
Guinea-Bissau *country* W Africa 56
Guiyang China 111 B6
Guizhou *province* China *var.* Kuei-chou, Kweichow, Qian 111 B6
Gujarāt *state* India 116 C4
Gujrānwāla Pakistan 116 C2
Gujrāt Pakistan 116 C2
Gulf, The *sea feature* Arabian Sea *var.* Persian Gulf 122 B2
Gulfport Mississippi, USA 30 C3
Gulu Uganda 55 B6
Gumbinnen *see* Gusev
Gunnbjørn Fjeld *mountain* Greenland 64 D4
Guri, Embalse de *Reservoir* Venezuela 41 E2
Gusau Nigeria 57 F3
Gusev Kaliningrad, Russian Federation *prev.* Gumbinnen 88 B4
Gushgy *see* Serhetabat
Guwāhāti India 117 G3
Guyana *country* NE South America 41
Gwalior India 116 D3
Gwangju South Korea *prev.* Kwangju 111 E4
Gyandzha *see* Gäncä
Gyangzê China 108 C5
Győr Hungary *Ger.* Raab 81 C6
Gyumri Armenia *Rus.* Kumayri, *prev.* Leninakan, Aleksandropol'99 F2
Gyzylarbat *see* Serdar

H

Ha'apai Group *islands* Tonga 127 F5
Haapsalu Estonia *Ger.* Hapsal 88 C2
Haarlem Netherlands 68 C3
Haast New Zealand 133 B6
Hachijō-jima *island* Japan 113 D5
Hachinohe Japan 112 D3
Hadejia *river* Nigeria 57 G3
Ḩaḑramawt *Mountain range* Yemen 103 C7
Hagåtña Guam 126 B1
Hague, The *see* 's-Gravenhage
Haibowan *see* Wuhai
Haicheng China 110 D4
Haifa *see* Hefa
Ḩā'il Saudi Arabia 102 B4
Hailar *see* Hulun Buir
Hainan *island* China *var.* Hainan Dao 106 D3 111 C8
Hainan *province* China *var.* Qiong 111 C7
Hainan Dao *see* Hainan Dao
Hai Phong Vietnam 118 D3
Haiti *country* West Indies 36
Hajdarken *see* Khaydarkan
Hakodate Japan 112 D3
Ḩalab Syria 100 B2
Hala'ib Triangle *disputed region* NE Africa 54 C3
Ḩalānīyāt, Juzur al *Island group* Oman 103 D6
Halden Norway 67 B6
Halfmoon Bay New Zealand 133 A7
Halifax Canada 21 F4
Halle Germany 76 C4
Hallein Austria 77 D7
Halls Creek Australia 128 D3
Halmahera, Pulau *island* Indonesia 121 F3
Halmahera Sea *Sea* Indonesia 121 F4
Halmstad Sweden 67 B7
Ha Long Vietnam *prev.* Hông Gai 118 E3
Hamada Japan 113 B5
Hamadān Iran 102 C3
Ḩamāh Syria 100 B3
Hamamatsu Japan 113 C5
Hamar Norway 67 B5
Hamburg Germany 76 C3
Hämeenlinna Finland 67 D5
HaMelaḩ, Yam *see* Dead Sea
Hamersley Range *mountain range* Australia 128 B4
Hamhŭng North Korea 110 E4
Hami China 108 C3
Hamilton Canada 20 D5
Hamilton New Zealand 132 D3
Hamm Germany 76 B4
Hammerfest Norway 66 D2
Handan China 110 C4
HaNegev *desert region* Israel *Eng.* Negev 101 A6
Hangayn Nuruu *mountain range* Mongolia 108 D2
Hangzhou China 111 D5
Hannover Germany *Eng.* Hanover 76 B4
Hanoi *capital of* Vietnam 118 D3
Hanover *see* Hannover
Hanzhong China 111 B5
Hapsal *see* Haapsalu
Ḩaraḑ Yemen 103 C5
Harare *capital of* Zimbabwe 61 E3
Harbin China 110 E3
Hargeysa Somalia 55 D5
Hari *river* Indonesia 120 B4
Harīrūd *river* C Asia 104 D4
Harper Liberia 56 D5
Harrisburg Pennsylvania, USA 23 E4
Harstad Norway 66 C2
Hartford Connecticut, USA 23 G3
Har Us Nuur *lake* Mongolia 108 C2

Hasselt Belgium 69 D5
Hastings New Zealand 132 E4
Hastings Nebraska, USA 24 E4
Hatay *see* Antakya
Hatteras, Cape *coastal feature* North Carolina, USA 31 G1
Hattiesburg Mississippi, USA 30 C3
Hat Yai Thailand 119 C7
Haugesund Norway 67 A6
Hauraki Gulf *gulf* New Zealand 132 D2
Havana *capital of* Cuba *Sp.* La Habana 36 B2
Havelock North Carolina, USA 31 G1
Havre Montana, USA 24 C1
Havre-Saint-Pierre Canada 21 F3
Hawaii *state* USA 135 E2
Hawai'ian Islands *islands* USA 125 F1
Hawai'ian Ridge *undersea feature* Pacific Ocean 134 D2
Hawera New Zealand 132 D4
Hawke Bay *bay* New Zealand 132 E4
Hawlēr *see* Arbīl
Hawthorne Nevada, USA 27 C6
Hay River Canada 19 E4
Hays Kansas, USA 25 E4
Hazar Turkmenistan *prev.* Cheleken 104 A2
Heard & McDonald Islands *islands* Indian Ocean 123 C7
Hebei *province* China *var.* Hopeh, Hopei, Ji; *prev.* Chihli 110 C4
Hebron West Bank *var.* Al Khalīl, El Khalil, *Heb.* Ḥevron 101 D7
Heerenveen Netherlands 68 D2
Heerlen Netherlands 69 D6
Hefa Israel *prev.* Haifa 101 A5
Hefei China 111 D5
Hei *see* Heilongjiang
Heidelberg Germany 77 B5
Heilbronn Germany 77 B5
Heilongjiang *province* China *var.* Hei, Hei-lung-chiang 110 E3
Hei-lung-chiang *see* Heilongjiang
Helena Montana, USA 24 B2
Hells Canyon *valley* Idaho/ Oregon USA 26 C3
Helmand *river* Afghanistan 104 C5
Helmond Netherlands 69 D5
Helsingborg Sweden 67 B7
Helsinki *capital of* Finland 67 D6
Henan *province* China *var.* Honan, Yu 111 C5
Hengduan Shan *mountain range* China 111 A6
Hengelo Netherlands 68 E3
Hengyang China 111 C6
Henzada *see* Hinthada
Herāt Afghanistan 104 C4
Hermansverk Norway 67 A5
Hermosillo Mexico 32 B2
Herning Denmark 67 A7
Heywood Islands *island group* Australia 128 C3
Hiiumaa *island* Estonia *Ger.* Dagden, *Swed.* Dagö 88 C2
Hildesheim Germany 76 C4
Hilversum Netherlands 68 C3
Himalayas *mountain range* S Asia 106 B2
Himora Ethiopia 54 C4
Ḥimş Syria 100 B3
Hinchinbrook Island *island* Australia 130 D3
Hindu Kush *mountain range* C Asia 105 E4
Hinthada Myanmar *prev.* Henzada 118 A4
Hiroshima Japan 113 B5
Hitachi Japan 112 D4
Hjørring Denmark 67 A7
Hlybokaye Belarus *Rus.* Glubokoye 89 D5
Hobart Tasmania 131 C8
Hobbs New Mexico, USA 29 E3
Hô Chi Minh Vietnam *var.* Ho Chi Minh City, *prev.* Saigon 119 E6
Ho Chi Minh City *see* Hô Chi Minh
Hodeida *see* Al Ḩudaydah
Hoek van Holland Netherlands 68 B4
Hoggar *see* Ahaggar
Hohe Tauern *mountain range* Austria 77 C7
Hohhot China 109 F3
Hokitika New Zealand 133 B5
Hokkaidō *island* Japan 112 D2
Holguín Cuba 36 C2
Holland *see* Netherlands
Hollabrunn Austria 77 E6
Holon Israel 101 A5
Holyhead Wales, UK 71 C5
Hombori Mopti, Mali 57 E3
Homyel'/Gomel' Belarus *Rus.* Gomel' 89 E7
Honan *see* Henan
Honduras *country* Central America 34-35
Honduras, Gulf of *sea feature* Caribbean Sea 34 C2
Hønefoss Norway 67 B6
Hông Gai *see* Ha Long
Hong Kong *special administrative region* China, E Asia 111 C6
Honiara *capital of* Solomon Islands 126 C3
Honshū *island* Japan 112 D3
Hoorn Netherlands 68 C2
Hopa Turkey 99 E2
Hopedale Canada 21 F2
Hopeh *see* Hebei
Hopei *see* Hebei
Hopkinsville Kentucky, USA 22 B5
Horki Belarus *Rus.* Gorki 89 E5
Horlivka Ukraine *Rus.* Gorlovka 90 G3
Horn, Cape *see* Hornos, Cabo
Hornos, Cabo *Eng* Cape Horn *coastal feature* Chile 47 C8
Horsham Australia 131 C7
Hospitalet *see* L'Hospitalet de Llobregat
Hot Springs Arkansas, USA 30 B2
Houston Texas, USA 29 G4
Hovd Mongolia 108 C2
Hövsgöl Nuur *lake* Mongolia 108 D1

Hradec Králové Czech Republic *Ger.* Königgrätz 81 B5
Hrodna/Grodno Belarus *Rus.* Grodno 89 B5
Huacho Peru 42 A3
Huainan China 111 D5
Huambo Angola 60 B2
Huancayo Peru 42 B3
Huang He *river* China *Eng.* Yellow River 110 C4
Huánuco Peru 42 B3
Huaraz Peru 42 B3
Hubei *province* China 111 C5
Hubli India 114 C2
Hudson *river* NE USA 23 F3
Hudson Bay *sea feature* Canada 16 C4
Hudson Strait *sea feature* Canada 19 H3
Huê Vietnam 118 E4
Huehuetenango Guatemala 34 B2
Huelva Spain 74 C4
Huesca Spain 75 F2
Hughenden Australia 130 C4
Hull *see* Kingston upon Hull
Hulun Buir China *var.* Hailar 109 F1
Hulun Nur *lake* China 109 F1
Humboldt *river* W USA 27 C5
Hunan *province* China *var.* Xiang 111 C6
Hungarian Plain *plain* C Europe 85 E2
Hungary *country* C Europe 81
Huntington Beach California, USA 27 C8
Huntington West Virginia, USA 22 D5
Huntsville Alabama, USA 30 D2
Hurghada Egypt 54 B2
Huron, Lake *lake* Canada/USA 22 D2
Hurunui *river* New Zealand 133 C5
Húsavík Iceland 65 E4
Huvadhu Atoll *island* Maldives 114 C5
Hvar *island* Croatia 82 B4
Hyargas Nuur *lake* Mongolia 108 D2
Hyderābād India 114 D1, 116 B3
Hyères, Îles d' *islands* France 73 D6

I

Iaşi Romania 90 D3
Ibadan Nigeria 57 F4
Ibagué Colombia 40 B3
Ibarra Ecuador 40 A4
Iberian Peninsula *peninsula* SW Europe 84 B3
Ibérico, Sistema *Mountain range* Spain 75 F2
Ibiza *island* Spain *Cat.* Eivissa 75 G4
Ica Peru 42 B4
İçel *see* Mersin
Iceland *country* Atlantic Ocean 65 E4
Idaho *state* USA 26
Idaho Falls Idaho, USA 26 E3
Idfū Egypt 54 B2
Idlib Syria 100 B2
Ieper Belgium *Fr.* Ypres 69 A6
Ifôghas, Adrar des *upland* Mali *var.* Adrar des Iforas 57 F2
Iforas, Adrar des *see* Ifôghas, Adrar des
Iglau *see* Jihlava
Iglesias Italy 79 A5
Iguaçu *River* Argentina/Brazil 44 C3
Iguîdi, 'Erg *desert* Algeria/ Mauritania 56 D1
Ihavananthapuram *island* Maldives 114 C4
Ihosy Madagascar 61 G4
Iisalmi Finland 66 E4
IJssel *river* Netherlands 68 D3
IJsselmeer *lake* Netherlands *prev.* Zuider Zee 68 D2
Ikaría *island* Greece 87 D5
Iki *island* Japan 113 A6
Ilagan Philippines 121 E1
Ilebo Dem. Rep. Congo 59 C6
Ili *River* China/Kazakhstan 94 D3
Iligan Philippines 121 F2
Illapel Chile 46 B3
Illinois *state* USA 22 B4
Iloilo Philippines 121 E2
Ilorin Nigeria 57 F4
İluh *see* Batman
Imatra Finland 67 E5
Imperatriz Brazil 43 F2
Impfondo Congo 59 C5
Imphāl India 117 H4
Independence Missouri, USA 25 F4
India *country* S Asia 114-115, 116-117
Indian Ocean 122-123
Indiana *state* USA 22 C4
Indianapolis Indiana, USA 22 C4
Indigirka *river* Russian Federation 95 F2
Indonesia *country* SE Asia 120-121
Indonesian Borneo *see* Kalimantan
Indore India 116 D4
Indus *river* S Asia 116 C1
Indus Cone *see.* Indus Fan
Indus Fan *var.* Indus Cone. *Undersea feature* Arabian Sea 122 B3
Indus, Mouths of the *wetlands* Pakistan 116 B4
Ingolstadt Germany 77 C6
Inguri *see* Enguri
Inhambane Mozambique 61 E4
Inn *river* C Europe 77 D6
Innaanganeq *headland* Greenland 64 C1
Inner Islands *islands* Seychelles 61 H1
Inner Mongolia *autonomous region* China 109 F3
Innsbruck Austria 77 C7
I-n-Sâkâne, Erg *Desert* Mali 57 E2
I-n-Salah Algeria 52 D3
Insein Myanmar 118 B4
Inukjuak Canada *prev.* Port Harrison 20 D2
Inuvik Canada 19 E3
Invercargill New Zealand 133 A7

Inverness Scotland, UK 70 C3
Investigator Ridge *undersea feature* Indian Ocean 122 D4
Ioánnina Greece 86 A4
Iónia Nisiá *island group* Greece *Eng.* Ionian Islands 87 A5
Ionian Islands *see* Iónia Nisiá
Ionian Sea Mediterranean Sea 87 A6
Íos *island* Greece 87 D6
Iowa *state* USA 25 F3
Ipoh Malaysia 120 B3
Ipswich England, UK 71 E6
Iqaluit Canada *prev.* Frobisher Bay 19 H3
Iquique Chile 46 B1
Iquitos Peru 42 B2
Irákleio Greece 87 D7
Iran *country* SW Asia 102-103
Iranian Plateau *upland* Iran 102 D4
Iraq *country* SW Asia 102
Irbid Jordan 101 B5
Ireland *country* W Europe 70-71
Irian Jaya *see* Papua
Irish Sea British Isles 71 C5
Irkutsk Russian Federation 97 E4
Iron Mountain Michigan, USA 22 B2
Ironwood Michigan, USA 22 B1
Irrawaddy *river* Myanmar 118 B2
Irrawaddy, Mouths of the *wetlands* Myanmar 118 A4
Irtysh *River* Asia 94 C3
Iruña *see* Pamplona
Ishim *River* Kazakhstan/Russian Federation 94 C3
Isiro Dem. Rep. Congo 59 E5
İskenderun Turkey *Eng.* Alexandretta 98 D4
Iskŭr *river* Bulgaria 86 C1
Iskŭr, Yazovir *Reservoir* Bulgaria 86 C2
Islay *island* Scotland, UK 70 B4
Islāmābād *capital of* Pakistan 116 C1
Ismaila *see* Al Ismā'īlīya
Isnā Egypt 54 B2
Isparta Turkey 98 B4
Israel *country* SW Asia 100-101
Issyk-Kul, Ozero *lake* Kyrgyzstan 105 G2
İstanbul Turkey *var.* Stambul, *prev.* Constantinople, Byzantium, *Bul.* Tsarigrad 98 B2
İstanbul Boğazi *see* Bosporus
Itabuna Brazil 43 G4
Itagüí Colombia 40 B2
Italy *country* S Europe 78-79
Ittoqqortoormiit Greenland 65 E3
Iturup *island* Japan/Russian Federation (disputed) 112 E1
Ivanhoe Australia 131 C6
Ivano-Frankivs'k Ukraine 90 C2
Ivanovo Russian Federation 92 B4
Ivittuut Greenland 64 B4
Ivory Coast *see* Côte d'Ivoire
Ivujivik Canada 20 D1
Iwaki Japan 112 D4
Izabal, Lago de *lake* Guatemala 34 C2
Izhevsk Russian Federation 93 C5 96 B3
İzmir Turkey *prev.* Smyrna 98 A3
İzmit Turkey *var.* Kocaeli 98 B2
Izu-shotō *island group* Japan 113 D6

J

Jabal ash Shifā *desert* Saudi Arabia 102 A4
Jabalpur India 116 E4
Jackson Mississippi, USA 30 C2
Jacksonville Florida, USA 31 E3
Jacksonville Texas, USA 29 G3
Jacmel Haiti 36 D3
Jaén Spain 75 E4
Jaffna Sri Lanka 115 E3
Jagdaqi China 109 G1
Jiangxi *province* China 111 C6
Jaipur India 116 D3
Jajce Bosnia & Herzegovina 82 C4
Jakarta *capital of* Indonesia 120 C5
Jakobstad Finland 66 D4
Jakobstadt *see* Jēkabpils
Jalālābād Afghanistan 105 E4
Jalal-Abad *see* Dzhalal-Abad
Jalandhar India 116 D2
Jalapa *see* Xalapa
Jamaame Somalia 55 D6
Jamaica *country* West Indies 36
Jamālpur Bangladesh 117 G4
Jambi Indonesia 120 B4
James Bay *sea feature* Canada 20 C4
Jammu & Kashmir *disputed region* India/Pakistan 116 D2
Jāmnagar India 116 B4
Jan Mayen *external territory* Norway, Arctic Ocean 65 F3
Japan *country* E Asia 112-113
Japan, Sea of Pacific Ocean 112 B3
Jarvis Island *unincorporated territory* USA, Pacific Ocean 125 F2
Java *see* Jawa
Java Sea Pacific Ocean *var.* Laut Jawa 122 D4
Java Trench *undersea feature* Indian Ocean 122 D4
Jawa *island* Indonesia *var.* Java 120 C5
Jawa, Laut *see* Java Sea
Jayapura Indonesia 121 H4
Jaz Mūrīān, Hāmūn-e *lake* Iran 102 E4
Jedda *see* Jiddah
Jefferson City Missouri, USA 25 G4
Jeju-do *island* South Korea *prev.* Cheju-do 111 E5
Jeju Strait *sea feature* South Korea *prev.* Cheju Strait 111 E5
Jēkabpils Latvia *Ger.* Jakobstadt 88 C4
Jelgava Latvia *Ger.* Mitau 88 C3
Jember Indonesia 120 D5
Jena Germany 76 C4

Jenīn *var.* Janīn, Jinīn; *anc.* Engannim. West Bank 101 D6
Jérémie Haiti 36 D3
Jerevan *see* Yerevan
Jericho West Bank 101 B5
Jerid, Chott el *salt lake* Africa 84 D4
Jersey *British Crown Dependency* Channel Islands 71 D8
Jerusalem *capital of* Israel 101 B5
Jhelum Pakistan 116 C2
Ji *see* Hebei
Ji *see* Jilin
Jiangsu *province* China *var.* Chiang-su, Kiangsu, Su 111 D5
Jiangxi *province* China *var.* Chiang-hsi, Gan, Kiangsi 111 C6
Jiaxing Zhejiang, China 111 D5
Jibuti *see* Djibouti
Jiddah Saudi Arabia *Eng.* Jedda 103 A5
Jiftlik Post West Bank 101 D7
Jihlava Czech Republic *Ger.* Iglau 81 B5
Jilin *province* China *var.* Chi-lin, Girin, Ji, Kirin 110 E3
Jilin China 110 E3
Jīma Ethiopia 55 C5
Jin *see* Shanxi
Jinan China 111 C4
Jingdezhen China 111 D5
Jinhua China 111 D5
Jining *see* Ulan Qab
Jinotega Nicaragua 34 D3
Jinsha Jiang *river* China 108 D5
Jinzhou China 110 D4
Jīzān Saudi Arabia 103 B6
João Pessoa Brazil 43 H3
Jodhpur India 116 C3
Joensuu Finland 67 E5
Johannesburg South Africa 60 D4
Johnston Atoll *US unincorporated territory* Pacific Ocean 125 E1
Johor Bahru Malaysia 120 C3
Joinville Brazil 44 D3
Joliet Illinois, USA 22 B3
Jönköping Sweden 67 B7
Jonquière Canada 21 E4
Jordan *country* SW Asia 100-101
Jordan *river* SW Asia 101 B5
Joseph Bonaparte Gulf *gulf* Australia 128 D2
Jos Plateau *upland* Nigeria 57 G4
Juan Fernandez, Islas *islands* Chile 46 A4
Juàzeiro Brazil 43 G3
Juàzeiro do Norte Brazil 43 G3
Juba *capital of* South Sudan 55 B5
Júcar *river* Spain 75 E3
Judenburg Austria 77 D7
Juigalpa Nicaragua 34 D3
Juiz de Fora Brazil 43 G5 45 F2
Juneau Alaska, USA 18 D4
Junggar Pendi *desert* China 108 C2
Junín Argentina 46 D4
Jura *mountains* France/ Switzerland 77 A7
Jura *island* Scotland, UK 70 B4
Jurbarkas Lithuania *Ger.* Jurburg, *var.* Georgenburg 88 B4
Jurburg *see* Jurbarkas
Juruá *river* Brazil/Peru 42 C2
Juticalpa Honduras 34 D2
Jutland see Jylland
Juventud, Isla de la *island* Cuba 36 B2
Jylland *peninsula* Denmark *Eng.* Jutland 67 A7
Jyväskylä Finland 67 D5

K

K2 *peak* China/Pakistan *Eng.* Mount Godwin Austen 116 D1
Kaachka *see* Kaka
Kaakhka *see* Kaka
Kabale Uganda 55 B6
Kabinda Dem. Rep. Congo 59 D7
Kābol *see* Kabul
Kabul *capital of* Afghanistan *Per.* Kabol 105 E4
Kachch, Gulf of *sea feature* Arabian Sea 116 B4
Kachch, Rann of *wetland* India/ Pakistan *var.* Rann of Kutch 116 B4
Kadugli Sudan 54 B4
Kaduna Nigeria 57 G4
Kaédi Mauritania 56 C3
Kâgheţ *Physical region* Mauritania 56 D1
Kagoshima Japan 113 A6
Kahramanmaraş Turkey *var.* Marash, Maraş 98 D4
Kai, Kepulauan *island group* Indonesia 121 G4
Kaifeng China 111 C5
Kaikohe New Zealand 132 C2
Kaikoura New Zealand 133 C5
Kainji Reservoir *Reservoir* Nigeria 57 F4
Kairouan Tunisia 53 E1
Kaiserslautern Germany 77 B5
Kaitaia New Zealand 132 C2
Kajaani Finland 66 E4
Kaka Turkmenistan *prev.* Kaakhka, *var.* Kaachka 104 C3
Kakhovka Ukraine 91 F4
Kakhovs'ka Vodoskhovyshche *Reservoir* Ukraine 91 F3
Kalahari Desert *desert* southern Africa 60 C4
Kalamariá Greece 86 C3
Kalámata Greece 87 B6
Kalāt *see* Qalāt
Kalbarri Australia 129 A5
Kalemie Dem. Rep. Congo 59 E7
Kalgoorlie Australia 129 C6
Kalimantan *geopolitical region* Indonesia *Eng.* Indonesian Borneo 120 D4
Kaliningrad *external territory* Russian Federation 96 A2
Kaliningrad Kaliningrad, Russian Federation *prev.* Königsberg 88 A4
Kalinkavichy Belarus *Rus.* Kalinkovichi 89 D7

Kalinkovichi *see* Kalinkavichy
Kalisch *see* Kalisz
Kalispell Montana, USA 24 B1
Kalisz Poland *Ger.* Kalisch 80 C4
Kalmar Sweden 67 C7
Kalpeni Island *island* India 114 C3
Kama *river* Russian Federation 92 D4
Kamchatka *peninsula* Russian Federation 97 H3
Kamchiya *river* Bulgaria 86 E2
Kamina Dem. Rep. Congo 59 D7
Kamishli *see* Al Qāmishlī
Kamloops Canada 19 E5
Kampala *capital of* Uganda 55 B6
Kâmpóng Cham Cambodia 119 D6
Kâmpóng Chhnăng Cambodia 119 D5
Kâmpóng Saôm *see* Sihanoukville
Kâmpôt Cambodia 119 D6
Kampuchea *see* Cambodia
Kam"yanets'-Podil's'kyy Ukraine 90 C3
Kananga Dem. Rep. Congo 59 D7
Kanazawa Japan 112 C4
Kandahār Afghanistan *var.* Qandahār 104 D5
Kandi Benin 57 F4
Kanivs'ke Vodoskhovyshche *Reservoir* Ukraine 91 E2
Kandy Sri Lanka 115 E3
Kanestron, Ákra *see* Palioúri, Akrotírio
Kangaroo Island *island* Australia 131 B7
Kangertittivaq *region* Greenland 64 E3
Kangikajik *headland* Greenland 65 E4
Kanjiža Serbia 82 D2
Kankan Guinea 56 D4
Kano Nigeria 57 G4
Kānpur India *prev.* Cawnpore 117 E3
Kansas *state* USA 24-25
Kansas City Kansas, USA 25 F4
Kansas City Missouri, USA 25 F4
Kansk Russian Federation 97 E4
Kansu *see* Gansu
Kaohsiung *see* Gaoxiong
Kaolack Senegal 56 B3
Kapfenberg Austria 77 E7
Kaposvár Hungary 81 C7
Kapsukas *see* Marijampolė
Kapuas *river* Indonesia 120 D4
Kara-Balta Kyrgyzstan 105 F2
Karabük Turkey 98 C2
Karāchi Pakistan 116 B4
Karaganda *see* Karagandy
Karagandy Kazakhstan *prev.* Karaganda 96 C4
Karakol Kyrgyzstan *prev.* Przheval'sk 105 G2
Kara Kum *see* Garagum
Karakumskiy Kanal *see* Garagum Kanaly
Karakumy *see* Garagum
Karamay China 108 C2
Karamea Bight *gulf* New Zealand 133 C5
Karasburg Namibia 60 C4
Kara Sea *see* Karskoye More
Kardítsa Greece 86 B4
Kariba, Lake *lake* Zambia/ Zimbabwe 60 D3
Karimata, Selat *strait* Indonesia 120 C4
Karkinits'ka Zatoka *sea feature* Black Sea 91 E4
Karl-Marx-Stadt *see* Chemnitz
Karlovac Croatia 82 B3
Karlovy Vary Czech Republic *Ger.* Karlsbad 81 A5
Karlsbad *see* Karlovy Vary
Karlskrona Sweden 67 C7
Karlsruhe Germany 77 B5
Karlstad Sweden 67 B6
Karnātaka *state* India 114 D1
Kárpathos *island* Greece 87 E7
Kars Turkey 99 F2
Karshi Uzbekistan *prev.* Bek-Budi, *Uzb.* Qarshi 104 D3
Karskoye More Arctic Ocean *Eng.* Kara Sea 137 H3
Kasai *river* Dem. Rep. Congo 59 C6
Kasama Zambia 61 E2
Kaschau *see* Košice
Kāshān Iran 102 C3
Kashi China 108 A3
Kasongo Dem. Rep. Congo 59 E6
Kassa *see* Košice
Kassala Sudan 54 C4
Kassel Germany 76 B4
Kastamonu Turkey 98 C2
Katanning Australia 129 B6
Kateríni Greece 86 B4
Katha Myanmar 118 B2
Katherine Australia 128 E2
Kathmandu *capital of* Nepal 117 F3
Katsina Nigeria 57 G3
Katowice Poland 81 C5
Kauen *see* Kaunas
Kaunas Lithuania *Ger.* Kauen, *Pol.* Kowno, *Rus.* Kovno 88 B4
Kavadarci Macedonia 82 E5
Kavála Greece 86 C3
Kavaratti Island *island* India 114 C3
Kavīr, Dasht-e *Salt pan* Iran 102 D3
Kawasaki Japan 113 D5
Kayan *river* Indonesia 120 D3
Kayes Mali 56 C3
Kayseri Turkey 98 D3
Kazakhstan *country* C Asia 96
Kazan' Russian Federation 96 B3
Kazandzhik *see* Bereket
Kazanlŭk Bulgaria 86 D2
Kecskemét Hungary 81 D7
Kediri Indonesia 120 D5
Keetmanshoop Namibia 60 C4
Kefalloniá *island* Greece *Eng.* Cephalonia 87 A5
Keá *see* Tziá
Kelang *see* Klang
Kelmė Lithuania 88 B4
Kelowna Canada 19 E5
Kemerovo Russian Federation 96 D4
Kemi Finland 66 D4

Kemi *river* Finland 66 D3
Kemijärvi Finland 66 D3
Kendari Indonesia 121 E4
Këneurgench *see* Köneürgench
Kénitra Morocco 52 C2
Kennewick Washington, USA 26 C2
Kenora Canada 20 A3
Kentucky *state* USA 22 C5
Kenya *country* E Africa 55
Kerala *state* India 114 D3
Kerch Ukraine 91 G4
Kerguelen *island group* Indian Ocean 123 C7
Kerguelen Plateau *undersea feature* Indian Ocean 123 C7
Kerki *see* Atamyrat
Kérkira *see* Kérkyra
Kérkyra Greece 86 A4
Kérkyra *island* Greece *prev.* Kérkira, *Eng.* Corfu 86 A4
Kermadec Islands *island group* Pacific Ocean 125 E4
Kermadec Trench *undersea feature* Pacific Ocean 125 E4
Kermān Iran *var.* Kirman 102 D4
Kermānshāh Iran *prev.* Bākhtarān 102 C3
Kerulen *river* China/Mongolia 109 E2
Ketchikan Alaska, USA 18 D4
Key West Florida, USA 31 E5
Khabarovsk Russian Federation 97 G4
Khanka, Lake *lake* China/ Russian Federation 110 E3
Khankendy *see* Xankändi
Kharkiv Ukraine *Rus.* Khar'kov 91 G2
Khar'kov *see* Kharkiv
Khartoum *capital of* Sudan *var.* Al Khurţūm 54 B4
Khāsh Iran 102 E4
Khaskovo Bulgaria 86 D2
Khaydarkan Kyrgyzstan *var.* Khaydarken, Hajdarken 105 E2
Khaydarken *see* Khaydarkan
Kherson Ukraine 91 E4
Kheta *river* Russian Federation 94 D2
Khíos *see* Chíos
Khirbet el 'Aujā et Tahtā West Bank 101 D6
Khmel 'nyts'kyy Ukraine 90 D2
Khodzhent *see* Khŭjand
Khojend *see* Khŭjand
Khokand *see* Qo'qon
Kholm *see* Khulm
Khon Kaen Thailand 118 C4
Khorog *see* Khorugh
Khorugh Tajikistan *Rus.* Khorog 105 F3
Khouribga Morocco 52 C2
Khudzhand *see* Khŭjand
Khŭjand Tajikistan *var.* Khodzheut, Khojend, *Rus.* Khudzhand *prev.* Leninabad 105 E2
Khulna Bangladesh 117 G4
Khulm Afghanistan *prev.* Kholm 105 E3
Khvoy Iran 102 B3
Kiangsi *see* Jiangxi
Kiangsu *see* Jiangsu
Kičevo Macedonia 83 D5
Kiel Germany 76 C2
Kielce Poland 80 D4
Kiev *capital of* Ukraine *Ukr.* Kyyiv 91 E2
Kiffa Mauritania 56 C3
Kigali *capital of* Rwanda 55 B6
Kigoma Tanzania 55 B7
Kikládhes *see* Kyklades
Kikwit Dem. Rep. Congo 59 C6
Kilimanjaro *peak* Tanzania 55 C7
Kilkís Greece 86 B3
Killarney Ireland 71 A6
Kimberley South Africa 60 D4
Kimberley Plateau *upland* Australia 128 D3
Kindia Guinea 56 C4
Kindu Dem. Rep. Congo 59 D6
King Island *island* Australia 131 C7
Kingissepp *see* Kuressaare
Kingman Reef *unincorporated territory* USA, Pacific Ocean 125 F2
King Sound *sound* Australia 128 C3
Kingsport Tennessee, USA 31 E1
Kingsville Texas, USA 29 G5
Kingston Canada 20 C5
Kingston *capital of* Jamaica 36 C3
Kingston upon Hull England, UK *var.* Hull 71 E5
Kingstown St Vincent & The Grenadines 36 G4
King William Island *island* Canada 19 F3
Kinneret, Yam *see* Tiberius, Lake
Kinshasa *capital of* Dem. Rep. Congo *prev.* Léopoldville 59 B6
Kirghizia *see* Kyrgyzstan
Kiribati *country* Pacific Ocean 127
Kirin *see* Jilin
Kiritimati *island* Kiribati *var.* Christmas Island 127 G2
Kirkenes Norway 66 E2
Kirklareli Turkey 98 A2
Kirksville Missouri, USA 25 F4
Kirkūk Iraq 102 B3
Kirkwall Scotland, UK 70 C2
Kirman *see* Kermān
Kirov Russian Federation 92 C4 96 B3
Kirovabad *see* Gäncä
Kirovakan *see* Vanadzor
Kirovohrad Ukraine 91 E3
Kiruna Sweden 66 C3
Kisangani Dem. Rep. Congo *prev.* Stanleyville 59 D5
Kishinev *see* Chişinău
Kismaayo Somalia 55 D6
Kisumu Kenya 55 C6
Kitakyūshū Japan 113 A5
Kitami Japan 112 D2
Kitchener Canada 20 C5
Kitwe Zambia 60 D2
Kivu, Lake *lake* Rwanda/Dem. Rep. Congo 55 B6 59 E6
Kızıl Irmak *river* Turkey 98 C2
Kizyl-Arvat *see* Serdar

Kladno Czech Republic 81 A5
Klagenfurt Austria 77 D7
Klaipėda Lithuania *Ger.* Memel 88 B4
Klamath Falls Oregon, USA 26 B4
Khang Malaysia *var.* Kelang 120 B2
Ključ Bosnia & Herzegovina 82 B3
Knin Croatia 82 B4
Knoxville Tennessee, USA 31 E1
Knud Rasmussen Land *region* Greenland 64 D1
Kōbe Japan 113 C5
Koblenz Germany 77 B5
Kobryn Belarus 89 B6
Kocaeli *see* İzmit
Kočani Macedonia 83 E5
Kōchi Japan 113 B6
Kochi India *see* Cochin 114 D3
Kodiak Alaska, USA 18 C3
Kodiak Island *island* Alaska, USA 18 C3
Koedoes *see* Kudus
Kohīma India 117 H3
Kohtla-Järve Estonia 88 D2
Kokand *see* Qo'qon
Kokchetav Kazakhstan 96 C4
Kokkola Finland 66 D4
Koko Nor *see* Qinghai
Koko Nor *see* Qinghai Hu
Kokshaal-Tau *mountain range* Kyrgyzstan 105 G2
Kola Peninsula *see* Kol'skiy Poluostrov
Kolguyev, Ostrov *island* Russian Federation 92 D2
Kolhumadulu Atoll *island* Maldives 114 C5
Kolka Latvia 88 C3
Kolkata India *var.* Calcutta 117 F4
Köln Germany *Eng.* Cologne 76 B4
Kol'skiy Poluostrov *peninsula* Russian Federation *Eng.* Kola Peninsula 63 F1 92 C2
Kolwezi Dem. Rep. Congo 59 D8
Kolyma *river* Russian Federation 95 G2
Kommunizma, Pik *see* Communism Peak
Komoé *river* Côte d'Ivoire 57 E4
Komotiní Greece 86 D3
Komsomol'sk-na-Amure Russian Federation 97 G4
Kondoz *see* Kunduz
Konduz *see* Kunduz
Köneürgench Turkmenistan *prev.* Kunya-Urgench, *prev.* Këneurgench 104 C2
Kong Christian IX Land *region* Greenland 64 D4
Kong Christian X Land *region* Greenland 64 E3
Kong Frederik VI Kyst *region* Greenland 64 C4
Kong Frederik VIII Land *region* Greenland 64 E2
Kong Frederik IX Land *region* Greenland 64 C3
Kong Karls Land *island group* Svalbard 65 G2
Kong Oscar Fjord *fjord* Greenland 65 E3
Konia *see* Konya
Königgrätz *see* Hradec Králové
Königsberg *see* Kaliningrad
Konispol Albania 83 D7
Konjic Bosnia & Herzegovina 82 C4
Konya Turkey *prev.* Konia 98 C4
Kopaonik *mountains* Serbia 83 D4
Koper Slovenia 77 D8
Koprivnica Croatia 82 B2
Korçë Albania 83 D6
Korčula *island* Croatia 82 B4
Korea Bay *bay* China/North Korea 110 D4
Korea Strait *sea feature* Japan/ South Korea 110-111 E5
Korinthiakós Kólpos *sea feature* Greece *Eng.* Gulf of Corinth 87 B5
Kórinthos Greece *Eng.* Corinth 87 B5
Kōriyama Japan 113 D4
Korla China 108 C3
Korosten' Ukraine 90 D1
Kortrijk Belgium 69 A6
Kos *island* Greece 87 E6
Kosciusko, Mount *peak* Australia 131 D7
Košice Slovakia *Ger.* Kaschau, *Hung.* Kassa 81 D6
Köslin *see* Koszalin
Kosovo *country* SE Europe 83 D5
Kosovska Mitrovica *see* Mitrovicë/Mitrovica
Kosrae *island* Micronesia 126 C2
Kossou, Lac de *lake* Côte d'Ivoire 56 D4
Kostanay Kazakhstan *var.* Kustanay 96 C4
Kostyantynivka Ukraine 91 G3
Koszalin Poland *Ger.* Köslin 80 B2
Kota India 116 D4
Kota Bharu Malaysia 120 B3
Kota Kinabalu Malaysia 120 D3
Kotka Finland 67 E5
Kotlas NW Russia 92 C4
Kotuy *river* Russian Federation 95 E2
Koudougou Burkina Faso 57 E4
Kourou French Guiana 41 H2
Kousséri Cameroon 58 B3
Kouvola Finland 67 E5
Kovel' Ukraine 90 C1
Kovno *see* Kaunas
Kowno *see* Kaunas
Kozáni Greece 86 B4
Kozhikode India *see* Calicut 114 D2
Kra, Isthmus of *coastal feature* Myanmar/Thailand 119 B6
Kragujevac Serbia 82 D4
Krakau *see* Kraków
Kraków Poland *Eng.* Cracow, *Ger.* Krakau 81 D5
Kralendijk Bonaire 37 E5
Kraljevo Serbia 82 D4
Kranj Slovenia 77 D7
Krasnodar Russian Federation 93 A6

Krasnovodsk *see* Türkmenbaşy
Krasnoyarsk Russian Federation 96 D4
Krasnyy Luch Ukraine 91 H3
Kremenchuk Ukraine 91 F2
Kremenchuts'ke Vodoskhovyshche *Reservoir* Ukraine 91 E2
Krems an der Donau Austria 77 E6
Kretinga Lithuania *Ger.* Krottingen 88 B3
Krichev *see* Krychaw
Krishna *river* India 114 C1
Kristiansand Norway 67 A6
Kristianstad Sweden 67 B7
Kríti *island* Greece *Eng.* Crete 87 C7
Kritikó Pélagos *see* Crete, Sea of
Krivoy Rog *see* Kryvyy Rih
Krk *island* Croatia 82 A3
Kroonstad South Africa 60 D4
Krottingen *see* Kretinga
Krung Thep *see* Bangkok
Kruševac Serbia 83 E4
Krušné Hory *see* Erzgebirge
Krychaw Belarus *Rus.* Krichev 89 E6
Kryms'kyy Pivostriv *peninsula* Ukraine *var.* Crimea 90 F4
Kryvyy Rih Ukraine *Rus.* Krivoy Rog 91 E3
Kuala Lumpur *capital of* Malaysia 120 B3
Kuala Terengganu Malaysia 120 B3
Kuang-tung *see* Guangdong
Kuantan Malaysia 120 C3
Kuba *see* Quba
Kuching Malaysia 120 C3
Kuçovë Albania *prev.* Qyteti Stalin 83 D6
Kudus Indonesia *prev.* Koedoes 120 D5
Kuei-chou *see* China Guizhou
Kugluktuk Canada *prev.* Coppermine 19 E3
Kuito Angola 60 C2
Kuldīga Latvia *Ger.* Goldingen 88 B3
Kullorsuaq Greenland 64 C2
Kŭlob Tajikistan *Rus.* Kulyab 105 E3
Kulyab *see* Kŭlob
Kum *see* Qom
Kuma *river* Russian Federation 93 B7
Kumamoto Japan 113 B6
Kumanovo Macedonia 83 E5
Kumasi Ghana 57 E5
Kumayri *see* Gyumri 99 F2
Kumo Nigeria 57 G4
Kumon Range *mountain range* Myanmar 118 B1
Kunashir *island* Japan/Russian Federation (disputed) 112 E1
Kunduz Afghanistan *var.* Kondoz, Konduz, Qondūz 105 E3
Kunja-Urgenč *see* Köneürgench
Kunlun Mountains *see* Kunlun Shan
Kunlun Shan *mountain range* China *Eng.* Kunlun Mountains 106 B4
Kunming China 111 B6
Kununurra Australia 128 D3
Kupang Indonesia 120 E5
Kür *see* Kura
Kura *river* Azerbaijan/Georgia *Az.* Kür 99 G2
Kurashiki Japan 113 B5
Kurdistan *region* Turkey 99 F4
Küre Dağları *mountains* Turkey 98 C2
Kuressaare Estonia *prev.* Kingissepp, *Ger.* Arensburg 88 C2
Kurgan–Tyube *see* Qŭrghonteppa
Kuril Islands *islands var.* Kurile Islands Pacific Ocean 112 E1
Kurile Islands *see* Kuril Islands
Kuril Trench *undersea feature* Pacific Ocean 134 C2
Kurnool India 114 D2
Kushiro Japan 112 E2
Kushka *see* Serhetabat
Kustanay *see* Kostanay
Kütahya Turkey *prev.* Kutaiah 98 B3
Kutaiah *see* Kütahya
Kutaisi Georgia 99 F2
Kutch, Rann of *see* Kachch, Rann of
Kuujjuaq Canada 21 E2
Kuujjuarapik Canada *prev.* Poste-de-la-Baleine 20 D2
Kuusamo Finland 66 E3
Kuwait *country* SW Asia 102 C4
Kuwait City *capital of* Kuwait 102 C4
Kuytun China 108 C2
Kvitøya *island* Svalbard 65 G1
Kwangju *see* Gwangju
Kwango *river* Dem. Rep. Congo 59 C7
Kwangtung *see* Guangdong
Kweichow *see* Guizhou
Kykládes *island group* Greece *prev.* Kikládhes, *Eng.* Cyclades 87 D6
Kyrenia *see* Girne
Kyrgyzstan *country* C Asia *var.* Kirghizia 105
Kýthira *island* Greece 87 B6
Kyushu-Palau Ridge *undersea feature* Pacific Ocean 124 B1
Kyyiv *see* Kiev
Kyyivs'ke Vodoskhovyshche *Reservoir* Ukraine 91 E1
Kyōto Japan 113 C5
Kyūshū *island* Japan 113 B6
Kyzylorda Kazakhstan 96 B5

L

Laâyoune Western Sahara 52 B3
Labé Guinea 56 C4
Laborca *see* Laborec
Laborec *river* Slovakia *Hung.* Laborca 81 E5
Labrador *region* Canada 21 F2
Labrador Sea Atlantic Ocean 64 B5
Laccadive Islands *see* Lakshadweep
La Ceiba Honduras 34 D2
Lachlan River *river* Australia 131 C6
La Coruña *see* A Coruña

La Crosse Wisconsin, USA 22 A2
Ladoga, Lake *see* Ladozhskoye Ozero
Ladozhskoye Ozero *lake* Russian Federation *Eng.* Lake Ladoga 92 B3
Ladysmith Wisconsin, USA 22 A2
Lae Papua New Guinea 126 B3
La Esperanza Honduras 34 C2
Lafayette Louisiana, USA 30 B3
Laghouat Algeria 52 D2
Lagos Nigeria 57 F5
Lagos Portugal 74 C4
Lagouira Western Sahara 52 A4
La Grande Oregon, USA 26 C3
La Habana *see* Havana
Lahore Pakistan 116 C2
Laï Chad 58 C4
Laila *see* Laylá
Lajes Brazil 44 D3
Lake Charles Louisiana, USA 30 B3
Lake District *region* England, UK 71 C5
Lakewood Colorado, USA 24 D4
Lakshadweep *island group* India *Eng.* Laccadive Islands 114 B2
La Ligua Chile 46 B4
La Louvière Belgium 69 B6
Lambaré Paraguay 44 B3
Lambaréné Gabon 59 B6
Lamía Greece 86 B4
Lancaster England, UK 71 D5
Lancaster California, USA 27 C7
Lancaster Sound *sea feature* Canada 19 F2
Landsberg *see* Gorzów Wielkopolski
Land's End *coastal feature* England, UK 71 C7
Landshut Germany 77 D6
Lang Sơn Vietnam 118 D3
Länkäran Azerbaijan *Rus.* Lenkoran' 99 H3
Lansing Michigan, USA 22 C3
Lanzarote *island* Spain 52 B3
Lanzhou China 110 B4
Laon France 72 D3
La Oroya Peru 42 B3
Laos *country* SE Asia 118
La Palma *island* Spain 52 A3
La Paz *legislative & administrative capital of* Bolivia 42 C4
La Paz Mexico 32 B3
La Pérouse Strait *sea feature* Japan 112 D1
Lapland *region* N Europe 66 C3
La Plata Argentina 46 D4
Lappeenranta Finland 67 E5
Laptev Sea *see* Laptevykh, More
Laptevykh, More Arctic Ocean *Eng.* Laptev Sea 97 F2
L'Aquila Italy 78 C4
Laramie Wyoming, USA 24 C4
Laredo Texas, USA 29 F5
La Rioja Argentina 46 C3
Lárisa Greece 86 B4
Lārkāna Pakistan 116 B3
Larnaca Cyprus *var.* Larnaka, Larnax 98 C5
Larnaka *see* Larnaca
Larnax *see* Larnaca
La Rochelle France 72 B4
La Roche-sur-Yon France 72 B4
La Romana Dominican Republic 36 E3
Las Cruces New Mexico, USA 28 D3
Las Piedras Uruguay 44 C5
La Serena Chile 46 B3
La Spezia Italy 78 B3
Las Tablas Panama 35 F5
Las Vegas Nevada, USA 27 D7
Latakia *see* Al Lādhiqīyah
Latvia *country* NE Europe 88
Launceston Tasmania 131 C8
Laurentian Basin *see* Canada Basin
Laurentian Mountains *upland* Canada 16 D4
Lausanne Switzerland 77 A7
Laut, Pulau *prev.* Laoet. *Island* Indonesia 120 D4
Laval France 72 B4
Lawton Oklahoma, USA 29 F2
Laylá Saudi Arabia 103 C5
Lazarev Sea *sea* Antarctica 136 B2
Lebanon *country* SW Asia 100-101
Lebu Chile 47 B5
Lecce Italy 79 E5
Leduc Canada 19 E5
Leeds England, UK 71 D5
Leeuwarden Netherlands 68 D1
Leeward Islands *see* Sotavento, Ilhas de
Lefkáda *island* Greece *prev.* Levkás 87 A5
Lefkoşa *see* Nicosia
Lefkosia *see* Nicosia
Legaspi *see* Legazpi City
Legazpi City Philippines *var.* Legaspi 120 E2
Legnica Poland *Ger.* Liegnitz 80 B4
Le Havre France 72 B3
Leicester England, UK 71 D6
Leiden Netherlands 68 C3
Leipzig Germany 76 D4
Lek *river* Netherlands 68 C4
Le Léman *see* Geneva, Lake
Lelystad Netherlands 68 D3
Léman, Lac *see* Geneva, Lake
Le Mans France 72 B4
Lemesos *see* Limassol
Lemnos *see* Límnos
Lena *river* Russian Federation 97 F3
Leninabad *see* Khŭjand
Leninakan *see* Gyumri
Leningrad *see* St Petersburg
Leninsk *see* Türkmenabat
Lenkoran' *see* Länkäran
León Mexico 33 E4
León Nicaragua 34 C3
León Spain 74 D1
Léopoldville *see* Kinshasa
Lepel' *see* Lyepyel'
Le Puy France 73 C5
Lérida *see* Lleida
Lerwick Scotland, UK 70 D1
Lesbos *see* Lésvos
Leshan China 111 B5

Leskovac Serbia 82 E4
Lesotho *country* southern Africa 60
Lesser Antilles *island group* West Indies 37 G4
Lésvos *island* Greece *Eng.* Lesbos 86 D4
Lethbridge Canada 19 E5
Leti, Kepulauan *island group* Indonesia 121 F5
Leuven Belgium 69 C6
Leverkusen Germany 76 A4
Levin New Zealand 132 D4
Levkás *see* Lefkáda
Lewis *island* Scotland, UK 70 B2
Lewiston Idaho, USA 26 C2
Lewiston Maine, USA 23 G2
Lexington Kentucky, USA 22 C5
Lezhë Albania 83 D5
Lhasa China 108 C5
Lhazê China 108 C4
L'Hospitalet de Llobregat *var.* Hospitalet. Spain 75 G2
Liao *see* Liaoning
Liaoning *province* China *var.* Liao, Shengking; *hist.* Fengtien, Shenking. Admin. region 110 D3
Libau *see* Liepāja
Liberec Czech Republic *Ger.* Reichenberg 80 B4
Liberia *country* W Africa 56
Liberia Costa Rica 34 D4
Libreville *capital of* Gabon 59 A5
Libya *country* N Africa 53
Libyan Desert *desert* N Africa 50 C3
Lichuan China 111 B5
Liechtenstein *country* C Europe 77 B7
Liège Belgium 69 D6
Liegnitz *see* Legnica
Lienz Austria 77 D7
Linz Austria 77 D7
Liepāja Latvia *Ger.* Libau 88 B3
Liffey *river* Ireland 71 B5
Ligurian Sea Mediterranean Sea 78 A3
Likasi Dem. Rep. Congo 59 E8
Lille France 72 D2
Lillehammer Norway 67 B5
Lilongwe *capital of* Malawi 61 E2
Lima *capital of* Peru 42 B4
Limassol Cyprus *var.* Lemesos 98 C5
Limerick Ireland 71 A6
Límnos *island* Greece *var.* Lemnos 86 D4
Limoges France 72 C5
Limón Costa Rica 35 E4
Limpopo *river* southern Africa 60 D3
Linares Chile 46 B4
Linares Spain 75 E4
Linchuan *see* Fuzhou
Lincoln England, UK 71 D5
Lincoln Nebraska, USA 25 F4
Lincoln Sea Arctic Ocean 64 E1
Linden Guyana 41 G2
Lindi Tanzania 55 C8
Line Islands *island group* Kiribati 127 G2
Linköping Sweden 67 C6
Linz Austria 77 D6
Lion, Golfe du *sea feature* Mediterranean Sea 73 D6
Lipari, Isola *island* Italy 79 D6
Lipari Islands *see* Isole Eolie
Lira Uganda 55 B6
Lisbon *capital of* Portugal *Port.* Lisboa 74 B3
Litani *river* SW Asia 91 B4
Lithuania *country* E Europe 88-89
Little Andaman *island* India 115 G2
Little Minch *sea feature* Scotland, UK 70 B3
Little Rock Arkansas, USA 30 B2
Liuzhou China 111 C6
Liverpool England, UK 71 D5
Livingstone Zambia 60 D3
Livno Bosnia & Herzegovina 82 B4
Livorno Italy 78 B3
Ljubljana *capital of* Slovenia 77 D7
Ljusnan *river* Sweden 67 B5
Llanos *region* Colombia/ Venezuela 41 E2
Lleida Spain *Cast.* Lérida 75 F2
Lobatse Botswana 60 D4
Lobito Angola 60 B2
Locarno Switzerland 77 B7
Lodja Dem. Rep. Congo 59 D6
Łódź Poland *Rus.* Lodz 80 D4
Lofoten *island group* Norway 66 B3
Logroño Spain 75 E2
Loire *river* France 72 B4
Loja Ecuador 40 A5
Lokitaung Kenya 55 C5
Loksa Estonia *Ger.* Loxa 88 D2
Lombok, Pulau *island* Indonesia 120 D5
Lomé *capital of* Togo 57 E5
Lomond, Loch *lake* Scotland, UK 70 C4
London Canada 20 C5
London *capital of* UK 71 E6
Londonderry Northern Ireland, UK 70 B4
Londonderry, Cape *coastal feature* Australia 128 D2
Londrina Brazil 44 D2
Long Beach California, USA 27 C8
Long Island *island* The Bahamas 34 D2
Long Island *island* NE USA 23 G3
Longreach Australia 130 C4
Long Strait *Strait* Russian Federation 95 H2
Longview Texas, USA 29 G3
Longview Washington, USA 26 B2
Longyearbyen Svalbard 65 F2
Lop Nur *lake* China 108 C3
Lorca Spain 75 E4
Lord Howe Island *island* Australia 124 C4
Lord Howe Rise *undersea feature* Pacific Ocean 124 D4

Lorient France 72 A4
Los Alamos New Mexico, USA 28 D1
Los Angeles California, USA 27 C7
Loslau *see* Wodzisław Śląski
Los Mochis Mexico 32 C3
Losonc *see* Lučenec
Losontz *see* Lučenec
Lot *river* France 73 B5
Louangphrabang Laos 118 C3
Loubomo Congo 59 B6
Louisiana *state* USA 30 B3
Louisville Kentucky, USA 22 C5
Louisville Ridge *undersea feature* Pacific Ocean 125 E4
Lovech Bulgaria 86 C2
Lower California *see* Baja California
Lower Hutt New Zealand
Loxa *see* Loksa
Loyauté, Îles *island group* New Caledonia 126 D5
Loznica Serbia 82 C3
Lu *see* Shandong
Luanda *capital of* Angola 60 B1
Luanshya Zambia 60 D2
Lubango Angola 60 B2
Lubbock Texas, USA 29 E2
Lübeck Germany 76 C3
Lublin Poland *Rus.* Lyublin 80 E4
Lubny Ukraine 91 F2
Lubumbashi Dem. Rep. Congo 59 E8
Lucapa Angola 60 C1
Lucena Philippines 120 E2
Lučenec Slovakia *Hung.* Losonc, *Ger.* Losontz 81 D6
Lucerne *see* Luzern
Lucknow India 117 E3
Lüderitz Namibia 60 C4
Ludhiāna India 116 D2
Lugano Switzerland 77 B7
Lugo Spain 74 C1
Luhans'k Ukraine 91 H3
Luleå Sweden 66 D4
Lumsden New Zealand 133 A7
Lüneburg Germany 76 C3
Luninyets Belarus 89 C6
Luoyang *var.* Honan, Lo-yang. China 110 C4
Lusaka *capital of* Zambia 60 D2
Lushnjë Albania 83 D6
Lūt, Baḩrat *see* Dead Sea
Luts'k Ukraine 90 C1
Luxembourg *country* W Europe 69 D8
Luxembourg *capital of* Luxembourg 69 D8
Luxor *see* Al Uqşur
Luzern Switzerland *Fr.* Lucerne 77 B7
Luzon *island* Philippines 121 E1
Luzon Strait *sea feature* Philippines/Taiwan 107 E3
L'viv Ukraine *Rus.* L'vov 90 C2
L'vov see L'viv
Lyepyel' Belarus *Rus.* Lepel' 89 D5
Lyon France 73 D5
Lyublin *see* Lublin

M

Ma'ān Jordan 101 B6
Maas *see* Meuse
Maastricht Netherlands 69 D6
Macao *special administrative region* China, E Asia *var.* Macau 111 C7
Macapá Brazil 43 F1
Macau *see* Macao
Macdonnell Ranges *mountains* Australia 130 A4
Macedonia *country* SE Europe officially Former Yugoslav Republic of Macedonia, *abbrev.* FYR Macedonia 83
Maceió Brazil 43 H3
Machala Ecuador 40 A5
Mackay Australia 130 D4
Mackay, Lake *lake* Australia 128 D4
Mackenzie *river* Canada 19 E4
Mackenzie Bay *sea feature* Atlantic Ocean 136 D3
Macleod, Lake *lake* Australia128 A4
Mâcon France 72 D5
Macon Georgia, USA 31 E2
Madagascar *country* Indian Ocean 61
Madagascar Basin *undersea feature* Indian Ocean 123 B5
Madagascar Plateau *undersea feature* Indian Ocean 123 A6
Madang Papua New Guinea 126 B3
Madeira *river* Bolivia/Brazil 42 D2
Madeira *island group* Portugal 52 A2
Madhya Pradesh *state* India 117 E4
Madison Wisconsin, USA 22 B3
Madiun *prev.* Madioen. Indonesia 120 D5
Madona Latvia *Ger.* Modohn 88 D3
Madras *see* Chennai
Madre de Dios *river* Bolivia/Peru 42 C3
Madrid *capital of* Spain 75 E3
Madurai India 114 D3
Magadan Russian Fed. 97 G3
Magallanes *see* Punta Arenas
Magallanes, Estrecho de *see* Magellan, Strait of
Magdalena *river* Colombia 40 B2
Magdeburg Germany 76 C4
Magelang Indonesia 120 C5
Magellan, Strait of *sea feature* S South America *Sp.* Estrecho de Magallanes 47 B8
Maggiore, Lake *lake* Italy/Switzerland 78 B2
Mahajanga Madagascar 61 G3
Mahalapye Botswana 60 D4
Mahanādi *river* India 117 F5
Mahārashtra *state* India 116 D5
Mahé *island* Seychelles 61 H1
Mahilyow/Mogilëv Belarus *Rus.* Mogilëv 89 E6
Mährisch-Ostrau *see* Ostrava

Maicao Colombia 40 C1
Maiduguri Nigeria 57 H4
Maīmanah Afghanistan *prev.* Meymaneh 104 D4
Maine *state* USA 23 G1
Maine, Gulf of *gulf* USA 23 G2
Mainz Germany 77 B5
Maio *Island* Cape Verde 56 A3
Maíz, Islas del *islands* Nicaragua 35 E3
Majorca *see* Mallorca
Majuro *island* Marshall Islands 126 D1
Makarska Croatia 82 B4
Makarov Basin *undersea feature* Arctic Ocean 137 G3
Makassar Indonesia *prev.* Ujungpandang 121 E4
Makassar Strait *strait* Indonesia 120 D4
Makeyevka *see* Makiyivka
Makhachkala Russian Federation 93 B7 96 A4
Makiyivka Ukraine *Rus.* Makeyevka 91 G5
Makkah Saudi Arabia *Eng.* Mecca 103 A5
Makkovik Canada 21 F2
Malabo *capital of* Equatorial Guinea 59 A5
Malacca, Strait of *sea feature* Indonesia/ Malaysia 106 C4 119 C8 120 B3
Maladzyechna Belarus *Rus.* Molodechno, *Pol.* Molodeczno 89 C5
Málaga Spain 74 D5
Malakal South Sudan 55 B5
Malang Indonesia 120 D5
Malanje Angola 60 C2
Malatya Turkey 99 E3
Malawi *country* southern Africa 61
Malay Peninsula *peninsula* Malaysia/Thailand 119 D8
Malaysia *country* Asia 120
Malden Island *atoll* Kiribati 125 F2
Maldives *country* Indian Ocean 114 C4
Male' *capital of* Maldives 114 C4
Malekula *island* Vanuatu 124 D3
Mali *country* W Africa 57
Malindi Kenya 55 C7
Mallorca *island* Spain *Eng.* Majorca 75 H3
Malmö Sweden 67 B7
Malta *country* Mediterranean Sea 79 C8
Malta Montana, USA 24 C1
Malta Channel *sea feature* Mediterranean Sea 79 C7
Maluku *island group* Indonesia *var.* Moluccas 107 E4 121 F4
Maluku, Laut Pacific Ocean *Eng.* Molucca Sea 121 F4
Mamberamo *river* Indonesia 121 H4
Mamoudzou *capital of* Mayotte 61 G2
Man, Isle of *British Crown Dependency* UK 71 C5
Manado Indonesia 121 F3
Managua *capital of* Nicaragua 34 D3
Manama *capital of* Bahrain *Ar.* Al Manāmah 103 C5
Mananjary Madagascar 61 G3
Manaus Brazil 42 D2
Manchester England, UK 71 D5
Manchester New Hampshire, USA 23 G2
Manchurian Plain *plain* E Asia 107 E1
Mandalay Myanmar 118 B3
Mangalia Romania 90 D5
Mangalore India 114 C2
Manicouagan, Réservoir *Reservoir* Canada 21 E3
Manihiki *atoll* Cook Islands 125 F3
Maniitsoq Greenland 64 C3
Manila *capital of* Philippines 121 E1
Manisa Turkey *prev.* Saruhan 98 A3
Manitoba *province* Canada 19 G4
Manizales Colombia 40 B3
Manjimup Australia 129 B7
Mannar Sri Lanka 115 E3
Mannar, Gulf of *sea feature* Indian Ocean 114 D3
Mannheim Germany 77 B5
Manono Dem. Rep. Congo 59 E7
Mansel Island *island* Canada 20 C1
Mansfield Ohio, USA 22 D4
Manta Ecuador 40 A4
Mantes-la-Jolie France 72 C3
Mantova Italy *Eng.* Mantua 78 B2
Mantua *see* Mantova
Manurewa New Zealand 132 D3
Manzhouli China 109 F1
Mao Chad 58 B3
Maoke, Pegunungan *mountains* Indonesia 121 H4
Maputo *capital of* Mozambique 61 E4
Mar, Serra do *mountains* Brazil 38 D4
Maracaibo Venezuela 40 C1
Maracaibo, Lago de *inlet* Venezuela 40 C1
Maracay Venezuela 40 D1
Maradi Niger 57 F3
Marāgheh Iran 102 C3
Marajó, Ilha de *island* Brazil 43 F2
Marañón *river* Peru 42 B2
Maraş *see* Kahramanmaraş
Marash *see* Kahramanmaraş
Marbella Spain 74 D5
Marble Bar Australia 128 B4
Mar Chiquita, Laguna *salt lake* Argentina 46 C3
Mardān Pakistan 116 C1
Mar del Plata Argentina 47 D5
Mardin Turkey 99 E4
Margarita, Isla de *island* Venezuela 41 E1
Māragow, Dasht-e- *desert* Afghanistan 104 C5
Mariana Trench *undersea feature* Pacific Ocean 124 B1 126 B1
Marías, Islas *islands* Mexico 32 C4

Maribor Slovenia 77 E7
Marie Byrd Land *region* Antarctica 136 B4
Mariehamn Finland 67 D6
Marijampolė Lithuania *prev.* Kapsukas 88 B4
Marília Brazil 44 D2
Maringá Brazil 44 D2
Marion, Lake *lake* South Carolina, USA 31 F2
Mariscal Estigarribia Paraguay 44 B2
Maritsa *river* SE Europe 86 D3
Mariupol' Ukraine *prev.* Shdanov 91 G3
Marka Somalia 55 D6
Marmara, Sea of *see* Marmara Denizi
Marmara Denizi Turkey *Eng.* Sea of Marmara 98 B2
Marne *river* France 72 D3
Marotiri *Island group* French Polynesia 125 F4
Maroua Cameroon 58 B3
Marowijne *river* French Guiana/Suriname 41 H3
Marquesas Fracture Zone *tectonic feature* Pacific Ocean 125 G3
Marquesas Islands *island group* French Polynesia *Fr.* Îles Marquises 125 G3
Marquette Michigan, USA 22 B1
Marquisas, Îles *see* Marquesas Islands
Marrakech Morocco *Eng.* Marrakesh 52 C2
Marrawah Australia 131 C8
Marree Australia 131 B5
Marsala Italy 79 C6
Marseille France 73 D6
Marshall Islands *country* Pacific Ocean 126-127
Martin Slovakia *prev.* Turčianský Svätý Martin, *Ger.* Sankt Martin, *Hung.* Turócszentmárton 81 C5
Martinique *overseas department* France, West Indies 37
Mary Turkmenistan *prev.* Merv 104 C3
Maryborough Australia 131 E5
Maryland *state* USA 23 F4
Masai Steppe *grassland* Tanzania 55 C7
Mascarene Basin *undersea feature* Indian Ocean 123 B5
Mascarene Islands *island group* Indian Ocean 61 H4
Mascarene Plain *undersea feature* Indian Ocean 123 B5
Mascarene Plateau *undersea feature* Indian Ocean 123 B5
Maseru *capital of* Lesotho 60 D4
Mas-ha Bank 101 D6
Mashhad Iran *var.* Meshed 100 E3
Masindi Uganda 55 B6
Maşīrah, Jazīrat *Island* Oman 103 E6
Maşīrah, Khalīj *bay* Oman 103 E6
Mason City Iowa, USA 25 F3
Masqaţ *see* Muscat
Massachusetts *state* USA 23 G3
Massawa *see* Mits'iwa
Massif Central *upland* France 73 C5
Massoukou Gabon 59 B6
Masterton New Zealand 133 D5
Matadi Dem. Rep. Congo 59 B7
Matagalpa Nicaragua 34 D3
Matamoros Mexico 33 E2
Matanzas Cuba 36 B2
Matara Sri Lanka 115 E4
Mataram Indonesia 120 D5
Mataró Spain 75 G2
Mato Grosso *upland* Brazil 43 E3
Matosinhos Portugal 74 C2
Matsue Japan 113 B5
Matsuyama Japan 113 B5
Matterhorn *peak* Italy/ Switzerland 77 B7
Maturín Venezuela 41 E1
Maun Botswana 60 D3
Mauritania *country* W Africa 56
Mauritius *country* Indian Ocean 61 H4 123 B5
Mawlamyine Myanmar *prev.* Moulmein 118 B4
Mayaguana *island* The Bahamas 36 D2
Mayfield New Zealand 133 C6
Mayotte *overseas department* France, Indian Ocean 61 G2
Mayyit, Al Baḩr al *see* Dead Sea
Mazār-e Sharīf Afghanistan 104 D3
Mazatlán Mexico 32 C3
Mažeikiai Lithuania 88 B3
Mazury *region* Poland 80 D3
Mazyr Belarus *Rus.* Mozyr' 89 D7
Mbabane *capital of* Swaziland 61 E4
Mbaké Senegal 56 B3
Mbala Zambia 61 E1
Mbale Uganda 55 C6
Mbandaka Dem. Rep. Congo 59 C5
Mbeya Tanzania 55 B8
Mbuji-Mayi Dem. Rep. Congo 59 D7
McKinley, Mount *peak* Alaska, USA *var.* Denali 18 C3
Mead, Lake *lake* SW USA 28 A1
Mecca *see* Makkah
Mechelen Belgium 69 C5
Mecklenburger Bucht *bay* Germany 76 C2
Medan Indonesia 120 B3
Medellín Colombia 40 B2
Médenine Tunisia 53 F2
Medford Oregon, USA 26 A4
Medina *see* Al Madīnah
Mediterranean Sea Atlantic Ocean 84-85
Meekatharra Australia 129 B5
Meerut India 116 D3
Megísti *island* Greece 98 B4
Mek'elē Ethiopia 54 C4
Mekong *river* SE Asia 106 D3
Mekong, Mouths of the *wetlands* Vietnam 119 D6
Melanesia *region* Pacific Ocean 126 C3
Melanesian Basin *undersea feature* Pacific Ocean 134 C3

Melbourne Australia 131 C7
Melbourne Florida, USA 31 F4
Melghir, Chott *Salt lake* Algeria 53 E2
Melilla *external territory* Spain, N Africa 52 C1
Melitopol' Ukraine 91 F4
Melo Uruguay 44 C4
Melville Island *island* Australia 128 E2
Melville Island *island* Canada 19 E2
Memel *see* Klaipėda
Memel *see* Neman
Memphis Tennessee, USA 30 C1
Mendaña Fracture Zone *tectonic feature* Pacific Ocean 135 G3
Mende France 73 C6
Mendeleyev Ridge *undersea feature* Arctic Ocean 137 G2
Mendocino Fracture Zone *tectonic feature* Pacific Ocean 134 D2
Mendoza Argentina 46 B4
Menengiyn Tal *plain* Mongolia 109 F2
Menongue Angola 60 C2
Menorca *island* Spain *Eng.* Minorca 75 H3
Metairie Louisiana, USA 30 C3
Mentawai, Kepulauan *island group* Indonesia 120 B4
Meppel Netherlands 68 D2
Merced California, USA 27 B6
Mercedes Uruguay 44 B5
Mergui *see* Myeik
Mergui Archipelago *island chain* Myanmar 119 B6
Mérida Mexico 33 H3
Mérida Spain 74 D3
Mérida Venezuela 40 C2
Meridian Mississippi, USA 30 C2
Merredin Australia 129 B6
Mersin Turkey *var.* İçel 98 C4
Meru Kenya 55 C6
Merv *see* Mary
Mesa Arizona, USA 28 B2
Meshed *see* Mashhad
Messina Italy 79 D6
Messina, Stretto di *sea feature* Ionian Sea/Tyrrhenian Sea 79 D7
Mestre Italy 78 C2
Meta *river* Colombia/Venezuela 40 C2
Metković Croatia 82 C4
Metz France 72 E3
Meuse *river* W Europe *var.* Maas 72 D3
Mexicali Mexico 32 A1
Mexico *country* North America 32-33
México, Golfo de *see* Mexico, Gulf of
Mexico, Gulf of *sea feature* Atlantic Ocean/Caribbean Sea 48 A4
Mexico City *capital of* Mexico *Sp.* Ciudad de México 33 E4
Meymaneh *see* Maīmanah
Mezen' *river* Russian Federation 92 D3
Miami Florida, USA 31 F5
Miami Beach Florida, USA 31 F5
Mianyang China 111 B5
Michigan *state* USA 22 C2
Michigan, Lake *lake* USA 17 C5
Micronesia *country* Pacific Ocean 126 B2
Micronesia *region* Pacific Ocean 126
Mid Atlantic Ridge *undersea feature* Atlantic Ocean 48 B4
Middelburg South Africa 60 D5
Middle Andaman *island* India 115 G2
Middlesbrough England, UK 71 D5
Mid-Indian Basin *undersea feature* Indian Ocean 122 C4
Mid-Indian Ridge *undersea feature* Indian Ocean 123 C5
Midland Texas, USA 29 E3
Mid-Pacific Mountains *var.* Mid-Pacific Seamounts. *Undersea feature* Pacific Ocean 124 C1
Mid-Pacific Seamounts *see* Mid-Pacific Mountains
Midway Islands *US territory* Pacific Ocean 134 D2
Mikhaylovka Russian Federation 93 B6
Milagro Ecuador 40 A4
Milan *see* Milano
Milano Italy *Eng.* Milan 78 B2
Mildura Australia 131 C6
Millennium Island *island* Kiribati *prev.* Caroline Island 127 H3
Miles Australia 131 D5
Miles City Montana, USA 24 C2
Milford Haven Wales, UK 71 C6
Milford Sound New Zealand 133 E6
Milford Sound *inlet* New Zealand 133 A6
Mílos *island* Greece 87 C6
Milwaukee Wisconsin, USA 22 B3
Min *see* Fujian
Minatitlán Mexico 33 G4
Minch, The *Strait* Scotland, UK 70 C3
Mindanao *island* Philippines 121 F2
Mindoro *island* Philippines 121 E2
Mindoro Strait *sea feature* South China Sea/Sulu Sea 121 E2
Mingäçevir Azerbaijan *Rus.* Mingechaur 99 G2
Mingechaur *see* Mingäçevir
Minho *river* Portugal/Spain *Sp.* Miño 74 C2
Minicoy Island *island* India 114 C3
Minneapolis Minnesota, USA 23 F2
Minnesota *state* USA 25 F2
Miño *river* Portugal/Spain *Port.* Minho 74 C1
Minorca *see* Menorca
Minot North Dakota, USA 24 D1
Mīnā' Qābūs Oman 122 B3
Minsk *capital of* Belarus 89 C5
Minto, Lake *lake* Canada 20 D2

Miranda de Ebro Spain 75 E1
Mirim, Lake *see* Mirim Lagoon
Mirim Lagoon *lagoon* Brazil/ Uruguay *var.* Mirim, Lake 44 C5
Mirtóo Pelagos *sea feature* Mediterranean Sea 87 C6
Miskitos Cayos *islands* Nicaragua 35 E2
Miskolc Hungary 81 D6
Mişrātah Libya 53 F2
Mississippi *state* USA 30 C2
Mississippi *river* USA 16 C5
Mississippi Delta *wetlands* USA 30 C4
Missoula Montana, USA 24 B2
Missouri *state* USA 25 G4
Missouri *river* USA 17 C5
Mistassini, Lake *lake* Canada 20 D3
Mitau *see* Jelgava
Mitchell S Dakota, USA 25 E3
Mitchell River *river* Australia 130 C3
Mitilíni Greece 86 D4
Mito Japan 112 D4
Mitrovica *see* Mitrovicë/ Mitrovica
Mitrovicë/Mitrovica Kosovo *Serb.* Mitrovica, *prev.* Kosovska Mitrovica 83 D5
Mits'iwa Eritrea *var.* Massawa 54 C4
Mitumba, Monts *Mountain range* Dem. Rep. Congo 59 E7
Miyazaki Japan 113 B6
Mjøsa *lake* Norway 67 B5
Mljet *island* Croatia 83 C5
Mmabatho South Africa 60 D4
Mo Norway 66 C3
Mobile Alabama, USA 30 C3
Moçambique Mozambique 61 F2
Mocímboa da Praia Mozambique 61 F2
Mocoa Colombia 40 B4
Mocuba Mozambique 61 E3
Modena Italy 78 B3
Modesto California, USA 27 B6
Modohn *see* Madona
Modriča Bosnia & Herzegovina 82 C3
Mogadiscio *see* Mogadishu
Mogadishu *capital of* Somalia *Som.* Muqdisho, *It.* Mogadiscio 55 D6
Mogilëv *see* Mahilyow/Mogilëv
Mo i Rana Norway 66 C3
Mojave California, USA 27 C7
Mojave Desert *desert* W USA 27 C7
Moldavia *see* Moldova
Molde Norway 67 A5
Moldova *country* E Europe *var.* Moldavia 90
Molodechno *see* Maladzyechna
Molodeczno *see* Maladzyechna
Molotov *see* Perm'
Moluccas *see* Maluku
Molucca Sea *see* Maluku, Laut
Mombasa Kenya 55 C7
Monaco *country* W Europe 73 E6
Monclova Mexico 33 E2
Moncton Canada 21 F4
Mongo Chad 58 C3
Mongolia *country* NE Asia 108-109
Monroe Louisiana, USA 30 B2
Monrovia *capital of* Liberia 56 C5
Mons Belgium 69 B6
Montague Seamount *undersea feature* Atlantic Ocean 45 H1
Montana *state* USA 24 C2
Montauban France 73 C6
Mont Blanc *peak* France/Italy 62 D4
Mont-de-Marsan France 72 B6
Monte Cristi Dominican Republic 37 E3
Montego Bay Jamaica 36 C3
Montenegro *Country* SE Europe 83 D5
Monterey California, USA 27 B6
Montería Colombia 40 B2
Montero Bolivia 42 D4
Monterrey Mexico 33 E2
Montes Claros Brazil 43 G4
Montevideo *capital of* Uruguay 44 C5
Montgomery Alabama, USA 30 D2
Monthey Switzerland 77 A7
Montpelier Vermont, USA 23 F2
Montpellier France 73 C6
Montréal Canada 21 E4
Montserrat *overseas territory* UK, West Indies 37
Monywa Myanmar 118 A3
Monza Italy 78 B2
Moora Australia 129 B6
Moore, Lake *lake* Australia 129 B6
Moorhead Minnesota, USA 25 E2
Moosonee Canada 20 C3
Mopti Mali 57 E3
Morava *river* C Europe 82 E4
Moravská Ostrava *see* Ostrava
Moray Firth *inlet* Scotland, UK 70 C3
Moree Australia 131 D5
Morelia Mexico 33 E4
Morena, Sierra *mountain range* Spain 74 D4
Murghāb, Daryā-ye *river* Afghanistan/Turkmenistan 104 D4
Morioka Japan 112 D3
Mornington Abyssal Plain *undersea feature* Pacific Ocean 135 G5
Morocco *country* N Africa 52
Morogoro Tanzania 55 C7
Mörön Mongolia 108 D2
Morondava Madagascar 61 F3
Moroni *capital of* Comoros 61 F2
Morotai, Pulau *island* Indonesia 121 F3
Morova *river* Poland 80 C6
Morris Jesup, Kap *headland* Greenland 65 E1
Moscow *capital of* Russian Federation *Rus.* Moskva 92 B4 96 B2
Mosel *river* W Europe *Fr.* Moselle 77 A5

Moselle *river* W Europe *Ger.* Mosel 72 E4
Mosgiel New Zealand 133 B7
Moshi Tanzania 55 C7
Moskva *see* Moscow
Mosquito Coast *coastal region* Nicaragua 35 E3
Moss Norway 67 B6
Mossendjo Congo 59 B6
Mossoró Brazil 43 H2
Most Czech Republic *Ger.* Brüx 80 A4
Mostaganem Algeria 52 D1
Mostar Bosnia & Herz. 82 C4
Mosul *see* Al Mawşil
Motril Spain 75 E5
Motueka New Zealand 133 C5
Moulins France 72 C4
Moulmein *see* Mawlamyine
Moundou Chad 58 C4
Mount Gambier Australia 131 B7
Mount Isa Australia 130 B4
Mount Magnet Australia 129 B5
Mount Vernon Illinois, USA 22 B5
Mouscron Belgium 69 A6
Moyobamba Peru 42 B2
Moyu China 108 B2
Mozambique *country* SE Africa 61
Mozambique Channel *sea feature* Indian Ocean 61 F3
Mozyr' *see* Mazyr
Mpika Zambia 61 E2
Mtwara Tanzania 55 C8
Muang Không Laos 119 D5
Muang Xaignabouri *see* Xaignabouri
Mudanjiang China 110 E3
Mufulira Zambia 60 D2
Muğla Turkey 98 A4
Mulhouse France 72 E4
Mull *island* Scotland, UK 70 B3
Muller, Pegunungan *mountains* Indonesia 120 C3
Multān Pakistan 116 C2
Mumbai India *var.* Bombay 117 C5
München Germany *Eng.* Munich 77 C6
Muncie Indiana, USA 22 C4
Munich *see* München
Münster Germany 76 B4
Muqdisho *see* Mogadishu
Mur *river* C Europe 77 E7
Murchison River *river* Australia 129 B5
Murcia Spain 75 F4
Mures *river* Hungary/Romania 81 D7
Murfreesboro Tennessee, USA 30 D1
Murgab Tajikistan 105 F3
Murgap *river* Turkmenistan *var.* Murghab 104 C3
Murghab *see* Murgap
Müritz *lake* Germany 76 D3
Murmansk Russian Federation 92 C2 96 C1
Murray *river* Australia 131 B6
Murray Fracture Zone *tectonic feature* Pacific Ocean 135 E2
Murray Ridge *Undersea feature* Arabian Sea 122 B3
Murwillumbah Australia 131 E5
Murzuq Libya 53 F3
Muş Turkey 99 F3
Muscat *capital of* Oman *Ar.* Masqaţ 103 E5
Musgrave Ranges *mountain range* Australia 129 D5
Musters, Lago *lake* Argentina 46 C6
Mu Us Shadi *Desert* China 109 E3
Mvonioälv *river* Finland/ Sweden 66 D3
Mwali *island* Comoros 61 F2
Mwanza Tanzania 55 B6
Mwene-Ditu Dem. Rep. Congo 59 D7
Mweru, Lake *lake* Dem. Rep. Congo/Zambia 59 D7
Myanmar *country* SE Asia *var.* Myanmar 118-119
Myeik Myanmar *prev.* Mergui 119 B5
Mykolayiv Ukraine *Rus.* Nikolayev 91 E4
Mykonos *island* Greece 87 D5
Mysore India 114 D2
Mzuzu Malawi 61 E2

N

Naberezhnyye Chelny Russian Federation *prev.* Brezhnev 93 C5
Nablus West Bank *var.* Năbulus, *Heb.* Shekhem 101 D6
Năbulus *see* Nablus
Nacala Mozambique 61 F2
Naga Philippines 120 E2
Nagano Japan 112 C4
Nagasaki Japan 113 A6
Nāgercoil India 114 D3
Nagorno-Karabakh *region* Azerbaijan 99 G2
Nagoya Japan 113 C5
Nāgpur India 116 D4
Nagqu China 108 C5
Nagykanizsa Hungary *Ger.* Grosskanizsa 81 C7
Nagyszombat *see* Trnava
Naha Japan 113 A8
Nain Canada 21 F2
Nairobi *capital of* Kenya 55 C6
Najaf *see* An Najaf
Najrān Saudi Arabia 103 B6
Nakamura Japan 113 B6
Nakhichevan' *see* Naxçıvan
Nakhon Ratchasima Thailand 119 C5
Nakhon Sawan Thailand 119 C5
Nakhon Si Thammarat Thailand 119 C6
Nakuru Kenya 55 C6
Nal'chik Russian Federation 96 A4
Namangan Uzbekistan 105 E2
Nam Co *lake* China 108 C4
Nam Đinh Vietnam 118 D3
Namib Desert *desert* Namibia 60 B3
Namibe Angola 60 B2
Namibia *country* southern Africa 60
Nampa Idaho, USA 26 C3

Namp'o North Korea 110 E4
Nampula Mozambique 61 F2
Namur Belgium 69 C6
Nanchang China 111 C5
Nancy France 72 D3
Nānded India 116 D5 114 D1
Nanjing China 111 D5
Nanning China 111 B6
Nanortalik Greenland 64 C5
Nansen Basin *undersea feature* Arctic Ocean 137 G4
Nantes France 72 B4
Napier New Zealand 132 E4
Naples *see* Napoli
Napo *river* Ecuador/Peru 42 B2
Napoli Italy *Eng.* Naples 79 D5
Narbonne France 73 C6
Nares Strait *sea feature* Canada/Greenland 64 C1
Narew *river* Poland 80 E3
Narmada *river* India 116 D4
Narva Estonia 88 E2
Narva *river* Estonia/Russian Federation 88 E2
Narva Bay *sea feature* Gulf of Finland *Est.* Narva Laht, *Rus.* Narvskiy Zaliv 88 E2
Narva Laht *see* Narva Bay
Narvik Norway 66 C3
Narvskiy Zaliv *see* Narva Bay
Naryn Kyrgyzstan 105 G2
Nāshik India 116 C5
Nashville Tennessee, USA 30 D1
Nâşir, Buḩeiret *see* Nasser, Lake
Nassau *capital of* The Bahamas 36 C1
Nasser, Lake *reservoir* Egypt *var.* Nâşir, Buḩeiret 54 B2
Natal Brazil 43 H3
Natal Basin *Undersea feature* Indian Ocean 123 A5
Natitingou Benin 57 E4
Naturaliste Plateau *undersea feature* Indian Ocean 123 E6
Natzrat Israel *Eng.* Nazareth 101 A5
Nauru *country* Pacific Ocean 126 D3
Navapolatsk/Novopolotsk Belarus *Rus.* Novopolotsk 89 D5
Navassa Island *unincorporated territory* USA, West Indies 36 D3
Navoiy Uzbekistan *Uzb.* Nawoly 104 D2
Nawābshāh Pakistan 116 B3
Nawoly *see* Navoiy
Naxçıvan Azerbaijan *Rus.* Nakhichevan' 99 G3
Náxos *island* Greece 87 D6
Nay Pyi Taw *capital of* Myanmar 118 B3
Nazareth *see* Natzrat
Nazca Peru 42 B4
Nazrēt Ethiopia 55 C5
Nazwá Oman 103 E5
N'Dalatando Angola 60 B2
Ndélé Central African Republic 58 C4
N'Djaména *capital of* Chad 58 B3
Ndola Zambia 60 D2
Nebitdag *see* Balkanabat
Nebraska *state* USA 24-25 E3
Neches *river* S USA 29 H3
Neckar *river* Germany 77 B5
Necochea Argentina 47 D5
Neftezavodsk *see* Seýdi
Negēlē Ethiopia 55 C5
Negev *see* HaNegev
Negro, Río *river* Argentina 47 C5
Negro, Rio *river* Brazil/Uruguay 44 C4
Negro, Rio *river* N South America 40 C1
Neiva Colombia 40 B3
Nellore India 115 E2
Neman *river* NE Europe *Bel.* Nyoman, *Lith.* Nemunas, *Ger.* Memel, *Pol.* Niemen 88 B4
Nemunas *see* Neman
Nemuro Japan 112 E2
Nepal *country* S Asia 117
Neris *river* Belarus/Lithuania *Bel.* Viliya, *Pol.* Wilja 88 C4
Ness, Loch *lake* Scotland, UK 70 C3
Netherlands *country* W Europe *var.* Holland 68-69
Netze *see* Noteć
Neubrandenburg Germany 76 D3
Neuchâtel, Lac de *lake* Switzerland 77 A7
Neumünster Germany 76 C2
Neuquén Argentina 47 C5
Neusiedler See *lake* Austria/Hungary 77 E6
Neusohl *see* Banská Bystrica
Neutra *see* Nitra
Nevada *state* USA 26-27
Nevers France 72 C4
Nevşehir Turkey 98 C3
New Amsterdam Guyana 41 G2
Newark New Jersey, USA 23 F3
New Britain *island* Papua New Guinea 126 B3
New Brunswick *province* Canada 21 F4
New Caledonia *special collectivity* France, Pacific Ocean 126 C5
New Caledonia *island* Pacific Ocean 124 D3
New Caledonia Basin *undersea feature* Pacific Ocean 124 D4
Newcastle Australia 131 D6
Newcastle upon Tyne England, UK 70 D4
New Delhi *capital of* India 116 D3
Newfoundland & Labrador *province* Canada 21 F2
Newfoundland *island* Canada 21 G3
Newfoundland Basin *undersea feature* Atlantic Ocean 48 B3
New Georgia Islands *island group* Solomon Is 126 C3
New Guinea *island* Pacific Ocean 126 B3
New Hampshire *state* USA 23 G2
New Haven Connecticut, USA 23 G3

New Ireland *island* Papua New Guinea 126 C3
New Jersey *state* USA 23 F4
Newman Australia 128 B4
New Mexico *state* USA 28-29
New Orleans Louisiana, USA 30 C3
New Plymouth New Zealand 132 D3
Newport Oregon, USA 26 A3
Newport News Virginia, USA 23 F5
New Providence *island* The Bahamas 36 C1
Newry Northern Ireland, UK 71 B5
New Siberian Islands *see* Novosibirskiye Ostrova
New South Wales *state* Australia 131 C6
New York *state* USA 23 F3
New York New York, USA 23 F3
New Zealand *country* Pacific Ocean 132-133
Neyshābūr Iran 102 D3
Ngaoundéré Cameroon 58 B4
Ngerulmud *capital of* Palau 126 A1
N'Giva Angola 60 C3
N'Guigmi Niger 57 H3
Nha Trang Vietnam 119 E5
Niagara Falls *waterfall* Canada/ USA 23 E3
Niamey *capital of* Niger 57 F3
Niangay, Lac *lake* Mali 56 E3
Nias, Pulau *island* Indonesia 120 B3
Nicaragua *country* Central America 34-35
Nicaragua, Lago de *lake* Nicaragua 34 D3
Nice France 73 E6
Nicobar Islands *island group* India 115 H3
Nicosia *capital of* Cyprus *var.* Lefkosia, *Turk.* Lefkoşa 98 C5
Nicoya, Península de *peninsula* Costa Rica 34 D4
Niemen *see* Neman
Nieuw Amsterdam Suriname 41 H2
Niğde Turkey 98 D4
Niger *country* W Africa 57
Niger *river* W Africa 56-57 D3
Niger, Mouths of the *delta* Nigeria 57 F5
Nigeria *country* W Africa 57
Niigata Japan 112 C4
Nijmegen Netherlands 68 D4
Nikolayev *see* Mykolayiv
Nikopol' Ukraine 91 F3
Nile *river* N Africa 54 B3
Nile Delta *wetlands* Egypt 54 B1
Nîmes France 73 D6
Ninetyeast Ridge *undersea feature* Indian Ocean 123 C5
Ningbo China 111 D5
Ningxia *autonomous region* China 110-111 B4
Nioro Mali 56 D3
Nipigon, Lake *lake* Canada 20 B4
Niš Serbia 82 E4
Nitra Slovakia *Ger.* Neutra, *Hung.* Nyitra 81 C6
Nitra *river* Slovakia *Ger.* Neutra, *Hung.* Nyitra 81 C6
Niue *asociated territory* New Zealand, Pacific Ocean 127 F4
Nizāmābād India 114 D1
Nizhnevartovsk Russian Federation 96 D3
Nizhniy Novgorod Russian Federation *prev.* Gor'kiy 93 C5 96 B3
Nkongsamba Cameroon 58 B4
Norak Tajikistan 105 E3
Nord Greenland 65 E2
Nordaustlandet *island* Svalbard 65 G1
Norfolk Virginia, USA 23 F5
Norfolk Island *external territory* Australia, Pacific Ocean 124 D4
Nori'lsk Russian Federation 96 D3
Norfolk Ridge *undersea feature* Pacific Ocean 124 D4
Norman Oklahoma, USA 28 F2
Normandie *region* France *Eng.* Normandy 72 B3
Normandy *see* Normandie
Normanton Australia 130 C3
Norrköping Sweden 67 C6
Norseman Australia 129 C6
North Albanian Alps *mountains* Albania/ Montenegro 83 D5
North America 16-17
North Andaman *island* India 115 G2
North Atlantic Ocean 64-65
North Australian Basin *undersea feature* Indian Ocean 124 A2 128 A2
North Bay Canada 20 D4
North Cape *coastal feature* New Zealand 132 C1
North Cape *coastal feature* Norway 66 D2
North Carolina *state* USA 31 F1
North Dakota *state* USA 24-25 D2
North Fiji Basin *undersea feature* Coral Sea 124 D3
Northern Cook Islands *islands* Cook Islands 127 G4
Northern Cyprus, Turkish Republic of *disputed region* Cyprus 98 C5
Northern Dvina *river* Russian Federation *see* Severnaya Dvina 63 G2
Northern Ireland *province* UK 70-71
Northern Mariana Islands *commonwealth territory* USA, Pacific Ocean 124 C1
Northern Sporades *see* Vóreies Sporádes
Northern Territory *territory* Australia 130 A3
North European Plain *region* N Europe 62 E3
North Frisian Islands *islands* Denmark/Germany 76 B2
North Island *island* New Zealand 132 G2
North Korea *country* E Asia 110

North Little Rock Arkansas, USA 30 B1
North Platte Nebraska, USA 25 E4
North Platte *river* C USA 24 D3
North Pole *ice feature* Arctic Ocean 137 G3
North Sea Atlantic Ocean 70 E2
North Siberian Lowland *lowlands* Russian Federation 94-95
North Taranaki Bight *gulf* New Zealand 132 D3
North Uist *island* Scotland, UK 70 B3
Northwest Territories *territory* Canada 19 E3
Norway *country* N Europe 66-67
Norwegian Sea Arctic Ocean 137 G5
Norwich England, UK 71 E6
Noteć *river* Poland *Ger.* Netze 80 C3
Nottingham England, UK 71 D6
Nottingham Island *island* Hudson Strait 20 D1
Nouâdhibou Mauritania 56 B2
Nouakchott *capital of* Mauritania 56 B2
Nouméa *capital of* New Caledonia 126 D5
Nova Gradiška Croatia 82 C3
Nova Iguaçu Brazil 43 F5 45 F2
Novara Italy 78 B2
Nova Scotia *province* Canada 21 F4
Novaya Zemlya *islands* Russian Federation 137 H4
Novaya Zemlya Trench *see* East Novaya Zemlya Trench
Novi Sad Serbia 82 D3
Novokuznetsk Russian Federation *prev.* Stalinsk 96 D4
Novopolotsk see Navapolatsk/ Novopolotsk
Novosibirsk Russian Federation 96 D4
Novosibirskiye Ostrova *islands* Russian Federation *Eng.* New Siberian Islands 95 F1
Novo Urgench *see* Urgench
Novyy Margilan *see* Farg'ona
Nsanje Malawi 61 E3
Nsawam Ghana 57 E5
Nubian Desert *desert* Sudan 54 B3
Nu'eima West Bank 101 D7
Nuevo Laredo Mexico 33 E2
Nuku'alofa *capital of* Tonga 127 F5
Nukus Uzbekistan 104 C2
Nullarbor Plain *region* Australia 129 D6
Nunap Isua Island *coastal region* Greenland *var.* Uummannaruaq *Dan.* Kap Farvel 64 C5
Nunavut *Territory* Canada 19 F3
Nunivak Island *island* Alaska, USA 18 B2
Nuoro Italy 79 A5
Nuremberg *see* Nürnberg
Nürnberg Germany *Eng.* Nuremberg 77 C5
Nusa Tenggara *islands* East Timor / Indonesia 120 E5
Nuuk Greenland *var.* Godthåb 64 C4
Nyainqêntanglha Shan *mountain range* China 108 D5
Nyala Sudan 54 A4
Nyasa, Lake *lake* E Africa 51 D5
Nyeri Kenya 55 C6
Nyima China 108 C4
Nyíregyháza Hungary 81 E6
Nyitra *see* Nitra
Nykøbing Denmark 67 B8
Nyköping Sweden 67 C6
Nyngan Australia 131 D6
Nyoman *see* Neman

O

Oakland California, USA 27 B6
Oakley Kansas, USA 25 E4
Oamaru New Zealand 133 B7
Oaxaca Mexico 33 F5
Ob' *river* Russian Federation 96 D4
Oban Scotland, UK 70 C4
Obihiro Japan 112 D2
Obo Central African Republic 58 D4
Oceania 124-125
Ocean Island *see* Banaba
Oceanside California, USA 27 C8
Ochamchira *see* Och'amch'ire
Ochamchire Georgia prev. Och'amch'ire, *Rus.* Ochamchira 99 E1
Och'amch'ire *see* Ochamchire
Ödenburg *see* Sopron
Odense Denmark 67 B7
Oder *river* C Europe 80 C4
Odesa Ukraine *Rus.* Odessa 91 E4
Odessa see Odesa
Odessa Texas, USA 29 E3
Odienné Côte d'Ivoire 56 D4
Oesel *see* Saaremaa
Ofanto *river* Italy 79 D5
Offenbach Germany 77 B5
Ogaden *plateau* Ethiopia 55 D5
Ogallala Nebraska, USA 24 D4
Ogbomosho Nigeria 57 F4
Ogden Utah, USA 24 B3
Ogdensburg New York, USA 23 F2
Oger *see* Ogre
Ogre Latvia *Ger.* Oger 88 C3
Ogulin Croatia 82 B3
Ohio *state* USA 22 D4
Ohio *river* N USA 22 B5
Ohrid Macedonia 83 D6
Ohrid, Lake *lake* Albania/ Macedonia 83 D6
Ohře *river* Czech Republic/ Germany *Ger.* Eger 81 A5
Ōita Japan 113 B6
Okavango *river var.* Cubango southern Africa 60 C3
Okavango Delta *wetland* Botswana 60 C3
Okayama Japan 113 B5
Okazaki Japan 113 C5
Okeechobee, Lake *lake* Florida, USA 31 F4
Okhotsk Russian Federation 97 G3

Okhotsk, Sea of Pacific Ocean 134 C1
Okinawa *island* Japan 113 A8
Oki-shotō *island group* Japan 113 B5
Oklahoma *state* USA 29 F1
Oklahoma City Oklahoma, USA 29 F2
Okushiri-tō *island* Japan 112 C2
Okāra Pakistan 116 C2
Öland *island* Sweden 67 C7
Olavarría Argentina 46 D4
Olbia Italy 79 B5
Oldenburg Germany 76 B3
Oleksandriya Ukraine *Rus.* Aleksandriya 91 E3
Olenëk Russian Federation 97 E3
Ölgiy Mongolia 108 C2
Olhão Portugal 74 C4
Olita *see* Alytus
Olmaliq *see* Almalyk
Olmütz *see* Olomouc
Olomouc Czech Republic *Ger.* Olmütz 81 C5
Olsztyn Poland *Ger.* Allenstein 80 D2
Olt *river* Romania 90 B5
Olympia Washington, USA 26 B2
Omaha Nebraska, USA 25 F4
Oman *country* SW Asia 103 D6
Oman, Gulf of *sea feature* Indian Ocean 103 E5, 122 B3
Omdurman Sudan 54 B4
Omsk Russian Federation 96 C4
Onega *river* Russian Federation 92 C4
Onega, Lake *see* Onezhskoye Ozero
Onezhskoye Ozero *lake* Russian Federation *Eng.* Lake Onega 92 B3
Ongole India 115 E2
Onitsha Nigeria 57 F5
Onslow Australia 128 A4
Ontario *province* Canada 18 B3
Ontario, Lake *lake* Canada/USA 17 D5
Oostende Belgium *Eng.* Ostend 69 A5
Opole Poland *Ger.* Oppeln 80 C4
Oporto *see* Porto
Oppeln *see* Opole
Oradea Romania 90 B3
Oran Algeria 52 D1
Orange River *river* southern Africa 60 C4
Oranjestad Aruba 37 E5
Orantes *River* Asia 100 B3
Ordu Turkey 98 D2
Ordzhonikidze *see* Vladikavkaz
Örebro Sweden 67 C6
Oregon *state* USA 26
Orël Russian Federation 83 A5
Orem Utah, USA 24 B4
Orenburg Russian Federation 93 C6 96 B4
Orense *see* Ourense
Orestiáda Greece 86 D3
Orinoco *river* Colombia/ Venezuela 41 E3
Oristano Italy 79 A5
Orkney *islands* Scotland, UK 70 C2
Orlando Florida, USA 31 E4
Orléans France 72 C4
Örnsköldsvik Sweden 67 C5
Orantes *river* SW Asia 100 B3
Orosirá Rodópis *see* Rhodope Mountains
Orsha Belarus 89 E5
Orsk Russian Federation 93 D6 96 B4
Oruro Bolivia 42 C4
Ōsaka Japan 113 C5
Osborn Plateau *undersea feature* Indian Ocean 123 C5
Ösel *see* Saaremaa
Osh Kyrgyzstan 105 F2
Oshawa Canada 20 D5
Oshkosh Wisconsin, USA 22 B2
Osijek Croatia 82 C3
Oslo *capital of* Norway 67 B6
Osmaniye Turkey 98 D4
Osnabrück Germany 76 B3
Osorno Chile 47 B5
Oss Netherlands 68 D4
Ossora Russian Federation 97 H2
Ostend *see* Oostende
Östersund Sweden 67 C5
Ostrava Czech Republic *Ger.* Mährisch-Ostrau, *prev.* Moravská Ostrava 81 C5
Ostrołęka Poland 80 D3
Ostrowiec Świętokrzyski Poland 80 D4
Ōsumi-shotō *island group* Japan 113 A7
Otago Peninsula *peninsula* New Zealand 133 B7
Otaru Japan 112 D2
Oti *river* Africa 57 E4
Otranto, Strait of *sea feature* Albania/Italy 79 E5
Ottawa *capital of* Canada 20 D4
Ottawa *river* Canada 20 D4
Ou *river* Laos 118 C3
Ouachita *river* SE USA 30 B2
Ouagadougou *capital of* Burkina Faso 57 E3
Ouarâne *desert* Mauritania 56 D2
Ouargla Algeria 53 E2
Ouessant, Île d' *island* France 72 A3
Ouésso Congo 59 C5
Oujda Morocco 52 D2
Oulu Finland 66 D4
Oulu *river* Finland 66 D4
Oulujärvi *lake* Finland 66 E4
Ounasjoki *river* Finland 66 D3
Our *river* W Europe 69 E7
Ourense Spain *Cast.* Orense 74 C2
Ourinhos Brazil 44 D2
Ourthe *river* Belgium 69 D6
Outer Hebrides *island group* UK *var.* Western Isles 70 B3
Outer Islands *island group* Seychelles 61 H2
Ouyen Australia 131 C6
Oviedo Spain 74 D1
Owando Congo 59 C6
Owen Fracture Zone *tectonic feature* Arabian Sea 122 B3
Owensboro Kentucky, USA 22 B5

Oxford England, UK 71 D6
Oxnard California, USA 29 C7
Oyem Gabon 59 B5
Oyo Nigeria 57 F4
Ozark Plateau *plain* Arkansas/ Missouri, USA 25 G5
Ózd Hungary 81 D6

P

Paamiut Greenland 64 B4
Pachuca Mexico 33 E4
Pacific-Antarctic Ridge *undersea feature* Pacific Ocean 136 B5
Pacific Ocean 134-135
Padang Indonesia 120 B4
Paderborn Germany 76 B4
Padova Italy *Eng.* Padua 78 C2
Padre Island *island* Texas, USA 29 G5
Padua *see* Padova
Paducah Kentucky, USA 22 B5
Paeroa Waikato, New Zealand 132 D3
Pafos *see* Paphos
Pag *island* Croatia 82 A3
Pago Pago *capital of* American Samoa 127 F4
Paide Estonia *Ger.* Weissenstein 88 D2
Paihia New Zealand 132 D2
Painted Desert *desert* SW USA 28 C1
País Valenciano *cultural region* Spain 75 F3
Pakistan *country* S Asia 116
Pakokku Myanmar 118 A3
Palagruza *island* Croatia 83 B5
Palau *country* Pacific Ocean *var.* Belau 124 B2 126
Palawan *island* Philippines 121 E2
Palawan Passage *passage* Philippines 121 E2
Paldiski Estonia *prev.* Baltiski, *Eng.* Baltic Port, *Ger.* Baltischport 88 C2
Palembang Indonesia 120 C4
Palencia Spain 74 D2
Palermo Italy 79 C6
Palikir *capital of* Micronesia 126 C2
Palioúri, Akrotírio *coastal feature* Greece *var.* Akra Kanestron 86 C4
Palk Strait *sea feature* India/Sri Lanka 115 E3
Palliser, Cape *headland* New Zealand 133 D5
Palm Springs California, USA 27 D8
Palma Spain 75 G3
Palmer Land *physical region* Antarctica 136 A3
Palmerston North New Zealand 132 D4
Palmyra *see* Tudmur
Palmyra Atoll *incorporated territory* USA, Pacific Ocean 125 F2
Palu Indonesia 121 E4
Pamir *river* Afghanistan/ Tajikistan 105 F3
Pamirs *mountains* Tajikistan 105 F3
Pampa Texas, USA 29 E2
Pampas *region* South America 46 C4
Pamplona Spain *var.* Iruña 75 F1
Pānāji India 114 C2
Panama *country* Central America 35
Panamá, Golfo de *sea feature* Panama 35 F5
Panama Canal *canal* Panama 35 F4
Panama City *capital of* Panama 35 F5
Panama City Florida, USA 30 D3
Pančevo Serbia 82 D3
Panevėžys Lithuania 88 C4
Pantanal *region* Brazil 38 C4
Pantelleria *island* Italy 79 B7
Papeete *capital of* French Polynesia 127 H4
Paphos Cyprus *var.* Pafos 98 C5
Papua *province* Indonesia *prev.* Irian Jaya 121 H4
Papua New Guinea *country* Pacific Ocean 126
Paracel Islands *disputed territory* Asia 120 D1
Paragua *river* Venezuela 41 E3
Paraguay *country* South America 44
Paraguay *river* C South America 38 C4 44 B2
Parakou Benin 57 F4
Paramaribo *capital of* Suriname 41 G2
Paraná Argentina 46 D4
Paraná *river* C South America 46 D3
Paranaíba Brazil 43 G2
Paraparaumu New Zealand 132 D4
Pardubice Czech Republic *Ger.* Pardubitz 81 B5
Pardubitz *see* Pardubice
Parepare Indonesia 121 E4
Paris *capital of* France 72 C3
Paris Texas, USA 29 G2
Parma Italy 78 B3
Pärnu Estonia *Rus.* Pyarnu, *prev.* Pernov, *Ger.* Pernau 88 C2
Páros *island* Greece 87 D6
Pasadena California, USA 27 C7
Pasadena Texas, USA 29 G4
Passo Fundo Brazil 44 D3
Pasto Colombia 40 B4
Patagonia *region* S South America 47 C6
Pathein Myanmar *prev.* Bassein 118 A4
Patna India 117 F3
Patos, Lagoa dos *lagoon* Brazil 44 D4
Pátra Greece 87 B5
Pattani Thailand 119 C7
Pattaya Thailand 119 C5
Patuca *river* Honduras 34 D2
Pau France 73 B6
Pavlodar Kazakhstan 96 C4
Pavlograd *see* **Pavlohrad**
Pavlohrad Ukraine *Rus.* Pavlograd 91 G3
Paysandú Uruguay 44 B4

Pazardzhik Bulgaria *prev.* Tatar Pazardzhik 86 C2
Pearl *river* SE USA 30 C3
Peawanuck Canada 20 C2
Peć *see* Pejë/Peć
Pechora *river* Russian Federation 92 D3
Pecos Texas, USA 29 E3
Pecos *river* SW USA 28 D2
Pécs Hungary *Ger.* Fünfkirchen 81 C7
Pegasus Bay *bay* New Zealand 133 C5
Pegu *see* Bago
Peipsi Järv *see* Peipus, Lake
Peipus, Lake *lake* Estonia/ Russian Federation *Est.* Peipsi Järv, *Rus.* Chudskoye Ozero 88 D2
Peiraías Greece *var.* Piraiévs, *Eng.* Piraeus 87 C5
Pejë/Peć Kosovo *Serb.* Peć 83 D5
Pekalongan Jawa, Indonesia 120 C4
Pekanbaru Indonesia 120 B3
Peking *see* Beijing
Pelagie, Isola *island* Italy 79 B8
Peloponnese *see* Pelopónnisos
Pelopónnisos *peninsula* Greece *Eng.* Peloponnese 87 B5
Pelotas Brazil 44 C4
Pelotas *river* Brazil 44 C3
Pematangsiantar Indonesia 120 B3
Pemba *island* Tanzania 51 E5
Pendleton Oregon, USA 26 C2
Pennines *hills* England, UK 70 D4
Pennsylvania *state* USA 23 E3
Penong Australia 131 A6
Penonomé Panama 35 F5
Penrhyn *atoll* Cook Islands 125 F3
Penrhyn Basin *undersea feature* Pacific Ocean 135 E2
Pensacola Florida, USA 30 D3
Penza Russian Federation 93 B5
Penzance England, UK 71 C7
Peoria Illinois, USA 22 B4
Percival Lakes *lakes* Australia 128 C4
Pereira Colombia 40 B3
Périgueux France 73 B5
Perm' Russian Federation *prev.* Molotov 93 D5 96 B3
Pernau *see* Pärnu
Pernik Bulgaria *prev.* Dimitrovo 86 C2
Pernov *see* Pärnu
Perpignan France 73 C6
Persian Gulf *sea feature* Arabian Sea *var.* The Gulf 122 B2
Perth Australia 129 B6
Perth Scotland, UK 70 C3
Perth Basin *undersea feature* Indian Ocean 123 E6
Peru C South America 42
Peru-Chile Trench *undersea feature* Pacific Ocean 135 G3
Perugia Italy 78 C4
Pescara Italy 78 D4
Peshāwar Pakistan 116 C1
Petah Tikva Israel 101 A5
Peterborough England, UK 71 E6
Peterborough Canada 20 D5
Peter the First Island *island* Antarctica 136 A4
Petra see Wādī Mūsā
Petrich Bulgaria 86 C3
Petroaleksandrovsk *see* To'rtko'l
Petrograd *see* St Petersburg
Petropavlovsk Russian Federation 96 C4
Petropavlovsk-Kamchatskiy Russian Federation 97 H3
Petrozavodsk Russian Federation 92 B3
Pevek Russian Federation 97 G1
Pforzheim Germany 77 B6
Phangan, Ko *island* Thailand 119 C6
Philadelphia Pennsylvania, USA 23 F4
Philippine Basin *undersea feature* Pacific Ocean 124 B1
Philippine Trench *undersea feature* Philippine Sea 124 A2
Philippines *country* Asia 121
Philippine Sea Pacific Ocean 121 F1 124 A1
Philippopolis *see* Plovdiv
Phnom Penh *capital of* Cambodia 119 D6
Phoenix Arizona, USA 28 B2
Phoenix Islands *island group* Kiribati 127 F3
Phôngsali Laos 118 C3
Phuket Thailand 119 B7
Phuket, Ko *island* Thailand 119 B7
Phumĭ Sâmraông Cambodia 119 D5
Piacenza Italy 78 B2
Piatra-Neamţ Romania 90 C3
Piave *river* Italy 78 C2
Picton New Zealand 133 C5
Pielinen *lake* Finland 66 E4
Pierre South Dakota, USA 25 E3
Piešťany Slovakia *Ger.* Pistyan, *Hung.* Pöstyén 81 C6
Pietermaritzburg South Africa 60 D4
Pihkva Järv *see* Pskov, Lake
Piła Poland *Ger.* Schneidemühl 80 C3
Pilar Paraguay 44 B3
Pilchilemu Chile 46 B4
Pilcomayo *river* C South America 44 B2 46 D2
Pilsen *see* Plzeň
Pinar del Río Cuba 36 A2
Píndos *mountain range* Greece *Eng.* Pindus Mountains 86 A4
Pindus Mountains *see* Píndos
Pine Bluff Arkansas, USA 30 B2
Pine Creek Australia 128 E2
Pinega *river* Russian Federation 92 C3
Pineiós *river* Greece 86 B4
Pínes, Akrotírio *coastal feature* Greece 86 C4
Ping, Mae Nam *river* Thailand 118 C4
Pinsk Belarus *Pol.* Pińsk 89 B4
Piraeus *see* Peiraías
Piraiévs *see* Peiraías

Pisa Italy 78 B3
Pisco Peru 42 B4
Pishpek *see* Bishkek
Pistyan *see* Piešťany
Pitcairn, Henderson, Ducie & Oeno Islands *overseas territory* UK, Pacific Ocean 125 G4
Piteå Sweden 66 D4
Piteşti Romania 90 C4
Pittsburgh Pennsylvania, USA 23 E4
Piura Peru 42 A2
Pivdennyy Bug *river* Ukraine 91 E3
Plasencia Spain 74 D3
Plata, Rio de la *river* Argentina/ Uruguay *var.* River Plate 44 B5 46 D4
Plate, River *see* **Plata, Rio de la**
Platte *river* C USA 25 E4
Plattensee *see* Balaton
Plenty, Bay of *bay* New Zealand 132 E3
Pleven Bulgaria 86 C1
Płock Poland 80 D3
Ploieşti Romania 90 C4
Plovdiv Bulgaria *Gk.* Philippopolis 86 C2
Plungė Lithuania 88 B4
Plymouth *capital of* Montserrat 37 G3
Plymouth England, UK 71 C7
Plzeň Czech Republic *Ger.* Pilsen 81 A5
Po *river* Italy 78 B2
Pocatello Idaho, USA 26 E4
Po Delta *wetland* Italy 78 C3
Podgorica *capital of* Montenegro 83 C5
Pohnpei Island *island* Micronesia 126 C2
Pointe-Noire Congo 59 B6
Poitiers France 72 B4
Poland *country* E Europe 80-81
Polatsk Belarus 89 D5
Pol-e Khomrī *see* Pul-e Khumrī
Poltava Ukraine 91 F2
Poltoratsk *see* Aşgabat
Polynesia *region* Pacific Ocean 127
Pomeranian Bay *bay* Germany/ Poland 80 B2
Pompano Beach Florida, USA 31 F5
Ponca City Oklahoma, USA 29 G1
Pondicherry India 115 E2
Ponta Grossa Brazil 44 D2
Pontevedra Spain 74 C1
Pontianak Indonesia 120 C4
Poona *see* Pune
Poopó, Lake *lake* Bolivia 42 C5
Popayán Colombia 40 B3
Poprad Slovakia *Ger.* Deutschendorf 81 D5
Porbandar India 116 B4
Pori Finland 67 D5
Porsgrunn Norway 67 B6
Portalegre Portugal 74 C3
Port Angeles Washington, USA 26 A1
Port Arthur Texas, USA 29 H4
Port Augusta Australia 131 B6
Port-au-Prince *capital of* Haiti 36 D3
Port Blair India 115 G2
Port Douglas Australia 130 D3
Port Elizabeth South Africa 60 D5
Port-Gentil Gabon 59 A6
Port Harcourt Nigeria 57 F5
Port Hardy Canada 18 D5
Port Harrison *see* Inukjuak
Port Hedland Australia 128 B4
Portland Australia 131 B7
Portland Maine, USA 23 G2
Portland Oregon, USA 26 B2
Port Lincoln Australia 131 A6
Port Louis *capital of* Mauritius 61 H4
Port Macquarie Australia 131 E6
Port Moresby *capital of* Papua New Guinea 126 B3
Porto Portugal *Eng.* Oporto 74 C2
Porto Alegre Sao Tome and Principe 44 D4
Port-of-Spain *capital of* Trinidad & Tobago 37 G5
Porto-Novo *capital of* Benin 57 F5
Porto Velho Brazil 42 C3
Portoviejo Ecuador 40 A4
Port Said *see* Būr Saʿīd
Portsmouth England, UK 71 D7
Port Sudan Sudan 54 C3
Portugal *country* SW Europe 74
Port-Vila *capital of* Vanuatu 126 D5
Porvenir Chile 47 B7
Posadas Argentina 46 E3
Posen *see* Poznań
Poste-de-la-Baleine *see* Kuujjuarapik
Pöstyén *see* Piešťany
Potenza S Italy 79 D5
Poti Georgia 99 E2
Potosí Bolivia 42 C5
Potsdam Germany 76 D4
Póvoa de Varzim Portugal 74 C2
Powder *river* N USA 24 C2
Powell, Lake *lake* SW USA 24 B5
Poza Rica Mexico 33 F4
Poznań Poland *Ger.* Posen 80 C3
Pozo Colorado Paraguay 44 B2
Pozsony *see* Bratislava
Prag *see* Prague
Prague *capital of* Czech Republic *Cz.* Praha, *Ger.* Prag 81 B5
Praha *see* Prague
Praia *capital of* Cape Verde 56 A3
Prato Italy 78 B3
Pratt Kansas, USA 25 E5
Preschau *see* Prešov
Prescott Arizona, USA 28 B2
Presidente Prudente Brazil 44 D2
Prešov Slovakia *Ger.* Eperies, *var.* Preschau, *Hung.* Eperjes 81 D5
Prespa, Lake *lake* SE Europe 83 D6 86 A3
Presque Isle Maine, USA 23 G1

Pressburg *see* Bratislava
Preston England, UK 71 D5
Pretoria *judicial capital of* South Africa 60 D4
Préveza Greece 86 A4
Prijedor Bosnia & Herzegovina 82 B3
Prilep Macedonia 83 E5
Prince Albert Canada 19 F5
Prince Edward Island *province* Canada 21 F4
Prince Edward Islands *island group* South Africa 123 A7
Prince George Canada 19 E5
Prince of Wales Island *island* Canada 19 F2
Prince Rupert Canada 18 D4
Princess Charlotte Bay *bay* Australia 130 C2
Princess Elizabeth Land *region* Antarctica 136 C3
Príncipe *island* Sao Tome & Principe 59 A5
Pripet *river* Belarus/Ukraine 90 C1
Pripet Marshes *wetlands* Belarus/Ukraine 90 C1
Prishtinë *capital of* Kosovo 83 D5
Prizren Kosovo 83 D5
Prome *see* Pyay
Prossnitz *see* Prostějov
Prostějov Czech Republic *Ger.* Prossnitz 81 C5
Provence *region* France 73 D6
Providence Rhode Island, USA 23 G3
Providencia, Isla de *island* Colombia 35 E3
Provo Utah, USA 24 B4
Prudhoe Bay Alaska, USA 18 D2
Przheval'sk *see* Karakol
Pskov Russian Federation 92 A4
Pskov, Lake *lake* Estonia/ Russian Federation *Est.* Pihkva Järv, *Rus.* Pskovskoye Ozero 88 D3
Pskovskoye Ozero *see* Pskov, Lake
Ptich' *see* Ptsich
Ptsich *river* Belarus *Rus.* Ptich' 89 D6
Pucallpa Peru 42 B3
Puebla Mexico 33 F4
Pueblo Colorado, USA 22 D4
Puerto Aisén Chile 47 B6
Puerto Barrios Guatemala 34 C2
Puerto Carreño Colombia 40 D2
Puerto Cortés Honduras 34 C2
Puerto Deseado Argentina 47 C6
Puerto Maldonado Peru 42 C4
Puerto Montt Chile 47 B5
Puerto Natales Chile 47 B7
Puerto Plata Dominican Republic 37 E3
Puerto Princesa Philippines 120 E2
Puerto Rico *commonwealth territory* USA, West Indies 37 F3
Puerto San Julián Argentina 47 C7
Puerto Suárez Bolivia 42 D4
Puerto Vallarta Mexico 32 D4
Pula Croatia 82 A3
Pul-e Khumrī Afghanistan *prev.* Pol-e Khomrī 105 E4
Pune India *prev.* Poona 114 C1
Puno Peru 42 C4
Punta Arenas Chile *prev.* Magallanes 47 B7
Puntarenas Costa Rica 34 D4
Purmerend Netherlands 68 C3
Purus *river* Brazil/Peru 42 C3
Pusan *see* Busan
Putrajaya *administrative capital of* Malaysia 120 B3
Putumayo *river* NW South America 38 B3
Pyapon Myanmar 118 B4
Pyarnu *see* Pärnu
Pyay Myanmar *prev.* Prome 118 A4
Pyongyang *capital of* North Korea 110 E4
Pyramid Lake *lake* Nevada, USA 27 C5
Pyrenees *mountain range* SW Europe 62 C4

Q

Qaanaaq Greenland *var.* Thule 64 D1
Qābatiya West Bank 101 D7
Qaidam Pendi *basin* China 108 D4
Qalāt Afghanistan *prev.* Kalāt104 D5
Qalqīlya West Bank 101 D7
Qamdo China 108 D5
Qandahār *see* Kandahār
Qaqortoq Greenland 64 C4
Qara Qum *see* Karakumy
Qarshi *see* Karshi
Qasigiannguit Greenland 64 C3
Qatar *country* SW Asia 103 D5
Qattara Depression *see* Qaţţārah, Munkhafaḑ al
Qaţţārah, Munkhafaḑ al *desert basin* Egypt *Eng.* Qattara Depression 54 A1
Qausuittuq *see* Resolute
Qeqertarsuaq Greenland 64 B3
Qeqertarsuaq *island* Greenland 64 B3
Qian *see* Guizhou
Qilian Shan *mountain range* China 108 A4
Qimusseriarsuaq *bay* Greenland 64 C2
Qinā Egypt 54 B2
Qingdao China 110 D4
Qinghai *province* China *var.* Chinghai, Koko Nor, Qing, Tsinghai 108 D4
Qinghai Hu *lake* China *var.* Koko Nor 108 D4
Qingzang Gaoyuan *plateau* China *Eng.* Plateau of Tibet 110 A4
Qiong *see* Hainan
Qiqihar China 110 D3
Qira China 108 B4
Qitai China 108 C3

Qom Iran *var.* Kum 102 C3
Qondūz *river* Afghanistan 105 E4
Qondūz *see* Kunduz
Qo'qon Uzbekistan prev. Kokand, *var.* Khokand, 105 E2
Quba Azerbaijan *Rus.* Kuba 99 H2
Québec Canada 21 E4
Québec *province* Canada 20 D3
Queen Charlotte Islands *islands* Canada 18 D4
Queen Charlotte Sound *sea feature* Canada 18 D5
Queen Elizabeth Islands *islands* Canada 19 F1
Queensland *state* Australia 130 C4
Queenstown New Zealand 133 B6
Quelimane Mozambique 61 E3
Querétaro Mexico 33 E4
Quetta Pakistan 116 B2
Quezaltenango Guatemala 34 B2
Quibdó Colombia 40 B2
Quimper France 72 A3
Quy Nhơn Vietnam 119 E5
Qing *see* Qinghai
Quito *capital of* Ecuador 40 A4
Qŭrghonteppa Tajikistan *Rus.* Kurgan–Tynbe 105 E3
Qyteti Stalin *see* Kuçovë

R

Raab *see* Győr
Raab *see* Rába
Rába *river* Austria/Hungary *Ger.* Raab 81 C7
Rabat *capital of* Morocco 52 C2
Race, Cape *coastal feature* Canada 21 H4
Rach Gia Vietnam 119 D6
Radom Poland 80 D4
Radviliškis Lithuania 88 C4
Ragusa Italy 79 D7
Rahīmyār Khān Pakistan 116 C3
Raipur India 117 E5
Rājahmundry India 115 E1
Rājasthān *state* India 116 C3
Rājkot India 116 C4
Rājshāhi Bangladesh 117 G4
Rakaia *river* New Zealand 133 C6
Rakvere Estonia *Ger.* Wesenberg 88 D2
Raleigh North Carolina, USA 31 F1
Ralik Chain *islands* Marshall Islands 126 D1
Râmnicu Vâlcea Romania *prev.* Rîmnicu Vîlcea 90 B4
Ramallah West Bank 101 D7
Ramree Island *island* Myanmar 118 A3
Rancagua Chile 46 B4
Rānchi India 117 F4
Randers Denmark 67 A7
Rangiora New Zealand 133 C6
Rangitikei *river* New Zealand 132 D4
Rangoon *see* Yangon
Rankin Inlet Canada 19 G3
Rapid City South Dakota, USA 24 D3
Rarotonga *island* Cook Islands 127 G5
Rasht Iran 102 C3
Ratak Chain *islands* Marshall Islands 126 D1
Ratchaburi Thailand 119 C5
Rat Islands *island group* Alaska, USA 18 A2
Raukumara Range *mountain range* New Zealand 132 E3
Rauma Finland 67 D5
Ravenna Italy 78 C3
Rāwalpindi Pakistan 116 C1
Rawson Argentina 47 C6
Razgrad Bulgaria 86 D1
Reading England, UK 71 D6
Rebecca, Lake *lake* Australia 129 C6
Rebun-tō *island* Japan 112 D1
Rechytsa Belarus 89 D7
Recife Brazil 43 H3
Recklinghausen Germany 76 G4
Red Deer Canada 19 E5
Redding California, USA 27 B5
Red River *river* S USA 30 B3
Red River *river* China/ Vietnam 118
Red Sea Indian Ocean 122 A3
Reefton New Zealand 133 C5
Regensburg Germany 77 C5
Reggane Algeria 52 D3
Reggio di Calabria Italy 79 D6
Reggio nell' Emilia Italy 78 B3
Regina Canada 19 F5
Rehoboth Namibia 60 C4
Reichenberg *see* Liberec
Reid Australia 129 D6
Reims France *Eng.* Rheims 72 D3
Reindeer Lake *lake* Canada 17 C4
Reni Ukraine 90 D4
Rennes France 72 B3
Reno Nevada, USA 27 B5
Resistencia Argentina 46 D3
Reşiţa Romania 90 B4
Resolute Canada *Var.* Qausuittuq 19 F2
Réunion *overseas department* France, Indian Ocean 123 B5
Reus Spain 75 G2
Reutlingen Germany 77 B6
Reval *see* Tallinn
Revel *see* Tallinn
Revillagigedo, Islas *island* Mexico 32 B4
Rey, Isla del *island* Panama 35 F5
Reykjavík *capital of* Iceland 65 E5
Reynosa Mexico 33 E2
Rēzekne Latvia *Ger.* Rositten, *Rus.* Rezhitsa 88 D4
Rezhitsa *see* Rēzekne
Rheims *see* Reims
Rhine *river* W Europe 62 D3
Rhode Island *state* USA 23 G3

Rhodes *see* Ródos
Rhodope Mountains *mountain range* Bulgaria/Greece *Gk.* Orosirá Rodópis, *Bul.* Despoto Planina 86 C3
Rhône *river* France/Switzerland 62 C4
Ribeirão Preto Brazil 45 E1
Riberalta Bolivia 42 C3
Rîbniţa Moldova 90 D3
Richfield Utah, USA 24 B4
Richland Washington, USA 24 C2
Richmond Kentucky, USA 22 C5
Richmond New Zealand 133 C5
Richmond Virginia, USA 23 E5
Richmond Range *mountain range* New Zealand 133 C5
Ricobayo, Embalse de *reservoir* Spain 74 D2
Riga *capital of* Latvia *Latv.* Rīga 88 C3
Riga, Gulf of *sea feature* Baltic Sea 88 C3
Riihimäki Finland 67 D5
Rijeka Croatia *It.* Fiume 82 A3
Rimah, Wādī ar *dry watercourse* Saudi Arabia 103 B5
Rimini Italy 78 C3
Rîmnicu Vîlcea *see* Râmnicu Vâlcea
Riobamba Ecuador 40 A4
Rio Branco Brazil 42 C3
Río Cuarto Argentina 46 C4
Rio de Janeiro Brazil 45 F2
Río Gallegos Argentina 47 C7
Rio Grande Brazil 44 D4
Rio Grande *river* N America 16 B6
Rio Grande Rise *undersea feature* Atlantic Ocean 49 C6
Río Verde Mexico 33 E3
Rishiri-tō *island* Japan 112 D1
Rivas Nicaragua 34 D3
Rivera Uruguay 44 C4
Riverside California, USA 27 C8
Riverton New Zealand 133 A7
Rivne Ukraine *Rus.* Rovno 90 C2
Riyadh *capital of* Saudi Arabia *Ar.* Ar Riyāḑ 103 C5
Rize Turkey 99 E2
Rkîz Mauritania 56 C3
Road Town *capital of* British Virgin Islands 37 F3
Roanne France 73 D5
Roanoke Virginia, USA 23 E5
Roanoke *river* SE USA 31 G1
Robinson Range *mountain range* Australia 129 B5
Rochester Minnesota, USA 25 F3
Rochester New York, USA 23 E3
Rockford Illinois, USA 22 B3
Rockhampton Australia 130 D4
Rock Island Illinois, USA 22 B3
Rock Springs Wyoming, USA 24 C3
Rockstone Guyana 41 G2
Rocky Mountains *mountain range* Canada/USA 18-19 D4
Rodez France 73 C6
Ródhos *see* Ródos
Ródos *island* Greece *var.* Ródhos, *Eng.* Rhodes 87 E6
Ródos Greece *Eng.* Rhodes 87 E6
Rodosto *see* Tekirdağ
Roeselare Belgium 69 A5
Roma Australia 131 D5
Roma *see* Rome
Romania *country* SE Europe 90
Rome *capital of* Italy *It.* Roma 78 C4
Rome Georgia, USA 30 D2
Rønne Denmark 67 B8
Ronne Ice Shelf *ice feature* Antarctica 136 B3
Roosendaal Netherlands 68 C4
Rosario Argentina 46 D4
Roseau *capital of* Dominica 37 G4
Rosenau *see* Rožňava
Rositten *see* Rēzekne
Ross Ice Shelf *ice feature* Antarctica 136 B4
Ross Sea Antarctica 136 B4
Rostak *see* Ar Rustāq
Rostock Germany 76 C2
Rostov-na-Donu Russian Federation 96 A3
Roswell New Mexico, USA 28 D2
Rotorua New Zealand 132 D3
Rotorua, Lake *lake* New Zealand 132 D3
Rotterdam Netherlands 68 C4
Rouen France 72 C3
Rovaniemi Finland 66 D3
Rovno *see* Rivne
Rovuma *river* Mozambique/Tanzania 61 F2
Roxas City Philippines 121 E2
Rožňava Slovakia *Ger.* Rosenau, *Hung.* Rozsnyó 81 D6
Rozsnyó *see* Rožňava
Ruatoria New Zealand 132 E3
Ruawai New Zealand 132 D2
Rudnyy Kazakhstan 96 C4
Rudolf, Lake *see* Lake Turkana
Rügen *headland* Germany 76 D2
Rukwa, Lake *lake* Tanzania 55 B7
Rumbek South Sudan 55 B5
Rundu Namibia 60 C3
Ruoqiang China 108 C3
Ruse Bulgaria 86 D1
Russian Federation *country* Europe/Asia 92-93 96-97
Rustavi Georgia 99 F2
Rutland Vermont, USA 23 F2
Rutog China 108 B4
Rwanda *country* C Africa 55
Ryazan' Russian Federation 93 B5 96 B3
Rybinskoye Vodokhranilishche *Reservoir* Russian Federation *Eng.* Rybinsk Reservoir 92 B4
Rybnik Poland 81 C5
Ryūkyū-rettō *island group* Japan 113 A8

Ryukyu Trench *Undersea feature* East China Sea 134 B2
Rzeszów Poland 81 E5**Saale** *river* Germany 76 C4

Saarbrücken Germany 77 A5
Saare *see* Saaremaa
Saaremaa *island* Estonia *var.* Saare, Sarema, *Ger.* Ösel, *var.* Oesel 88 C2
Šabac Serbia 82 C3
Sabadell Spain 75 G2
Sabah *cultural region* Borneo 120 D3
Sab'atayn, Ramlat as *desert* Yemen 103 C7
Sabhā Libya 53 F3
Sabzevār Iran 102 D3
Sacramento California, USA 27 B6
Şa'dah Yemen 103 B6
Sado *island* Japan 112 C4
Safi Morocco 52 B2
Saginaw Michigan, USA 22 C3
Sahara *desert* N Africa 50 B3
Sahel *region* W Africa 50 B3
Saïda Lebanon *anc.* Sidon 100 B4
Saidpur Bangladesh 117 G3
Saigon *see* Hô Chi Minh
Saimaa *lake* Finland 67 E5
Saint-Brieuc France 72 A3
Saint Catherines Canada 20 D5
Saint-Chamond France 73 D5
St Christopher & Nevis *see* St Kitts & Nevis
St Cloud Minnesota, USA 25 F2
St-Denis *capital of* Réunion 61 H4
Saintes France 72 B5
Saint-Étienne France 73 D5
Saint George Australia 131 D5
St. George's *capital of* Grenada 37 G5
St Helena *overseas territory* UK, Atlantic Ocean 49 D5
St Helier *capital* Jersey 71 D8
Saint-Jean, Lake *lake* Canada 21 E4
Saint John Canada 21 F4
St John's *country capital* Antigua and Barbuda 37 G3
Saint John's Canada 21 H3
St Joseph Missouri, USA 25 F4
St Kitts & Nevis *country* West Indies *var.* St Christopher & Nevis 37
St.-Laurent-du-Maroni French Guiana 41 H2
Saint Lawrence *river* Canada 21 E4
Saint Lawrence, Gulf of *sea feature* Canada 21 F3
St. Lawrence Island *island* Alaska, USA 18 C2
Saint-Lô France 73 B3
Saint Louis Senegal 56 B3
St Louis Missouri, USA 25 G4
St Lucia *country* West Indies 37
Saint-Malo France 72 B3
Saint-Nazaire France 72 B4
Saint Paul Minnesota, USA 25 F2
St-Paul, Île *island* French Southern and Antarctic Lands 123 C6
St Peter Port *capital of* Guernsey 71 D8
St Petersburg Russian Federation *Rus.* Sankt-Peterburg, *prev.* Leningrad, Petrograd 92 B3 96 B2
St Petersburg Florida, USA 31 E4
Saint Pierre & Miquelon *overseas collectivity* France, Atlantic Ocean 21 G4
St Vincent, Cape *see* São Vicente, Cabo de
St Vincent & The Grenadines *country* West Indies 37
Saipan *island country capital* Northern Mariana Islands 124 B1
Sakākah Saudi Arabia 102 B4
Sakakawea, Lake *lake* North Dakota, USA 24 D2
Sakarya *see* Adapazarı
Sakhalin *island* Russian Federation 97 H4
Sal *island* Cape Verde 56 A2
Salado *river* Argentina 46 C3
Şalālah Oman 103 D6
Salamanca Spain 74 D2
Sala y Gómez *island* Chile, Pacific Ocean 135 F4
Saldus Latvia *Ger.* Frauenburg 88 B3
Salekhard Russian Federation 96 D3
Salem India 114 D2
Salem Oregon, USA 26 A3
Salerno Italy 79 D5
Salerno, Golfo di *sea feature* Italy 79 D5
Salihorsk Belarus *Rus.* Soligorsk 89 C6
Salima Malawi 61 E2
Salinas California, USA 27 B6
Salisbury England, UK 71 D7
Salisbury Island *island* Canada 20 D1
Salonica *see* Thessaloníki
Salso *river* Italy 79 C7
Salt *see* As Salţ
Salta Argentina 46 C2
Saltillo Mexico 33 E2
Salt Lake City Utah, USA 24 B4
Salto Uruguay 44 B4
Salton Sea *lake* California, USA 27 D8
Salvador Brazil 43 G4
Salween *river* SE Asia 111 A6
Salzburg Austria 77 D6
Salzgitter Germany 76 C4
Samara Russian Federation 93 C6 96 B3
Samarinda Indonesia 121 E4
Samarkand Uzbekistan 104 D2
Sambre *river* Belgium 69 B7
Samoa *country* Pacific Ocean 127 F4
Samobor Croatia 82 B3
Sámos *island* Greece 87 D5
Samothrace *see* Samothráki
Samothráki *island* Greece *Eng.* Samothrace 86 D3
Samsun Turkey 98 D2

Samui, Ko *island group* Thailand 119 C6
San *river* Poland 81 E5
Saña Peru 42 A3
Sana *capital of* Yemen *var.* Şan'ā' 103 B7
Sanandaj Sinneh. Iran 102 C3
San Andrés, Isla de *island* Colombia 35 E3
San Angelo Texas, USA 29 F3
San Antonio Chile 46 B4
San Antonio Texas, USA 29 F4
San Antonio *river* S USA 29 G4
San Antonio Oeste Argentina 47 C5
Sanāw Yemen 103 C6
San Bernardino California, USA 27 C7
San Carlos Uruguay 44 C5
San Carlos de Bariloche Argentina 47 B5
San Clemente Island *island* W USA 27 C8
San Cristóbal Venezuela 40 C2
San Diego California, USA 27 C8
Sandwich Island *see* Efate
San Fernando Trinidad & Tobago 37 G5
San Fernando Venezuela 40 D2
San Fernando de Noronha *island* Brazil 43 H2
San Francisco California, USA 27 B6
Sangir, Kepulauan *island group* Indonesia 121 F3
San Ignacio Belize 34 C1
San Joaquin Valley *valley* W USA 27 B6
San José *capital of* Costa Rica 34 D4
San Jose California, USA 27 B6
San José del Guaviare Colombia 40 C3
San Juan Argentina 46 B3
San Juan *river* Costa Rica/ Nicaragua 34 D4
San Juan *capital of* Puerto Rico 37 F3
San Juan Bautista Paraguay 44 B3
San Juan de los Morros Venezuela 40 D1
Sankt Martin *see* Martin
Sankt-Peterburg *see* St Petersburg
Sankt Pölten Austria 77 E6
Şanlıurfa Turkey *prev.* Urfa 98 E4
San Lorenzo Honduras 34 C3
San Luis Potosí Mexico 33 E3
San Marino *country* S Europe 78 C3
San Matías, Golfo *sea feature* Argentina 39 C6
San Miguel El Salvador 34 C3
San Miguel de Tucumán Argentina 46 C3
San Nicolas Island *island* W USA 27 B8
San Pedro Sula Honduras 34 C2
San Remo Italy 78 A3
San Salvador *capital of* El Salvador 34 C3
San Salvador de Jujuy Argentina 46 C2
San Sebastián *see* Donostia/ San Sebastián
Santa Ana El Salvador 34 B2
Santa Ana California, USA 27 C8
Santa Barbara California, USA 27 B7
Santa Catalina Island *island* W USA 27 C8
Santa Clara Cuba 36 B2
Santa Cruz Bolivia 42 D4
Santa Cruz California, USA 27 B6
Santa Cruz Islands *island group* Solomon Islands 126 C4
Santa Fe Argentina 46 D3
Santa Fe New Mexico, USA 28 D2
Santa Maria Brazil 44 C4
Santa Marta Colombia 40 C1
Santander Spain 75 E1
Santanilla, Islas *islands* Honduras 35 E1
Santarém Brazil 43 E2
Santarém Portugal 74 C3
Santaren Channel *Channel* The Bahamas 36 C2
Santa Rosa Argentina 47 C4
Santa Rosa California, USA 27 A6
Santa Rosa de Copán Honduras 34 C2
Santa Rosa Island *island* W USA 27 B8
Santiago *island* Cape Verde 56 A3
Santiago *capital of* Chile 46 B4
Santiago Dominican Republic 37 E3
Santiago Panama 35 F5
Santiago de Compostela Spain 74 C1
Santiago de Cuba Cuba 36 C3
Santiago del Estero Argentina 46 C3
Santo Antão *island* Cape Verde 56 A2
Santo Domingo *capital of* Dominican Republic 37 E3
Santo Domingo de los Colorados Ecuador 40 A4
Santoríni *island* Greece 87 D6
Santos Brazil 45 E2
São Borja Brazil 44 C3
São Francisco *river* Brazil 43 G3
São José do Rio Preto Brazil 44 D1
São Luís Brazil 43 G2
São Nicolau *island* Cape Verde 56 A2
Saône *river* France 72 D4
São Paulo Brazil 43 F5 45 E2
São Tomé *capital of* Sao Tome & Principe 59 A5
São Tomé *island* Sao Tome & Principe 59 A5
Sao Tome & Principe *country* W Africa 59
São Vincente *island* Cape Verde 56 A2
São Vicente, Cabo de *coastal feature* Portugal *Eng.* Cape St Vincent 74 B4
Sapele Nigeria 57 F5
Sapporo Japan 112 D2
Saragossa *see* Zaragoza

Sarajevo *capital of* Bosnia & Herzegovina 82 C4
Sarandë Albania 83 D6
Saransk Russian Federation 93 B5
Saratov Russian Federation 93 B6
Sarawak *state* Malaysia 120 D3
Sardegna *island* Italy *Eng.* Sardinia 79 A5
Sardinia *see* Sardegna
Sarema *see* Saaremaa
Sargasso Sea Atlantic Ocean 48 B4
Sargodha Pakistan 116 C2
Sarh Chad 58 C4
Sārī Iran 102 D3
Saruhan *see* Manisa
Sasebo Japan 113 A6
Saskatchewan *province* Canada 19 F5
Saskatchewan *river* Canada 19 F5
Saskatoon Canada 19 F5
Sassandra *River* Côte d'Ivoire 56 D5
Sassari Italy 79 A5
Satu Mare Romania 90 B3
Saudi Arabia *country* SW Asia 102-103
Sault Sainte Marie Canada 20 C4
Sault Sainte Marie Michigan, USA 22 C1
Saurimo Angola 60 C2
Sava *river* SE Europe 82 C3
Savannah Georgia, USA 31 F3
Savannah *river* SE USA 31 E2
Savissivik Greenland 64 C2
Savona Italy 78 A3
Savu Sea *sea* Indonesia 120 E5
Sawḩāj Egypt *var.* Sohâg 54 B2
Şawqirah Oman 103 D6
Saýat Turkmenistan 104 D3
Sayhūt Yemen 103 D7
Saynshand Mongolia 109 E2
Say 'ūn Yemen 103 C6
Scandinavia *geophysical region* Europe 48 D2
Schaffhausen Switzerland 77 B6
Schaulen *see* Šiauliai
Schefferville Canada 21 E2
Scheldt *river* W Europe 69 B5
Schiermonnikoog *island* Netherlands 68 D1
Schneidemühl *see* Piła
Schwäbische Alb *mountains* Germany 77 B6
Schwarzwald *Forested mountain region* Germany *Eng.* Black Forest 77 B6
Schwerin Germany 76 C3
Scilly, Isles of *islands* UK 71 B7
Scotia Sea Atlantic Ocean 136 A1
Scotland *national region* UK 70
Scottsbluff Nebraska, USA 24 D3
Scottsdale Arizona, USA 28 B2
Scranton Pennsylvania, USA 23 F3
Scutari, Lake *lake* Albania/ Montenegro 83 C5
Seddon New Zealand 133 C5
Seattle Washington, USA 26 B2
Ségou Mali 56 D3
Segovia Spain 75 E2
Segura *river* Spain 75 E4
Seikan Tunnel *tunnel* Japan 112 D3
Seinäjoki Finland 67 D5
Seine *river* France 72 C3
Sejong City *administrative capital of* South Korea 110 E4
Selfoss Iceland 65 E5
Semara *see* Smara
Semarang Indonesia 120 D4
Semey Kazakhstan *prev.* Semipalatinsk 96 D4
Semipalatinsk *see* Semey
Sendai Japan 112 D4
Senegal *country* W Africa 56
Senegal *river* Africa 56 C3
Sên, Stœng *river* Cambodia 119 D5
Seoul *capital of* South Korea *Kor.* Sŏul 110 E4
Sept-Iles Canada 21 F3
Seraing Belgium 69 D6
Seram, Pulau *island* Indonesia 121 F4
Serbia *country* SE Europe 82 D3
Serdar Turkmenistan *prev.* Gyzylarbat, prev. Kizyl-Arvat 104 B2
Serhetabat Turkmenistan *prev.* Gushgy, Kushka 104 C4
Serov Russian Federation 96 C3
Serpent's Mouth, The *sea feature* Trinidad & Tobago/ Venezuela *Sp.* Boca de la Serpiente 41 F1
Serra do Mar *mountains* Brazil 44 D3
Sérres Greece 86 C3
Setesdal *valley* Norway 67 A6
Sétif Algeria 53 E1
Setúbal Portugal 74 C4
Seul, Lake *lake* Canada 20 A3
Sevana Lich *lake* Armenia 99 G2
Sevastopol' Ukraine 91 F5
Severn *river* Canada 20 B3
Severn *river* England/Wales, UK 71 D6
Severnaya Dvina *river* Russian Federation *Eng.* Northern Dvina 92 C3
Severnaya Zemlya *island group* Russian Federation 137 H3
Sevilla Spain *Eng.* Seville 74 D4
Seville *see* Sevilla
Seychelles *country* Indian Ocean 61 122 B4
Seyðisfjörður Iceland 65 E4
Seýdi Turkmenistan *prev.* Neftezavodsk 104 D2
Seyhan *see* Adana
Sfax Tunisia 53 F2
's-Gravenhage *capital of* Netherlands *Eng.* The Hague 68 B3
Shaan *see* Shaanxi
Shaanxi *province* China *var.* Shaan, Shan-hsi, Shaanxi Sheng, Shenshi, Shensi 111 C5

Shaanxi Sheng *see* Shaanxi
Shache China 108 A3
Shackleton Ice Shelf *ice feature* Antarctica 136 D3
Shandong *province* China *var.* Lu, Shantung 110 D4
Shanghai China 111 D5
Shangrao China 111 D6
Shan-hsi *see* Shaanxi
Shannon *river* Ireland 71 B5
Shan Plateau *upland* Myanmar 118 B3
Shantou China 111 D6
Shantung *see* Shandong
Sharjah *see* Ash Shāriqah
Shawnee Oklahoma, USA 29 G2
Shdanov *see* Mariupol'
Shebeli *river* Ethiopia/Somalia 55 D5
Sheberghān *see* Shibirghān
Sheffield England, UK 71 D5
Shengking *see* Liaoning
Shenking *see* Liaoning
Shenshi *see* Shaanxi
Shensi *see* Shaanxi
Shenyang China 110 D3
Sherbrooke Canada 21 E4
Sheridan Wyoming, USA 22 C2
's-Hertogenbosch Netherlands 68 C4
Shetland *islands* Scotland, UK 70 D1
Shevchenko *see* Aktau
Shihezi China 108 C2
Shijiazhuang China 110 C4
Shikoku *island* Japan 113 B6
Shikoku Basin *undersea feature* Philippine Sea 134 B2
Shikotan *island* Japan/Russian Federation (disputed) 112 E2
Shikārpur Pakistan 116 B3
Shimonoseki Japan 113 A5
Shinano-gawa *river* Japan 112 C4
Shingū Japan 113 C5
Shinyanga Tanzania 55 B7
Shiquanhe *see* Gar
Shibirghān Afghanistan *prev.* Sherberghān 104 D3
Shīrāz Iran 102 D4
Shkodër Albania 83 D5
Shostka Ukraine 91 E1
Shreveport Louisiana, USA 30 A2
Shrewsbury England, UK 71 D6
Shumen Bulgaria 86 D2
Shymkent Kazakhstan *prev.* Chimkent 96 B5
Šiauliai Lithuania *Ger.* Schaulen 88 B4
Šibenik Croatia 82 B4
Siberia *region* Russian Federation 97 E3
Siberut, Pulau *island* Indonesia 120 B4
Sibiu Romania 90 B4
Sibolga Indonesia 120 B3
Sibu Malaysia 120 C3
Sibut Central African Republic 58 C4
Sibuyan Sea *sea* Philippines 121 E2
Sichuan *province* China *var.* Chuan, Ssu-ch'uan, Szechwan 111 B5
Sichuan Pendi *depression* China 111 B5
Sicilia *island* Italy *Eng.* Sicily 79 C7
Sicily, Strait of *sea feature* Mediterranean Sea 79 B7
Sicily *see* Sicilia
Sidi Bel Abbès Algeria 52 D1
Sidon *see* Saïda
Siednesibirskoye Ploskogor'ye *plateau* Russian Federation *Eng.* Central Siberian Plateau 97 E3
Siegen Germany 76 B4
Siena Italy 78 B3
Sierra Leone *country* W Africa 56
Sierra Madre del Sur *mountain range* Mexico 33 E5
Sierra Madre Occidental *mountain range* Mexico *var.* Western Sierra Madre 17 B6
Sierra Madre Oriental *mountain range* Mexico *var.* Eastern Sierra Madre 32 D2
Sierra Nevada *mountain range* Spain 75 E4
Sierra Nevada *mountain range* W USA 27 B6
Sighişoara Romania 90 C4
Siglufjörður Iceland 65 E4
Siguiri Guinea 56 D4
Sihanoukville Cambodia *var.* Kâmpóng Saôm 119 D6
Siirt Turkey 99 F3
Siling Co *lake* China 108 C5
Silkeborg Denmark 67 A7
Sillein *see* Žilina
Šilutė Lithuania 88 B4
Simeulue, Pulau *island* Indonesia 120 A3
Simferopol' Ukraine 91 F5
Simpson Desert *desert* Australia 130 C4
Sinai *desert* Egypt 54 B1
Sincelejo Colombia 40 B1
Sines Portugal 74 B4
Singapore *country* SE Asia 120
Singapore *capital of* Singapore 120 C3
Sinkiang *see* Xinjiang Uygur Zizhiqu
Sinnamary French Guiana 41 H2
Sinop Turkey 98 D2
Sint-Niklaas Belgium 69 B5
Sintra Portugal 74 B3
Sion Switzerland 77 B7
Sioux City Iowa, USA 25 F3
Sioux Falls South Dakota, USA 25 E3
Siracusa Italy *Eng.* Syracuse 79 D7
Siret *river* Romania/Ukraine 90 C4
Sirikit Reservoir *Reservoir* Thailand 118 C4
Sirte, Gulf of *see* Surt, Khalīj
Sisak Croatia 82 B3
Sisimiut Greenland 64 C3
Sittoung *river* Myanmar 118 B4
Sittwe Myanmar *prev.* Akyab 118 A3
Sivas Turkey 98 D3
Sjælland *island* Denmark 67 B7
Skagerrak *sea feature* Denmark/Norway 67 A6

Skellefteå Sweden 66 D4
Skopje *capital of* Macedonia 83 E5
Skövde Sweden 67 B6
Skovorodino Russian Federation 97 F4
Skye *island* Scotland, UK 70 B3
Slavonski Brod Croatia 82 C3
Sligo Ireland 71 B5
Sliven Bulgaria 86 D2
Slonim Belarus 89 C6
Slovakia *country* C Europe 81
Slovenia *country* SE Europe 77
Slov'yans'k Ukraine 91 G3
Słupsk Poland *Ger.* Stolp 78 C2
Slutsk Belarus 89 C6
Smallwood Reservoir *reservoir* Canada 21 E3
Smara Western Sahara *var.* Semara 52 B3
Smederevo Serbia 82 D3
Smolensk Russian Federation 92 A4
Smyrna *see* İzmir
Snake *river* NW USA 26 D4
Snowdonia *mountains* Wales, UK 71 C5
Sobradinho, Represa de *Reservoir* Brazil 43 G3
Sochi Russian Federation 93 A7 96 A3
Société, Îles de la *islands* French Polynesia *Eng.* Society Islands 127 H4
Society Islands *see* Société, Îles de la
Socotra *see* Suquţrá
Sodankylä Finland 66 D3
Sofia *capital of* Bulgaria *var.* Sofija, *Bul.* Sofiya 86 C2
Sofija *see* Sofia
Sofiya *see* Sofia
Sognefjorden *inlet* Norway 67 A5
Sohâg *see* Sawhāj
Sokhumi Georgia *Rus.* Sukhumi 99 E1
Sokodé Togo 57 E4
Sokoto Nigeria 57 F3
Sokoto *river* Nigeria 57 F3
Solāpur India 116 D5 114 D1
Sol, Costa del *coastal region* Spain 75 E5
Soligorsk *see* Salihorsk
Solomon Islands *country* Pacific Ocean 126
Solomon Islands *island group* PNG/Solomon Islands 124 C3
Solomon Sea Pacific Ocean 126 B3
Somalia *country* E Africa 54-55
Somali Basin *undersea feature* Indian Ocean 122 A4
Somaliland *Disputed territory* E Africa 55 D5
Sombor Serbia 82 C3
Somerset Island *island* Canada 19 F2
Somme *river* France 72 C3
Somoto Nicaragua 34 D3
Songea Tanzania 55 C8
Songkhla Thailand 119 C7
Sonoran Desert *see* Altar, Desierto de
Sopron Hungary *Ger.* Ödenburg 81 B6
Soria Spain 75 E2
Sorocaba Brazil 43 F5 45 E2
Sorong Indonesia 124 G4
Sotavento, Ilhas de *island group* Cape Verde *var.* Leeward Islands 56 A3
Soûr Lebanon *anc.* Tyre 100 A4
Sousse Tunisia 53 F1
South Africa *country* southern Africa 60-61
South America 38-39
Southampton England, UK 71 D7
Southampton Island *island* Canada 17 G3
South Andaman *island* India 115 G2
South Australia *state* Australia 131 A5
South Australian Basin *undersea feature* Southern Ocean 124 B5
South Bend Indiana, USA 22 C3
South Carolina *state* USA 31 F2
South Carpathians *see* Carpaţii Meridionali
South China Sea Pacific Ocean 119 E7
South Dakota *state* USA 24-25 E3
South East Point *coastal feature* Australia 131 C7
Southeast Indian Ridge *undersea feature* Indian Ocean 123 E6
Southeast Pacific Basin *undersea feature* Pacific Ocean 135 E5
Southend-on-Sea England, UK 71 E6
Southern Alps *mountain range* New Zealand 133 B6
Southern Cook Islands *islands* Cook Islands 127 G5
Southern Cross Australia 129 B6
Southern Ocean *ocean 123 D7*
Southern Upland *mountain range* Scotland, UK 70 C4
South Fiji Basin *undersea feature* Pacific Ocean 124 D4
South Geomagnetic Pole *pole* Antarctica 136 C3
South Georgia *overseas territory* UK, Atlantic Ocean 136 A1
South Indian Basin *undersea feature* Indian Ocean 123 E7
South Island *island* New Zealand 133 D5
South Korea *country* E Asia 110-111
South Orkney Islands *islands* Antarctica 136 A2
South Pole *ice feature* Antarctica 136 B3
South Sandwich Islands *overseas territory* UK, Atlantic Ocean 136 A1
South Shetland Islands *islands* Antarctica 136 A2
South Sudan *country* NE Africa 55 B5
South Taranaki Bight *bight* New Zealand 132 C4
South Uist *island* UK 70 B3
South West Cape *headland* New Zealand 133 A8

Southwest Indian Ridge *undersea feature* Indian Ocean 123 B6
Southwest Pacific Basin *undersea feature* Pacific Ocean 125 F4
Soweto South Africa 60 D4
Spain *country* SW Europe 74-75
Sparks Nevada, USA 27 B5
Sparta *see* Spárti
Spartanburg South Carolina, USA 31 E2
Spárti Greece *Eng.* Sparta 87 B6
Spencer Gulf *gulf* Australia 131 B6
Spitsbergen *island* Svalbard 65 F2
Split Croatia 82 B4
Spokane Washington, USA 26 C2
Spratly Islands *islands* South China Sea 120 D2
Spree *river* Germany 76 D4
Springfield Illinois, USA 22 B4
Springfield Massachusetts, USA 23 G3
Springfield Missouri, USA 23 F5
Springfield Oregon, USA 26 A3
Srebrenica Bosnia & Herzegovina 82 C4
Srednesibirskoye Ploskogor'ye *var.* Central Siberian Uplands, *Eng.* Central Siberian Plateau. *mountain range* Russian Federation 97 E3
Sri Jayewardenapura Kotte *legislative capital of* Sri Lanka115 E4
Sri Lanka *country* S Asia *prev.* Ceylon 115
Srinagarind Reservoir *Reservoir* Thailand 119 C5
Srpska, Republika *republic* Bosnia and Herzegovina 82 C3
Ssu-ch'uan *see* Sichuan
Stalinabad *see* Dushanbe
Stalingrad *see* Volgograd
Stalin Peak *see* Communism Peak
Stalinsk *see* Novokuznetsk
Stambul *see* İstanbul
Stanley *capital of* Falkland Islands 47 D7
Stanleyville *see* Kisangani
Stara Planina *see* Balkan Mountains
Stara Zagora Bulgaria 86 D2
Starbuck Island *island* Kiribati 125 F2
Stavanger Norway 67 A6
Stavropol' Russian Federation 93 A7 96 A3
Steinamanger *see* Szombathely
Steinkjer Norway 66 B4
Stepanakert *see* Xankändi
Stettin *see* Szczecin
Stewart Island *island* New Zealand 133 A8
Štip Macedonia 83 E5
Stirling Scotland, UK 70 C4
Stockholm *capital of* Sweden 67 C6
Stockton California, USA 27 B6
Stœng Treng Cambodia 119 D5
Stoke-on-Trent England, UK 71 D6
Stolp *see* Słupsk
Storfjorden *fjord* Norway 65 F2
Stornoway Scotland, UK 70 B2
Stralsund Germany 76 D2
Stranraer Scotland, UK 70 C4
Strasbourg France *Ger.* Strassburg 72 E4
Stratford New Zealand 132 D4
Stratford-upon-Avon England, UK 71 D6
Stratonice Czech Republic 81 A5
Stromboli *island* Italy 79 D6
Struma *see* Stymonas
Strumica Macedonia 83 E5
Strymonas *river* Bulgaria/ Greece *var.* Struma 86 C3
Studholme New Zealand 133 B6
Stuhlweissenburg *see* Székesfehérvár
Stuttgart Germany 77 B6
Subotica Serbia 82 D2
Suceava Romania 90 C3
Sucre *legal capital of* Bolivia 42 C5
Sudan *country* NE Africa 54 B3
Sudbury Canada 20 C4
Sudd *region* South Sudan 55 B5
Sudeten *mountains* Central Europe *var.* Sudetes, Sudetic Mountains, *Cz./Pol.* Sudety 81 B5
Sudetes *see* Sudeten
Sudetic Mountains *see* Sudeten
Sudety *see* Sudeten
Suez *see* As Suways
Suez, Gulf of *sea feature* Red Sea 101 A8
Suez Canal *canal* Egypt *Ar.* Qanāt as Suways 54 B1
Şuḩār Oman 103 D5
Sühbaatar Mongolia 109 E1
Suhl Germany 76 C5
Sukabumi Indonesia 120 C5
Sukhumi *see* Sokhumi
Sukkur Pakistan 116 B3
Sula, Kepulauan *island group* Indonesia 121 F4
Sulawesi *island* Indonesia *Eng.* Celebes 121 E4
Sulu Archipelago *island group* Philippines 121 E3
Sülüktü *see* Sulyukta
Sulu Sea Pacific Ocean 121 E2
Sulyukta Kyrgyzstan *Kir.* Sülüktü 105 E2
Sumatra *island* Indonesia 120 B4
Sumba, Selat *island* Indonesia 121 E5
Sumbawanga Tanzania 55 B7
Sumbe Angola 60 B2
Sumgait *see* Sumqayıt
Sumqayıt Azerbaijan *Rus.* Sumgait 99 H2
Sumy Ukraine 91 F1
Sunda, Selat *strait* Indonesia 120 D5
Sunderland England, UK 70 D4
Sundsvall Sweden 67 C5
Suntar Russian Federation 97 F3

Sunyani Ghana 57 E4
Superior Wisconsin, USA 22 A1
Superior, Lake *lake* Canada/ USA 16 C5
Suquţrá *island* Yemen *var.* Socotra 103 D7 122 B3
Şūr Oman 103 E5
Surabaya Indonesia 120 D5
Surakarta Indonesia 120 D5
Sūrat India 116 C5
Surat Thani Thailand 119 C6
Sûre *river* W Europe 69 D7
Surfers Paradise Australia 131 E5
Surinam *see* Suriname
Suriname *country* NE South America *var.* Surinam 41
Surkhob *river* Tajikistan 105 E3
Surt Libya *var.* Sidra 53 G2
Surt, Khalīj *sea feature* Mediterranean Sea *Eng.* Gulf of Sirte, Gulf of Sidra 85 E4
Surtsey *island* S Iceland 65 E5
Susanville California, USA 27 B5
Suways, Qanāt as *see* Suez Canal
Suva *capital of* Fiji 127 E4
Svalbard *external territory* Norway, Arctic Ocean 65 G2
Svay Riĕng Cambodia 119 D6
Sverdlovsk *see* Yekaterinburg
Svetlogorsk *see* Svyetlahorsk/ Svetlogorsk
Svyataya Anna Trough *undersea feature* Kara Sea 137 H4
Svyetlahorsk/Svetlogorsk Belarus *Rus.* Svetlogorsk 89 D6
Swakopmund Namibia 60 B3
Swansea Wales, UK 71 C6
Swaziland *country* southern Africa 61
Sweden *country* N Europe 66-67
Sweetwater Texas, USA 29 F3
Swindon England, UK 71 D6
Switzerland *country* C Europe 77
Sydney Australia 131 D6
Sydney Canada 21 G4
Syeverodonets'k Ukraine 91 G1
Syktyvkar Russian Federation 92 D4 96 C3
Sylhet Bangladesh 117 G4
Syracuse *see* Siracusa
Syracuse New York, USA 23 E3
Syr Darya *river* C Asia 104 D1
Syria *country* SW Asia 100-101
Syrian Desert *desert* SW Asia *Ar.* Bādiyat ash Shām 101 C5
Szczecin Poland *Ger.* Stettin 80 B3
Szczeciński, Zalew *bay* Germany/Poland 80 A2
Szechwan *see* Sichuan
Szeged Hungary *Ger.* Szegedin 81 D7
Szegedin *see* Szeged
Székesfehérvár Hungary *Ger.* Stuhlweissenburg 81 C6
Szekszárd Hungary 81 C7
Szolnok Hungary 81 D6
Szombathely Hungary *Ger.* Steinamanger 81 B6

T

Tabariya, Bahrat *see* Tiberius, Lake
Tábor Czech Republic 81 B5
Tabora Tanzania 55 B7
Tabrīz Iran 102 C2
Tabuaeran *island* Kiribati 127 G2
Tabūk Saudi Arabia 102 A4
Tacloban Philippines 120 F2
Tacna Peru 42 C4
Tacoma Washington, USA 26 B2
Tacuarembó Uruguay 44 C4
Tadmur *see* Tudmur
Taegu *see* Daegu
Taejŏn *see* Daejeon
Tafassâsset, Ténéré du *desert* Niger 57 G2
Taguatinga Brazil 43 F3
Tagus *river* Portugal/Spain *Port.* Tejo, *Sp.* Tajo 74 C3
Tahiti *island* French Polynesia 127 H5
Tahoe, Lake *lake* W USA 27 B5
Tahoua Niger 57 F3
Taibei *capital of* Taiwan *var.* Taipei111 D6
T'aichung *see* Taizhong
Taieri *129* New Zealand 133 B7
Taihape New Zealand 132 D4
T'ainan *see* Tainan
Tainan Taiwan *prev.* T'ainan111 D6
Taipei *see* Taibei
Taiping Malaysia 120 B3
Taiwan *country* E Asia *prev.* Formosa 111
Taiwan Strait *sea feature* East China Sea/South China Sea *var.* Formosa Strait 111 D7
Taiyuan China 110 C4
Taizhong Taiwan *prev.* T'aichung 111D6
Ta'izz Yemen 103 B7
Tajikistan *country* C Asia 105
Tajo *see* Tagus
Takapuna New Zealand 132 D2
Takla Makan *see* Taklimakan Shamo
Taklimakan Shamo *desert region* China *var.* Takla Makan 108 B3
Talamanca, Cordillera de *mountains* Costa Rica 35 E4
Talas Kyrgyzstan 105 F2
Talaud, Kepulauan *island group* Indonesia 121 F3
Talca Chile 46 B4
Talcahuano Chile 46 B4
Taldykoigan Kazakhstan 96 C5
Tallahassee Florida, USA 30 D3
Tallinn *capital of* Estonia *prev.* Revel, *Ger.* Reval, *Rus.* Tallin 88 D2
Talsen *see* Talsi
Talsi Latvia *Ger.* Talsen 88 B3
Tamale Ghana 57 E4
Tamanrasset Algeria 53 E4
Tambo Australia 130 C4
Tambov Russian Federation 93 B5
Tamil Nādu *state* India 114 D2
Tampa Florida, USA 31 E4
Tampere Finland 67 D5

Tampico Mexico 33 F3
Tamworth Australia 131 D6
Tanami Desert *desert* Australia 128 E3
Tananarive *see* Antananarivo
Tanega-shima *island* Japan 113 B7
Tanga Tanzania 55 C7
Tanganyika, Lake *lake* E Africa 51 D5
Tanger Morocco *var.* Tangiers 52 C1
Tanggula Shan *mountain range* China 108 C4
Tangiers *see* Tanger
Tangra Yumco *lake* China 108 B5
Tangshan China 110 D4
Tanimbar Islands *see* Tanimbar, Kepulauan
Tanimbar, Kepulauan *island group* Indonesia *Eng.* Tanimbar Islands 121 F5
Tanjungkarang *see* Bandar Lampung
Tan-Tan Morocco 52 B3
Tanzania *country* E Africa 55
Taoudenni Mali 57 E2
Tapa Estonia *Ger.* Taps 88 D2
Tapachula Mexico 33 G5
Tapajós *river* Brazil 43 E2
Taps *see* Tapa
Ţarābulus *see* Tripoli, Lebanon
Ţarābulus al-Gharb *see* Tripoli, Libya
Taranto Italy 79 E5
Taranto, Golfo di *sea feature* Mediterranean Sea 79 E5
Tarapoto Peru 42 B2
Tarawa *island* Kiribati 127 E2
Taraz Kazakhstan *prev.* Dzhambul, Zhambyl 96 C5
Tarbes France 73 B6
Tarcoola Australia 131 A5
Târgovişte Romania *prev.* Tîrgovişte 90 C4
Târgu Mureş Romania *prev.* Tîrgu Mureş 90 C4
Tarija Bolivia 42 C5
Tarim Basin *basin* China 108 B3
Tarim He *river* China 108 B3
Tarn *river* France 73 C6
Tarnów Poland 81 D5
Tarragona Spain 75 G2
Tarsus Turkey 98 D4
Tartu Estonia *prev.* Yur'yev, *var.* Yurev, *Ger.* Dorpat 88 D3
Ţarţus Syria 100 B3
Tashauz *see* Daşoguz
Tashkent *capital of* Uzbekistan *var.* Taškent, *Uzb.* Toshkent 105 E2
Taškent *see* Tashkent
Tasman Bay *inlet* New Zealand 132 C4
Tasmania *state* Australia 131 C8
Tasman Basin *undersea feature* Tasman Sea 124 D5
Tasman Plateau *undersea feature* Pacific Ocean 124 C5
Tasman Sea Pacific Ocean 134 C4
Tassili-n-Ajjer *desert plateau* Algeria 53 E4
Tatabánya Hungary 81 C6
Tatar Pazardzhik *see* Pazardzhik
Taubaté Brazil 43 F5 45 E2
Taumarunui New Zealand 132 D3
Taunggyi Myanmar 118 B3
Taunton England, UK 71 D7
Taupo New Zealand 132 D3
Taupo, Lake *lake* New Zealand 132 D3
Tauragė Lithuania 88 B4
Tauranga New Zealand 132 D3
Taurus Mountains *mountain range* Turkey *see* Toros Dağları 94 D4
Tavoy *see* Dawei
Tawau Malaysia 120 D3
Taymyr, Ozero *lake* Russian Federation 97 E2
Taymyr, Poluostrov *peninsula* Russian Federation *Eng.* Taymyr Peninsula 97 E2
Taymyr Peninsula *see* Taymyr, Poluostrov
Tbilisi *capital of* Georgia *prev.* Tiflis 99 F2
Te Anau New Zealand 133 A7
Te Anau, Lake *lake* New Zealand 133 A7
Tedzhen *see* Tejen
Tegal Indonesia 120 C5
Tegucigalpa *capital of* Honduras 34 C2
Teheran *see* Tehrān
Tehrān *capital of* Iran *prev.* Teheran 102 C3
Tehuacán Mexico 33 F4
Tehuantepec, Golfo de *sea feature* Mexico 33 G5
Tejen Turkmenistan *prev.* Tedzhen 104 C3
Tejo *see* Tagus
Te Kao New Zealand131 C1
Tekirdağ Turkey *It.* Rodosto 98 A2
Te Kuiti Waikato, New Zealand 132 D3
Tel Aviv-Yafo Israel 101 A5
Teles Pires *river* Brazil 43 E3
Tell Atlas *plateau* Africa 84 C3
Telschen *see* Telšiai
Telšiai Lithuania *Ger.* Telschen 88 B4
Temuco Chile 47 B5
Ténéré *physical region* Niger 57 G2
Tenerife *island* Spain 52 A3
Tennant Creek Australia 130 A3
Tennessee *state* USA 30 D1
Tennessee *river* SE USA 31 C1
Tepelenë Albania 83 D6
Tepic Mexico 32 D4
Teplice Czech Republic *Ger.* Teplitz, *prev.* Teplice-Šanov, *Ger.* Teplitz-Schönau 80 A4
Teplice-Šanov *see* Teplice
Teplitz *see* Teplice
Teplitz-Schönau *see* Teplice
Teraina *island* Kiribati 127 G2
Teresina Brazil 43 G2
Termez Uzbekistan 105 E3
Terneuzen Netherlands 69 B5
Terni Italy 78 C4

Ternopil' Ukraine *Rus.* Ternopol' 90 C2
Ternopol' *see* Ternopil'
Terrassa Spain 75 G2
Terre Haute Indiana, USA 22 B4
Terres Australes et Antarctiques Françaises *see* French Southern and Antarctic Lands
Terschelling *island* Netherlands 68 C1
Teruel Spain 75 F3
Teseney Eritrea 54 C4
Tessalit Mali 57 E2
Tete Mozambique 61 E3
Tétouan Morocco 52 C1
Tetovo Macedonia 83 D5
Tetschen *see* Děčín
Tevere *river* Italy 78 C4
Texas *state* USA 28-29 F3
Texarkana Arkansas, USA 30 A2
Texas City Texas, USA 29 G4
Texel *island* Netherlands 68 C2
Thailand *country* SE Asia 118-119
Thailand, Gulf of *sea feature* South China Sea 119 C6
Thames *river* England, UK 71 D6
Thar Desert *desert* India/Pakistan 116 C3
Tharthār, Buḩayrat ath *lake* Iraq 102 B3
Thásos *island* Greece 86 C3
Thaton Myanmar 118 B4
Theiss *see* Tisza
Thermaic Gulf *see* Thermaïkós Kólpos
Thermaïkós Kólpos *sea feature* Greece *Eng.* Thermaic Gulf 86 B4
Thessaloníki Greece *var.* Salonica 86 B3
The Valley *dependent territory capital* Anguilla 37 G5
Thimphu *capital of* Bhutan 117 G3
Thionville France 72 E3
Thiruvananthapuram India *see* Trivandrum 114 D3
Thompson Canada 19 F4
Thorn *see* Toruń
Thorshavn *see* Tórshavn
Thracian Sea Greece *Gk.* Thrakikó Pélagos 86 D3
Thrakikó Pélagos *see* Thracian Sea
Three Kings Islands *island group* New Zealand 132 C1
Thule *see* Qaanaaq
Thunder Bay Canada 20 B4
Thuner See *lake* Switzerland 77 B7
Thurso Scotland, UK 70 C2
Tianjin China *var.* Tientsin 110 D4
Tiberias, Lake *lake* Israel *var.* Sea of Galilee, *Heb.* Yam Kinneret, *Ar.* Bahrat Tabariya 101 B5
Tibesti *mountains* Chad/Libya 50 C3
Tibet *autonomous region* China *Chin.* Xizang 108 C5
Tibet, Plateau of *see* Qingzang Gaoyuan
Tienen Belgium 69 C6
Tien Shan *mountain range* C Asia 105 G2
Tientsin see Tianjin
Tierra del Fuego *island* Argentina/Chile 47 C8
Tiflis *see* Tbilisi
Tighina Moldova *prev.* Bendery 90 D4
Tigris *river* SW Asia 94 B4
Tijuana Mexico 32 A1
Tiki Basin *undersea feature* Pacific Ocean 135 E3
Tiksi Russian Federation 97 F2
Tilburg Netherlands 68 C4
Timaru New Zealand 133 B6
Timişoara Romania 90 A4
Timmins Canada 20 C4
Timor *island* Indonesia 121 F5
Timor Sea Indian Ocean 121 F5
Tindouf Algeria 52 B3
Tínos *island* Greece 87 D5
Tirana *capital of* Albania 83 D6
Tiraspol Moldova 90 D4
Tîrgovişte *see* Târgovişte
Tîrgu Mureş *see* Târgu Mureş
Tirol *region* Austria *var.* Tyrol 77 C7
Tiruchchirāppalli India 114 D3
Tisa *see* Tisza
Tisza *river* E Europe *Ger.* Theiss, *Cz./Rom./SCr.* Tisa 81 D6
Titicaca, Lake *lake* Bolivia/Peru 42 C4
Tlemcen Algeria 52 D2
Toamasina Madagascar 61 G3
Toba, Danau *lake* Indonesia 120 B3
Tobago *island* Trinidad and Tobago 37 G5
Toba Kākar Range *mountains* Pakistan 116 B2
Tobruk *see* Ţubruq
Tocantins *river* Brazil 43 F3
Tocopilla Chile 46 B2
Togo *country* W Africa 57 E4
Tokat Turkey 98 D3
Tokelau *dependent territory* New Zealand, Pacific Ocean 127 F3
Tokmak Kyrgyzstan 105 F2
Tokuno-shima *island* Japan 113 A8
Tokushima Japan 113 B5
Tokyo *capital of* Japan 113 D5
Toledo Spain 75 E3
Toledo Ohio, USA 22 C3
Toledo Bend Reservoir *Reservoir* S USA 29 H3
Toliara Madagascar 61 E3
Tol'yatti *prev.* Stavropol' Russian Federation 93 C5
Tomakomai Japan 112 D2
Tombouctou Mali 57 E3
Tombua Angola 60 B2
Tomini, Gul of *sea feature* Indonesia 121 E4
Tomsk Russian Federation 96 D4
Tonga *country* Pacific Ocean 127 E5
Tongatapu *island* Tonga 125 E3
Tongking, Gulf of *see* Tonkin, Gulf of

Tongliao China 109 G2
Tongtian He *river* China 108 C4
Tonkin, Gulf of *sea feature* South China Sea *var.* Gulf of Tongking 111 B7
Tônle Kông *river* Cambodia/ Vietnam 118 E5
Tônlé Sap *lake* Cambodia 119 D5
Tonopah Nevada, USA 27 C6
Toowoomba Australia 131 D5
Topeka Kansas, USA 25 F4
Top Springs Australia 130 A3
Torino Italy *Eng.* Turin 78 A2
Tornio Finland 66 D4
Tornionjoki *river* Finland/ Sweden 66 D3
Toronto Canada 20 D5
Toros Dağları *mountain range* Turkey *Eng.* Taurus Mountains 98 C4
Torre del Greco Italy 79 D5
Torrens, Lake *lake* Australia 131 B5
Torreón Mexico 32 D2
Torres Strait *sea feature* Arafura Sea/Coral Sea 126 B4
Torrington Wyoming, USA 24 D3
Tórshavn *capital of* Faroe Islands *Dan.* Thorshavn 65 F5
To'rtko'l Uzbekistan *prev.* Petroaleksandrovsk, *prev.* Turtkul', *Uzb.* Türtkŭl 104 C2
Tortoise Islands *see* Galapagos Islands
Tortosa Spain 75 F2
Toruń Poland *Ger.* Thorn 80 C3
Toscana *region* Italy *Eng.* Tuscany 78 B3
Toscano, Archipelago *island group* Italy 78 B4
Toshkent *see* Tashkent
Tottori Japan 113 B5
Touggourt Algeria 53 E2
Toulon France 73 D6
Toulouse France 73 B6
Toungoo Myanmar 118 B4
Tournai Belgium 69 B6
Tours France 72 C4
Townsville Australia 130 D3
Toyama Japan 112 C4
Tozeur Tunisia 53 E2
Trâblous *see* Tripoli, Lebanon
Trabzon Turkey *Eng.* Trebizond 99 E2
Tralee Ireland 71 A6
Trang Thailand 119 C7
Transantarctic Mountains *mountain range* Antarctica 136 B3
Transnistria *region* Moldova 90 D3
Transylvania *region* Romania 90 B3
Transylvanian Alps *see* Carpaţii Meridionali
Trapani Italy 79 C6
Traralgon Australia 131 C7
Trasimeno, Lago *Lake* Italy 78 C4
Traverse City Michigan, USA 22 C2
Travis, Lake *lake* Texas, USA 29 F4
Trebinje Bosnia & Herzegovina 83 C5
Trebizond *see* Trabzon
Trelew Argentina 47 C6
Trenčín Slovakia *Ger.* Trentschin *Hung.* Trencsén 81 C6
Trencsén *see* Trenčín
Trento Italy *Ger.* Trient 78 C2
Trenton New Jersey, USA 23 F4
Trentschin *see* Trenčín
Tres Arroyos Argentina 47 D5
Treviso Italy 78 C2
Trient *see* Trento
Trieste Italy 78 D2
Tríkala Greece 86 B4
Trincomalee Sri Lanka 115 E3
Trindade *external territory* Brazil, Atlantic Ocean 49 C6
Trinidad Bolivia 42 C4
Trinidad Uruguay 44 B5
Trinidad *island* Trinidad & Tobago 38 C2
Trinidad & Tobago *country* West Indies 37 G5
Trípoli Greece 87 B5
Tripoli Lebanon *var.* Trâblous, Ţarābulus 100 B4
Tripoli *capital of* Libya *Ar.* Ţarābulus al-Gharb 53 F2
Tristan da Cunha *overseas territory* UK, Atlantic Ocean 49 D6
Trivandrum India *see* Thiruvananthapuram 114 D3
Trnava Slovakia *Ger.* Tyrnau, *Hung.* Nagyszombat 81 C6
Trois-Rivières Canada 21 E4
Trollhättan Sweden 67 B6
Tromsø Norway 66 C2
Trondheim Norway 66 B4
Trondheimsfjorden *inlet* Norway 66 B4
Troyes France 72 D4
Trujillo Honduras 34 D2
Trujillo Peru 42 A3
Tsarigrad *see* İstanbul
Tschenstochau *see* Częstochowa
Tselinograd *see* Astana
Tsetserleg Mongolia 108 D2
Tshikapa Dem. Rep. Congo 59 C7
Tsinghai *see* Qinghai
Tsumeb Namibia 60 C3
Tsushima *island* Japan 113 A5
Tuamotu Fracture Zone *tectonic feature* Pacific Ocean 125 H3
Tuamotu Islands *island group* French Polynesia 125 G3
Tubmanburg Liberia 56 C4
Ţubruq Libya *Eng.* Tobruk 53 H2
Tucson Arizona, USA 28 B3
Tucupita Venezuela 41 F1
Tucuruí, Represa de *Reservoir* Brazil 43 F2
Tudmur Syria *var.* Tadmur, *Eng.* Palmyra 100 C3
Tuguegarao Philippines 121 E1

Tuktoyaktuk Canada 137 E2
Tula Russian Federation 93 B5 96 A3
Tulancingo Mexico 33 E4
Tulcán Ecuador 40 B4
Tulcea Romania 90 D4
Tūlkarm West Bank 101 D7
Tully Australia 130 D3
Tulsa Oklahoma, USA 29 G1
Tundzha *river* Bulgaria 86 D2
Tungaru *island group* Kiribati *prev.* Gilbert Islands 127 E2
Tunis *capital of* Tunisia 53 F1
Tunisia *country* N Africa 53 F2
Tunja Colombia 40 C2
Tupiza Bolivia 42 C5
Turan Lowland *lowland* Turkmenistan/Uzbekistan *var.* Turan Plain, *Rus.* Turanskaya Nizmennost' 104 C2
Turan Plain *see* Turan Lowland
Turanskaya Nizmennost' *see* Turan Lowland
Turčianský Svätý Martin *see* Martin
Turin *see* Torino
Turkana, Lake *lake* Ethiopia/ Kenya *var.* Lake Rudolf 50 D4 55 C5
Turkey *country* SW Asia 98-99
Türkmenabat Turkmenistan *prev.* Chardzhev, *prev.* Chardzhou, *prev.* Leninsk, *Turkm.* Chärjew 104 D3
Türkmenbaşy Turkmenistan *prev.* Krasnovodsk 104 A2
Turkmenistan *country* C Asia 104
Turks & Caicos Islands *overseas territory* UK, West Indies 37
Turku Finland 67 D5
Turnagain, Cape *headland* New Zealand 132 E4
Turnhout Belgium 69 C5
Turnu Severin *see* Drobeta-Turnu Severin
Turócszentmárton *see* Martin
Turpan China 108 C3
Turtkul' *see* To'rtko'l
Tŭrtkŭl *see* To'rtko'l
Tuscany *see* Toscana
Tuvalu *country* Pacific Ocean 127 E3
Tuxtla Mexico 33 G5
Tuz Gölü *lake* Turkey 98 C3
Tuzla Bosnia & Herz. 82 C3
Tver' Russian Federation 92 B4
Twin Falls Idaho, USA 26 D4
Tyler Texas, USA 29 G3
Tyre *see* Soûr
Tyrnau *see* Trnava
Tyrol *see* Tirol
Tyrrhenian Sea Mediterranean Sea 78 C6
Tyup Kyrgyzstan 105 G2
Tziá *island* Greece *prev.* Kéa 87 C5

U

Ubangi *river* C Africa 59 C5
Uberaba Brazil 43 F5, 45 E1
Uberlândia Brazil 43 F5, 45 E1
Ubon Ratchathani Thailand 119 D5
Ucayali *river* Peru 42 B3
Uchkuduk Uzbekistan *Uzb.* Uchquduq 104 D2
Uchquduq *see* Uchkuduk
Udine Italy 78 C2
Udon Thani Thailand 118 C4
Uele *river* Dem. Rep. Congo 58 D5
Ufa Russian Federation 96 B3
Uganda *country* E Africa 55
Uíge Angola 60 B1
Ujungpandang *see* Makassar
Ukhta Russian Federation 92 D4
Ukiah California, USA 27 A5
Ukmergė Lithuania 88 C4
Ukraine *country* E Europe 90-91
Ulaanbaatar *see* Ulan Bator
Ulaangom Mongolia 108 C2
Ulan Bator *capital of* Mongolia *var.* Ulaanbaatar 109 E2
Ulanhad *see* Chifeng
Ulan Qab China *var.* Jining 109 F3
Ulan-Ude Russian Federation 97 E4
Ullapool Scotland, UK 70 C3
Ulm Germany 77 C6
Ulster *region* Ireland/UK 71 B5
Ulungur Hu *lake* China 108 C2
Uluru *peak* Australia *var.* Ayers Rock 129 E5
Ul'yanovsk Russian Federation 93 C5
Umeå Sweden 66 D4
Umnak Island *island* Alaska, USA 18 B3
Una *river* Bosnia & Herzegovina/Croatia 82 B3
Unalaska Island *island* Alaska, USA 18 B3
Ungava, Péninsule d' *peninsula* Canada 20 D1
Ungava Bay *sea feature* Canada 21 E1
United Arab Emirates *country* SW Asia 103 D5
United Kingdom *country* NW Europe 70-71
United States of America *country* North America 16-17
Uppsala Sweden 67 C6
Ural *river* Kazakhstan/Russian Federation *Kaz.* Zhayyk 96 B4
Ural Mountains *mountain range* Russian Federation *var.* Ural'skiy Khrebet, Ural'skiye Gory 92-93
Ural'sk Kazakhstan 96 B3
Ural'skiy Khrebet *see* Ural Mountains
Ural'skiye Gory *see* Ural Mountains
Urfa *see* Şanlıurfa

Urganch *see* Urgench
Urgench Uzbekistan *prev.* Novo Urgench, *Uzb.* Urganch 104 C2
Uroševac *see* Ferizaj/Uroševac
Ŭroteppa Tajikistan 105 E2
Uruapan Mexico 33 E4
Uruguaiana Brazil 44 B4
Uruguay *country* SE South America 44
Uruguay *river* S South America 46 D3
Urumchi *see* Ürümqi
Ürümqi China *prev.* Urumchi 108 C3
Usa *river* Russian Federation 92 D3
Uşak Turkey *prev.* Ushak 98 B3
Ushak *see* Uşak
Ushuaia Argentina 47 C8
Ust'-Chaun Russian Federation 97 G1
Ustica, Isola de *island* Italy 79 C6
Ústí nad Labem Czech Republic *Ger.* Aussig 80 A4
Ust'-Kamchatsk Russian Federation 97 H2
Ust'-Kamenogorsk Kazakhstan 96 D5
Ustyurt Plateau *upland* Kazakhstan/Uzbekistan 104 B1
Usumacinta *river* Guatemala/ Mexico 34 B1
Usumbura *see* Bujumbura
Utah *state* USA 24 B4
Utena Lithuania 88 C4
Utica New York, USA 23 F2
Utrecht Netherlands 68 C3
Uttar Pradesh *state* India 117 E3
Uummannarsuaq *see* Nunap Isua
Uvs Nuur *lake* Mongolia 108 C2
Uyo Nigeria 57 G5
Uyuni Bolivia 43 C5
Uzbekistan *country* C Asia 104-105
Uzhgorod *see* Uzhhorod
Uzhhorod Ukraine *Rus.* Uzhgorod 90 B2

Vaal *river* South Africa 60 D4
Vaasa Finland 67 D5
Vadodara India 116 C4
Vaduz *capital of* Liechtenstein 77 B7
Vág *see* Váh
Váh *river* Slovakia *Ger.* Waag, *Hung.* Vág 81 C6
Valdés, Península *peninsula* Argentina 47 C5
Valdez Alaska, USA 18 D3
Valdivia Chile 47 B5
Valdosta Georgia, USA 31 E3
Valence France 73 D5
Valencia Spain 75 F3
Valencia Venezuela 40 D1
Valencia *region* Spain 75 F3
Valera Venezuela 40 C1
Valga Estonia *Ger.* Walk 88 D3
Valladolid Spain 74 D2
Valledupar Colombia 40 C1
Vallenar Chile 46 B3
Valletta *capital of* Malta 79 C8
Valley, The *capital of* Anguilla 37 G3
Valmiera Latvia *Ger.* Wolmar 88 C3
Valparaíso Chile 46 B4
Van Turkey 99 F3
Van, Lake *see* Van Gölü
Vanadzor Armenia *prev.* Kirovakan 99 F2
Vancouver Canada 19 E5
Vancouver Washington, USA 26 B2
Vancouver Island *island* Canada 18 D5
Vänern *lake* Sweden 67 B6
Vangaindrano Madagascar 61 G4
Van Gölü *lake* Turkey *Eng.* Lake Van 99 F3
Vantaa Finland 67 D5
Vanua Levu *island* Fiji 127 E4
Vanuatu *country* Pacific Ocean 126 D4
Vārānasi India 117 E3
Varaždin Croatia 82 B2
Vardar *river* Greece/Macedonia *prev.* Axios 83 E6
Vardø Norway 66 E2
Varkaus Finland 67 E5
Varna Bulgaria 86 E2
Västerås Sweden 67 C6
Vatican City *country* S Europe 78 C4
Vättern *lake* Sweden 67 B6
Vava'u Group *island group* Tonga 127 F4
Vawkavysk Belarus *Rus.* Volkovysk, *Pol.* Wołkowysk 89 B5
Växjö Sweden 67 C7
Vaygach, Ostrov *island* Russian Federation 92 E3
Veles Macedonia 83 E5
Velikaya *river* Russian Federation 95 G2
Velikiye Luki Russian Federation 92 A4
Velikiy Novgorod Russian Federation 92 B4 96 B2
Velingrad Bulgaria 86 C2
Vellore India 114 D2
Venezia Italy *Eng.* Venice 78 C2
Venezuela *country* N South America 40-41
Venezuela, Gulf of *sea feature* Caribbean Sea 40 C1
Venice *see* Venezia
Venice, Gulf of *sea feature* Adriatic Sea 78 C2
Venlo Netherlands 69 D5
Venta *river* Latvia/Lithuania 88 B3
Ventspils Latvia *Ger.* Windau 88 B3
Vera Argentina 46 D3
Veracruz Mexico 33 F4
Verkhoyanskiy Khrebet *mountain range* Russian Federation *Eng.* Verkhoyansk Range 97 F3

Verkhoyansk Range *see* Verkhoyanskiy Khrebet
Vermont *state* USA 23 F2
Vernon Texas, USA 29 F2
Véroia Greece 86 B3
Verona Italy 78 C2
Versailles France 72 C3
Verviers Belgium 69 D6
Vesoul France 72 D4
Veszprém Hungary *Ger.* Veszprim 81 C7
Veszprim *see* Veszprém
Viana do Castelo Portugal 74 C2
Viareggio Italy 78 B3
Vicenza Italy 78 C2
Vichy France 73 C5
Victoria *state* Australia 131 C7
Victoria Canada 18 D5
Victoria *capital of* Seychelles 61 H1
Victoria Texas, USA 29 G4
Victoria *river* Australia 128 D3
Victoria, Lake *lake* E Africa *var.* Victoria Nyanza 55 B6
Victoria Falls *waterfall* Zambia/Zimbabwe 51 C6
Victoria Island *island* Canada 19 F2
Victoria Land *region* Antarctica 137 C4
Victoria Nyanza *see* Victoria, Lake
Vidin Bulgaria 86 B1
Viedma Argentina 47 C5
Vienna *capital of* Austria *Ger.* Wien 77 E6
Vientiane *capital of* Laos 118 C4
Vietnam *country* SE Asia 118-119
Vigo Spain 74 C2
Vijayawāda India 115 E1
Vila Nova de Gaia Portugal 74 C2
Vila Real Portugal 74 C2
Viliya *see* Neris
Viljandi Estonia *Ger.* Fellin 88 D2
Villach Austria 77 D7
Villahermosa Mexico 33 G4
Villa Mercedes Argentina 46 C4
Villarrica *peak* Chile 39 B6
Villavicencio Colombia 40 C3
Villeurbanne France 73 D5
Vilna *see* Vilnius
Vilnius *capital of* Lithuania *Pol.* Wilno, *Ger.* Wilna, *Rus.* Vilna 89 C5
Viña del Mar Chile 46 B4
Vinh Vietnam 118 D4
Vinnitsa *see* Vinnytsya
Vinnytsya Ukraine *Rus.* Vinnitsa 90 D2
Virgin Islands *unincorporated territory* USA, West Indies 37 F3
Virginia Minnesota, USA 25 F2
Virginia *state* USA 22-23
Virovitica Croatia 82 C3
Virtsu Estonia *Ger.* Werder 88 C2
Visākhapatnam India 117 E5
Visalia California, USA 27 C7
Visby Sweden 67 C7
Viscount Melville Sound *sea feature* Arctic Ocean 19 F2
Viseu Portugal 74 C3
Vistula *see* Wisła
Vitebsk *see* Vitsyebsk/Vitebsk
Viterbo Italy 78 C4
Viti Levu *island* Fiji 127 E4
Vitim *river* Russian Federation 95 E3
Vitória Brazil 43 G5 45 G1
Vitória da Conquista Brazil 43 G4
Vitoria-Gasteiz Spain 75 E1
Vitsyebsk/Vitebsk Belarus *Rus.* Vitebsk 88 E5
Vjosës, Lumi i *river* Albania 83 D6
Vladikavkaz Russian Federation *prev.* Ordzhonikidze, Dzaudzhikau 93 B7
Vladimir Russian Federation 93 B5
Vladimirovka *see* Yuzhno-Sakhalinsk
Vladivostok Russian Federation 97 G5
Vlieland *island* Netherlands 68 C1
Vlissingen Netherlands *Eng.* Flushing 69 B5
Vlorë Albania 83 D6
Vojvodina *region* Serbia 82 D3
Volga *river* Russian Federation 96 A3
Volgograd Russian Federation *prev.* Stalingrad 93 B6, 96 A3
Volkovysk *see* Vawkavysk
Vologda Russian Federation 96 B2
Vólos Greece 86 B4
Volta *river* Ghana 57 E4
Volta, Lake *lake* Ghana 57 E4
Volta Redonda Brazil 45 E2
Vóreies Sporádes *island group* Greece *Eng.* Northern Sporades 86 C4
Vorkuta Russian Federation 92 E3 96 C2
Vormsi *island* Estonia *Ger.* Worms, *Swed.* Ormsö 88 C2
Voronezh Russian Federation 93 B5
Võru Estonia *Ger.* Werro 88 D3
Vosges *mountain range* France 72 E4
Vostochno-Sibirskoye More Arctic Ocean *Eng.* East Siberian Sea 137 G2
Vostok Island *island* Kiribati 127 H4
Vrangel'ya, Ostrov *island* Russian Federation *Eng.* Wrangel Island 97 G1
Vratsa Bulgaria 86 C2
Vršac Serbia 82 D3
Vukovar Croatia 82 C3
Vulcano, Isola *island* Italy 79 D6
Vyatka *river* Russian Federation 93 C5

W

Wa Ghana 57 E4
Waag *see* Váh
Waal *river* Netherlands 68 D4
Wabash *river* C USA 22 B4

Waco Texas, USA 29 G3
Waddeneilanden *island group* Netherlands *Eng.* West Frisian Islands 68 C1
Waddenzee *sea feature* Netherlands 68 D1
Wadi Halfa Sudan 54 B3
Wādī Mūsā Jordan *var.* Petra 101 B6
Wad Medani Sudan 54 B4
Wagga Wagga Australia 131 C6
Wagin Australia 129 B6
Wahai Indonesia 121 F4
Wahībah, Ramlat Āl *Desert* Oman 103 E5
Waiau *river* New Zealand 133 A7
Waipawa New Zealand 132 E4
Wairau *river* New Zealand 133 C5
Wairoa New Zealand 132 E3
Waitaki *river* New Zealand 133 B6
Waiuku New Zealand 132 D3
Wakatipu, Lake *lake* New Zealand 133 D7
Wakayama Japan 113 C5
Wake Island *atoll* Pacific Ocean 124 D1
Wake Island *US unincorporated territory* Pacific Ocean 134 C2
Wakkanai Japan 112 D1
Wałbrzych Poland *Ger.* Waldenburg 80 B4
Waldenburg *see* Wałbrzych
Wales *national region* UK *Wel.* Cymru 71
Walgett Australia 131 D5
Walk *see* Valga
Walla Walla Washington, USA 26 C2
Wallis & Futuna *overseas collectivity* France, Pacific Ocean 127 E4
Walnut Ridge Arkansas, USA 30 B1
Walvis Bay Namibia 60 B4
Walvis Ridge *undersea feature* Atlantic Ocean 49 D6
Wan *see* Anhui
Wanaka New Zealand 133 B6
Wanaka, Lake *lake* New Zealand 133 B6
Wandel Sea Arctic Ocean 137 G4
Wanganui New Zealand 132 D4
Wanlaweyn Somalia 55 D6
Warangal India 117 E5
Warkworth New Zealand D2
Warrnambool Australia 131 C7
Warsaw *capital of* Poland *Pol.* Warszawa, *Ger.* Warschau 80 D3
Warschau *see* Warsaw
Warszawa *see* Warsaw
Warta *river* Poland *Ger.* Warthe 80 C4
Warthe *see* Warta
Wash, The *inlet* England, UK 71 E5
Washington *state* USA 26
Washington, D.C. *capital of* USA 23 E4
Waterford Ireland 71 B6
Watertown New York, USA 23 E2
Watertown South Dakota, USA 25 E2
Wau South Sudan 55 B5
Waukegan Illinois, USA 22 B3
Wawa Canada 20 C4
Weddell Plain *undersea feature* Atlantic Ocean 136 B2
Weddell Sea Antarctica 136 A2
Weichsel *see* Wisła
Weissenstein *see* Paide
Wellesley Islands *island group* Australia 130 B3
Wellington *capital of* New Zealand 133 D5
Wellington, Isla *island* Chile 47 B7
Wells, Lake *lake* Australia 129 C5
Wels Austria 77 D6
Wenden *see* Cēsis
Wenzhou China 111 D6
Werder *see* Virtsu
Werro *see* Võru
Wesenberg *see* Rakvere
Weser *river* Germany 76 B3
Wessel Islands *island group* Australia 130 B2
West Antarctica *region* Antarctica 134 B3
West Bank *disputed territory* SW Asia 101 A5
West Bengal *state* India 117 F4
Western Australia *state* Australia 128-129
Western Dvina *river* E Europe *Bel.* Dzvina, *Ger.* Düna, *Latv.* Daugava, *Rus.* Zapadnaya Dvina 88 C4
Western Ghats *mountain range* India 106 B3, 114 C1
Western Isles *see* Outer Hebrides
Western Sahara *region occupied by Morocco* N Africa 52 A3
Western Sierra Madre *see* Sierra Madre Occidental
Westerschelde *inlet* Netherlands 69 B5
West Falkland *island* Falkland Islands 47 D7
West Frisian Islands *see* Waddeneilanden
West Indies *island group* North America 48 A4
West Palm Beach Florida, USA 31 F4
Westport New Zealand 133 C5
West Siberian Plain *see* Zapadno-Sibirskaya Ravnina
West Virginia *state* USA 22-23
Wetar Strait *sea feature* Indonesia 121 F5
Wexford Ireland 71 B6
Whakatane New Zealand 132 E3
Whangarei New Zealand 132 D2
Wharton Basin *undersea feature* Indian Ocean 123 D5
Wheeling Ohio, USA 22 D4
Whitehorse Canada 18 D4
White Nile *river* Sudan / South Sudan 55 B5
White Sea *see* Beloye More

White Volta *river* Burkina Faso /Ghana 57 E4
Whitianga New Zealand 132 E3
Whitney, Mount *peak* W USA 27 C6
Whitsunday Group *island group* Australia 130 D3
Whyalla Australia 131 B6
Wichita Kansas, USA 25 E5
Wichita Falls Texas, USA 29 F2
Wicklow Mountains *mountains* Ireland 71 B5
Wien *see* Vienna
Wiener Neustadt Austria 77 E6
Wiesbaden Germany 77 B5
Wight, Isle of *island* England, UK 71 D7
Wilcannia Australia 131 C6
Wilhelm, Mount *peak* Papua New Guinea 126 B3
Wilja *see* Neris
Wilkes Land *region* Antarctica 137 C4
Willemstad Curaçao 37 E5
Williamsport Pennsylvania, USA 23 E3
Williston North Dakota, USA 24 D1
Wilmington Delaware, USA 23 F4
Wilmington North Carolina, USA 31 G2
Wilna *see* Vilnius
Wilno *see* Vilnius
Windau *see* Ventspils
Windhoek *capital of* Namibia 60 C3
Windorah Australia 130 C4
Windsor Canada 20 C5
Windward Islands *see* Barlavento, Ilhas de
Winisk *river* Canada 20 B3
Winnemucca Nevada, USA 27 C5
Winnipeg Canada 19 G5
Winnipeg, Lake *lake* Canada 19 G5
Winston-Salem North Carolina, USA 31 F1
Winton Australia 130 C4
Wisconsin *state* USA 22 B2
Wismar Germany 76 C3
Wisła *river* Poland *Ger.* Weichsel, *Eng.* Vistula 63 E3 80 D4
W.J. van Blommesteinmeer *Reservoir* Suriname 41 H3
Włocławek Poland 80 C3
Wodzisław Śląski Poland *Ger.* Loslau 81 C5
Wolfsburg Germany 76 C3
Wollongong Australia 131 D6
Wolmar *see* Valmiera
Woods, Lake of the *lake* Canada/USA 20 A3
Woodville New Zealand 132 D4
Worcester England, UK 71 D6
Worcester Massachusetts, USA 23 G3
Worms *see* Vormsi
Wołkowysk *see* Vawkavysk
Wrangel Island *see* Vrangel'ya, Ostrov
Wrocław Poland *Ger.* Breslau 80 C4
Wuday 'ah Saudi Arabia 103 C6
Wuhai China *var.* Haibowan 109 E3
Wuhan China 111 C5
Wuliang Shan *mountain range* China 111 A6
Wuppertal Germany 76 A4
Würzburg Germany 77 C5
Wuxi China 111 D5
Wyndham Australia 128 D3
Wyoming *state* USA 24 C3

X

Xaignabouli Laos *prev.* Muang Xainabouri 118 C3
Xalapa Mexico *var.* Jalapa 118 C3
Xai-Xai Mozambique 61 E4
Xalapa Mexico 33 F4
Xam Nua Laos 118 D3
Xankändi Azerbaijan *Rus.* Khankendy, *prev.* Stepanakert 99 G2
Xánthi Greece 86 C3
Xiamen China 111 D6
Xi'an China 111 B5
Xiang *see* Hunan
Xiao Hinggan Ling *mountain range* China 110 D2
Xilinhot China 109 F2
Xingu *river* Brazil 43 E2
Xingxingxia China 108 D3
Xining China 109 E4
Xinjiang Uygur Zizhiqu *autonomous region* China *var.* Sinkiang 108 B3
Xinxiang China 110 C4
Xixón *see* Gijon
Xizang Zizhiqu *see* Tibet
Xuzhou China 111 D5

Y

Yafran Libya 53 F2
Yakima Washington, USA 26 B2
Yaku-shima *island* Japan 113 B7
Yakutsk Russian Federation 97 F3
Yala Thailand 119 C7
Yalong Jiang *river* China 111 A5
Yalta Ukraine 91 F5
Yamaguchi Japan 113 B5
Yambio South Sudan 55 B5
Yambol Bulgaria 86 D2
Yamdena, Pulau *island* Indonesia 121 G5
Yamoussoukro *capital of* Côte d'Ivoire 56 D5
Yamuna *river* India 117 E3
Yana *river* Russian Federation 95 F2
Yangon Myanmar *Eng.* Rangoon 118 B4
Yangtze *see* Chang Jiang
Yaoundé *capital of* Cameroon 59 B5
Yap *island* Micronesia 126 A1
Yap Trench *undersea feature* Philippine Sea 124 B2
Yaqui *river* Mexico 32 B2
Yarmouth Canada 21 F4
Yaroslavl' Russian Federation 96 B2

Yazd Iran 102 D4
Yazoo *river* SE USA 30 C2
Yecheng China 108 A3
Yekaterinburg Russian Federation *prev.* Sverdlovsk 96 C3
Yelisavetpol *see* Gäncä
Yellowknife Canada 19 E4
Yellow River *see* Huang He
Yellow Sea Pacific Ocean 110-111
Yellowstone *river* NW USA 24 C2
Yemen *country* SW Asia 103 C7
Yenakiyeve Ukraine 91 G3
Yengisar China 108 A3
Yenisey *river* Russian Federation 96 D3
Yerevan *capital of* Armenia *var.* Erevan, Jerevan, *Eng.* Erivan 99 F2
Yevpatoriya Ukraine 91 F4
Yinchuan China 110 B4
Yining China 108 B2
Yogyakarta Indonesia 120 D5
Yokohama Japan 113 D5
Yopal Colombia 40 C2
York England, UK 71 D5
York, Cape *headland* Australia 130 C1
Yorkton Canada 19 F5
Youngstown Ohio, USA 22 D3
Ypres *see* Ieper
Yu *see* Henan
Yuba City California, USA 27 B5
Yucatan Channel *channel* Caribbean Sea 36 A2
Yucatan Peninsula *peninsula* Mexico 33 H4
Yue *see* Guangdong
Yueyang China 111 C5
Yukon *river* Canada/USA 18 C2
Yukon Territory *territory* Canada 18 D3
Yuma Arizona, USA 28 A3
Yun *see* Yunnan
Yunnan *province* China *var.* Yun, Yun-nan 111 B6
Yun-nan *see* Yunnan
Yurev *see* Tartu
Yur'yev *see* Tartu
Yushu China 108 D4
Yuzhno-Sakhalinsk Russian Federation *var.* Vladimirovka 97 H4
Yverdon Switzerland 77 A7

Z

Zacapa Guatemala 34 C2
Zacatecas Mexico 32 D3
Zadar Croatia 82 A4
Zagreb *capital of* Croatia 80 B3
Zāgros, Kuhhā-ye *mountain range* Iran/Iraq 102 D4
Zāhedān Iran 102 E4
Zahlé Lebanon 100 B4
Zaire *country see* Dem. Rep. Congo
Zaire *river see* Congo
Zaječar Serbia 82 E4
Zákinthos *see* Zákynthos
Zákynthos *island* Greece *prev.* Zákinthos 87 A5
Zalaegerszeg Hungary 81 B7
Zambezi Zambia 60 D2
Zambezi *river* southern Africa 60 D3
Zambia *country* southern Africa 60-61
Zamboanga Philippines 120 E3
Zamora Spain 74 D2
Zanda Xizang Zizhiqu, W China 108 B4
Zanjān Iran 102 C3
Zanzibar Tanzania 55 C7
Zaozhuang China 111 D5
Zapadnaya Dvina *see* Western Dvina
Zapadno-Sibirskaya Ravnina *Eng.* West Siberian Plain. *Plain* Russian Federation 96 C3
Zapala Argentina 47 B5
Zaporizhzhya Ukraine *Rus.* Zaporozh'ye 91 F3
Zaporozh'ye *see* Zaporizhzhya
Zarafshon Uzbekistan 104 D2
Zaragoza Spain *Eng.* Saragossa 75 F2
Zaranj Afghanistan 104 C5
Zaria Nigeria 57 G4
Zaysan, Ozero *lake* Kazakhsta 94 D3
Zeebrugge Belgium 69 A5
Zenica Bosnia & Herzegovina 82 C4
Zeravshan *river* C Asia 105 E3
Zeya *river* Russian Federation 95 F3
Zhambyl *see* Taraz
Zhayyk *see* Ural
Zhdanov *see* Mariupol'
Zhe *see* Zhejiang
Zhejiang *province* China *var.* Che-chiang, Chekiang, Zhe 111 D5
Zhengzhou China 111 C5
Zhezkazgan Kazakhstan *prev.* Zdhezkazgan 96 C4
Zhitomir *see* Zhytomyr
Zhlobin Belarus 89 D6
Zhodzina Belarus 89 D5
Zhytomyr Ukraine *Rus.* Zhitomir 90 D2
Zibo China 110 D4
Zielona Góra Poland *Ger.* Grünberg in Schlesien 80 B5
Zigong China 111 B6
Žilina Slovakia *Hung.* Zsolna, *Ger.* Sillein 81 C5
Zimbabwe *country* southern Africa 60-61
Zinder Niger 57 C3
Zoetermeer Netherlands 68 C4
Zomba Malawi 61 E2
Zonguldak Turkey 98 C2
Zouérat Mauritania 56 C1
Zrenjanin Serbia 82 D3
Zsolna *see* Žilina
Zug Switzerland 77 B7
Zuider Zee *see* IJsselmeer
Zürich Switzerland *Eng.* Zurich 77 B6
Zurich *see* Zürich
Zürichsee *lake* Switzerland 77 B7
Zuwārah Libya 53 F2
Zvornik Bosnia & Herzegovina 82 C3
Zwedru Liberia 56 D5
Zwickau Germany 76 D4
Zwolle Netherlands 68 D3